Law and Economics

The Law and Economics approach to law dominates the intellectual discussion of nearly every doctrinal area of law in the United States and its influence is growing steadily throughout Europe, Asia, and South America. Numerous academics and practitioners are working in the field with a flow of uninterrupted scholarship that is unprecedented, as is its influence on the law.

Academically, every major law school in the United States has a Law and Economics program and the emergence of similar programs on other continents continues to accelerate. Despite its phenomenal growth, the area is also the target of an ongoing critique by lawyers, philosophers, psychologists, social scientists, even economists since the late 1970s. While the critique did not seem to impede the development of the field, it certainly has helped it to become more sophisticated, inclusive, and mature. In this volume some of the leading scholars working in the field, as well as a number of those critical of Law and Economics, discuss the foundational issues from various perspectives: philosophical, moral, epistemological, methodological, psychological, political, legal, and social.

The philosophical and methodological assumptions of the economic analysis of law are criticized and defended, alternatives are proposed, old and new applications are discussed.

The book is ideal for a main or supplementary textbook in courses and seminars on legal theory, philosophy of law, jurisprudence, and (of course) Law and Economics.

Aristides N. Hatzis is an Associate Professor of Legal Theory at the University of Athens, Greece.

Nicholas Mercuro is Professor of Law in Residence at the Michigan State University College of Law and Member of the Faculty of James Madison College, Michigan State University, USA.

The economics of legal relationships
Sponsored by Michigan State University College of Law
Series Editors:
Nicholas Mercuro
Michigan State University College of Law
Michael D. Kaplowitz
Michigan State University

* The first three volumes listed above are published by and available from Elsevier

Law and Economics

Philosophical issues and fundamental questions

Edited by Aristides N. Hatzis and Nicholas Mercuro

Routledge
Taylor & Francis Group

LONDON AND NEW YORK

First published 2015
by Routledge
2 Park Square, Milton Park, Abingdon, Oxon OX14 4RN

and by Routledge
711 Third Avenue, New York, NY 10017

First issued in paperback 2017

Routledge is an imprint of the Taylor & Francis Group, an informa business

British Library Cataloguing in Publication Data
A catalogue record for this book is available from the British Library

Library of Congress Cataloging in Publication Data
Law and economics: philosophical issues and fundamental questions/ edited by Aristides N. Hatzis, Nicholas Mercuro.
    pages cm. – (The economics of legal relationships)
    Includes bibliographical references and index.
    1. Law and economics–Philosophy. I. Hatzis, Aristides N., editor.
    II. Mercuro, Nicholas, editor.
    K487.E3L3877 2015
    343.0701–dc23   2014030954

ISBN 13: 978-1-138-08162-8 (pbk)
ISBN 13: 978-0-415-40410-5 (hbk)

Typeset in Times New Roman
by Wearset Ltd, Boldon, Tyne and Wear

Contents

Contributors

Brian H. Bix, Frederick W. Thomas Professor of Law and Philosophy, University of Minnesota, USA.

Daniel A. Farber, Sho Sato Professor of Law, University of California, Berkeley School of Law, USA.

Lawrence M. Friedman, Marion Rice Kirkwood Professor of Law, Stanford Law School, USA.

Allan C. Hutchinson, Distinguished Research Professor, Osgoode Hall Law School, York University, Toronto, Canada.

Gerrit De Geest, Charles F. Nagel Professor of International and Comparative Law, Director of the Center on Law, Innovation & Economic Growth, Washington University at St. Louis, USA.

Douglas H. Ginsburg, Senior Judge, United States Court of Appeals for the District of Columbia Circuit, Professor of Law, George Mason University School of Law, USA.

Aristides N. Hatzis, Associate Professor of Philosophy of Law and Theory of Institutions, Department of Philosophy & History of Science, University of Athens, Greece.

Jonathan Klick, Professor of Law, University of Pennsylvania Law School, USA.

Elisabeth Krecké, Professor of Economics, Aix Marseille Université, Faculté d'Economie et de Gestion, CERGAM, France.

Steven G. Medema, Department of Economics, University of Colorado at Denver, USA.

Nicholas Mercuro, Professor of Law in Residence, Michigan State University College of Law, James Madison College, Michigan State University, USA.

Martha C. Nussbaum, Ernst Freund Professor of Law and Ethics, Law School, Philosophy Department, and Divinity School, University of Chicago, USA.

Francesco Parisi, Oppenheimer Wolff and Donnelly Professor of Law, University of Minnesota Law School, USA, Professor of Economics, University of Bologna, Italy.

Richard A. Posner, Judge, US Court of Appeals for the Seventh Circuit; Senior Lecturer, University of Chicago Law School, USA.

Edward Rubin, University Professor of Law and Political Science, Vanderbilt University, USA.

Thomas S. Ulen, Swanlund Chair Emeritus, University of Illinois at Urbana-Champaign, and Professor Emeritus of Law, University of Illinois College of Law, USA.

Joshua D. Wright, Commissioner, US Federal Trade Commission, Professor of Law (on leave), George Mason University School of Law, USA.

Preface

There is no approach to law that is more influential in the United States today than Law and Economics; in economics departments, it is a standard course offering. The literature in the field continues to influence the intellectual discussion of nearly every doctrinal area of law. Outside of the United States its ideas and impact on law grow steadily.

It has been more than 40 years since the publication of Richard Posner's *Economic Analysis of Law*, the book that helped launch the Law and Economics movement. The ninth edition of the book was published in early 2014, this time competing against over thirty textbooks, edited collections, and casebooks on Law and Economics. Today, law review articles that incorporate the "economic way of thinking" are numerous; economics departments and law schools routinely offer at least one Law and Economics course; and major law schools feature well-funded and well-established Law and Economics programs/centers. The ideas and concepts that constitute Law and Economics are now being transmitted to successive generations of graduates in both economics and the law.

This is no doubt a success story, especially in the legal academia where the change of paradigms is not exactly a frequent occurrence given the fact that doctrinalism continues to hold sway. And one must not forget that all of this happened even though Law and Economics initially faced an unprecedented attack by almost everyone in American and English legal theory. If not formally marginalized, Law and Economics scholars created a tension among their doctrinally trained colleagues who were left wondering what exactly did Pareto Optimality, Kaldor–Hicks efficiency, and welfare economics have to do with their "law". Thirty five years ago, in the famous "twin symposia" on "efficiency" and "wealth maximization" in legal theory (*Journal of Legal Studies*, 9:2, March 1980 and *Hofstra Law Review*, 8:3–4 Spring-Summer 1980), the foundational assumptions and the deductive approach proffered by Law and Economics was harshly criticized and its future seemed somewhat uncertain. Nobody could have anticipated that it would move forward against this full-scale attack. A look back suggests that those practicing Law and Economics have proven to be quite resilient and adept at surviving.

Today, even though Law and Economics remains somewhat controversial, it is now securely niched within the legal academy. Those working in the field are busy producing an immense body of work – in the contiguous subdisciplines of New Institutional Economics, Public Choice Theory, Behavioral Law, and Economics, even Austrian Law and Economics – some of which pushes back on the early assumptions and models based on rational choice. It now exerts an even greater influence if only by its sheer volume.

But fundamental questions remain: Is Law and Economics a utilitarian, market-friendly legal theory? Or is it a new legal paradigm which, despite its intellectual debts, has managed to realize the promise of Sociological Jurisprudence and Legal Realism? ... Or is it both?

More than fifty years after the formulation of the Coase theorem and Guido Calabresi's work on torts; forty years after the presentation of the Posnerian research program, and thirty five years after Henry Manne began his Economics Institute for Law Professors and Law Institutes for Economics Professors, the movement is now distinctly different yet at the same time less controversial and, dare we say, almost mainstream. Because of this, we thought the time had come to revisit the question of values in Law and Economics. We were interested in what others thought about such questions as: What are the norms and values underlying this impressive body of research? ... and ... What are the philosophical issues and fundamental question confronting this evolving discipline? We were fortunate enough to solicit contributions from those in Anglo-Saxon and continental legal theory and some of the leading experts in Law and Economics from various generations and representatives from different schools of thought. We are grateful for their willingness to participate and hope this book continues to solidify the field within the legal academy.

Aristides N. Hatzis and Nicholas Mercuro
January 2015

1 Norms and values in the economic approach to law

Richard A. Posner*

The economic approach to law ("law and economics," "economic analysis of law") embodies norms of two types: procedural or epistemological norms, the norms of scientific inquiry; and moral or political norms, which come into play when the economic approach is used as a basis for making proposals for legal reform. The two types of norms correspond to the conventional distinction between "positive" and "normative" analysis, but the conventional distinction is confusing because norms enter into positive analysis, merely norms of a different type.

Let me set the stage by reviewing briefly the history and current scope and direction of the economic approach to law. Some of the basic economizing properties of law had been perceived since antiquity, notably the function of property in creating investment incentives; but the first notable explicit application of economics to law was Bentham's economic theory of crime and punishment, revived two centuries later by Gary Becker. Bentham didn't just make the point that (in modern terminology) people balance benefits and costs in making decisions, even "nonmarket" decisions such as whether to commit a crime, and that punishment is a type of cost; he made a host of less obvious economic points.[1] Why he failed to extend the analysis to other areas of law, such as tort law, which by imposing liability might be thought to be imposing a punishment cost closely akin to that imposed by the criminal law, and why economists did not take a serious interest in the law until the twentieth century, is an abiding mystery. For whatever reason, it was until quite recently much easier for legal thinkers to understand the regulatory character of criminal law than the regulatory character of civil law; as late as Holmes's great work *The Common Law* (1881), tort law was seen as a matter of shifting losses in accordance with moral norms rather than of optimizing the number and severity of deliberate and accidental injuries. (Holmes did, however, have an insight into the economic character of contract law.)

Scattered work of economists (such as John R. Commons, Frank Knight, Robert Hale, and, in England, A.C. Pigou) and of economically minded lawyers (such as William O. Douglas) in the early decades of the twentieth century were the as-yet unrecognized portents of a law and economics movement that began to be recognized as such in the 1950s as a result of a growing body of economic analysis of antitrust and public utility–common carrier regulation. That work reached new levels of intellectual sophistication in the 1950s in the hands of Aaron Director and his protegés, including Robert Bork; George Stigler, who did the first serious statistical studies of the effect of regulation; and Ronald Coase, in his studies of marginal cost pricing and other aspects of public utility and common carrier regulation. The *Journal of Law and Economics*, founded in 1958 by Director and edited first by him and then by Coase, gave the movement a name and a forum for publication. Meanwhile, the economics of income taxation had been launched with the work of Henry Simons (who also contributed to the economic analysis of labor unions), and the economics of corporate law had been launched with work by Henry Manne against a background of the theory of the firm developed by Coase in the 1930s, and with the pathbreaking article on corporate financial structure by Modigliani and Miller.

The scholarship that I have been describing had in common a focus on bodies of law that regulate explicitly economic behavior. Much of law, however, regulates nonmarket behavior, as Bentham had recognized. Gary Becker's doctoral thesis on the economics of racial discrimination, published in 1957, was a milestone in the expansion of the nascent "law and economics" movement to the legal regulation of nonmarket behavior; and his students, notably Isaac Ehrlich and William Landes, were later to do important studies of the economics of discrimination, crime, and procedure. (Becker himself contributed importantly to the economics of crime in his 1968 article on crime and punishment, reviving, modernizing, and extending Bentham.) The 1960s opened with Coase's revolutionary article on social cost and Guido Calabresi's first article on the economics of accident law; and later I and others chimed in.

By 1973, when the first edition of my textbook-treatise *Economic Analysis of Law* was published, a comprehensive law and economics movement could be said to exist, centered at the University of Chicago and predominantly conservative (in the free-market sense) politically. It was very heavily invested, however, in a relatively few fields, primarily antitrust, public utility regulation, and torts; the literature dealing with the other fields of law was as yet skimpy. Economic analysis of law at this time was not only topically limited but also methodologically simple. Most studies employed a straightforward (to an economist!) model of human behavior as being rationally self-interested. Mathematical formalization was limited, formal game theory was infrequently employed, and quantitative empirical analysis was extremely rare.

That was forty years ago. In the intervening period the law and economics movement has become geographically, politically, thematically, and methodologically diverse – as well as much larger, more specialized, more rigorous, more influential, more orthodox. There are now seven English-language journals that specialize in the economic analysis of law, and in addition many economic studies of law are published in conventional law journals and conventional economic journals. No field of law has remained immune from intensive economic scrutiny (including, besides formal law, a variety of informal norms viewed as law substitutes), not even family law, public international law, ancient and primitive law, or the speech and religion clauses of the First Amendment; and some subfields of law and economics, such as bankruptcy, antitrust, common carrier regulation, and intellectual property, have spawned immense literatures. Increasingly the practitioners of economic analysis of law have economics Ph.D.s, with or without a J.D. as well, and employ the formalizations now typical, though sometimes regretted, of modern economics. The simple model of rationally self-interested behavior of decades earlier has been enriched by greater attention to altruism (where Becker was again the principal pioneer), and challenged by institutional economists, such as Oliver Williamson, and by behavioral economists, such as Christine Jolls; the behavioral economists draw heavily on the work of the psychologist Daniel Kahneman. The University of Chicago remains an important site of the law and economics movement, but is no longer dominant.

Against this background, I begin my consideration of the norms and values of economic analysis of law with what I have termed procedural or epistemological norms – the norms of scholarly inquiry to which a particular field, here economic analysis of law, is committed. Although there is a good deal of casual, sloppy, and tendentious economic analysis of law, most of the academic practitioners of economic analysis of law are committed to norms of a broadly scientific character. These norms include the explicit statement of assumptions, a practice facilitated by formal models; an insistence that the analysis be logically coherent, another practice facilitated by formal models, with their explicit logical (mathematical) relations; and a belief that theory should issue in hypotheses that can be falsified by data that are objective in the sense that observers can be induced to agree on them regardless of the preferences, background, ideology, or other personal (or group) characteristics of the observer.

These are the norms that guide inquiry in the natural sciences, on which modern economists model their own research. The achievements of economics, including its subfield of economic analysis of law, lag the aspirations and pale beside the achievements of fields like physics and biology; but they are not trivial. The principal difficulties that obstruct scientific economics are the complexity of human behavior and institutions and the fact the data relevant to economic analysis, and in particular to many areas of economic analysis of law (such as crime, litigation, accidents, the family, and the behavior of judges), are difficult to quantify or to manipulate experimentally. The latter problem can be mitigated but not entirely solved by means of statistical analysis that tries to isolate causal factors.

But I am not centrally concerned with how successful economics in general or economic analysis in particular has been in overcoming the obstacles to a rigorously scientific approach. I am interested, rather, in the spirit in which this work is conducted. The aspiration to the rigor and objectivity of the natural sciences provides a model lacking in most areas of legal research. My particular *bête noire*, constitutional law, presents the most striking but not the only contrast to economic analysis of law. The most salient characteristics of academic research on constitutional law are its politicization,[2] its absence of empirical content or even curiosity (so that such fundamental issues as the effect of major constitutional decisions on public attitudes, social structure, and even policy outcomes remain unilluminated[3]), and, as a consequence of the first two points, its *interminability* – the same arguments are repeated in slightly different form year after year, decade after decade, generation after generation. No tendency is discernible for issues to be resolved and inquiry to move on to new issues. There is lively debate and often impressive rhetoric, but there is no intellectual *progress* in constitutional law. The major exceptions are, unsurprisingly, the application to constitutional law of the methods of other fields, notably the political scientist's interest precisely in the consequences of constitutional doctrine (for which Gerald Rosenberg's research is justly renowned[4]) and the economic analyst's endeavor to view constitutional law through the lens of public-choice theory.

The late philosopher Richard Rorty, though by no means an enthusiast for science, the claim of which to have a pipeline to objective knowledge of the external world he thought (as a pragmatist in the tradition of Charles Sanders Peirce) overblown – thought in fact continuous with the exploded claims of religion – admired the *ethics* of scientific inquiry, namely the commitment to resolve disputes in an open, disinterested manner in which evidence is valued, the possibility of falsification of one's beliefs is accepted (this acceptance we might call anti-dogmatism), and an effort is made to forge agreement not through force or mystification but through conversation, observation, and, in short, rational inquiry. Rorty believed, rightly in my view, that the ethics of scientific inquiry and not merely the amenability of the physical world to human understanding has played an important role in the success of science in increasing mankind's power to predict and control physical processes. Science was for him a *moral* success; and in just the same way economic analysis of law can modestly congratulate itself on its efforts, however imperfect, to emulate the ethics of the natural sciences.

The norms of science are oriented toward discovery, toward learning how to do things; their domain is positive analysis. And one of the dividends of the economic approach to law is its encouragement of positive analysis, of understanding the structures, concepts, procedures, and institutions of the law – a useful corrective to the overwhelming emphasis of legal scholarship on reform. (Again, constitutional law is the exemplar of traditionalism; constitutional law scholarship is almost entirely normative.) But economics in general, and economic analysis in particular, are also heavily normative. People aren't as curious about the economic system or the legal system as they are about the stars, or the descent of man from monkeys, or the structure of numbers. Their interest in the economic and legal systems is practical; it is an interest in making these systems work better. It would be, in contrast, highly presumptuous to orient astronomy toward getting the stars to shine more brightly! Of course, much scientific work is also oriented toward "making things better," but generally, though with important exceptions, "better" is a technical rather than a moral concept in science, though it may be freighted with moral concern. One can design a "better" bomb without concerning oneself with the moral implications of one's action. But economic and legal reform is all about making things better in a moral sense, and as a result normative analysis in these fields, and in their intersection in the economic analysis of law, thrusts the reformer, the normative economic analyst of law, into controversies in moral and political philosophy.

This is not something new in economics by any means. Economics has always had a strong, even dominant, normative component. From Adam Smith's advocacy of free trade, to Bentham's criticism of usury laws, to Keynes's advocacy of deficit spending in depressions, to Milton Friedman's advocacy of monetarism, a volunteer army, and a negative income tax, economists have thought it natural to translate their diagnoses of economic pathologies into prescriptions for cure. And yet they have rarely thought it necessary to construct a bridge between "is" and "ought" – that is, to lay philosophical foundations for the use of economics as a normative rather than merely a positive science. The branch of economics that addresses the issue of the normativity of economics rigorously, "welfare economics," although it has engaged the attention of a number of distinguished economists, such as Paul Samuelson and Amartya Sen, has always been rather peripheral to the discipline, just as medical ethics is peripheral to medicine. Economists can get away with being casual about the normativity of their subject because they can usually appeal to a generally accepted goal, such as maximizing the value of a nation's output, rather than having to defend the goal. By showing how a change in economic policy or arrangements would move us closer to that goal, they can make a normative statement without having to defend their fundamental premises. They can keep debate at the technical level where reasoning is over means rather than ends. No one feels pressed to offer a *philosophical* defense of his views whose normative aspirations are modest. A watch repairer doesn't need philosophy to justify his saying that a broken watch ought to be fixed and an economist doesn't need philosophy to justify advocating measures for increasing a nation's rate of economic growth or reducing inflation or unemployment. The economist must be careful not to neglect unwanted side-effects of the measures he proposes – but then the watch repairer has to consider the cost of repairing the watch.

Let me offer an example of modest normativity in the economic analysis of law. Almost all economists believe that price-fixing conspiracies should be forbidden, because such conspiracies tend to reduce the efficiency with which scarce resources are used. The conspirators generate supracompetitive profits for themselves by raising their price above cost, thus deflecting some consumers (those who refuse to pay the higher price) to substitutes that may cost more to produce but that look cheaper because they are being sold at a price equal to their cost.[5] In other words, price fixing confronts consumers with false alternatives (goods that seem cheaper but really aren't) that cause them to buy goods that are more costly than what they have given up, so there is a net social loss. The loss is magnified by whatever costs the conspirators incur in creating and maintaining their conspiracy, since the conspiracy does not produce a product commensurate with the costs, or indeed any product at all except to transfer wealth from consumers to the conspirators. (The firms are productive; the conspiracy itself is not.)

Some of the terms that I am using, such as "efficiency," "social loss," or even "wealth," are loaded from a moral or political standpoint. One may ask, for example, why the increased costs created by the conspiracy are not offset by the transfer of wealth from consumers to producers – maybe the latter obtain greater utility from wealth than the former, or are worthier people, or use their wealth in a way that benefits society as a whole in a sense that economic concepts may not capture, such as by contributing to cultural or political activities. Yet somehow these possibilities do not (at least nowadays) seem to bother many of the people who think about antitrust. They are content, most of them, with focusing on the narrowly, perhaps arbitrarily, "economic" consequences of price fixing – and they feel no need to explore the foundations of the view that those consequences are indeed "bad."

The antitrust example illustrates an important category of normative economic analysis of law – the category of reforms (whether already adopted, as in the case of the prohibition of price fixing, or proposed) that do not seem to require difficult tradeoffs because the benefits are all or pretty much all on one side and the costs on another, even when the terms "benefits" and "costs" are used in the broadest possible sense, to encompass all the pros and cons that an observer might care to consider. In the case of prohibiting price fixing, although in principle all sorts of noneconomic costs and benefits might be brought into the picture, the relevant community, consisting of those who have a professional interest in antitrust, is content both to limit attention to the narrowly economic benefits and costs and to find the latter decisively outweighed by the former. So it becomes an easy case for normative law and economics, more precisely a *relatively* easy case because there are some situations in which price fixing is an element of an arrangement that seems on balance beneficial, but I needn't go into that here.

The difficult cases, the cases in which normative economic analysis of law becomes problematic, are of two kinds. First are cases in which the benefits or the costs, or both, associated with some rule or doctrine or practice are simply very difficult to measure. Second are cases in which the economic model itself seems to leave out of account normatively important considerations. The first category, although very important, is not very interesting insofar as the only problem is measurement, a problem that one might expect to be overcome eventually. It becomes interesting when measurement is contended to be impossible, as in the case of valuing a human life for purposes of determining a cost-justified precaution against a life-threatening condition. Even in such cases the tough normative issue can sometimes be finessed – in the example just given by asking not what a life is worth but how much people disvalue the small risks that are ordinarily in question. If the question is how much to invest in a safety precaution that might eliminate a one in 100,000 risk of death, we might ask what costs people incur in their daily life to avoid such risks, for example when they are deciding whether to cross the street against the light or fasten an automobile seat belt or fly in a private plane.

But after all such ingenious finessing, one is left with a large class of cases in which economic proposals are resisted on the ground that the economic approach leaves important normative considerations out of account. Many of these cases arise from economists's forays into areas traditionally regarded as not economic – a commonplace in economic analysis of law. To say that an area is not traditionally regarded as "economic" is to say that suggestions for orienting it toward efficiency or other economic values are likely to jar because it is assumed that noneconomic values dominate issues that are not explicitly economic. And then what is the economist to do? Can he say more than that he's shown that policy X would increase efficiency but that he can't speak to X's ultimate merit?

Not without hitching economic values to some more comprehensive source or concept of value; and historically that has largely meant hitching economic science to utilitarian philosophy. Modern economics makes heavy use of utilitarian terminology, in such key expressions as "expected utility," "marginal utility," and "utility maximization." But in practice normative economics is rarely utilitarian in any rigorous sense. Remember in the price-fixing example that while the conspiracy will reduce the value of output it will also transfer wealth from consumers to producers, and if producers happen to obtain more utility from money than consumers do, the wealth transfer brought about by the conspiracy may generate utility gains that exceed the loss of utility caused by the fall in the value of output. Modern economics has given up on trying to measure utility, because such measurement requires information about people's preferences and emotions that seems unobtainable.[6] The historical linkage between economics and utilitarianism thus has largely been severed. The practical significance of utility in modern economics is mostly limited to attitudes toward risk, which can drive a wedge between wealth and utility. A risk-averse person, for example, will by definition prefer a certainty of receiving $10 to a 10 percent chance of obtaining $100, even though the chance and the certainty would be valued equally by a person who was indifferent to risk. The chance and the certainty differ in utility but are identical in "value" as that term is usually understood.

It turns out, moreover, that utilitarianism is not a reliable guide to social policy, all measurement problems to one side.[7] The basic reasons are fourfold. First, few people actually believe – and there is no way to prove them wrong – that maximizing happiness, or contentment, or joy, or preference satisfaction, or the excess of pleasure over pain, or some other version of utility is or should be one's object in life. Happiness is important to most people, but it isn't everything. How many of us would be willing to take a pill that would put us into a blissfully happy dreamlike trance for the rest of our lives, even if we were absolutely convinced of the safety and efficacy of the pill and the trance? Even today, when science has brought close to reality many of the technological marvels that Aldous Huxley in *Brave New World* (1932) projected 600 years into the future – feel-good drugs (his *soma* is our Prozac), comprehensive cosmetic surgery, elimination of the ills of old age, the divorce of reproduction from sex, consumerism, and so forth – most of us would side with "Mr. Savage" in rejecting the Utopian lives of the "normals."

Second, and closely related, there is a question about the authenticity of preferences. Preferences are shaped by information and by psychology, for example by the natural desire to adjust one's aspirations to one's circumstances. A person who having been born into a low caste cannot aspire to rise beyond the rank of a ditch digger will be ill-advised to bewail his fate. He will be happier if he accepts the system and sees his place in it as dictated by a higher law or power from which he may expect to receive posthumous justice. Having scaled down his preferences to his condition he may be content with the status quo and resist change. Women confined by caste-like restrictions to household production may adapt to that condition by embracing it as their natural state. They may be happy to play the role to which their parents, reflecting the values of their society, have predestined them.

Third, by aggregating utility across persons, utilitarianism treats people as cells in the overall social organism rather than as individuals. This is the source of the familiar barbarisms of utilitarian ethics, such as the deliberate sacrifice of innocents to maximize the total amount of happiness in the society (or the world, or the universe), or the "utility monster" whose capacity for sadistic pleasure so far exceeds the capacity of his victims to experience pain that utility is maximized by allowing him to commit rape and murder. Defenders of utilitarianism seek to deflect such criticisms by pointing out that lack of trust in officials would defeat any effort to empower the state to attempt to maximize utility on an individual basis. The only regime that would *dependably* be utility maximizing in the real world would be a form of rule utilitarianism that limited the power of government and so would rule out, for example, the kind of authoritarian regime, well-intentioned but sinister (a techno-futuristic version of the reign of the Grand Inquisitor described in *The Brothers Karamazov*), depicted in Huxley's novel. But practical objections to the logical implications of utilitarianism miss the point. The logic itself is repulsive. Even if we assume away all the problems of implementation, and contemplate the result – the inducement of blissful trances by utterly benign, democratically responsive officials – we still don't like it.

Fourth, utilitarianism has no boundary principles, except possibly sentience. Peter Singer, the leading philosophical advocate of animal liberation, is a utilitarian.[8] Animals feel pain, and even more clearly do foreigners, so that utilitarianism collides with powerful intuitions that our social obligations are (usually) greater to family and close friends than to strangers, greater to the people of our own society than to outsiders, and greater to human beings than to (other) animals.

The weaknesses of utilitarianism may seem very damaging to the project of normative economics. Most economists, to the extent that they propose reforms and thus use economics as a normative rather than purely positive tool of analysis, are easily caricatured as unreflective utilitarians, ignorant not only of their own philosophical tradition but also of the criticisms of utilitarianism that philosophers have made and of alternative conceptions of the good life and the good society to those propounded in the utilitarian tradition. Economists tend to take preferences as given and to conceive it to be the function of government to create and protect free-market institutions that will allow those preferences to be gratified to the maximum extent possible. They tend to assume that all preferences can be monetized and that measures of strictly economic welfare, such as gross national product (GNP), are reasonable proxies for the total preference satisfaction achieved in the society. So as between two societies, the one that has the higher GNP per capita is given the palm as being "better" in the economic sense of having maximized utility or economic welfare (treated as synonyms) more successfully than the other society.

Such an approach is attacked as unrealistic in ignoring the role of adaptive and otherwise inauthentic preferences, and as resting on an impoverished conception of human welfare. As I have already noted, people's preferences often do not coincide with what a neutral observer would think good for them or what they would think good for themselves if they lived in a different kind of society or just if they knew more about alternative ways of living. Yet economists's hesitancy to penetrate beneath the surface indications of preference that they call "revealed preference" (that is, preference revealed by behavior), or to deal with nonmonetizable phenomena (a reluctance that is changing, however), may be regrettable, but it is not the product of philosophical commitment, or of confusion either. It is a consequence of the character of economics as a discipline. The assumptions that preferences are stable and are reliably revealed by behavior (by "putting your money where your mouth is"), and that monetary values, express or imputed, are a meaningful index to a meaningful concept of human welfare, enable economists to formulate testable hypotheses about behavior. Economists may cling too tightly to these assumptions, but if so it is for methodological rather than philosophical reasons. The commitment is not to utilitarianism, but to a certain model of inquiry – what economists regard as scientific and their critics as scientistic – and thus of the methodological norms with which I began my discussion of the norms and values of economic analysis of law. Moreover, economists are not as blinkered as the discussion to this point may have suggested. There is a long tradition in economics of distinguishing between monetary and real phenomena; indeed, from Adam Smith's advocacy of fair trade onward, an important function of the economist has been to remind people of the difference.

Some of the objections to utilitarianism can be elided by substituting wealth for utility as the maximand. "Wealth" is to be understood in this context not in strictly monetary terms but rather as the summation of all the valued objects, both tangible and intangible, in society, weighted by the prices they would command if they were to be traded in markets. In other words, the market transaction is taken as paradigmatic of morally appropriate action. This view, though anathema to anyone who retains even residual socialist sympathies in this era of triumphalist capitalism, can be defended (though how successfully remains to be seen) by reference to notions both of express and of implied consent. If A sells B his stamp collection for $1,000, this implies that the stamp collection is worth less than $1,000 to A and more than $1,000 to B. Let us suppose that it is worth $900 to A (that is, he would have thought himself better off at any price above that) and $1,200 to B (the most he would have paid for it). The transaction is wealth-maximizing because before it took place A had something worth $900 to him and *B* had $1,000 in cash, while afterward *A* has $1,000 and *B* has something worth $1,200 to him; so aggregate wealth has increased by $300 ($1,000 + $1,200 − $1,000 + $900). The increase in wealth has been brought about by consent rather than coercion; and provided that the transaction has no third-party effects, it has made two people better off and no one worse off. It thus is the product of free, unanimous choice.

Wealth maximization meets some of the objection that I discussed earlier to utility maximization. Value is easier to measure than utility; no position is taken on what people want or should want, such as happiness; the scope of permissible coercion is less (though, as we are about to see, not zero) because the right to act on one's desires is limited by willingness to pay (*B* can't grab *A*'s stamp collection just because it gives him more pleasure than it gives *A*); the boundary problem is solved because the community is defined as those who have money to back their desires; and noneconomic values such as freedom and autonomy are preserved. The last point is particularly important. It allows the economist to hitch his wagon to a fashionable philosophical star, that of Kant and his avatars. The individual has more dignity and autonomy under wealth maximization than under utilitarianism, because his interests, or some them at any rate, cannot be taken or destroyed without his express or implied consent. We might think of wealth maximization, therefore, as a political philosophy that, recognizing the enduring influence of both utilitarian and Kantian ethics, draws on both to provide practical, feasible guidance to the formation and administration of public policy in a modern democratic state. We might think of it as a graceful bow to the irreducible moral pluralism of the United States, which might be thought to require of any widely acceptable political philosophy that it borrow strands from different moral traditions even if incompatible.

Granted, there's a risk of falling between stools with this kind of hybrid ethical system. Consider a forced uncompensated transfer of a television set from a poor person to a rich person. The transfer would be opposed by a utilitarian on the ground that, given diminishing marginal utility of income, it is highly unlikely that the rich person will derive as much utility from the television set as the poor person; therefore the involuntary uncompensated transfer is not utility maximizing. That argument is not available to the wealth maximizer. And yet it is apparent that the transaction would not be wealth maximizing, either, when one considers the incentive effects, on rich and poor alike, of allowing such transfers, compared to the alternative of forcing the rich person to transact with the poor person. The example does suggest, however, that willingness to accept payment rather than willingness to pay should be the measure of value when the policy of which the costs and benefits are being measured takes away property rights, as in the case of the television, or where farmland will be flooded as a result of the building of a dam. A willingness-to-accept requirement better protects property rights, which not only have an important economizing role in a market economy but also protect a person's economic independence.

Serious problems remain, however, though the fundamental objection to wealth maximization as an ethical norm is not, as might be supposed, that most transactions have third-party effects (assumed away in my previous examples) and that the economy cannot be organized on a purely voluntarist basis. It is true that coercion is indispensable to prevent a number of serious market failures and, in the form of taxation, to finance the coercive measures needed to prevent those market failures. But it is possible to design methods of regulation that bring about the approximate results that the free market would bring about when, as in my example of the sale of a stamp collection, transaction costs do not prevent a market from functioning. Much economic analysis of law is directed at suggesting "market mimicking" forms of regulation to deal with monopoly, externalities, and other conditions that prevent the market from working well because they cannot feasibly be contracted around.[9]

The fundamental objection to wealth maximization as an ethical norm is not its operability, but the dependence of market outcomes on the distribution of wealth. *A* may have valued his stamp collection at only $900, and *B* have valued it at $1,200, not because *A* loves stamps less than *B* – he may love them much more – and not because there is any appealing concept of desert to which *B* might appeal to validate his claim to be able to buy the collection at the price at which *A* agrees to sell it him. *A* may simply be destitute and have to sell his stamp collection in order to eat, and *B*, while not passionate about stamps – while indeed, let us assume, indifferent to them – wishes to diversify his enormous wealth by holding a variety of collectibles. These circumstances are not at all inconsistent with the sale's making both *A* and *B* better off; on the contrary, they explain *why* it makes both better off. But they sap the moral foundations of a social system oriented to wealth maximization. For after the paradise of optimality is attained, and all society's institutions have been brought into conformity with the requirements of wealth maximization and so consist of free markets supplemented by market-mimicking governmental interventions, the pattern of consumption and production will be strictly derivative from an underlying distribution of wealth. If that distribution is unjust, the pattern of economic activities derived from it will not have a strong claim to be regarded as just either. And insofar as the distribution of wealth is itself largely determined by the market, the justice of the market cannot be derived from some independent notion of the just distribution.

There is another indeterminacy at work: When a good is, or is equal to, a large part of the wealth of an individual, the wealth-maximizing allocation of the good may be indeterminate. If *A* and *B* each have only $100, and the question is whether some good is worth more to one of them than to the other, the answer may depend on who receives it and in that case the criterion of wealth maximization cannot be used to determine who shall receive it. If the good is worth $200 and is given to *A*, *A* will value it more to *B* because *B* will not be willing (if only because unable) to pay more for it; but if instead it is given to *B*, *B* will value it more because *A* will not be able to afford to buy it from *B*.

Some of these problems can be bracketed – the one just mentioned by observing that it makes the criterion of wealth maximization unusable only in cases in which the good to be allocated is a large part of the wealth of the contenders for it. The argument that legal decision making should be guided by that criterion does not require taking a position on its ultimate merits. Provided that wealth is a genuine social value, though not necessarily the only or even the principal such value, that it is one that judges are in a good position to promote, and that issues of economic equality are more efficiently or legitimately addressed by other organs of government, there is no compelling normative objection to using it to guide the common law. We might even think it Pareto efficient, a more powerful normative criterion than wealth maximization. A state of affairs is Pareto optimal if it cannot be changed without making at least one person worse off, and it is Pareto superior to another state of affairs if it makes at least one person better off and no one worse off. In either case the criterion, essentially, is unanimity, and the outcome of a unanimous choice has considerable moral appeal. If common law shaped by wealth maximization has the attractive features that I think it does, perhaps it is not too far off base to think that it would command almost unanimous consent *ex ante* if there were a mechanism for eliciting that consent.

Obviously, judge-made law does not exhaust the universe of potential legal reform; nor is the economic analyst of law content to advise on that law. The law wants to influence legislative and administrative policy as well, where (especially in the case of legislation) distributive considerations cannot be bracketed by being assigned to another branch of government. However, although economics cannot generate or validate a theory of distributive justice, it can make some descriptive points that may contribute to debates over redistributive measures or consequences. Most obviously the economist can point out that income and wealth[10] are unevenly distributed in our society, though he will quickly add that much of the inequality reflects choice – I would be wealthier had I not accepted an appointment as a judge many years ago – including the choice of what level of financial risk to assume. *This* degree of inequality satisfies the Pareto criteria. And much inequality simply reflects the different stages of the life cycle, a pretty neutral determinant. (Almost all children are "poor" in measured money terms – but, in a wealthy country, most are not poor in any meaningful sense.) Much inequality of income and wealth reflects character and effort, but now we get into deep waters, because these are products, in part anyway (maybe ultimately in whole, if one rejects free will), of a "natural lottery" – differences in innate characteristics, including brains, energy, and a predisposition to good health, rather than of choice.

Much inequality of wealth reflects sheer luck, even if one's natural endowment of character and intelligence is considered an entitlement rather than a product of the random sorting of genes. There is the luck of being born in a wealthy versus a poor country, the luck of being a beneficiary or casualty of unpredictable shifts in consumer demands and labor markets, the luck of inheritance, the luck of the financial markets, the luck of whom you know, and the luck of your parents's ability and willingness to invest in your human capital. Determinists think that it's all luck, that deservedness has nothing to do with how rich or poor anyone is.

A point that reinforces skepticism about the justice of the income distribution and has received less attention than it should is that a market system tends to *magnify* differences in innate ability, driving a wedge between the natural lottery and income. The cause is the "superstar" phenomenon.[11] Consider two concert pianists, one (*A*) slightly better than the other (*B*). Suppose that most of the income of a concert pianist nowadays derives not from performing or teaching but from recording. Since recordings of the same piece of music are close substitutes, a consumer has no reason to buy recordings made by *B* rather than those made by *A* unless there is a significant difference in price, and there need not be; even if *A* receives a higher royalty from his contract with the record company than *B* could command, the added cost to the record company may be offset by the economies of a larger output. *A* may thus end up with a very substantial income from recording and *B* with a zero income from it, though *A* may be only a 2 percent better pianist and the difference in quality may be discernible by only a small percentage of the music-loving public. There need be nothing "unjust" in this outcome; but neither can it be referred to the difference in the quality of the individuals. It illustrates, rather, the moral *arbitrariness* of many of the wealth differences among individuals. A system of wealth maximization ratifies and perfects an essentially arbitrary distribution of wealth.

The justification for such a system, if there is one, is not ethical but pragmatic. I have come to believe that in a morally diverse society, such as that of the United States, pragmatism is the ultimate arbiter. To develop the argument that leads to this conclusion would lead me too far afield.[12] My subject is the economic analysis of law. I am content to argue that economic analysis of law promotes certain scholarly virtues that are sorely needed in legal scholarship and that it has a broad scope of relatively uncontroversial normative application. But I do not believe that it can resolve conflicts over ends, the sort of thing one encounters in debates over abortion rights, assisted suicide, affirmative action, homosexual marriage, capital punishment, and the sale of body parts. Not that these issues are undiscussable; not, indeed, that economic analysis has nothing to contribute to the discussion. Even the most impassioned proponents of a legal reform, though their passion be rooted in values that cannot be validated or challenged by an economist, are rarely indifferent to considerations of efficacy and of cost.

In closing let me mention briefly the effort by Professor Kaplow and Shavell, in a book-length article, to defend, in part against objections of a distributional character to the wealth-maximization approach, a "social welfare function" approach to normative issues in the economic analysis of law.[13] The concept of a social welfare function is central to certain versions of welfare economics. A social welfare function of the kind that Kaplow and Shavell discuss expresses social welfare, which is the maximand in welfare economics, as the sum of the individual welfare of the persons comprising the community whose welfare we wish to maximize: for example, all persons living in the United States. If individual welfare is defined as utility, the social welfare function is utilitarian; maximizing social welfare is equated to maximizing aggregate utility.

Kaplow and Shavell do not, however, limit their conception of the social welfare function to the utilitarian version. They define the social welfare function as the aggregate of the well-being of individuals, but they permit the concept of "well-being" to be defined differently from pure utility, so that, for example, utilities of individuals are weighted to reflect value judgments, for example, a preference for the utility of the poor over the utility of the rich.[14] One objection to this approach is that the value judgments that deflect the Kaplow–Shavell social welfare function from pure utility maximization are exogenous to their analysis; this opens up the possibility that the source or justifications of the value judgments might overthrow the social welfare function approach itself. Another objection is that distributional considerations to one side, the social welfare function approach is open to the (other) standard objections to utilitarianism. Against this it must be pointed out, however, that Kaplow and Shavell are really arguing not for the social welfare function *über alles* but merely for its superiority over notions of "fairness," such as corrective justice and redistribution, for guiding legal decision making. And on this more practical level, in which the case they make for the social welfare function resembles the case for wealth maximization, they may well be right.

Notes

* Judge, US Court of Appeals for the Seventh Circuit; Senior Lecturer, University of Chicago Law School. This chapter draws in part on chapter 3 of my book *Frontiers of Legal Theory* (2001b). Chapter 1 of that book is a brief introduction to the economic analysis of law; for fuller discussion, see my *Economic Analysis of Law* (8th edn., 2011). The chapter was originally written more than a decade ago; I have updated it only slightly

1 Namely, that to deter crime the punishment must impose sufficient pain that when added to any other pain anticipated by the criminal it will exceed the pleasure that he anticipates from the crime; that punishment greater than this should not be imposed, because the result would be to create pain (to the undeterrable criminal) not offset by pleasure (benefits) to the potential victims of crime; that the schedule of punishments must be calibrated in such a way that if the criminal has a choice of crimes he will commit the least serious; that fines are a more efficient method of punishment than imprisonment because they confer a benefit as well as impose a detriment; and that the less likely the criminal is to be caught, the heavier the punishment must be, to maintain an expected cost great enough to deter.

2 See, for example, (Posner 2001a, chapter 4).

3 As some constitutional scholars are beginning to complain. See references and discussion in "Introduction" to (Posner 2001b); also see (Klarman 2000).

4 See, in particular (Rosenberg 1991).

5 To put this differently, but perhaps more perspicuously, price fixers generate supra-competitive profits for themselves by restricting their output, forcing price up; the resulting loss of output, denying consumers goods whose full costs they would gladly cover (the competitive price would cover those costs), is a social loss.

6 Some economists say that comparing different people's utility is "meaningless," but they are wrong. Parents, for example, are constantly making guesses, often pretty good ones, about the relative effect on their utility and their children's utility of transferring money to the children. This is a general feature of altruism, and altruism both within and outside the family is common.

7 The literature on the relation between economics and utilitarianism is vast. For a useful anthology, see (Farian *et al.* 1996).

8 See (Singer 1990).
9 As Coase's classic article on social cost showed, if transaction costs are low the market will internalize externalities (Coase 1960). Similarly, if transaction costs in a monopoly setting are low the victims of the monopoly will pay the monopolist to expand his output to the competitive level. There will still be a transfer of wealth to the monopolist, but, at least as a first approximation, the allocation of resources will be efficient because the output of the monopolized market will be the same as it would be under competition.
10 Income is the flow, wealth the stock; since each can be converted into the other, I use them essentially interchangeably.
11 See (Rosen 1981).
12 It is developed at length in my books (Posner 1990, 1995, 1999).
13 See (Kaplow and Shavell 2001: esp. 976–999).
14 Ibid., 987–989.

References

Coase, R.H. 'The problem of social cost', *Journal of Law and Economics* 3, 1960: 1–44.

Farian, F., Hahn, F., and Vannucci, S. (eds.) (1996) *Ethics, Rationality, and Economic Behaviour*, New York: Oxford University Press.

Kaplow, L. and Shavell, S. 'Fairness versus welfare', *Harvard Law Review* 114, 2001: 961–1388.

Klarman, M.J. 'Review essay: rethinking the history of American freedom', *William and Mary Law Review* 42, 2000: 265–288.

Posner, R.A. (1990) *The Problems of Jurisprudence*, Cambridge, MA: Harvard University Press.

Posner, R.A. (1995) *Overcoming Law*, Cambridge, MA: Harvard University Press.

Posner, R.A. (1999) *The Problematics of Moral and Legal Theory*, Cambridge, MA: Harvard University Press.

Posner, R.A. (2001a) *Breaking the Deadlock: The 2000 Election, the Constitution, and the Courts*, Princeton, NJ: Princeton University Press.

Posner, R.A. (2001b) *Frontiers of Legal Theory*, Cambridge, MA: Harvard University Press.

Posner, R.A. (2011) *Economic Analysis of Law* (8th edn.), New York: Aspen Publishers.

Rosen, S. 'The economics of superstars', *American Economic Review* 71, 1981: 845–858.

Rosenberg, G.N. (1991) *The Hollow Hope: Can Courts Bring about Social Change?* Chicago, IL: University of Chicago Press.

Singer, P. (1990) *Animal Liberation* (rev. edn.), New York: Harper Collins.

2   Flawed foundations

The philosophical critique of (a particular type of) economics

Martha C. Nussbaum*

Introduction

The success of Law and Economics obscures, to some extent, a striking fact: The movement has virtually ignored criticisms of its foundations that are increasingly influential in mainstream economics, and by now commonplace (at least as points to grapple with) in utilitarian philosophy. These criticisms are hardly new – indeed, in philosophy most of them have been around since the fourth century BC, when Aristotle criticized Plato's ambitious attempt to propose a "science of measurement" dealing with ethical value. By not informing itself about, and confronting, these criticisms, Law and Economics, which typically sees itself as a forward-looking and scientific movement, risks being stuck in the confusions that plagued philosophy during that interesting century.

Law and Economics could be understood as involving simply a commitment to bring economics to bear upon law. So understood, the project would involve no particular claims about the proper foundations for economics. It would be as compatible with Amartya Sen's neo-Aristotelian conceptions as with those used by the "Chicago School," as hospitable to Adam Smith's complex cognitive analyses of emotion (based on Aristotle and the Stoics) as to the various views of preference and desire more commonly found in neoclassical economics. But in fact, although recently the movement has become somewhat broader, taking more account of approaches such as those of Sen and Smith, Law and Economics has been built on a particular set of conceptual foundations. These involve at least the following ideas: that rational agents are self-interested maximizers of utility; that utility can best be understood (for explanatory/predictive purposes) as a single item varying only in quantity; that utility is best analyzed in terms of the satisfaction of preferences; that preferences are exogenous, i.e., not significantly shaped by laws and institutions; and that the ends adopted by an agent cannot themselves be the subject of rational deliberation, although agents may deliberate about instrumental means to ends. All these ideas were at one time unchallenged in mainstream neoclassical economics; all are currently contested, in part as the result of pressure from philosophy and its history.

The topic of endogenous preferences has received considerable discussion within the Law and Economics movement, and has by now become a major topic of the work of Gary Becker, one of the movement's mentors. I shall therefore discuss it here only where it impinges on one of my other topics. I do think it significant, however, that the endogeneity of preferences has been recognized by almost all the major writers on emotion and desire in the history of Western philosophy, including Plato, Aristotle, the Epicureans, the Stoics, Thomas Aquinas, Spinoza, and Adam Smith, not to mention countless contemporary writers in philosophy and in related fields (such as anthropology and cognitive psychology). It is therefore a sign of the problem I am discussing that Becker and others entertained this idea only recently, when work on phenomena such as addiction made its importance obvious, despite the fact that it had importance as well for earlier work on human capital formation.[1] Adam Smith evidently believed that a pretty good way for an economist to spend his life was to teach and read a great deal of philosophy; he may have been right.

Let me now, however, turn to seven issues less frequently discussed where the same problem, I believe, obtains: powerful philosophical arguments that cast doubt on current foundations are being ignored. As we proceed, it is important to bear in mind that Law and Economics is, in effect, both an explanatory/predictive and a normative theory. Typically it presents itself as explanatory/predictive; but through a certain characteristic use of the concept of rationality, it ends up making normative judgments as well. Thus Richard Posner, for example, both characterizes (most) human behavior as rational in the precise descriptive sense he gives to that term, and then, shifting over to a normative use of the same term, blames certain other agents for not conforming their behavior to those standards.[2] I shall attempt to distinguish these two uses of the theory wherever that is possible and relevant. My economic examples will generally be drawn from the areas with which my work has made me most familiar: development and welfare.

Plural utility and non-commensurability

A commitment to the commensurability of all an agent's ends runs very deep in the Law and Economics movement. Even when a plurality of distinct ends is initially recognized, the underlying view that agents are "maximizers of satisfactions," and that satisfaction is something that varies in degree rather than in kind, leads the theorist rapidly back to the idea that distinctions among options should be understood in terms of the quantity of utility they afford, rather than in terms of any basic qualitative differences. (Thus Posner, having identified three distinct ends of sexual activity, proceeds to treat choices and tradeoffs between them as if they were choices between differing amounts of a homogeneous good.[3]) Even though this is not offered as an account of how agents internally view their choices, it is assumed that casting choices this way will allow us to make correct predictions about the behavior of most people.

Plato (and Henry Sidgwick, following his lead) proceeded in just this way, holding that we would have an adequate ethical science only if we did establish it as a "science of measurement," in which all the diverse values that people ordinarily pursue were understood as merely different quantities of a single over-arching value.[4] They took this course because they believed that only in this way could human action be systematized and rendered lawlike.[5] But they portrayed their project from the start as radically revisionary, rather than explanatory of current behavior: they were offering people a tool by which they could think and act more "scientifically," and hence behave differently – not offering an accurate way of explaining and predicting what real people think and do.[6] Indeed, according to Plato's highly persuasive account, the genuine recognition of values as commensurable would change human action utterly, removing the passionate longing for distinct individuals that gives much of human life a messy character, and even removing the common phenomenon of *akrasia*, in which an agent judges one course of action better than another but does the worse. Plato convincingly argued that a person who recognized no qualitative distinctions in value would never have this problem, and would therefore behave very differently on a number of important occasions. Following his lead, later philosophers had a great deal to say about the "therapeutic" advantages of commensurability in altering human behavior, removing, for example, many grounds for emotions such as jealousy and anger that currently explain a great deal of human action. Sidgwick, too, insisted that a true utilitarian agent would choose differently from most people, although for complicated reasons he thought that society, to be well coordinated, should contain only a small number of such agents.[7]

If we consider some central texts in Law and Economics, the Plato/Sidgwick claim is borne out: we see the world remade, not the world we live in. For example, Posner's descriptions of human sexuality, in *Sex and Reason*, do not convey the sense that we are looking at sex the way people generally look at it; instead, a perspective of lofty detachment has flattened and simplified things that are usually messy and real. More important, it would appear that Plato and Sidgwick are correct about the magnitude of the differences: they seem sufficient to affect greatly the model's predictive value.[8]

This criticism (put more generally) is by now a common point in mainstream economics. Invoking John Stuart Mill's version of this ancient point, Amartya Sen, for example, has argued that welfare economists, to have an adequate predictive theory, should understand utility "primarily as a vector (with several distinct components), and only secondarily as some homogeneous magnitude." Such a view will offer, he claims, "a significantly richer descriptive account of a person's well-being," in ways that make better predictions possible.[9] Whether these predictive differences are significant enough to affect the usefulness of models remains, of course, an empirical question; the answer may well vary from one area of economics to another. Sen has made a good case, however, for the conclusion that welfare and development economists must confront this issue and produce arguments that either refute his position by applying utility theory to predict messy real-world human behavior, or incorporate plural vectors in models that better predict real-world behavior.

Sen's challenge remains unanswered. Sen's criticism does not rely on the idea that assumptions must be realistic. Milton Friedman long ago correctly argued that positive economics, like other sciences, can and should use simple assumptions that do not in all respects correspond to the complex phenomenology of real human action.[10] What is at issue is the question of whether the assumptions are too crude, so oversimple that they fail to single out those aspects of the world that are most salient for predictive purposes. Here the Law and Economics movement has tended to follow the views of Karl Popper, who held that even extremely crude assumptions are frequently aids to scientific progress: as experience falsifies them, they are re-formulated and progress is made.[11] But Popper had an extravagant admiration for the hypotheses of the ancient Greek pre-Socratic philosophers. Thales's dictum that the world is made of water and Heraclitus's opposing claim that everything is fire were to Popper bold conjectures that promoted good prediction and scientific discovery![12] Sen's point, in essence, I think, is that the assumption of commensurability is all too like Thales's assumption: too simple to lead to illuminating and pertinent prediction.

If commensurability leads to inadequate explanation and prediction, does it still, as Plato and Sidgwick thought, offer us a normative theory of rationality that will help us remake our world? Again, the philosophical tradition from Aristotle to Mill has given us many reasons to question this idea. Complex accounts of reasonable choosing put forward in Aristotle, Mill, and other more recent philosophers show us that there is no good reason to suppose that commensurability is a prerequisite of rational choice in the normative sense.[13] Furthermore, they show us that to make two ends commensurable when there are good reasons for thinking them distinct in quality is itself a piece of irrationality, one that can frequently be explained just as Plato and Sidgwick explain it: as a reaction against the complexity of life and as the expression of a desire for a purer and cleaner existence. But such reactions are not always rational in the normative sense: they may express hatred of a world that contains surprise and suffering, and a desire to punish those elements of the world that occasion surprise by refusing them the recognition that their qualitative distinctness urges.

One area in which the refusal to recognize plural ends has been especially pernicious is development economics, by now heavily intertwined with law and normative public policy. Until rather recently, "the quality of life" in a nation was assessed simply by enumerating GNP per capita. This crude norm did not even make salient the distribution of wealth and income, and thus routinely gave high marks to nations such as South Africa, with its tremendous inequalities. Still less did it ask about the connection of GNP to other areas of human functioning that are important indicators of quality of life: areas such as life expectancy, infant mortality, educational attainment, and the presence or absence of political liberties.[14] More recently, a plural-valued approach inspired by Aristotle has begun to have considerable influence on the ways in which international agencies make normative assessments.[15] This progress needs to be acknowledged in areas of Law and Economics that deal with human welfare.

One corollary of the recognition of qualitatively distinct ends is the recognition of contingent moral dilemmas, conflicts in which one cannot satisfy all the distinct claims that legitimately demand recognition. Once again, this is an issue that has inspired a large literature in philosophical and, by now, economic accounts of rationality.[16] It seems reasonable to think that the recognition of such contingent conflicts is both an important part of daily life, influencing behavior in ways that are significant, and also an important part of a normative account of social rationality. Conflicts in which the competing concerns are not *in principle* irreconcilable, but in which the conflict arises from the structure of a particular situation, can alert us to the presence of irrationality and/or injustice in our social institutions.[17] We notice, for example, that although women and men in our own world face many painful conflicts between the demands of child care and the demands of work, this conflict is not intrinsic to the goods involved, and could be either reduced or removed in a world with more public support for parental leave and child care, and less hostility to parenthood in the established structure of careers.

Notice that this kind of recognition of moral dilemmas entails the rejection of the economic principle of the *independence of irrelevant alternatives*: we make progress by comparing our present set of options (unfavorably) with another imaginable set, in which agents could fulfill all their deepest commitments without conflict.[18]

There are many deep questions here; I have only gestured toward them. They need to be debated in any adequate merger of economics with law.

Well-being and agency

Suppose we now supply Law and Economics with a richer account of utility: is that the end of the problem? There are many reasons to think it is not. Utility is standardly considered (for example, by Posner) as a state of the agent, a state of satisfaction. Here Law and Economics follows both Jeremy Bentham and Sidgwick; even if we add a Millean account of the plurality of satisfactions, we are still dealing only with states of well-being. But agents also act and choose, and this makes an explanatory and a moral difference. In addition to states of well-being, people value and pursue their own agency. They do not typically view as equivalent two states of the world, one produced by their own agency and the other not. Aristotle argued that for most people the main thing that makes life worth living is voluntary action, and that people would not choose any amount of contentment if it were not accompanied by space for choice and practical reason: to do so would be to "choose the life of dumb grazing animals."[19] Criticizing Bentham, Mill similarly spoke of the difference between Socrates unsatisfied and a pig satisfied.[20] Any theory that ignores this distinction thus courts gross explanatory inadequacy. (It makes it very difficult to understand why people struggle so hard for various types of freedom and agency, as they clearly do, why for many people in the world of my childhood the slogan "Better dead than Red" had profound explanatory significance, and so forth.) It might be claimed that the value of choice and practical reason can be cashed out in terms of a "psychic good" that can be understood to be a part of utility. But such arguments need to be made; they certainly run the risk of making the concept of utility utterly vacuous and lacking in predictive value. Any approach along these lines must show how it can solve this problem.[21] Once again, the problem may be more serious for some areas of Law and Economics than for others, but it needs to be addressed.

If a focus on well-being to the exclusion of agency offers inadequate explanations, it seems even more clearly inadequate as a normative theory of rational choice. For it seems normatively irrational (and seems so, indeed, to many of the founders of the Law and Economics movement, with their strong libertarian affiliations) to consider two states of the world equivalent when one involves the liberty of action and the other does not. Again, it is not my contention that Law and Economics cannot meet this challenge; economics has done so already, in quite a few ways.[22] But the challenge cannot simply be ignored, and the answer will need to be subtle enough to grapple with the considerable philosophical literature that by now exists on this question.[23]

Like the plurality of ends, the distinct importance of agency is by now routinely recognized in development economics. The dominant approaches of both Amartya Sen and Partha Dasgupta (along with Sudhir Anand, Jean Drbze, and many others) make it a matter of course to recognize distinct domains of human *functioning* and *capability* that are not commensurable along a single metric, and with regard to which choice and liberty of agency play a fundamental structuring role.[24] Moreover, far from being recondite philosophical subtleties, these notions are in common use by international agencies, structuring their ways of measuring welfare and quality of life.[25] This shows that taking conceptual distinctions seriously does not hobble science or policy; it actually enables both to progress in humanly useful directions.

Neglect of agency brings with it a common corollary: neglect of the separateness of persons as an important issue in personal and social choice.[26] Sidgwick, for example, proceeded as if the satisfactions of all rational agents could be regarded, for purposes of choice, as fused into a single system; the boundaries between agents were not regarded as salient when one considered how to augment society's total welfare. No philosopher I know of has ever argued that this kind of boundary-neglect provides an adequate explanatory theory, and it is obvious that it does not.

People care deeply about the difference between a pain in their own life and a pain in China (to use Adam Smith's graphic example).[27] Even Buddhism, in which this disregard of individuation is regarded as normatively superior, presents itself as a revisionary theory that does not offer good accounts of actual behavior. What might, however, be argued is that neglect of boundaries provides a normatively superior theory, by breaking down a kind of irrational egoism that leads us unjustly to rig things in favor of our own position. This is one of the most difficult issues in moral and political philosophy; I cannot even adequately describe its complexity here. Suffice it to say, however, that much good argument suggests that neglect of boundaries is not the best way to ensure the most relevant and justice-producing impartiality.

The separateness of one person from another can be strongly defended as a basic fact for ethics and politics, one that will stop a normative account from justifying one group's extreme misery by pointing to the extreme satisfaction of another group, as classical utilitarians often do.[28] There are certainly arguments on both sides here; many thinkers in Law and Economics will probably wish to defend Sidgwick's normative views against the criticisms of John Rawls, T.M. Scanlon, Brian Barry, and others.[29] But then they will need to grapple with the arguments; this has not yet been done.

Libertarianism, utilitarianism, Paretianism

Practitioners of Law and Economics typically rely on the ideas of utilitarianism, for example, the idea of wealth maximization. They typically also portray themselves as libertarians, committed to giving personal liberty of choice a strong degree of priority. Finally, they characteristically endorse Pareto optimality as a normative criterion of social choice. But these three views are not all consistent. Insofar as utilitarianism is committed to aggregating utilities across persons and pursuing the greatest total (or average) utility, it is committed to respecting liberty rather less than most libertarians (and most liberals) would wish to do. If infringing political liberties and liberties of expression, speech, and conscience turns out to be what in fact, in some circumstance, maximizes utility, the utilitarian favors that course as best. (Obviously, we are focusing on normative issues here.) Libertarians, by contrast, are committed to giving liberty priority even when that does not maximize welfare. It has long been recognized that in this respect the two positions are on a collision course.[30] One may grant, along with Mill, that liberty frequently does enhance social welfare;[31] but once one grants the distinction it is implausible to suppose things will always be thus. And if one tries dogmatically to rig things so that restrictions on liberty always result in more utility losses than gains, one is simply robbing the idea of utility-maximizing of any predictive value. This has been belatedly recognized in at least some parts of the Law and Economics movement. For example, Posner has recently stated that his economic approach to the regulation of sexuality is in tension with the normative libertarianism he espouses.[32] But why did we have to rediscover the wheel? Once again, grasping established distinctions in philosophy would have made more progress possible sooner.

As for the relationship between Pareto optimality and libertarianism, it is much debated. The huge literature by now responding to Amartya Sen's *The Impossibility of a Paretian Liberal*[33] has shown, at any rate, that there is no easy way of resolving the tension between the two principles, so long as we do not exclude nosy preferences from the social choice function. Many different approaches have been tried by many philosophers and economists, and we would expect writers in Law and Economics to acquaint themselves with those debates more than they have in fact done.

Rational deliberation about ends

It is a dogma of neoclassical economics, and of rational choice theory, that we can deliberate rationally only about the instrumental means to ends, and not about the content of ends themselves. This dogma, which relies on the idea that our ends are hard-wired by exogenously given tastes, has been seriously shaken by the recognition of the endogeneity of preferences. The recognition that we have some control over the shaping of our tastes (both through the shaping of laws, policies, and institutions, and through personal self-shaping and the educating of children) must at least make us ponder the question of whether this shaping can be done more or less well. But Law and Economics has not deeply investigated this question.

In terms of both explanation and normative argument, this is a flaw. People do deliberate about ends all the time. To give an example close to home, a student who aims at becoming a lawyer does certainly deliberate about instrumental means to that goal: about how to get a good score on the LSAT, about which law schools to apply to, about how to do well once there. But he or she typically deliberates in another way as well, asking what *counts as* being a good lawyer – is it a matter of making money, or serving the poor, or seeking intellectual stimulation, or some complex mixture of more than one of these? Such deliberations, which seek to *specify* the content of a vague end, do not have the simple vertical structure of means–ends deliberation. They typically proceed by moving horizontally, consulting other ends the person may have. How much importance does money have in her life? What commitments does she have to social justice? Does she want to have children? And so forth. Notice that all of this will not only lead to a more precise specification of the end, but also to a more refined selection of instrumental means: for it seems plausible to suppose that it will influence her choice of law school and courses of study. At the same time, her deliberations about lawyering will probably also cast new light on her other ends, giving her a sense, for example, of how she might want to specify the vague ends of "having children," "serving justice," and so forth. And of course, in the context of deliberation about other ends – say, having children or serving justice – she may also ask about the whole end of being a lawyer, as to whether it is one she really wishes to pursue. This is how we really do deliberate in life, in this holistic manner that seeks broad coherence and fit among our ends considered as a group. This picture of deliberation was first advanced by Aristotle, and it has recently been prominently revived in some excellent work by David Wiggins and Henry Richardson.[34]

Work by Wiggins, Richardson, and others has made it very plausible to suppose that considering the concrete specification of plural, interconnected ends provides a very good description of how real people deliberate, and a fact so central that it seems unlikely to be irrelevant to a model's predictive value.[35] At any rate, if some area of Law and Economics wants to show that it is predictively insignificant, the argument needs to be made. It also seems clear that we can describe normative criteria for rationality within this type of deliberation. Indeed, it would appear that any deliberation that doesn't include this kind of specificationist approach is bound to be blinkered and (normatively) *irrational*. Moreover, it can easily be extended to interpersonal deliberation, and thus to social choice.[36] Once again, Law and Economics cannot afford to proceed as though all these arguments do not exist. If it wishes to rebut them, on either the explanatory or the normative plane, it must first confront them.

Preference, desire, emotion, intention, action

Law and Economics typically recognizes a rather reduced number of explanatory entities behind human action. Indeed, the capacious category "preference" seems to cover all of the psychological underpinnings of action, both cognitive and conative. At least there is a distinction made between preference and action: following Becker rather than Paul Samuelson, Law and Economics has typically treated preferences as items that have psychological reality and can be individuated to some extent independently of the actions they explain. By proceeding in this way, it has avoided some of the conceptual quagmire that characterizes the Samuelson revealed-preference approach.[37]

But what an impoverished repertory of explanatory entities! Western philosophers, ever since Plato and Aristotle, have agreed that the explanation of human action requires quite a few distinct concepts; these include the concepts of belief, desire, perception, appetite, and emotion – *at the very least*. Some contemporary philosophers have felt that Aristotle was basically right, and that we do not need any categories other than those he introduced.[38] Others have not been so satisfied. The Stoics introduced a further notion of *impulse* (*hormê*), in the belief that the Aristotelian categories did not altogether capture the innate tendency of things to preserve their being. In a related move, Spinoza introduced the idea of *conatus*, and gave it great prominence. Kant was partial to the notion of *inclination* (*Neigung*), feeling that it captured features of emotion and desire not fully included in the Aristotelian/medieval framework. Recently some philosophers have argued that the concept of *intention* is both irreducible to any of the others and an essential part of explaining action.[39] And of course others have shown an interest in the concepts introduced by psychoanalysis.

These concepts are introduced as basic to *explanation and prediction*, not simply as concepts that agents actually use.[40] In addition to these rich beginnings, there have been centuries of very subtle work on each of the Aristotelian notions, asking about the relationship between emotion and belief, between both of these and desire, and so forth.[41] This work makes the two claims both normative and predictive, saying both what emotions, desires, appetites, and beliefs will sway an ideally rational agent and also how the behavior of someone who is moved by an emotion, for example grief or compassion, is likely to differ from the behavior of a person who is moved by an appetite with no cognitive content – or by rational self-interest. Some especially important predictive consequences lie in the area of education. Philosophers claim that emotions respond to education in a way that is very different from the way in which intellectual calculations and non-cognitive appetites respond, and they predict accordingly the results of different educational strategies.[42]

Here, more than anywhere else, the foundations of Law and Economics look as yet underdeveloped and crude. If we do not even bother to sort out the many different ways in which people (and other animals[43]) are moved, how can we hope to have an adequate descriptive, much less a normative, theory? Law and Economics has just barely reached the point at which it is able to distinguish between Becker and Samuelson (and this was not always the case); it has not yet put itself onto the map of conceptually respectable theories of human action. This was not so, of course, in the early days of political economy: Adam Smith is one of the greatest thinkers about the relationship between emotion and action, and he seems to have thought that this inquiry (both predictive and normative) was an important part of thinking about the economy and public policy, besides being of intrinsic interest.

The complexity of ethical motivation

If Law and Economics is ignorant of the theories of human action that have been painstakingly elaborated over the course of 2,400 years, it is not terribly likely that it will see all the complexities of the ways in which people are moved by ethical considerations. And in fact it does not. *Homo economicus* is a self-interested maximizer of his own satisfactions (or, occasionally, a classical utilitarian maximizer of social welfare). Altruism tends to be reduced to a type of egoism, in which people get reputational or psychic goods for themselves. For some time it has been influentially argued within economics that this approach is inadequate, even for predictive purposes: we need to recognize sympathy and commitment as independent sources of motivation.[44] This is hardly a surprising claim, because it is one that has been argued throughout the history of Western philosophy – starting, again, with Aristotle, who argued that people who die for their friends or family cannot plausibly be said to do so for satisfaction, because they are risking or forfeiting, in the process, all prospect of future satisfaction. A theory that focuses on satisfaction will therefore make bad predictions about what they will do.[45] Recently these ideas have been receiving striking empirical confirmation: it has been powerfully argued that economic theories could not have predicted that anyone would risk life, family, comfort, and reputation to rescue Jews during the Holocaust. And yet a significant number of people did.[46] Again, this does not mean that practitioners of Law and Economics need agree with these results, nor does it entail that they cannot show that for their particular purposes in a given project these facts are predictively irrelevant. But then they have some work to do, both empirical and conceptual, to show how they will explain the behavior of such altruists without new conceptual resources.

Modeling the family

All of the conceptual complexities discussed above arise in a strange and fascinating way in the model of the family most influential in the Law and Economics movement, namely Gary Becker's. Whereas for the most part altruism plays a small role in accounts of economic motivation (or is, as I said, reduced to something else), in Becker's account of the family it plays a stunningly central role.

The head of the household is assumed to be a beneficent altruist who will adequately take cognizance of all the interests of all family members, in the process of maximizing the utility of the household as a whole. It is likely that altruism is to be understood as elsewhere in Becker's work, as a variety of self-interest;[47] nonetheless, its centrality here is striking.

What we have said so far gives us several reasons to be uneasy with this approach, as either an explanatory or a normative account of the way things are. It assumes a rather slender number of motives. (And Becker now says as much. In his 1992 Nobel Prize lecture he points out that "[m]any economists, including me, have excessively relied on altruism to tie together the interests of family members." He suggests that he should have included, as well, motives such as fear, guilt, "and other attitudes."[48]) The model treats the concerns of all as an aggregate and the household as a single organic whole, thus neglecting the salience of boundaries between persons. We cannot even find out how A or B are doing, we can only find out how the whole household is doing – and yet we are assured that all is well, because no tradeoffs that slight any member's interests will be made. The potential conflict between maximization of well-being and making some members do badly is not stated or faced. What this means is that the model offers no predictions at all, much less correct ones, about a number of very real questions, such as: When there is a food shortage, which children will be fed? How is domestic violence likely to be correlated with household income? What influence does education have on the nutrition of female children? Should we expect the health status of widows in India to be higher or lower than that of widowers?[49]

The fact is that the household is far from being a harmonious unit, even when, as may be the case in families, its members love each other. (Oddly, this also is not how economics assumes people *usually* are, so we have a complex problem of consistency on our hands as well.) Real families contain much altruism, but they also contain conflicts over resources, and different bargaining positions that situate agents differently with respect to those conflicts. We must understand these different bargaining positions before we can make any prediction at all about a wide range of urgent questions of well-being and agency. Such an understanding is also crucial to an adequate normative account of family law, because law is one of the factors that most decisively structures the bargaining positions of such agents – saying who can marry, what divorce involves, what rights wives have against domestic violence and marital rape, what rights children do and don't have, and so forth. In short, the defects in the standard economic model of the family have enormous explanatory and predictive significance, as well as great normative significance when public policy attempts to address these problems.

As Richard Posner valuably recognized in his remarks, this has been a major area of feminist criticism against Law and Economics, and a valid area of criticism.[50] Moreover, it is not only feminists who have pressed these claims; it is, by now, a large part of the economics profession, where bargaining models have more or less displaced the older organic models as the standard ways of modeling family interactions. As I say, Becker himself has recognized that his model is seriously flawed, although he has not, to my knowledge, endorsed a bargaining model as opposed to an organic model.

These shortcomings are closely bound up with other shortcomings in Law and Economics's conception of its foundations. Neglect personal boundaries, the distinction between agency and well-being, and the diverse varieties of human motivation, and you are very likely to come out with an impoverished theory of the family. Law and Economics should address this important area of human life, and economists interested in law are doing so already.[51] If practitioners of Law and Economics ignore this work, it will continue to go forward without them.

Conclusion

Aristotle thought that there was conceptual progress in political thought. For when we sit down and sort through all the good and bad arguments our major predecessors have made, we will learn a lot:

> Some of these things have been said by many people over a long period of time, others by a few distinguished people; it is reasonable to suppose that none of them has missed the target totally, but each has gotten something or even a lot of things right.[52]

Furthermore, we will also be enabled to avoid their errors. Finally, perhaps, we will ourselves make a little progress beyond them. Aristotle also noticed, however, that the passion for science and simplicity frequently lead highly intelligent people into conceptual confusion and an impoverished view of the human world. So he did not think that progress was inevitable, and one of his great arguments for reading was that it could remind us of conceptual complexities we might otherwise efface, in our zeal to make life more tractable than it is.

Science does not have to be impoverished; in fact, it must not be, if it is to deliver perspicuous descriptions, adequate predictions, and, perhaps, helpful normative recommendations. But Law and Economics is currently still somewhat impoverished. It is impoverished because it did not proceed in the way that Aristotle recommends, sitting down with the arguments of eminent predecessors to see what can be learned from their years of labor. Let us hope that this process will soon begin. There would seem to be no better place for it to begin than in Chicago.

Notes

* Ernst Freund Professor of Law and Ethics, University of Chicago Law School, Philosophy Department, and Divinity School. I would like to thank Douglas Baird, Richard Posner, Mark Ramseyer, and Cass Sunstein for their helpful comments on an earlier draft, and Ross Davies for invaluable research assistance. This chapter was originally published in *University of Chicago Law Review* 64, 1997: 1197–1214.

1 Becker now states that discrimination on the basis of race and sex can cause people to form low aspirations and hopes, and therefore to underinvest in their human capital. See (Becker 1993). We should not congratulate people for rediscovering something whose predictive importance has already been discovered and convincingly defended by others, if the arguments of those others were publicly available.

2 See, for example (Posner 1983), where Posner first makes the assumption that people are "rational maximizers of their satisfactions," ibid. at 1, and then goes on to criticize Supreme Court privacy decisions for not conforming to rationality, as he has previously defined it, calling the privacy decisions a "topsy-turvy world." Ibid., at 345.

3 (Posner 1992), recognizing three distinct ends; ibid. at 115–142, discussing tradeoffs in quantitative terms. See also (Nussbaum 1992).

4 See (Nussbaum 1986, chapter 4).

5 The best discussion of Sidgwick's philosophical motivations is in (Richardson 1994, chapter 5).

6 On Plato, see (Nussbaum 1990, chapter 3); on Sidgwick, see my discussion in (Nussbaum 1986) at 112–117. See also (Richardson 1994, chapter 5).

7 See (Nussbaum 1990) at 113. See also (Wiggins 1980a).

8 See (Nussbaum 1992) arguing this point in detail.

9 See (Sen 1980); see also (Sen and Williams 1982, "Introduction"), for related criticisms of economic utilitarianism.

10 (Friedman 1984). Interestingly enough, Friedman held that the science of sociology does require realistic assumptions. Ibid., at 236.

11 See (Popper 1974); see also (Popper 1959).

12 (Popper 1974), at 136–165.

13 See (Richardson 1994, chapter 6). On Aristotle, see (Nussbaum 1986, chapter 10) and (Nussbaum 1990, chapter 2). On Mill's normative critique of Bentham, see (Sen 1980), at 193.

14 See (Nussbaum and Sen 1993, "Introduction"). United Nations Development Programme, Human Development Reports have used a plural measure based on Sen's work since 1993. See, for example (United Nations Development Programme, Human Development Report 1995: 15–23).

15 See, for example, the (United Nations Development Programme, Human Development Report 1995).

16 For a long, but only partial, list of modern philosophers who have addressed this concern, see (Nussbaum 1986), at 27 and note 6. See also (Nussbaum 1990, chapter 2); and (Gowans 1994). In economics, see (Sen 1987).

17 This point was well made by (Hegel 1920). For contemporary discussion, see (O'Neill 1996) and (Marcus 1980).

18 See my discussion of Arrow in (Nussbaum 1990) at 64–65 and note 23. See also (Sen 1987); and (Richardson 1994), chapter 5 at 111–118.

19 (Aristotle 1894) at 1096a1–2, 1098b33–1099a7, 1176a33–35. (Aristotle 1991) at 1215b22–31, 1216a3–8. See also (Nussbaum 1995).

20 (Mill 1950, "Utilitarianism"). Mill's example actually makes two points: one about qualitative differences within satisfactions, and the other about the need to move beyond satisfaction in seeking to understand what agents have reason to pursue.

21 On Aristotle's approach, see (Nussbaum 1986, chapter 10) and, more generally, (Sen 1985a).

22 See (Sen 1985a). See also (Sen 1982), and, for implications in development economics, see (Sen 1984). See also the role played by liberty in (Dasgupta 1994).

23 Within the utilitarian tradition recently, see (Griffin 1986).

24 See (Sen 1984, 1985b, 1994); (Drze and Sen 1995); (Dasgupta 1994). See also the (United Nations Development Programme's Human Development Report 1995).

25 For an independent defense of similar concepts, see (Allardt 1993); (Erikson 1993).

Sen's approach has structured the United Nations Development Programme's Human Development Reports since 1993, with Anand as co-consultant. See (United Nations Development Programme's Human Development Report 1995).

26 This is clearly an issue for well-being too, not just for agency. For reasons of economy, I consider it only here.
27 See (Smith 1984), at 136–137. See also (Coase 1976).
28 See (Rawls 1971) §§5, 30.
29 See, for example, ibid.; (Scanlon 1975); (Barry 1995).
30 The materials for this point are already in Aristotle and the Stoics, but its clearest formulations are modern. One excellent treatment is in (Rawls 1971) at §§28–29, for whom that clash is the central reason for rejecting utilitarianism.
31 (Mill 1950, "On Liberty").
32 (Posner 1995) at 23–24, granting that economic thinking has "illiberal implications" and that we "cannot make [them] disappear by judicious assignment of rights.
33 (Sen 1982, chapter 13).
34 See (Wiggins 1980b); (Richardson 1994, chapter 10). Both give detailed arguments about Aristotle's views that point the reader to all the relevant passages in Aristotle.
35 See (Richardson 1994).
36 Ibid., chapter 11.
37 See, for example (Sen 1993).
38 See, for example (von Wright 1963); (Davidson 1980).
39 See (Bratman 1987). See also (Anscombe 1969).
40 Frequently they will not correspond straightforwardly to the way agents see their actions, and some of the beings whose actions are being explained, such as nonhuman animals, are not thought to have concepts at all.
41 Emotions are standardly thought to involve complex cognitive content and to be modifiable by the modification of belief; many desires have less cognitive content, and some may resist modification.
42 We can add that non-Western philosophical traditions also have contributed a great deal along these lines. See, generally (Marks and Ames 1995) and (Matilal 1986).
43 See Aristotle's *De Motu Animalium*, proposing a common schema for the explanation of all animal motion.
44 See (Sen 1977).
45 (Aristotle 1894), at 1174a4–8, 1117b10 *et seq.*, 1169a18–b2.
46 See (Monroe 1996).
47 See, for example, (Becker 1976). See also the critique in (Monroe 1996), at 162–164.
48 (Becker 1993), at 400.
49 Becker's recent remarks do not indicate that he intends to disaggregate the family into its separate components; apparently he still prefers an organic model in which the motives of the head of the household stand in for the whole, though these motives are now made more complex.
50 See (Sen 1990); (Agarwal 1997); (Lundberg and Pollak 1996); (Dasgupta 1994, chapter 11).
51 See, for example (Agarwal 1994, 1997).
52 (Aristotle 1894), at 1098b28–30.

References

Agarwal, B. (1994) *A Field of One's Own: Gender and Land Rights in South Asia*, Cambridge: Cambridge University Press.
Agarwal, B. (March 1997) '"Bargaining" and gender relations: within and beyond the household', FCND Discussion Paper, International Food Policy Research Institute.
Allardt, E. (1993) 'Having, loving, being: an alternative to the Swedish model of welfare

research', in M. Nussbaum and A. Sen (eds.), *The Quality of Life*, Oxford: Oxford University Press.

Anscombe, G.E.M. (1969) *Intention*, (2nd edn.), Ithaca, NY: Cornell University Press.

Aristotle (1894) *Nicomachean Ethics* (I. Bywater, ed.) Oxford: Oxford University Press.

Aristotle (1991) *Eudemian Ethics* (R.R. Walzer and J.M. Mingay, eds.) Oxford: Oxford University Press.

Barry, B. (1995) *Justice as Impartiality*, New York: Oxford University Press.

Becker, G.S. (1976) *The Economic Approach to Human Behavior*, Chicago, IL: University of Chicago Press.

Becker, G.S. 'Nobel lecture: the economic way of looking at behavior', *Journal of Political Economy* 101, 1993: 385–409.

Bratman, M.E. (1987) *Intentions, Plans, and Practical Reason*, Cambridge, MA: Harvard University Press.

Coase, R.A. 'Adam Smith's view of man', *Journal of Law and Economics* 19, 1976: 529–546.

Dasgupta, P. (1994) *An Inquiry Into Well-Being and Destitution*, Oxford: Clarendon Press.

Davidson, D. (1980) *Essays on Actions and Events*, Oxford: Oxford University Press.

Drze J. and Sen, A. (1995) *India: Economic Development and Social Opportunity*, Oxford: Oxford University Press.

Erikson, R. (1993) 'Descriptions of inequality: the Swedish approach to welfare research', in M. Nussbaum and A. Sen (eds.), *The Quality of Life*, Oxford: Oxford University Press.

Friedman, M. (1984) 'The methodology of positive economics', in D.M. Hausman, (ed.), *The Philosophy of Economics: An Anthology*, Cambridge: Cambridge University Press.

Gowans, C.W. (1994) *Innocence Lost: An Examination of Inescapable Moral Wrongdoing*, Oxford: Oxford University Press.

Griffin, J. (1986) *Well-Being: Its Meaning, Measurement, and Moral Importance*, Oxford: Oxford University Press.

Hegel, G.W.F. (1920) 'Antigone: the philosophy of fine art – vol. 4', translation by P.B. Osmaston (London; G. Bell and Sons), reprinted in *Hegel on Tragedy*, A. Paolucci and H. Paolucci (eds.) New York: Harper & Row, 1975.

Lundberg, S. and Pollak, R. 'Bargaining and distribution in marriage', *Journal of Economic Perspectives* 10, 1996: 139–158.

Marcus, R.B. 'Moral dilemmas and consistency', *Journal of Philosophy* 77, 1980: 121–136.

Marks, J. and Ames, R.T. (eds.) (1995) *Emotions in Asian Thought: A Dialogue in Comparative Philosophy*, Albany, NY: State University of New York Press.

Matilal, B.K. (1986) *Perception: An Essay on Classical Indian Theories of Knowledge*, Oxford: Oxford University Press.

Mill, J.S. (1950) *Utilitarianism, Liberty, and Representative Government*, New York: E.P. Dutton & Co.

Monroe, K.R. (1996) *The Heart of Altruism: Perceptions of a Common Humanity*, Princeton, NJ: Princeton University Press.

Nussbaum, M.C. (1986) *The Fragility of Goodness: Luck and Ethics in Greek Tragedy and Philosophy*, New York: Cambridge University Press.

Nussbaum, M.C. (1990) *Love's Knowledge: Essays on Philosophy and Literature*, New York: Oxford University Press.

Nussbaum, M.C. '"Only grey matter"? Richard Posner's cost–benefit analysis of sex', *University of Chicago Law Review* 59, 1992: 1689–1734.

Nussbaum, M.C. (1995) 'Aristotle on human nature and the foundations of ethics', in J.E.J. Altham and R. Harrison (eds.) *World, Mind, and Ethics: Essays on the Ethical Philosophy of Bernard Williams*, Cambridge: Cambridge University Press.

Nussbaum, M.C. and Sen, A. (eds.) (1993) *The Quality of Life*, New York: Oxford University Press.

O'Neill, O. (1996) *Towards Justice and Virtue: A Constructive Account of Practical Reasoning*, Cambridge: Cambridge University Press.

Popper, K. R (1959) *The Logic of Scientific Discovery*, London: Hutchinson & Co.

Popper, K.R. (1974). *Conjectures and Refutations: The Growth of Scientific Knowledge*, London: Routledge.

Posner, R.A. (1983) *The Economics of Justice*, Cambridge, MA: Harvard University Press.

Posner, R.A. (1992) *Sex and Reason*, Cambridge, MA: Harvard University Press.

Posner, R.A. (1995) *Overcoming Law*, Cambridge, MA: Harvard University Press.

Rawls, J. (1971) *A Theory of Justice*, Cambridge, MA: Belknap Press.

Richardson, H.S. (1994) *Practical Reasoning About Final Ends*, Cambridge: Cambridge University Press.

Scanlon, T.M. 'Preference and urgency', *Journal of Philosophy* 72, 1975: 655–669.

Sen, A. 'Rational fools: a critique of the behavioral foundations of economic theory', *Philosophy and Public Affairs* 6, 1977: 317–344; reprinted in Sen, A. (1982) *Choice, Welfare, and Measurement*, Oxford: Basil Blackwell.

Sen, A. 'Plural utility', *Proceedings of the Aristotelian Society* 81, 1980: 193–215.

Sen, A. (1982) *Choice, Welfare, and Measurement*, Oxford: Basil Blackwell.

Sen, A. (1984) *Resources, Values, and Development*, Cambridge, MA: Harvard University Press.

Sen, A. 'Well-being, agency and freedom: the Dewey lectures – 1984', *Journal of Philosophy* 82, 1985a: 169–221.

Sen, A. (1985b) *Commodities and Capabilities*, Oxford: Elsevier.

Sen, A. (1987) *On Ethics and Economics*, Oxford: Basil Blackwell.

Sen, A. (1990) 'Gender and cooperative conflicts', in I. Tinker (ed.), *Persistent Inequalities: Women and World Development*, New York: Oxford University Press.

Sen, A. 'Internal consistency of choice', *Econometrica* 61, 1993: 495–521.

Sen, A. 'Freedoms and needs: an argument for the primacy of political rights', *New Republic* 31, January 10 and 17, 1994.

Sen, A. and Williams, B. (eds.) (1982) *Utilitarianism and Beyond*, Cambridge: Cambridge University Press.

Smith, A. (1759, reprint 1984) *The Theory of Moral Sentiments* (reprint 1984) Indianapolis, IN: Liberty Fund.

United Nations Development Programme (1995) *Human Development Report*, Oxford: Oxford University Press.

von Wright, G.H. (1963) *The Varieties of Goodness*, London: Routledge.

Wiggins, D. (1980a) 'Weakness of will, commensurability, and the objects of deliberation and desire', in A.O. Rorty (ed.), *Essays on Aristotle's Ethics*, Berkeley, CA: University of California Press.

Wiggins, D. (1980b) 'Deliberation and practical reason', in A.O. Rorty (ed.), *Essays on Aristotle's Ethics*, Berkeley, CA: University of California Press.

3 Norms and values in the study of law

*Lawrence M. Friedman**

There is a lot to like in Richard Posner's take on the economic approach to law – especially the cautious claims he makes for his field. He has certainly done more than anybody else to *create* law and economics; and to apply economic insights to law. His chapter, which is the basis of the first part of this collection, is quite admirable, as far as it goes. I would like, however, to make a modest claim on behalf of the other social sciences, and their approach to the study of law and the legal system. Posner hardly mentions them; I say this without rancor, since it was, after all, not the subject he was addressing. In this chapter I want to make a few remarks about the sociology (if you will) of law and economics, its position in the legal academy; and to suggest (at least on theoretical grounds) that the law and society movement, and perhaps behavioral law and economics, have a good case for claiming a similar status. Right now, these movements are like ships passing in the night. This is not, I believe, an ideal situation.

A word of caution: those of us who are not economists, and who study the legal system from the angle of other social sciences or of socio-legal history, have to be careful to avoid feelings of sheer jealousy. Economics is the gorilla in the room. Tons of students in our universities major in economics; their numbers dwarf those who major in sociology, political science, or psychology. Economics seems a better bet in the job market. Perhaps it is. I doubt that many Fortune 500 companies are looking for anthropologists, any more than they are looking for people who majored in Latin and Greek.

Economists (dare I say this?) tend to be people, on the whole, who have a great deal of self-confidence (at least this is my experience). Economists are proud of their field; they consider it a true real-life science; many of them also think that the other social sciences simply do not measure up. The President has his Council of Economic Advisors. It is an important body; presumably it helps the President run the country by advising him about the economy, taxation, the business cycle, banking, finance policy, and a flock of other issues. Nobody is going to argue that the government should *not* concern itself with such matters. Coping with economic problems is something a modern government simply *must* do. If the economy stumbles, the government may stumble too. If the economy takes a serious fall, the regime is likely to be booted out of office.

But there is more to society than an economic system; and there are a great many other things that a government has to deal with. Along with the Council of Economic Advisers, a President could have, one supposes, a Council of Social Science Advisors. A council of this sort, made up of social scientists, could give advice and make pronouncements on crime policy, education policy, immigration, and a great many other subjects. Of course, the government does in fact deploy whole flocks of experts in all of these fields; they play a big role in the civil service, they serve on commissions, and so on. Politicians in general are positively addicted to one branch of applied social science, public opinion polling. Nonetheless, the social sciences (apart from economics) somehow lack visibility. They have no *official* status. Nor do they have a Nobel Prize, even a pseudo-Nobel Prize. On the plane of symbolism and in the world of academic prestige, clearly economics rocks. The rest of us, in the social sciences and the humanities, are distinctly in second place. We are a little bit like ragged orphan children, pressing our noses against shop windows filled with luxury goods we are far too destitute to buy.

Economics claims to be a science, and a hard science at that. This is not empty talk. As Posner tells us, the claim relates both to method and to attitude. Economists state their assumptions explicitly. They advance hypotheses: hypotheses which flow out of rigorous theorizing, and which can be proved true or false on the basis of real data. And the data are handled rigorously, making use of the latest statistical tools.

The rigor, however, may come at a price. Human beings are devilishly complex, in mind and body and attitude and behavior. It is one thing to gather statistics on market phenomena, on GNP, on rates of employment and unemployment. It is quite another to try to pin numbers on issues of crime, family life, love and sex, accidents, happiness and depression, mental illness and health, and, in general, the way most people navigate through life. Economists try to cope with complexity, either by ignoring it, or by making radical assumptions about behavior and attitudes. They try to strip away noise that interferes with the pursuit of scientific rigor. Most notoriously, they base their work on some fundamental assumptions about human nature, and the way people are supposed to behave. Of course, economists know that these assumptions are not really the truth, the whole truth, and nothing but the truth. But they feel these assumptions are not *too* unrealistic; that their strategies do not bring about *too* radical a distortion of life; and that their techniques have paid off in a big way.

And, to be sure, many economists are not simply resting on traditional laurels. Some, indeed, are making a valiant attempt to add to the tool chest of assumptions. Behavioral economics (and its offshoot, behavioral law and economics) is a growing field; and a very promising one. Many economists are taking a close look at the pathbreaking work of Daniel Kahnemann and Amos Tversky (1979). This work calls into question some basic assumptions about the way people think and act which have been part of the structure of economic theory. It has stimulated some economists – including some who deal with the legal system – to build models based on more realistic assumptions. One of these assumptions is that people fall prey to many cognitive biases that lead to behavior that is not "rational" in the classical economic sense but nonetheless systematic and predictive.

Some economists have also noticed that social norms have an effect on the way people behave, in complicated ways that their models did not take into account. They also began to prick up their ears and listen to what law and society scholars were telling them about the law in action, the living law, which is never quite what the formal models suggest – whether it was the behavior of ranchers in California (the subject of an important study by Robert Ellickson [1991]) or the study of Wisconsin businessmen in the classic article by Stewart Macaulay (1963). They absorbed lessons from the sociology of law, which helped them to understand that people were not just maximizing their utility in response to legal rewards and punishments: that individuals did not speed on the highway, did not avoid their tax obligations, or did not pollute solely because they were afraid of the long arm of the law. Something was missing from the models.

All this ferment from sociology and psychology has done a lot of good; and yet, my impression is that on the whole, economists cling tenaciously to their classical assumptions – at least as a starting point. They see no real alternative. It is a kind of life-raft in an ocean of crashing waves and fearful complexity. Maybe the models can be pruned and refined and added to, they imagine. There is no reason to throw them overboard.

Not that I think they *should* be thrown overboard. They are, after all, extremely useful. But there are limits to their utility. Take ideas about rationality, self-interest, and maximization. *Homo economicus*, the man (or woman) who acts on the basis of rational self-interest, is still a person at the critical core of the economic science. He may be a robot; but like many modern robots, he is useful, and he can perform all sorts of jobs. The other social sciences lack anything similar – they really have no conceptual superstructure, nothing that they can turn into working models on the scale and type of economic models. There are some core ideas, but they do not lend themselves to mathematical modeling, for the most part. Some sociologists, psychologists, and political scientists have tried to build theory in a serious way; but the results are either controversial or unsuccessful or both. Some social scientists have decided that, if you can't beat them, you ought to join them; and the result is a kind of political science, sociology, or psychology that looks a lot like economics lite. The field of economics, indeed, casts a very long shadow.

In point of fact, there are other perfectly sensible ways to start off the study of human behavior. Suppose one began with axioms that are, in a way, diametrically opposed to the axioms of economics. Suppose we began, for example, by assuming that *everything* we do is based on custom, norms, habits, and traditions, rather than rational choice or the like. If we began that way, we would not necessarily reject ideas about rational self-interest and the like, but we would use them only if all other explanations failed.

Does this seem absurd? Not if you pause to think about what life is really like. Consider your own behavior on any particular day. Or the behavior of most people, ordinary people. They get up in the morning, they dress, they eat eggs or cereal, they drink coffee, they go to work, they talk to people, they drive cars or ride the bus; they interact with families, parents, friends, they buy things at the store, they work, they play, they make love. What all of us do, say, and think, during the course of the days and weeks and months and years doesn't resemble very much our friend, *Homo economicus*, at least not in any realistic sense. Much of the behavior is routine. Much of it is unthinking, habitual, responsive to hidden and unconscious cues. Some of it is dictated by fashion. Some of it is dictated by ideology. Some by religious faith. Or by desire, prejudice, hatred, love – you name it. To be sure, you can, if you wish, analyze much of this, and the behavior that depends on these emotions (or non-emotions) in terms of self-interest, but this ends up leading nowhere. The Trappist monk is maximizing something, and so is the serial killer, and so are all of us, but this turns the whole idea into a useless tautology. The embezzler embezzles, you can say, when the expected gain exceeds the risks and losses, but this tells us absolutely nothing about what makes embezzlers tick and why they behave as they do.

I am, of course, talking about people, not hedge funds, corporations, mortgage houses, stock exchanges, and the like. Frankly, I think we could probably explain a lot of what happens in the business world, too, and even in "the market," by invoking ideas about ritual, custom, social norms, habits, tastes, and other things equally fuzzy. But I hesitate to invade this particular province.

Certainly, there are areas of life, where we have free choice; a rich domain, where people can and do make decisions that are (they suppose) in their interests. But even this domain is constrained in ways most people are completely unaware of. Most of us are just plain folks, not trained anthropologists. And just plain folks are, on the whole, blind to the ways convention, habit, and tradition run their lives; they have little or no idea about the forces that constrain their choices and limit their options. I like to compare us to animals born and raised in a zoo. Inside its cage or enclosure, the zoo animal has freedom of movement. It may be, in a way, unaware of the limits, which have always been there, and which it hardly notices. And of course the animal has no idea of the big outside world, the jungle where others of his species spend their lives.

When I go to a restaurant, the waiter hands me a menu, and I decide what I want to order – whether to skip the appetizers, whether to order chicken or fish, whether to have dessert or not. But of course the menu totally limits my choices. When I go to the supermarket to buy food, I buy exactly what I want, but I never ask why the butcher doesn't stock goat meat or tripe, why nobody eats a dormouse any more, why locusts and grasshoppers and grubs are not for sale. Indeed, why am I wearing a shirt and pants, and not a toga? Modern societies have made the long journey from status to contract – we know that – and yet a cage of constraints still encloses all of us. Of course, the zone of choice has gotten bigger, compared to earlier times; the menu is larger, it has more items on it; life is less limited than it was in ancient times, or, for that matter, the way it still is for some tribes in the Amazon jungle. Nonetheless, the cage of custom is powerful everywhere.

To be sure, expressive individualism and choice are hallmarks of modernity, at least in the club of rich, developed countries. You cannot make sense of the way we live now except in terms of the primacy of individual choice. A market system, democracy, the rule of law, representative government – all of them assume what I have called the republic of choice (Friedman 1990). Nonetheless, we have to recognize powerful and often unconscious constraints that bind everyone in various ways. There *is* a realm of free choice, and even a realm of rational behavior. The realm can expand or contract. It is important, politically and morally. It has to be nourished and protected. But it also has to be understood for what it is, what it has been, and what its boundaries are. There is a huge difference between people's *perception of freedom of choice*; and freedom of choice as a social reality.

The goal of economics, and of all social sciences, is to understand what makes people and societies tick. Economics has made a lot of progress in our times in doing exactly that. It does some things very well. But on the other hand, it does a pretty bad job (or no job at all) in explaining many big and small aspects of human behavior. It has little or nothing to say about fashion and taste. It fails to explain, much less predict, why sushi is all the rage, even though no red-blooded American would have dreamed of eating such a thing in the past; or for that matter why the Japanese now eat cheese and yogurt which they once found disgusting. No econometric formula can tell us why or when skirt lengths go up and down; why people wear T-shirts with slogans and advertisement; and why they put bumper stickers on cars. It has no formula to explain why religious fundamentalism, in many different faiths, seems to have enjoyed some sort of upsurge; or for that matter, it has no explanation for terrorists and suicide bombers. Not that other social sciences can honestly claim to answer these questions. But the others are at least *curious* about all sorts of phenomena which economics either ignores or deals with inadequately, brushing them off as "taste" (which defies explanation), or trying to squeeze them into the strait-jacket of utility maximization. Changes in laws and legal fashions are also hard to explain: why no-fault divorce swept the country after 1970, or why crime rates rise and fall, for no apparent reason; or why drug laws get passed when they do; or why gay marriage gains popularity; or why there is a sudden passion for historic preservation laws. On the other, a respectable literature in legal sociology and socio-legal history does at least try to grapple with these issues. Successfully? Sometimes yes, sometimes no.

The point is simply this: some human behavior is culturally determined, and all human behavior is culturally grounded. So much of it depends on time and place. That pure, sterile, abstract world which can be modeled mathematically is not the world we live in (for the most part). A predictive science of human behavior, which can tell us what people (generally or individually) are going to do, is not even on the horizon. Hard scientists can tell us precisely when Halley's comet will next appear. Doctors are at least fairly good at predicting how people will respond to a particular drug. But human behavior does not lend itself, right now, to this kind of prediction. Philosophers of science argue about whether a true science of human behavior, a predictive science, a deterministic science, is even within the realm of the possible. No matter; science has, as yet, no way of knowing when the next big earthquake is coming to California, or even how much rain will fall in the state next year. And human behavior is way more challenging than weather.

I would never suggest throwing away mathematical models of behavior. In their place, they work. They probably work a lot better for stock exchanges and business corporations than for people, as I said. But all of the social sciences, including economics, seem to need more and better theories about social change – theories about how and why society moves up, down, sideways, and in what direction. Our times are times of especially rapid (and drastic) social change. I have the impression that social science, including economics, does its best job telling us why things are the way they are; but they are less good at telling us how we got there, and hopeless on where we are going. The legal system is never static; the law changes as society changes; it is extremely responsive to alterations in what I call legal culture, that is, patterns of demands and expectations (Friedman 1975). But, unfortunately, there are far too many variables that can influence or affect the legal culture. Technology is one of these variables. Consider, for example, the incredible way in which the railroad, the automobile, and air travel have impacted society. Or think of the consequences of modern medicine, especially antibiotics. More recently, the computer and the internet have just about turned everything upside down.

The revolutions in science and technology, it seems to me, are intimately connected with the rise and expansion of capitalism, as cause, or effect, or something in between. And the capitalist system (in various shades and dimensions), which dominates all of the rich, developed countries, has a powerful influence on the way people think, work, and live. Old habits and constraints, old traditions and ways of life, have fallen away like tenpins; we live in a new world, a world of clocks and machines, a world which has redefined concepts of time and space, a world in which knowledge grows exponentially, a world of fresh possibilities – but also a world of new constraints and dislocations.

Even human personality has been affected. This is an age of individualism. The individual is the focus of life, not the family, the clan, the group, at least relative to other times and other places. Human beings are, after all, social animals; they do not thrive in isolation. But the modern citizen of Finland or Australia has wide scope for individual choice, even given all the constraints, compared to the medieval serf or ancient peasant; and possibly even compared to the nobles and gentry of the past.

Choice is, among other things, the product of the economic system. Capitalism depends on making and buying and selling; choice is central to capitalism; decisions made by people to buy products and services. Companies, factories, stores all need sales to survive; they need customers who want to use or buy their wares. Hence the primacy of advertising. All advertising, whatever the subject, addresses itself to the individual: it tells him or her that he or she would be richer, happier, sexier, more fulfilled, if he or she would only listen to the message. Modern societies are societies of consumers, societies of desire and fulfillment. The *legal* culture of the modern economic state is a culture of individual rights and the free market. It is also, perhaps paradoxically, and in complex ways, also the culture of the modern welfare and regulatory state. This, at any rate, is the way we live now. What makes our society function is of course beyond the scope of this chapter. But a society of advertising, a society of desire and permission, of discipline and constraint, a society as varied and unpredictable as the weather, is beyond the scope of hard science. At least so far.

The social sciences, in any event, are practically newborn babies. Social science in any meaningful sense really dates from the last century or two; you can always scrape together some sort of precursor, an essay by Montesquieu, a few lines from Aristotle; but in a real sense you can hardly trace serious social science back beyond the nineteenth century. Economic science has the same short history, more or less. There is not much point looking for economics before, say, Adam Smith. In any event, the assumptions of economics are the assumptions of contemporary minds. Nobody in feudal Japan or ancient Egypt could have imagined such a science.

Or the other social sciences. Anthropology, sociology, and psychology were not disciplines taught in medieval Bologna or Oxford. These are new disciplines; they demand a kind of cool cultural relativity; and this is a distinctly modern attitude. The anthropologist must be willing to stand back and look at other cultures with detachment: to see them in context, and as coherent wholes. The anthropologist does not dismiss native peoples as primitive pagans, whose cultures and traditions are not worthy of a second thought. European powers in the past ruthlessly destroyed old cultures. The Spaniards leveled Aztec cities. Natives were to be subjugated, converted to Christianity, and, if resistant, killed. Sociology, too, as a discipline, really has little more than a century or so to its credit. It depends on a willingness to suspend judgment about social facts, unless and until they are poked, prodded, and measured. These include the facts of the very society the sociologist inhabits. Sociology, not unlike psychology, can be, and often is, rigorous and quantitative; at other times it may seem fuzzy and biased, and no doubt some of the work *is* fuzzy and biased. But the methodologies used are not that different from the ones Richard Posner describes (and praises) in economics.

Law and economics is a late development in economics;[1] similarly, the law and society movement is about two generations old. In the past, sociology paid very little attention to law, with some famous and honorable exceptions. The most important exception, of course, was Max Weber, whose writings on the sociology of law are still a fruitful source of insights. Sociology tended to pay more attention to social norms and informal processes; legal norms often seemed irrelevant. Law schools, of course, had hardly any interest in how society worked at all. They peddled their dry, didactic concept of law.

The situation began to change after the end of World War II. One influence, perhaps, was the work of the Warren court – the striking series of Supreme Court cases which broke new (legal) ground, especially the school segregation case.

If nothing else, the bold decisions of the court pushed the legal system into the sociological spotlight. Maybe formal law mattered after all. Maybe courts mattered. Foundations, too, took notice – money from a foundation, for example, paid for a classic study of the jury system, carried out at the University of Chicago in the 1960s (Kalven and Zeisel 1966). A significant center of study was the University of Wisconsin; Professor J. Willard Hurst, founder of the modern school of socio-legal history, had an important influence on law and society in general. Hurst's brand of legal history was something new for the United States; it shifted attention from doctrine to the social and economic roots of legal arrangements, and their impact on society (see, for example, Hurst 1956).

Meanwhile, a small group of youngish scholars, mostly sociologists, got together in 1964 and founded what became the Law and Society Association. The Association began to hold annual meetings, and in 1967 launched an important journal, *The Law and Society Review*. Social scientists whose work focused on the legal system more or less made the Association their intellectual base; they were joined by like-minded law professors. The annual meetings today have grown in size; more than 2,000 people attended the 2013 meeting in Boston: law professors, sociologists, anthropologists, political scientists, psychologists, historians, and others. About a quarter of the members are from outside the United States. Economists are, unfortunately, underrepresented in the Association. But a few do join – particularly those who are interested in behavioral economics.

The law and society movement is, in other words, something of a success. On the other hand, it is much more fragmented than, say, the law and economics movement, and it never had the money that some foundations – the Olin Foundation, for example – plowed into law and economics, in a number of law schools. Within the law and society movement there is not much of a common core or canon. I doubt if you could rally the members around a single group of propositions and assumptions. About all that they have in common is a belief that legal systems are not autonomous, and perhaps a few other very basic, very abstract propositions. They also (like economists) reject legal formalism; and what at least one scholar has called "magic legalism," that is, the belief that legal rules, statutes, doctrines automatically translate into behavior. There is much less agreement on methodology than in economics. And the field, unlike economics, does not seem particularly cumulative. Sometimes it seems, in fact, to be going in circles. I personally am inclined to be a bit more positive; I think of the circles as spirals, going upwards (slowly). But not everybody would agree.

Has the law and society movement influenced the academy? Somewhat. Law schools, however, are rather resistant. Economics, so far, has had much greater influence. Some elite law schools have as many as four or five faculty members with Ph.D.s in economics; my impression is that only a few law schools have even one sociologist, psychologist, or political scientist on their faculty. There are international law and economics associations in many countries;[2] some also have law and society associations as well.[3] Some fields – anti-trust; business law in general – are practically economic fiefdoms; and economic precepts creep into many other fields and thus into law school courses, including such basic ones as torts and contracts.

Yet I think there is a great deal to learn from the law and society movement. The subjects it studies have a lot of potential. They provide valuable insights and understanding for many areas of law. When I was interested in studying criminal justice, I found the economic literature dead, dry, jejune. I felt I learned a lot more from a study that interviewed real burglars who were working in St. Louis – insight on what makes these people tick and why they behave as they do (Wright and Decker 1994). Maybe my preferences are the result of bias. Or even, as I suggested, envy. I leave this to the reader to assess.

Law and economics is certainly here to stay, in one form or another. Economic analysis is essential for at least *some* aspects of law; and useful for many of the others. Yes, I wish some of its practitioners were more empirical and less interested in "theory." I wish some of them were less imperialistic. I wish some of them would open their minds more to what sociologists, psychologists, historians, and other social scientists are trying to say to them. I am willing to admit that they would hear a lot of noise, and a lot of wrong-headed, sloppy, and foolish things; and would be exposed, no doubt, to slip-shod methods off and on. But there is bad scholarship in every field.

Richard Posner thinks law and economics is, in fact, getting broader and more ecumenical. I think he is right. Behavioral economics seems to be flourishing. Many economists are now interested in institutions of governance and how they work, for instance, those working in new institutional economics. Posner himself is a paradigm; he has written on an amazing range of subjects, including of all things sex (Posner 1992) Perhaps some sort of synthesis, between *all* social sciences, including economics, is on the way. That would certainly be welcome: imagine the achievement, if there were such a thing as a unified social science of law.

Law and economics, legal sociology, and socio-legal history, would make a great team, if practitioners could find a way to work together, or at least talk to each other. There is, after all, a common enemy: traditional legal scholarship. Despite a good deal of progress, the social sciences (including economics) have not really succeeded in slaying this particular dragon. Legal scholarship of the bad old kind has a tight and tough core that resists reform and revolution. When Posner complains about legal scholarship, because it lacks rigor and objectivity, I can only say amen. Law reviews publish thousands of pages every year of arid doctrinalism, work that is blind to social reality, false to history, incurably solipsistic and inbred. Posner is particularly biting and critical with regard to scholarship in constitutional law. The field, he says, lacks any empirical content, or even curiosity about such content; and it fails to make any intellectual progress. Here too I think he is entirely right. "Con law" is the high citadel of punditry; its practitioners have the most prestige in law schools; they get quoted in the newspapers; and appear at times on talk shows. Scholars spin out their own pet theories, based on nothing much, and pass these off as some sort of eternal truth.

If not eternal truth, then the truth about what the constitution really means or should mean. As a legal historian, I am particularly irritated by the pseudo history that defaces the field. The "originalists," on or off the bench, are the biggest offenders, but not the only ones.

Legal scholars are, on the whole, blithely indifferent to impact – that is, whether their doctrines and decisions make any difference in the real world. Political scientists are responsible for most of the rather small group of "impact studies." And yet, isn't impact vitally important? This of course is true not only for constitutional doctrines; it is true of law in general. Does a loyalty oath really have a "chilling" effect on speech? Did the "one man one vote" doctrine change the way legislatures behaved? Do easy divorce laws have an effect on family disintegration? If you increase the penalty for burglary, on the books, will burglaries decline, and if so, by how much? Do medical malpractice cases induce doctors to practice "defensive medicine"? You could spin out an endless list of questions. Not many of them have answers so far.

Law and economics, sociology of law, and behavioral law and economics do seem to begin from different premises. Still, I think they are committed to a similar goal: to understand how law works in society; and why. They are even, in large part, committed to the same cluster of methods. They have or should have the same ideology of rigor and objectivity. Nobody, I suppose, is truly objective, in an absolute sense – but still, there is a world of difference between normative hot air and wild guesses, on the one hand; and carefully structured research on the other. In any event, in a perfect world, economics and the other social sciences would be allies and brothers. This perfect world, of course, is not yet here.

Richard Posner is a judge, a legal scholar, and a person of many interests. He has been a commanding figure in the law and economics movement. He is also deeply interested in normative issues – in the great issues of jurisprudence. He has particularly argued for the principle of wealth maximization, as a touchstone of policy. Of course, people who read his work would surely prefer to live in a country like Finland, rather than (say) as a garment worker in Bangladesh, slaving away for pennies in a filthy and unsafe factory. But whether *in* Finland policy A is necessarily better than policy B, because it is wealth maximizing – that seems to me something of a leap.

Of course, philosophies, values, and ideologies make a difference in the world of scholarship, as they do elsewhere. Economists, on the whole, are more conservative than (say) sociologists or psychologists; more committed to free-market solutions to problems; less troubled by social inequalities; more suspicious of government programs. Political orientation is a key influence on the questions a person chooses to study – it constructs the frame of reference – and very often it influences how the data are analyzed. But consensus on *how* the work is done, on the rigor of the method, should be, one hopes, a lot less elusive.

42   *L.M. Friedman*

Notes

* Marion Rice Kirkwood Professor of Law, Stanford Law School.
1 The usual launch date is said to be 1960 with the publication of articles by Coase (1960) and Calabresi (1961).
2 This website identifies ten of the leading international law and economics associations: www.amlecon.org/alea-otherAssociations.html.
3 This website identifies several of the leading international law and society associations: http://lawandsocietyworld.org/members/search.

References

Calabresi, G. 'Some thoughts on risk distribution and the law of torts', *Yale Law Journal* 70, 1961: 499–553.
Coase, R. 'The problem of social cost', *Journal of Law and Economics* 3, 1960: 1–44.
Ellickson, R. (1991) *Order Without Law: How Neighbors Settle Disputes*, Cambridge, MA: Harvard University Press.
Friedman, L. (1975) *The Legal System: A Social Science Perspective*, New York: Russell Sage Foundation.
Friedman, L. (1990) *The Republic of Choice*, Cambridge, MA: Harvard University Press.
Hurst, J. (1956). *Law and the Conditions of Freedom in the Nineteenth-Century United States*, Madison, WI: University of Wisconsin Press.
Kahneman, D. and Tversky, A. 'Prospect theory: an analysis of decision under risk', *Econometrica* 47, 1979: 263–291.
Kalven, H. and Zeisel, H. (1966) *The American Jury*, Boston, MA: Little, Brown and Company.
Macaulay, S. 'Non-contractual relations in business: a preliminary study', *American Sociological Review* 28, 1963: 55–67.
Posner, R. (1992) *Sex and Reason*, Cambridge, MA: Harvard University Press.
Wright, R. and Decker, S. (1994) *Burglars on the Job: Streetlife and Residential Break-ins.* Boston, MA: Northeastern University Press.

4   The dominance of norms

Edward Rubin*

Introduction

The effort to take account of social norms represents the most sophisticated and productive response of microeconomic theorists to the attack on rational choice theory (Cooter 1989; Dau Schmidt 1997; Ellickson 1998; Katz 1996; Posner 2000). In answer to the claim that people are subject to a much wider and more complex set of motivations – claims supported by an entire century of empirical and epistemological research (Brown *et al.* 2012; Green and Shapiro 1994; Mansbridge 1990) – microeconomists have strived to incorporate social norms into their field's behavioral model, and to adjust that model in cases where incorporation proves impossible. For perfectly good reasons, however, they have been unwilling to abandon their model, which has produced such impressive results, and also unwilling to abandon their delicious sense that other social sciences lack the rigor that microeconomics has achieved through its mathematical methodology. To anyone approaching the debate with even a modicum of neutrality, the arguments against rational choice theory at the most general level are powerful, but it seems difficult to believe that the impressive edifice of modern microeconomics is truly built on sand.

This chapter revisits the debate about rational choice theory and attempts to resolve this dilemma by adopting a cultural and historical perspective. Its argument is that the social science approach to human motivation is correct in general, that people respond to a wide and varied range of motivations. In our society, however, one of the most powerful motivations is the one that microeconomists have identified, that is, people's desire to maximize their material self-interest through rational action. Thus, the microeconomic theory of rational choice has powerful explanatory value for us, but that is not because rational choice is the dominant norm of all societies. The reason, rather, is that it is our particular norm, and occupies the same place for us that the desire for honor, for salvation, or for some other value has occupied for previous societies (Rubin 2015).

Rational choice theory is not irrelevant to prior periods of history, of course. To begin with, the social norms of most earlier societies have endorsed or allowed the behaviors that this theory describes within limited domains. In addition, human psychology generates a wide range of individualized variation.

There have been opportunistic and materialistic people in the most sacerdotal societies, just as there are many truly altruistic individuals within our own. Among the very few rules of human behavior that can be regarded as true universals, one is that people's behavior will always be strongly determined by prevailing social norms, and another is there are always individuals who will violate whatever social norms prevail.

This leads to an important epistemological consideration that will constitute the second major theme of this discussion. As we gaze across the great expanse of human history, it will always be possible to find cases of behavior that conform to the rational choice model. But there is a great danger of over-interpreting these cases, and thereby misinterpreting prior societies in general, because rational choice is such a strong norm in our own society. In other words, when we look at other societies, we interpret them according to our own normative framework; we see them through rational-choice-colored glasses. We tend to over-emphasize the importance of individuals whose sensibility is most similar to our own because we find those individuals most comprehensible, we tend to interpret behaviors that are foreign to our sensibility as secondary to some deeper, more familiar motivation, and we tend to treat people's own efforts to explain or justify their behavior in terms other than rational choice as conscious or unconscious insincerity.

These mindsets feed into our tendency to conceive of ourselves as a culmination of human history, perched at a lofty height above our predecessors, and able to look down on them with a detached, quasi-divine sense of perspective borne of superior knowledge and rationality. That only demonstrates that we are subject to the same illusions as the societies over which we claim superiority. We may be the only society with motorcycles and personal computers, but we experience the same conceptual constraints as others and we are victims of the same particularized perceptions. Thus, we cannot fully trust ourselves to judge whether these other societies are governed by norms that are the same as or different from our own. That does not mean that we must abandon the inquiry, but rather that we must approach the entire subject with a sense of self-awareness and humility.

The first part of this chapter will explain the way in which people in societies different from our own were subject to other motivations in situations where rational choice would tend to dominate in our society. It will further explain how we tend to interpret their behavior in rational choice terms, and why this tendency is unreliable. The explanation will proceed by considering three examples, one drawn from our predecessor society, Ancient Rome, one from an earlier period of our own society, the High Middle Ages, and one from a contemporary non-Western culture, the Ugandan Ik. These examples are the flight of the *curiales*, the reconstruction of Chartres Cathedral, and the Ik's response to the disruption of their nomadic patterns.

The second part of the chapter will then discuss the reason why rational choice became a dominant motivation in the High Modern era of Western society. Two of the most famous works of historical sociology, Max Weber's *The Protestant Ethic and the Spirit of Capitalism*, originally published in 1904–5

(Weber 2002) and R.H. Tawney's *Religion and the Rise of Capitalism*, originally published in 1926 (Tawney 1954), attribute this development to Calvinism. Despite its formidable pedigree, this hypothesis suffers from serious defects. The argument offered here will be that the modern sensibility resulted from much broader, longer-acting trends, specifically commercialization, urbanization, centralized government, and secularization. The final section of the chapter explores the relationship between the West's prevailing norm of rational action and the additional norms that have been discussed in microeconomic theory. It argues that some of these norms are internal to the prevailing one, and are thus explicable in terms of rational choice, as microeconomic analysis asserts, but that others reflect additional norms in the general society that exist alongside, and sometimes in competition with, the prevailing norm. The historically based view that rational choice is a prevailing norm, not a human universal, allows these other norms to be acknowledged in a plausible and realistic manner, rather than being explained away by a Procrustean, and ultimately unconvincing effort to fit them into a unitary model of human motivation.

Prevailing norms in other societies

In attempting to place our modern, economically oriented motivation system within a cultural and historical framework, it is important to be clear about its meaning. A standard way to do so is to rely on John Ferejohn's distinction between thin and thick rationality (Ferejohn 1991). Thin rationality asserts that people's behavior displays certain formal or structural attributes: it attempts to maximize the actor's utility (that is, the actor's own objectives), it is consistent and transitive (that is, if the actor prefers A to B and B to C, she prefers A to C), and it is oriented to the individual (that is, self-regarding rather than altruistic or other regarding). Thick rationality makes the further assertion that behavior displays substantive features as well, the most important being that the form of utility that the actor is trying to maximize is material advantage or self-interest.

While thin rationality is a useful concept for analyzing or designing decision making within a single society, it does not provide a sufficient grounding for the claims that microeconomists advance. Those claims necessarily rely on the thick rationality assertion that people attempt to maximize their material self-interest. The need for this further, substantive assertion becomes apparent as soon as one engages in the sort of cross-cultural analysis that this chapter will pursue. Thin rationality defines utility to encompass efforts to achieve any goal, including heavily symbolic ones such as honor and supernatural ones such as salvation. As I argue in a forthcoming book, those are in fact the goals that people in earlier eras of the Western world explicitly identified as the basis of their actions (Rubin 2015). Including goals of this sort destroys any possibility of relying on revealed preferences to determine people's choices, because any behavior can be explained as a rational effort to achieve symbolic or supernatural goals. Only efforts to achieve a goal that leads to observable results, such as material wealth, can be assessed by an external observer.

Worse still, including symbolic or supernatural goals not only renders goal attainment unmeasurable, but it also undermines the formal attributes of thin rationality, and thus does not qualify as a theory of rational action in any sense. Most obviously, it eliminates the feature of individualist orientation. One can certainly say that an individual actor is striving to secure his own honor, or his own salvation, as an individual interest, but both of these value systems can readily demand purely altruistic behavior. Second, these goals undermine the feature of maximization, since they allow the individual to secure the goal at the moment of death, having lived an entire life according to a different pattern of behavior (Dante 2003: 302–307; Judges 16: 28–31).[1] Finally, such goals even call transitivity into question, because they are so abstract. An actor who prefers honor to money (he is willing to engage in extensive philanthropy) and money to sex (he marries a woman he does not love for her money) might prefer sex to honor (he frequents houses of ill repute). This is possible because abstract goals, unlike wealth, are sufficiently malleable to be adjusted in accordance with one's circumstances or desires. In short, to say that people try to maximize their utility, rather than their material self-interest, is only to say that people try to get what they want. Even that is not a human universal to be sure; as Harry Frankfurt argued (1988) and Dostoyevsky dramatized (1959), people can contain within themselves different and contradictory levels of desire. But the desire to get what one wants is generally dominant, and it is too widespread, too ill-defined and, most important, too unobservable a motivation to function as the basis of a definitive theory of human behavior.

The claim of microeconomic theory is that people seek to maximize their material self-interest. This is generally easy to determine in a money economy because we do not need to inquire into the reason people have particular preferences, that is, particular definitions of their own material self-interest (Hardin 1996). In Ancient Egypt, which had no monetary system, it might be difficult to determine whether a particular shoemaker was trading the shoes he made on a rational basis because we would not know his subjective valuation of the commodities he received in exchange. While people may be motivated to misrepresent their preferences under certain circumstances (Kuran 1997), values established through a medium of exchange provide good evidence of self-interest maximization. If the shoemaker trades his product for the most money he can get, we can conclude that he has acted rationally, without further inquiry into his preferences about the way he spends the money (Coleman 1990: 775–784).

Is rational choice, in the form of material self-interest maximizing, a prevailing norm in all societies? The question can be pursued in the abstract, in which case it involves the entire range of human behavior, or it can be pursued by a systematic account of history, in which case it involves the entire range of human experience. For the present, it will be pursued by example. This approach is subject to a variety of well-known hazards, of course, but the goal here is to be illustrative, rather than definitive, to demonstrate that people in different societies seem subject to motivations different from our own, and to explore our tendency to interpret their behavior in accordance with our own, familiar motivations.

Three examples

The flight of the curiales in Ancient Rome

In the Ancient Greek cities, public works and festivals were often financed by liturgies, that is, payments by wealthy citizens for specified purposes.[2] These often resembled modern sponsorships; typical liturgies were maintaining a warship for one year, producing a theatrical performance, or giving a banquet for one's tribe (Joint Association of Classical Teachers 1984: 228–229; Ober 1989: 195–234). When Rome conquered Greece, it made no effort to alter the internal governance of the Greek cities, but simply incorporated them into the Empire, the major change being the imposition of peace and termination of their independent foreign policy. It taxed the conquered cities, but the taxes were imposed on the city as a whole, that is, as tribute, rather than directly on the city's residents (Bringmann 2007: 107–111; Gruen 2004: 262–266; Wells 1992: 143–151). Very often, the money for these tribute payments came from wealthy citizens, and thus took the form of liturgies.

When Rome conquered the non-urbanized Celtic areas in the West – Gaul, Hispania, the Netherlands, and Britain – it chose to use the Greek city-state as the model of local governance.[3] The new cities were laid out by the legions in a uniform pattern with two long, straight perpendicular streets, a forum at their intersection and a fort on the periphery (Blair 1963: 101–113; Heather 2006: 37–40, 123–151; Wells 1992: 246–251). In place of the somewhat staggering variety of Greece's city constitutions,[4] Rome imposed a political structure as uniform as their urban design. "[T]here was one basic constitution composed in Rome, which all these towns adopted, changing just a few details to suit their own circumstances" (Heather 2006: 39). In place of the long-established, generally aristocratic elites that formed the governing class of the Greek cities, the Romans appointed wealthy individuals to serve on the governing body, or *curia*. These *curiales* were then expected to support the city through liturgies, sponsoring festivals, building public works, and paying the tributary taxes that the Empire imposed on each of its newly minted cities (Fox 1986: 50–57; Veyne 1987: 106–115; Wells 1992: 143, 146).

The flight of the *curiales* began almost as soon as this system was put in place. In pre-Roman Greece, cities were self-contained political entities, the arena for all political activity, social life, and personal reputation. The city's territory of course included the surrounding agricultural land, but anywhere beyond the limits of that territory was generally claimed by another city or a non-Hellenic tribe, and even if unoccupied, was distinctly unsafe in these unsettled times. Once the *pax Romana* was imposed, however, this situation changed dramatically. The open land outside the cities was simply another region of the same imperial province, and was just as safe as the cities. Political advancement depended upon Rome, not one's own particular city, and social or cultural life was increasingly imperial in scope and character (Brown 1989: 24–41; Heather 2006: 117–118; Wells 1992: 223–254; Wickham 2009: 27–36). In these circumstances, the obligation to contribute to the city's tax or maintenance expenses was increasingly seen as a burden to be avoided, rather than an obligation to be accepted or an honor to be sought. As a result, the wealthy withdrew from the cities, preferring to lavish their resources on their own private villas than contribute to the welfare of the cities where they had previously served (Blair 1963: 121–130; Heather 2006: 35–36; Salway 1981: 588–614; Wells 1992: 178–182). This flight of the *curiales* undermined the Empire's entire system of local governance. By the second century, Roman authorities were attempting to prop it up by legal mechanisms, such as prohibitions on departure; by the fourth century, they had largely abandoned it, and moved to the direct taxation of individuals and to the establishment of bureaucratic city government (Geary 1988: 26–28; Goldsworthy 2009: 168–171).

The reconstruction of Chartres cathedral

On the night of June 10–11, 1194, a great fire destroyed the city of Chartres, including the entirety of its famous cathedral with the exception of the front, or west façade.[5] This cathedral, which was dedicated to the Virgin Mary, was reputed to have been founded a century prior to her birth, in response to an oracle. It held one of the most treasured relics in Christendom, the Sacred Tunic that Mary had worn when she gave birth to Christ (Simson 1988: 160). By the time of the fire, the worship of Mary, which had been relatively minor element in Early Medieval Christianity, was rising toward its High Medieval acme (Adams 1986: 87–105, 237–268; Cantor 1994: 341; Markale 1987: 176–201). As a result, Chartres, having bet on the winning doctrinal horse, had become one of the most important pilgrimage destinations in Western Europe, and its cathedral one of Europe's most important shrines.

The people's response to the calamity that had overtaken them is narrated in dramatic terms by a contemporary source. It recounts that the Cardinal of Pisa, who happened to be residing in Chartres at that time, persuaded both the religious leaders of the diocese and an assembly of the people that the cathedral must be rebuilt. As he addressed the populace, some church officials appeared with the Sacred Tunic, which they reported had miraculously escaped the fire's destruction. In a surge of religious enthusiasm, the church officials and people agreed to donate all the funds they could possibly spare to the reconstruction project. They themselves participated in the process, working long hours on a voluntary basis (Simson 1988: 161–178).

Despite this effort, the community's ability to finance the project was exhausted after three years – Chartres was a wealthy town, but it had no more than 10,000 people – and those in charge of the project were forced to issue a general appeal for help. Deputations of preachers, accompanied by lesser relics than the Tunic, were sent throughout France and beyond to garner contributions for continuation of the work. Queen Blanche, the mother of St. Louis, donated an enormous sum, as did the Duke of Burgundy, an ally of the crown and probably the wealthiest French baron of the time, but so did Richard the Lionhearted, although he happened to be at war with France, and so did many less exalted individuals. The vast, elaborately embellished edifice that these efforts produced is generally considered to be the most magnificent of all Gothic cathedrals (Adams 1986: 87, 186; Simson 1978: 178–182).

The Ik tribe in northern Uganda

The story of the Ik is told by Colin Turnbull, an anthropologist who had previously studied the pygmies of the Ituri Forest in the Congo. The pygmies, according to Turnbull, revere this seemingly ominous jungle and it sustains their highly integrated and largely rewarding lives (Turnbull 1968). The Ik are different. They were originally semi-nomadic hunters, circulating through the adjoining regions of northern Uganda, Kenya, and Sudan in pursuit of prey, and spending the majority of their year in Uganda's fertile, game-rich Kidepo Valley. Independence rigidified the previously permeable boundaries between the quondam colonies, and then Uganda declared the Kidepo a national park. Now restricted to the small, most mountainous and least fertile portion of their former range, the Ik's opportunity to hunt has been dramatically reduced and their ability to raise crops instead is insufficient in all but the most drought-free years (Turnbull 1972: 20–33).

The result, as Turnbull describes it, is that the Ik turned nasty. In their effort to get food, they beg from strangers, steal from each other, trample their own parents, and pry food out of elderly people's mouths, all without the slightest indication of remorse (Turnbull 1972: 151–154, 261). They farm their meager fields in isolation, and either eat or hide the small amount they harvest, leaving their traditional granaries empty. When one of them succeeds in killing an animal (often illegally), he gorges himself on the meat before any other members of the tribe, including his relatives, can find him (Turnbull 1972: 81–89). The Ik's tiny villages are criss-crossed by thatched walls that allow each family to get outside the village, often by means of narrow corridors, without being required to see or interact with any of their neighbors (Turnbull 1972: 115–122). They ignore personal hygiene, allow their homes to be overrun with lice and roaches, and defecate at the doorway of each other's compounds. Young girls trade sex for food, sometimes with Ik males, sometimes with herdsmen from other tribes who pass through their territory (Turnbull 1972: 254–255). They lose their looks early as a result of the harsh conditions, and if they have failed to marry, are often abandoned and die before they reach their thirties. When they succeed in marrying and having children, these children are sent out of the home when they turn three years old and left to fend for themselves (Turnbull 1972: 121, 135–138). Turnbull describes one child, in some way impaired, who found herself incapable of managing and returned to her parents's compound to be fed. Her parents locked her in the compound without food and left her alone. They returned after she had starved to death and threw her shrunken body out as garbage (Turnbull 1972: 131–132).

Whatever culture the Ik possessed in past years has disappeared. They ignore their sacred tree, which serves only as a target for cow dung thrown by visiting herdsmen (Turnbull 1972: 62, 91). Because their previous traditions prescribed that both wedding and funerals must be accompanied by a feast provided by the celebrating or grieving family, marriages are no longer celebrated and deaths are concealed, often by dumping the dead body in a hole (Turnbull 1972: 85–86, 123–124, 130, 194–196). Although they occasionally aid each other in building homes, they neither hunt nor farm together. Much of their time is spent sitting on a raised platform that adjoins the village, scanning the horizon and either ignoring or annoying the other people on the platform (Turnbull 1972: 87).[6]

Interpreting the examples

Anyone who has attended a group decision-making session, such as a faculty meeting, must acknowledge that the motivations of other people, even when they are members of the same society, come from similar backgrounds, and are engaged in the same enterprise, can be difficult to discern. It thus seems advisable to approach the task of explaining the behavior of people as remote from ourselves as the *curiales*, the re-builders of Chartres, and the Ik with a sense of humility. In particular, we should guard against a tendency to assimilate their motivations to our own, to discount explanations that we deem implausible and to ignore apparently discordant facts. To do so is to recognize that explaining human behavior is a matter of interpretation, with all the attendant complexities that modern philosophy, literary criticism, and social science have discussed. It deals with the mental frameworks that determine people's behavior, the meaning that they give to observed events, and their own possibilities for action (Berger and Luckmann 1966; Goodman 1978; Habermas 1987: 113–197, 301–373; Winch 1958).

Of these three examples, the flight of the *curiales* seems most readily explicable in terms of the material self-interest that, as described above, necessarily grounds microeconomic theory. It can be seen as resulting from the disappearance of the observable conditions that enforced performance of the liturgies in the original Greek cities. In the intense, constrained conditions that those original cities created, wealthy individuals had little choice but to contribute to the city in the socially accepted manner. Anyone who failed to do so would be ostracized and his material position would deteriorate as a result.[7] Withdrawal from the city was simply not an option. The *curiales* were able to withdraw, or flee, from the Roman colonies because these conditions no longer prevailed. Their revealed preferences – the fact that they escaped from their social obligation to contribute to their city as soon as it was advantageous for them to do so – seem to indicate that they in fact were motivated by material self-interest.

This rational choice explanation cannot be definitively disproved, but it suffers from empirical difficulties. To begin with, it was not the way that the Greeks themselves understood the liturgies. The wealthy citizens of Greek cities certainly sought to retain and expand their wealth, and fully understood the social sanctions that would follow from their failure to contribute to the city. But they identified their primary motivation as maximizing their honor, not their wealth, and in fact saw wealth as a means of securing honor, rather than the opposite (Finley 1965; Joint Association of Classical Teachers 1984: 134–142; MacIntyre 1984: 121–145). The claim that they were being insincere necessarily assumes the proposition that it attempts to prove, namely that self-interest is the most basic explanation for human behavior, and that one must probe behind any assertion of a contrary motivation until the true, material self-interest maximizing behavior is revealed.

In addition to this failure to account for people's subjective attitudes, the rational choice explanation for the flight of the *curiales* also fails to account for other observable behaviors. The urban elite in the Eastern or Greek part of the Empire did not withdraw from their cities to nearly the same extent. For the most part, they remained, even though they enjoyed the equivalent protection of the *pax Romana* (Brown 1989: 42–45, 139–143; Wickham 2009: 25, 263–265).[8] As Peter Brown notes, mid-fifth century Christian bishops in the Eastern Empire often defended themselves from charges of heresy with the same argument that Athenian plutocrats had used in the fifth century BC to defend themselves from charges of disloyalty, namely that they had "embellished their city by building an aqueduct and the public porticoes" (1989: 44). That is probably a major reason why the eastern part of the Empire survived so much longer, and was not only able to weather the Germanic and Slavic invasions, but also retain its core territory in the face of the more sudden and antagonistic eruption of the Arabs.[9]

The problem in the Western Empire was that the urban mode of governance was a transplant. As a result, the sense of belonging or commitment that the Greeks felt toward their long-established, individually distinctive cities was greatly attenuated in the colonial cities of the Latin West. These manufactured entities were simply not able to confer the non-material benefits on their wealthy citizens that their originals in the East provided. It thus seems more likely that the flight of the *curiales* was not primarily motivated by self-interest, but rather by a normative system centered on a distinctive form of honor that was connected with their role as citizens of cities. To be sure, it was also motivated by self-interest, but only secondarily. The *curiales* withdrew because the primary motivation had become too attenuated to counter-balance this secondary one. The political configuration of the Latin West, with its pacified countryside and increasingly uniform culture, provided them with the opportunity to withdraw, but it was the weakness of the transplanted Greek model, and the Roman inability to replace it, that removed the non-material motivation to remain.

In contrast to the flight of the *curiales*, the heroic efforts to rebuild Chartres seem to reveal a preference for other-directed action, the sacrifice of material wealth motivated by religious fervor. It is perhaps inaccurate to describe this behavior as altruistic. The people who donated time and money to the reconstruction of the Cathedral were motivated by a highly specific desire to benefit themselves, but the benefit they sought was the salvation of their immortal souls. In their view, they were maximizing their utility, but not by any effort related to their material well-being here on Earth, that is, any behavior that would support the rational choice theory of human behavior. Thus, the way to place their behavior and ours within a single explanatory framework is not to assert that all people are motivated by material self-interest, but rather that they are motivated by norms; ours is material and theirs was sacerdotal.

To be sure, it is possible to re-interpret the behaviors that the prelates and townspeople of Chartres exhibited in material self-interest maximizing terms. With the growth of Marianism in the High Middle Ages, Chartres became a major pilgrimage center, and by the late twelfth century it was hosting four large trade fairs coinciding with the four feasts of the Virgin.[10] The destruction of the cathedral threatened to end these highly remunerative events, and its reconstruction was seen as necessary for the town's continued precedence and prosperity (Simson 1988: 164–169). There can be little doubt that everyone in Chartres was fully aware of this issue, and relatively little doubt that it functioned as a motivating factor. But before accepting an interpretation that self-interest was the primary motivation, we need to recognize that it is our own primary motivation and that no one in our society, no matter how devout, believes in God the way virtually everyone did in the High Middle Ages. Here again, interpreting the people's behavior as based on material self-interest maximizing denies their own account of their behavior. Not only would they have indignantly rejected the assertion that their religious fervor in reconstructing their cathedral was a façade, but they probably valued the prosperity that the pilgrimages and trade fairs brought as a sign of grace, as well as a source of revenue.

As in the case of the *curiales*, the economic interpretation of the cathedral's restoration also presents empirical difficulties. If a completed cathedral was seen as essential to the revival of pilgrimage and trade fairs, the townspeople must also have known that they would not live to benefit from their contributions and exertions. Chartres Cathedral is famous for having been rebuilt so quickly, which explains its well-known architectural unity, but even so it was about thirty years before the side walls were raised, and a full sixty before the choir was finished. No adult who participated in the original reconstruction effort was alive, or could reasonably have expected to be alive, when the cathedral was completed.

Self-interested behavior tends to be short-term, even today, due to rational discounting; surely the discount rate was substantially higher in the Middle Ages, given shorter life expectancies and greater political instability. Is it really plausible that self-interested people would devote the proverbial "best years of their lives" to an enterprise that would only benefit the next generation? And even if they could have been induced to do so, why would they not have erected a simpler structure that would have taken less effort, been finished more quickly, and still provided the necessary setting for the Sacred Tunic that was apparently the primary magnet for pilgrims and traders? Instead, they lavished enormous physical and artistic effort on a vast structure alive with sculptured figures, aglow with stained glass panels, and universally recognized as one of the world's architectural masterpieces. In addition, people from all over France and elsewhere contributed to the cathedral's reconstruction. Yet many of them might have derived material benefit from the decline of Chartres and the transfer of trade to their own communities, while those who were more remote, like King Richard, would probably not have been affected one way or the other.

The rebarbative Ik might appear at first to provide support for both the universality of material self-interest motivation and a condemnation of its consequences. Deprived by political developments of all but a meager and uncertain subsistence, they seem to have responded rationally in abandoning all morality and aesthetics in their dogged determination to survive. While much of the social norms literature in rational choice theory consists of efforts to explain cooperative or altruistic behavior in terms of material self-interest, the Ik seem to render these admittedly challenging efforts unnecessary. Confronted by the need for brute survival, they have apparently jettisoned the norms that govern more prosperous societies, which suggests that those norms are luxury goods, and thus much easier to explain or to explain away. Turnbull seems to subscribe to this interpretation. In the semi-hysterical peroration with which he ends his otherwise descriptive account, he suggests that the Ik's society is the one that lies in wait for all of us as we abandon the values that once constrained us (1972: 287–295). Material self-interest, he suggests, is the one true motivation, the skeleton inside human behavior that will be revealed when moral decline has burned the flesh away.

This self-interest interpretation of the Ik's behavior occurs naturally to us, and may well be the explanation they themselves provide for it, although Turnbull is not entirely clear about this point. But it is called into question by several features of his own account that he passes over without emphasis. The year after he completed his initial study, he returned and found that atypically heavy rainfalls had enabled the Ik to produce abundant crops (268–270). But "every crop, in every field, was rotting through sheer neglect.... [G]rubs and caterpillars were everywhere, and some fields had been destroyed by baboons" (1972: 269). Instead of spending the additional time in the fields that the bumper crop would render profitable, they continued to sit on the village platform, ignoring or annoying each other. The people's explanation for this behavior was that they had enough food for the time being, and saw no reason to expend any additional effort. But if self-interest had motivated the Ik in being so remorselessly cruel toward each other when they were starving, one would think that it would motivate them to maximize their food production in more favorable times and save the excess in physical or monetary form. Their lack of interest in doing so suggests that they are in fact demoralized, in both senses of the term. They have no morals but, more importantly, they have no motivation. They are a small tribe, with what seems to have been a rather rudimentary culture that was closely tied to their migration pattern and its physical setting. The complete disruption of this pattern and their exclusion from their primary hunting grounds administered a seemingly fatal blow to their ability to maintain a functional society.

On reflection, the selfish, brutal, and life-shortening behavior of the Ik is not self-interest maximizing at all. Interpreting it as such reflects not only our own cultural orientation, but also a certain self-hatred for having adopted it, and thus a willingness to see it exemplified, as Turnbull does, in an obviously dysfunctional society. Clearly, it would be in the Ik's material self-interest to cooperate with one another in a variety of tasks. They appear to have had such a social norm in the past, but it has become vestigial, surviving only as a vague sense that favors must be repaid, something the Ik try to avoid by walling off their homes and hunting or farming by themselves so that no one is in a position to do favors for them.

The social norms literature tries to explain how self-interest generates cultural patterns of cooperation, the basic idea being that these norms enable people to overcome immediate calculations of self-interest and work together to maximize their well-being in the longer term. James Coleman, for example (1990: 309–310) notes Turnbull's observation that Ik people sometimes provide assistance to a member of the tribe against that member's will, and speculates that they are creating obligations at times of ease that must then be recompensed at times of hardship. This does not really explain how such a norm would develop, however. Even more significantly, his interpretation is unconvincing because there is such a strong likelihood that the obligee will defect. It seems more plausible that the people providing the unrequested assistance are simply being mean, that they enjoy the discomfort that the obligee will experience in both witnessing their efforts and then breaching the weakened but still existent norm by failing to reciprocate. What prevents the Ik from cooperating with each other when it would be truly beneficial to do so, as their failure to take advantage of a bumper crop suggests, is not self-interest. It is meanness, a savage anger or resentment toward each other born of their exile from their favored hunting grounds and their former way of life.

In other words, norms of cooperation are not reflections of self-interest. They are norms. They function differently in different societies depending on the way they fit with the normative structure of those societies. In our society, they do indeed serve as ways to counteract short-term self-interest, because self-interest maximizing is a prevailing norm in our society. In Ancient Greek society, and for some period of time in Roman society as well, they served as means of maintaining urban culture and enhancing the individual's sense of honor, one particular manifestation being the liturgies, or private sponsorship of public functions. In Medieval Europe, norms of cooperation served to support religious institutions and secure people's confidence in their individual salvation. The Ik society's norms had broken down, not because they were exceptionally self-interested, or inveterately short-term thinkers, but because they had come to hate each other, and perhaps themselves as well.

Material self-interest maximizing as Western modernity's prevailing norm

Although the model of material self-interest maximizing does not succeed very well in interpreting behavior of people in many societies, it does succeed in ours. By using it, impressive insights about the modern Western world have been achieved. The purpose of this section is to explain why the success of the model in explaining behavior in our own society does not prove that self-interest maximizing is a human universal, and why social norms should not be regarded as mere adjustments to an otherwise successful model of behavior based on material self-interest, but rather as the overarching framework within which that model operates. As in the examples discussed above, that explanation depends in part on the cultural differences between our own society and others. This section adds a specifically historical account to the largely cultural one of the preceding section. That is, considering the historical development of the material self-interest norm in our own society not only indicates that this norm is a distinctive one, but demonstrates how it emerged as a result of particular historical trends, trends that did not operate, at least in the same way, in other societies.

As we look back on the historical development of our current society, sometimes described as High Modernity, it seems apparent that our current belief in the legitimacy of self-interest maximizing behavior is a relatively recent development. Well into the Early Modern era, charging interest on a loan was regarded as a serious offense, prices were expected to be just or fair, rather than being determined by the market, artisanal output and hours of work were restricted by the guilds, and the pursuit of wealth was regarded with suspicion or outright condemnation (Le Goff 1980a, 1980b; Schama 1997: 323–329; Tawney 1954). Explicit statements of these principles were regularly repeated, with virtually no dissent. Their basis was the religious ideology that dominated discourse in this period, particularly when the rules of social behavior were at issue. As late as the seventeenth century, Tawney notes (1954: 146), the general view, as expressed by Archbishop Laud, was that "the self-interest which leads the individual to struggle for riches and advancement" is a demon to be exorcised. The contrast with contemporary norms is unmistakable. Clearly a major change in the prevailing belief and value system separates us from our predecessors.

There has been much discussion in the historiography of Western society about the rise of the so-called capitalist spirit. Weber (2002) and Tawney (1954) conclude that the crucial factor was Calvinism, and consequently that the turning point was the Protestant Reformation. As these authors and others, such as Ernst Troeltsch (1912), describe it, the capitalist spirit is not exactly equivalent to rational self-interest maximizing. Weber, for example, characterizes it as "this-worldly asceticism," and associates it with intense hard work, with self-denial and with Benjamin Franklin's strictures against wasting time, rather than simply as the desire to amass material wealth (2002: 14–22, 53–101). Many psychologically, aesthetically, or sybaritically oriented people might argue that the joyless life thus conjured up is not in any individual's self-interest. But if we recognize that microeconomic theory and its political theory analogue of public choice are based not simply on self-interest, but on material self-interest, the difference between the two decreases markedly. The asceticism that Weber describes represents a convincing strategy, in all likelihood the best strategy, for maximizing one's material conditions. Thus, while it may not be true that all material self-interest maximizers behave like modern capitalists, it seems accurate to assert that modern capitalists tend to be rational self-interest maximizers.

This is an impressive theory, but it presents some difficulties in connection with the present inquiry. These are not empirical; while Weber's and Tawney's evidence has been challenged, it has held up reasonably well to a century of scrutiny. Rather, one difficulty is to explain why Calvin produced the momentous impact that Weber and Tawney ascribe to him. Given that he did not wield any direct power,[11] his influence depended solely on the persuasive quality of his work. That work was largely theological, of course. Although Calvin's penetrating intellect led him to the conclusion that lending money at reasonable rates served a useful economic purpose, he was as disparaging of commerce as other Christian writers, so that the economic implications of his work depended on active interpretation by others (Schama 1997: 329–343; Tawney 1954: 145–149, 177–180). A still greater difficulty is that Calvinism, even given its most wide-ranging interpretation, affirmatively demands hard work and frugality, and approves of wealth only as a consequence and emblem of those virtues. A brilliant inventor who makes a fortune on the basis of a sudden, electrifying insight, and then spends the remainder of her life in languid luxury, would horrify a Calvinist. In contrast, the modern ethos of material self-interest maximizing sees the desire for wealth as an intrinsic engine of prosperity, and regards the retired inventor as having earned her leisure by the market value of her contribution.

However original and startling it may be to attribute the modern mentality of wealth maximization to the austere and acetic Calvinists, a better explanation is to treat this mentality as the culmination of deeper and more familiar social trends: commercialization, urbanization, centralized government, and secularization. While neither trade nor artisanal activity disappeared in the latter part of the Early Middle Ages (AD 800–1000), the level of commercial activity was substantially lower than it had been during the late Empire (Lopez 1966: 103–111; Pirenne 1954; Ward-Perkins 2005; Wickham 2009: 529–551); after that it steadily revived. Its growth was fueled in part by a pre-Reformation desire for wealth, but at least equally by the desire for liberty, since the cities provided the only refuge from the feudal system where non-noble people could be free (Bartlett 1993: 106–132; Geis and Geis 1969: 199–210; Lopez 1966: 126–148; Mundy and Riesenberg 1958; Pirenne 1952), and urban populations can only feed and clothe themselves through commerce. The revival of centralized governance was a parallel and interacting trend. Kings could grant these cities the charters that conferred freedom on their residents, and the cities then became the natural allies of the centralizing monarchs in their centuries-long struggle with the feudal and essentially agricultural lords (Bartlett 1993: 167–196; Hay 1966: 81–166). As the monarchs triumphed they disarmed the lords and turned them into courtiers; the order that the process imposed upon the area within the monarch's jurisdiction produced the collateral benefit of facilitating commerce (Elias 1994: 441–475; Ogg 1960: 275–311). The resulting commerce then financed the monarchs and encouraged their increasing political ambitions, which in turn created an increased need for funds, and thus a further incentive to support the cities and impose order on the nation.

The parallel process of secularization is both too complex and too familiar to be described in any detail in this discussion. For present purposes, it is sufficient to note that the Roman Empire's collapse left Western Europe with a universal church and particularized political regimes.[12] After 1000 this mismatch generated an inevitable tension between the church and the centralizing monarchs. In this case, as in the case of their conflict with the feudal lords, the monarchs gradually prevailed. The intellectual developments now identified as the Renaissance weakened Christianity's hold on people's minds to some extent; the troubled century that preceded it (1309 to 1418) featuring the Avignon Papacy, when the Church was dominated by the French monarchy, and the Great or Western Schism, when two or more people claimed to be Pope (Hay 1989: 288–304; Renouard 1970) probably produced an even greater impact. At first, the Reformation seemed to signal a revival of religious feeling, but its long-term effects were to fractionate institutional Christianity, which placed both the newly established Protestant Churches and the newly depleted Catholic Church still more securely under national control, and to raise doubts about the certainty of Christian doctrine (MacCulloch 2003; Skinner 1978). Europe's exposure to non-Christian cultures during the sixteenth and seventeenth centuries, and the Scientific Revolution of the latter period, further undermined religious doctrine and belief. By the eighteenth century, skepticism and genuinely secular attitudes were becoming prevalent (Gay 1977), and by the nineteenth and twentieth centuries they were predominant (Bruce 2002; Chadwick 1975).

These trends, operating continuously, slowly undermined the religious, salvation-oriented mode of thought that prevailed in the Christian West and prepared the way for the modern belief in the legitimacy and value of material self-interest maximizing. The crucial figure in effecting this transition, the person who definitively rejected the Medieval view and articulated the Modern one, is exactly the person who is conventionally identified as having done so, namely Adam Smith. It is important, however, to recognize the meaning of Smith's work in context, as well as its significance in retrospect. As modern scholars have emphasized, Smith saw himself as an ethicist, rather than an economist (Herman 2001: 204–210; Himmelfarb 2005: 35–38, 53–70). This is not only because his other major work was *A Theory of Moral Sentiments* (1976), but also because *The Wealth of Nations* (1986) was itself concerned with ethics. It was written against the background of Bernard de Mandeville's *Fable of the Bees.*

At the beginning of the eighteenth century, Mandeville published a poem entitled "The Grumbling Hive," or "Knaves Turn'd Honest," which he then incorporated into the *Fable of the Bees, or Private Vices, Publick Virtues*, a lengthy monograph (Mandeville 1988). As the title suggests, Mandeville's argument is that avaricious, inconsiderate behavior that is condemned on moral grounds combines to produce social good (1988: 24–25):

Thus every part was full of Vice
Yet the whole mass a Paradise;...
The root of Evil, Avarice

> That dam'd, ill-natur'd baneful Vice
> Was Slave to Prodigality
> That noble Sin; whilst Luxury
> Employ'd a million of the Poor,
> And odious Pride a million more:
> Envy it self, and Vanity,
> Were ministers of Industry;

Mandeville was himself a social reformer, but he was also among the first of a group of eighteenth-century thinkers who delighted in satirizing traditional religion and morality. Smith offers a much more complex and thoughtful version of Mandeville's insight, turning it from satire into economics, but he also reformulates its moral implications in a momentous way. Selfish, or what we now called self-interested, behavior is not a vice that ironically produces public benefit according to Smith. He does not go so far as to call it a virtue, as he is still sufficiently immersed in traditional society, but he describes it as natural behavior, the rational and blameless pursuit of one's interest that can be approved because of the good results that it produces. "It is not from the benevolence of the butcher, the brewer, or the baker that we expect our dinner, but from their regard to their own interest. We address ourselves, not to their humanity but to their self-love" (Smith 1986: 119). Being natural, in the eighteenth century, was essentially equated with being good, in at least a quasi-moral sense, and thus Smith begins the modern tradition of treating rational self-interest maximizing as a dominant norm.

At the very least, then, it seems clear that Western society did not regard material self-interest maximizing as an acceptable form of behavior until the late eighteenth century. It is, of course, quite possible to argue that the prevailing social norms in pre-modern times had no effect on behavior, that people were as motivated by material self-interest in those times as they are at present. These assertion runs up against some formidable difficulties, however. First, it assumes that a prevailing social norm can exist for an extended time, at least 800 years in this case, without affecting behavior. Second, it ignores a wide range of social practices that seem contrary to our notion of self-interest maximizing, attempting to explain them in terms of institutional constraints that themselves remain unexplained. Third, and most significant, because it is our norm, we must recognize that we will tend to interpret people's behaviors in those terms, that we will seize on the behavior of those who deviated from the prior, different norm as typical, and search for other motivations to explain the behavior of those who apparently conformed to it.

There is, moreover, strong collateral evidence to suggest that Smith's work reflects a true normative transformation in society. The late eighteenth century was an era of truly epochal change. It saw two wide-ranging revolutions, in America and France, and the advent of large-scale or mass democracy in America as a result of that revolution and in Britain, as a result of the cabinet system triggered, ironically perhaps, by that same revolution.[13] It saw as well the initiation of modern administrative governance in revolutionary America and France, but also in Britain, as a result of Pitt's reforms, in Austria, through the efforts of a benevolent despot, Emperor Joseph II, and in Prussia, as a result of the Stein–Hardenberg reforms supported by a less benevolent despot, Frederick William III (Rubin 2005: 22–36). During the same period, the Industrial Revolution can be said to have truly begun, although its transformative effects would not be felt for several decades. All these changes can be regarded as related to the normative framework of material self-interest maximizing. Democracy, after all, is based on the premise that people voting in their own interests should determine government policy, rather than its being determined by a monarch who, at least in theory, acts on their behalf, based on his own judgment about what is good for them. Administrative governance conceives its purposes as serving the people's material needs, providing economic prosperity and social welfare through consciously developed policy.[14] And the Industrial Revolution was not only spear-headed by entrepreneurs who were free of traditional constraints and focused on obtaining as much wealth as possible, but also enabled them to achieve that wealth by producing mass-market goods that appealed to the material desires of the populace.

In short, material self-interest maximizing became a prevailing norm in the Western world at the end of the eighteenth century. Its origins can be traced to readily identifiable political, social, and intellectual trends, and its ascendency associated with closely allied developments in other aspects of society. These trends and developments are unique; no other society has experienced the same process of commercialization, nationalization, and secularization, nor has any other society developed mass democracy, administrative governance, and industrialization except as a result of Western influence. This explanation provides additional evidence for the proposition that self-interest maximizing is a specific feature of our own society, and not a human universal. In examining these societies, such as Ancient Rome, Medieval Europe, and the Ik, we see that it is difficult to interpret the behavior of people in other societies as primarily motivated by material self-interest maximizing. In examining our own society, we find that people's behavior can in fact be interpreted as motivated in this way. But that reflects particular and identifiable developments that emphasize its distinctiveness. In short, material self-interest maximizing is itself a norm. We engage in it, and do so to a unique extent, because it is our norm, not because it resides with the genetic program of the human race.

Prevailing norms and the social norms literature

As stated at the outset, modern microeconomic theory recognizes the role of social norms and attempts to take account of them within the framework of its rational choice analysis. The argument thus far is that norms, not rational choice, constitute the framework, and that material self-interest maximizing, the form of rational choice theory that serves as the basis of microeconomics, is simply the particular norm that prevails in our own society. But if that is the case, then what is the status of the norms that microeconomic analysis has incorporated, and how do they relate to the larger norm that valorizes self-interested behavior? The answer that this section will suggest is that at least some of these norms reflect other aspects of society's normative structure, and appear within the realm of economic activity when the prevailing norm, for one reason or another, does not comprehensively control people's actions.

If a norm is defined as a rule that is not enforced by law but is nonetheless obeyed (Posner 2002), then a good deal of norm-driven behavior, like a good deal of law-abiding behavior, can be explained by the rational actor model. There is no great difficulty in explaining, from a rational choice perspective, why contemporary Europeans, unlike their Early Medieval predecessors, no longer use armed force to resolve disputes over real property; we need only observe the modern state's reliable imposition of severe punishment for such behavior. Equally severe sanctions can also be imposed by non-official or non-legal actors. Thus, if all the members of a given commercial community, like diamond merchants or theatrical producers, will stop dealing with a person who engages in a certain type of behavior, then no rational actor who wanted to make a living in that field would engage in the prohibited behavior unless she thought she could escape detection (Bernstein 1992, 1996; Cooter 1996; Rock and Wachter 1996). In other words, some norm-driven behavior is generated within the structure of material self-interest maximizing behavior, and demands no reference to any other norm.

There are, however, other norm-driven behaviors that are not so easy to explain. One such set of behaviors are those where the sanctions are weak or non-existent. The microeconomically based literature on social norms focuses on cases of this kind, such as the norm that one should vote in national elections or give tips to certain types of service providers (Ferejohn and Fiorina 1974; Green and Shapiro 1994; Kostristsky 2013; Levmore 2000). Another, and perhaps more serious problem, is to explain why people, if they are indeed concerned with maximizing their own self-interest, do not defect from intermittently enforced norms on a more regular basis (Eisenberg 1999; MacCauley 1963), that is, why social norms can be so stable over long periods of time. A frequent response to both apparent contradictions has been to construct post hoc accounts demonstrating that maintenance of the norm is in fact instrumentally rational, that tipping is a way of monitoring service, or that the economy will function better if norms of fair dealing and trust are maintained. But this approach leaves an explanatory gap. The power of microeconomic theory lies in its solid reliance on methodological individualism, its insistence that collective patterns and results must be explained in terms of the behavior of discrete individuals (Coleman 1990: 1–23), and not by reference to vague or posited concepts that sound good in German, like zeitgeist, weltanschauung, or gessellschaft. From this perspective, however, it becomes difficult to explain why material self-interest maximizers would engage in action that only produces collective benefits and not benefits to themselves as individuals (Cooter 2000; Kostritsky 2013).

Some of the efforts to close this gap have been heroic, but they suffer from the overelaborate quality of the Ptolemaic spheres. This is not to deny that many of these explanations are informative about the way that social norms function, particularly in economic settings, nor even to assert that they can be definitively proven wrong. The difficulty is again epistemological; these explanations reveal the same weakness as the effort to explain the flight of the *curiales*, the reconstruction of Chartres, and the miseries of the Ik in self-interest maximizing terms. They not only seem to be trying too hard, but what they are trying to do is to assimilate behaviors that appear to be based on other motivations into our own society's prevailing norm. This produces the same sense of discomfort that one senses when observing that a medical specialist invariably diagnoses patients as suffering from the particular disease in which he specializes, no matter what the presenting symptom may be.

The alternative is similar to the alternative in the three examples offered above. In those cases, the more plausible approach is to explain the observed behavior in terms of other social norms, such as honor, religious belief, or vindictiveness. This jettisons the claim that all behavior is based on material self-interest maximizing, but retains the more defensible epistemological stance of methodological individualism. The alternative norms are experienced, and in most cases internalized, by the individual actors, not as a result of calculation, but through the process that Husserl described as intersubjectivity (Husserl 1962: 93–95, 388–390; 1970: 252–257). This means, very roughly, that it is learned at the very basic level where one learns how to function as a member of a particular society, that the only way for the individual to understand the rules of proper behavior and even coherent thought within the society is to incorporate certain norms into her belief system.

James Coleman (1990) argues against such explanations, and specifically refers to Weber's theory of the Protestant Ethic in making his case (1990: 6–10). While apparently willing to accept the idea that macro-level social conditions can generate or influence individual attitudes, he challenges the claim that individual attitudes, which occur at the micro level, can aggregate to produce social conditions, and demands that any such explanation must trace an institutional path, that is, must show how individuals influenced a specific social actor and how that actor then affected the society in general. This sounds rigorous, especially given the peremptory way that Coleman presents it. But it cannot withstand analysis because it assumes the point he is trying to demonstrate, namely that individual attitudes cannot aggregate to produce social conditions. He is certainly entitled to demand a mechanism by which such a process can occur, but his study rejects, or rather assumes away, the one that is being argued for here and that most social scientists accept. This is some version of intersubjectivity, the idea that individual attitudes, which would include norms and also related interpretive or epistemological views of nature (which we generally call descriptions) structure the possibilities for social action, the range of behaviors that any individual can pursue, and the meaning of those behaviors for herself and other members of society.[15]

A thought experiment can illustrate the implausibility of Coleman's argument. If a group of people from a particular society were to be marooned on an isolated but habitable island, the idea that the society they created there would respond only to the prevailing conditions, and would not mirror their culture of origin in basic ways, is inconceivable. The experiment has actually been performed a few times on a small scale, such as Pitcairn Island, and more times on a larger one, such as the foundation of colonial regimes in North America, Australia, and lower South America (that is, in places where there was not a significant mixing of incoming and indigenous cultures). Such examples provide strong evidence that attitudes will shape culture even in the absence of institutional structures.

In the case of our society, the most plausible reason why people do not always seem to act as material self-interest maximizers is that there are other norms in the society beside the dominant or prevailing one, that different areas of life are controlled by different norms that bleed into one another. Their existence provides a well-recognized critique of rational actor theory (Cho 2012; Edelman 2004; Green and Shapiro 1994) This multiplicity of motivation might seem unsatisfying to someone committed to the microeconomic model, or to an a priori demand that theories of behavior operate universally. But if the pattern of behavior on which that model rests is itself a norm and not a human universal, as argued above, then reference to one norm is no worse than reference to another. In other words, once we recognize that rational self-interest maximizing is the particular norm of our society, there is no reason why we should not have other norms as well, and no reason why reference to those other norms is a less satisfactory explanation for human behavior than reference to the prevailing one.

In fact, it is quite clear that our society has norms other than material self-interest maximizing, however significant and distinctive that particular norm may be. Two brief examples will suffice. It certainly appears that the High Modern West is more commercial, or economically oriented, than its Medieval predecessor, but the norms involving marriage have moved in the opposite direction. During the Middle Ages, marriages were arranged as economic alliances, whether it was two noble families uniting their estates, a nobleman with a good name marrying a merchant's daughter with a good inheritance, or a peasant with a horse marrying another peasant with a wagon (Coontz 2005: 88–122; Duby 1978; Geis and Geis 1987; Thomas 2009: 214–220). This was not only a pragmatic arrangement but a social norm. The Catholic Church insisted that marriage must be based on consent, but parents extracted that consent from their children (or a grown man might extract it from a twelve-year-old girl's parents) and relied on the prevailing norm to secure it (Brundage 1987; Duby 1978). In the modern world, the idea of a just price is scorned and guild restrictions regarded as a type of superstition, but people marry for love (Coontz 2005; Hetherington 2003). This is not to say that they never take economic factors into account, but rather that there is a strong social norm against choosing a marital partner on that basis.

The second example is the one given by Judge Posner in his contribution to this volume. It is presumably in the material self-interest of many academics, particularly in fields such as law, political science, economics, and sociology that involve active controversies, to adopt pro-industry positions. Doing so would help them obtain private grants, remunerative consultancies, and greater opportunities for employment if they decided to leave academia. In addition, it might help them obtain tenure in certain cases, or attract contributions to their universities for which equally mercenary deans and provosts might reward them with salary increases or summer grants. But strong social norms demand that academics base their work on their best judgment. There may well be some academics who alter their views to achieve material rewards, but there are very few who would admit to doing so, which is perhaps the best evidence for the existence of a robust social norm.

In other words, although material self-interest maximizing is a prevailing norm in our society, it is not the only norm. It certainly determines a good deal of observed behavior, but because it is a norm, and not a human universal, it can be readily altered or alloyed by other norms when circumstances render those considerations operative. Thus, behavior that cannot be explained, at least without heroic and ultimately unconvincing efforts, as rational choice should not be regarded as enigmatic lapses into irrationality. Rather, it represents the natural interplay of varying attitudes that any complex society displays, the range of behavior resources that individuals within such a society will naturally draw upon in daily life. The modern individual who scorns advice to seek a wealthy spouse and marries instead for love or passion will then ignore affection or belief when she leaves the house for her job at the bank. The scholar who sincerely adopts his academic stance on the basis of personal ideology will then jump from the institution that gave him tenure to one offering a higher salary with no thought of institutional loyalty. Each particular motive may require explanation, but the fact that they are mixed together does not. It is only the unlikely case of a single motivation, a norm so powerful that it controls everything a person does, that should elicit our astonishment.

Notes

* University Professor of Law and Political Science, Vanderbilt University. I want to thank my research assistant, Lara Assaf, for her assistance with this chapter.
1 Manfred, King of Sicily, 1258–66, was a libertine and an enemy of the Church all his life, but, at least according to Dante, he repented as he lay dying on the battlefield and thereby earned a place in Purgatory, which is of course salvation ("Horrible were my sins, but infinite is the abiding Goodness which holds out, Its open arms to all who turn to It") (Dante 2003: 306). Judges 16 recounts the death of Samson, whose brothers bury him in his father's tomb, recognizing that he has either redeemed his honor or earned salvation.
2 The term "liturgy" means public service in Greek. It came to be associated with the ceremony in which a Catholic priest officiated (or specifically with the Eucharist in the Eastern Church) because this ceremony was public, as opposed to the devotions in private homes that prevailed in early Christianity. Modern English continues to use the word "service" in this dual capacity of a public function and a religious ceremony. The practice of providing liturgies is sometimes referred to as evergetism (Veyne 1987: 107–110).
3 Some of these areas, such as Sicily, modern Provence, and parts of Spain's Mediterranean coast, were already Hellenized, so that Roman administration could be imposed on an existing city-state structure, as it was in the East (Wells 1992: 146–148).

4 Aristotle and his students apparently documented the constitutions of some 170 different city-states. Only one survives, the one about Athens purportedly written by Aristotle himself (Aristotle 1952: 553).

5 The South Tower (to your right as you face the façade), which originally stood free but was incorporated into the façade by the reconstruction, is generally considered an architectural masterpiece for its elegant solution to the problem of placing an octagonal fleche that meets the sky on top of a square base that rests on the ground (Adams 1986: 62–68).

6 Turnbull's account of the Ik ends with the completion of his book in 1971. A somewhat later academic article notes that there has been no follow-up study (Heine 1985) and, so far as I have been able to determine, there is none to date. A recent feature news story suggests that the Ik have survived, although just barely (Musasizi 2013); it does not reveal whether their culture remains the same as the one Turnbull observed.

7 In notoriously litigious Athens, the defendant in a lawsuit could point to his performance of a liturgy as evidence that the citizen jury should find in his favor (there being no rules of evidence). Moreover, someone who was expected to perform a liturgy could insist that another person, who was wealthier but doing less, perform it in his place (Joint Association of Classical Teachers 1984: 229). These enforcement mechanisms certainly made the liturgy less voluntary, but Athens was probably exceptional, being so much larger and more commercial than any other mainland Greek city. More importantly, these mechanisms are all based on an underlying ethos of obligation.

8 Of course, wealthy people in the East, as in the West, built lavish rural villas. It is always nice to have a country house if you can afford it. But in the East, as in the West at an earlier time, people tended to use their rural residences as second homes, not as ways of withdrawing from urban life.

9 Unlike the Arabs, the German conquerors were not particularly antagonistic to Roman civilization. Many were Christianized before they entered the Empire, and nearly all had extensive economic and cultural contact with it. Having arrived, those so-called barbarians that were not already Christianized converted rapidly, and saw themselves as successors to the Roman rulers. The Arabs, of course, followed a rival religion that was equally sophisticated as Christianity. They never converted, and they regarded themselves as displacing Roman rule with a new and superior culture (Brown 1989: 189–203; Lewis 2008: 57–84; Ward-Perkins 2005: 81–82; Wickham 2009: 279–297).

10 In addition to the Nativity, these were the Presentation (in the Temple), or Candlemas, on February 2, the Annunciation, on March 25, and the Assumption (Mary's direct ascent into Heaven) on August 15.

11 To be sure, he was a religious leader of a rather remarkable theocracy in one small European principality – Geneva – but he only obtained that position because he had been invited by the civil authorities (Godfrey 2009: 57–59; Gordon 2009: 121–125).

12 There was a brief historical moment, when Charlemagne ruled most of Western Christendom and was crowned Emperor by the Pope, that the reestablishment of a unified political and religious regime seemed possible. But Charlemagne's Empire broke apart during the ninth century, and the Imperial Crown shifted to one of its component parts, corresponding roughly to modern Germany, which then became the Papacy's most determined opponent.

13 When Lord North resigned his Prime Ministership in 1782 because of the failure to subdue the revolution in the Thirteen Colonies, all the other ministers resigned along with him, the first time such a thing had happened. This meant that they were not the king's ministers but part of an elected government that stood or fell on the basis of the electorate's confidence.

14 I have elaborated this argument in two books, *Beyond Camelot* (2005) and *Soul, Self and Society* (forthcoming, 2015).

15 A striking feature of Coleman's massive and often informative study is his absolute refusal to engage with any of the numerous and well-known modern thinkers who argue in favor of social constructivism. From this entire literature, which directly challenges his theory, I was able to find only one passing reference to Habermas (Coleman 1990: 636) on a minor point.

References

Adams, H. (1986) [1904] *Mont Saint Michel and Chartres*, New York: Penguin.
Aristotle (1952) 'The Athenian Constitution' (F. Kenyon, trans.), in *The Works of Aristotle*, Chicago, IL: Encyclopedia Britannica.
Bartlett, R. (1993) *The Making of Europe: Conquest, Colonization and Cultural Change 950–1350*, Princeton, NJ: Princeton University Press.
Berger, P. and Luckmann, T. (1966) *The Social Construction of Reality: A Treatise in the Sociology of Knowledge*, New York: Anchor Books.
Bernstein, L. 'Opting out of the legal system: extra-legal contractual relations in the diamond industry', *Journal of Legal Studies* 21, 1992: 115–157.
Bernstein, L. 'Merchant law in a merchant court: rethinking the code's search for immanent business norms', *University of Pennsylvania Law Review* 144, 1996: 1765–1821.
Blair, P. (1963) *Roman Britain and Early England, 55 B.C.–A.D. 871*, New York: W.W. Norton.
Bringmann, K. (2007) *A History of the Roman Republic* (W.J. Smyth, trans.), Cambridge: Polity Press.
Brown, P. (1989) *The World of Late Antiquity*, New York: W.W. Norton.
Brown, S., Brown, R., and Penner, L. (2012) *Moving Beyond Self-Interest: Perspectives from Evolutionary Biology, Neuroscience, and the Social Sciences*, Oxford: Oxford University Press.
Bruce, S. (2002) *God is Dead: Secularization in the West*, Malden, MA: Blackwell Publishing.
Brundage, J. (1987) *Law, Sex, and Christian Society in Medieval Europe*, Chicago, IL: University of Chicago Press.
Cantor, N. (1994) *The Civilization of the Middle Ages*, rev. edn., New York: Harper Perennial.
Chadwick, O. (1975) *The Secularization of the European Mind in the 19th Century*, Cambridge: Cambridge University Press.
Cho, S. 'Beyond rationality: a sociological construction of the World Trade Organization', *Virginia Journal of International Law* 52, 2012: 321–354.
Coleman, J. (1990) *Foundations of Social Theory*, Cambridge, MA: Belknap Press.
Coontz, S. (2005) *Marriage, a History: How Love Conquered Marriage*, New York: Penguin Books.
Cooter, R. 'The best right laws: value foundations of the economic analysis of law', *Notre Dame Law Review* 64, 1989: 817–837.
Cooter, R. 'Decentralized Law for a Complex Economy: The Structural Approach to Adjudicating the New Law Merchant, *University of Pennsylvania Law Review* 144, 1996: 1643–1696.
Cooter, R. 'Three effects of social norms on law: expression, deterrence, and internalization', *Oregon Law Review* 79, 2000: 1–22.
Dante Alighieri (2003) *The Divine Comedy* (J. Ciardi, trans.), New York: New American Library.

Dau-Schmidt, K. 'Economics and sociology: the prospects for an interdisciplinary discourse on law', *Wisconsin Law Review* 3, 1997: 389–420.

Dostoyevsky, F. (1959) [1866], *Crime and Punishment* (C. Garnett, trans.), New York: Dell Publishing.

Duby, G. (1978) *Medieval Marriage: Two Models from Twelfth Century France* (Elborg Forster, trans.), Baltimore, MD: Johns Hopkins University Press.

Edelman, L. (2004) 'Rivers of law and contested terrain: a law and society approach to economic rationality', *Law and Society Review* 28, 2004: 181–197.

Eisenberg, M. (1999) 'Corporate law and social norms', *Columbia Law Review* 99, 1999: 1253.

Elias, N. (1994) [1939] *The Civilizing Process*, Oxford: Blackwell.

Ellickson, R. (1994) *Order Without Law: How Neighbors Settle Disputes*, Cambridge, MA: Harvard University Press.

Ferejohn, J. (1991) 'Rationality and interpretation: parliamentary elections in early Stuart England', in *The Economic Approach to Politics: A Critical Reassessment of the Theory of Rational Action* (Kristen Monroe, ed.), New York: Harper Collins.

Ferejohn, J. and Fiorina, M. (1974) 'The paradox of not voting: a decision theory analysis', *American Political Science Review* 68, 1974: 525–536.

Finley, M.I. (1965) *The World of Odysseus*, rev. edn., New York: Viking Press.

Fox, R.L. (1986) *Pagans and Christians*, New York: Harper & Row.

Frankfurt, H. (1988) *The Importance of What We Care About: Philosophical Essays*, Cambridge: Cambridge University Press.

Gay, P. (1977) *The Enlightenment: The Rise of Modern Paganism*, New York: W.W. Norton.

Geary, P. (1988) *Before France and Germany: The Creation and Transformation of the Merovingian World*, Oxford: Oxford University Press.

Gies, F. and Gies, J. (1987) *Marriage and the Family in the Middle Ages*, New York: Harper Perennial.

Gies, J. and Gies, F. (1969) *Life in a Medieval City*, New York: Harper & Row.

Godfrey, W. (2009) *John Calvin: Pilgrim and Pastor*, Wheaton, IL: Crossways Books.

Goldsworthy, A. (2009) *How Rome Fell: Death of a Superpower*, New Haven, CT: Yale University Press.

Goodman, N. (1978) *Ways of Worldmaking*, Indianapolis, IN: Hackett Publishing.

Gordon, B. (2009) *Calvin*, New Haven, CT: Yale University Press.

Green, D. and Shapiro, I. (1994) *Pathologies of Rational Choice Theory: A Critique of Applications in Political Science*, New Haven, CT: Yale University Press.

Gruen, E. (2004) 'Rome and the Greek world', in *The Cambridge Companion to the Roman Republic* (H. Flower, ed.), New York: Cambridge University Press.

Habermas, J. (1987) *The Theory of Communicative Action, vol. 2: Lifeworld and System: A Critique of Functionalist Reason* (Thomas McCarthy, trans.), Boston, MA: Beacon Press.

Hardin, R., 'Magic on the frontier: the norm of efficiency', *University of Pennsylvania Law Review* 144, 1996: 1987–2020.

Hay, Denys (1989) *Europe in the Fourteenth and Fifteenth Centuries*, London: Longman.

Heather, P. (2006) *The Fall of the Roman Empire: A New History of Rome and the Barbarians*, Oxford: Oxford University Press.

Heine, B. 'The mountain people: some notes on the Ik of Northern Uganda', *Africa* 55, 1985: 3–16.

Herman, A. (2001) *How the Scots Invented the Modern World*, New York: Three Rivers Press.

Hetherington, E. (2003) *For Better or For Worse: Divorce Reconsidered*, New York: W.W. Norton.

Himmelfarb, G. (2005) *The Roads to Modernity: The British, French, and American Enlightenments*, New York: Vintage.

Husserl, E. (1962) *Ideas: General Introduction to Pure Phenomenology* (W.R. Boyce Gibson, trans.), New York: Collier Books.

Husserl, E. (1970) *The Crisis of the European Sciences and Transcendental Phenomenology: An Introduction to Phenomenological Philosophy* (David Carr, trans.), Evanston, IL: Northwestern University Press.

Joint Association of Classical Teachers (1984) *The World of Athens: An Introduction to Classical Athenian Culture*, Cambridge: Cambridge University Press.

Katz, A., 'Taking private ordering seriously', *University of Pennsylvania Law Review* 144, 1996: 1745–1763.

Kostritsky, J., 'The law and economics of norms', *Texas International Law Journal* 48, 2013: 465–505.

Kuran, T. (1997) *Private Truths, Public Lies: The Social Consequences of Preference Falsification*, Cambridge, MA: Harvard University Press.

Le Goff, J. (1980a) 'Merchant's time and church's time in the Middle Ages', in *Time, Work and Culture in the Middle Ages* (A. Goldhammer, trans.), Chicago, IL: University of Chicago Press.

Le Goff, J. (1980b) 'Licit and illicit trades in the Medieval West' in *Time, Work and Culture in the Middle Ages* (A. Goldhammer, trans.), Chicago, IL: University of Chicago Press.

Levmore, S., 'Norms as supplements', *Virginia Law Review* 86, 2000: 1989.

Lewis, D. (2008) *God's Crucible: Islam and the Making of the Europe, 570–1215*, New York: W.W. Norton.

Lopez, R. (1966) *The Birth of Europe*, New York: M. Evans & Co.

Macaulay, S. 'Non-contractual relations in business: a preliminary study', *American Sociological Review* 28, 1963: 55–72.

MacCulloch, D. (2003) *The Reformation: A History*, New York: Penguin Books.

MacIntyre, A. (1984) *After Virtue*, 2nd edn. Notre Dame, IN: University of Notre Dame Press.

Mandeville, B. (1988) [1724] *The Fable of the Bees, or Private Vices, Publick Benefits*, Indianapolis, IN: Liberty Fund, Inc.

Mansbridge, J. (1990) *Beyond Self-Interest*, Chicago, IL: University of Chicago Press.

Markale, J. (1987) *Courtly Love: The Path of Sexual Initiation*, Rochester, VT: Inner Traditions.

Mundy, J. and Riesenberg, P. (1958) *The Medieval Town*, Princeton, NJ: D. Van Nostrand Co.

Musasizi, S., 'Meet the Ik: Karamoja's original tribe on the verge of extinction', *Observer*, 2013, http://observer.ug/index.php?option=com_content&view=article&id=27912:meet-the-ik-karamojas-original-tribe-on-verge-of-extinction&catid=73:highlights&Itemid=70 (accessed January 13, 2014).

Ober, J. (1989) *Mass and Elite in Democratic Athens: Rhetoric, Ideology and the Power of the People*, Princeton, NJ: Princeton University Press.

Ogg, D. (1960) *Europe in the Seventeenth Century*, New York: Collier Books.

Pirenne, H. (1952) *Medieval Cities: Their Origins and the Revival of Trade*, Princeton, NJ: Princeton University Press.

Pirenne, H. (1954) *Mohammed and Charlemagne*, London: George Allen & Unwin.

Posner, E. (2002) *Law and Social Norms*, Cambridge, MA: Harvard University Press.

Renouard, Y. (1970) *The Avignon Papacy 1305–1403*, London: Faber and Faber.

Rock, E. and Wachter, M., 'The enforceability of norms and the employment relationship', *University of Pennsylvania Law Review* 144, 1996: 1913–1952.

Rubin, E. (2005) *Beyond Camelot: Rethinking Politics and Law for the Modern State*, Princeton, NJ: Princeton University Press.

Rubin, E. (2015) *Soul, Self, and Society: The New Morality and the Modern State*, New York: Oxford University Press.

Salway, P. (1981) *Roman Britain*, Oxford: Oxford University Press.

Schama, S. (1997) *The Embarrassment of Riches: An Interpretation of Dutch Culture in the Golden Age*, New York: Vintage Books.

Simson, O. (1978) *The Gothic Cathedral*, Princeton, NJ: Princeton University Press.

Simson, O. (1988) *The Gothic Cathedral: Origins of Gothic Architecture and the Medieval Concept of Order*, 3rd edn., Princeton, NJ: Princeton University Press.

Skinner, Q. (1978) *The Foundations of Modern Political Thought, vol. 2: The Age of Reformation*, Cambridge: Cambridge University Press.

Smith, A. (1986) [1776] *The Wealth of Nations: Books I–III*, London: Penguin Books.

Smith, A. (1976) [1959] *The Theory of Moral Sentiments*, Oxford: Oxford University Press.

Tawney, R.H. (1954) *Religion and the Rise of Capitalism*, New York: Mentor Books.

Thomas, K. (2009) *The Ends of Life: Paths to Fulfillment in Early Modern England*, Oxford: Oxford University Press.

Troeltsch, E. (1912) *Protestantism and Progress: A Historical Study of the Relation of Protestantism to the Modern World* (W. Montgomery, trans.), New York: G.P. Putnam's Sons.

Turnbull, C. (1968) *The Forest People*, New York: Simon & Schuster, Inc.

Turnbull, C. (1972) *The Mountain People*, New York: Simon & Schuster, Inc.

Veyne, P. (1987) 'The Roman Empire', in *A History of Private Life, vol. 1: From Pagan Rome to Byzantium* (P. Veyne, ed.; A. Goldhammer, trans.), Cambridge, MA: Belknap Press.

Ward-Perkins, B. (2005) *The Fall of Rome and the End of Civilization*, Oxford: Oxford University Press.

Weber, M. (2002) [1904–5] *The Protestant Ethic and the Spirit of Capitalism* (S. Kalberg, trans.), Los Angeles, CA: Roxbury.

Wells, C. (1992) *The Roman Empire*, 2nd edn., Cambridge, MA: Harvard University Press.

Wickham, C. (2009) *The Inheritance of Rome: Illuminating the Dark Ages 400–1000*, New York: Viking.

Winch, P. (1958) *The Idea of a Social Science and its Relation to Philosophy*, London: Routledge & Kegan Paul.

5 From dismal to dominance?

Law and economics and the values of imperial science, historically contemplated

Steven G. Medema*

Introduction

The (hi)story of the economic analysis of law is one of success, whether "success" is measured by the field's explanatory power or by its professional entrenchment. On the economics side, its journals have significant status within the profession at large, the subject matter has its own *JEL* code, and texts and courses have proliferated at the undergraduate and graduate levels. Within the legal realm, the economic approach still has its detractors, and some might argue that it is no less controversial now than at its inception, or even at the time of the *Hofstra Law Review* symposium that this volume commemorates. It is unquestionable, though, that the economic analysis of law has become an established player within legal theory and, institutionally, within American law schools,[1] while Critical Legal Studies, its ostensible challenger in the race to upset the mainstream apple cart, has splintered into a number of ineffectual "critical X" groups that have little impact on legal training and scholarship.

The economic approach, while retaining much of its original flavor, has not remained static; rather, it has evolved to encompass a somewhat broader perspective than evidenced in its formative years. This broadening owes, of course, to the influence of work being done in behavioral law and economics and the analysis of social norms, movements that seem to be generating a natural, and even predictable, melding of certain facets of the economic and traditional legal approaches.[2] Even with this slight broadening of perspective, though, the values of the economic analysis of law remain pretty much unchanged. Its values are those of a particular definition of economics and of the economic imperialism that this definition has engendered, and – in certain quarters at least – of a particular normative perspective: efficiency, or wealth maximization.[3] Gary Becker is the person perhaps most closely associated with this view of economics and Richard Posner, in the minds of most, with the application of these values with the legal arena.

Economics as imperial science

It is useful to begin with a little history.[4] "Law and economics" scholarship – the analysis of the interrelations between legal and economic processes – extends back long before Richard Posner, Gary Becker, Guido Calabresi, Ronald Coase, or even Aaron Director arrived on the scene. Adam Smith devoted more than a little discussion to the topic of the appropriate legal framework for an economic system, and economic or quasi-economic approaches to the analysis of law can be traced back at least to the utilitarian efforts of Jeremy Bentham and Henry Sidgwick that book-ended the nineteenth century.[5] Legal Realist lawyer-economists such as Walton Hamilton and Robert Lee Hale (who were economists on law school faculties before that tradition got started at Chicago) engaged in a great deal of legal-economic analysis, although neither they nor law-minded economists such as John R. Commons had anything to do with inspiring the economic analysis of law – at least not directly.[6]

The development of law and economics at Chicago is actually an "old" law and economics story, one that involves the analysis of the impacts of various regulatory statutes – including those in the area of antitrust – that impact the functioning of the economic system. This was the law and economics of Director and Coase, and the type of work that filled the pages of the *Journal of Law and Economics* in the 1960s. That the analysis was carried out using a Marshallian brand of price theory does not negate its "old" character. Indeed, in a methodological sense it is very much consistent with the policy analysis that one finds in the work of Alfred Marshall and his disciple, that bane of the Chicago tradition, A.C. Pigou.[7] That there may well be a difference in perceptions regarding benefits and costs on the normative side – and thus regarding the form that law should take – does not negate this essential analytical continuity.

While the Chicago School is just one of many players in the law and economics tradition, the birth of the *economic analysis of law* is very much a Chicago story, one centering on Becker and Posner, with the works of Coase and Calabresi serving as important stimuli.[8] The rise of the economic analysis of law – a rather more narrow enterprise than "law and economics" – is a product of the collision of two forces within economics.[9] The first is the gradual narrowing of economic method in the post-WWII era,[10] one artifact of which was the transformation of law and economics into the economic analysis of law.[11] The neoclassical turn of economics in the post-war era engendered a methodological mindset, and accompanying toolkit, that gave economics a degree of homogeneity that would have been unthinkable in the highly pluralistic interwar period.[12] While scholars are of different minds on the utility of this neoclassicizing process, what is clear is that many of the problems that occupied scholars in the inter-war period – including some that dealt with the legal–economic nexus – were effectively ruled out of bounds by the nature of the new methodology.

The second of the larger professional forces within economics that provided impetus for the development of the economic analysis of law is the expansion of the boundaries of economics that began in the 1960s. Gary Becker is central to this part of the story, as he and his students set to analyzing all manner of social phenomena with a combination of price theory and econometric analysis. Such is the range of this work that almost no area of the social sciences and almost no aspect of human conduct remains free from being carved up by the scalpel of economics.[13] This extension of economic analysis beyond its traditional bound-aries made the economic analysis of *law* a part of the rule rather than the excep-tion to it. Scholars such as Posner (Chapter 1, this volume), Becker (1976), and Edward Lazear (2000) argue that this has brought much-needed intellectual rigor to these fields of study. Critics, in turn, charge rigor mortis.

While the rational choice revolution across the social sciences is a many-faceted phenomenon,[14] the artistic license for economists to cross over into sub-jects traditionally noneconomic in nature came via Lionel Robbins's *Essay on the Nature and Significance of Economic Science* in 1932. Rejecting the extant notion that the boundaries between "economics" and "not economics" are set by behavior that is or is not directed toward the enhancement of material welfare, Robbins argued that economics focuses on the form of behavior "imposed by the influence of scarcity." In particular, "Economics is the science which studies human behaviour as a relationship between ends and scarce means which have alternative uses." Robbins went on to note the implications of this definition:

> It follows from this, therefore, that in so far as it offers this aspect, any kind of human behaviour falls within the scope of Economic Generalizations. We do not say that the production of potatoes is economic activity and the pro-duction of philosophy is not. We say rather that, in so far as either kind of activity involves the relinquishment of other desired alternatives, it has its economic aspect. There are *no limitations* on the subject-matter of Eco-nomic Science save this.
>
> (Robbins 1932: 16, emphasis added)

When writing "no limitations," Robbins almost certainly did not anticipate how the boundaries of economics would be stretched in the years to come. Nor, it would seem, did anyone else who read the essay at the time, given that it took more than three decades for scholars to begin seriously extending the economic paradigm. The practice of economics continued to reflect the "old" view that economics is the study of the economic system – the same view that character-ized the "old" law and economics – even as it assimilated the idea that it is choice under scarcity within that context that defines what economists analyze.

There can be no question, however, that Robbins defined economics in a manner that naturally allowed for its extension beyond the analysis of standard market phenomena. The gradual institutionalization of an economics defined as the analysis of choice under scarcity meant that it was only a matter of time before we began to see the "economic analysis of" a whole lot of things,[15] with work in this area variously described as "the economics of non-market behav-ior," "the analysis of non-market decision making," and "economic imperial-ism." The common denominator, according to Lazear (2000: 100–102) is that economics has brought increasing scientific rigor to a host of academic areas and attendant analyses of social phenomena. In Lazear's words, "The power of eco-nomics lies in its rigor. Economics is scientific; it follows the scientific method of stating a formal refutable theory, testing the theory, and revising the theory based on the evidence" (p. 102). This rigor, in turn, "allows complicated concepts to be written in relatively simple, abstract terms" that "strip away complexity."

In economics, this abstraction comes via a trinity of attributes: (1) the assumption that individuals are rational maximizers; (2) the notion of equilibrium; and (3) the assessment of equilibria based upon their efficiency properties (Lazear 2000: 100–102). While some of those working in these other fields have lamented what they see as excessive abstraction in the economic approach, Lazear argues that complexity, while perhaps adding descriptive richness "also prevents the analyst from seeing what is essential" (pp. 99–100). In fact, he says, it is this very abstraction that makes economics succeed "where other social sciences fail" (p. 102) because it allows for "analysis" in a way that the other social sciences do not (p. 103).

Lazear finds the case for the success of economic imperialism unambiguous, that the widespread application of the economic paradigm has left the social sciences in a much stronger position:

> Economists generally believe in the market test. Economic imperialism can be judged to be successful only if it passes this test, which means that the analyses of the imperialists must influence others. The effort to extend the field measures its success by inducing others to adopt the economic approach to explore issues that are not part of classical economics. One possibility is that scholars outside of economics use economic analyses to understand social issues. Political scientists, lawyers, and sociologists come to use the methods of economics to answer the questions that are of interest in their fields. Another possibility is that economists expand the boundaries of economics and simply replace outsiders as analysts of "noneconomic" issues, forcing noneconomists out of business, as it were, or at least providing them with competition on an issue in which they formerly possessed a monopoly.
>
> (Lazear 2000: 104)

Lazear (p. 104) maintains that both of these routes have been successful, and that "[t]he fact that there have been so many successful efforts in so many different directions attests to the power of economics" (p. 142).

Others may wish to contest Lazear's assertions,[16] but our purpose here is not to analyze or debate the explanatory power of the economic paradigm either in general or in its various specific applications. As we noted at the outset, however, it would be difficult to conclude that the economic analysis of law – and the same can be said of public choice – is anything other than a success, certainly within economics and most probably within law.

Posner and the imperial values of the economic analysis of law

By Robbins's definition, the analysis of legal issues falls squarely within the scope of economics. Law is unambiguously about rights, and rights, by their very nature, exist because of the problem of scarcity. After all, if rights are not scarce, why is there competition over them? If all goods (defined in the broadest possible sense) were unlimited in supply, there would be no need to define rights over them, even if the definition of rights were a costless process – which it is not. And, unless one wishes to dismiss neoclassical economics as utterly irrelevant to anything – and there are some who do – phenomena with a scarcity component are, *prima facie*, amenable to analysis using price theory.

The question, then, is not *whether* economics is an appropriate vehicle for analyzing legal relationships, but *what form* the relationship between economics and law should take and the implications of this for legal scholarship and, perhaps ultimately, the law. There are any number of answers being given to this question,[17] although there is no mistaking the fact that contemporary law and economics is dominated by the approach and direction that has its roots in Chicago.

The success of the economic analysis of law has hinged crucially on the effectiveness of two streams of argument.[18] The first was the demonstration of how economic analysis can inform legal thinking – in particular, how the assumption of *Homo economicus* responding to the incentives created by legal rules assists us in understanding the potential effects of alternative legal rules, and the assessment of these rules and associated outcomes based upon their efficiency properties.[19] The second stream of argument central to the success of the law and economics movement was making the case for "efficiency as justice."

Posner, of course, has been instrumental on both of these fronts. Among his voluminous writings, Posner's *Economic Analysis of Law* has done the most to facilitate the development and spread of the economic way of looking at legal rules. First published in 1973, its pages, like the rings of a tree, mark the development of the field over the past four decades.[20] Its contents span virtually the entire range of law and, as Posner calls it, "the legal regulation of non-market behavior" (p. xix). What is perhaps most surprising is the enormous percentage of this material present already in the first edition of the book. Even though the field was in its infancy, Posner was able to show the tremendous possibilities of the application of economic theory to legal analysis and to outline a framework for a field of analysis – a framework that he and others quickly began to fill in.

Interestingly, though, Posner began his law and economics career with his feet planted rather solidly in the "old" law and economics camp.[21] He was an associate professor of law at Stanford in the late 1960s when he came into contact with Aaron Director, who introduced him to the "Chicago" economic approach to analyzing legal rules. Director, of course, was old school. His work was not concerned with expanding the boundaries of economics, but with analyzing how legal rules impact economic performance. His published writings were few, but he had institutionalized law and economics at Chicago via his teaching and the success of the *Journal of Law and Economics*, of which Director was the founding editor. His influence on Posner is not surprising given that Posner's early scholarship was in the area of antitrust.[22] This was an area long the province of economists and economic approaches, but which Director had imbued with a distinctive Chicago price-theoretic flavor. It is also, of course, the area where the Chicago School can claim its greatest success on the law-making front.

Posner's transformation from someone focused on "old" law and economics to developer of the economic analysis of law really came via the influence of Gary Becker. Becker's economic theory of crime and punishment showed that economics was not a one-hit wonder (antitrust) when it came to using economics to analyze the law. Taken as a lens through which to view legal issues, it also suggested that Coase's "The Problem of Social Cost" was something more than an exercise in externality theory. When the Beckerian framework for analysis was combined with Coase's pregnant statement about judges perhaps having something like efficiency in mind when making legal decisions, Posner was off and running. It would be safe to say that he has not slowed down.

If I am correct in suggesting that the economic analysis of law resulted from the "Beckerization" of Posner, then it is reasonable to assert that the values of the economic analysis of law are the values of economic imperialism. One version of this is that, as such, the values here are those of value-free science, a sort of agnostic theorizing process that takes as its mission the description and explanation of legal phenomena and the analysis of the consequences of alternative legal rules. Of course, theory choice itself is a value-laden process, and the assumptions about individual behavior add another layer on the values front. Likewise, the (positive) assessment of equilibria based on their efficiency properties leaves out the rather messy question of what happens on the road to equilibrium and begs the question of impacts beyond efficiency. Viewed from this perspective, the economic analysis of law, while not exactly value free, embodies values that are no different than those underlying the analysis of a host of other policy issues (e.g., taxation and public goods) on the traditional economic front.

Posner (1987) has suggested that this new and more rigorous approach came to law at a time when it was in an unsettled state and engaged in a search for moorings. This provided an opening for and a receptiveness to new ideas that might not have been present at other points in law's intellectual history. Within economics, we have already noted the beginnings of boundaries expansion in the 1960s, but this process itself needs to be explained. Why, in the present instance, did economists suddenly begin to analyze legal topics? Robbins's definition certainly seems to have allowed for it, but since the time of Robbins's writing, economists had continued to confine their work pretty much exclusively to topics traditionally considered economic. One possible explanation is that these forays into other disciplines, including law, provided a creative scholarly outlet for those economists with a broader intellectual curiosity. A second possibility is that these disciplines, including law, served as an area to be colonized by those who considered economics as the queen of the social sciences and felt that these fields, like weakened corporations, were primed for takeover.

A third possibility, one not remarked upon in the literature, is that these fields offered fertile ground for generating refereed publications at a time when publication pressures within economics were increasing substantially. Looked at from this perspective, the first edition of Posner's *Economic Analysis of Law* was a 700-page suggestion in search of applied theorists and econometricians. Posner had offered a paradigm that was relatively easy for others to extend once the foundation had been laid. Insights were mathematized, models tweaked, and regressions run. The last aspect has been enhanced in recent years by developments in computing power and in data set availability, which allows any punter under publication pressure to do empirical work in the field. This should not be taken to imply that applied econometric work in the economic analysis of law is unsophisticated. However, the level of originality, sophistication, and insight varies greatly here, as it does in so many other areas of economics. To the extent, though, that publication pressure is a driving force behind the growth of economics literature, it is not unreasonable to suggest that such pressure is one of the chief values underlying work in the economic analysis of law these days.[23] The proportions of this work that have generated heat as opposed to light is another question entirely and awaits the judgment of history.

Going normative: Posner and the case for efficiency as justice

The second stream of argument central to the success of the economic analysis of law has been its ability to gain a measure of acceptance for the application of the efficiency criterion in legal thinking. Of course, the fact that economic analysis may be able to enlighten our understanding of the implications of alternative legal rules does not imply that the criterion of efficiency should be applied to determine the appropriate rights assignment. To pretend otherwise – whether because one is in favor of the use of the efficiency criterion or opposed to it – is to confuse an "is" with an "ought."

Efficiency's normative role in economic imperialism is most prominently displayed in law and economics, and here, too, Posner has been the central figure. The attempt to make the case for "efficiency as justice" was done both historically and philosophically. The historical aspect was accomplished by arguing that common law rules tend to exhibit an underlying economic logic – that is, consciously or not, the decisions reached by judges over time have had a tendency to promote wealth maximization. This idea was first hinted at by Ronald Coase in "The problem of social cost" (1960) but was more extensively developed by Posner and others in the 1970s and 1980s. Posner's position is that "The logic of the common law is an economic logic" (Landes and Posner 1987: 312), and, in an extensive body of published analysis, he worked to build the case empirically.[24] The argument is not that all common law rules are efficient or that the application of rules from common law precedents is always efficient; the point, for Posner, is that "the law creates incentives for parties to behave efficiently," not that people actually do so (Landes and Posner 1987: 312). Like most collections of facts, the general sweep of common law case and doctrinal history shows consistency with multiple possible stories; nevertheless, the arguments for the efficiency theory have their compelling aspects.

The philosophical component involved making the case for the use of the efficiency (or wealth maximization) criterion in legal decision making, as against other principles that could inform judicial reasoning. Here, Posner has played a particularly interesting role over time. In *The Economics of Justice* (1981: 48–115), he both distances wealth maximization from utilitarianism (see also Posner 2001a: 96–98) and attempts to ground an ethical defense of wealth maximization in the notion of consent, operating via the Pareto criterion. That is, a wealth-maximizing legal change is one where, with appropriate side payments as necessary, one or more parties are made better off and no one is made worse off. Such a change would command unanimous consent among rational agents. Of course, wealth maximization differs from the Pareto criterion in that it does not preclude losers. But, argues Posner, compensation comes *ex ante* or, at the very least, the wealth-maximizing set of rules is one that would command unanimous consent among rational agents *ex ante*.[25]

That the ethical case for efficiency as justice has its controversial, and even problematic, aspects is no secret.[26] And, in recent years, Posner has moved away from, even rejected, the ethical defense of wealth maximization – practically, because of the questions regarding the relationship between efficiency and the distribution of wealth,[27] and philosophically because his pragmatism now causes him to reject the idea of an underlying ethical basis for law. Posner nevertheless finds pragmatic justification for the wealth-maximization criterion on multiple fronts. First, political stability and average income in society tend to be positively correlated; that is, wealth maximization as a legal decision rule will tend to promote political stability (Posner 2001a: 102ff.). Beyond this, Posner argues that wealth maximization and the benefit–cost analysis that underlies it are operationally valid, tend to be more immune from political prejudices and pressures than are other decision rules, and can enhance the quality of government decision making (2001a: 123).[28] While Posner no longer attempts to ground wealth maximization ethically in the idea of consent, he does continue to hold the view that a wealth-maximizing rule for common law decision making might command something like unanimous consent *ex ante* if some method existed for voting on the issue. And, notably, he did not give up his insistence that efficiency "is perhaps the most common" meaning of "justice" (Posner 1992: 27).

The debate over application of the efficiency criterion raises a number of issues that are too often under-appreciated by one side or the other – or both – in this debate. First, it is a selective imposition of values – the values associated with efficiency. However, every definition of justice privileges some particular set of values over others; the question is, whose values are to count? It is equally wrongheaded to pretend either that efficiency does not involve the imposition of values or that it involves the imposition of values that are, a priori, inappropriate.

Second, efficiency is simply a particular form of benefit–cost analysis, one in which wealth values are weighted and other values are not. "Fairness," however defined, is nothing more than another and different case of benefit–cost analysis, one where the values in the benefit–cost analysis are denominated differently than in the case of efficiency judgments. More to the point, *all* adjudication involves some form of benefit–cost analysis, dollar-valued or otherwise.

A third, and related, point is that all of these various forms of benefit–cost calculation involve a choice as to what counts as a benefit or cost, and how much. That is, all of the decision rules mark out a certain group of variables for inclusion in the evaluation and assign weights to those variables. These choices of variables and weights to be applied to them are inherently selective and involve the imposition of the values of those doing the choosing. This is no more or less true of the efficiency criterion than of the various fairness, "natural" rights, or other criteria that critics of the economic analysis of law would champion. Finally, all of these benefit–cost processes involve selective perception in the identification and assessment of magnitude of the variables in question.

Note that none of these points is meant in a pejorative way; this is simply an inevitable cost of doing business when one is making choices among alternatives, and to pretend otherwise is to obfuscate the mechanisms of choice.[29] The question that remains, then, is whether there is an appropriate role for efficiency-based normative analysis in the economic analysis of law. Posner argues in the affirmative on pragmatic grounds. I will offer a different defense, one that relies on the positive side of the economic analysis of law, outlined above.

Are Posner's values everyone's values? The Coase theorem and justice as "doing what comes naturally"

In a market system, resources tend to gravitate to their highest-valued uses. And, as scholars such as Wesley Hohfeld (1913) and John R. Commons (1924, 1925) showed us nearly a century ago, the resources at stake are rights. That is, market "transactions" are not over goods and services, but over *rights over* goods and services. At their core, that is, input and output markets are vehicles for the transfer of legal rights between agents. To say that the market ought not to be the arbiter of legal rights, then, is to say that markets ought not to exist. If we use market principles to allocate rights over, e.g., apples and oranges, clothing, automobiles, housing, etc., why not also rights over contractual performance, unobstructed views, the environment, liability for bodily harm, human organs, the human genome, and fetuses? There is a legitimate question as to why, given that the vast majority of rights within a market system are allocated through the pricing mechanism, this is not true of *all* rights. The onus is to some extent on those opposed to the efficiency criterion to make the case here.

The relevance of market principles for the law in general is nicely illustrated by the Coase theorem, The theorem tells us that if rights are fully specified and transaction costs are zero, parties arrive at an efficient and invariant allocation of rights regardless of how those rights are initially assigned by the courts.[30]

The Coase theorem shows us the market for legal rights working in its purest form; it is the vacuum of physics brought into the social realm. And, in spite of the many claims to the contrary, the theorem is correct. It may be a tautology, as some have claimed, and it may be completely unrealistic, given that transaction costs are always positive, but that does not make it any less correct as a conclusion derived from a set of initial premises.[31] It is also a positive statement, rather than a normative one. The theorem dispenses completely with the notion of efficiency as a *goal* for legal-economic policy and says instead that, try as they might, it is impossible for courts to engender inefficient outcomes because rights will always end up in their highest-valued uses – if transaction costs are zero.

In spite of the Coase theorem's positive nature, it is here that we find the case for the application of the efficiency criterion. The theorem tells us that parties will bargain to the efficient outcome, regardless of how rights are initially assigned, *if* they are not precluded from doing so. It thus shows us the allocation of rights to which the parties would agree voluntarily. Unfortunately, transaction costs of various sorts often get in the way. The "mimic the market" approach to adjudication suggests that the judge facilitate this (otherwise unattainable) outcome in his or her ruling. The efficiency criterion, then, does nothing more than allow parties to reach the allocative arrangement that they would have arrived at via mutual agreement if transaction costs had not precluded it. Here, law becomes a vehicle that allows conflicts to be resolved in the manner that the disputants would themselves mutually demonstrate that they prefer.

While this grounding of efficiency may seem identical to Posner's original consent-oriented defense, it is in fact different. Posner's Paretian approach legitimizes the result on the grounds that something which makes everyone better off, at least in potential, would command unanimous consent (in potential). The Coase theorem-based defense argues that the judge is simply facilitating that which the individuals themselves *would do* if external forces did not prevent them from doing so. The difference is one of an outcome worked out among the parties themselves as against one worked out by someone else and consented to by the parties involved.

It must be acknowledged that this "doing what comes naturally" basis for the efficiency criterion turns on the validity of the theorem's depiction of individual behavior. The question, then, is to what extent this behavioral model accurately describes behavior within the legal arena. The experimental and empirical literature examining the propensity of agents to bargain along the lines suggested by the Coase theorem has generated very mixed returns.[32] Among other things, this literature suggests that distribution *does* matter and that social norms cause people to value things in ways not necessarily consistent with efficiency or with the predictions of rational choice theory.[33] However, the jury remains out on all of this.

Finding value in the past: realism, institutionalism, and Chicago

Having thus far focused primarily on the economic analysis of law as a subfield of economics, we should now spend a little time looking at it from the side of law. If the hallmark of economic analysis is prediction, then perhaps it is Holmes who is the greatest of all law and economics scholars. It was Holmes, of course, who made "the man of the future ... the man [and woman, as it happens!] of statistics and the master of economics." The future, it would seem, is now. But where has this left us? Modern Chicago economic analysis of law has become a dominant force in the legal arena as well as a thriving sub-field within economics. Meanwhile, legal realism is long dead, though its banner is carried by the law and society movement and the various contemporary "critical" approaches. The "old" Institutional law and economics survives, but as a heterodox rather than mainstream movement. Certain aspects of the "old" Chicago approach are now found in the New Institutional Economics, with its substantial Coasean component. What, if anything, can be said about the relationship between these strands of thought?

To begin with, there is good reason for suspicion about the traditional historical narrative surrounding Chicago law and economics.[34] This narrative tells the story in strictly internalist terms, essentially denying any link to or commonalities with and overtly attempting to distance itself from other legal-economic movements of the twentieth century – in particular, legal realism and institutional law and economics. Milton Friedman's response to the attempt to link legal realism and institutional law and economics of the 1920s and 1930s with the early stages of Chicago law and economics is typical:

> You have a paradox that comes out of what all of you have been saying. You're saying that the real antecedent to the conjunction of law and economics was the institutional economists and the legal realists who wanted to intervene from a particular point of view, who were trying to reshape society, and then you come to the next stage in which ... Henry Simons ... represented all of the opposite tendencies. The natural development of legal economics at the University of Chicago then centered on a person who was opposed to almost everything that institutionalists and legal realists stood for.
>
> (Kitch 1983: 176)

Edmund Kitch, a Chicago-trained legal scholar (1961–4) and later the Director of the Law and Economics Program at the University of Chicago Law School, sums up the Chicago attitude toward realism quite nicely: "The only thing that seems to tie these people together was an agreement that conventional legal scholarship as it had been practiced by their predecessors was inadequate and provided an insufficient understanding of the way law works" (Kitch 1983: 165). Posner (1995: 393) likewise criticizes realism for what he sees as its "lack of method," as well as for its "naïve enthusiasm for government." On the former point, Posner suggests that it "was not their fault," that the realists

> knew what to do – think things not words, trace the actual consequences of legal doctrines, balance competing policies – but not how to do any of these things.... The tools of economics, statistics, and other pertinent sciences were insufficiently developed to enable a social-engineering approach to be taken to law.

The similarity between the Chicago perspectives on realism and institutionalism is striking. Stigler's assessment of institutionalism is typical:

> I would say that the institutional school failed in America for a very simple reason. It had nothing in it except a stance of hostility to the standard theoretical tradition. There was no positive agenda of research, there was no set of problems or new methods they wanted to invoke.
>
> (Kitch 1983: 170)

Friedman, in a similar vein, called institutionalism "empty of content" and "highly normative" (Kitch 1983: 171, 172). Even Coase (1984: 230), whose work is so similar to that of the institutionalists in so many ways,[35] claims that institutionalism is "a dreary subject" and that "the American Institutionalists were not theoretical but anti-theoretical, particularly where classical economic theory was concerned. Without a theory they had nothing to pass on except a mass of descriptive material waiting for a theory or a fire."[36] The equation of "theory" and "theoretical" with a particular (neoclassical) form of price theory is made clear in Ward Bowman's assertion that:

> It seems to me that economics as a part of so-called institutionalism was a very ambiguous thing, and except for Chicago it didn't have anything to do with price theory. If you look at the way Yale, in that period, thought of an economist it was no different from how they thought of a sociologist. As far as I can remember, it was only at Chicago that you had what we call economics put into law in that way. Henry Simons was the economist at Chicago, but Walton Hamilton was the economist at Yale, and that speaks for itself.
>
> (Kitch 1983: 176)

Given that Hamilton had been, among other things, the President of the American Economic Association, Bowman's characterization here might be considered a bit too dismissive.

There is no question that the institutionalists and the segment of Chicago that became dominant in the second half of the century marched to different drummers. Frank Knight and Jacob Viner were the economists who had the most impact on Chicago law and economics in both its old and new varieties. Viner brought the Marshallian approach that has come to be associated so closely with the Chicago price-theoretic tradition that underlies, really, both the old and the new Chicago perspectives.[37] Knight, too, played an important role in the Chicago price theory tradition, but his greatest legacy may be on the attendant philosophical perspective that he imparted to his students – including Milton Friedman, George Stigler, and Aaron Director – that, within a liberal democracy, the pursuit of economic self-interest by economic actors is a given, competition is inherent within and intrinsic to economic life, and market-generated outcomes tend to be superior to those resulting from government interference with the market mechanism. While the efficacy of the market was being increasingly questioned within the profession at large during the middle third of the twentieth century, the market-oriented views of a formidable group of economists at Chicago set the Chicago perspective apart from much of the rest of the profession.

The neoclassical method and anti-interventionist stance of the Chicago School *does* stand in stark contrast to the institutional approach.[38] Perhaps not surprisingly, then, an a- or anti-theoretical methodology and highly interventionist ideology are the common themes of the Chicago criticisms of realism and institutionalism. Harold Demsetz suggests that these two factors are actually linked – that "the antitheoretical bent" of institutionalism is "politically motivated" and "explainable by the desire to be shorn of the constraints that the theory did impose on political action" – that is, "highlighting the indirect effects in a way that those who want to intervene would like to be without" (Kitch 1983: 175, 174).

There are least two ironies associated with this perspective. One is that institutional and early Chicago law and economics were, at their roots, more similar than dissimilar, being focused on the elaboration of the legal underpinnings of the competitive market system – in both the positive (what is) and normative (what is most appropriate) senses. That one group was more focused on the language of marginal benefits and marginal costs than the other does not negate the fact that they were both looking at the same legal-economic issues. Second, the attempt to label realism and institutionalism "politically motivated" is more than a little interesting coming from the Chicago School, which has itself both had this label applied to it by its critics and, at times, carried it as a banner when extolling the virtues of the market system. The normative nature of this criticism illustrates the contrasting values that underlie the Chicago and realist/institutional approaches. But the fact that one side extols the virtues of markets operating within the context of one system of rights and the other a different rights structure does not make one side any more interventionist or politically motivated than the other.[39] The larger point here is that while the realist/institutionalist and Chicago programs were poles apart politically, and even methodologically, the missions behind them (and the New Institutional Economics) bear striking similarities. That those on each side of these debates continue to attempt to minimize commonalities (as if there is guilt by association running in every direction) does not negate this essential continuity.

82   S.G. Medema

While the ideological element looms large here, there is good reason to doubt the critics who suggest that impetus for the development of law and economics at Chicago was anti-interventionism. Kitch (1983: 175–176) perhaps best described the thrust of law and economics at Chicago and other law schools during the first half of the century when he said that:

> My impression from what I've been able to find on Chicago is that the interest that law schools had in economics did not come out of any anti-interventionist thinking. It essentially came out of the idea that the legal system is going to be doing this [i.e., overtly dealing with economic issues] now and that means we need to learn how to do it right and maybe econo-mists know something about how to do it right.... There is a great legiti-macy given to the idea that government is going to be doing these things and we in the law schools should try to help the government do it right.
>
> (Kitch 1983: 175–176)

The diversity that characterized the economics department for so long and the relatively small place of economics within the law school at Chicago in the early years would not have allowed for any large, concerted political agenda. Indeed, Stigler (1988: 148) has argued that "There was no Chicago School of Economics ... at the end of World War II."[40]

Nor, indeed, of law and economics. Prior to the arrival of Coase in 1964, the law school never had more than one economist on the faculty, although there were some faculty with sympathies for examining antitrust cases, regulatory issues, and so on through the lens of economic analysis, enough, in fact, that a small reading group of economics and legal faculty was formed. And the pres-ence of scholars such as Karl Llewellyn on the faculty managed to ensure that there was always strong resistance to expansion of the influence of neoclassical economics in the 1950s. Henry Manne has reported that the neoclassical eco-nomic analysis that was in the air "infuriated" Llewellyn, particularly when stu-dents would use it in the attempt to refute positions that Llewellyn would take in the classroom (Kitch 1983: 184), and Llewellyn went so far as to question whether Chicago was doing a proper job of training lawyers (p. 191). Edward Levi, as Dean, protected and encouraged law and economics,[41] but as Director has pointed out, on the whole there was neither "any great resistance" to nor "any great enthusiasm for" law and economics – at least until it was proposed that a second economist be hired (Kitch 1983: 186). The status of economics in the law school even then was such that Coase's initial appointment was partially in the business school. But Chicago in that period was a fairly fertile and decen-tralized place, where doing new, different, and non-traditional things was encouraged.

What all of this points to is that the ferment of legal realism – which opened up law and legal theory to the influence of the social sciences – was a big reason why law and economics could gain a foothold at Chicago and eventually sprout and spread in new form. The idea that the march from the "old" Chicago law and economics of Henry Simons, Aaron Director, and Ronald Coase to the "new" economic analysis of law of Richard Posner and Gary Becker was a natural progression cannot sustain the weight of the fact; Chicago law and economics was transformed and moved in a very different (and no less interesting or illuminating) direction in the 1970s. The legal realism to which Chicago is so hostile, though, helped to spawn the older approach and facilitated the development of the new. In doing so, it opened a door that could not be closed. Posner's repeated attempts to dismiss such a link miss the point:

> The "crits" worry that the practitioners of law and economics will contest with them the mantle of legal realism. They needn't worry. We economic types have no desire to be pronounced the intellectual heirs of ... William Douglas, Jerome Frank, or Karl Llewellyn. The law and economics movement owes little to legal realism – perhaps nothing beyond the fact that Donald Turner and Guido Calabresi, pioneering figures in the application of economics to law, graduated from Yale Law School and may have been influenced by the school's legal-realist tradition to examine law from the perspective of another discipline. Although the legal realist Robert Hale anticipated some of the discoveries (inventions?) of law and economics, most modern law and economics scholars were unaware of his work until recently. It is difficult to measure and therefore treacherous to disclaim influence, but, speaking as one who received his legal education at the Harvard Law School between 1959 and 1962, I can attest that to a student the school seemed untouched by legal realism. And none of the legal and economic thinkers who since law school have most shaped my own academic and judicial thinking – Holmes, Coase, Stigler, Becker, Director, and others – was himself a product in whole or in part of legal realism.
>
> (Posner 1995: 3)

But this is beside the point. That Coase, Stigler, Becker, and Director *could* shape and influence the perspective, scholarship, and judicial opinions of one of the most influential legal scholars of the late twentieth century, and, by extension, stimulate the development of a new approach to legal inquiry is not only a legacy of realism but perhaps its foremost one.

Notes

* Department of Economics, University of Colorado at Denver, CB 181, Denver, Colorado 80217–3364, USA. Instructive comments on earlier versions of this chapter were received from Alain Marciano, Sophie Harnay, Christian Barrère, and participants in the seminar on "Richard Posner and the Economic Analysis of Law" at the University of Reims Champagne Ardenne, and from Philippe Fontaine and participants in the H2S/EconomiX seminar at the École normale supérieure de Cachan and the University of Paris X – Nanterre. I am particularly grateful for the stimulating discussions on this topic with Alain Marciano during my visit to Reims.
1 The situation is very different in European law schools. See (Garoupa and Ulen 2006) for a discussion.

2 See, e.g., (Jolls 2007) and the essays in (Sunstein 2000). Of course, law has always had norms at its heart: The "reasonable" individual of traditional legal analysis is one socialized into and acting in accordance with the norms and customs of society.

3 The values of "law and economics" – a much more diverse enterprise – are much broader, reflective of its greater diversity. For an elaboration of "law and economics" in its broader sense, see (Mercuro and Medema 2006). It is also the case that not all practitioners of the economic analysis of law agree that wealth maximization is an appropriate normative criterion.

4 This discussion draws on (Medema 2006).

5 On Bentham, see (Posner 1981; 2001b). On Sidgwick, see (Medema 2007). Heath · Pearson (1997) provides an excellent discussion of various nineteenth-century continental traditions.

6 Samuels (1998) offers a nice selection of this literature, while Samuels (1993) presents a survey.

7 On the place of Marshallian price theory in Chicago law and economics, see (Medema 2011). On Pigou as a Chicago foil, see (Medema 1996) and (Aslanbeigui and Medema 1998).

8 The classic citations here are (Coase 1960; Becker 1968; Posner 1973; and Calabresi 1961). On the history of Chicago law and economics, see (Kitch 1983; Coase 1993; and Medema 2010a; 2011). For a discussion of Calabresi's contributions, see the articles in the 2005 symposium on Calabresi, published in the *Maryland Law Review*.

9 Posner (1987) offers an account of what was happening on the legal scholarship side.

10 See, e.g., (Morgan and Rutherford 1998).

11 See (Medema 1998) for discussion.

12 I do not mean to suggest here that post-war mainstream economics is homogeneous, for it was not and is not. In fact, there is even heterogeneity within the Chicago School itself. That having been said, there is far less pluralism in the post-war period than existed in the inter-war period.

13 The reader who attributes a pejorative tone to that metaphor would do well to remember that the surgeon's scalpel generally makes the patient better off than before said scalpel was applied.

14 See, e.g., (Amadae 2004).

15 See (Raditzky and Berholz 1987; Lazear 2000) for surveys.

16 Ronald Coase (1977), for one, predicted that economic imperialism was doomed to failure because of economists's lack of knowledge of these other fields. So far, though, that has not proved to be a deterrent to economists.

17 See, e.g., (Mercuro and Medema 2006) for a survey.

18 This discussion draws on (Medema 2010a).

19 This, of course, matches the attributes of economic imperialism set out by Lazear.

20 Weighing in at roughly 400 pages and 170,000 words in its first edition, *Economic Analysis of Law* has grown to 510,000 words (700 pages of much finer print) – a three-fold increase over the five subsequent editions.

21 On this point, see also (Marciano 2006; Medema 2010b).

22 Virtually all of the dozen or so articles that Posner published from 1969 to 1971 were in the area of antitrust and related areas of regulatory policy. Posner's views on antitrust are best seen in his 1976 book *Antitrust Law: An Economic Perspective*, a second edition of which was published in 2001.

23 Some support for the idea of refereed publication as a leading value driving economic research can be found in (Colander 2005). One could argue that a similar process has gone on in any number of other areas within economics – e.g., human capital analysis and the new trade theory. A small number of scholars do the heavy lifting at the outset, and then the masses move in to do analyses, the marginal product of which is very small as compared to the early work in the area.

24 Posner is by no means alone here, and there is an extensive parallel literature offering theoretical explanations for *why* the common law might have evolved efficiently. See, e.g., (Posner 2003) or (Mercuro and Medema 2006, chapter 2) for a discussion of this literature.

25 The commonality with the Rawlsian veil of ignorance and with James Buchanan's constitutional economics should not be lost on the reader. On the former, see (Posner 1981: 99–101). On the significant departure between the larger perspectives of Buchanan and Posner, see (Marciano 2006).

26 See, e.g., the "Symposium on efficiency as a legal concern," *Hofstra Law Review* 8 (1980).

27 The distributional issues are two: first, wealth maximization results based on an unjust underlying distribution of income may not themselves have credible claims to being just; second, there are issues regarding willingness/ability to pay and the resulting impact on valuation.

28 The operational validity claim is called into question by the circularity of efficiency-based reasoning – that is, the idea that efficiency is a function of rights, and not the other way around. See, for example, (Bromley 1990; Samuels 1981; and Veljanovski 1981).

29 See (Medema and Samuels 2000).

30 The Coase theorem has actually been stated in several ways – with not unimportant variations – over time. See (Medema and Zerbe 2000) for an extensive discussion of the Coase theorem literature.

31 One of the truly silly criticisms of law and economics is that its practitioners all believe that the Coase theorem describes reality. A moment's thought reveals that, if this were actually true in reality, the entire economic analysis of law enterprise would never have left the ground – indeed, would be nonsensical. There would be no need to analyze the efficiency properties of alternative legal rules nor to advocate particular legal rules based upon their efficiency properties. Interestingly, Posner has stayed away from the long-running debate over the Coase theorem. His only discussion of it comes in *Economic Analysis of Law*, where he presents it as one of the building blocks of the economic approach to law.

32 See, e.g., (Ellickson 1991; Farnsworth 1998; Hoffman and Spitzer 1982, 1985, 1986; Harrison *et al.* 1987), and the analysis of this literature in (Medema and Zerbe 2000).

33 Interestingly, if we actually lived in the zero transaction costs world contemplated by the theorem, and the theorem's behavioral underpinnings were accurate depictions of agent behavior, judges could indulge their distributional preferences by assigning rights to whomever they pleased, with no negative efficiency consequences, no efficiency–equity tradeoffs. Unfortunately, the real world does not afford us this luxury.

34 See, e.g., (Kitch 1983; Coase 1993; and Posner 1995). For an alternative view, see (Medema 1998).

35 See (Medema 1996) for a discussion of the commonalities between the law and economics of Coase and the institutionalists.

36 Interestingly, this contrasts with his comment, in response to a disparaging remark about American institutionalists by Richard Caves, that "we have less to fear from institutionalists who are not theorists than from theorists who are not institutionalists" (Coase 1964: 196). It may or may not be coincidental that this remark was made in an AEA conference session in December 1963, while Coase was still a faculty member at the University of Virginia. There is also no little irony in the fact that Posner has leveled a similar criticism at Coase following Coase's attempts to distance himself from the economic analysis of law and claim the New Institutional Economics as his intellectual progeny. See, e.g., (Coase 1993: 251) and his remarks in (Kitch 1983: 192), as well as (Posner 1993a, 1993b).

37 Becker's price theory has more of a hard-nosed rational choice flavor than does Viner's, but there is a basic continuity – one that is not surprising given that Friedman

learned his price theory from Viner, and Becker his from Viner and from Friedman. See (Medema 2011).
38 In contrast to what Friedman implies, however, this is somewhat less true of Henry Simons, who advocated forceful government intervention to promote atomistic competition.
39 In fact, one could flip Demsetz's argument around and suggest that the use of a particular definition of "economic science" by Chicago economists allows them to dismiss that with which they have fundamental ideological disagreements.
40 Stigler may have been shading the truth a bit here, for he used the term "Chicago school" in 1949. See (Medema 2014) for a discussion of the origins and diffusion of the term "Chicago School."
41 This after several years of serving as the foil for Director's economic critique of the received approach to antitrust analysis. See, e.g., (Kitch 1983).

References

Amadae, S. (2004) *Rationalizing Capitalist Democracy: The Cold War Origins of Rational Choice Liberalism*, Chicago, IL: University of Chicago Press.

Aslanbeigui, N. and Medema, S.G. 'Beyond the dark clouds: Pigou and Coase on social cost', *History of Political Economy* 30, 1998: 601–625.

Becker, G.S. 'Crime and punishment: an economic approach', *Journal of Political Economy* 76, 1968: 169–217.

Becker, G.S. (1976) *The Economic Approach to Human Behavior*. Chicago, IL: University of Chicago Press.

Bromley, D.W. 'The ideology of efficiency: searching for a theory of policy', *Journal of Environmental Economics and Management* 19, 1990: 86–107.

Calabresi, G. 'Some thoughts on risk distribution and the law of torts', *Yale Law Journal* 70, 1961: 499–553.

Coase, R.H. 'The problem of social cost', *Journal of Law and Economics* 3, 1960: 1–44.

Coase, R.H. 'Discussion', *American Economic Review* 54(3), 1964: 192–197.

Coase, R.H. (1977) 'Economics and contiguous disciplines', in Mark Perlman (ed.) *The Organization and Retrieval of Economic Knowledge*, Boulder, CO: Westview Press.

Coase, R.H. 'The new institutional economics', *Journal of Institutional and Theoretical Economics* 140, 1984: 229–231.

Coase, R.H. 'Law and economics at Chicago', *Journal of Law and Economics* 36, 1993: 239–254.

Colander, D. 'Economics as an ideologically challenged science', *Revue de Philosophie Économique* 11, 2005: 9–30.

Commons, J.R. (1924) *Legal Foundations of Capitalism*. Reprint. Clifton, NJ: Augustus M. Kelley, 1974.

Commons, J.R. 'Law and economics', *Yale Law Journal* 34, 1925: 371–382.

Ellickson, R.C. (1991) *Order Without Law: How Neighbors Settle Disputes*, Cambridge, MA: Harvard University Press.

Farnsworth, W. 'Do parties to nuisance bargain after judgment? A glimpse inside the cathedral', *University of Chicago Law Review* 66, 1998: 373–436.

Garoupa, N. and Ulen, T.S. (2006) 'The market for legal innovation: law and economics in Europe and in the United States', Working Paper, New University of Lisbon and University of Illinois College of Law.

Harrison, G.W., Hoffman, E., Rutström, E.E., and Spitzer, M.L. 'Coasian solutions to the externality problem in experimental market', *Economic Journal* 97, 1987: 388–402.

Hoffman, E. and Spitzer, M.L. 'The Coase theorem: some experimental tests', *Journal of Law and Economics* 25, 1982: 73–98.

Hoffman, E. and Spitzer, M.L. 'Entitlements, rights, and fairness: an experimental examination of subjects' concepts of distributive justice', *Journal of Legal Studies* 14, 1985: 259–297.

Hoffman, E. and Spitzer, M.L. 'Experimental tests of the Coase theorem with large bargaining groups', *Journal of Legal Studies* 15, 1986: 149–171.

Hohfeld, W.N. 'Some fundamental legal conceptions as applied in judicial reasoning', *Yale Law Journal* 23, 1913: 16–59.

Jolls, C. (2007) 'Behavioral law and economics', in P. Diamond and H. Vartiainen (eds.) *Behavioral Economics and Its Applications*, Princeton, NJ: Princeton University Press.

Kitch, E.W. 'The fire of truth: a remembrance of law and economics at Chicago, 1932–1970', *Journal of Law and Economics* 26, 1983: 163–233.

Landes, W. and Posner, R.A. (1987) *The Economic Structure of Tort Law*, Cambridge, MA: Harvard University Press.

Lazear, E.P. 'Economic imperialism', *Quarterly Journal of Economics* 115, 2000: 99–146.

Marciano, A. (2006) 'Public choice, new law and economics and the economic analysis of law', Working Paper, University of Reims Champagne Ardenne.

Medema, S.G. 'Of Pangloss, Pigouvians, and pragmatism: Ronald Coase on social cost analysis', *Journal of the History of Economic Thought*, 18, 1996: 96–114.

Medema, S.G. 'Wandering the road from pluralism to Posner: the transformation of law and economics, 1920s–1970s', *The Transformation of American Economics: From Interwar Pluralism to Postwar Neoclassicism – History of Political Economy Annual Supplement* 30, 1998: 202–224.

Medema, S.G. (2006) 'Alfred Marshall meets law and economics: rationality, norms, and theories as tendency statements', in C. Krecke and E. Krecke (eds.) *The Cognitive Revolution in the Social Sciences*, a special issue of *Advances in Austrian Economics* 9: 235–252.

Medema, S.G. 'Sidgwick's utilitarian analysis of law: a bridge from Bentham to Becker?' *American Law and Economics Review* 9, 2007: 30–47.

Medema, S.G. (2010a) 'The Chicago school of law and economics', in Ross Emmett (ed.) *The Elgar Companion to the Chicago School*, Aldershot: Edward Elgar Publishing.

Medema, S.G. (2010b) 'Richard A. Posner', in Ross Emmett (ed.) *The Elgar Companion to the Chicago School*, Aldershot: Edward Elgar Publishing.

Medema, S.G. (2011) 'Chicago price theory and Chicago law and economics', in Rob Van Horn, Philip Mirowski, and Thomas Stapleford (eds.) *Building Chicago Economics: New Perspectives on the History of America's Most Powerful Economics Program*, Cambridge: Cambridge University Press.

Medema, S.G. (2014) 'On the origins and diffusion of the term, "Chicago school"', Working Paper, University of Colorado, Denver.

Medema, S.G. and Samuels, W.J. 'The economic role of government as, in part, a matter of selective perception, sentiment, and valuation: the cases of Pigovian and Paretian welfare economics', *American Journal of Economics and Sociology* 59, 2000: 87–108.

Medema, S.G. and Zerbe, R.O., Jr. (2000) 'The Coase theorem', in Boudewijn Bouckaert and Gerrit De Geest (eds.) *Encyclopedia of Law and Economics*, Volume I, Cheltenham: Edward Elgar.

Mercuro, N. and Medema, S.G. (2006) *Economics and the Law: From Posner to Post Modernism and Beyond*, 2nd edition, Princeton, NJ: Princeton University Press.

Morgan, M. and Rutherford, M. (eds.) *The Transformation of American Economics: From Interwar Pluralism to Postwar Neoclassicism – History of Political Economy Annual Supplement*, 30, 1998.

Pearson, H. (1997) *Origins of Law and Economics: The Economists' New Science of Law, 1830–1930*, Cambridge: Cambridge University Press.

Posner, R.A., 'The new institutional economics meets law and economics', *Journal of Institutional and Theoretical Economics* 149(1), 1963a: 73–87.

Posner, R.A. 'Nobel Laureate: Ronald Coase and methodology', *Journal of Economic Perspectives* 7(4), 1963b: 195–210.

Posner, R.A. (1973) *Economic Analysis of Law*, Boston, MA: Little, Brown and Company.

Posner, R.A. (1976) *Antitrust Law: An Economic Perspective*, Chicago, IL: University of Chicago Press. Second edition, 2001.

Posner, R.A. (1981) *The Economics of Justice*, Cambridge, MA: Harvard University Press.

Posner, R.A. 'The decline of law as an autonomous discipline: 1962–1987', *Harvard Law Review* 100, 1987: 761–780.

Posner, R.A. (1992) *Economic Analysis of Law*, 4th edition, Boston, MA: Little, Brown and Company.

Posner, R.A. (1995) *Overcoming Law*, Cambridge: MA: Harvard University Press.

Posner, R.A. (2001a) *Frontiers of Legal Theory*, Cambridge, MA: Harvard University Press.

Posner, R.A. (2001b) 'The law and economics movement: from Bentham to Becker', in *Frontiers of Legal Theory*, Cambridge, MA: Harvard University Press.

Posner, R.A. (2003) *Economic Analysis of Law*, 6th edition, New York: Aspen Publishers.

Raditzky, G. and Berholz, P. (1987) *Economic Imperialism: The Economic Method Applied Outside the Field of Economics*, New York: Paragon.

Robbins, L. (1932) *An Essay on the Nature and Significance of Economic Science*, London: Macmillan.

Samuels, W.J. 'Maximization of wealth as justice: an essay on Posnerian law and economics as policy analysis', *Texas Law Review* 60, 1981: 147–172.

Samuels, W.J. (1993) 'Law and economics: some early journal contributions', in Warren J. Samuels, Jeff Biddle, and Thomas W. Patchak-Schuster, *Economic Thought and Discourse in the Twentieth Century*, Aldershot: Edward Elgar Publishing.

Samuels, W.J. (1998) *Law and Economics: The Early Journal Literature*, 2 vols. London: Pickering and Chatto.

Stigler, G.J. (1988) *Memoirs of an Unregulated Economist*, New York: Basic Books.

Sunstein, C.R. (2000) *Behavioral Law and Economics*, New York: Cambridge University Press.

Veljanovski, C. 'Wealth maximization, law and ethics: on the limits of economic efficiency', *International Review of Law and Economics* 1, 1981: 5–28.

6   Beyond the law-and-economics approach

From dismal to democratic

*Allan C. Hutchinson**

"Adam, Adam, Adam Smith/Listen what I charge you with/didn't you say/In class one day/That selfishness was bound to pay?/Of all the doctrines that was the Pith/Wasn't it, wasn't it, wasn't it, Smith?"

Stephen Leacock

Introduction

Oliver Wendell Holmes, Jr. has proven to be the most prescient of commentators. In 1897, he could already predict that Richard Posner would be "the man of the future" – "for the rational study of the law, the black-letter man may be the man of the present, but the man of the future is the man of statistics and the master of economics" (Holmes 1920: 187). While Posner has assumed many varied *personae* in his professional career, he has remained most closely associated with the law-and-economics approach; he was its most uncompromising practitioner and proselytizer, if not its founding figure. He might no longer be the law-and-economics fundamentalist of decades gone by, but he remains an enthusiastic supporter and promoter of its value "for the rational study of law." In short, Posner is an enthusiastic, if more skeptical and chastened, supporter of the law-and-economics approach.

Posner's continuing fondness for law-and-economics has much to do with his commitment to the appeal of a more scientific method of studying law and related phenomena. He maintains that reliance upon an approach that lends itself more readily to empirical validation and analytical rigor can allow legal study to distance itself better, if not entirely, from the ideological and political quagmire of more traditional and popular modes of jurisprudential inquiry. In this way, Posner believes that "the rational study of law" can be more useful, more dependable, more realistic, and less contested. Accordingly, despite his general shift to a more pragmatic orientation, he has kept faith with law-and-economics's central idea that normative and intellectual progress can be achieved by basing legal study on a "simple model of rationally self-interested behavior" (Posner, this volume: p. 2). Although he recognizes that this model needs to be more enriched, sophisticated, problematized, complicated, flexible, and focused from its more simplistic and unquestioning beginnings, he holds that this model can and should be the basis for "the rational study of law."

In this chapter I intend to challenge the viability and legitimacy of the law-and-economics approach as a mode of rational or scientific study. If Posner's watered-down version of law-and-economics can be shown to be unconvincing, then the extravagant claims of a more doctrinaire and less pragmatic law-and-economics will be rendered equally unpersuasive. As so often, it is not the case that law-and-economics has nothing to offer to the study of law, but that it over-reaches and makes broader claims for itself than can be defended or substantiated. When Posner concedes that economists and, therefore, law-and-economists "cling too tightly" to the assumptions implicit in "a model of rationally self-interested behavior," he insists that this is "for methodological rather than philosophical reasons" (Posner, this volume: p. 9). In contrast, I want to suggest that any "clinging," tightly or loosely, to such a model is wrongheaded. I contend that it is the philosophical – and, by extension, the political – reasons that loom largest in his enterprise. As such, Posner's continuing attachment to the law-and-economics approach as a scientific hedge against political contestation and disagreement is misplaced.

Throughout this chapter I want to recommend a philosophical shift from the "dismal" pseudo-science of law-and-economics to the more encouraging insights of a democratic sensibility as a means for evaluating the performance and promise of law. In the first section I will introduce the bare bones of the law-and-economics approach and its methodological assumptions; the emphasis will be upon explaining the dependence on the model of rationally self-interested behavior. The second section will take a step back to revisit the inspirational writings of Adam Smith; this offers a way of hoisting law-and-economists by their own petard and revealing the moral and political commitments of their allegedly neutral methodological assumptions. In the third part I survey the main failings of law-and-economics in terms of social fairness; their contribution to perpetuating social inequality is highlighted. The fourth section focuses on the corrosive effects of positing markets as being distinct from government regulation; this brings into sharper relief the political dimensions of law-and-economics. Finally, in the fifth section I suggest a different way of thinking about economics and politics; law-and-economists would play an important, but more modest, role in democratic emancipation.

An ill-wind from Chicago

For better and worse, a Chicago-style economic analysis has been accepted as a standard tool for engaging in both descriptive and prescriptive study of legal rules and institutions. However, as with the blues, Chicago offers only one economic version of a much broader phenomenon and tends to pass off this local variant as the "best" or "only" version of economic analysis. Its adherents explain or critique law in terms of economic logic; law is viewed as a series of incentives and disincentives to influence the behavioral choices of people who are viewed as rational and self-interested competitors for society's scarce resources. As a mode of positive analysis, it evaluates the empirical impact of different legal rules as price-setting devices in terms of their allocative efficiency and distributive justice. More controversially, as a mode of normative analysis, it evaluates whether any particular change in legal doctrine will increase *economic efficiency*. Although there is considerable debate within law-and-economics about the precise contours of this vital concept, there are two principal standards at work – a proposed shift in circumstances will be efficient either because it makes someone better off without making anyone else worse off (Pareto efficiency) or because it will generate sufficient gains to pay off the losers, at least hypothetically, and still leave gains for the winners (Kaldor–Hicks efficiency).

The basic commitment that ties together the different defenses of economic efficiency or wealth-maximization as the underlying rationale for the present or revised arrangements and operation of law is a faith in the efficiency-generating qualities of the market. Defenders of the status quo argue that a market economy is still thought to offer the most dependable institutional device by which to coordinate productive endeavors and meet the mixed needs of its participants; it emphasizes personal choice and voluntary consent to extant arrangements and affairs. In this law-and-economics world, much legal regulation is considered to be a largely technical matter which is readily accessible to the objective expert and which implicates no real political or broader judgmental issues. The role of law is facilitative – to provide the default or standard rules to enhance transactions or to step in where the market has been prevented from operating perfectly (e.g., lack of information, unequal power). Most adherents to this approach maintain that there is enough of an ideal market in operation (i.e., transactions costs approximate to zero and genuine competition exists) to warrant reliance on its analytical authority and normative predictions in designing legal institutions and doctrines.

The theoretical and assumptive backdrop to this law-and-economics approach is a model of rationally self-interested behavior. People will interact with others so as to satisfy their existing preferences. Because people's preferences are individual and not amenable to some cross-social hierarchical ordering or once-and-for-all collective calibration, the market recommends itself as a neutral clearing-house: people can make choices about how much they value their competing preferences and how much they are prepared to bid for their satisfaction. If the government were to intervene too freely in this process, it would be making illegitimate moral and political choices for its citizens. However, a fully-functioning market obviates such interference and adopts a neutral stance toward people's preferences and life plans. At its most unadulterated, law-and-economics suggests that the market is somehow a natural or self-evidently moral arena of social behavior that both needs almost no moral justification in itself, but also works as the moral underwriter for what is done in its name: "the perfect market, were it realized, would constitute a morally free zone, a zone within which the constraints of morality would have no place" (Trebilcock 1994: 29).

However, the confidence which law-and-economics scholars place in the capacity of market forces to fulfill these onerous responsibilities seems extravagant and suspect. At bottom, this is because the world-view that informs law-and-economics is so attractive to the established order in its simplicity and self-serving tendencies: it offers a superficially coherent, partially representative, and ideologically comfortable approach to the resolution of difficult dilemmas. Yet, although it is not entirely fictional in its depictions, it is far-fetched to imagine and assume that this is not only a realistic description of actual human behavior, but also a normative template for its justification and regulation. The "model of rationally self-interested behavior" is a metaphor (a limited and "defunct" one at that) to help understand a much more complex and multifaceted reality. To treat it as if it actually captured fully and faithfully the real-world interactions and motivations of people is misleading. It establishes an entirely private world in which the public interest has and can have no role at all: State intervention is presumptively illegitimate except as a last-resort replicator when there is a demonstrable breakdown or otherwise irremediable imperfection in the operation of the marketplace.

Within such a world-view, democracy has little purchase or relevance; it is reduced to a peripheral or partial role that is subservient to the expansive operation of the market. This is an undeserved diminishment of the democratic imperative. For present purposes, it is sufficient to note that democracy can better be understood as a way of life as well as a system of government that seeks to maximize the opportunities for people to participate in framing and fulfilling the terms and conditions of their own lives in all their dealings. It embraces people's private activities as well as their public interactions.[1]

Back to Adam

The central idea that the unhindered operations of a competitive market will ensure that private endeavor translates into public good is, of course, traceable to the pioneering work of Adam Smith, the Scottish father of modern economics. His monumental *The Wealth of Nations*, published in 1776, the same year as the American Declaration of Independence, was intended primarily as an assault on the protectionist and monopolist policies of the British eighteenth-century government. In so doing, he explained the power of a free-enterprise system to regulate economic activity in a socially beneficial manner. He reasoned that, because individuals acting separately can have only a small effect on prices and overall production, the "invisible hand" of the market would make a public virtue (i.e., optimal production) out of private vices (i.e., self-interest and acquisitiveness) (Smith and Cannan 2000: 485). These basic ideas have been jumped on by modern economists and political commentators to bolster the claim that the best way to serve society at large is by relying on the facility of markets to orchestrate private economic activity for the public good. However, according to Smith – and this is absolutely crucial – such unplanned coordination would only occur if certain conditions were in place:

> that the competitive market was anchored by an appropriate legal and institutional framework;

that economic activity was supported by a genuine sense of community well-being; and

that the economy was primarily comprised of small and local merchants.

Yet, the basic truth is that these enabling pre-conditions have been conveniently ignored or overlooked by modern marketeers. Once they are taken into account, the use to which Smith's work has been put and the persisting faith in the disciplinary power of markets are fatally subverted.

First, while it is true that Smith was generally no friend of government, his primary criticisms of government were directed as much to their particular protectionist polices against free-trade as to the general involvement of government in commerce and business. Unlike many contemporary marketeers', Smith's was not a campaign against government per se. He understood that it was not only the right, but also the responsibility of government to ensure that the market was able to function fairly and properly. Government's task was to establish appropriate rules of property and contract-formation as well as to ensure that competition and fair-dealing would flourish; this required more than a hands-off mentality that characterizes much modern theorizing. Smith did not subscribe blindly to the notion that "the government which governs least is the government that governs best." He was much less dogmatic and more strategic in his proposals. Moreover, although Smith could not be labeled as any kind of socialist, there is no reason to assume that he would not have accepted and even welcomed considerable government regulation in the complex and dense economic conditions of the early twenty-first century. This stands as a major difference between the real Adam Smith and the imagined Adam Smith of Friedrich Hayek, Milton Friedman, and their law-and-economics kin.

Second, in championing the merits of a robust market economy, Smith was clear that "it is not from the benevolence of the butcher, the brewer, or the baker that we expect our dinner, but from their regard to their own interest" (Smith 2000: 15). However, by self-interest he did not mean a crass disregard for the welfare of others; there is a difference between a strong self-interest and an unmitigated selfishness or greed. Not only did Smith write with compassion about the workers's plight in an industrial society, but he also demonstrated a genuine egalitarian instinct, distinctly lacking in his latter-day disciples. It was Smith's belief that the market system can only work if there existed what he called "sympathy" or the willingness to take care of neighbors and to share gains with the less fortunate. While dependence on the "benevolence" of others was ill-founded, he did not foreclose the important need for such benevolence. Smith's was a caution, not a castigation. He understood that, for his "invisible hand" to direct free markets, there had to be a cohesive, morally disciplined and socially benevolent social system in place: "[the rich] are led by *an invisible hand* to make the same distribution of the necessities of life, which would have been made, had the earth been divided into equal portions among all its inhabitants" (Smith 1759: 273). For him, the market did not operate independently of morals, but required a pre-existing moral context which valued fellow-feeling and communal generosity: "the wise and virtuous man is at all times willing that his own private interest should be sacrificed to the public interest of his own particular order or society" (Smith 1759: Part VI, s.2, ch.III, 295). In effect, Smith grasped, unlike his contemporary faux-imitators, that the strengths of "market capitalism" (which are considerable) are as much to be found in its limits as in its central idea.

Third, and perhaps most strikingly in regard to the situation of modern economies, Smith had little time for "the mean rapacity, the monopolizing spirit of merchants and manufacturers, who neither are, nor ought to be, the rulers of mankind" (Smith and Cannan 2000: 527). In offering his defense of free markets, Smith's idea of commerce was of small-scale, low-personnel, and relatively private businesses competing in local markets and engendering benevolent communities. He envisaged small manufacturing businesses, like pin-makers, which comprised ten or so artisans who, with a different set of specialized skills, could be molded into an efficient workforce: the owners were not only the managers, but also often part of the workforce itself. Smith opposed any form of economic concentration on the ground that it hampers the natural ability of the market's invisible hand to ensure that prices and bargains are fairly made and to advance the public good. Indeed, Smith was sufficiently far-sighted to recognize that the great manufacturers and merchants of the day were "an order of men, whose interest is never the same as the public" (Smith and Cannan 2000: 250) Growing in size and unconnected to one particular community or locality, the corporation would begin to serve its own interests at the expense of everyone else's.[2] In short, Smith considered that large corporations perverted rather than personified the entrepreneurial spirit of a market economy. Almost 160 years before Berle and Means, he saw that companies "scarce[ly] ever fail to do more harm than good" (Smith and Cannan 2000: 818) and that "the pretense that corporations are necessary to the better government of the trade is without foundation" (Smith and Cannan 2000: 149).[3]

In the real world

To echo some wags in the world of science, the "great tragedy" of economics, like so many other academic disciplines, is that beautiful theories are brought to their knees by ugly facts. And there are very many ugly facts and unsightly failings, according to its critics, that law-and-economics chooses to ignore – it is reductionist in its insistence in viewing all social conduct in terms of market behavior; it manages, by giving everything a monetary value, to overvalue and undervalue much of human interaction; its leading concepts (voluntariness, transaction costs, etc.) are theoretically vague and practically indeterminate; it is ethically bankrupt in that it takes all personal preferences at face value and refuses to distinguish among them; it is self-serving in that it treats all personal preferences as independent of the social or market system in which they are generated and satisfied; it ignores the distinction between willingness to pay and ability to pay; and it celebrates individual autonomy over communal attachment.[4] Nevertheless, law-and-economics scholarship does focus attention on the important economic function of legal rules and obliges lawyers to attend to the instrumental consequences of different legal regimes and reforms. Perhaps more than most theories of law, its fatal flaw is that it overreaches itself and, instead of being content with offering a partial insight into the operation of law and society, it claims to provide a total and hegemonic account of law. As such, it reveals itself as a political ideology as much as a philosophical theory.

There is much to be said about how the workings of market economies fail to live up to the assumptions, expectations, and predictions of its defenders. Yet, it is also the case that, even when the market is working as well as it can or even approximating to the ideal conditions postulated by its theoretical adherents, there remain grave problems with its basic operating assumptions. This is particularly so in regard to what counts as efficient and, therefore, just outcomes when viewed from a staunchly democratic standpoint. At the heart of the problem are the vital definitions of "wealth" and "efficiency" which are so limited and limiting that they fail to capture and weigh the full social costs of different ways of acting and organizing. By only counting money-based preferences and by treating each dollar as always being worth the same value (rather than assessing its worth relative to how many other dollars a person has), market economics reduces almost all social interactions into little more than a discrete series of economic calculations; this elides as much as it illuminates. Of course, treating market transactions as being matters of economic reckoning is not so odd or unexpected; any approach that did not account for their obvious economic dimensions would be found severely wanting. However, the real difficulty arises when this bottom-line mentality is the only one in play.

Under the prevailing economic mind-set, the simple standard for assessing and comparing different economic situations is that of cost–benefit analysis: Will it be more efficient to move from the status quo to a future proposed arrangement? Will the potential gains of doing so outweigh the potential losses because overall wealth will thereby be increased? This sounds an entirely sensible approach; it would seem silly to refuse to change simply because losses resulted as long as the gains made were greater. So, for example, faced with the prospect of a business decision about whether to introduce a new manufacturing process in its plants, a corporation would be expected to decide in favor of doing so, if any losses (cost of machinery, re-training, etc.) in that process would be more than made up for by the anticipated profits from such a change. Indeed, under present models of corporate governance, the management would likely be derelict in its responsibilities not to adopt such a course of action that promised to do this.

Despite its initial and almost intuitive appeal, there are considerable problems with such an economic analysis. One of the most significant, when viewed from a more democratic perspective, is that there is no concern for who bears the loss or who receives the gain as long as the calculation results in an overall enhancement in social wealth. In this two-dimensional universe of the market, the emphasis is on social utility rather than social fairness: "the ideal capitalist firm is relentlessly engaged in profit maximization" (Williamson 1996: 167). However, this efficiency calculation is a hypothetical one in that, as long as gains are greater than losses, the changes should be made. Even if there is enough of a gain to indemnify the losers (e.g., laid-off workers) and still come out ahead, there is no expectation in the law-and-economists's frame of reference that the losers will be so compensated. So, shareholders are entitled to take the full benefit of the gains even though those who suffer the losses are expected to absorb the full extent of the losses. It is only with a distinctly nonmarket intervention by the state (e.g., legislated redundancy payments) that the corporation is obliged to ensure that the gains will be sufficient to provide *actual* compensation and still make a profit.

If the losses which resulted from business decisions were random or, at least, tended to be rotated over time among various groups, including shareholders, the outcome of any particular calculation might be less troublesome; claims that economic efficiency was tantamount to social fairness might be more palatable. However, the fact is that most losses tend to be carried by those groups (e.g., working families and local communities) who are least able to carry them and who have no or little participation in the decision-making process itself. In this constant tilting of the equational balance, the gap between winners and losers will steadily increase. Further, lest it be thought that these critical observations are merely abstract and hypothetical, the Canadian corporate economy in the last couple of decades has followed exactly this kind of pattern. Not only has the income and wealth gap between rich/executive and poor/workers widened, but the harsh logic of economic efficiency has been utilized to justify enhanced corporate profits by laying-off workers, selling off assets, cutting back on research, neglecting long-term planning, and even buying up their own shares. For instance, according to the Canadian Centre for Policy Alternatives, between 1988 and 1996, thirty-three major corporations increased their combined revenues by $40 billion and, at the same time, reduced their workforces by 35 percent or 216,000 jobs.[5] Some of the more notable examples are: Petro-Canada reported a very successful turn-around by laying off 700 employees, boosting dividends, and increasing stock price; General Motors Canada shed 2,500 workers and increased its profits by 35 percent; Bank of Montreal laid off 1,400 employees and increased its profits by 20 percent; Canadian National reduced its labor force by almost 10,000 and its stock tripled in value.

Markets and governments

The fatal flaw in the law-and-economics approach is the claim that it is meaningful to talk about free markets in contrast to schemes of government regulation – that there is some important sense in which a market can be said *not* to be a form of governmental regulation. However, this is an entirely misconceived representation of the market, its relation to governmental regulation, and its moral status. It is never a question of contrasting market allocation with government distribution because the market is one form of government regulation. Contrary to many law-and-economists's assertions and assumptions, government regulation is not a separate and independent institutional response. On the contrary, it is the *sine qua non* of a free market's operation. Without the existence of an authoritative state process to define property entitlements, enforce contracts, prevent involuntary transactions, maintain a circulating medium, and curtail monopoly and anti-competitive behavior, there exists no market in any real or meaningful sense. Moreover, the choice is never between the allocation of goods by a decentralized market or through centralized government administration. It is a choice between various supporting rationales and arguments about those choices. And there is no neutral, non-moral, or apolitical standard by which to make those kinds of choices; it is the stuff of politics, not a respite from it.

Many implications flow from law-and-economists's refusal or reluctance to recognize this vital insight. From a democratic perspective, the most troubling aspect of this tendency to naturalize the market is its effect upon the all-important question of the identity of market actors and their preference-formation. Traditional economics takes preferences as exogenous givens and treats their satisfaction as being presumptively good. Of course, more sophisticated and pragmatic theorists, like Posner, reject such crude assumptions. Nevertheless, he insists that, while "economists' hesitancy to penetrate beneath the surface indications of preference that they call 'revealed preference' ... or to deal with non-monetizable phenomena ... may be regrettable," there remains genuine merit and validity in assuming that preferences are "stable and reliably revealed by behavior" so as to "enable economists to formulate testable hypotheses about behavior."[6] However, that said, he and like-minded scholars fail to grasp the debilitating implications of the recognition that preferences are not stable and adaptive in, at least, two important respects.

First of all, although many law-and-economics types accept that rich and poor develop their preferences, at least in part, as a result of their relative positions in the market, they still manage to treat the poor as if being poor was somehow *outside and independent of* the market's operation. Moreover, there also seems to be an assumption among some that, once it is recognized that many individual choices reflect adaptive preferences, the challenge is to predict the kind of choices that people would make if they were not constrained by the social, economic, legal, or other contexts in which they live.[7] However, this misses the major force of the critics's observation – people are never outside or unconstrained by such contexts. Indeed, without such informing contexts there would be no basis on which to generate preferences or to choose between them. History shows that people interact with and adapt to their socio-historical contexts as they also struggle to transform and adapt them. The real challenge, therefore, is not to wish away the informing context and then hazard a guess at what hypothetical choices would be made, but to work toward negotiating a context in which people can fully develop and experiment with their preferences. Democracy is the best process through which to do this. To understand this is to appreciate that freedom is not an absence of constraints, but is realized in a particular and changing set of constraints.

Pushed a little further, this insight leads to the second limitation of law-and-economics's reliance on a simple model of rationally self-interested behavior. People's identities are affected by their micro-social environments (such as family, friends, colleagues, etc.) and macro-social environments (such as nationality, class, ethnicity, religion, etc.). Consequently, in a society permeated by economic logic and market imagery, the type of economic arrangements that exist not only influence the substantive preferences that people generate and seek to fulfill, but also help shape the kind of persons that people become. For example, within the classic vision of market actors as "preference maximizers," there is little possibility of nurturing a social good that is more than the aggregate of private preferences. Further, such a model inculcates a consumer mentality and tutors people to develop and abide by a certain economic rationality. This is a very sterile and one-dimensional version of human activity and its potentiality. Market actors are deemed to be cognitively supreme and highly rational; they are able to analyze vast amounts of information about alternative courses of action, to prioritize them in terms of their expected utility, and to do so in an entirely consistent way. Such an account fails to appreciate that the market creates this utility-monster as much as its acquired or adaptive preferences. To paraphrase Oscar Wilde, marketeers know "the price of everything and the value of nothing."[8]

It is not that citizens act irrationally, but that they follow different and often conflicting rationalities that cannot be reduced to a set of simple-minded directives: "efficiency is not an end, but a means to achieve valued ends ... [and] when it's used as an end in itself, it becomes a cult" (Stein 2001: 6). Insofar as a market model of human activity simplifies these multiplex calculations, citizens are reduced to little more than fungible consumers. Rather than taking the market as a given, it needs to be justified as a particular kind of government regulation among a larger mix of schemes and arrangements. It is not exchange in and of itself that should be encouraged, but the kind of participation that is not exhausted by an act of market exchange. By reducing participation to exchange, people begin to think of themselves as consumers in all they do, even when they are not in an overtly economic situation. While people are economic consumers some of the time, they are political citizens all of the time. Whereas the market obtains its authority from people's consuming decisions, the practice of citizenship involves a more expanded notion of participation. Markets allow only for differences counted in terms of dollars and, therefore, the primary difference is between those who have and those who have-not. Democratic politics allows for an expanded recognition of differences that can be counted and debated in many different ways including, but not limited to, dollars.

In calling for the abandonment of markets as the theoretical and organizational paradigm for civic interaction, I am not to be taken to be making some commitment to a discredited and disavowed model of a state-planned economy. Any lingering faith in the possibility that a planned distribution of goods and services through bureaucratic channels might be the best alternative to a free market ideology is to be thoroughly debunked and discarded; such polarized thinking is entirely antithetical to a democratic way of proceeding. Ironically, the notions of unified economic actors with fixed preferences, instrumental causality, and objective rationality are also pre-occupations of Marxian economic thought.[9] At different times and in different ways, policy-makers must be prepared to experiment with a variety of strategies and interventions. This cannot be achieved through the dismal method of law-and-economics, but through the more vibrant possibilities of full-blown democracy.

Beyond efficiency

In offering this robust critique of a law-and-economics approach, the intention has not been to advance the position that productivity or profit-making is all bad or even inherently bad. This would be plain silly. There is nothing wrong with productivity, efficiency, etc. Indeed, they are essential values for any modern society to embrace and foster. But it is the elevation of such values to a cluster of meta-values by which all social processes and other values must be judged that is the problem. For example, it is entirely fair and appropriate that investors should be entitled to a reasonable return on their capital investment and that their capital is worthy of protection. However, there is equally no reason why that must always be at the entire expense of or in essential priority to the interests of all others. As both a matter of historical record and as an issue of public policy, it is mistaken to suggest, as many law-and-economics commentators do, that making as much money and profits as possible is or ought to be the sole or primary goal of the business corporation. This would be, as an incredulous critic notes, "to define the business corporation ... as a kind of shark that lives off the community rather than as an important agency in the construction, maintenance, and transformation of our shared lives" (White 1985: 1419). While a cost–benefit analysis is necessary and desirable, it ought to be only the first step in making decisions, not the first, last, only, or primary consideration.

The search for a suitable and simple calculus by which to achieve some degree of commensurable comparison between different proposals or states of affairs is a sleeveless errand; there is no algorithm, be it economic or political, that can do such work. Law-and-economists are wrong to believe that not only is "efficiency" a measurable and exclusive standard by which to adjudge competing states of social affairs, but also that such efficiency is only realizable in a free and unregulated market. If the law-and-economics approach has any appeal, it is in its stark and beguiling simplicity, not its subtle and nuanced sophistication; a limited number of variables can be fed into an equally limited number of equations, which, in turn, will produce a limited number of policy recommendations. As seductive as this appears, it is the stuff of fantasy.

In contrast, a democratic approach rejects the claim that there is one simple equation by which to settle upon the best course to follow for all time. Being pragmatic and practical, it eschews resort to mechanical formulae and places its faith in the power of real people in real situations grappling with the best way to proceed for them at that time. Democracy is less about once-and-for-all accounting and more about a contingent doing-the-best-we-can. The process for formulating benefits and entitlements is important in itself under a democratic theory as much as the results it produces; an in-depth appreciation of the rich social context within which individuals exist and thrive is essential. Most importantly, it will allow due weight to be given to the fact that so much economic activity takes places against a background of starkly maldistributed resources and wealth which will presumptively invalidate the legitimacy of many (and even most) outcomes reached.

A simple example serves to illustrate the anti-democratic thrust of law-and-economics. In the law of torts, Learned Hand's famous formula for determining negligence liability is considered to be the jewel in law-and-economics's crown. It will be remembered that it asserted that liability should only be imposed on an actor when the discounted costs of the accident are greater than the cost of precautions necessary to avoid it or $B < PL$ (i.e., where B is the cost of taking safety precautions; P is the probability of an accident occurring; and L is the amount of damages caused by the accident if it occurred).[10] To incentivize people to invest more in safety than the discounted costs of the injuries caused by the resulting accident is to encourage a wasteful use of scarce resources and is, therefore, inefficient. While there is much to recommend this efficiency analysis from a law-and-economics's perspective (and as a rationale for extant negligence law), its democratic shortcomings are manifest. Manufacturers and other corporate actors are charged with settling upon an efficient level of accidents, whereas the harms caused to workers, consumers, and others are simply variables in a general calculation: The victims of accidents are left with no control over or input into their own fate. From a democratic perspective, it is not that there should be a commitment to achieve an accident-free world – an impossible and undesirable goal. Instead, the democratic ambition is to allow each person to participate in and determine the extent of risk to which they are exposed. Not only does law-and-economics give no particular weight or value to such involvement and accountability, it works against it.

Consequently, although trumpeted as a simple route to freedom and social justice, so-called market fundamentalism is as potent and as misguided an ideology as any other.[11] Yet, while most ideologies, like Marxism and fascism, have been recognized as the failures that they were, market fundamentalism still manages to hold sway and, therefore, to wreak its own havoc on the world. Despite efforts by its protagonists, there is simply no reason to be persuaded that capitalism and democracy are somehow synonymous. Indeed, the link between capitalism and democracy is weak at best and counter-productive at worst. If capitalism is to remain, then it must serve rather than master the interests of democracy. Citizens are entitled to basic economic protections by virtue of their membership in society, not only through their economic successes. Democrats appreciate that, while everything has a cost, this is not the sole measure of value. Citizens are not only consumers – *I buy, therefore, I am*. And democracy is not only or best sold in the marketplace. Indeed, as Amy Chua has noted, "markets concentrate wealth, often spectacular wealth, in the hands of the market-dominant minority, while democracy increases the political power of the impoverished majority" (Chua 2003: 6). The obvious challenge, therefore, is to ensure that politics is played out throughout social life and not merely confined to areas outside the economic sphere; people are entitled to participation and accountability in their economic dealings as much as with their political engagement. To accept less would be to eviscerate the emancipatory potential of democracy and to concede authority to the corporate elite alone.

One of Adam Smith's most oft-cited expressions is that "it is not from the benevolence of the butcher, the brewer, or the baker that we expect our dinner, but from their regard to their own interest" (Smith 2000: 15). This sits very uncomfortably with the contemporary role and dominance of mega-corporations. Today's conglomerates are hardly analogous with the local butchers, brewers, or bakers of Smith's eighteenth-century Scotland. It is simply not the case that, orchestrated by the market's "invisible hand," such corporate entities are working for the public good. The fabled "invisible hand" is more likely sponsored by these corporations and its palm greased by their marketing efforts. If social approval is to be given to rationally self-interested behavior, it must be because it is shown to be of social benefit in that the invisible hand is working sufficiently well; it must be capable of coordinating competition among self-interested marketeers so as to result in a stable and balanced economic system. Self-interest is not a vice, but its excessive and unbalanced pursuit threatens to overwhelm the virtue of social cohesion to which it is supposed to contribute: the market ethic will bite the "invisible hand" that coordinates it and undermine the whole rationale for the market in the first place. It is less the idea that butchers, brewers, and bakers will rule the world, but more that they will do so as butchers, brewers, and bakers rather than as citizens.

Nevertheless, it is not enough to simply be against something: one must be *for* something. And democracy is the best and most effective alternative. The democratic citizen is not only one species of *Homo economicus*. Relying exclusively on the jargon of economics as the language of citizenship tends to make us think of ourselves as only consumers, competitors, enemies, etc. rather than as occasional colleagues, neighbors, friends, etc. When people begin to talk of themselves as market actors and consumers, they begin to act out their allotted roles in a script and voice that is not of their own choosing. It is not profits and wealth that should be given social priority, but the kind of participation that is not exhausted by an act of market exchange. The political ambition must surely be to ensure that, while people are economic actors some of the time, they are democratic citizens all of the time.[12]

Whereas law-and-economists have a marked tendency to put representative democracy in the service of private values, participatory citizens accept that the relation between public virtue and private values is open to revisable articulation. Indeed, the attraction of democracy is its potential to keep politics permanently open and fluid. As such, citizenship under radical democracy need not be committed to one common good (i.e., economic efficiency), and a limited one at that, but to an engaged practice of civility in which a good life consists of public-spirited engagement with others over the shape and substance of "the good life." Within this democratic understanding, it is possible to integrate

Homo economicus into a much broader and deeper conversational context. The notion of the "free market" and its abstract denizens would not be outside or beyond political authority, but would be within its bailiwick. Whereas law-and-economists view people as existing in an abstract realm of optional interactions with anonymous others, the citizen is located at a historical time and in a local place where personal and social living are situated in a web of connections between real people. So understood, it might mean that, in exercising their rights and making claims, people would take into account their responsibilities to others, particularly those less fortunate and more vulnerable than themselves.

Conclusion

In a rare (or indiscrete) concession, two leading practitioners of law-and-economics acknowledged that "culture and ideology, not only value maximization and self-interest, might influence" a society's choice of laws and legal arrangements (see Bebchuk and Roe 1999: 168). This may seem obvious to many, but it is an insight that eludes or is trivialized by most law-and-economics scholars. "Value maximization and self-interest" are themselves cultural and ideological artifacts that are passed off by their defenders as something both technical and apart from culture and ideology. Law-and-economics, therefore, must be adjudged as much as a political probe as a technical inquiry. When this is done, it is revealed to be a very elite and self-serving mode of analysis. In its single-minded emphasis on profits and wealth, it manages to present most civic interactions not only as something outside of democratic politics, but also as somehow beyond its legitimate bailiwick. While it might well be a desirable goal to be more economically efficient than not, that should only be embraced as a means to achieve more expansive and democratically determined ends. As Adam Smith reminded us (if only to be selectively ignored), a person "is certainly not a good citizen who does not wish to promote by every means in his power the welfare of the whole society of his fellow citizens" (Smith 1759: 290).

Notes

* Distinguished Research Professor, Osgoode Hall Law School, York University, Toronto, Canada. I am grateful to friends and colleagues for critical assistance and intellectual support.
1 See below in the section entitled *Beyond efficiency*; also see generally (Hutchinson 2008).
2 See also (Galbraith 2001).
3 See also (Berle and Means 1932).
4 For a good summary, see (Ashford 2002).
5 See generally (Harmes 2004).
6 See (Posner, this volume: p. 9); see also (Trebilcock 1994: 267 – "scholars need to take more seriously the proposition that many individual preferences are socially constructed and are amenable to revision").
7 On this point, see (Trebilcock 1994: 267).
8 Wilde (1892) was talking about cynics.

9 On this point, see (Amariglio and Ruccio 1994: 21).
10 See *U.S.* v. *Carroll Towing*, 159 F.2d 169 (2d Cir. 1947). Ironically, Learned Hand was described by one of his biographers (Frank 1957: 668) as "par excellence, the democratic aristocrat."
11 A sophisticated attempt to portray "market economics" as an (American) article of faith is provided by (Nelson 2001); see also (Soros 2000).
12 On this point, see (Kay 2003).

References

Amariglio, J. and Ruccio, D., 'Postmodernism, Marxism, and the critique of modern economic thought', *Rethinking Marxism* 7, 1994: 7–35.

Ashford, R., 'The socio-economic foundation of corporate law and corporate social responsibility', *Tulane Law Review* 76, 2002: 1187–1206.

Bebchuk, L. and Roe, M., 'A theory of path dependence in corporate ownership and governance', *Stanford Law Review* 52, 1999: 127–170.

Berle, A. and Means, G. (1932) *The Modern Corporation and Private Property*, New York: Commerce Clearing House.

Chua, A. (2003) *World on Fire: How Exporting Freemarket Democracy Breeds Ethnic Hatred and Global Instability*, New York: Doubleday.

Frank, J. 'Some reflections on judge Learned Hand', *University of Chicago Law Review* 24, 1957: 666–705.

Galbraith, J.K. (2001) 'The founding faith: Adam Smith's *Wealth of Nations*', in A.D. Williams (ed.) *The Essential Galbraith*, Boston, MA: Houghton Mifflin: 153–168.

Harmes, A. (2004) *The Return of the State: Protesters, Power-Brokers, and the New Global Compromise*, Berkeley, CA: Douglas & McIntyre.

Holmes, O.W. Jr. (1920) *Collected Legal Papers*, edited by P. Smith, Clark: The Lawbook Exchange, Ltd.

Hutchinson, A.C. (2008) *The Province of Jurisprudence Democratized*, New York: Oxford University Press.

Kay, J. (2003) *The Truth about Markets: Their Genius, Their Limits, Their Foibles*, New York: Penguin Books.

Nelson, R. (2001) *Economics as Religion: From Samuelson to Chicago and Beyond*, University Park, PA: Pennsylvania State Press.

Smith, A. (1759) *The Theory of Moral Sentiments*, London: A. Millar, and A. Kincaid and J. Bell.

Smith, A. (2000 [1776]) *An Inquiry into the Nature and Causes of the Wealth of Nations*, London: Methuen & Co., Ltd).

Smith, A. and Cannan, E. (eds.) (2000) *The Wealth of Nations*, New York: Modern Library.

Soros, G. (2000) *Open Society: Reforming Global Capitalism*, London: Little, Brown.

Stein, J.G. (2001) *The Cult of Efficiency*, Toronto: House of Anansi Press.

Trebilcock, M. (1994) *The Limits of Freedom of Contract*, Cambridge, MA: Harvard University Press.

White, B. 'How should we talk about corporations? The languages of economics and of citizenship', *Yale Law Journal* 94, 1985: 1416–1425.

Wilde, O., *Lady Windermere's Fan, A Play About a Good Woman*, produced February 22, 1892, St James's Theatre in London.

Williamson, O. (1996) *The Mechanisms of Corporate Governance*, New York: Oxford University Press.

7 Functional law and economics

The search for value-neutral principles of lawmaking

*Jonathan Klick and Francesco Parisi**

Introduction

During its relatively short history, the law and economics movement has developed three distinct schools of thought. The first two schools of thought – the positive school and the normative school – developed almost concurrently. The positive school, historically associated with the early Chicago School, restricts itself to the descriptive study of the incentives produced by the legal system largely because its adherents believe that efficient legal rules evolve naturally. On the other hand, the normative school, historically associated with the early contributions of the Yale School, sees the law as a tool for remedying "failures" that arise in the market.

The subsequently developed functional school of law and economics draws from public choice theory and the constitutional paradigm of the Virginia school of economics, and offers a third perspective which is neither fully positive nor fully normative. Recognizing that there are structural forces that often impede the development of efficient legal rules, the functional school allows for the possibility of using insights from public choice economics to remedy faulty legal rules at a meta level. However, unlike the normative school, the functional school also recognizes that there are failures in the political market that make it unlikely that changes will be made on a principled basis. Also, it is difficult to identify all of the ultimate consequences of corrective legal rules. This skepticism causes the functional school to focus on using economic theory to design legal meta-rules that lead to efficiency *ex ante*. Achieving this *ex ante* efficiency requires the design of legal institutions that induce individuals to internalize the effects of their private activities, as well as inducing them to reveal their true preferences in situations where collective decisions must be made.

In addition to these over-arching differences about the role of law and economics in the design of legal institutions, there are other methodological differences among these schools of thought. These differences are illustrated by the debate on how to define efficiency at the individual decision level and in the aggregate. Specifically, the schools often take different stances on how social preferences should be evaluated and what exactly should be maximized to achieve an optimal legal system. In the sections that follow, we lay out the development of these schools of thought, detailing where they differ methodologically.

Common tools, different methods

Most practitioners of law and economics believe that there is an important common ground unifying all scholars in the discipline, regardless of their ideology – a search for new insights in the law by applying economic concepts and theories (MacKaay 2000). Despite this common statement of purpose, various schools of law and economics can be identified, each with an elaborate research program and a distinct methodological approach.

Positive versus normative approaches to law and economics

During the early period of the discipline, law and economics scholarship was labeled as Chicago-style or Yale-style.[1] These labels made reference to the respective dominant positive or normative approach utilized by each school.[2] The origins of the Chicago and Yale Schools of law and economics are attributable to the early work of a handful of scholars, including the pioneering work of Ronald Coase and Guido Calabresi in the early 1960s.

A difference in approach is detectable between the law and economics scholarship of the early 1960s and that of the 1970s. The earlier studies appraised the effects of legal rules on the normal functioning of the economic system. By contrast, the subsequent generation of studies used economic analysis to achieve a better understanding of the legal system. Indeed, in the 1970s a number of important applications of economics to law gradually exposed the economic structure of basically every aspect of a legal system, from its origin and evolution to its substantive, procedural, and constitutional rules.

In many respects, the impact of law and economics has exceeded its original ambitions. One effect of the incorporation of economics into the study of law was to transform traditional legal methodology irreversibly. Legal rules began to be studied as an organic system. Economics provided the analytical rigor necessary for the study of the vast body of rules present in a modern legal system. This intellectual revolution came at an appropriate time, when legal academia was actively searching for a tool that permitted critical appraisal of the law, rather than merely strengthening the dogmatic consistencies of the system.

At this point, methodological differences came to surface with substantive practical differences. The Chicago School laid most of its foundations on the work carried out by Richard Posner in the 1970s. An important premise of the Chicago approach to law and economics is the idea that the common law is the result of an effort, conscious or not, to induce efficient outcomes. This premise is known as the efficiency of the common law hypothesis. According to this hypothesis (first intimated by Coase [1960] and later systematized and greatly extended by Posner), common law rules attempt to allocate resources in either a Pareto or Kaldor–Hicks efficient manner.[3]

Posner endorses a scientific approach which uses economics to objectively study the legal system and the behavior it regulates. He believes that positive economic analysis is immune to most abuse and misuse because it is merely used to explain or predict incentives which guide individuals and institutions under alternative legal rules.

The primary hypothesis advanced by positive economic analysis of law is the notion that efficiency is the predominant factor shaping the rules, procedures, and institutions of the common law. Posner contends that efficiency is a defensible criterion in the context of judicial decision-making because "justice" considerations, on the content of which there is no academic or political consensus, introduce unacceptable ambiguity into the judicial process. In arguing for positive use of economics, Posner is not denying the existence of valuable normative law and economics applications. In fact, law and economics often has many objective things to say that will affect one's normative analysis of a policy.[4]

Despite the powerful analytical reach of economic analysis, Chicago scholars acknowledged from the outset that the economist's competence in the evaluation of legal issues was limited. While the economist's perspective could prove crucial for the positive analysis of the efficiency of alternative legal rules and the study of the effects of alternative rules on the distribution of wealth and income, Chicago-style economists generally recognized the limits of their role in providing normative prescriptions for social change or legal reform.[5]

Conversely, the Yale School of law and economics, often described as the "normative" school, believes that there is a greater need for legal intervention in order to correct for pervasive forms of market failure.[6] Distributional concerns are central to the Yale-style literature. The overall philosophy of this group is often presented as more value-tainted and more prone to policy intervention than the Chicago law and economics school.

Unlike its Chicago counterpart, this school has attracted liberal practitioners who employ the methodology of the Chicago School but push it to formulate normative propositions on what the law ought to be like (MacKaay 2000).[7] Given the overriding need to pursue justice and fairness in distribution through the legal system, most Yale-style scholars would suggest that efficiency, as defined by the Chicago School, could never be the ultimate end of a legal system.

The functional approach and individual-centered economic analysis

As the domain of law and economics has expanded, its perspective on methodological issues has not been stagnant.[8] In the 1990s, a new generation of literature, developed at the intersection of law, economics, and public choice theory, pushed the boundaries of economic analysis of law, studying the origins and formative mechanisms of legal rules. The resulting approach, which we describe as the "functional" approach to legal analysis, is quite skeptical of both the normative and the positive alternatives.[9] The systematic incorporation of public choice theory into the economic approach to law may serve to bridge the gap between conflicting normative perspectives in law and economics, at least by bringing the debate onto the more solid ground of collective choice theory.

The functional approach is wary of the generalized efficiency hypothesis espoused by the positive school.[10] In this respect, the functionalists share some of this skepticism of the normative school. There is little empirical support for a generalized trust in the efficiency of the law in all substantive areas. The functional school of law and economics is even more vocally skeptical of a general efficiency hypothesis when applied to sources of the law other than common law (e.g., legislation or administrative regulations).

The functional approach is also critical of the normative extensions and ad hoc corrective policies which are often advocated by the normative schools. Economic models are a simplified depiction of reality. Thus, functionalists think it is generally dangerous to use such tools to design corrective or interventionist policies. In this respect, the functionalists are aligned with the positive school in their criticism of the normative approach. According to both the positivists and the functionalists, normative economic analysis often risks overlooking the many unintended consequences of legal intervention.

Public choice theory in general, and constitutional political economy in particular, provide strong methodological foundations for the functional school of law and economics. The findings of public choice theory, while supporting much of the traditional wisdom, pose several challenges to neoclassical law and economics. In spite of the sophisticated mathematical techniques of economic analysis, judges and policymakers in many situations still lack the expertise and methods for evaluating the efficiency of alternative legal rules.[11] Therefore, courts and policymakers should undertake a functional analysis. Such an analysis requires them to first inquire into the incentives underlying the legal or social structure that generated the legal rule, rather than directly attempting to weigh the costs and benefits of individual rules.[12] In this way, the functionalist approach to law and economics can extend the domain of traditional law and economics inquiry to include both the study of the influence of market and non-market institutions (other than politics) on legal regimes, and the study of the comparative advantages of alternative sources of centralized or decentralized lawmaking in supplying efficient rules.

With this focus on the underlying legal and social structure, there is less impetus to micro-manage individual legal and policy decisions. Such micromanagement is likely to suffer from the rent-seeking activities of interested parties. Much of the intellectual foundation for this structural focus can be found in the seminal writings of James Buchanan.[13] Buchanan (1987: 243) eloquently describes the constitutional political economy research program in his Nobel Prize address by saying: "I sought to make economic sense out of the relationship between the individual and the state before proceeding to advance policy nostrums."

Individual preferences, collective choices: Pareto, Bentham, and Rawls

The need to make comparative evaluations between different rules motivates much of law and economics. Consequently, the second methodological problem in law and economics deals with the choice of criteria for carrying out such comparative analysis. In practical terms, this problem is concerned with the method of aggregation of individual preferences into social preferences, and is not unique to law and economics. It is part of a much larger methodological debate in economic philosophy and welfare economics.

As early as 1881 Edgeworth (1881: 7–8) stated the moral dilemma of social welfare analysis, observing that a moral calculus should proceed with a comparative evaluation of "the happiness of one person with the happiness of another.... Such comparison can no longer be shirked, if there is to be any systematic morality at all." The problem obviously arises from the fact that economists do not have any reliable method for measuring individuals's utility, let alone make inter-personal comparisons of utility.

Economic analysis generally utilizes one of the three fundamental criteria of preference aggregation set out below.

Ordinality and Pareto

The first criterion of social welfare is largely attributable to Italian economist and sociologist Vilfredo Pareto. The Pareto criterion limits the inquiry to *ordinal* preferences of the relevant individuals. According to Pareto, an optimal allocation is one that maximizes the well-being of one individual relative to the well-being of other individuals being constant.[14] In normal situations there are several possible solutions that would qualify for such a criterion of social optimality. For example, if the social problem is that of distributing a benefit between two parties, any hypothetical distribution would be Pareto optimal, since there is no possible alternative redistribution that would make one party better off without harming another party.

The Pareto criterion has been criticized for two main reasons: (1) it is status quo dependent, in that different results are achieved depending on the choice of the initial allocation; and (2) it only allows *ordinal* evaluation of preferences, since it does not contain any mechanism to induce parties or decision makers to reveal or evaluate *cardinal* preferences (i.e., the intensity of preferences). As a result of these shortcomings, scholars (e.g., Calabresi 1991) have questioned the usefulness of the Pareto criterion in its applications to law and economics.

Utilitarian measures: Bentham and Kaldor–Hicks

In the nineteenth and early twentieth centuries, economists and philosophers developed welfare paradigms according to what degree all affected individuals had to be taken into account in any comparative evaluation of different states of the world. This methodological trend, related to utilitarian philosophy, is best represented by philosophers and jurists such as Bentham (1839), and later economists such as Kaldor (1939) and Hicks (1939), who in different ways formulated criteria of social welfare that accounted for the *cardinal* preferences of individuals.

In *Principles of Moral and Legislation*, Bentham (1789) presents his theory of value and motivation. He suggests that mankind is governed by two masters: "pain" and "pleasure." The two provide the fundamental motivation for human action. Bentham notes that not all individuals derive pleasure from the same objects or activities, and not all human sensibilities are the same.[15] Bentham's moral imperative, which has greatly influenced the methodological debate in law and economics, is that policymakers have an obligation to select rules that give "the greatest happiness to the greatest number." As pointed out by Kelly (1998: 158) this formulation is quite problematic, since it identifies two maximands (i.e., degree of pleasure and number of individuals) without specifying the tradeoff between one and the other. Bentham's utilitarian approach is thus, at best, merely inspirational for policy purposes.

Later economists, including Kaldor (1939), Hicks (1939), and Scitovsky (1941), formulated more rigorous welfare paradigms which avoided the theoretical ambiguities of Bentham's proposition. However, these formulations presented a different set of difficulties in their implementation. The core idea of their approach is that state A is to be preferred to state B if those who gain from the move to A gain enough to compensate those who lose. The test is generally known as the Kaldor–Hicks test of potential compensation. It is one of "potential" compensation because the compensation of the losers is only hypothetical and does not actually need to take place.[16] In practical terms, the Kaldor–Hicks criterion requires a comparison of the gains of one group and the losses of the other group. As long as the gainers gain more than the losers lose, the move is deemed efficient. Mathematically, both the Bentham and the Kaldor–Hicks versions of efficiency are carried out by comparing the aggregate payoffs of the various alternatives and selecting the option that maximizes such summation.

Multiplicative social preferences: Nash and Rawls

Other paradigms of social welfare depart from the straight utilitarian approach, suggesting that social welfare maximization requires something more than the maximization of total payoffs for the various members of society. Societies are formed by a network of individual relations and there are some important interpersonal effects that are part of individual utility functions. Additionally, human nature is characterized by diminishing marginal utility, which gives relevance to the distribution of benefits across members of the group.

Imagine two hypothetical regimes: (1) in which all members of society eat a meal a day; and (2) in which only a random one-half of the population gets to eat a double meal while the other unlucky half remains starving. From a

Kaldor–Hicks perspective, the two alternatives are not distinguishable from the point of view of efficiency because the total amount of food available remains unchanged. In a Kaldor–Hicks test, those who get a double meal have just enough to compensate the others and thus society should remain indifferent between the two allocational systems. Obviously, this indifference proposition would leave most observers unsatisfied. In the absence of actual compensation, the criterion fails to consider the diminishing marginal benefit of a second meal and the increasing marginal pain of starvation. Likewise, the randomized distribution of meals fails to consider the interpersonal effects of unfair allocations. Fortunate individuals suffer a utility loss by knowing that other individuals are starving while they enjoy a double meal. Because of the diminishing marginal utility of wealth and interpersonal utility effects, from an *ex ante* point of view, no individual would choose allocation system (2), even though the expected return from (2) is equal to the return from (1).

Scholars that try to evaluate the welfare implications of distributional inequalities generally do so by invoking Rawls's (1971)[17] theories of justice or by using Nash's (1950)[18] framework of welfare.

The intuition underlying these criteria of welfare is relatively straightforward; the well-being of a society is judged according to the well-being of its weakest members. The use of an algebraic product to aggregate individual preferences captures that intuition. As the strength of a chain is determined by the strength of its weakest link, so the chain of products in an algebraic multiplication is heavily affected by the smallest multipliers. Indeed, at the limit, if there is a zero in the chain of products, the entire grand total will collapse to zero. This means that the entire social welfare of a group approaches zero as the utility of one of its members goes to zero.

In the law and economics tradition, these models of social welfare have not enjoyed great popularity. This is not due to an ideological preconception but rather is a result of a combination of several practical reasons. These reasons include the general tendency to undertake a two-step optimization in the design of policies, and the difficulties of identifying an objective criterion for assessing interpersonal utility and diminishing marginal utility effects. From a methodological point of view, distributional concerns are generally kept separate from the pursuit of efficiency in policymaking. Such separation has been rationalized on the basis that the legal system is too costly an instrument for distribution, given the advantage of the tax system for wholesale reallocation of wealth (e.g., Kaplow and Shavell 1994).

Some of the tension among these three social welfare standards is dissipated by the functional school's focus on *ex ante* welfare. That is, ideally, legal meta-rules should be designed to maximize expected welfare, not realized welfare. From the *ex ante* perspective, there is no tension between the Pareto and the Hicks–Kaldor standard.[19] Further, while the *ex ante* perspective does not require the generalized risk aversion posited in the Rawlsian veil of ignorance decision rule, it does allow for the protection of the "worst off" member of society along dimensions where a representative individual would rationally choose such protections *ex ante*. This notion is implicit in the Buchanan and Tullock (1962) derivation of optimal constitutional rules, which serves as part of the foundation of functional law and economics.

What is the maximand?

There is a third methodological problem: What should the legal system try to maximize? In this debate, even strict adherents to the instrumentalist view of the law may question whether the objective of the law should be the maximization of aggregate wealth or the maximization of aggregate utility.

If the scholars involved in this debate could look at the issue as neutral spectators, consensus could be reached on the idea that the ultimate policy goal is the maximization of human happiness and well-being. Consequently, the human dimension cannot be by-passed in policy evaluation. Regardless of such an observation, economic analysis of law rarely uses utility-based methods of evaluation. The reason for this is mostly pragmatic. Unlike wealth (or quantities of physical resources), utility cannot be objectively measured. Furthermore, interpersonal comparisons of utility are impossible, rendering any balancing across groups or individuals largely arbitrary. These limitations make utility maximization unviable for practical policy purposes.

Given the above limitations, practitioners of economic analysis of law have departed from the nineteenth-century utilitarian ideal of utility maximization.[20] Instead, they have increasingly used a paradigm of wealth maximization. Posner is the most notable exponent of the wealth maximization paradigm. Under wealth maximization principles, a transaction is desirable if it increases the sum of wealth for the relevant parties (where wealth is meant to include all tangible and intangible goods and services).

The early years of law and economics were characterized by some uneasiness in accepting the notion of wealth maximization as an ancillary paradigm of justice. Most of the differences proved to be largely verbal, and many others were dispelled by the gradual acceptance of a distinction between paradigms of utility maximization and wealth maximization. However, two objections continue to affect the lines of the debate.

The first objection relates to the need for specifying an initial set of individual entitlements or rights as a necessary prerequisite for operationalizing wealth maximization. In this context, one can think of the various criticisms of wealth maximization by property right advocates who perceive the social cost of adopting such a criterion of adjudication as very high, given wealth maximization's instrumentalist view of individual rights and entitlements. These critics argue that rights have value that must be accounted for outside of how useful they might be to the accumulation of wealth. Along similar lines, these critics suggest that the wealth maximization criterion of economic analysis is comparable to the methodological approach of economics prior to the advent of public choice theory, insofar as an understanding of "political failures" was missing from the study of collective decision making (Buchanan 1974; Rowley 1989).

The second objection springs from the theoretical difficulty of defining the proper role of efficiency as an ingredient of justice, vis-à-vis other social goals. Legal scholars within the law and economics tradition (see, e.g., Calabresi 1980) have claimed that an increase in wealth cannot constitute social improvement unless it furthers some other social goal, such as utility or equality. Denying that one can tradeoff efficiency against justice, these scholars argue instead that efficiency and distribution are equally essential elements of justice, which is seen as a goal of a different order than either of its constitutive elements.

Posner stands as the most notable defender of the criterion of wealth maximization addressing these important questions and justifying wealth maximization as a worthy standard for evaluating legal rules. Posner (1987) explicitly advocates wealth maximization as a criterion that should guide judicial rule making. Making the case for wealth maximization, he defines it and compares it with the alternative theories of utilitarianism and libertarianism. As mentioned earlier, wealth maximization occurs when a transaction increases the total amount of goods and services, weighted by offer prices and demand prices.[21] Because of the market's ability to capture subjective values and preferences, wealth maximization is a comprehensive measure of social welfare.[22]

Wealth maximization as a social value

Much of the criticism of law and economics lies in the mistaken belief that wealth maximization is a form of utilitarianism. Prior to his important article on utilitarianism and legal theory (Posner 1979a), Posner himself had been wrongly characterized as acknowledging utilitarianism as the inspiration of law and economics. Posner (1979a) distinguishes utilitarianism from the methodological premises of law and economics, arguing in favor of wealth maximization as a superior normative theory of law.

According to Posner, utilitarianism holds that the worth of a law should be judged by its effect in promoting the surplus of pleasure over pain ("happiness") across society. Normative economics holds that a law should be judged by its effects in promoting social welfare, a term which when broadly defined almost means the same as utilitarian happiness. In this context, Posner suggests that economists's use of "utility" as a synonym for "welfare" adds to the confusion.

Utilitarianism is distinct from wealth maximization because it seeks to maximize aggregate "happiness" while wealth maximization seeks to maximize aggregate economic utility, called "wealth." While happiness is a philosophical concept that cannot be easily measured, wealth is more practical and measurable (Posner 1979a; 1987). More fundamentally, happiness is an insufficient social goal because happiness is passive and focuses on consumption. Wealth maximization, on the other hand, is dependent on productive effort. While being aware of the limits of a concept of wealth as a good in itself, Posner believes that wealth maximization results in a work ethic that is in fact necessary for utilitarian happiness to be brought about, and thus is an important mechanism for the advancement of society. While not precluding an instrumentalist maximization of wealth, Posner's theory does not rely on utilitarianism as a necessary methodological assumption.[23]

There is a possible intuitive justification of wealth maximization. This intuitive foundation was first emphasized by Posner (1979a), who argued that wealth maximization can be regarded as a superior ethical principle because it is more consistent with ethical intuitions, provides for a more sound theory of justice, and yields more definite results than the alternative economic views on justice. By promoting the efficient use of resources, wealth maximization encourages traditional capacities, such as intelligence, and traditional virtues, such as honesty.[24]

An important part of the debate on the paradigm of wealth maximization relates to its ethical and normative justification. This foundational work in law and economics has been described as a form of normative analysis that "turns the mirror of analysis inward," attempting to answer the fundamental question of "why the law or public policy should promote efficiency" (Coleman 1982). Advocates of wealth maximization generally offer two basic arguments in support of such a normative goal: a teleological justification and a consent justification.[25] These justifications have come under the scrutiny of well-known legal and economic theorists.

According to (Coleman 1982), wealth maximization is a form of Kaldor–Hicks maximization in disguise. The practical advantages of wealth maximization over utility maximization relate to the fact that it is easier to ascertain actual changes in wealth as opposed to utility. In spite of such practical superiority, Posner's normative criterion remains subject to several of the shortcomings of the Kaldor–Hicks criterion, including its difficult moral defensibility. Posner's defense of wealth maximization has been further criticized for building upon notions of implied, rather than actual, consent. Coleman (1982) recognizes the usefulness of tests of hypothetical consent a là Rawls, but questions the uniqueness of wealth maximization as a dominant criterion of justice from the perspective of *ex ante* social choice. The indeterminacy of such hypothetical social choice poses a challenge to the consent-based moral justification of wealth maximization.

Economic theories of justice

In spite of the articulate defense of the criterion of efficiency in legal and policy decisions, most law and economic scholars do not argue that efficiency concerns should replace morality. However, whenever moral or ethical theories of justice fail to generate unambiguous results that could guide policy choices and, more generally, in the absence of thumping moral or ethical concerns, efficiency provides the most appropriate criterion for allocating limited resources among competing claims.

Legal scholars (e.g., Malloy 1988), however, have often argued that efficiency-based and utilitarian theories of justice promote "disrespect for individual liberty," are "indeterminative and elitist," and "can hardly be viewed as anything other than amoral, if not immoral." Posner (1988), in his reply to Malloy, once again, takes issue. He suggests that these critiques miss the mark, in that they treat the methodology of law and economics as a political theory. Indeed, Posner (1988), while arguing that wealth maximization is the best normative and positive theory of common law rights and remedies, never suggested that wealth maximization should be the only social value or principle of justice.[26]

Even the most extreme advocates of wealth maximization do not contend that such a criterion should override moral concerns. The preference for wealth maximization over other criteria of welfare derives from the general suspicion against paternalistic governmental intervention (which would unavoidably be triggered if morality was recognized as the sole criterion of legal interpretation and judicial action) and the risks involved in shifting the burden to the judiciary in asking judges to decide controversies on the basis of distributive considerations.

Wealth maximization sometimes runs contrary to moral guides such as natural rights. The natural rights perspective views society as a compact, in which people surrender just enough of their own natural liberties as is necessary to protect everyone else's equal natural liberties. Posner believes that because the notion of natural rights can be expanded so readily, it is too unstable a foundation to build upon. He also believes that it is fundamentally anti-democratic because it holds that the more rights people have, the smaller the permissible scope of public policy deliberation.

Many of the arguments made by natural rights proponents rely on examples for which there is moral consensus. Posner points out that the power of natural rights's moral discourse runs out when one faces controversial moral issues. Thus, paradoxically, whenever an analytical perspective is most needed to frame policy questions, natural rights emerge as non-dispositive and thus hardly valuable instruments of adjudication.

Preference revelation as decision criterion

Functional law and economics bypasses the wealth/utility divide by focusing on choice or revealed preference as the criterion of decision. That is, by designing mechanisms through which parties are induced to reveal their subjective preferences, the functional law and economics approach obviates the need for third parties, such as judges or legislators, to decide between wealth and utility as the appropriate maximand. The institutions favored by the functional approach minimize the impediments to the full revelation of the subjective preferences of the parties to a transaction by focusing on incentive compatibility mechanisms. This mechanism design approach tends to align individual and social optimality.

The mechanism design perspective of economics attempts to channel the intrinsic behavioral tendencies of individuals to reach a desired social outcome. That is, rather than attempting to alter individual behavior, functional law and economics suggests that institutions should provide incentives, such that individuals will naturally act in a desired way without any external monitoring or coercion. This necessarily requires that individuals have the ability and incentive to reveal their own subjective values and preferences, and that all costs and benefits generated by an individual's actions accrue to that individual. This implies that individuals will only achieve socially optimal outcomes when they act for their own gain, and incentives are not attenuated by principal agent problems whereby an individual is directed to fulfill some social goal directly.

Examples of research in this area include the functional law and economics explanations for the cooperation that underlies much of human interaction. Cooperative behavior is an empirical regularity that proves puzzling from both the positive and normative perspectives. Cooperation does not easily fit within either of the original law and economics perspectives. Unbridled competition is what drives the supposedly efficient outcomes predicted by the positive school, while the normative school prescribes external limits or alterations on the natural competition that arises among individuals. However, Fon and Parisi (2003) show how social norms evolve to solve various prisoner's dilemma games by internalizing reciprocity constraints on individual action, improving the welfare of participants relative to the purely competitive outcome. Laboratory evidence of the internalization of these reciprocity norms is provided by McCabe *et al.* (2003). This individual-centered focus also solves another seemingly intractable problem encountered in a corporate approach to law. Utility maximization necessarily requires that subjective values be attributed to human action. However, it is not possible for an outside observer to evaluate these subjective values and draw the appropriate legal or policy conclusions to maximize social welfare. To avoid this information problem, the functional law and economics approach relies on institutions that provide individuals with the opportunity to express their own values truthfully. These revealed preferences are then granted complete validity in normative terms, with law- and policymakers taking them as a given.

Conclusion

Functional law and economics avoids paternalism and methodological imperialism by formulating value-neutral principles of collective choice. It builds upon the methodological premises of normative individualism, giving greatest freedom to individual choice, and fostering socially desirable human action by establishing structural principles that induce individuals to take into account private information and subjective values and truthfully reflect such information and values in their behavioral choices. Functional law and economics represents a mode of analysis that bridges (and, in some sense, improves upon) both the positive and normative schools of thought in law and economics. Through its *ex ante* perspective, the functional school focuses on mechanism design issues to explain the origins of law, capturing both the efficiency and non-efficiency perspectives of the other two schools.

116   *J. Klick and F. Parisi*

Notes

* Jonathan Klick is a Professor of Law at the University of Pennsylvania Law School; Francesco Parisi is the Oppenheimer Wolff and Donnelly Professor of Law at the University of Minnesota Law School, and a Professor of Economics at the University of Bologna. An earlier version of this chapter initially appeared in the *Chicago-Kent Law Review*: "Functional law and economics: the search for value-neutral principles of law making," Jon Klick and Francesco Parisi, *Chicago-Kent Law Review*, 79(2): 431–450 (2004). We thank the editors of *Chicago-Kent Law Review* for allowing us to reprint a slightly revised version of the article now in chapter format.

1 The institution-based distinction is no longer salient as Yale has many positivist law and economics scholars on its faculty, just as Chicago has scholars who can be categorized in the normative school. For a more extensive discussion of functional law and economics and its role within the landscape of analytical methods in law and economics, see (Parisi 2003).

2 Despite some notable antecedents, it was not until the mid-twentieth century, through the work of Henry Simon, Aaron Director, Henry Manne, George Stigler, Armen Alchian, Gordon Tullock, and others, that the links between law and economics became an object of serious academic pursuit.

3 Further, common law rules are said to enjoy a comparative advantage over legislation in fulfilling this task because of the evolutionary selection of common law rules through adjudication. Several important contributions provide the foundations for this claim; the scholars who have advanced theories in support of the hypothesis are, however, often in disagreement as to its conceptual basis.

4 Posner offers crime as an example. Positive law and economics can help explain and predict how various punishments will affect the behavior of criminals. It might determine that a certain sanction is more likely to deter a certain crime. While this analysis does not by itself mean that the law should be adopted, it can be used to influence normative analysis on whether the law would be beneficial to society.

5 Recognition of the positive nature of the economic analysis of law was not sufficient to dispel the many misunderstandings and controversies in legal academia engendered by the law and economics movement's methodological revolution. As (Coase 1978) indicated, the cohesiveness of economic techniques makes it possible for economics to move successfully into another field, such as law, and dominate it intellectually. But methodological differences played an important part in the uneasy marriage between law and economics. The Popperian methodology of positive science was in many respects at odds with the existing paradigms of legal analysis. Rowley (1981) characterizes such differences, observing that positive economics follow the Popperian approach, whereby testable hypotheses (or models) are derived by means of logical deduction, and then tested empirically. Anglo-American legal analysis, on the other hand, is generally inductive: lawyers use individual judgments to construct a general premise of law. Much work has been done in law and economics despite these methodological differences, with a reciprocal enrichment of the analytical tools of both disciplines.

6 MacKaay (2000) observes that the Yale School considers market failures to be more pervasive than Chicago scholars are willing to admit. Legal intervention is believed to be the appropriate way of correcting such failures, although it may not succeed in all circumstances.

7 Posner (1979b) acknowledges that normative economic analysis, i.e., the use of economics to argue for what law should be, is susceptible to criticism. On the other hand, he notes that while economic analysis assesses the costs and benefits of a proposed rule, it is the noneconomic weighting of the economic factors which is vulnerable to subjective ideology.

8 Some degree of controversy still surrounds several of the methodological, normative,

and philosophical underpinnings of the economic approach to law. However, most of the ideological differences tend to lose significance because their operational paradigms often lead to analogous results when applied to real cases. However, some scholars perceive the current state of law and economics as comparable to the state of economics prior to the advent of public choice theory, insofar as an understanding of "political failures" was missing from the study of market failures (Buchanan 1974; Rowley 1989). Public choice may indeed inject a skeptical, and at times disruptive, perspective into the more elegant and simple framework of neoclassical economics, but this added element may well be necessary to understand a complex reality.

9 For a brief intellectual history of the three approaches to law and economics, see (Posner and Parisi 1998).

10 See (Tullock 1971) for an early systematic treatment of the law from the functionalist perspective. In that work, Tullock raises a good deal of skepticism regarding the efficiency of prevailing legal systems, pleading in the book's preface (Tullock 1971: vi): "Our present legal system cries out for reform."

11 An important premise of the functional approach to law and economics is its reliance on methodological individualism. According to this paradigm of analysis, only individuals choose and act (see, e.g., Buchanan [1990] and the various contributions the Virginia School of political economy). The functional approach to law and economics is informed by an explicit recognition that whatever social reality we seek to explain at the aggregate level ought to be understood as the result of the choices and actions of individual human beings who pursue their goals with an independently formed understanding of the reality that surrounds them (Vanberg 1994: 1). Normative individualism further postulates that only the judgment of the single individuals can provide a relevant benchmark against which the merits of alternative rules can be evaluated.

12 On this point see (Cooter 1994), introducing the similar idea of structural adjudication of norms.

13 A good summary of Buchanan's structural vision of government and society can be found in (Brennan and Buchanan 2000).

14 As a corollary, a change to a Pareto superior alternative makes someone better off without making anyone worse off.

15 See (Posner 1998) for an interesting discussion on Bentham and his influence on the law and economics movement.

16 One should note that, if actual compensation were carried out, any test satisfying the Kaldor–Hicks criterion of efficiency would also satisfy the Pareto criterion.

17 Notable scholars have considered the conditions under which principles of justice can emerge spontaneously through the voluntary interaction and exchange of individual members of a group. As in a contractarian setting, the reality of customary law formation relies on a voluntary process through which members of a community develop rules that govern their social interaction by voluntarily adhering to emerging behavioral standards. In this setting (Harsanyi 1955) suggests that optimal social norms are those that would emerge through the interaction of individual actors in a social setting with impersonal preferences. The impersonality requirement for individual preferences is satisfied if the decision makers have an equal chance of finding themselves in any one of the initial social positions and they rationally choose a set of rules to maximize their expected welfare. Rawls (1971) employs Harsanyi's model of stochastic ignorance in his theory of justice. However, the Rawlsian "veil of ignorance" introduces an element of risk aversion in the choice between alternative states of the world, thus altering the outcome achievable under Harsanyi's original model, with a bias toward equal distribution (i.e., with results that approximate the Nash criterion of social welfare). Further analysis of the spontaneous formation of norms and principles of morality can be found in (Sen 1979; Ullmann-Margalit 1977; and Gauthier 1986).

18 According to the Nash criterion, social welfare is given by the product of the utility of the members of society (Nash 1950). See (Mueller 1989: 379–382), attributing the multiplicative form of the social welfare function to Nash.

19 See (Klick and Parisi 2003) for an exposition of this point.

20 Already, Bentham (1839) challenged the use of objective factors, such as wealth or physical resources, as a proxy for human happiness. Despite the difficulties in quantification of values such as utility or happiness, the pursuit of pleasure and happiness and the avoidance of pain are the motivating forces of human behavior. Wealth, food, and shelter are mere instruments to achieve such human goals.

21 For intangible goods for which there are no explicit markets, Posner suggests that shadow prices serve equally well as tools of objective evaluation.

22 In a methodological comparison of the various criteria of social choice Posner (1987) considers the value of wealth maximization as a criterion for guiding judicial rule making and adjudication. Even if no moral or ethical argument can be established in its favor, wealth maximization or efficiency is still a valuable tool for normative analysis. Posner (1979a; 1990) further points out that economics can, with a morally neutral approach, provide an evaluation of the costs of any proposed action. Economics can provide direction to any decision, particularly one in which efficiency is a prevailing value.

23 In order to evaluate the ethical argument for efficiency rather than utilitarianism, (Posner 1979a) acts on the presumption that any ethical theory is valid unless rejected, and he evaluates both utilitarianism and wealth maximization on two principal grounds for rejecting an ethical theory: its logical inadequacy, or its incongruence with widely shared ethical intuitions. Posner regards utilitarianism as somewhat illogical and inconsistent with generally accepted notions of individual rights. Its logical and moral shortcoming rests in its boundless insistence that we maximize the total amount of happiness in the universe, even beyond human utility, which can only be attained by making many people unhappy. In this way, Posner attacks traditional utilitarianism for its indefiniteness.

24 Posner (1979a) suggests that wealth maximization also supports the creation of a system of exclusive rights that extends to all valued things that are scarce, with the initial right vesting in those who are likely to value them the most and a free market for those rights once assigned (resembling Adam Smith's system of "natural liberty"). It relies on traditional capacities and virtues to reduce the cost of transacting those rights. Further, wealth maximization requires legal rules to promote hypothetical bargains where transaction costs are prohibitive. It also requires legal remedies to deter and redress the invasion of rights. Thus, a market economy regulated according to wealth-maximizing principles fosters empathy and benevolence without destroying individuality.

25 Libertarianism challenges the wholesale endorsement of wealth-maximization because of the libertarian interest in personal autonomy over social welfare and its opposition to coercive exchanges, be them explicit or disguised. Posner (1979a) notes that when compensation is considered *ex ante*, much coercive exchange is essentially voluntary – thus satisfying libertarian concerns.

26 In a similar context, Posner (1990) describes himself as a "pragmatic economic libertarian." He is libertarian in that he is suspicious of public intervention and favors small government. He uses economic theory to define what he sees as the appropriate role of the government to intervene and correct serious market failures. He is pragmatic in the sense that he does not derive these free-market views from dogmatic or philosophical underpinnings. Instead, he uses wealth maximization to operationalize his economic libertarianism.

References

Bentham, J. (1789) *An Introduction to the Principles of Morals and Legislation*, London: Payne and Son.
Bentham, J. (1839) *A Manual of Political Economy*, New York: G.P. Putnam.
Brennan, G. and Buchanan, J. (2000) *The Reason of Rules: Constitutional Political Economy*, Indianapolis, IN: Liberty Fund, Inc.
Buchanan, J. 'Good economics: bad law', *Virginia Law Review*, 60, 1974: 483–492.
Buchanan, J. 'The constitution of economic policy', *American Economic Review*, 77(3), 1987: 243–250.
Buchanan, J. 'The domain of constitutional economics', *Constitutional Political Economy* 1, 1990: 1–18.
Buchanan, J. and Tullock, G. (1962) *The Calculus of Consent*, Ann Arbor, MI: University of Michigan Press.
Calabresi, G. 'About law and economics: a letter to Ronald Dworkin', *Hofstra Law Review* 8, 1980: 553–562.
Calabresi, G. 'The pointlessness of Pareto: carrying Coase further', *Yale Law Journal* 100, 1991: 1211–1237.
Coase, R. 'The problem of social cost', *Journal of Law and Economics* 3, 1960: 1–44.
Coase, R. 'Economics and contiguous disciplines', *Journal of Legal Studies* 7, 1978: 201–211.
Coleman, J. 'The normative basis of economic analysis: a critical review of Richard Posner's *The Economics of Justice*', *Stanford Law Review* 34, 1982: 1105–1131.
Cooter, R. 'Structural adjudication and the new law merchant: a model of decentralized law', *International Review of Law & Economics* 14, 1994: 215–227.
Edgeworth, F. (1881) *Mathematical Psychics*, London: C. Kegan Paul.
Fon, V. and Parisi, F. 'Reciprocity-induced cooperation', *Journal of Institutional and Theoretical Economics* 159, 2003: 76–92.
Gauthier, D. (1986) *Morals by Agreement*, Oxford: Clarendon Press.
Harsanyi, J. 'Cardinal welfare individualistic ethics, and interpersonal comparisons of utility', *Journal of Political Economy* 63, 1955: 309–321.
Hicks, J. 'The foundations of welfare economics', *Economic Journal* 49, 1939: 696–712.
Kaldor, N. 'Welfare propositions of economics and inter-personal comparisons of utility', *Economic Journal* 49, 1939: 549–552.
Kaplow, L. and Shavell, S. 'Why the legal system is less efficient than the income tax in redistributing income', *Journal of Legal Studies* 23, 1994: 667–681.
Kelly, P. (1998) 'Bentham, Jeremy', in P. Newman (ed.) *New Palgrave Dictionary of Economics and the Law*, London: Palgrave.
Klick, J. and Parisi, F. 'The disunity of unanimity' *Constitutional Political Economy* 14, 2003: 83–94.
McCabe, K.A., Rigdon, M., and Smith, V. 'Positive reciprocity and intentions in trust games', *Journal of Economic Behavior and Organization* 52, 2003: 267–275.
MacKaay, E. (2000) 'History of law and economics', in B. Bouckaert and G. De Geest (eds.) *Encyclopedia of Law and Economics*. Cheltenham: Edward Elgar.
Malloy, R. 'The merits of the Smithian critique: a final word on Smith and Posner', *University of Kansas Law Review* 36, 1988: 266–274.
Mueller, D. (1989) *Public Choice II*. Cambridge: Cambridge University Press.
Nash, J. 'The bargaining problem' *Econometrica* 18, 1950: 155–162.

120   *J. Klick and F. Parisi*

Parisi, F. (2003) 'The origins of the law and economics movement', in C.K. Rowley and F. Schneider (eds.) *Encyclopedia of Law and Economics*, Dordrecht: Kluwer.

Posner, R. 'Utilitarianism, economics, and legal theory', *Journal of Legal Studies*, 8, 1979a: 103–140.

Posner, R. 'Some uses and abuses of economics in law', *University of Chicago Law Review*, 46, 1979b: 281–306.

Posner, R. 'The justice of economics', *Economia delle Scelte Pubbliche*, 1, 1987: 15.

Posner, R. 'The ethics of wealth maximization: reply to Malloy' *Kansas Law Review*, 36, 1988: 261–265.

Posner, R. 'Law and economics is moral', *Valparaiso University Law Review*, 24, 1990: 163–173.

Posner, R. 'Bentham's influence on the law and economics movement' *Current Legal Problems*, 51, 1998: 425–439.

Posner, R. and Parisi, F. 'Scuole e Tendenze nella Analisi Economica del Diritto' *Biblioteca della Liberta* 147, 1998: 3–20.

Rawls, J. (1971) *A Theory of Justice*. Cambridge, MA: Harvard University Press.

Rowley, C. 'Social sciences and the law: the relevance of economic theories', *Oxford Journal of Legal Studies* 1, 1981: 391–405.

Rowley, C. 'The common law in public choice perspective: a theoretical and institutional critique', *Hamline Law Review* 12, 1989: 355–383.

Scitovsky, T. 'A note on welfare propositions in economics', *Review of Economic Studies*, 9, 1941: 77–88.

Sen, A. (1979) 'Rational fools: a critique of the behavioural foundations of economic theory', in F. Hahn and M. Hollis (eds.) *Philosophy and Economic Theory*. Oxford: Clarendon Press.

Tullock, G. (1971) *The Logic of the Law*. New York: Basic Books.

Ullmann-Margalit, E. (1977) *The Emergence of Norms*. Oxford: Clarendon Press.

Vanberg, V. (1994) *Rules and Choice in Economics*. London: Routledge.

8 Law and economics

Systems of social control, managed
drift, and the dilemma of rent-seeking
in a representative democracy

Nicholas Mercuro*

Introduction

Within a representative democracy, many policymakers (executives, legislators, regulators, agents of nonprofits, and bureaucrats) set public policies in place under a flawed perspective that does not make clear the meaningful alternatives available to society. This perspective emanates from many of the core principles of law and economics (here meant to include Chicago law and economics, public choice theory, and New Institutional Economics [NIE]). It is a perspective that views public policy through a common lens, but one that is quite narrow. For instance, when a public policy or change in law is being contemplated, one would ask: What impact will it have on our nation (or region)? That question can be analyzed through the lens of the law, thus asking whether the law will be just or fair and/or whether it will be "reasonable" in that it conforms to the norms and conventions of the community and/or the "settled" common law. Alternatively, that question can be analyzed through the lens of law and economics, thus asking whether the outcome of the policy or change in law will be efficient.

How does the lens of law and economics shape the thinking of policymakers? In brief, from Chicago law and economics we learn that since market outcomes are efficient, we need smaller government and less regulation – public policy should cease intervening in the play of free markets. Whenever the market falls short of providing an efficient allocation of resources due to externalities or some other form of market failure, one can rely on the common law and damage measures, which proponents of Chicago contend have been demonstrated to be composed of rules and doctrines that produce efficient court outcomes. Thus, society need not rely on the legislative branch to adopt regulatory statutes or bureaucratic mechanisms to remedy these problems. All one needs to do is maintain a narrow lens as to the scope of market failure and then, when market failure is observed, rely on the common law to generate efficient outcomes.[1] Any policymaker hesitant to go the full free-market route and who contemplates a larger role for the public sector is quickly counseled by proponents of public choice that: (1) their representative democracy is populated with rationally ignorant individuals;[2] and (2) most (if not all) contemplated public policy initiatives that expand the scope of the public sector will soon end in failure with an inevitable wasteful and inefficient allocation of society's resources. The latter is a theory whose quest is to (intentionally or otherwise) undermine any credible commitment to the public sector.[3] Thus, executive office holders, legislators, regulators, corporate leaders, leaders of political parties, agents of nonprofits, and bureaucrats are left with the prescriptions of Chicago law and economics to place a heavier reliance on markets to allocate resources efficiently as the lead play, with public choice emphasis on public sector failure serving as the trump card – both sides covered!

NIE jumps into the fray by relaxing some of the assumptions of both Chicago law and economics and public choice, and takes on the task to expand the role of the state, but mostly to provide a credible commitment to pro-market institutions. The result of their combined efforts (particularly for the *institutional environment* branch of NIE) is to narrow the list of public policy options for those within a representative democracy – the focus becomes market-oriented public solutions with a disregard of the meaningful alternatives.

The argument here is that what is needed is a different conceptual model – a lens with a broader perspective and thus discussion of more and varied policy options. The driving force behind this conceptual model is the need to come to grips with the interrelations among legal, social, and economic processes. In this regard, the fundamental question that needs to be addressed is: What are the most significant drivers that impact the character and fabric of the economic life and the well-being of its citizens? In short, what drives a nation's political-economic performance? The contention of this chapter is that there are a variety of factors and forces at work that give rise to the performance of the political economy, particularly in the context of a representative democracy.[4] The first section of this chapter focuses on the several sectors of a nation state and their predicate underlying structure of rights through which scarce resources are channeled, namely: the *market sector*, the *public sector*, the *nonprofit sector*, the *communal sector*, and the *open sector*. The second section of the chapter will include a discussion of public policy formation as well as drift policy. The third section will include an abbreviated treatment of the role of social norms and standards on the character and fabric of economic life. The final section will explore the meaning, role, and implications of so-called rent-seeking behavior within a representative democracy.[5]

Systems of social control

Introduction

Conceptually, it is useful to begin with the notion of five distinct sectors through which a nation state organizes, channels, and controls the allocation and distribution of its scarce resources. The several sectors of a nation state and their predicate underlying structure of rights through which scarce resources are channeled are: (1) the private property rights that underlie the *market sector*; (2) working rules and status rights that underlie the *public sector*; (3) complex rights that underlie the *nonprofit sector*; (4) common property that underlies the *communal sector*; and (5) the *open sector*, where there are no property rights. Taken together, the combined collection of rights and rules define the limits of social behavior within each sector and, in so doing, determine what can and cannot be done by individuals and institutions in the society. Initially, here, each sector is treated as if it exists separate and apart from the other sectors. In actuality, in a market economy organized by a representative democracy, all five systems operate contemporaneously to allocate a nation state's scarce resources.

It must be clear from the outset that government has an important and ongoing role in setting these sectors in place – in that effort, it must make a deliberate and transparent credible commitment to each sector. In addition, in light of ever-changing economic, technological, and political realities, legal and institutional change within a nation state is inevitable. As parties of interest work out those changes, the relative size and scope of the market, public, nonprofit, communal, and the open-access sectors is altered. Further, it is also clear that government, in all of its executive, legislative, bureaucratic, and judicial manifestations, over time helps fashion legal-economic drivers, in particular, (1) formal rules, (2) working rules and status rights, (3) political parties, (4) social norms, and (5) the design of standards. As these fundamental drivers operate and as the relative size and scope of the market, public, nonprofit, communal, and the open-access sectors are reworked, the combined net effect is to impact the character and fabric of economic life, and thus, a nation state's economic, social, and political well-being.

Market sector

In the pure market sector, all property rights are held privately as bundles of fee simple absolute rights. According to the conventional legal-economic definition of private property rights, what are owned by individuals are not goods or resources, but the rights to use goods and resources. When individuals in a representative democracy, acting through their political-legal institutions, make the choice to use the market sector as the preferred system of social control, they must, antecedently, use government to define, assign, and enforce a structure of private property rights to establish the market. At the same time, to help ensure market success, the government must make a credible commitment to its market sector. In this idealized sector, once rights are defined and assigned, it is then possible for the individuals to further enhance their welfare by specializing and engaging in exchange through trade and realigning the use of resources in production. This process of trade is conventionally viewed as a purely voluntary endeavor (as no individual will engage in a trade that leaves him worse off) and, as characterized here, it is what is said to transpire in the market sector.[6] Thus, given defined private property rights together with some government-determined initial distribution of those rights, barring major problems with information, enforcement, public goods, and externalities, ideally, a purely competitive, perfectly functioning market will, in both exchange and production, allow individuals in the economy to exhaust all gains from trade and thereby provide a Pareto-efficient allocation of resources (consistent with the duality theorem). It is important to reemphasize that an efficient market-sector allocation of resources is predicated upon both (1) the government's deliberate and transparent credible commitment to that sector; and (2) the initial assignment of property rights from which trade can begin (so as to be able to exhaust the subsequent gains from trade). In a representative democracy, this commitment comes about by those asserting their interests through government to define property rights, assign property rights, enforce property rights, and foster contracts in each product and factor market.

The credible commitment to markets manifests itself as government sets legal institutions in place to lubricate trade so as to allow an economy to exhaust all gains from trade. The development and support of a variety of market-augmenting activities and institutions costs a nation state some its scarce resources – namely, market transaction costs (Coase 1960). Such activities include: having the government provide a medium of exchange, underwriting the entire infrastructure of common (or civil) law courts, and maintaining a system to collect taxes. In addition, the state must spend resources to provide a legal infrastructure whose fundamental purpose is to oversee the proper functioning of markets – for example, (1) a system of antitrust laws and agencies to promote competition and to detect and punish fraud in markets, or (2) regulatory agencies that work to ensure that near-full information requirements are met in both product and factor markets. Without government-sanctioned and -enforced private property rights to resources and goods, as well as the concomitant credible commitment of government to support markets, there would be no incentive to realign resource use and nothing to exchange on the market.[7]

The government's market-augmenting activities are sometimes pejoratively labeled by some (extreme) market proponents as "government regulation" and denigrated accordingly. Their bluster notwithstanding, it is never a question of a market for any good or factor of production with government regulations or without government regulations. A vibrant market for any good or resource exists because of the market-augmenting, government-structured definition, assignment, and enforcement of rights that shape the market – all markets are complemented by government. Further, as political, technological, and economic change comes about and as market performance unfolds, citizens in a representative democracy, both individually and collectively, act through their representatives to revise the market-augmenting structure of rights and rules to refashion the political-legal arena within which the markets actualize. Indeed, the American institutional economist Ayres observed this long ago in arguing that it was the organizational structure of society – the ongoing nexus between the government and the market economy – that determined the allocation and distribution of resources – *not merely the market*. He wrote:

> The object of dissent is the conception of the market as the guiding mechanism of the economy, or more broadly, the conception of the economy as

organized and guided by the market. It simply is *not true* that scarce resources are allocated among alterative uses by the market. The real determinant of whatever allocation occurs in any society is the organizational structure of that society – in short, its institutions.... *By focusing attention on the market mechanism, economists have ignored the real allocation mechanism.*

(Ayres 1957: 26; emphasis added)

Some, though thankfully few, in law and economics have tried to lay out a vision that the market somehow existed and flourished during some pre-political state of nature and thus, the way to make markets work is to remove all (most) government "intrusions" or "regulations." Oddly, their rhetoric suggests that somehow the market is an alternative to government. Simply put, this is a fabrication. Mature policymakers understand that the market sector is not part of a parallel universe; it does not stand above and apart and predate the activities of human lawmakers; neither does it does have a "natural" legitimacy that rests with either reason or divine inspiration; and, importantly, there is nothing natural or spontaneous in the development of markets.[8] They further recognize that it costs society some of its scarce resources to credibly commit to and maintain its market sector. It is those markets that have the state's sanction, those that are aided, abetted, and fostered by government (for additional examples, the securities markets, the commodities markets, and the financial markets) that are ultimately embraced by nations who adopt capitalistic markets. And it was Coase (who reiterated Ayres point some four decades later) who wrote: "It is the institutions of a country ... its legal system, its political system, its social system, its educational system, its culture and so on ... that govern the performance of the economy" (Coase 1998: 73).

In summary, adopting markets as the preferred system of social control for allocating scarce resources is a product of careful thought and deliberation by many parties of interest, resulting in what are termed here *institutionalized markets* – where markets are viewed as a function of the nation's political-legal institutions, including its constitution, it legislature, its bureaucracy, its political parties, and its judiciary, and the power structures which form and continually operate through them. In a representative democracy, individuals – corporate leaders, agents of nonprofits, shape shifters, lobbyists, and shrewd politicians – are regularly working through government to advance their individual and/or group interests to expand or contract the size, scope, and nature of its market sector.

Of course, as outlined in the Introduction, aggregate economic performance is driven by all five systems of social control, of which the government-augmented market sector is but one. We now turn to the public sector through which a nation state also allocates its scarce resources.

Public sector

The public sector is yet another arena for organizing and controlling the allocation and distribution of scarce resources in a society. In this idealized sector, selected goods, services, and factors of production will be allocated through the state by use of formal rules, institutional working rules, status rights, and legal doctrines. As with the market sector, here too, for this sector's success, the government has an important and ongoing role to play by making a credible commitment to its public sector. And again, as with the market sector, it costs a nation state some its scarce resources – namely, government-related transaction costs – to support the various units of government that comprise the public sector.

Formal rules, status rights, institutional working rules, legal doctrines

In a representative democracy, when individuals or groups in society, acting through their political-legal institutions, make the choice to use the public sector as the preferred system of social control they must institutionally set in place the *formal rules* to govern the allocation of those resources. In the United States the formal rules governing the public sector are promulgated under federal law in accordance with the Administrative Procedures Act (or under state regulations in the case of state rules).[9] Under the Act, depending upon the specificity of the statute governing the resources to be allocated by the public sector, rules are set forth (under a system of "notice and comment") which provide the government agency the mechanism (the authority and the procedure) to allocate public-sector goods, services, or factors of production.

In addition, the relevant government agency must define and assign *status rights* which are, in effect, eligibility requirements for individuals to gain access to goods, services, and resources (typically, such requirements are not specified in the authorizing statute). Status rights are rights to goods, services, and resources which are exclusive, nontransferable, and are provided to individuals at the discretion of either the local, state, or federal government (or, typically, some combination thereof).[10] These status rights for selected goods and service or factors of production can be conceived of as "the rules for government provision" in its broadest sense. Over the past several decades many goods and services have been provided through this sector.[11]

Closely related to the public sector status rights are the institutional *working rules* – the complex set of rules that give rise to the governance of the institutional decision-making processes that are adopted by and within all branches of government and across government agencies, departments, and commissions. For example, these would include the more formal rules of the US House of Representatives and the US Senate, including the rules drawn from nineteenth- and twentieth-century precedents. Oftentimes, these working rules of governance are formally worked out by the institution itself in developing its own rules and bylaws; they include rulings of presiding officers or a variety of established and customary practices, or ad hoc arrangements crafted to meet specific circumstances. And, while much more subtle and indirect, the many working rules and bylaws have a direct bearing on the nation's character of economic life.

In common law, *legal doctrines* emerge as the judiciary, over time, decides cases and produces judge-made law (and thus precedent). The common law is replete with examples that support the case for recognizing that in revising legal doctrines, judges do indeed "make the law." This was nicely summed up by Friedman (2000: 3, 104), who correctly observed that:

> [M]uch of the law is a creation not of the legislatures but of judges, embedded in past precedents that determine how future cases will be decided.... One of the startling discoveries that students make in the first year of law school is how much of law is created, modified, and in some cases later repealed, entirely by judges.

Beyond the evolution of judge-made law, there is a significant cadre of Chicago law and economic scholars who contend that not only does judge-made common law evolve, but that (under a variety of different theories) it evolves into doctrines which turn out to be efficient or wealth maximizing.[12] It should be pointed out that on this topic there is a significant divide between Chicago and public choice scholars. While Chicago embraces the more romantic efficiency position, public choice is quick to denigrate the outcomes of the common law courts/judges. No one better expressed the disdain for the common law and the principles involved than one of its founding fathers, Tullock, who wrote:

> The common law system is ... a socialistic bureaucracy in which attorneys essentially lobby government officials – judges and juries – much in the same way that special interest groups lobby the legislature.... [T]he invisible hand of the market does not have its counterpart in the disinterest of the judge. Rather, its counterpart is the visible boot of the politically active judge and the bony knees and elbows of the semi-blindfolded, intellectually lame jury.
>
> (Tullock 2005a: 472–473)

While space does not allow for an extended discussion of the evolution of common law (efficient or otherwise), suffice it to say that, like rules and status rights, the court's legal doctrines do in fact evolve over time, and as the courts jettison old doctrines and create and apply new doctrines, the result is to alter the character of economic life of a nation state.

Evolving political parties and institutions of governance

The political/legal institutions that make up the public sector are in a constant (though gradual and incremental) state of flux. One of the prime purveyors of public policy are, of course, the nation's political parties, which help provide the nation (directly and indirectly) with its legislators, agendas, policy guidance, appointed regulators (through consent requirements), etc. The political parties are an unstable, loose collection of parties of interest gathered together to compete with each other to create or affirm certain principles and put policies and people in place. The parties internally evolve by the activities of shape shifters.[13] The line of literature that inspired the concept of "shape shifters" begins with Issacharoff and Karlan's (1999) discussion of the response of political parties to campaign finance reforms. Their article is narrowly concerned with the "hydraulics of campaign finance" and the means and manner by which political actors engage in regulatory avoidance as they work around new campaign finance laws. Merge that idea with Aldrich's characterization (Aldrich 1995) of the legal apparatus of political parties "as an endogenous institution," shaped by party actors as they see fit, and Fiorina's observations (Fiorina 2002) that the party actors reshape the internal organizational forms, rules, and strategies of their party in response to legal and political demands as they arise, and you have the basis for *shape shifting*.[14]

In extending the analysis, Kang first challenges the judicial practice of formal law's treatment of political parties as discrete entities – as legally identifiable actors within the official party apparatus, such as officeholders, party committees, and official party organizations. He argues that to truly comprehend the nexus between regulations and the political parties, a political party is best understood in "supralegal" terms that transcend the usual notion of parties; he jettisons the judicial practice of treating them as having a formal legal structure and identity.[15] In addition, Kang believes that Issacharoff and Karlan's (1999) earlier work that also focused on campaign finance is too narrow, inasmuch as campaign finance is but a sub-category of the regulation of political parties. In advancing the idea of the "hydraulics of party regulation," he argues more broadly that various types of government regulation of political parties (beyond campaign finance reform) encourage political leaders to find new, more effective private means of effectuating the results that they achieved previously through their party. This can be accomplished because, behind the party's formal legal entities, stands a larger, supralegal party coalition. And so, any attempts to regulate political parties in formal, doctrinal terms (that is, the treatment of political parties as discrete legal entities with actors engaged in official activities), will rarely be able to keep pace with the ever-changing forms and practices of the supralegal political party. As such, since the supralegal party remains outside of the regulatory reach, there are ample opportunities for regulatory avoidance. In short, political parties find new ways to accomplish their goals even when old ways of achieving those goals have been cut off by the passage of regulations (whether by bureaucratic regulation, legislative statute, or court decision). Kang describes the hydraulics of party regulation as follows:

> The real hydraulics problem is more profound and rises above the fungibility of money or the specifics of campaign finance.... Leaders act through a political party because it offers a certain package of costs and benefits.

However, when regulation significantly raises the cost of acting via the party structure, leaders seek alternate means of doing business at lower cost. Attempts at regulating (constraining) what leaders can do officially through the party encourages the party leaders to step back and devise new, more private, creative means outside the legal apparatus in order to accomplish the same end.

(Kang 2005: 149, 148)

In a further elaboration of this process, Gerken (2014: section II) also observed that political parties (entities integral to the public sector) were hard to regulate as they were constantly evolving. Her reasoning centers on the rise of dark money and the concomitant rise of shadow parties whose shape shifters revamp intraparty power relations, influence party politics, and ultimately fashion public policy. Shape shifters transfer political activity from the more public, transparent sphere of the political party's legal structure to the less regulated, private/nonprofit sphere. Within this less-regulated arena accountability and transparency are far less, and so supra-legal activities are pushed ever deeper into the quiet background of everyday politics, shielding the public from the real exercise of power in the supra-legal shadow party (Kang 2005: 158).

For our purposes here, the role of shape shifters can be extended beyond campaign finance and even beyond political parties, to political institutions in general. As Gerken observed: "They are shape shifters. Each time we try to regulate a particular type of political institution, political entrepreneurs find new outlets to channel their energies, new institutions to occupy, new means of exercising power" (Gerken 2014: 110). The point of emphasis is that as shape shifters maneuver to take hold of power in the political arena across political institutions, the size and scope of the public sector can be altered.

In summary, taken together, in a representative democracy, whenever the public sector is selected as the preferred system of social control, the formal rules, the working rules and status rights, the legal doctrines, regulations, and the emergent political parties have a direct impact on the allocation and distribution of society's scarce resources. Within the public sector, none of these are set in stone, but rather are themselves a response to economic and social needs and, as such, can and do undergo revisions. In today's modern administrative state, individuals – grass-roots activists, political operatives, corporate leaders, lobbyists, shape shifters of all stripes – are continuously working through government to advance their individual and/or group interests, and in so doing, will determine the relative size and scope of its public sector. Their collective actions determine: (1) which goods, services, and factors of production will be publicly provided together with the respective eligibility requirements; (2) the rules of governance (formal and working rules) of its public sector; (3) the legal doctrines that will guide court rulings that impact the sector; and (4) the intraparty power relations of political parties.

Unlike the market-sector resource allocations, there is no duality theorem present that helps to ensure that government decision makers will formulate public policies, regulations, or rights, rules, or doctrines that will yield economically efficient results. This problem is partially offset by the extent to which such public-sector decision making and decisions are based on benefit–cost calculations – in such cases, public-sector decisions can be said to approach a Kaldor–Hicks efficient allocation of resources.[16]

Nonprofit sector

While the lion's share of a nation's allocation of scarce resources is channeled through its market and public sectors, the nonprofit sector has its own role to play. As recently characterized, "[In the United States] the sector is big and sprawling, plays an indispensable role in society and the economy, and faces daunting financial and operating challenges" (Cohen 2010; see also Sherlock and Gravelle 2009). In the United States nonprofits employ roughly 9 percent of the workforce and account for approximately 5 percent of US economic activity (GDP). "Nonprofits" is a term used to describe a broad array of private, nonprofit organizations and nongovernmental institutions composed of individuals acting voluntarily in pursuit of the nonprofit's mission.

As with both the market and public sectors, the government has an important and ongoing role to play in its credible commitment to its nonprofit sector. In the United States, the sector has been given legitimation through government with nonprofits grounded in law, economics, and politics; they are now firmly situated in various sectors of the economy including education, health, social services (broadly defined), arts and culture, religion, civil rights, labor unions, political parties, social clubs, international aid, and, the environment and natural resources.

Nonprofits are private, voluntary, and self governing; they are run by boards (typically, though not always, exclusive of government officials). Nonprofits are institutionalized by securing legal standing as corporations under state corporate law; in addition, they must obtain recognition as a nonprofit organization from the IRS under federal tax law. Being a state corporate entity enables them to enter into contracts and frees individual officers from any responsibility from the nonprofit's financial commitments. Nonprofits are not dedicated to earning profits – they do not distribute excess revenues. If a surplus is earned, it is either (1) retained (as reserves, as temporarily restricted funds, or as part of the nonprofit's endowment); or (2) reinvested (in organizational expansion or redirected back into the organization to pursue its mission). This so-called "nondistribution constraint" has become a defining characteristic of nonprofit organizations. Over the years, with changes to the IRS Code and subsequent tax law revisions and related court decisions, an elaborate classificatory scheme was established that accorded different kinds of tax privileges and various degrees of regulatory oversight to various categories of nonprofits.[17]

Nonprofits exist without simple, clear lines of ownership and accountability. As Frumkin has observed, "[L]ittle is known about the underlying purposes and values that animate nonprofits … or the vehicles through which these values and purposes are channeled." This is due in part to the fact that the activities of non-profits "reflect a confusing agglomeration of strongly held private values as well as a set of complex public purposes" (Frumkin 2002: 8–9). That is, donors to nonprofits, as well as the granting agencies and the individuals who run the non-profit, may have different conceptions as to the exact mission of a nonprofit and, in fact, that conception may evolve over time.[18] Beyond the vagaries of owner-ship and thus accountability, a further characteristic that complicates analysis of the nonprofit sector is the fact that many nonprofit organizations acquire funding not only from their own earned revenues (typically from fees for service), but they also acquire significant funds from foundations, corporations, and the government. Since most nonprofits are governed by members of their governing boards (with members being non-owners and thus with substantial leeway in decision making), their actions are guided by the general notion to act in line with the nonprofit's mission as well as their version of the public interest or their vision of the public good.

US law generally permits a nonprofit to pursue almost any purpose so long as the nondistribution constraint is observed. Over time, nonprofit law has had to address the nondistribution constraint issue and the difficulties in controlling the managers of nonprofits with respect to so-called self-dealing transactions (Brody and Cordes 2006: 142). As Hansmann describes it, the difficulty arises because "[W]e have long relied on [federal] tax law to police the conduct of nonprofit managers because nonprofit corporate law has defaulted in this role." Indeed, he went on to state that "the federal tax code virtually mandates that individual states adopt them as part of their nonprofit corporation law," and with respect to self-dealing he observed that "[I]t has been the [federal] tax code, regulations, [court] rulings, and cases – not the corporate law duty of loyalty – that has defined the limits on self-dealing transactions by nonprofit managers" (Hansmann 2001: 263). In effect, what has happened is that the federal tax law rules have become the corporations code/law for nonprofit corporations. This default IRS regulation of nonprofits is not an insignificant point. The present oversight and regulation is partly skewed or distorted in that the interests and policy posture of the IRS (in their capacity to oversee the nation's federal tax laws) do not necessarily coincide with the interests of the members (or the mission) of the nonprofits or, for that matter, the interests of the general public (Hansmann 2001: 263).

Economic rationale underlying nonprofits

In competitive markets, when certain situations or circumstances arise, market failures will ensue. In such instances, the economy will experience externalities, under-supplied public goods, and/or contract failure – each of which provides an economic rationale as to why nonprofits emerge. Typically, to correct for these instances of market failure some form of remedy is called for. Following the Pigovian mind-set, with respect to externalities, the solution becomes one of having the government impose taxes, provide subsidies, or regulate through command and control, all in an effort to internalize the positive or negative externality. Or, where there is an expressed need for a public good, the government would take the necessary steps to overcome the free-rider problem and provide the public good and thereby avoid the persistent underallocation of resources

However, through active neglect or drift (see discussion below regarding Type I, II, or III drift), the present government may opt to live with persistent misallocation of resources. It is in this political-economic context that the non-profit emerges in an effort to meet demands for particular types of goods or services that some individuals and/or groups in society feel are not being adequately met within the market sector or by the public sector. It is the combined (1) market failure and (2) government's subsequent failure to implement public-sector remedies that can potentially shift the provision of certain goods and services into the nonprofit sector. Thus, the nonprofits can be conceived of as "gap-filling entities" or "gap-filling organizations." This combined economic/political failure becomes the economic *raison d'etre* for nonprofits and has been aptly described by Salamon:

> By forming nonprofit organizations, smaller groupings of people can begin addressing needs that they have not yet convinced others to support. In short, it is not market failure alone that leads to a demand for nonprofit organizations. Rather it is the failure of both the market and the state to supply collective goods desired by a segment of the populations, but not by enough to trigger a government response.

(Salamon 1999: 12)

In addition to externality and public-good market failures, Hansmann describs a third instance – what he terms "contract failure" (Hansmann 1980). Contract failure can lead to a rise or expansion of nonprofit activity in the following way. Within the market sector, due to the market circumstances and/or the nature of the good or service being provided by the for-profit firm, the consumer may feel that (s)he is unable to accurately evaluate the attributes or quality of the good or service. Such informational asymmetries for some goods and services can arise due to either (1) the inability of the consumer to correctly assess the quantity or quality of the product or service, and/or (2) the high transaction costs involved in making an accurate assessment. Given that asymmetry, the for-profit firms in the market sector have both the opportunity and the incentive to provide consumers less service than that which was promised and paid for. That recognized, non-profit organizations can emerge as a more trustworthy alternative to provide the good or service.

Nonprofits and their relationship with government

It is important to understand the nonprofits's policy relationship to government. Here, the literature identifies three alterative relationships most commonly observed – supplementary, complementary, and adversarial (Young 2006). First, in their supplementary role, nonprofits are seen as fulfilling a demand for government goods left unsatisfied after partial or limited government action. In short, the government has simply not done enough, leaving some citizens or groups unsatisfied with the actual government provision. It is this group of citizens who can potentially mobilize into a nonprofit in order to provide additional – "supplementary" – levels of some public good, or additionally abate negative externalities or enhance the resources going to goods providing positive externalities.

Second, in their complementary role nonprofits are seen as partners to government by entering into an informal partnership or contractual relationship with some government entity. In this relationship, nonprofits typically deliver the public good or direct resources to abate a negative externality but are largely financed by the government to do so. Aspects of the theory of the firm and transactions costs economics suggest that, in certain instances, it is more efficient for the government to delegate delivery of such services to nonprofits, thereby expanding the complementary relationship between the two organizational entities. Indeed, as characterized by Hall (2006: 53), following World War II, the then new nonprofits became an integral part of government, with Hall observing that "[nonprofits] increasingly became – if not extensions of government itself – an intrinsic part of the organizational field of public governance." Nonprofits also have an ever-growing relationship with political parties. As the federal government (legislature and the courts) set laws in place to regulate political parties, shape shifters have turned to the nonprofit sector to help accomplish their goals and missions – witness the pairing of 501(c)(4) nonprofits with their sister super PACs.

Finally, nonprofits may take on an adversarial role with respect to government over issues related to (1) governance, (2) public policy, and (3) the regulation and oversight of nonprofits. With respect to the first, in a representative democracy, in their effort to shape public policy, nonprofits advocate and lobby government to revise its institutions – its entrenched working rules of governance that directly affect nonprofits. Second, nonprofits advocate for public polices that advance the nonprofit's goals, as well as the interests of their constituents, which may be at odds with the official status quo government policy positions. And third, with respect to the regulation and oversight of nonprofits, government is tasked with ensuring nonprofits's trustworthiness. That being said, nonprofits are not neutral as to their preferred regulatory oversight and, in a representative democracy, the impacted parties of interest will lobby accordingly to get their preferred regulatory arena set in place.

Thus, there is an ongoing nexus between nonprofits and the government. It is significant and, in part, represents the government's credible commitment to the nonprofit sector. It manifests itself through (1) the evolving US tax code for nonprofits; (2) the government's partial funding of some nonprofits; and (3) individuals in society (including the members of nonprofits) regularly working through government to expand the size and scope of the nonprofit sector. There remains the difficult question as to whether nonprofits enhance efficiency. While beyond the scope of this chapter, it should be noted that in assessing the performance of nonprofits, the results remain ambiguous though a majority of studies do conclude that nonprofits are somewhat less efficient that their private-sector counterparts (Steinberg 2006: 128). But one must be careful in reaching for a definitive conclusion – there are many difficulties in making the comparison.[19] That being said, in a representative democracy, nonprofits work through government and the courts to revise the legal-economic arena in which they operate and to shape government policies that impact their sector, whether in a supplementary, complementary, or an adversarial role.

Communal sector

Individuals in a society, acting through their political-legal institutions, may decide that commodities or resources will be communally owned (*res communes*) and allocated through the nation state's communal sector. Like the other systems of social control, common property is successful in allocating scarce resources only to the extent to which government credibly commits to the communal sector. In essence, common property is private property owned by a group of co-owners where all members of the group are subject to accepted rules that are transparent to all. The groups may vary in size and have their own internal governance structure. Collectively, the group of individuals has the rights to use and transfer the resource and, importantly, also reserves the right to exclude nonmembers. Typically, a management group oversees the manner by which a common property resource can be used. And, with reserving the right to exclude nonmembers, depending upon the group rules used to manage the resource, communal property may well result in an efficient allocation of resources.[20]

In light of problems relating to negative externalities or the depletion of a resource, with the potential for a common-property remedy in hand, policy makers have less of a knee-jerk response to merely choose between command and control state remedies (public-sector solutions) or privatization of the resource (market-sector solutions). They instead have the option of channeling the resources through the communal sector. This more informed view is in marked contrast to the previously held position held by many legal-economic policymakers that, somehow, common property was inferior to private property. Of course, such policymakers were never clearly wrong since the essence of common property was never made clear to them.[21] The emergence of the literature on common property as an alternative policy option was nicely summed up by Stiglitz (2009: B-1), observing that:

> Conservatives used the tragedy of the commons to argue for [private] property rights, and efficiency was achieved as people were thrown off the commons.... What Ostrom has demonstrated is the existence of social control mechanisms that regulate the use of commons without having to resort to [private] property rights.

As a result, the communal sector has become a viable option in many public policy debates and analysis.

The communal sector option has become more attractive as communal-sector research demonstrates that communal arrangements compare favorably with public- or market-sector remedies on efficiency grounds (Agrawal 2001: 1650).[22] This research has shown that common property generally is most effective when: (1) the group tends to be small, with a clearly defined and identifiable membership; (2) where the individuals are located not far from the resource; and (3) where they have some regular interaction (i.e., a continuing relationship/ past experiences in cooperating). Such groups tend to have common social and cultural norms, and have established an effective mechanism of enforcement.[23]

Open-access resource sector

Finally, individuals in a nation state, acting through their political-legal institutions, may decide that commodities or resources will be owned by no one, equally available to all (*res nullius*). In this sector, by definition, there are no property rights to the commodity or resource and so it will belong to the party to first exercise control over the commodity or resource The resulting open-access allocation of the resource would be allocatively efficient only if supply exceeds demand at a zero price. If supply does not exceed demand at a zero price and society nonetheless continues to allocate the commodity or resource through the open-access sector, the resource will be overused/destroyed.[24]

While there are only a few instances for which no rights to a resource formally exist – the atmosphere, the oceans (beyond stipulated boundaries from land), the international seabeds, outer space, and Antarctica[25] – in fact, much of public policy centers precisely on the recognition that few resources can be left in open access. This recognition presents a necessity of choice in selecting one of the alternative systems of social control since all such resources will be subject to the "tragedy of the commons" – destruction! Thus, the fundamental public policy challenge is to intelligently decide whether to allocate those resources through the market, public, nonprofit, or the communal sector. Two other possible alternatives would be to agree to all-inclusive treaties that are established and enforced to allocate an open-access good, commodity, or resource, or perhaps to have the good or resource allocated through the prevailing social norms of the community beyond the reach of the law.

Public policy: legal change and managed drift

One of the crucial questions is how, in a representative democracy, does a nation state accomplish legal change sufficient to keep up with the ever-changing technological and economic environment. Public policy debates typically revolve around the question: "In what direction shall we change the law/the statute/the regulation/legal doctrines/past court rulings?" To the extent that changes in law affect incentives, the field of law and economics helps to provide a systematic way to think about this question.

Legal centralist approach to public policy

First, the field recognizes that much of public policy involves altering the law – where law is conceived in its broadest sense and has no singular origin. That is, public policy may come about by altering the Constitution, statutes, formal rules, working rules, regulations, or the judicial doctrines or findings of the courts.[26] Such changes may come through the executive branch, the legislature, the courts, or a government agency or department. Second, policymakers and alert parties of interest understand that the goals of public policy will *not* be realized by changing the law willy-nilly or in an ad hoc manner under some vague claim of justice, fairness, or in the name of the public interest or for the common good. They know policy goals will be reached by structuring and adopting those specific laws, rights, rules, doctrines, and regulations for which there is a known nexus between the said change in law and the desired outcome. Third, in fashioning public policy it is essential to understand that the impact of legal change is relevant whenever (1) a change in the law will alter the incentive structure confronting individuals and groups in society (often); and (2) when the public policy does not run counter to the social norms of the engaged community.

Under these conditions, the "legal centralist" approach to public policy suggests each legal change alters the incentives confronting individuals and groups in society and thereby alters their behavior and, in the aggregate, the new behavior results in a different economic performance. The efforts of those engaged in positive, legal-economic research are devoted to trying to describe the exact nexus between policy options and the expected outcomes; that is, bringing forth accurate answers to the question: What performance will result from a change in law? Peculiar to law and economics, that economic performance is typically measured or evaluated in terms of Pareto efficiency in exchange and production, or Kaldor–Hicks efficiency. Law typically makes reference to fairness or justice and doctrines related to reasonableness in accordance with social norms.[27]

Managed drift

This is not to suggest that public policy always involves actively and purposefully changing the law. In fact, public policy can be accomplished by "drift" – the failure of government (intentional or otherwise) to respond to the ever-present social, technological, and/or economic changes. By failing to take action, policy-/lawmakers work to maintain the status quo regime of laws, rights, rules, doctrines, and regulations together with the related allocation and distribution of resources.[28] Policy by drift can accomplished in a variety of ways. First, what is termed here Type-I drift can be conceived of as public policy where passive ignorance is in play. Here, when the technological/economic environment (within which individual consumers and producers make choices) changes over time, the government may simply be ignorant of, or in fact, choose to ignore the new realities. For example, the government may choose not to increase the level of the national minimum wage so that, over time, its real value diminishes with annual inflation. Such Type-I drift would have direct economic consequences for those impacted.

Alternatively, the government may proceed to adopt a policy of Type II-drift. Here, the government, aware of the new technological/economic realities, actively engages in public policies to alter the formal rules, the institutional working rules, and the rules of governance, and to do so in a manner that effectively erects political and procedural barriers to hinder active governance. For example, the government may start requiring super majorities in the legislature or instituting a filibuster rule to promote Type II-drift. Such institutional changes that lock-up governance serve to accomplish drift by putting an effective stop to (or slowing the adoption of) public policy reforms or initiatives. Type-II drift policy can also include the selective non-enforcement of new or existing laws and/or regulations (e.g., environmental laws and regulations or antitrust laws and regulations). Like the erection of barriers to hinder active governance, under this scheme the net effect is the same – to effectively maintain the status quo regime of law, rights, rules, doctrines, and regulations with all of its economic implications. Finally, Type II-drift can also be accomplished through a public–private policy innovation – the active fostering of public ignorance, purposefully created by special interest groups in an effort to create confusion and suppress the truth; this has been given the moniker "agnotology."[29] Here, agnotological-induced drift comes about when think-tanks, lobbying firms, shape shifters, news outlets, political parties, and corporations (acting in conscious parallelism) combine their efforts to foster the public's ignorance by promoting spurious science and dubious intelligence in an effort to intentionally manufacture doubt and create uncertainty in areas of public policy where there otherwise exists widespread consensus and agreement (Mirowski and Nik-Khan 2013: 282–284; Foucart 2011). The desired effect is to stifle public policy by contrivance and thereby preserve the status quo. Mirowski and Nik-Khan (2013: 283) identify some of the drift-promoting techniques and schemes:

> from the accusation of opponents of dealing in "junk science" to the manipulation of the media through various public relations techniques, to the magnification of "uncertainties," the circumvention of various prior academic outlets and peer review structures, attacks on the legitimacy of existing experts, and appeals for "balance" to accord credibility to otherwise fringe explanations.
>
> (Mirowski and Nik-Khan 2013: 283)

One of the most visible public manifestations of agnotology goes something like the following. A party of interest finds some partially reputable figure(s) to come forward and manufacture an alternative proposition that runs contrary to the widely accepted knowledge that underlies a proposed public policy, noting that while their alternative proposition is largely unfounded, it is often in line with the interests of the lobbyists, corporate leaders, media magnates, and shape shifters of a particular bent. Once these figures are identified, some journalism outlets exhibit the unfortunate tendency to treat a proposition as "true" as long as someone in a position of authority can be found and is willing to be quoted saying it. All of the parties involved try to muddle objectivity and manufacture doubt and uncertainty by presenting "two sides" to an issue, pitting jousting "authorities" against one another. The net effect of proffering a fake "balanced" debate (and then to imply that it is "fair" because it was "balanced") is to simply manufacture ignorance. It fosters the illusion of doubt over the proposed policy in question (1) in the minds of a segment of a rationally ignorant public; and (2) in the minds of policy-/lawmakers who were searching for any dubious fact to support their predetermined position; or (3) in the minds of sincere policymakers who are in search of genuine information – all of which eventually leads to drift.[30]

Finally, parties of interest may work through government to adopt Type-III drift – a series of public policies designed broadly to pursue legislation and/or rules that will drastically reduce the aggregate size and scope of government programs. Type-III drift is accomplished through the issuance of executive orders, the passage of legislation, the curtailment of government regulations, the implementation of non-enforcement strategies,[31] etc., all of which leaves fewer resources for government, and, being smaller, gives it a reduced capacity to respond to existing or new technological and economic realities of the day. Simply put, Type-III drift is an across-the-board government contraction policy.

Of course, law and economics policymakers are aware that such "policy by contraction" runs counter to the universal optimization principle of microeconomics (what they teach their students). The principle suggests that, to attain an optimal/efficient level of the program under scrutiny, the government should be utilizing resources – for example, expanding or contracting the scope of the level of pollution abatement, public education, or public infrastructure projects – up to the point where the program's marginal benefit is equal to its marginal cost. When parties of interest are successful in implementing Type-III drift, it forces government to adhere to an across-the-board policy by contraction that systematically results in across-the-board inefficient allocations of society's scarce resources, with all its economic implications.

Summary to systems of social control and public policy

Typically, a nation state is structured so that its scarce resources are allocated and the character of economic life is determined by its market sector, public sector, nonprofit sector, and communal sector (and rarely left as an open-access resource). Those interested in public policy must recognize, first, there are no "single-sector" solutions – no nation state operates with one sector and, for policy makers, little is learned by narrowing your lens to solution-by-markets. Society bears high opportunity costs by engaging in any form of "single institutionalism" based policy. As Komesar (1994: 6) observed: "The correct question is whether, in any given setting, the market is better or worse than its available alternatives or the political process is better or worse that its available alternatives." A singular solution (relying only on the market sector or the public sector) to legal-economic issues reflects only one particular set of value premises and one particular construction of the benefits and costs at issue. Second, policy-makers should be reminded of Buchanan's admonition that "man must look to all institutions as potentially improvable. Man must adopt the attitude that he can control his fate; he must accept the necessity of choosing" (Buchanan 1977: 136). Institutionalized markets are but one option and are a function of the institutions and power structures which form and operate through them. The market sector should not be the assumed superior and substitute for all other sectors. Third, the success of any of the four sectors depends, in part, on the extent to which government makes a deliberate and transparent credible commitment to that sector. Fourth, in a representative democracy, in light of ever-changing economic, technological, and political realities, legal and institutional change within a nation state is inevitable. As parties of interest – including various interest groups, lobbyists, shape shifters, think-tanks, etc. – work to change the formal rules, property rights, working rules, and status rights, the relative size and scope of the market, public, nonprofit, and communal sectors are altered and with that a new economic performance unfolds.

A valid question is: How do various types of institutional arrangements perform comparatively when confronted with policy options that involve difficult resource allocation questions? Importantly, the performance (and the criteria to evaluate performance) of any one of the sectors needs to be compared to the performance of other sectors in actual field settings and not ideologically presumed.[32] As Komesar stated: "Whether and to what extent the structures of government thought to support the market do in fact enhance transacting, increase resource allocation efficiency, or promote any other social goal are issues too important and difficult to be assumed" (Komesar 1994: 114). With respect to sector performance (especially between the market versus the public sectors), Stone (1997: 61–85) has pointed out that the measurement of efficiency in the public sector is marked with some very difficult issues (to an extent these same issues are raised in the context of the nonprofit and communal sectors). What constitutes efficiency in each sector of the economy is predicated, in part, on: (1) who determines what is the correct output goal or program objective; (2) how we value and compare multiple objectives; (3) how different objectives or outputs benefit different constituencies or groups; (4) how we count inputs that are simultaneously outputs to somebody else; (5) how we decide which of the many benefits/outputs of any input to count; and (6) how we count the virtually unlimited opportunity costs of resources used as inputs (Stone 1997: 66). She goes on to argue that "to go beyond the vague [efficiency] slogans and apply the concept to a concrete policy choice requires making assumptions about who and what counts as important" (Stone 1997: 65). Very much in line with Knight (see below), Stone wrote:

There are no correct answers to these questions to be found outside the political process. The answers built into supposedly technical analyses of efficiency are nothing more than political claims. By ordering different assumptions, sides in a conflict can portray their preferred outcomes as being efficient.

(Stone 1997: 65)

Beyond its direct impact on law and legal policy, the government also impacts economic performance and a nation's character and fabric of economic life by fashioning social norms and by creating and designing standards for its goods, services, and factors of production – following is a brief mention of both.

Social norms and standards[33]

Social norms

In addition to the various legal relations governing society, the evolving habits, customs, mores, and social norms of a community also influence or regulate behavior and thus impact a nation's economic performance.[34] The law and economics literature on social norms argues for the inclusion of social norms into the analysis to develop more robust explanations of behavior in order to predict more accurately the effects of changing law. The genesis of social norms analysis in law and economics is often attributed to Ellickson's 1991 pathbreaking book, *Order Without Law*. In the ensuing years the scholarship in this area grew exponentially and reflects several different perspectives on the analysis and role of norms for legal and public policy.

Social norms set in place a separate set of incentives (separate from the legal-based incentives) – incentives that also induce certain patterns of preference formation and thus impact behavior and ultimately economic performance. As McAdams described it, "laws affect behavior not only by making the behavior more costly, but also by affecting social norms and, consequently, by changing an individual's preferences for undertaking particular acts" (McAdams 2000: 389). So, while individuals may respond to the legal incentives (threats of fines and/or imprisonment) not to pollute, not to cheat on their taxes, not to speed on the highway, to some extent the presence of societal norms can also explain why some individuals do not pollute, do not cheat on their taxes, and do not speed on the highway. Social norms can impact performance in several ways. First, social norms can matter because they sometimes control individual behavior to the exclusion of prevailing law.[35] Second, norms and law may work independently to influence behavior in the same direction.[36] And third, law may intentionally influence social norms themselves.[37]

For public policy, the impact of a proposed change in law will likely vary, depending on whether the legal change is neutral, running with, running against, or altering prevailing social norms. The point to be emphasized is that, in attempting to alter economic performance through legal change, policymakers that rely on neoclassical models populated with "unsocialized individuals" (Ellickson's term) are apt to neglect law's interaction with social norms. When the behavior of individuals in a community is systematically influenced by social norms in ways that are not considered by public policymakers who focus exclusively on law, the public policy predictions are likely to overstate or understate the behavioral response to proposed change in law and thereby incorrectly predict future economic performance – with the follow-on claim of "unintended consequences" not far off.

Further, recognition of the fact that laws could change social norms spawned what is termed "New Chicago." Contributors to this facet of social norms literature emphasized the fact that law can and does affect social norms. And since law can strengthen the norms it embodies and weaken those norms it condemns, the government is in the unique position of being able to advance desirable norms and undermine unwanted ones (see Sunstein 1996). For public policy, the significance of the fact that the government can influence social norms cannot be overstated – far from diminishing the role of the government (à la Chicago and public choice), this fact offers an expanded opportunity for state activity or regulation – here, to alter social norms, and ultimately economic performance, in ways that will enhance social welfare.

Standards

If laws, rights, rules, legal doctrines, and social norms are the driving forces that give rise to a nation's character of economic life by impacting the allocation of its scarce resources, it is standards that give rise to the fabric of that life. Up until a decade ago, standards were often considered rather benign. It was commonly observed that "One of the interesting aspects is that [standards] have largely escaped consistent attention ... the work of creating them is often invisible or deleted in descriptions of their development" (Lampland and Star 2009: 9). In suggesting why, Krislov observed that "the recognition of standards has been stunted by the amorphousness and innocuousness of the label" (Krislov 1997: 7). "Standards" refer to the standards for products, processes, practices, and people, as well as certifications and accreditations of all sorts. The concern here is with formal standards that require a governing authority to legitimate and stand behind the standard – this can be done under the auspices of the state or, as is often the case in the United States, under the auspices of a private entity (Busch 2011).

Standards fall somewhere between the law and social norms, although they typically overlap with both. They are a means for governing a nation (both people and things).

The provision of standards is an essential means for handling a wide variety of issues. At the most elementary level, we are talking about weights and measures or the matching of threads for nuts and bolts. But standards also provide a nation with the technical regularity and compatibility of physical objects, electricity generation and transmission, telecommunications, the gauges of railroad tracks, food safety, environmental protection, safe transportation, worker health and safety, as well as quality education and healthcare. Standards are embodied in a variety of technical documents and reference materials (that characterize and specify certain technical objects used to calibrate other objects). They also include a variety of "good practices" in manufacturing, medicine, accounting, or agriculture; and in the ethical codes covering a wide range of professions, and the ratings of colleges and universities.

The focus on standards here is not to imply a quest for homogeneity of products, services, or factors of production. Standards provide integrity for both homogeneous and differentiated products and processes and thus impact a nation's economic performance. Some standards are promulgated by government agencies (federal, state, and/or local) under relevant standard-setting statutes and/or regulations. In the United States standard setting that takes place under federal law is done in accordance with the Administrative Procedures Act. The Act sets forth a few general background procedures (constraints) within which standard setting then takes place.[38] More often (particularly in the United States), standards are set forth by individual firms and/or industry associations, by entities formed under the umbrella of hundreds of industry- or sector-based standards development organizations (SDOs) which develop and publish industry-specific standards. To complete the process, the SDOs work together with third-party certifiers (TPCs) and national accreditation bodies (NABs).

Standards give rise to the fabric of life by defining the very nature of the factors of production and the goods and services produced in an economy. They help to make each other's actions comprehensible and comparable; they define the essence of that which passes through the market, public, nonprofit, and communal sectors. One is not just buying a tire, having a blood test, enrolling in college, building a tunnel, etc. Meeting a standard (or not) may affect one's ability to sell a particular product, to provide a particular service, to enter a profession, to employ a particular production process, or to build a certain structure in a particular way. All of these activities are predicated upon (1) the design of the standards; (2) the integrity of the processes used in setting the standards; and (3) the enforcement of standards that underlie each. Once established, they enable individuals to better engage in forms of beneficial cooperation in commerce and trade and provide a zone of safety. In short, standards (as metrics) provide a nation a means to determine whether its policies are enhancing or undermining the fabric of life and thus, the welfare of its citizens.

Summary

In a dynamic setting, individuals in a representative democracy, acting both individually and collectively, will attempt to promote their economic welfare: (1) by changing the rights structures that underlie the systems of social control, and thereby revise the relative size and scope of each sector; (2) by altering laws, rules, legal doctrines, and regulations in an effort to enhance their welfare; (3) following New Chicago, work to change social norms; and (4) through both government and industry associations, redesign and update standards and the standard-setting processes, all impacting the character and fabric of economic life.

Rent seeking in the context of systems of social control

Introduction

This part of the chapter attempts to identify a fundamental problem that confronts law and economics-inspired market advocates who argue against rent-seeking activities (hereafter MSAs). In short, it is the problem of how proponents of the market sector perceive and treat – both theoretically and in actual policy – what they selectively choose to label as "rent-seeking activities" and then identify and bemoan the associated "wastes of rent seeking."[39] It is an effort wherein they purport to positively describe and analyze resource-wasting activities of individuals and groups seeking to *obtain* (with less emphasis on *maintain*) wealth transfers through government.

Setting the market in place: MSAs's frame of reference

To understand those who are critical of rent-seeking activities, one must understand their frame of reference – their starting point. It starts with a vision of an ideal market (described above in the section *Market sector*) and seems to suggest that at an early point in time, the market almost spontaneously emerged – distinct from government. It was pure and stood alone, above and apart from the activities of human lawmakers. In this context, proponents of the MSAs (inspired by Chicago law and economics) make every effort to see that the market sector is selected as the preferred system of social control. At center stage is the concept of wealth-maximizing gains from trade across all product and factor markets. At the same time, the public choice advocates continue to remind policymakers of each and every public-sector failure – falling nicely into their attempt to undermine the government's credible commitment to its public sector. Once these idealized markets are conceptually set in place, MSAs then engage in an effort that purports to be objective and positive to selectively observe individuals, interest groups, lobbyists, and shape shifters routinely working through government to effect transfers to themselves (more typically their clients) from the larger population. Such behavior was labeled "rent seeking" with a particular focus on monopoly power transfers. The moniker and the concept gained immediate traction, being invoked by economists, lawyers, policymakers, and even journalists. Over time, the scope of activities expanded from a somewhat narrow economic focus on monopoly to a broader set of government activities (described below). As will be seen, for some MSAs, in order to establish their critique of rent-seeking activities, it required them to repress the legitimacy of (1) many government programs even though they were established through representative democracy; (2) the common law as it evolved; and even (3) history, all in their effort to identify and denigrate the outcomes of certain government actions, policies, and programs as the product of rent-seeking behavior and to bemoan the waste of society's scarce resources. It appears clean but it is flawed!

Rent seeking made simple

Within the market sector, entrepreneurs pursue rents by (1) enhancing the demand for their product through creative advertising and product development; (2) inventing new products; (3) acquiring better technology to produce their product; and (4) finding ways to reduce the costs of their factors of production that go into making the product – all of which, if successful, serves to provide an entrepreneur with short-term economic profits. Neoclassical price theory predicts that profits tend to be equalized by the flow of investments across a wide variety of opportunities. So, if an opportunity for substantially higher profits emerges, we can expect that it will attract investment until the returns are driven down to a level equal to those generally available throughout the rest of the economy. As long as the market economy is sufficiently competitive, these profits (temporary rents) will be dissipated in the long run and consumers will have an efficiently produced bundle of goods and services from which to select at competitive prices.

In economics, the term *rent* has several meanings used sometimes to describe (1) the price paid for one of the factors of production – namely, land; (2) the price paid for those resources fixed in supply (which eliminates any incentive function as the supply of the resource does not respond to a change in price); (3) the price paid for non-reproducible assets (for example, the payments made for the works of expired artists or payments for unique skills in sports); and/or (4) the return to monopolists – monopoly rents, which while resulting in wealth transfers, do not serve any productive purposes. Early on, MSAs concern was with the waste of scarce resources that successfully established monopoly-like entities that resulted in dead-weight losses to society. So, if a rent-seeking initiative proves successful, "the monopolist gains a monopoly right, but citizens lose because the resources which could have been used to produce goods and services are channeled into nonproductive rent seeking and rent-protecting activities" (Johnson 1991: 331). It is important to note that in the public choice literature the focus of the analysis is not on the rents themselves, or even on the resource misallocations associated with the rent-generating positions; rather, it is on the "waste of resources" used to acquire the rents.

Not long thereafter, the definition of rent seeking was generalized to "the resource-wasting activities of individuals in seeking transfers of wealth through the aegis of the state" (Buchanan *et al.* 1980: ix). As Buchanan described it:

> Rent seeking analysis can be applied to many activities of the modern state, including the making of money transfers to specified classes of recipients. If mothers with dependent children are granted payments for being mothers, we can predict that we shall soon have more such mothers. If the

unemployed are offered higher payments, we predict that the number of unemployed will increase. Or, if access to membership in recipient classes is arbitrarily restricted [for example, when the state licenses an occupation or allocates TV spectra etc.], ... we must expect that the utility-maximizing behavior of individuals will lead them to waste more resources in trying to secure the "rents" or "profits" promised by government.

(Buchanan 1988: 8)

More recently, the concept has covered a wide array of government activities and programs including not only those activities that produce monopoly-like positions, but within the broader political arena rents may take the form of any special privilege or other forms of government transfers granted to certain individuals or groups, and so we read: "Rent-seeking is what economists call a special type of money making: the sort made possible by political connections" (*The Economist* 2014: 13). MSAs's rent-seeking concerns now focus more on such programs as welfare payments, public housing, and food stamps. In part and thanks to presidential candidate Romney, it gained its most recent formulation. During the 2012 campaign, Romney argued that 40 percent of all income taxes come from 1 percent of taxpayers and (in his now infamous observation) that 47 percent of Americans who pay no income tax are people who consider themselves "victims" who feel entitled to government handouts. Essentially, the argument is that government programs redistribute far too much from a shrinking pool of "makers" to a vast number of "takers," and now almost all programs that produce a group in society that can be labeled "takers" are termed rent-seeking programs, identified as such, and denigrated accordingly. More recently, to the credit of a group who self-identify as libertarians, the list is now expanded to include all programs including the former "untouchables" – the agriculture takers and military takers, with some hesitation to take on the oil industry takers. Given their zeal, one can only speculate that if the US Supreme Court were to make up yet another category and find that "States are people" (as they found "corporations to be people"), we would soon find that the states of Mississippi and Louisiana were labeled "rent seekers" by the MSAs (as they are surely the nation's "takers," with approximately 45 percent of each of their state's budget paid for by donor states – the nation's "makers")?[40]

With that said, the purpose here is to see what is being overlooked or covered up in the name of "rent seeking." Indeed, this section of the chapter is written in the spirit of what Pasour wrote (inspired by the words of the father of the Chicago School of economics):

In the words of Knight, (1935, p. 311) "The question whether any type of political machinery will work 'better' or 'worse' than another is ... a matter of opinion." And, since opinions vary widely, the identification of rent-seeking activities is inevitably based on value judgments (*often concealed ones*).

(Pasour 1987: 135; emphasis added)

Fundamental issues for MSAs

Omnipresent rents

Rent seeking becomes a major problem for MSAs for several reasons. First, as Mueller observed, rents are "omnipresent." Specifically, they "exist wherever information and mobility asymmetries impede the flow of resources. They exist in private good markets, factor markets, asset markets, and political markets. When rents exist rent seeking can be expected to exist" (Mueller 1989: 245). What gets concealed is the selective choice as to which activities in which of these markets are to be MSAs's focus of concern when rents are in fact omnipresent – what is the concealed principle to make that choice? Or did Knight have it right?

These are rational political investments

Second, to complicate matters, public choice recognizes that the wastes associated with rent seeking are the product of political investments that are consistent with rational behavior on the part of all participants in the political economy (Buchanan 1980: 9). Individuals come to each sector – the market, public, non-profit, and communal sectors of the economy – with a common motivation, to maximize their utility. As Buchanan reminded us time and again, in elaborating his notion of methodological closure:

> [The] approach requires only the simple assumption that the same individuals act in both relationships. Political decisions are not handed down from on high by omniscient beings who cannot err. Individuals behave in market interactions, in political-governmental interactions, in cooperative-nongovernmental interactions, and in other arrangements. *Closure of the behavioral system*, as I am using the term, means only that analysis [individual utility maximization] must be extended to the actions of persons in their several separate capacities.
>
> (Buchanan 1972: 12, emphasis added)[41]

Thus, rent seekers of all stripes and in all sectors are viewed as rational utility maximizers. The issue for MSAs is further complicated by virtue of the fact that some of these activities are, in fact, market-augmenting. For example, some corporate and industry interest groups work through government to support and enhance market-augmenting initiatives. As Bhagwati observed, rent-seeking behavior – for example, lobbying to restore free trade – is not necessarily wasteful. In fact, properly analyzed, such rent-seeking activities may be beneficial or harmful, depending upon whether "the resources used up in restoring free trade that is the lobby's economic advantage are socially more valuable than the social gains from free trade" (Bhagwati 1982: 997).

Political rent seeking is a market activity

The third observation, closely tied to the second, presents a real quandary for positive analysts bent on curtailing what they term rent seeking. The quandary presents itself due to the fact that most rent-seeking activity takes place in and thorough the nation's market sector, with the nonprofit sector becoming more and more involved in the game. While the MSAs typically argue for free, unregulated markets, to their puzzlement what they observe is that it is in and through their lauded free markets that these rent-seeking wealth transfers are accomplished – where "takers" are made. That is, rent seeking allocates society's scarce resources in and through the free markets for lobbyists, lawyers, corporate leaders, shape shifters, accountants, press agents, and economists – all scarce resources that their theory suggests could have instead been used in "economically productive activities" but are instead used by parties attempting to get a piece of those scarcity-induced rents (consistent with rational utility maximization – see above). Somehow, the paid efforts to those lawyers and lobbyists – with values established by free markets in a capitalist society – are "not productive" (though national income accounting does not differentiate). When national income accounts are aggregated, do they not treat incomes earned by rent-seeking lobbyists, lawyers, and shape shifters in the same manner as the incomes of hedge-fund operators and truck drivers? Do the MSAs think these market-sector factors of production should be identified and rewarded differently based on which markets they choose to operate in? Do they think their work contribution impacts our GDP differently? Are we really to take council from positive, market-sector analysts who, on the one hand, argue for free markets and, on the other hand, suggest that rent-seeking-related free-market activities (the market for lobbyists, lawyers, corporate leaders, shape shifters, accountants, press agents, and economists) are suspect and to be regulated or denigrated (perhaps disallowed)? Is this MSA rent-seeking policy – akin to an "industrial policy" – where they get to pick the new winners and losers? Buchanan might suggest they were playing God.[42] What gets concealed in their undertaking is the selective choice as to which of the activities within each free market are legitimate and which are labeled rent seeking and to be halted or curtailed. What is the concealed principle? Or did Knight have it right?

Selective identification: starting points in markets and law

Rent-seeking theory needs a starting point. MSAs need to be able to precisely state which are the government programs (which legal changes in the rights underlying the market, the public, the nonprofit, and the communal sectors) are the ones that transferred wealth from the makers to the takers that are wasting our resources. While there are a wide range of activities that MSAs normatively select to fall under the moniker of rent seeking, as will become evident, calling them names does not resolve some of the difficult problems raised. There is no doubt that in a representative democracy the increase in specialized pressure groups is a key factor in the rise in lobbying. What we observe are intelligent, disciplined, well-organized, well-funded groups in a representative democracy that use the power of the state to further their own economic ends by government (as described above), in and through the market sector. They do so far better than uneducated, disorganized, undisciplined, poorly funded groups. No doubt this phenomena is a problem for any democratic society, but the rent-seeking literature does nothing to resolve it.

There are two simple reasons. First, there is no identifiable common starting point as to what constituted some initial "legitimate market" they seem to believe spontaneously emerged and is distinct from government. The market has never been perfect and pure and there never was a market separate from government. As described above (under *Market sector*), given government's market-augmenting activities, all markets are complemented by government. Second, the legal relations governing society also have no baseline starting point – the laws that undergird much of our market, public, nonprofit, and communal sectors are constantly evolving. Thus, the effort by the MSAs (in their purported positive literature on rent-seeking) to objectively identify rent seeking behavior is in vain. As Pasour (1987: 132) observed: "Labeling the resource cost required to maintain legitimate political activity as rent-seeking waste ignores the problem of the 'ideal benchmark' in evaluating government activities." They cannot identify the unregulated market nor, more importantly, some baseline legal regime of laws, rights, rules, legal doctrines, and regulations from which to positively state: These are the legal changes in society that constitute rent seeking.

The selectivity in their approach is embarrassingly clear.[43] To highlight the selective identification process, take the example of the lobbying to maintain agricultural marketing orders. Marketing orders for fruits, vegetables, and specialty crops are provided to agricultural producers ostensibly as a tool for achieving "orderly marketing" conditions under the Federal Marketing Agreement Act of 1937.[44] Some positive economists offered evidence to justify this type of restriction on competition on the basis of economic efficiency (US Department of Agriculture 1981: 81). So, on the one hand, agricultural policy in general and agricultural marketing orders in particular can be considered to be an efficiency enhancing, legitimate function of government. If so determined, then the lobbying efforts to maintain the agricultural program or the marketing orders would not be considered rent-seeking waste. If, instead, MPAs and other parties of interest selectively identify the marketing orders as rent seeking, it is held that restrictions on competition of this type are not justified, the activity of obtaining or maintaining the marketing order would be considered rent-seeking waste.[45] There is no distinguishing principle – *where you start is where you end!*

More generally, with respect to the nexus between the economy and law, do MSAs really believe that the market, the public, the nonprofit, and the communal sectors moved through the 1800s and 1900s without any involvement with government? What is their benchmark "legal regime" to discern which legal changes were induced by rent seekers and which were the product of those acting responsibly through their representative democracy? Did not lobbyists, lawyers, corporate agents, shape shifters, accountants, press agents, and economists (virtually all employed in the market sector) work to (and continue today to) have their interests molded into laws and regulations? Did those from the Volker Fund, the Olin Fund, and Director, Simons, and von Hayek really think the laws and regulations in the United States they came upon were perfect and pure and to be left in place? Did they not act along with lobbyists and shape shifters of their day to try to (re)make the world according to Chicago in order to take hold of antitrust law and thereby produce a new set of winners and losers? Did not Baxter (Head of the Antitrust Division of the US Department of Justice under President Reagan) in the 1980s engage in across-the-board Type-II drift policies to limit the scope of antitrust laws and thereby produce a whole new set of winners and losers – makers and takers? The argument here is not whether what they did was good or bad; but to selectively suggest they were not rent seeking is simply not to be believed.

What history has observed is, as economic performance unfolds, as consumer demand shifts, as technologies change, as new resources are discovered and/or old ones move toward depletion, and as competition ensues, as new opportunities arise while past successes dwindle, the economy changes over time. In a dynamic economy, the new economic circumstances will invite new calls for changes in law and new policy initiatives, many impacting the rights underlying the market, the public, the nonprofit, and the communal sectors. Any history of the American economy will demonstrate the constantly evolving nexus between law (in all of its manifestations) and the economy – in almost every case there were winners and losers; there were makers and takers! The fact that public policy (changing law) has always produced winners and losers is longstanding and remains an important issue for economists. It is what inspired Kaldor, Hicks, and Scitovsky to take up their work on the compensation principle, and, at least for a time, have Posner adopt it in advocating for its use in law under the moniker "wealth maximization."[46] Thus, with no benchmark ideal market and no benchmark ideal law, one can legitimately ask: What is the concealed principle that enables the MSAs to positively identify rent-seeking legal changes in each sector from other legal changes? Or did Knight have it right?

Today's reality and conclusion

Ultimately, any rent-seeking theory that identifies society's takers and makers requires MSAs to work outside of their preferred positive analysis. In effect, what they are engaged in, is normatively targeting certain activities as "rent seeking" based on the arguments in their own personal utility functions (be they class-based, race-based, pure ideology, etc.). And so, they must learn from Knight and accept Buchanan's realization that they are just playing God and offer society nothing more than unrefined politics. In playing God (and politics), the MSAs's selective choice usually takes on the following contours. Typically, a government program or activity is set in place or enhanced by some interest group. If the program was normatively thought of as a legitimate function of the state (for example, new wealth transfers to the military, to agriculture, or to oil corporations – society's true takers), the critics of rent-seeking activities quietly remain in the background. In fact, the lobbying efforts to secure more funding for each of those sectors was typically looked on as "a good and efficient source of quality information" and hence not wasteful. The MSAs rarely attacked the lobbying and shape shifting associated with maintaining or enhancing those selective sectors – though some now have begun to do so occasionally, going after heretofore sacrosanct programs (military and agriculture), but never after the individual clients (the generals or the farmers). Alternatively, activities of other interest groups are presented by MSAs as questionable and suddenly the word "incentives" jumps to the forefront, as in the cases of public welfare or food stamps – and the program's clients become suspect. These programs are not illegal, but calls by some to expand them immediately invites MSAs to dwell on the "incentives" confronting the programs's recipients to behave in a manner they may find repugnant (typically based on agnotological conjecture). And so, consistent with Type-III drift policy – policy by contraction – the resources used to expand these programs are normatively labeled as wasteful rent seeking, the recipients denigrated, and political activities are undertaken to curtail (or eliminate) the programs. The economic implications of such policies are significant. If policy by contraction is the operational principle (as opposed to the universal optimization principle), then once the program is reduced, the principle suggests that upon further analysis the program should be further reduced, and further reduced, etc. It is not a guiding principle, and when followed it results in tragic misallocations of society's scarce resources.

In fact, most of the transfers brought about by government programs (whether or not labeled rent seeking) reflect and involve a mix of social norms, motives, and other choice-influencing factors. As simple logic dictates, making these choices in a representative democracy involves discerning the appropriate role of the state, which is profoundly normative. It is based on antecedent norms and changing circumstances and motives that lie outside of the analytical competence, training, and experience of those who propagate naming certain government activities as wasteful rent seeking and quietly view others as legitimate. What gets covered up in their ongoing effort is the operative principle used to distinguish the two. What is the concealed principle? They should be reminded, if and when *all* government programs and actions are defined by the MSAs as rent-seeking, that *naming everything the same thing under one theory, in fact, means you really have nothing*! The contention of this chapter was that there are a variety of factors and forces at work that give rise to the performance of the political economy through *all* of its sectors. Public policies that are set in place under the narrow lens and flawed perspective of law and economics does not make clear the meaningful alternatives available to society. The narrow focus on market-sector solutions to public policy issues is mind-numbingly narrow. Further, in a representative democracy, policymakers – executives, legislators, regulators, and bureaucrats – are going to be lobbied by lawyers, corporate leaders, agents of nonprofits, shape shifters, lobbyists, accountants, press agents, and economists. They want to be "represented" and the concept of rent seeking does nothing to inform society as to what they should or should not do, say, argue over, or argue for. As this section began with a quote from Pasour, I choose to end in the same way:

> In reality, then, there is no objective procedure either in determining which activities of the state are illegitimate, or in determining the extent of rent-seeking waste associated with activities considered to be legitimate. While economic theory is useful in explaining activities of individuals and groups in using the state to further their own ends, *it does not provide an objective procedure for determining inefficiency or rent-seeking waste....* [O]n strictly economic grounds, the [positive] economist cannot reject (or advocate) any public policy (Rothbard, 1982, p. 212). Economic theory, in this sense, is not a substitute for ethical or philosophical analysis.
>
> (Pasour 1987: 134)

Knight was right!

Notes

* Professor of Law in Residence, Michigan State University College of Law, and Professor, James Madison College, Michigan State University.
1 Halper (1993: 230–231) describes the same notion as follows:

> The Chicagoans argue that outcomes legitimate the superiority of the market as a form of collective decision-making – the market is the most efficient means to allocate resources.... [S]tate intervention in the market is warranted only to correct market failure, ... the common law, effectively the outcome of the day-to-day interactions of market participants, orders the market more efficiently than statutory law, the artificial creature of the legislative state.

2 The caricature of an individual behaving in a rationally ignorant manner is one of the benchmarks of public choice theory. The term was coined by Downs (1957: 244–246; 267–271) and remains an important element of public choice in promoting their theories of public-sector failure (see Shughart 2008).
3 See Simmons's (2011) recent book that dwells on the failure of the public sector; he's not alone (see also Tullock *et al.* 2002; Dolfsma 2013).
4 This chapter is an extension of an earlier work and a forthcoming chapter (Mercuro 2005; 2015).
5 It is clear that the economic performance of any nation state is impacted by more than the prevailing laws, rights, rules, legal doctrines, and regulations. As fully presented by Mercuro (2015), economic performance is also impacted by the social norms and standards adopted in the nation state. Both play an essential and important role in fashioning the character and fabric of economic life. Space limitations here only allow for an abbreviated treatment (see *Social norms and standards*, below).
6 A description of Pareto efficiency in exchange and production, as well as Kaldor–Hicks efficiency, is presented by Mercuro and Medema (2006). The duality theorem which demonstrates that a perfectly competitive economy will yield a Pareto-efficient allocation of resources is concisely explained by Feldman (1980: 1–4; 47–58). It should be underscored that this logical, systematic approach to public policy and assessing the outcomes of legal change is quite unique to the economic way of thinking as compared to the manner by which lawyers come up with public policy. This led Ackerman (1984: 22) to pose the question: "When they speak so resonantly of 'public policy,' do lawyers have the slightest idea what they're talking about?"

7 Hayek (1945: 111) emphasized this point, concluding that a well-functioning market "relies upon competition, which, if it is to be made effective, requires a good deal of government activity directed toward making it effective and toward supplementing it when it can not be made effective," with the implication that the mere existence of private property and freedom of contract were simply insufficient.

8 Not long ago Xu (2011: 1078), citing both Adam Smith (1763) and Ronald A. Coase (1992), wrote: "Markets ... do not develop spontaneously, ownership protection is not created independent of market development, and private ownership is insufficient for the market economy function." Simply put, without government functioning beyond the protection of property rights, there can be no market sector. This has become so obvious, even well-educated journalists have recognized the market–government nexus. The conservative columnist George Will (2000) has counseled his fellow conservative travelers:

> [I] will remind everyone – *some conservatives, painfully* – that a mature capital-ist economy is a government project. A properly functioning free market system does not spring spontaneously from society's soils as dandelions spring from suburban lawns. Rather *it is a complex creation of laws and mores* (emphasis added).

9 The procedures set forth in the Administrative Procedures Act are outlined by Bress-man *et al.* (2010: 400–402). The rule-making process for government agencies is mul-tifaceted in that (1) the initiating statute can range from being rather general (leaving the details left for the agency to fill in) or specific (with detailed provisions), or lie somewhere along the continuum of specificity; (2) agencies have leeway in fashion-ing their own agenda regarding the taking and timing of actions to be undertaken; and (3) agencies's actions are undertaken under the recognition that they are responsive and accountable to both Congress and the executive branch.

10 The use of the term *status rights* was first introduced by Dales (1972).

11 Some examples include: (1) public housing is provided to those who are eligible in accordance with the state or municipal promulgated status rights; (2) visits to state and national parks are allocated in accordance with the state or federal status rights; and (3) private, public, industrial, and commercial entities can use a nation's air and water resources under the state's stipulated rules and regulations (essentially eligibil-ity requirements to emit air emissions or water effluents).

12 With respect to legal doctrines, whether the common law *is* evolving efficiently or *should* evolve so as to yield an efficient stock of common law (as opposed to a just or fair law), is beyond the scope of this chapter. Much of this literature is discussed by Rubin (2006).

13 The moniker – shape shifters – was initiated by Gerken (2014: section A). This section of the chapter also borrows from Kang (2005).

14 This is Kang's characterization/description of the combined ideas of Aldrich (1995) and Fiorina (2002).

15 This section draws on Kang (2005: section III).

16 For example, a benefit–cost analysis for rules – major rules set forth by federal agen-cies – would have been required under the proposed (but never passed) US Senate Bill 981 – titled the Regulatory Improvement Act of 1997.

17 For example, the IRC §501(c)(3) describes organizations organized and operated exclusively for religious, charitable, scientific, testing for public safety, literary, or educational purposes, or to foster national or international amateur sports competition, also for the prevention of cruelty to children or animals as well as those dedicated to the environment and natural resources. The IRC §501(c) 4–27 calls for nonprofits to register by the specific nature of their activity – for example, 501(c)(4) are social welfare organizations; 501(c)(5) are for labor and agricultural organizations; 501(c) (6) are for business leagues; and 501(c)(7) are for social and recreation clubs.

18 On this point, see (Brown and Slivinski 2006: 141).
19 Two difficulties are mentioned here: First, as Steinberg (2006: 128) observed, "To the extent that nonprofits produce more unmeasured outputs, the costs of the unmeasured outputs will be overstated and nonprofits will seem less efficient." The second difficulty centers on the rationale for a nonprofit. This was addressed by Frumkin (2002: 124–125) where, beyond the cost assessment problem, he asserts that "the normative rationale for a nonprofit – far from residing in the ability of some nonprofit to deliver services efficiently – lies within the expressive character of the work within the sector." That is, nonprofits produce expressive outputs not easily quantifiable (in narrow efficiency calculations) but are, in fact, an important driving force that helps make nonprofits vibrant and innovative.
20 After an exhaustive review of a large number of studies, Baland and Platteau (2000: 175) came to the conclusion that "regulated common property and private property are equivalent from the standpoint of the efficiency of resource use."
21 On this point see (Ostrom 2000).
22 There are many studies that demonstrate the efficient outcomes of the communal sector. For example, see DeAlessi's discussion of the Maine lobster fishery and the lobstermen who fish outside controlled areas around Cozumel and Punta Allen Mexico (DeAlessi 1998: 18–19); the analysis of Fishermen's Dock Cooperative of Point Pleasant, New Jersey (McCay 1996: 118–119); and DeAlessi's (1998: 19–20) description of how ownership by a clan or group helped to prevent the destruction of the coral reefs in the South Pacific.
23 For a discussion of the conditions, see (Bromley 1991: 26–27) and (Agrawal 2001: 1653); see also (McCay 1996).
24 This was the essence of Garrett Hardin's seminal article "The tragedy of the commons" (1968).
25 These several examples are described by Soroos (1998).
26 These vehicles for implementing public policy have been recognized by the courts. For instance, a comparable list was set forth by Judge Albert L. Rendlen's decision in *Eyerman* v. *Mercantile Trust Co.* 524 S.W. 2d 210 (1975) at 217.
27 This is concisely described by Cooter and Ulen (1988: 11–12).
28 This concept of "drift" was explored in Walter Lippman's *Drift and Mastery*, first published in 1914. In his book, Lippman looks at the failure of government to respond to new economic realities and suggests that rational scientific governing can overcome forces of societal drift. It was Jacob S. Hacker and Paul Pierson's book, *Winner-Take-All Politics* (2010: 83–87), and their discussion of policy by drift, that inspired its inclusion into this section of the chapter.
29 The term was coined in 1992 by the linguist Iain Boal; for a concise introduction to agnotology and description as to how and why it came about, see Proctor (2008).
30 For example, the manufactured debates over global warming, evolution, vaccines, fluoridization of water, smoking as a cause of cancer, etc.
31 A notable example of managed drift occurred shortly after the 1980 election of President Ronald Reagan. He appointed William Baxter to take charge of the Antitrust Division of the US Department of Justice. Based on the ideas initially set forth by Aaron Director and others in advancing the Chicago School agenda for antitrust law, the antitrust policy agenda (later set in place by Baxter) has been described as a "breathtaking contraction in the scope of antitrust policy" (Posner 1979: 928); Baxter's efforts came to be known as the "Baxterization" of the Antitrust Division. This moniker for Baxter's nonenforcement approach is largely attributed to Victor H. Kramer (1981).
32 This conclusion is similar to conclusions drawn by Schlager and Ostrom (1992: 260).
33 An extended discussion of both social norms and standards and their respective impacts on the character and fabric of economic life in a nation state is contained in (Mercuro 2015).

34 This brief section of the chapter is drawn from Mercuro and Medema (2006: 306–340). Following the lead of many contributors to the literature, from this point on, the terms habits, customs, mores, and norms are conflated into the inclusive term "social norms."

35 Bernstein (1992), in a detailed analysis of the diamond industry, explains how the economic performance of that industry is influenced by social norms that work in place of formal law.

36 For example, in cases where the laws/public policies to have industry reduce air emissions and water effluents may run parallel with the social norm not to pollute.

37 For example, legal restrictions on public smoking may have strengthened an anti-smoking norm; or anti-littering laws may have enhanced the prevailing social norms not to litter.

38 State standards are set forth by the government under the same law/procedure cited above in note 9, using the system of "notice and comment" to provide the government agency the authority to create standards (see Breyer 1982).

39 The concept is said to have been first articulated by Tullock (1967); the term "rent seeking" was originally coined by Krueger (1974). Extensive discussions of rent-seeking can be found in (Buchanan *et al.* 1980; Mueller 2003: chapter 15; Tullock 1993, 2005b). While the terminology of rent-seeking is relatively recent, the behavior that it describes has been around at least since the advent of representative democracy (Buchanan 1980: 3).

40 These statistics are provided by Kiernan (2012).

41 Buchanan (1986: 23–24; 1988: 7) traces the roots of this movement toward closure to the work of Knut Wicksell, as well as a group of Italian public finance scholars of the late nineteenth and early twentieth centuries, including Antonio De Viti De Marco, Amilcare Puviani, Mauro Fasiana, and Matheo Pantaleoni.

42 Buchanan's caution to his fellow public choice economists to "avoid playing God" – the phrase he used to urge them to stay within their positive domain – is well known; see (Buchanan 2000; Kliemt 2002); also see (Davidson 2010).

43 These examples are borrowed from Pasour (1987).

44 This program is concisely described at: www.ams.usda.gov/AMSv1.0/FVMarketing OrderLandingPage.

45 Pasour offers another example – the case of labor unions (condensed here [Pasour 1987: 133]). Some claim the lobbying to raise wages as well as enhance labor conditions for union membership (with the unions established in law through the democratic process), can and do affect positively the functioning of the economic and social systems – therefore are not wasteful. Alternatively, he observed that others argue that the activities of labor unions can be selectively viewed as rent seeking and in so doing, selectively label the lobbying efforts associated with obtaining and maintaining unions and labor policies as rent seeking, the resources used up considered wastes, and unions denigrated accordingly. Another example includes public schools. If the public sector is thought to be the proper domain of K–12 education in a representative democracy, the use of resources devoted to lobbying efforts to improve schools and teachers's salaries would not necessarily be considered wasteful. However, if the MSAs have in mind as their benchmark view a view of the world where there are only private schools, then they can selectively label those lobbying resources used to enhance the quality of public schools as wasteful.

46 It should be noted that the compensation principle (the basis of benefit–cost analysis) can help guide the allocation of resources in an efficient direction. As described above, this is quite distinct from Type-III drift – policy by contraction – which is not a guiding principle, but an ideological assertion which, if followed (in particular, in areas such as schooling, transportation, airport infrastructure, etc.), will inevitably lead to misallocations of society's scarce resources.

References

Ackerman B. (1984) *Reconstructing American Law*, Cambridge, MA: Harvard University Press.

Agrawal, A. 'Common property institutions and sustainable governance of resources', *World Development* 29, 2001: 1649–1672.

Aldrich, J.H. (1995) *Why Parties? The Origin and Transformation of Political Parties in America*, Chicago, IL: University of Chicago Press.

Ayres, C.E. 'Institutional economics: discussion', *American Economic Review* 47, 1957: 13–27.

Baland, J.M. and Platteau, J.P. (2000) *Halting Degradation of Natural Resources: Is There a Role for Rural Communities?* Oxford: Oxford University Press.

Bernstein, L. 'Opting out of the legal system: extralegal contractual relations in the diamond industry', *Journal of Legal Studies* 21, 1992: 115–157.

Bhagwhati, J.N. 'Directly unproductive, profit-seeking (DUP) activities', *Journal of Political Economy* 1982, 1982: 988–1002.

Bressman, L.S., Rubin, E.L., and Stack, K.M. (2010) *The Regulatory State*, Aspen Publishers.

Breyer, S. (1982) 'Standard setting' in S. Breyer, *Regulation and Its Reform*, Cambridge, MA: Harvard University Press: 96–119.

Brody, E. and Cordes, J.J. (2006) 'Tax treatment of nonprofit organizations: a two-edged sword', in E.T. Boris and C.E. Steuerle (eds.) *Nonprofits and Government: Collaboration and Conflict*, Washington, DC: The Urban Institute Press: 141–180.

Bromley, D.W. (1991) *Environment and the Economy: Property Rights and Policy*, Cambridge, MA: Blackwell Publishers.

Brown, E. and Slivinski A. (2006) 'Nonprofit organizations and the market', in W.W. Powell and R. Steinberg (eds.) *The Nonprofit Sector: A Research Handbook*, New Haven, CT: Yale University Press: 140–158.

Buchanan, J.M. (1972) 'Toward analysis of closed behavioral systems', in J.M. Buchanan and R.D. Tollison (eds.) *Theory of Public Choice*, Ann Arbor, MI: The University of Michigan Press: 11–23.

Buchanan, J.M. (1977) 'Law and the invisible hand', in B.H. Siegan (ed.) *The Interaction of Economics and the Law*, Lexington, MA: Lexington Books, 127–138.

Buchanan, J.M. (1980) 'Rent seeking and profit seeking', in J.M. Buchanan, R.D. Tollison, and G. Tullock (eds.) *Toward a Theory of the Rent-Seeking Society*, College Station, TX: Texas A&M University Press: 3–15.

Buchanan, J.M. (1986) *Liberty, Market and State*. New York: New York University Press.

Buchanan, J.M. 'The economic theory of politics reborn', *Challenge* 31, 1988: 4–10.

Buchanan, J.M. (2000) 'Democratic values in taxation' (reprint) in *Debt and Taxes, The Collected Works of James M. Buchanan*, Volume 14, Indianapolis, IN: Liberty Fund: 36–45.

Buchanan, J.M., Tollison, R.D., and Tullock, G. (eds.) (1980) *Toward a Theory of the Rent-Seeking Society*, College Station, TX: Texas A&M University Press.

Busch, L. (2011) *Standards: Recipes for Reality*, Cambridge, MA: MIT Press.

Coase, R.H. 'The problem of social cost', *Journal of Law and Economics* 3, 1960: 1–44.

Coase, R.A. 'The institutional structure of production', *American Economic Review* 82, 1992: 713–719.

Coase, R.A. 'The new institutional economics', *American Economic Review* 88, 1998: 72–74.

Cohen, T. 'Nonprofit sector needs to be better understood', *Inside Philanthropy*, February 22, 2010. http://philanthropyjournal.blogspot.com/2010/02/nonprofit-sector-needs-to-be-better.html.

Cooter, R. and Ulen, T. (1988) *Law and Economics*. Glenview, IL: Scott, Foresman and Co.

Dales, J.H. (1972) 'Rights in economics', in G. Wunderlich and W.L. Gibson (eds.) *Perspectives on Property*, University Park, PA: Institute for Research on Land and Water Resources, Pennsylvania State University: 149–155.

Davidson, S. (2010) *Economists as Social Engineers*, Melbourne: Institute of Public Affairs: 1–12.

DeAlessi, M. (1998) *Fishing for Solutions*, London: Institute of Economic Affairs.

Dolfsma, W. (2013) *Government Failure: Society, Markets and Rules*, Cheltenham: Edward Elgar.

Downs, A. (1957) *An Economic Theory of Democracy*, New York: Harper & Brothers.

Economist, The 'The new age of crony capitalism', *Economist*, March 15, 2014: 13.

Ellickson, R. (1991) *Order Without Law*, Cambridge, MA: Harvard University Press.

Feldman, A.M. (1980) *Welfare Economics and Social Choice Theory*, Boston, MA: Martinus Nijhoff Publishing.

Fiorina, M.P. 'Parties and partisanship: a 40-year retrospective', *Political Behavior* 24, 2002: 93–115.

Foucart, S. 'When science is hidden behind a smokescreen', *Guardian Weekly*, June 28, 2011. www.guardian.co.uk/science/2011/jun/28/study-science-research-ignorance-foucart.

Friedman, D.D. (2000) *Law's Order*, Princeton, NJ: Princeton University Press.

Frumkin, P. (2002) *On Being Nonprofit: A Conceptual and Policy Primer*, Cambridge, MA: Harvard University Press.

Gerken, H.K. 'The real problem with citizens united: campaign finance, dark money, and shadow parties', *Marquette Law Review* 97, 2014: 101–118.

Hacker, J.S. and Pierson, P. (2010) *Winner-Take-All Politics*, New York: Simon & Schuster.

Hall, P.D. (2006) 'A historical overview of philanthropy, voluntary associations, and nonprofit organizations in the united states, 1600–2000', in W.W. Powell and R. Steinberg (eds.) *The Nonprofit Sector: A Research Handbook*, New Haven, CT: Yale University Press: 32–65.

Halper, L.A. 'Parables of exchange: foundations of public choice theory and the market formalism of James Buchanan', *Cornell Journal of Law and Public Policy* 2, 1993: 230–278.

Hansmann, H. 'The role of the nonprofit enterprise', *Yale Law Journal* 89, 1980: 835–901.

Hansman, H. (2001) 'Reform agenda for the law of nonprofit organizations', in K. Hopt and D. Reuter (eds.) *Stiftungsrecht in Europa*, Cologne: Carl Heymanns Verlag: 241–272.

Hardin, G. 'The tragedy of the commons', *Science* 162, 1968: 1243–1248.

Hayek, F.A. (1945 [1994]) 'A radio discussion: the University of Chicago Roundtable, April 22, 1945 – Discussants: Friedrich Hayek, Maynard C. Krueger, and Charles E. Merriman', in S. Kresge and L. Wenar (eds.) *Hayek on Hayek: An Autobiographical Dialogue*, London: Routledge: 108–123.

Issacharoff, S. and Karlan, P.S. 'The hydraulics of campaign finance reform', *Texas Law Review* 77, 1999: 1705–1708.

Johnson, D.B. (1991) *Public Choice: An Introduction to the New Political Economy*. Mountain View, CA: Bristlecone Books.

Kang, M.S. 'The hydraulics and politics of party regulation', *Iowa Law Review* 91, 2005: 131–187.

Kiernan, J.S. (2012) *States Most & Least Dependent on the Federal Government*. http:// wallethub.com/edu/states-most-least-dependent-on-the-federal-government/2700/# main-findings.

Kliemt, H. (2002) 'The art of the state, the state of the art', in J.M. Buchanan, G. Brennan, H. Kliemt, and R.D. Tollison (eds.) *Method and Morals in Constitutional Economics: Essays in Honor of James M. Buchanan*, New York: Springer: 98–102.

Komesar, N.K. (1994) *Imperfect Alternatives: Choosing Institutions in Law, Economics, and Public Policy*, Chicago, IL: University of Chicago Press.

Kramer, V.H. 'Antitrust today: the Baxterization of the Sherman & Clayton Acts', *Wisconsin Law Review* 1981, 1981: 1287–1302.

Krislov, S. (1997) *How Nations Choose Product Standards and Standards Change Nations*, Pittsburgh, PA: University of Pittsburgh Press.

Krueger, A.O. 'The political economy of rent seeking', *American Economic Review* 64, 1974: 291–303.

Lampland, M. and Star, S.L. (2009) 'Reckoning with standards', in M. Lampland and S.L. Star (eds.) *Standards and Their Stories: How Quantifying, Classifying, and Formalizing Practices Shape Everyday Life*, Ithaca, NY: Cornell University Press: 3–24.

Lippman, W. (1914) *Drift and Mastery*, Madison, WI: University of Wisconsin Press.

McAdams, R.H. 'An attitudinal theory of expressive law', *Oregon Law Review* 79, 2000: 339–390.

McCay, B.J. (1996) 'Common and private concerns', in S. Hanna, C. Folke, and K.G. Maler (eds.) *Rights to Nature*, Washington, DC: Island Press: 111–126.

Mercuro, N. (2005) 'A comparative institutional approach to law and economics: theory and environmental, natural resource, and land-use applications', in M. Oppenheimer and N. Mercuro (eds.) *Law and Economics: Alternative Economic Approaches to Legal and Regulatory Issues*, Armonk, NY: M.E. Sharpe, Inc.: 101–130.

Mercuro, N. (2015) 'Law, social norms, and standards: their nexus with government and their impact on the economic performance of nation states', in G.B. Ramello and T. Eisenberg (eds.) *Research Handbooks in Comparative Law*, Cheltenham: Edward Elgar.

Mercuro, N. and Medema, S.G. (2006) *Economics and the Law: From Posner to Post-Modernism and Beyond*, Princeton, NJ: Princeton University Press.

Mirowski, P. and Nik-Khan, E. 'Private intellectuals and public perplexity: the economics profession and the economic crisis', *History of Political Economy* 45 (suppl. 1) 2013: 279–311.

Mueller, D.C. (1989) *Public Choice II*, Cambridge: Cambridge University Press.

Mueller, D.C. (2003) *Public Choice III*, Cambridge: Cambridge University Press.

Ostrom, E. (2000) 'Private and common property rights', in B. Bouckaert and G. De Geest (eds.) *Encyclopedia of Law & Economics*, Cheltenham: Edward Elgar: 332–379.

Pasour, E.C. Jr. 'Rent seeking: some conceptual problems and implications', *The Review of Austrian Economics* 1, 1987: 123–143.

Posner, R.A. 'The Chicago school of antitrust analysis', *University of Pennsylvania Law Review* 127, 1979: 925–948.

Proctor, R. (2008) 'A missing term to describe the cultural production of ignorance (and its study)', in R. Proctor and L. Schiebinger (eds.) *Agnotology: The Making and Unmaking of Ignorance*, Stanford, CA: Stanford University Press: 1–33. www.indiana. edu/~kdhist/J400–2008–09-Spring-web/Agnotology-Introduction.pdf.

Rubin, P. (ed.) (2006) *The Evolution of Efficient Common Law*, Cheltenham: Edward Elgar.

Salamon, L. (1999) *America's Nonprofit Sector*, New York: The Foundation Center.

Schlager, E. and Ostrom, E. 'Property-rights regimes and natural resources: a conceptual analysis', *Land Economics* 68, 1992: 249–262.

Sherlock, M.F. and Gravelle, J.G. (2009) 'An overview of the nonprofit and charitable sector', CRS Report for Congress – Prepared for Members and Committees of Congress, November 17, 2009: 1–60.

Shughart II, W.F. (2008) 'Public choice', in *Concise Encyclopedia of Economics*, The Library of Economics and Liberty. www.econlib.org/library/Enc/PublicChoice.html.

Simmons, R. (2011) *Beyond Politics: The Roots of Government Failure*, Oakland, CA: The Independent Institute.

Smith, A. (1763) *Lectures on Justice, Police, Revenue and Arms*, Oxford: Clarendon Press (reprinted 1869).

Soroos, M.S. 'Preserving the atmosphere as a global commons', *Environment* 40, 1998: 7–13, 32–35.

Steinberg, R. (2006) 'Economic theories of nonprofit organizations', in W.W. Powell and R. Steinberg (eds.) *The Nonprofit Sector: A Research Handbook*, New Haven, CT: Yale University Press: 117–139.

Stiglitz, J. (quoted comment) in Uchitelle, L. 'Two americans are awarded nobel in economics', *New York Times*, October 13, 2009: B1.

Stone, D. (1997) *Policy Paradox: The Art of Political Decision Making*, New York: W.W. Norton.

Sunstein, C. 'On the expressive function of law', *University of Pennsylvania Law Review* 144, 1996: 2021–2053.

Tullock, G. 'The welfare costs of tarrifs, monopolies and theft', *Western Economic Journal* 5, 1967: 224–232.

Tullock, G. (1993) *Rent Seeking*, Oxford: Locke Institute.

Tullock, G. (2005a) 'The case against the common law', in F. Parisi and C.K. Rowley (eds.) *The Origins of Law and Economics: Essays by the Founding Fathers* Cheltenham: Edward Elgar: 464–474.

Tullock, G. (2005b) *Rent-Seeking Society*, in *The Selected Works of Gordon Tullock*, Volume 5, Indianapolis, IN: Liberty Fund.

Tullock, G., Seldon, A., and Brady, G.L. (2002) *Government Failure: A Primer in Public Choice*, Washington DC: Cato Institute.

US Department of Agriculture (1981) *A Review of Federal Marketing Orders for Fruits, Vegetables and Specialty Crops: Economic Efficiency and Welfare Implication*, Washington, DC: US Department of Agriculture.

Will, G. 'It's time Bush showed anger over Enron', *Jewish World News*, January 16, 2000: 3.

Xu, C., 'The fundamental institutions of China's reforms and development', *Journal of Economic Literature* XLIX, 2011: 1076–1151.

Young, D.R. (2006) 'Complementary, supplementary, or adversarial? Nonprofit–government relations', in E.T. Boris and C.E. Steuerle (eds.) *Nonprofits and Government: Collaboration and Conflict*, Washington, DC: The Urban Institute Press: 37–79.

Cases

Eyerman v. *Mercantile Trust Co.* 524 S.W. 2d 210 (1975).

9 Autonomy, welfare, and the Pareto principle

*Daniel A. Farber**

Few standards have more intuitive appeal than the Pareto principle.[1] The basic intuition is simple: If at least one person prefers a certain outcome, and no one else objects, society should favor that outcome. The Pareto principle is generally considered to be the "gold standard" for policy analysis. While much dispute exists about Kaldor–Hicks efficiency,[2] and about the relevance of distributional norms to law and economics,[3] practitioners of law and economics often take the Pareto principle as being beyond controversy. To quote Robert Cooter:

> [Economic models of law] ask whether legal resources can be reallocated so as to make at least one person better off without making anyone worse off. *Thus the economic analysis of law attempts to maximize the value of legal resources to the people who enjoy them.* For every wasteful law, a more efficient one could be substituted and the savings could be distributed among the people affected by the change so that some are made better off without making anyone worse off. Waste is, consequently, an irrationality to expunge from law and policy.
>
> (Cooter 1989: 822)

It is easy to confuse two very different arguments for the Pareto principle. One ground is that we should honor people's individual autonomy by respecting their preferences: "[a]ll participants would by definition consent to a transaction which left them better off, or as well off as before"; hence, "a moral analysis based on autonomy and consent would approve of transactions that were Pareto superior."[4] A second ground is that society should care about the welfare of its citizens and seek to promote their well-being. The Pareto principle is then simply an obvious application of utilitarianism, calling on society to adopt any policy that improves the welfare of at least one citizen while hurting no one else.

These two justifications for Pareto rest on two very different interpretations of preferences. In one interpretation, preference rankings correspond to objective welfare: one action is preferred over another if it produces an outcome with a higher level of individual welfare. Thus, preferences are defined as rankings of states of well-being. In the other conception, preferences reflect what action people would actually choose. As this distinction illustrates, the concept of preferences is more complex than it may initially appear (Kornhauser 2003a). Different definitions not only lead to different interpretations of the Pareto principle, but also connect differently with values of autonomy and welfare.

Under one view, the Pareto principle can be seen as an effort to create a kind of halfway stop between libertarianism and utilitarianism, because it gives weight to choices individuals would make but have not actually made – though only in the limited cases where these hypothetical choices do not conflict. This halfway solution turns out to be precarious. If we apply the Pareto principle based on what people would actually choose, we can end up with decisions that conflict with libertarianism, because they impose outcomes on people without actual consent. Decisions based on hypothetical consent may also conflict with utilitarianism (because they may not actually improve individual welfare).

The first part of this chapter considers the perplexities that arise in applying the concept of preferences in situations where what people would choose may not correspond with their actual welfare, where preferences change after a decision, or where there are flaws in preference formation due to limited rationality. These examples show that the Pareto principle can be based on how people would actually choose between policies only at the cost of eroding the connection of the Pareto principle with welfare. Thus, we must choose between a welfare-based and autonomy-based interpretation of the Pareto principle.

The second part of the chapter considers the relationship between the Pareto principle and social choice theory. It is here that we best see the connection between Pareto and utilitarianism. If we have enough information about preferences (however understood) to construct individual utility functions, the Pareto principle mandates that decisions maximize utility whenever there are no trade-offs between individuals. But agreeing to welfarism even in this narrow category of cases commits us to full-blown utilitarianism with only some very mild additional assumptions. To be sure, it is possible to dispute those additional assumptions, but doing so comes at a cost – for instance, we must assume that society's decisions can flip based on infinitely small changes in outcomes.

These considerations push strongly toward a utilitarian interpretation of the Pareto principle. Under a utilitarian view, the Pareto principle merely points to the most obvious situation where a decision increases social welfare. But classical utilitarianism is only contingently based on autonomy: It is based on what is good for people, not what they think is good for them or what they would choose themselves.

In short, welfarism rather than autonomy provides the most convincing account of the Pareto principle, and perhaps the only tenable account. Thus, the Pareto principle offers no halfway stop on the road to utilitarianism. The Pareto principle cannot fulfill the promise of a social choice criterion that simultaneously embodies rights-based views of autonomy and utilitarian views of welfare. For some, the "obvious" validity of the Pareto principle may seem to provide a knockdown argument for utilitarianism. But non-utilitarians need not accept the premise that decisions are necessarily morally right if they do not violate someone's preferences.

Issues relating to "preferences"

Choice versus welfare

Pareto principle is commonly rephrased in an appealing way: Society should take an action "if one person is better off, and no one else is worse off." But the principle can actually be understood in other terms, endorsing policies based on individual choices. On that reading, the Pareto principle upholds decisions if everyone in society would consent to them regardless of their reason. There is a fundamental logical distinction between welfare and consent. People often make choices that improve their well-being, but this will not always be the case. In this section we will delve more deeply into the concept of preferences to see why the autonomy-based interpretation of the Pareto principle is problematic in welfare terms. Indeed, even if we are content to define welfare as satisfying individual desires, autonomy-based interpretation of the Pareto principles raises some conundrums.

Preferences and individual welfare

Imagine a one-person society: Robinson Crusoe on his island. For him, the Pareto principle seems tautological: what Crusoe prefers, "society" (which is just another name for Crusoe himself) also prefers. But does this give us any reason to believe that what Crusoe prefers will actually increase his welfare? Is satisfying his preferences *necessarily* something we should consider a good thing for Crusoe?

Suppose a purely benevolent social planner – call her Crusoe's Mom – is hiding on the island. Is it given that Crusoe's Mom should try to arrange matters so Crusoe's preferences will be satisfied as much as possible under the circumstances? It is not at all certain that she should do so, as we will see. She might try to satisfy his preferences in order to make him feel happier or to make his life better (which might of course not be the same thing). Under some circumstances she may decide that his choices are the best indicator of what will make him better off. But the linkage between preferences and either happiness or welfare is contingent. She might well conclude that some of his choices are ill-informed or irrational in terms of his welfare.

It might seem obvious that satisfying preferences makes people happier, but this turns out to hold only in some circumstances. In reality, satisfying people's preferences might or might not make them happier (Bok 2010; Hovenkamp 1994). While most people have a preference for increased wealth, satisfying this preference may not in fact be a good way of making them happier (Bok 2010). In contrast, education "produces a greater sense of well-being than wealth equal to the education's price" (Hovenkamp 1994: 37–38). So to the extent that people focus on increasing wealth, they may not be choosing the best way to improve their future happiness.

Even if people's preferences corresponded with what makes them happy, happiness is not the same as welfare (Sen 1987: 60). The argument against equating the two, or otherwise defining well-being as a state of mind, is nicely summarized by Hausman and McPherson:

> Suppose there were an "experience machine" that could give people the highest quality experiences possible. These high-quality experiences might be intense sensations of pleasure or they might be experiences of climbing Everest or composing a symphony. Let them be whatever experiences mental-state theorists of well-being claim are ultimately and intrinsically good. The mental-state theorist would then have to say that all people would be better off permanently hooked up to a reliable experience machine rather than living their own lives and experiencing the decidedly mixed mental states that come with them. If one believes that those who are hooked up to the experience machine are missing out on some of the intrinsically good things in life ... then one cannot accept a mental-state view of well-being.
>
> (Hausman and McPherson 1996: 74–75)

The distinction between happiness and well-being is a classic issue regarding utilitarianism. Completely decisive philosophical arguments do not exist, but the argument against defining utility as a mental state seems to come close. Yet, if we reject happiness as the ultimate social goal, what do we use instead? Sen and others have argued for a richer conception of human flourishing, based on expanding human capabilities (Sen 1993: 30; Nussbaum 2001).[5] Whatever may be the merits of these or other efforts to define individual well-being objectively, we certainly cannot assume that what people want on any given occasion will actually promote their objective welfare. Thus, if we want to maintain a defense of the Pareto principle in terms of people being "better off," we must define the relevant preferences counterfactually, as the preferences people *would have had* if they understood their true welfare. If we want to understand preferences as choices, we cannot assume that the Pareto principle always serves welfare, even in the trivial case of a one-person society. Of course, it is not obvious how to define true welfare, but anyone with children knows that the child's choices do not always correspond with the child's welfare.

Preferences and social welfare

Apart from questioning the linkage between preferences and individual welfare, we might also question whether individual preferences invariably translate into some measure of societal well-being. There are three problems here: (1) some preferences may be inconsistent with the respect for individuals that underlies the autonomy-based argument for Pareto; (2) we may not be able to aggregate individual preferences over choices in a straightforward way; and (3) we may think that society's decision-making process should give people the opportunity to deliberate collectively over their preferences rather than simply taking existing preferences as given. We discuss these problems in turn.

As to the first problem, it has often been suggested that some preferences, such as those based on racism or sadism, do not deserve to be counted in making societal decisions (Hausman and McPherson 1996: 78–79). For example, Herbert Hovenkamp argues that some preferences must be considered irrelevant because they violate the premises of a constitutional democracy (Hovenkamp 1994: 63–64). The idea of laundering preferences is also endorsed by Matthew Adler, one of the leading law school advocates of welfarism (Adler 2000: 262–267).

In contrast to Hovenkamp, Lewis Kaplow and Steven Shavell argue that all preferences are equally entitled to respect, making it necessary to take preferences such as racism or sadism into account in calculating social welfare:

> [T]he moral force and appeal of welfare economics lies in promoting the actual well-being of people, not in advancing some hypothetical notion of satisfaction that is distinct from that of the individuals who are the objects of our concern. Furthermore, employing a cleansed version of preferences, rather than actual preferences may lead one to favor policies that make everyone worse off.
>
> (Kaplow and Shavell 2002: 419–420)

Thus, they say, "[t]he idea of an analyst substituting his or her own conception of what individuals should value for the actual views of the individuals themselves conflicts with individuals' basic autonomy and freedom" (Kaplow and Shavell 2002: 421–422). But this argument fails to confront a key question: Why should society give credence to individual values that themselves fail to honor the "basic autonomy and freedom" of other individuals? Thus, the harm principle seems like a plausible test for whether preferences should be respected.

One might argue on the basis of liberal tolerance that society should count all preferences equally, even intolerant ones. But this requires a very strong form of tolerance. It is one thing to argue against social intervention for the purpose of changing anti-social tastes. It is another to argue that society has a collective interest in actually advancing those tastes (at least when doing so does not harm other individuals) – for example, arguing that if people like telling racist jokes and society considers such jokes harmless, a liberal society should actively try to promote opportunities for racists to tell these jokes to each other in order to promote their happiness. (And if we assume continuity, the implication is that society should continue to promote those jokes even when they actually do some degree of harm to others.) Such an argument would not be impossible to make but seems far from the sort of self-evident validity that the Pareto principle originally seemed to promise.

Another problem with using the Pareto principle for making societal decisions also deserves mention. There are technical difficulties involved in applying the Pareto principle under conditions of uncertainty. It is quite possible that people are unanimous in their willingness to choose one policy over another, but have both varying views of the probability and value of different outcomes. Simply aggregating the preferences may be misleading (Hausman and

McPherson 1996: 88). Presumably, the solution to this problem is to apply the Pareto principle only to preferences about outcomes (or values), as opposed to preferences about decisions (see Kaplow and Shavell 2003: 358–359). The decision maker then applies her own best estimate of probabilities to determine whether a particular decision would be Pareto preferred if the participants shared his best estimate of the outcomes. But that increases the gap between the decisions that people would make themselves and those that are attributed to "society," undermining the autonomy justification for the Pareto principle.

A final difficulty in moving from individual preferences to social decisions is that we might not want to take those preferences as pre-political "givens." Communitarians believe that "communities, through their collective choices, may decide to adopt some new conception of the common good, and preferences are likely to adapt accordingly as individuals participate in this process of political reconceptualization of their community values" (Trebilcock 1993: 155–156). Going even further, some communitarians argue that private preferences are essentially irrelevant – what matters are not the preferences a person would express in market transactions, but rather the values she would express in her role as a citizen (Baron and Dunoff 1996: 440). The distinction is said to be that choices involve moral commitments and beliefs rather than merely wants and desires (Baron and Dunoff 1996: 443).

The temporal problem

In making decisions, we are concerned with two time periods – the time when the decision is made, and the later time when its effects will be felt. This opens the door to other perplexities about the Pareto principle – does the decision maker consider *ex ante* or *ex post* preferences? If we are utilitarians, we can balance welfare during the two periods in question. But if we seek an autonomy-based version of the Pareto principle, we find ourselves in real difficulties if people would have made different choices before the fact and after the fact.

If we think of preferences as being individual rankings of choices, preferences may change because people may discover that a policy they previously supported is now harming them. Alternatively, their values may change over time because their environment has changed, perhaps as a direct result of the decision in question. "That some nontrivial part of people's preferences is a product of their environment, rather than logically prior to all experience, seems so obvious that it is not worth debating" (Hovenkamp 1994: 51). Thus, some people

> may want things precisely because they cannot have them ("the grass is always greener on the other side of the fence"), while other people spurn what is beyond their reach, like the fox who judged the unobtainable grapes to be sour.
>
> (Hausman and McPherson 1996: 79)

Changing circumstances

Before the fact, the parties to a contract may think it will make them better off, but one or both of them may be wrong. As Trebilcock points out, from an *ex ante* perspective, this later regret is irrelevant, assuming the earlier decision was fully informed, rational, and voluntary. But from an *ex post* perspective, performance of the contract is no longer Pareto optimal. Trebilcock calls this the "Paretian dilemma" (Trebilcock 1993: 244). Economists strongly favor the *ex ante* perspective to select policies in the face of uncertainty (see Cooter 1989: 824; Easterbrook 1984: 19–33; Tullock 1980: 863). Others would favor the use of *ex post* preferences, at least when preferences have changed. Indeed, they say "the very point" of laws may be to "cultivate and elevate preferences" (Baron and Dunoff 1996: 455).

Although the *ex ante* perspective is not untenable, the normative case for it is far from straightforward in terms of autonomy.[6] Even where preferences have not changed, the *ex ante* perspective is not so obviously correct as some authors (Kaplow and Shavell 2003: 339) seem to believe. We will see in the second half of this chapter that a similar problem exists under the welfare-based view of Pareto: even if the *ex ante* perspective is correct for decision making under certainty, it may not be correct in cases of uncertainty.

To sharpen the issue, assume that the death penalty is a highly effective way to deter crime (a controversial assumption). For any citizen who is not actually sentenced to death, the crime control advantages outweigh the risk of being wrongfully executed in the future. John Doe, an innocent person, is now on death row. Suppose in the past he would have endorsed the death penalty, despite the inevitable possibility that innocent people would be mistakenly executed, if anyone had thought to ask him. Must we say that Doe has no reason to complain of being executed because of his past hypothetical consent to the policy?

The essential claim behind the *ex ante* perspective is that innocent defendants on death row would have accepted the gamble in advance so that it is fair to hold them to it now. But there are three possible arguments to the contrary, none of which can be dismissed out of hand. The first counter-argument is that, although these defendants *would* have consented to taking the risk of becoming victims, they did not actually give their consent. Hypothetical consent may not carry the same moral force as actual consent. To say that a person can be executed because he actually agreed to the institution of capital punishment at some earlier time is one thing; to say that he could be executed because he *would* have agreed seems much weaker. The second counter-argument is that even actual prior consent might not be enough. Perhaps the current preferences of innocent defendants should be considered; not just the preferences they had before the law was passed. The third counter-argument is that their consent lacks force because it was based on incomplete information – if they had known what the future had in store for them, they would never have consented to the law anyway.

Moreover, this example also poses the problem of identifying a unique moment in time when the *ex ante* perspective is to be applied. Doing so is easy if we assume that a policy is adopted at a single point in time, once and for all. But this is unrealistic. At any point in time, society has the option of either continuing the death penalty or replacing it with a maximum sentence of life in prison. Thus, the condemned prisoner can plausibly argue that the proper time for judging the death penalty is *now*, in which case it fails the Pareto test because it violates the prisoner's preferences for non-capital punishment.

If we are not prepared to accept the *ex ante* perspective universally or we cannot reliably pick out a single moment to use as a gauge, the Pareto principle becomes ambiguous in terms of autonomy. We might rescue the autonomy-based argument for the Pareto principle, perhaps, by applying it only when no one would object to an outcome at *any* point in time. But that seems to shrink the domain of the Pareto principle to the vanishing point. This by itself is not a fatal objection to the autonomy-based understanding of Pareto, but it is a significant complication.

Changing values and tastes

In the examples we have considered, individuals's basic values and tastes have remained unchanged; it is only the circumstances that have changed. Deeper problems are introduced when the transaction actually causes changes in values and tastes, making it difficult to determine which are the person's "true" values. When a person's goals have changed substantially, it is not at all clear that his or her earlier goals should be privileged over later ones. As Kronman says:

> From the standpoint of his present values, which he cannot shake off or suspend, his past actions may seem pointless or evil; in this respect, he is likely to regard his earlier decisions as a foreign element whose continuing influence appears senseless from the standpoint of his present goals.
>
> (Kronman 1983: 782)

Kaplow and Shavell argue that we should accept the *ex post* preferences in applying the Pareto principle. Thus,

> if it is discovered that individuals are able to adapt to certain physical disabilities more or less readily than is commonly supposed, the valuations employed in measuring tort damages or in performing cost–benefit analysis (for example, of highway safety improvements) should reflect actual harm rather than the victim's uninformed *ex ante* estimates.
>
> (Kaplow and Shavell 2002: 20)

The *ex post* stance is clearly welfare-based rather than autonomy-based. For instance, a woman might voluntarily enter into a surrogacy contract, and doing so might be a rational choice based on her current preferences. The autonomy-based approach to Pareto would presumably validate her choice. But after giving birth, she might find herself with a much different attitude toward giving up the child. This could conceivably be a completely unexpected change in attitude. She might even feel that, having gone through the birth experience, she is now a different person than she was when she entered into the contract. In any event, she may view enforcement of the rule as decreasing her welfare and perhaps the child's. A rule enforcing the surrogacy contract is Pareto optimal based on her *ex ante* preferences but not on the basis of her *ex post* preferences.

Policy-induced changes in values and tastes

A particular problem arises when the very existence of legal rules affects preferences (Sunstein 1986: 1129). Then, the policymaker must decide beforehand which set of preferences to favor, a decision that obviously cannot be made by looking at the preferences themselves (Hausman and McPherson 1996: 76–77). Instead, some objective gauge to welfare is needed, as opposed to the choices that individuals would make.

For instance, cognitive psychologists have established a recurring pattern in human behavior: people will demand more to sell something than they would be willing to pay to buy it. For example, in one experiment students who were randomly given a candy bar instead of a coffee mug were unwilling to trade for the mug, but those randomly receiving the mug were equally unwilling to trade for the candy bar. This "endowment" effect is strongest when people feel some moral entitlement to what they possess, even if the grounds for such a feeling are shaky (Kahman *et al.* 2000).

In this situation, the autonomy-based Pareto standard is indeterminate. If people happen to have coffee mugs initially, they universally prefer the mugs to the candy bars. Hence, it appears that possessing mugs is Pareto superior to possessing candy bars. If they happen to start off with candy bars, however, we find the opposite results. In particular, if we are in the position of assigning legal entitlements to mugs versus candy bars, we cannot apply the Pareto principle because the preferences depend on how we assign the entitlements.

Again, this is less of a difficulty if we adopt the paternalistic, welfare-based argument for Pareto rather than an autonomy-based one. From the paternalistic view, we need merely to decide which situation makes people happier or better off – how they rank alternatives themselves or which they would choose has no relevance except as evidence of what is really good for them.

Another instance of shifting preferences arises when adoption of a legal rule causes a conceptual shift in how people regard the relevant transaction. One concern is that legalizing certain market transactions will have harmful effects on how people view themselves and each other. The Pareto principle is strongly linked with the idea of market transactions. Assuming fully informed, rational, and voluntary decisions, an exchange must be a Pareto improvement – no one would agree to such an exchange unless it satisfied their preferences at least as well as the status quo. But society has always had doubts about certain exchanges, such as the sale of sexual services and human body organs. One objection is that we should not transform sexual activities, children, or body parts into commodities. Instead, we should view these things as integral to our definition of our selves, and thus incapable of being property (Radin 1987). A specific fear is that "permitting transactions such as these, along with the market rhetoric and manifestations that accompany them, may change and pervert the terms of discourse in which members of the community engage with one another" (Trebilcock 1993: 26). For example, "[o]ne concern with respect to legal sanctioning of *inter vivos* organ sales is that people will begin to view their organs entirely as commodities" (Trebilcock 1993: 35) Similarly, critics of surrogacy contracts fear that such contracts will reinforce oppressive gender roles (Trebilcock 1993: 50).

Of course, rather than being worried that a new legal rule will change preferences, we might welcome this result if we disfavor current preferences. One long-standing concern about basing social policy on existing preferences is that those preferences may be warped by oppressive institutions (Sen 1987: 48). For instance, women may adjust to sexist expectations and develop preferences for limited career options and dependence on men (Hausman and McPherson 1996: 79). But for these women, "liberties, high wages, and protection from domestic violence may make them better off than giving them what they prefer" (Hausman and McPherson 1996: 79). If the legal rules are changed, they will learn to value their new freedoms and benefits.

Cognitive limitations

Even if actual preferences are left unaffected by time or rule change, they may not provide a useful standard for societal decisions. It is no news, except perhaps to the most formalist economic theorists, that

> [p]eople's preferences are sometimes irrational in the sense that they are not mathematically consistent with other preferences or perhaps in the weaker sense that they simply do not seem intelligent in the light of the information that people have at the time they make a choice.
>
> (Hovenkamp 1994: 46)

Cognitive psychologists have documented an array of errors that human beings are prone to.[7] These errors make it harder to connect the proposition "individuals prefer *A* to *B*" to the proposition "society should choose *A* over *B*."

Thanks to the efforts of cognitive psychologists and behavioral economists, we now know a good deal about human intellectual limitations. For example, we know that humans make systematic errors in estimating risks. They tend to be overly optimistic, thinking they are less subject to risks than the average person. On the other hand, they overestimate risks based on the amount of attention given to the risks by the media. When an event has happened, they also overestimate the probability of its occurrence. Thus, people's decisions under uncertainty may reflect misperceptions of probabilities rather than true preferences about outcomes.

Preferences may also be less than rational for other reasons. When faced with complex tasks, people take shortcuts. For example, rather than trying to find the optimal outcome, they "satisfice" by settling for the first acceptable option rather than continue to search (Korobkin and Ulen 2000: 1078). Even when given correct probability information, people misprocess the information, ignoring information about base rates and focusing instead on the representativeness of an outcome (Korobkin and Ulen 2000: 1086–1090).

These deviations from the rational actor model clearly make practical application of the Pareto principle more difficult. We can no longer take completely for granted that voluntary, fully informed exchanges meet the Pareto principle. What is less clear is whether irrationality causes any normative difficulties for the Paretian. The effect of these cognitive difficulties is to take the analyst farther away from what people actually prefer regarding certain choices, and toward what people would prefer if their thinking met the economist's conception of rationality. Whether this is normatively troublesome depends on our degree of toleration for paternalism. In any event, we are once again pushed away from autonomy and preferences toward paternalism and objective welfare as the basis for applying and justifying the Pareto principle.

Preferences and bounded rationality

Reliance on preferences can also be problematic when people have incomplete or incoherent preferences, even at a single point in time. This leaves the Pareto principle incoherent to the extent we are really serious in phrasing it in terms of "preferences." To the extent that "preference" is really just shorthand for "what people would really prefer if they knew what was truly good for them," we can continue to endorse the Pareto principle, though only as a minimalist form of utilitarianism.

We can begin by considering situations in which people have seemingly inconsistent preferences. For example, they frequently use different discount rates for different time periods, resulting in preference reversals due to the mere passage of time (Korobkin and Ulen 2000: 1120). This leads to a situation in which it is rational to make a plan, which it will then be rational to abandon despite the absence of any change in preferences or circumstances. Similarly, people often demand more for accepting a delay than they would be willing to pay to accelerate the same event (Korobkin and Ulen 2000: 1122). Such situations, as well as those involving inadequate "will power," can be described by ascribing different "selves" to the same person at different moments in time – in effect, the self who decides on a diet is a different person than the self who later sneaks a candy bar. This is not problematic if our goal is welfare, but is a real problem if our goal is autonomy.

Other inconsistencies seem to show that preferences in some sense do not exist until people have reason to construct them, and that the results of the construction depend on the context. For example, the choices people make in pricing risky alternatives are not always consistent with their rankings of the outcomes

(Thaler 1992: 79–91). The general conclusion is that preferences are constructed based on the choices people are actually asked to make, rather than functioning as pre-existing tendencies regarding alternatives:

> The discussion of the meaning of preference and the status of value may be illuminated by the well-known exchange among three baseball umpires. "I call them as I see them," said the first. "I call them as they are," claimed the second. The third disagreed, "They ain't nothing till I call them." Analogously, we can describe three different views regarding the nature of values. First, values exist – like body temperature – and people perceive and report them as best they can, possibly with bias (I call them as I see them). Second, people know their values and preferences directly – as they know the multiplication table (I call them as they are). Third, values or preferences are commonly constructed in the process of elicitation (They ain't nothing till I call them). The research [on preference reversal] ... is most compatible with the third view of preference as a constructive, context-dependent process.
>
> (Thaller 1992: 90–91)

A somewhat similar problem of preference construction may exist when the choice is between sharply disparate values, such as money versus human life, or career versus family. Economists assume that preferences always exist between any two outcomes, so that a person can readily make a choice. But a number of philosophers insist on the incommensurability of values and our inability to give them all a common metric (Baron and Dunoff 1996: 486). To the extent that individuals share that view, it may not be possible to incorporate the full range of considerations they consider relevant into a simple preference ordering (Kornhauser 2003a).

If we support the Pareto principle because we truly care about fulfilling people's preferences, these findings present a real problem: people may not have any ascertainable preferences unless they are actually faced with a choice. If, instead, we are using Pareto as a stand-in for utilitarianism, we face some very difficult measurement problems. Essentially, in the instances where people find themselves stymied in making decisions for their own lives because of the difficulty of comparing radically different values, we must be prepared to make the comparison for them if we are to apply something like the Pareto principle.

We must also be willing to decide the "correct" way to frame specific choices, because what people prefer is often a function of framing. For example, people see a penalty for using credit cards differently from a bonus for using cash and respond differently to these two (McCaffery *et al.* 2000: 262). Yet, the economic substance of the two is identical. Framing can lead to inconsistent attitudes toward risk aversion, and can be affected by fairly small changes in presentation (Korobkin and Ulen 2000: 1104–1107).

A similar problem is presented by menu effects. If preferences are well behaved, whether A is preferred to B should not depend on how either one compares with C. Yet in many situations, individual choice turns out to be context dependent. For example, juries presented with certain facts might choose a verdict of murder over a verdict of voluntary manslaughter if those are the only two choices. But if they are also offered the choice of negligent homicide, they switch to finding voluntary manslaughter. This is exactly like always choosing chocolate over vanilla, except when strawberry is also on the menu, when you choose vanilla over chocolate (Kelman *et al.* 2000).

How are we to specify the "correct" setting for a decision, the one that will reveal what people "really" prefer? It is difficult to see any alternative except picking the frame that is most likely to lead people to the right choice, the choice that really furthers their welfare or happiness. So the framing problem reinforces our growing suspicion that the Pareto principle is really just a minimalist form of old-fashioned utilitarianism.

Preferences, autonomy, and social choice

The Pareto principle versus autonomy

Whichever interpretation of the Pareto principle we adopt, it is easy to see that it precludes giving weight to anything other than preferences even when the individuals involved are indifferent to a decision. Suppose, for example, that we believe that animals have rights but that those rights are highly subordinate to human welfare. Thus, animal rights become significant in making decisions as tiebreakers, when human welfare is unaffected. For example, one might consider the impact of a decision on animal rights when the affected humans have no preferences about the outcome one way or the other. This seems like a very modest and reasonable position, even for someone who does not put much stock in the idea of animal rights.

And yet, this position is incompatible with the Pareto principle, at least if we assume that the social choice function is continuous. Consider two outcomes, A and B, and assume that all the affected humans are indifferent between them (assign them the same utilities). Then society chooses outcome A. Now suppose instead that one individual has a minute preference for outcome B. If the social choice function is continuous, then this tiny preference shift should not change the result. So society still picks outcome A. But this violates the Pareto principle, for every affected person is either indifferent or prefers outcome B. Precisely the same argument applies to environmental values such as the preservation of endangered species,[8] or to the preservation of great works of art. Thus, the Pareto principles means that if everyone else is indifferent and one person has a faint distaste for Rembrandt, it is better for society to destroy all of the Rembrandts in the world. This is far from being an intuitively compelling conclusion. One might reasonably think that the world would be poorer if the last redwood or the last Rembrandt were destroyed, even if everyone alive were too insensitive to care. Perhaps it should not be too much of a surprise that the Pareto principle clashes with efforts to import non-individual-based values, even as a tiebreaker, given that such values conflict with both the autonomy and welfare-based grounds for adopting the Pareto principle.

It is more jarring to learn that the Pareto principle conflicts with individual autonomy. Much of the appeal of the Pareto principle rests on its apparent alignment with individual autonomy, although we have seen in the previous section that this linkage is problematic in other ways. It is disturbing to learn that there is a logical conflict between Pareto and autonomy. Amartya Sen proved that the following three conditions cannot be simultaneously satisfied by any method of selecting social policies:

1   *Universal applicability.* The method must be applicable to any possible array of individual preferences.
2   *Pareto.* The method respects the Pareto principle.
3   *Individual autonomy.* Each individual gets the final say about the choice between at least one set of alternatives (for example, whether that individual reads or does not read a specific book, everything else in the world being held constant).

Thus, Sen observed, the Pareto principle seems logically inconsistent with a minimal conception of liberalism in which individuals have the final say over even a single decision affecting themselves alone (Sen 1982b). A common response is to point out that the parties could bargain their way to a Pareto improvement, though of course this may not always be true, and even then enforcing the bargain might involve other rights violations (Katz 2006: 661–664).

Sen provided a seemingly contrived example of this paradox, in which two friends must decide whether one of them will read *Lady Chatterly's Lover*. Because of the nature of the example, it is not difficult to dismiss the paradox as a very clever but practically insignificant hypothetical (Sen 1982a: 288). Still, as Sen says, the logical implications are disturbing:

> [I]t turns out that a principle reflecting liberal values even in a very mild form cannot possibly be combined with the weak Pareto principle, given an unrestricted domain. If we do believe in these other conditions, then the society cannot permit even minimal liberalism. Society cannot then let more than one individual be free to read what they like, sleep they way they prefer, dress as they care to, etc., *irrespective* of the preferences of others in the community.
>
> (Sen 1982a: 290)

Sen concludes from such considerations that Pareto is "unacceptable as a universal rule" (Sen 1982b: 313).

This is one of a number of problems that arise if we do not distinguish between preferences relating to an individual's own interests and those relating to the interests of others (Kornhauser 2003b). If we do include those preferences in applying the Pareto principle, we drive a wedge between preference satisfaction and individual welfare. On the other hand, if we exclude them, we are then separating preference satisfaction from the actual decisions that people would make, undermining the autonomy basis for the Pareto principle.

Quite apart from Sen's technical result or the difficulty of interpreting "preferences" as equating with choices, the connection between the Pareto principle and the idea of personal autonomy is questionable. The Pareto principle does not merely mean that people are entitled to make choices. It also says that it is perfectly legitimate for society to make choices for them, if society believes that the affected individuals will like the results and no one else will be harmed. In this sense, the ultimate grounding of the Pareto principle is not autonomy but paternalism.

As a practical matter, the best paternalistic strategy may be to let people make their own decisions because they have better incentives or information about their own preferences. But this is a purely contingent result; there is nothing inherent in the welfare-based version of the Pareto principle to exclude the possibility that no individual would ever be allowed to make a decision about his own life because some supercomputer is better able to decide how to maximize their preferences. It is not surprising, therefore, that Sen was actually able to prove a logical inconsistency between Pareto and libertarianism. It is also unsurprising that libertarians are suspicious of the entire enterprise of welfare economics (Volokh 2011), of which the Pareto principle is a building block.

From Pareto to welfarism, and from welfarism to utilitarianism

Professors Kaplow and Shavell extend Sen's result to argue that Pareto is inconsistent with any nonwelfarist moral values such as fairness. They contend that:

> individuals will be made worse off overall whenever consideration of fairness leads to the choice of a regime different from that which would be adopted under welfare economics because, by definition, the two approaches conflict when a regime with greater overall well-being is rejected on grounds of fairness.
>
> (Kaplow and Shavell 2002: 52)

Intuitively, this result is related to the point made earlier: If a non-preference factor is even used as a tiebreaker, we must choose between violating the Pareto principle or introducing discontinuities into social choice.

In particular, when people are symmetrically situated *ex ante* – for example, equally likely to cause accidents or be accident victims – Kaplow and Shavell say that in this situation it is "*always* the case that everyone will be worse off when a notion of fairness leads to the choice of a different legal rule from that chosen under welfare economics" (Kaplow and Shavell 2002: 52). Their explanation is simply that:

> Because everyone is identically situated, whenever welfare economics leads to the choice of one rule over another, it must be that everyone is better off

under the preferred rule. Hence, whenever a notion of fairness leads one to choose a different rule from that favored under welfare economics, everyone is necessarily worse off as a result.

(Kaplow and Shavell 2002: 52)

By now, it should be clear how this argument glosses over difficulties about the relationship between welfare and preferences, and about the timing of policy evaluation (*ex ante* or *ex post*). It also brushes past the issue of autonomy – it may be that everyone will be better off but that they misguidedly would refuse to consent, so that imposing the rule makes them "worse off" in the sense of depriving them of liberty or of welfare as they themselves perceive it. It is little wonder, therefore, that the argument about symmetrical situations has failed to satisfy critics.

In an earlier work, however, Kaplow and Shavell make a more convincing argument that the Pareto standard necessarily implies welfarism (Kaplow and Shavell 2001). Given some additional but fairly modest assumptions about continuity and about the form of utility functions, they prove that the Pareto principle implies that social decisions can be made only by combining individual utility functions, eliminating any independent weight for concepts such as fairness or justice apart from their role in selecting a social welfare function.[9] For instance, Kantian theories of morality are ruled out by the Pareto principle (Kaplow and Shavell 2001).

Thus, modest and intuitively appealing as it may be, the Pareto principle potentially has far-reaching logical consequences.[10] If we give weight to any moral value that is independent of individual preferences, we must sometimes be willing to allow that value to trump all individual preferences, at least at the margin. But the Pareto principle combined with continuity rules out any decision that overrides individual preferences in this way, even to a small extent.[11] Admittedly, we could choose to dispense with continuity, but that essentially means that individuals can veto some decisions even when suffering only infinitesimal harm.

Shavell and Kaplow's argument does much to bridge the gap between the Pareto principle and welfare. A further argument does the same for the gap between welfarism and classical utilitarianism. Welfarism assumes that societal welfare is a function of individual utilities. But unless the function is utilitarian (gives equal weight to all utilities rather than favoring or disfavoring utility equality), serious problems arise in applying the Pareto standard in cases of uncertainty. In applying welfarism, we have a choice between maximizing the social welfare function as applied to the expected value of individual utilities in the future (an *ex ante* approach) or else calculating the social welfare function depending on how the future unfolds and then taking the expected value (*ex post*). If we use a non-utilitarian welfare function, the two results will differ, as a consequence of a mathematical rule about the expected values of non-linear functions. But this difference entangles us in difficulties, including potential tensions with the Pareto principle (Adler and Sanchirico 2006: 333–334).

There is a strong reason to adopt the *ex post* version of welfarism, using the expected value of social welfare as the decision standard. Failure to use the *ex post* version creates temporal inconsistencies unless we use a utilitarian welfare function. The alternative is to figure out the expected utility of a decision for each individual and then apply the social welfare function. Using the latter approach, we can find ourselves choosing a decision even though social welfare is expected to be lower after the decision than it would be with a different choice. Thus, adopting *ex ante* welfarism can lead to time inconsistencies. However, using *ex post* welfarism creates another problem, because it turns out that *ex post* welfarism is inconsistent with the *ex ante* Pareto principle (Adler and Sanchirico 2006: 333–334). Thus, it is possible that people unanimously would prefer one choice *ex ante* but that the policymaker would choose a different one based on the *ex post* use of the social welfare function even though preferences have not changed.

We might try to escape this dilemma by modifying the Pareto principle to apply only *ex post* as well. An *ex post* Pareto principle requires that if one choice leaves everyone better off (or alternatively, at least as well off) in every possible future state of the world, it will be favored by the decision maker.[12] If one choice is better than another in every state of the world, it can be said to be statewise dominant, so the *ex* post Pareto principle is equivalent to a principle favoring statewise dominant choices. If a policy is statewise dominant, its selection will also be endorsed by the *ex ante* Pareto principle, so the two are equivalent in the special situation of statewise dominance. But Policy A could be *ex ante* Pareto superior to Policy B without being statewise dominant. In that case, it is possible that *ex post* Pareto would reject the policy because, while it increases everyone's expected payoff, at least some realizations of the policy increase inequality enough to result in a lower expected value of the social welfare function.

This is not a logically impossible position, but it is an uncomfortable one. Consider Kaplow and Shavell's symmetrical situation, where a legal rule affects everyone identically *ex ante* because no one knows who will benefit or lose from the rule. (Note that this problem is distinct from the situation where preferences change, where Kaplow and Shavell would have the decision maker evaluate the policy based on *ex ante* expected welfare, but use *ex post* preferences in making that evaluation.) Kaplow and Shavell view it as obvious that in this situation society should adopt the rule if it increases expected utility because everyone in the population would, by their own lights, benefit from this rule. For instance, suppose everyone currently is at utility level 500. A proposed rule would have a 50 percent probability of moving any particular individual to a utility of 250, and a 50 percent chance of moving that individual to 752. That rule is *ex ante* Pareto superior to the status quo – every individual has an expected utility gain of one unit. Under the Kaplow and Shavell approach, we should adopt the rule. But a decision maker applying *ex post* welfarism might well reject it if the social welfare function is egalitarian, because the slight increase in average welfare is offset by a large increase in inequality. So we cannot have both *ex post* welfarism and *ex ante* Pareto.

Thus, we seem to be left with an unpleasant choice if we use a non-utilitarian social welfare function. We can adopt *ex ante* welfarism, accepting that we will possibly find ourselves adopting policies even if they are expected on average to result in a lower social welfare than alternatives. Or we can restrict ourselves to the much narrower *ex post* Pareto principle, meaning that we may sometimes find ourselves adopting policies that would be unanimously rejected by the individual members of the population *ex ante*. The only escape from this dilemma is to use a utilitarian social welfare function, which collapses the distinction between *ex post* and *ex ante* social welfare. Only by committing to a utilitarian social welfare function can we save *ex ante* Pareto without encountering time inconsistencies from *ex ante* welfarism.

Putting the results together, we see that the Pareto principle together with continuity implies welfarism, and welfarism together with time consistency and *ex ante* Pareto implies utilitarianism. Because of the need to imply additional assumptions, it would be an oversimplification to say that the Pareto principle mandates utilitarianism. But it does seem clear that the Pareto principle is tightly linked with the quasi-utilitarian approach of welfarism, and only a bit less tightly connected with utilitarianism itself.

This should not come as a great surprise in light of the earlier discussion. We have seen that if preferences are interpreted in nonwelfarist terms as simply standing for the choices that people would make between alternatives, the argument for the Pareto principle is not very strong. It would too often require giving effect to choices that are irrational, decrease their welfare, or conflict with the equally valid preferences between choices that people will have after the fact. To be blunt, the principle of giving people whatever they desire seems more appropriate for a candy store owner than a social planner.

If, however, we interpret the Pareto principle in terms of objective welfare, the argument for Pareto is much stronger. The arguments made in this section simply add weight to the argument that the Pareto principle is best understood as just an especially simple example of the utilitarian principle that society should always favor the outcome that increases total utility.[13]

Is the Pareto principle a knock-down argument for utilitarianism?

Kaplow and Shavell argue that the Pareto principle is inconsistent with giving independent weight to liberty, equality, or other moral values, which they use as an argument for rejecting these other values (except to the extent they might enter into choosing a social welfare function). But the argument can easily be reversed into a critique of the Pareto principle (Hocket 2009; Katz 2006). One principle is that a situation is always better if everyone prefers it. Another principle is that a situation is always worse if it violates human rights. If it turns out to be impossible to give universal effect to both principles, which should prevail? It is by no means clear which principle should be rejected, or whether we should perhaps be willing to tolerate small violations of each one in cases where they conflict, which might lead to some kind of threshold-based decision rules (Zamir and Medina

2008: 325). We may be loathe to give up on the Pareto principle, but that could be needed to maintain some even more important ethical principle.

As a matter of common sense, there seem to be a number of obvious attributes that any system for making social decisions should have. One of them is the Pareto principle. Another is that choices should be transitive: If society prefers *A* to *B* and *B* to *C*, then it should also prefer *A* to *C*. Still another is that a decision should not be affected by information about irrelevant alternatives: Eliminating the least favored alternative from the list of possibilities should not affect the ultimate choice between the other, more favored alternatives. (If someone prefers chocolate to vanilla ice cream, they should do so regardless of whether strawberry is also on the menu.) Alas, Arrow's Theorem is only one of a host of proofs that no mechanism of social choice can satisfy some very appealing set of characteristics.[14] Thus, in designing a mechanism for assessing societal decisions, we must sacrifice some desirable aspect of decision making or another. The only question is which one to sacrifice. There is no apparent reason why the Pareto principle should be immune.

If we think of the problem in terms of mechanisms for social choice (rather than as methods for policy assessment), we may not want the mechanisms to produce Pareto superior policies whenever such policies exist. Instead, we might want to block some Pareto improvements. For example, majority-voting systems are potentially subject to chaotic cycling, which could make the legal regime dangerously unstable. In order to attain stability, it may be useful to introduce some friction into the system, so that laws can only be passed if they make fairly large changes that possess wide popular support. But this friction may block changes that would help some small group of people without harming anyone else, or even changes that everyone would unanimously prefer (but only by a little bit) over the status quo. Such a sacrifice of the Pareto principle may be worthwhile in systemic terms.

Similarly, we might sacrifice the Pareto principle to reduce transaction costs. Eliminating waste sounds like a good idea, but like all good ideas, it may have diminishing returns. It may simply not be worth the trouble of searching out every possible Pareto improvement; we might do better to settle for an outcome that seems reasonably close to Pareto optimality. We might also bend the Pareto principle to ensure that outcomes have other desirable qualities. For example, in designing mechanisms for dividing goods among individuals, it may be impossible to find one where the results are guaranteed to be Pareto efficient and also leave each individual equally satisfied (Brams and Taylor 1996: 236).[15] We might choose to favor equity over efficiency.

Thus, in at least some circumstances, we might be willing to allow modest incursions on the Pareto principle, thereby tolerating a certain amount of economic inefficiency, because we would like the decision-making process to have other desirable attributes. An ideal system for making decisions would incorporate all of the features we desire, but unfortunately no such system is possible. The Pareto principle does not seem uniquely entitled to a sacrosanct status if such tradeoffs must be made.

In addition to these considerations, we may not want to respect the Pareto principle if we adhere to some non-utilitarian moral principle. As Sen showed, if we truly believe in individual autonomy, we may not be able to uphold the Pareto principle in all circumstances. Similarly, the upshot of Kaplow and Shavell's argument is that if we truly believe in human rights or other non-welfarist principles of justice, we may have to sacrifice the Pareto principle on occasion.

There is no reason why adherents to nonwelfarist ethical principles should be embarrassed by the need to violate the Pareto principle on occasion. Recall Cooter's characterization of the Pareto principle as essentially meaning that society should not waste resources (Cooter 1989: 822). But if we do believe in human rights or some similar moral principle, surely it is worth supporting that principle even if it unfortunately commits us to having to waste resources under some circumstances. A moral principle that is not strong enough to justify such a sacrifice is not much of a moral principle.

Conclusion

Perhaps the most important conclusion of this chapter is that the Pareto principle has no deep connection with individual autonomy or freedom. In terms of autonomy, Sen's paradox is not just a clever parlor trick, but the symptom of a profound gap between the Pareto principle and libertarianism. The libertarian believes that people should get what they choose for themselves; the Paretian believes that people should get what they *would* have chosen – under the most plausible interpretation, this means what they should have chosen to advance their own welfare rather than what they would actually have chosen.

The link that Kaplow and Shavell make between welfarism and Pareto further confirms that Pareto really rests on a utilitarian foundation, not a libertarian one.[16] The Paretian limits herself to the easiest cases for applying utilitarianism, those where the only utility changes are positive. But it turns out that once the utilitarian camel gets its nose in the tent this way, the rest is almost sure to follow. As we have seen, it takes only the addition of a few plausible assumptions to change the Paretian into a welfarist and then into a utilitarian.

As with utilitarianism more generally, the Pareto principle may in many circumstances be consistent with other moral principles – people probably do enjoy better welfare most of the time if society respects individual rights. But the relationship is contingent on circumstances. Thus, those who would give priority to individual rights and autonomy must be prepared to reject the Pareto principle – in other words, under at least some circumstances they must be prepared to reject outcomes even though no one in the relevant group would do so.

Much of the argument in this chapter can be encapsulated in the familiar example of the voluntary agreement to become a slave. Suppose that one person wants to become a slave of another, and the other agrees. Under the autonomy-based version of the Pareto principle, we have to uphold this agreement because it is the outcome both parties preferred. But this is not a very attractive position since it is easy to think of reasons why the agreement may not have been rational. A stronger case could be made for enforcement if we assume that the bargain increases the welfare of both parties. For this reason, the welfare-based interpretation of the Pareto principle is more attractive than the autonomy-based version. But under the welfare-based interpretation, the Paretian might even uphold slavery without the initial consent of the slave, if slavery would actually increase the slave's welfare (as in the situation where the other choice for a captured enemy was death). Thus, there is no guarantee that the welfare-based version of Pareto principle will respect autonomy – the slave may not have chosen slavery at any point in time.

We can also see from this example why the Pareto principle does not provide a knockdown argument against non-utilitarian moral principles. Suppose that the utility of the slave is higher than it would otherwise be, so that slavery satisfies the welfarist version of the Pareto principle. If we embrace the principle that the individual's right to autonomy can never be destroyed, then we are committed to rejecting slavery even though, from the perspective of their own values, both the slave owner and the slave are better off. But this is only to say that if we view freedom as inalienable, we must reject voluntarily assumed slavery even if the slave was fully informed, suffering from no cognitive deficiencies, etc. We might differ about whether it makes sense to view some rights as inalienable, but the fact that this stance involves violation of the Pareto principle is hardly a surprise. There is no reason for those who believe autonomy is inalienable to view Kaplow and Shavell's theorem as a further argument against their position, since those who embrace inalienable rights are indeed willing to sacrifice the preferences of both parties for a higher moral principle.

Thus, it is a mistake to view the Pareto principle as a non-controversial foundational principle for law and economics (or for welfare economics more generally). It is very closely tied to welfarism, and for that reason it may not be acceptable as a universal standard to nonwelfarists.

Still, for most of the problems that confront scholars in practice, the Pareto principle may remain very attractive. Although it is logically bound up in welfarism, it requires less information about preferences than full-blown welfarism. Thus, it can serve as a kind of rough-and-ready version of utilitarianism. And while other moral theories may be inconsistent with utilitarianism in some situations, many issues for economic analysis will not involve those situations. In addition, in many – though not all – situations, the welfare-based Pareto principle will lead to the same situation as the autonomy-based Pareto principle, so both welfare and autonomy are served. And finally, many situations do not involve anything that can plausibly be considered an inalienable right.

Thus, although it is not always an uncontroversial ethical standard, the Pareto principle can be used without fear of serious ethical dissension when certain requirements are met. Essentially, these are circumstances where the autonomy-based Pareto standard and the welfare-based standard coincide; impacts on wealth distribution are not large and preferences are stable (so the *ex ante* version of Pareto is acceptable), and no nonwelfarist value seems to be seriously in play. These conditions are satisfied, for instance, in much of business law.

Under those circumstances, the Pareto principle works perfectly well. Thus, the Pareto principle is likely to remain a useful tool. But we should not imagine that Professor Pareto showed us the way to normative bedrock, still less that his work provides an ironclad argument for utilitarianism.

Notes

* Sho Sato Professor of Law, University of California, Berkeley School of Law.
1 For definitions of the various Pareto standards, see (Bix 1999: 181).
2 This concept is defined in (Trebilcock 1993: 7).
3 See (Trebilcock 1993: 833–834) on redistribution.
4 As Bix points out, theorists such as Kant actually have a much narrower concept of autonomy than economists (Bix 1999: 181 n.13).
5 For a critique of Nussbaum's views, see (Lewis 2001).
6 For more extensive discussion of this point, see (Farber 2000).
7 A good survey can be found in (Korobkin and Ulen 2000).
8 See (Farber 1986: 346 n. 22) (arguing that the Pareto principle should be softened when individual preferences are only slightly in favor of the outcome which harms the environment).
9 Note, however, that additional assumptions are needed to derive the existence of a single social welfare function applicable to all combinations of possible utility profiles (Fleurbaey *et al.* 2003).
10 The assumption of continuity is clearly doing much of the work here. It essentially excludes the possibility of any bright-line moral rules.
11 This is not likely to faze anyone who does believe in an independent moral value, since such a person is presumably willing to favor implementing that value even if the cost is a small violation of the preferences of the people involved.
12 A weaker version would be to require that at least one person can be identified who is better off in each state of the world while no one else is ever worse off.
13 This formulation assumes that the population is fixed – otherwise, we must choose between total utility and some other measure like average utility.
14 For discussion of Arrow's Theorem and its implications for law, see (Farber and Frickey 1991: 38–40; Huang 2013: 154–156). Summaries of the leading impossibility results can be found in (Pattaanaik 1997; Huang 2013).
15 See (Brams and Taylor 1996: 236).
16 For this reason, Kaplow and Shavell's conclusions should be no surprise. If only welfarism can accommodate the Pareto principle, that is because the Pareto principle itself is welfarist to the core.

References

Adler, M.D., and Sanchirico, C.W. 'Inequality and uncertainty: theory and legal applications', *University of Pennsylvania Law Review* 155, 2006: 279–377.

Adler, M.D. 'Beyond efficiency and procedure: a welfarist theory of regulation', *Florida State University Law Review* 28, 2000: 241–338.

Baron, J.B. and Dunoff, J.L. 'Against market rationality: moral critiques of economic analysis in legal theory', *Cardozo Law Review* 17, 1996: 431–496.

Bix, B. (1999) *Jurisprudence: Theory and Context*, 2nd edition, Durham, NC: Carolina Academic Press.

Bok, D. (2010) *The Politics of Happiness: What Government Can Learn from the New Research on Well-Being*, Princeton, NJ: Princeton University Press.

Brams, S.J. and Taylor, A.D. (1996) *Fair Division: From Cake-Cutting to Dispute Resolution*, Cambridge: Cambridge University Press.

Cooter, R.D. 'The best right laws: value foundations of the economic analysis of law', *Notre Dame Law Review* 64, 1989: 817–837.

Easterbrook, F.H. 'The Supreme Court 1983 Term. Foreword: the court and the economic system', *Harvard Law Review* 98, 1984: 4–60.

Farber, D.A. 'From plastic trees to Arrow's theorem', *University of Illinois Law Review* 1986, 1986: 337–360.

Farber, D.A. (2000) 'Economic efficiency and the *ex ante* perspective', in S.J. Kraus and S.D. Walt (eds.) *The Jurisprudential Foundations of Corporate and Commercial Law*, Cambridge: Cambridge University Press.

Farber, D.A. and Frickey, P.P. (1991) *Law and Public Choice: A Critical Introduction*, Chicago, IL: University of Chicago Press.

Fleurbaey, M., Tungodden, B., and Chang, H.F. 'Any non-welfarist method of policy assessment violates the Pareto principle: a comment', *Journal of Political Economy* 111, 2003: 1382–1385.

Hausman, D.M. and McPherson, M.S. (1996) *Economic Analysis and Moral Philosophy*, Cambridge: Cambridge University Press.

Hocket, R.C. 'Why paretians can't prescribe: preferences, principles, and imperatives in law and policy', *Cornell Journal of Law and Policy* 18, 2009: 391–476.

Hovenkamp, H. 'The limits of preference-based legal policy', *Northwestern University Law Review* 89, 1994: 4–91.

Huang, P.H. 'Book review: Leo Katz, *Why Law is so Perverse*', *Journal of Legal Education* 63, 2013: 131–160.

Kahneman, D., Knetsch, J.L., and Thaler, R.H. (2000) 'Experimental tests of the endowment effect and the Coase theorem', in C.R. Sunstein (ed.) *Behavior Law and Economics*, Cambridge: Cambridge University Press.

Kaplow, L. and Shavell, S. 'Any non-welfarist method of policy assessment violates the Pareto principle', *Journal of Political Economy* 109, 2001: 281–286.

Kaplow, L. and Shavell, S. (2002) *Fairness versus Welfare*, Cambridge, MA: Harvard University Press.

Kaplow, L. and Shavell, S. (2003) 'Fairness versus welfare: notes on the Pareto principle, preferences, and distributive justice', *Journal of Legal Studies* 32, 2003: 331–362.

Katz, L. 'Choice, consent, and cycling: the hidden limitations of consent', *Michigan Law Review* 104, 2006: 627–670.

Kelman, M., Rottenstreich, Y., and Tversky, A. (2000) 'Context dependence in legal decision making', in C.R. Sunstein (ed.), *Behavior Law and Economics*, Cambridge: Cambridge University Press.

Kornhauser, L.A. 'Preference, well-being, and morality in social decisions', *Journal of Legal Studies*, 32, 2003a: 303–329.

Kornhauser, L.A. 'The domain of preference', *University of Pennsylvania Law Review* 151, 2003b: 717–746.

Korobkin, R.B. and Ulen, T.S. 'Law and behavioral science: removing the rationality assumption from law and economics', *California Law Review* 88, 2000: 1051–1144.

Kronman, A.T. 'Paternalism and the law of contracts', *Yale Law Journal* 92, 1983: 763–798.

Lewis, J. 'Giving way: Martha Nussbaum and the morality of privation', *University of Chicago Law School Roundtable* 8, 2001: 215–237.

McCaffery, E.J., Kahneman, D.J., and Spitzer, M.L (2000) 'Framing the jury: cognitive perspective on pain and suffering awards', in C.R. Sunstein (ed.) *Behavioral Law and Economics*, Cambridge: Cambridge University Press.

Nussbaum, M.C. (2001) *Women and Human Development: The Capabilities Approach*, Cambridge: Cambridge University Press.

Pattanaik, P.K. (1997) 'Some paradoxes of preference aggregation', in D.C. Mueller (ed.), *Perspectives on Public Choice: A Handbook*, Cambridge: Cambridge University Press.

Radin, M.J. 'Market-inalienability', *Harvard Law Review* 100, 1987: 1849–1937.

Sen, A. (1982a) 'The impossibility of a Paretian liberal', in A. Sen (ed.), *Choice, Welfare, and Measurement*, Cambridge, MA: Harvard University Press.

Sen, A. (1982b) 'Liberty, unanimity, and rights', in A. Sen (ed.), *Choice, Welfare, and Measurement*, Cambridge, MA: Harvard University Press.

Sen, A. (1987) *On Ethics & Economics*. Hoboken, NJ: Wiley-Blackwell.

Sen, A. (1993) 'Capability and well-being', in M.C. Nussbaum and A. Sen (eds.) *The Quality of Life*, New York: Oxford University Press.

Sunstein, C.R. 'Legal interference with private preferences', *University of Chicago Law Review* 53, 1986: 1129–1174.

Thaler, R.H. (1992) *The Winner's Curse: Paradoxes and Anomalies of Economic Life*, Princeton, NJ: Princeton University Press.

Trebilcock, M.J. (1993) *The Limits of Freedom of Contract*, Cambridge, MA: Harvard University Press.

Tullock, G. 'Two kinds of legal efficiency', *Hofstra Law Review* 8, 1980: 659–669.

Volokh, A. 'Rationality or rationalism? The positive and normative flaws of cost–benefit analysis', *Houston Law Review* 48, 2011: 79–98.

Zamir, E. and Medina, B. 'Law, morality, and economics: integrating moral constraints with economic analysis of law', *California Law Review* 96, 2008: 323–391.

10 Any normative policy analysis not based on Kaldor–Hicks efficiency violates scholarly transparency norms

Gerrit De Geest*

Introduction

Suppose I argue that legal rule *A* is better than legal rule *B*. When you ask me about my criteria for good rules, I mention one vague criterion, adding, "I have many more criteria, but today I apply only this one." When you then ask me about those other criteria, and about my meta-rule for solving conflicts among those criteria, I answer "I don't have to tell you." When you ask me about my definition for the vague term in the criterion I apply, I answer "I don't have to define it." And when you ask me about the empirical assumptions I make to conclude that rule *A* will effectively lead to the desired result, I answer "None of your business!"

If I really did this, I would violate clearly established scholarly norms. These norms hold that scholars who make a normative statement should reveal their normative framework (and their entire framework, not just a piece of it); that scholars who use a term must define it; and that scholars who make an empirical prediction must reveal the assumptions they have in mind. These scholarly transparency norms are so obvious that you may wonder why any scholar would ever want to violate them. The main point in this chapter is that any scholar who makes a normative statement that is not based on Kaldor–Hicks efficiency violates them.

The crux of my point is as follows. "Kaldor–Hicks efficiency" is a fancy term that essentially conveys two ideas. The first idea is that *all possible advantages and disadvantages* of a legal rule need to be taken into account – we cannot act as if some advantages or disadvantages do not exist.[1] The second idea is that to the extent these advantages and disadvantages lead to conflicting recommendations, all of them should be balanced, and therefore require translation into a common unit of measurement; this can be "dollars," "utility," "welfare," or "happiness," but it has to be something. Indeed, if you have conflicting goals you cannot decide ad hoc; you need a *meta-rule for* the conflicts. Kaldor–Hicks efficiency is based on the idea that there should not be a fixed ranking of values, but that the *conflicting values should be balanced*.[2] Since Kaldor–Hicks efficiency is, at its core, nothing else than these two ideas, any rejection of Kaldor–Hicks is a rejection of at least one of these two ideas.

Since these two ideas are commonsensical, my point is that all scholars who reject Kaldor–Hicks efficiency are, in practice, non-transparent. They cannot be consistently applying the criteria or meta-rules they articulate; implicitly, they must be using criteria or meta-rules that differ from the ones they articulate. Since it is not possible, in this brief chapter, to discuss in detail all previous attempts to reject Kaldor–Hicks efficiency, I will make a typology of alternatives, and show why each type is partly based on non-transparent reasoning.

When I discuss some of the alternatives to Kaldor–Hicks, I discuss not only fairness maxim-based criteria but also – and maybe surprisingly – the Pareto criterion. Indeed, a second point I want make in this chapter is that while the Kaldor–Hicks criterion is often framed as a variant of the Pareto criterion (the "potential Pareto superiority criterion"), it is at its core a very different criterion – so much that the Pareto criterion is more closely related to fairness maxim-based criteria than to the Kaldor–Hicks criterion. Indeed, there are two sorts of meta-norms – the *balancing meta-norms* that balance the conflicting values, and the *one-sided meta-norms* that categorically give priority to one value over the others. The Kaldor–Hicks criterion contains a balancing meta-norm; fairness maxim-based criteria contain one-sided meta-norms. The Pareto criterion contains a one-sided meta-norm in that categorical priority is given to the status quo. Indeed, if a proposed change makes someone worse off, the change cannot be implemented under the Pareto criterion. So the interests of those who are made worse off get categorical priority over the interests of those who are made better off – even if their gains would be a billion times higher than the losses of the loser. Since to my knowledge no scholar has ever defended such extreme positions, this means that those who defend the pure Pareto criterion are not fully transparent with respect to the criteria they are really applying. Relatedly, I argue that the assumptions made in a pure Pareto analysis can only be justified on the basis of Kaldor–Hicks.

At the outset, however, I need to make three important clarifications. The first is that I am not suggesting that scholars who reject Kaldor–Hicks efficiency are necessarily bad scholars or that their scholarship cannot contain any valuable elements. I am neither suggesting that law and economics scholars never violate transparency norms in practice, nor that law and economic papers should consider all advantages and disadvantages at the same time; as a matter of fact, they shouldn't (and they don't) because complex issues cannot be disentangled all at once. What I am really saying is that certain methodological positions cannot be defended, and that rejecting Kaldor–Hicks efficiency implies taking indefensible methodological positions – positions that violate fundamental scholarly norms.

The second clarification I need to make is that I use Kaldor–Hicks efficiency in its broad definition, in which the measure can be monetary units (dollars), utility units, welfare units, happiness units, or any other quantifiable measure. In its narrow (and original)[3] definition it refers to analyses in monetary units only ("willingness to pay"). Since willingness to pay depends on ability to pay, the narrowly defined Kaldor–Hicks criterion is biased by taking the existing distribution of income as given and ignoring the issue of optimal redistribution.

Moreover, narrowly defined Kaldor–Hicks analyses often take preferences as given (making the implicit assumption that individuals are always in the best position to determine their own preferences); in that case, the analysis is incomplete because it ignores the issue of optimal preferences. It is important to understand that criticism of the Kaldor–Hicks criterion is very often criticism of its narrow definition. As a matter of fact, the narrow Kaldor–Hicks criterion suffers from some of the same issues of one-sidedness as the Pareto criterion and all fairness maxim-based criteria.

The third clarification I need to make is that I do not say that it is impossible to reject Kaldor–Hicks without violating transparency norms. As a matter of fact, it is possible to reject Kaldor–Hicks and still be transparent by being completely unreasonable. To illustrate, suppose that a scholar takes the position that there is only one normative value (e.g., "honesty"), so that no meta-rule is required for solving conflicts between different values, and that she consistently argues that all policy questions in which honesty is not an issue (e.g. pollution issues) should be decided by flipping a coin (which is rational when there is no normative issue at stake). In that case, the Kaldor–Hicks criterion would not be applied, but the scholar would still be transparent and consistent. The position would be so normatively unreasonable, however, that I have never heard a scholar defend it. Therefore, my point is that scholars who reject Kaldor–Hicks (by arguing that there is only one value to be considered, or one value that always dominates the other values, or that there is no need for a meta-rule for balancing conflicting values) are in practice inconsistent. And since they do not consistently apply their explicit criteria, they are in practice applying criteria that are not articulated. Therefore, they are in practice non-transparent.

There is a vast literature on the relationship between economic efficiency and other values. While my chapter elaborates on some of the same themes as the "fairness versus welfare" literature, my arguments to reject "fairness" differ from the ones developed by Kaplow and Shavell (2001; 2002). Kaplow and Shavell argue that non-efficiency-based analyses are normatively unappealing (because they violate the Pareto criterion); I argue that such analyses violate fundamental norms of good scholarship. Kaplow and Shavell present the Pareto criterion as a normative ideal;[4] I argue that the Pareto criterion is at its core an unappealing criterion that has more similarities with fairness maxim-based criteria than with the Kaldor–Hicks criterion.

This chapter is organized as follows. I first discuss the fundamental scholarly norms of transparency, consistency, and completeness. Second, I show that fairness maxim-based normative systems are based on non-transparent reasoning. Next, I argue that those who reject the Kaldor–Hicks criterion in favor of the Pareto criterion are non-transparent and inconsistent by implicitly using the Kaldor–Hicks criterion. I also briefly comment on the argument that Kaldor–Hicks analyses are inconsistent or incomplete as well. I conclude by summarizing and by reflecting on the origin of the lack of consensus.

Fundamental scholarly norms

While there is no such a thing as an official code for good scholarship, it is none-theless safe to state that transparency is a fundamental scholarly norm. I discuss the origins and implications of this norm and its relationship with two other scholarly norms: consistency and (sufficient) completeness.

Transparency: make the unconscious conscious, reveal and justify implicit assumptions, define terms, reveal the whole normative framework

The duty to be transparent follows directly from the goal of scholarship: to advance knowledge in the fastest possible way. Transparency in essence means that scholars need to reveal why they reach certain conclusions; after all, knowledge advances faster when arguments are put on the table rather than remain hidden. So scholars cannot simply argue, "I believe that specific performance is a better remedy for contract breach than expectation damages because I have a gut feeling that it is better." They need to reveal why they think it is better. More specifically, they have to reveal what is their criterion for good law, how they define terms, what assumptions they are making, and what empirical evidence they possess.

One problem in this respect is that, in practice, human beings often make decisions on the basis of a gut feeling. For instance, many people cannot accu-rately explain why they fell in love with a certain other person. Since Sigmund Freud's writings, we know that a large part of our decision-making process takes place in the subconscious. Note that there is nothing wrong with that when the outcome works well. For instance, if a relationship that started with a subcon-scious choice turns out to work well, there is no need to analyze the selection criteria that were subconsciously used. But if relationships fail time and time again, it may be a good idea to bring the implicit selection criteria to the con-sciousness; only then can rational corrections be made.

Something similar holds for scholarly positions. Suppose I argue that when-ever someone causes harm by behaving differently from a reasonable person, she should pay damages under tort law. I do not define "reasonable person"; every time I decide a case, I rely on my "gut feeling" to determine what is reasonable. If all people in the legal community always have the same "gut feeling" there is no need to define reasonableness. But if some disagree, debate is needed, and the debate can only start if all the implicitly applied criteria (hidden behind the vague concept of "reasonableness") are made explicit. The subconscious of the scholars can no longer do the work; they need to bring their criteria to the consciousness.

Transparency means that we have to put all our arguments on the table – not only those in our consciousness but also those in our subconscious. More specifi-cally, the duty to be transparent implies defining the terms we are using, as well as revealing the assumptions we are making, all empirical evidence we have, and the normative framework we are applying when we make a normative statement.

Corollaries of transparency: consistency and completeness

Consistency is an obvious scholarly norm. We cannot say in one discussion on misrepresentation that lying is always bad and the next day in a discussion on insider trading that lying is sometimes good. Nor can we use arguments "ad hoc" – not consistently applied but only used to obtain a certain outcome.

While consistency is a fundamental scholarly norm on its own, it can also be seen as a corollary of the transparency norm. Indeed, whenever scholars are inconsistent – that is, when they are not consistently applying the criterion they articulate – they must implicitly be applying another criterion. (I am not suggesting here that such scholars are deliberately misrepresenting their criterion; much more likely, their true criterion is still in their subconscious). Therefore, the duty to be consistent forces the scholar to better articulate the truly applied criterion.

One difficulty with the duty to be consistent (and the prohibition on ad hoc arguments) is that a violation of this duty can only be discovered by observing many statements on slightly different topics. If someone only takes a position on one very specific topic (for instance, one single fact pattern on insider trading) inconsistency is hard to discover. Therefore, there is an implicit scholarly duty to consider extensions – or, to put it differently, to be sufficiently complete.[5] For instance, if someone argues "lying is always bad," the question may be asked whether lying to a criminal who asks us where a possible victim is hiding is bad. If the answer is "well, lying is good in that case," then "do not lie" turns out to be no more than a proxy for a higher norm. Completeness is therefore an important corollary of consistency. Inconsistencies in turn force the scholar to acknowledge that the truly applied criterion is different from the articulated criterion. In this sense, the duty to be sufficiently complete is a corollary of the duty to be transparent.

Normative analyses based on fairness maxims

The best-known resistance against Kaldor–Hicks efficiency comes from scholars who base their normative statements on fairness maxims. Such scholars may argue, for instance, that contracts should be enforceable because it is unfair to break a promise; that misrepresentation should invalidate the contract because it is unfair to lie; that patents should be awarded because it is unfair to free-ride on the research efforts of others; that pollution should be forbidden because it is unfair to harm others; that bankruptcy rules should not be too harsh because it is unfair to deny someone a new start (and not too soft because it is unfair not to keep a financial promise); that compensation should be paid to those whose property is taken under eminent domain because otherwise the taking would be theft and theft is immoral.

Fairness maxims have some appeal because they illuminate at least one side of the problem: they help us realize how frustrating an outcome is for one of the parties. If I promise you something and then I don't keep my promise, this is quite frustrating for you. So if we look at contract breach solely from the side of the promisee, we will probably conclude that contract breach is always a bad thing. If we look at pollution from the victim's side only, we may conclude that pollution is always a bad thing. If we look at patents from the inventor's perspective, we may conclude that free-ridership by another is always a bad thing, and that patents should be eternal.

But the flipside of fairness maxims is that they look at *only one side* of the problem. If we look at the other side, we may want to change our conclusion. If I promise to build a house for you but later I learn that it would cost ten times more than previously estimated because the land is unstable (something I could not reasonably have foreseen), should I really keep my promise? Making huge losses is quite frustrating for me; I may even go bankrupt, bringing financial trouble to my family.

When there is a conflicting (dis)advantage *on the other side*, there are four fundamental options, which will all be analyzed in the following subsections. The first is to simply ignore the other (dis)advantages; a scholar may say, for instance, "I don't care about the situation of promisors, I only care about the situation of promisees," and conclude that specific performance is the optimal rule and that impracticability should never be an excuse. In this case, the scholar's system avoids conflicts of values by having only one value. A specific case is where the one value is vague and general, so that at first glance it seems to make justifying any desirable outcome possible. The second fundamental option is that a scholar acknowledges both (dis)advantages, but formulates a fixed ranking order. She may say, for instance, "The interest of the promisee is always more important than the interest of the promisor," and reach the same conclusion. The third fundamental option is that the scholar acknowledges both (dis)advantages and balances them using a certain measure (such as monetary losses, utility losses, or happiness losses); since this is exactly what Kaldor–Hicks does, the scholar could only reject the specific measures that are being used under Kaldor–Hicks so far. The fourth and final fundamental option is that the scholar acknowledges the conflicting (dis)advantages but decides on the basis of a "gut-feeling" rather than on the basis of an explicit meta-criterion.

Normative systems with only one well-defined value

Normative systems with only one value have one advantage: they don't need a meta-rule to decide conflicts of values. Suppose, for instance, that my only value is "no pollution." As a logical consequence, I forbid even the slightest form of pollution. I do this irrespective of the benefit of the polluting activity because I do not care at all about those other benefits. Those benefits have zero value in my normative system.[6]

There are two major problems associated with having only one such value. The first is that it necessarily leads to extreme outcomes. For instance, if my only value is "no pollution," then I forbid all car-driving. Even ambulances are no longer allowed on the roads because they cause pollution – only modest pollution, but that does not matter.

The second major problem is that when choices consist of two alternatives that are not inconsistent with the only value that is considered, the logical conclusion is that these alternatives are equally good or bad. So if a factory has to choose between two activities that do *not* cause the slightest pollution, for instance one that generates an economic benefit of $100 million and one that generates only a $10 million benefit, neither outcome is to be normatively preferred. A legal rule that forbids the $100 million activity is equally good as a legal rule that permits it; as a matter of fact, if we were to vote on such a rule, we may as well flip a coin because it is normatively irrelevant which activity will take place. Similarly, if a scholar whose only value is "no pollution" has to decide contract cases, in which pollution is not at stake but the discussion is, for instance, on balancing "honesty" and "encouraging entrepreneurship," the scholar should just flip a coin.

In theory, a normative system with only one such value could be transparent and consistent. As mentioned earlier, someone could reject Kaldor–Hicks efficiency without violating transparency and consistency norms (the normative system would be highly unappealing, but it would still be transparent and consistent). In practice, however, I have never met a scholar who defends the extreme implications of such a normative system. Therefore, scholars who defend a system with only one value do not reveal their complete normative system. They are inconsistent (because they do not defend the logical implications of a taken position) and they are non-transparent (because they must be applying normative criteria that they do not articulate, possibly because it is subconscious).

Normative systems with only one vague and general value

A variant of the previous type is to have a normative system with only one value, but one that is sufficiently vague and general, so that it apparently captures all relevant considerations. For instance, a scholar could reject the Learned Hand formula (which requires judges to balance precaution costs and expected accident costs to determine whether an injurer should be liable for negligence, and which is a straightforward application of Kaldor–Hicks efficiency) and argue instead that people should behave "reasonably." Similarly, she could reject the notion that patent duration should depend on the balance of innovation benefits and monopoly costs, and defend non-eternal patents on the basis of the norm that "rights are a good thing but they should be reasonable." Or she could reject the notion that contract rules should maximize the joint surplus of the parties (something that requires constant balancing of costs and benefits) and argue instead that all contract rules should be based on the maxim that "parties should act in good faith."

At first glance, having only one vague value has two advantages. The first is that since there is only one value, value conflicts cannot occur, so that there is no need to articulate a meta-rule for solving such conflicts. The second is that keeping the one norm sufficiently vague and general seems to address all relevant considerations.

The problem, however, is that scholars have the fundamental duty to define terms. What is "reasonable" behavior in the context of accident prevention?

What is a "reasonable period" of IP protection? When the scholar does not defend corner solutions (such as a speed limit of 1 mph, or eternal patents) but interior solutions (such as 70 mph, or twenty years of patent protection), there must be a balancing criterion that is implicitly applied. Therefore, scholars who defend normative systems with undefined terms violate transparency norms – unless they always defend corner solutions when it comes to policy choices, but I am not aware of any scholar who does that consistently.

Many values with meta-criterion for fixed ranking

Those who defend a normative system with many values, but do not want to balance values, can in principle formulate a meta-criterion that ranks these values in an immutable order. This was the position taken by the German philosopher Max Scheler (1973: 104–110). In his system, values regarding "holiness" came first, followed by values regarding "culture" (including aesthetics and truthfulness), "vitality," and "utility"; values regarding "pleasure" came fifth and last. The higher values always ought to be preferred to the lower.

Here is how a fixed ranking of values works.[7] Suppose the government has a budget to spend, and the choice is between building a new cathedral and building a new highway. In this case, we have to ask which values the choices represent. Since religious values are more highly ranked than economic values, we should build the cathedral. (We may explain our decision by saying that "a virtuous life is more important than a life with many material goods.") The next time the government has a budget available, we ask the same questions, and decide to build another cathedral. And another one.

The problem with a fixed ranking is that it violates the principle of marginalism. How valuable an additional cathedral is depends on how many cathedrals there already are; how valuable a new highway is depends on how many highways there already are. To be sure, marginalism is an economic norm, and at first glance it is not inconsistent for a scholar who rejects economic efficiency to also reject marginalism. Moreover, a fixed ranking can be transparent. So once again, this shows that it is theoretically possible to reject Kaldor–Hicks without a violation of fundamental scholarly norms.

In practice, however, I have never met a person who rejects marginalism in her personal decision making. For instance, I know people who like apples and therefore buy some apples, but I have never met someone who spends 100 percent of her yearly income on buying apples. So, apparently, the value of apples must decrease at some point to make other goods more preferable.

Moreover, I have never seen a scholar categorically reject marginalism, likely because it leads to implications that no reasonable person would ever defend. Similarly, I have never heard of a policymaker who proposes spending 100 percent of the government budget on a single category, such as education, transport, or defense. This means that in practice scholars who defend a fixed value-ranking system are non-transparent, inconsistent, or both.

Many values; meta-criterion for weighing them

The Kaldor–Hicks criterion balances (dis)advantages in terms of monetary, utility, or happiness value. In principle, a scholar could reject these measures and develop a different measure that allows him to quantify and compare (dis)advantages. A condition for such a measure is that it is, in principle, empirically verifiable. "Empirically verifiable" is not synonymous with "easy to measure"; for instance, happiness is notoriously hard to measure. But there is a difference between hard to measure and non-measurable. For instance, suppose a scholar proposes "goodness units" as a measure. In the example of the pollution factory with +$100 of benefits and –$20 of pollution costs, she gives +5 goodness points to the benefits, –6 goodness points to the degree of pollution, and concludes that pollution should be forbidden. But the measure should be so defined that other scholars should be able to challenge the measurement by re-measuring it empirically.

My point is that those who reject Kaldor–Hicks but still balance values have a scholarly duty to reveal the balancing measure they are really applying. If it is not money, utility, happiness, or welfare, what is it? Of course, it is not impossible that, at some point in the future, someone will come up with a measure that is different from the ones that are currently used by economists. But the measure needs to be clearly defined. And even then, the normative system would essentially be just a variant of Kaldor–Hicks efficiency, since it would be based on the same ideas.

Many values, but no meta-criterion for solving conflicts

Suppose a scholar defends a normative system with several values (based on fairness maxims) but does not define a meta-criterion for when they are in conflict. The scholar may say, for instance, that "honesty is good" and "pollution is bad." In discussions on contract law, the scholar takes the position that there should be a duty to disclose all information one might have. In discussions on environmental law, she takes the position that activities should be forbidden as soon as they cause the slightest pollution. At first glance, these values do not seem to be in conflict, because pollution is not an issue in contract law and honesty is (usually) not an issue in environmental law.

But suppose there is a case in which the two values conflict. For instance, the seller of a house wants to make a copy of a document for the buyer but making this copy has a very small environmental cost. Which value should dominate?

Here are some other examples. A scholar defends twenty-year patents on the basis of the maxim that it is immoral to free-ride on the efforts of others (in this case, the research efforts of the inventors). When asked why patents should be limited to twenty years, the scholar answers that free competition is an important value as well. Clearly, this scholar is using an implicit criterion for balancing the conflicting values.

When the same scholar is asked why home sellers should reveal termite infestations, she answers "because honesty is an important value." When asked whether entrepreneurial information should be revealed by buyers (for instance, by art experts who have discovered a masterpiece at a flea market, or by mining companies who have discovered a mineral deposit after spending millions of dollars on research), she answers that they should not, because this would lead to free-ridership by the owner on the efforts of others. Since the two values (honesty and no free-ridership) were in conflict, she must be using an implicit meta-criterion.

So scholars who defend several potentially conflicting values and take a position when the values are in conflict, violate the transparency norm because they must be using a meta-criterion which is not revealed. (Note that scholars who refuse to take a position whenever the values are in conflict violate the completeness corollary in order to avoid violating the consistency requirement.)

Normative analyses based on (narrowly defined) Pareto efficiency instead of Kaldor–Hicks efficiency

Kaldor–Hicks efficiency has been criticized not only by scholars who prefer fairness maxims but also by economists. For instance, Buchanan (1979: 150–152) has argued that welfare economics should be based on Pareto efficiency, not cost–benefit analysis. Austrian economists have rejected straightforward cost–benefit analyses and proposed "structural efficiency" as an alternative criterion. Some others have argued that efficiency analysis is too ambitious from a scientific point of view, and that economists should limit themselves to explaining "what is going on" (e.g., Samuels and Schmid 1981: 1).

The point of many of these scholars seems to be that Pareto efficiency is ethically more appealing and less speculative than Kaldor–Hicks efficiency. I will now argue that Pareto efficiency is not ethically more appealing – to the contrary, its strict application may lead to morally shocking recommendations such as the reintroduction of censorship – and that Pareto analyses are not less speculative than Kaldor–Hicks. I will also show that even in a pure Pareto framework, the most common assumptions can only be justified on the basis of Kaldor–Hicks.

Kaldor–Hicks is based on a balancing meta-rule, Pareto on a one-sided meta-rule

Kaldor–Hicks efficiency is the optimality criterion that economists generally use. Technically, an activity is Kaldor–Hicks efficient if the winners could compensate the losers and still be better off. Since this is only possible if the benefits exceed the costs, a simpler formulation is to say that an activity is Kaldor–Hicks efficient if its benefits exceed its costs. Suppose that an industrial activity pollutes the air. A legal rule that simply permits this activity is Kaldor–Hicks efficient if the benefits of the activity exceed the pollution costs. Suppose that the benefit of the activity is +$100 and the pollution cost is –$20. The activity (and the legal rule that permits it) is considered economically desirable because its benefits exceed its costs. The activity makes the country +$80 wealthier.

An important feature of Kaldor–Hicks efficiency is that it forces policymakers to consider all (dis)advantages of activities. They cannot simply say "The activity has a pollution cost, so let's forbid it." They should also look at the advantage. Conversely, they cannot simply say "The activity has a benefit, so let's permit it." They should also consider the pollution cost.

Kaldor–Hicks means not only that all (dis)advantages should be identified and taken into consideration, but also that they should be weighed. This weighing requires a common measure. This measure is usually monetary value ("dollars") because this is the easiest to measure empirically, but it can also be another measure, such as "utility" or "happiness." Without a common measure, balancing (dis) advantages would not be possible, as it would be comparing apples and oranges.[8]

Pareto optimality is a very different criterion. A Pareto improvement is defined as an activity that makes at least one person better off and no person worse off.

This sounds great (who can be against an activity that has only advantages and no disadvantages?), but the positive framing only obscures the fact that the Pareto criterion is unreasonable. Consider again the pollution activity with a benefit of +$100 to the polluter and a pollution cost of –$20 to the neighbors. This activity is no Pareto improvement because it makes some people worse off. If policymakers strictly adhered to the Pareto criterion they would forbid the activity. The Pareto criterion permits only changes that have no disadvantages.[9]

According to the Pareto criterion, policymakers do not have to take all advantages and disadvantages into consideration. As a matter of fact they only have to pay attention to the disadvantages. If an activity has pollution costs, it should be forbidden – end of story. Policymakers should not examine whether the activity has advantages too, because these do not matter. Even if the benefits were a trillion times greater than the pollution costs, the activity would still not be a Pareto improvement.

Because the social benefits are ignored as soon as there are social costs, the Pareto criterion can lead to morally shocking conclusions. Suppose a political manifesto makes a society better but the king unhappy. Since one person is made worse off, the book should be censored.

The benchmarking problem

Another fundamental problem with the Pareto criterion is benchmarking – and it is important to see that this problem is caused by the fact that not all (dis)advantages of a problem receive weight under the Pareto criterion. Suppose I am considering two contractors to build a house. I eventually sign a contract with contractor A because he is cheaper than contractor B. I am happy about the deal, contractor A is happy about the deal, but contractor B is unhappy about not getting the deal. Is this a Pareto improvement? Only if we "benchmark" the status quo in a certain way. If the benchmark is the position in which all parties were before the house was built, then I am better off, contractor A is better off, and contractor B is no worse off. But then "Pareto optimality" is only informing us that it is better that the house is built by contractor A than not built at all; this is not so useful, because the interesting question is not so much whether the house should be built but whether A or B should build it.[10]

If we benchmark the status quo in such a way that expectations for the future do not count, then many changes that apparently generate losers become Pareto improvements. Abolishing a monopoly position or removing a dictator from power, for instance, then becomes a Pareto improvement. Sure, it makes the monopolist or dictator worse off compared to their expectations for the future, but if the benchmark is not their expectations but the money they had acquired (or the power they had exercised) until that point, they are not worse off by losing their privileged position. Under the same benchmark, even the taking of a house under eminent domain without compensation becomes a Pareto improvement. This taking makes the owner worse off but only in comparison to his expectations for the future, not in comparison to his enjoyment of the house in the past. Sure, one could try to change the benchmark in this case by saying that the owner's expectations for the future were reasonable since he owned the property. But this benchmarking is less natural than it may seem, because the question in a normative discussion is not whether he had a reasonable expectation under the law but which expectations the law should create.

My point here is not that benchmarking is important under the Pareto criterion. My point is that benchmarking is so important because Pareto optimality is, at its core, an unreasonable criterion. The Pareto criterion tells us to consider only some effects, and to completely ignore all other effects. Therefore, the choice of the effects that need to be considered does all the work. This is different under the Kaldor–Hicks criterion. Since there you have to consider all effects, it does not matter whether you consider, for instance, the pollution costs in light of the benefits, or the benefits in light of the pollution costs.

Are Pareto efficiency statements less speculative?

If the Pareto criterion, in its pure form, is unreasonable, why was it ever proposed? To understand this, we have to go back in time. In the early days of welfare economics, (dis)advantages were identified and balanced, though the unit was usually utility rather than dollars. In other words, the Kaldor–Hicks criterion was applied (very often in one of its broad definitions, measuring utility), even though Kaldor and Hicks had not published their papers yet.

But then Lionel Robbins (1932, 1938) and Austrian economists criticized this balancing for being speculative. They argued that it is next to impossible to compare interpersonal utility, that is, utility for different individuals. I know that I like apples more than oranges, but do I like apples more than you like apples? We don't have machines to measure how much each of us enjoys apples. Does the polluter benefit more from the activity than I suffer from the smoke? Well, my suffering is subjective. There is no way for other people than me to find out how much I really suffer. (Sure, they could ask me, but I have no incentive to honestly reveal my true losses.)

The Pareto criterion was an attempt to make optimality judgments without making interpersonal utility comparisons. If you are better off and I am not worse off, the activity is an improvement. There is no need to measure how much you are better off; whatever the magnitude is, it will always be larger than zero, and so the activity will remain desirable.

In practice, there will be very few activities that meet this criterion. If we were to strictly apply the Pareto criterion, the polluting factory that generates a benefit of +$100 but a pollution cost of –$20 must be closed. By the same token, the political manifesto that makes society better but hurts the feelings of the dictator must be censured. While the Pareto criterion has rhetorical appeal, it does not explain the normative choices most people make, and it would even be quite dangerous to really apply the Pareto criterion in practice.

Kaldor and Hicks then found a way to reframe the criterion economists had been using all along (balance costs and benefits) as a variant of the Pareto criterion. Their insight was that when the benefits outweigh the costs, the winners (who receive the benefits) could in theory compensate the losers (who bear the costs) and still be better off. The polluting factory could compensate the neighbors (paying them $20) and still have a net benefit of $80 ($100 minus the $20 compensation). The cost–benefit balancing criterion became the potential Pareto criterion.

This reframing had rhetorical appeal. If an activity makes not only winners but also losers, and you can frame it as if there are only winners, well, who can still be against it? (Though the fact that losers could be compensated does not make them compensated.)

But we are back to square one: The Pareto criterion was formulated because weighing (dis)advantages can be speculative but hypothetical Pareto compensations are as speculative as straightforward cost–benefit comparisons. Indeed, the advantage of the pure Pareto criterion was that it did not require interpersonal utility comparisons. The Pareto criterion did not require us to measure the magnitude of the costs but only their direction. If all point in a (weakly) positive direction, the outcome is an improvement. If the two parties are happy with the contract, the contract is an improvement; there is no need to find out how much each party gains. It is sufficient to know that both gain (or at least are not made worse off). But the hypothetical Pareto improvement loses this advantage. Indeed, winners could compensate losers and still be better off only if winners gain more utility than losers lose. To find that out, however, requires interpersonal utility comparison: we have to know that the winners's utility increase exceeds the losers's utility decrease.

If individual gains and losses are deemed too subjective to be measured scientifically, the only case in which we can really be sure that no party is made worse off is if both effectively approve the change – at least so it seems. For starters, this means that the application of the Pareto principle outside contract law is problematic. Consider taking of property under eminent domain. Since owners are in principle fully compensated, they are in principle not made worse off. But how can we know that they are fully compensated when compensation is decided by a third party – the judge? The same applies to other examples of what Calabresi and Melamed (1972) called liability rules. This does not mean that such transactions are not socially desirable – they may be, if we apply Kaldor–Hicks and estimate the error costs to be sufficiently small. But it is important to realize that the Pareto justification here is as speculative as the Kaldor–Hicks justification of the pollution case: a third party judges that the costs for one party are smaller than the benefits for another party.

Buchanan argued that constitutional political economy should be based on Pareto, not Kaldor–Hicks. In a sense, this is true: if political rules are agreed upon when all citizens are still in an original position à la John Rawls, before they know whether they will be winners or losers, then the later losers can be presumed to have consented to losing. But in the real world, constitutional amendments are not made in an original position and therefore the analysis can only be made using Kaldor–Hicks. Moreover, and more to the point here, even if analyses were based on Pareto, this use of the Pareto criterion would not make it any less speculative than when Kaldor–Hicks would have been used.

So we are left with one field of law – contracts. At first glance, contractual exchanges seem to be the poster-child of a Pareto improvement: The fact that a contract has been agreed to suggests that both parties are better off (at least *ex ante*, before chances are realized). But this conclusion can only be made if numerous assumptions are made – assumptions that to a large extent find their translation in contract doctrines. For instance, we must assume that there was no misrepresentation, no duress, no undue influence, no misunderstanding, no incapacity. Moreover, when written contracts are signed, we must assume that both parties read and understood the contract, or that judges are able to find out what was the true deal.

As it turns out, each of these contract doctrines involves some balancing of costs, and can therefore only be justified with Kaldor–Hicks efficiency. For instance, the misrepresentation requirement relates only to information that is "material," i.e., important enough to be disclosed or to require more care during the communication process. Whether information is material requires the balancing of the costs (of producing information, disclosing information, double-checking information) and the benefits of information. Since these costs are spread over the two parties, this balancing requires the acceptance of Kaldor–Hicks efficiency. Many other examples can be given. For instance, default rules in contract law are in principle chosen in such a way that they maximize the joint surplus for the parties in the majority of the contracts; since default rules are sticky, what is best for the majority cannot be simply derived from the choices of the majority but requires a Kaldor–Hicks balancing of costs and benefits. Or, to take another example, the duty to disclose is based on the least-cost-information-gatherer principle. The so-called "objective theory" penalizes the party that could have avoided misunderstanding at least cost. All these applications of the "least cost avoider" principle can only be justified using Kaldor–Hicks.

A second point is that empirical explanations, predictions, and, therefore, normative statements (which always have an implicit empirical element) are always based on a number of assumptions. These assumptions need to be justified, i.e., the scholar should explain why she believes that they are either realistic or that relaxing them would not change the outcome. But it nearly always requires Kaldor–Hicks to justify these assumptions. In other words, scholars who stick to the Pareto criterion cannot justify their assumptions.

For instance, a contract model typically assumes that there are no externalities (excluding a number of well-identified cases, such as cartel agreements, which have negative external effects on consumers, but for which the law can have targeted rules). In reality, there may be envy, altruism, and price externalities – none of which is addressed by specific contract doctrines. Consider a construction contract that creates a surplus of +$100, making the builder and the owner each +$50 better off. But now suppose that the neighbor of the owner is envious and suffers –$120 when he sees a house that is more beautiful than his. In that case, the contract makes society worse off. Or suppose that a competing builder, who is less efficient and can create only a surplus of +$80, has extremely empathetic parents who are +$40 better off when they see their son get the contract (but whose price nonetheless prevents them from subsidizing the contract price). In this case, the choice to work with the first builder makes society worse off compared to working with the second builder. Or suppose that the contract price itself changes the market price – making either future owners or future builders worse off.

Such externalities are typically assumed away in contract models; but how can these assumptions be justified? A scholar could argue that envy should not be taken into account because it is immoral, but this way the scholar introduces an exogenous norm to save an existing normative system. Moreover, the same argument could not be made about empathy externalities – it is hard to consider empathy immoral.

These assumptions could be justified, however, using Kaldor–Hicks. Contract rules are made for a general set of cases, and if empathy effects are stronger than envy effects, empathy will generally make the contract surplus stronger. Therefore, the best the legal system can do is to maximize the joint surplus of the parties – if the direct surplus is maximized, the indirect empathy surplus is also maximized. Even if envy would usually be stronger than empathy, the net surplus would still be maximized by maximizing the direct surplus, unless envy effects would be so strong that they dominate the direct effects plus the indirect empathy effects. But in that case, the best society would be one in which contracts were forbidden and misery were maximized. This does not look plausible.

By the same token, price externalities can be assumed away because they are overall zero-sum effects. If the market price goes down by $10, all sellers lose $10 and all consumers win $10. There can be a negative effect when the price (that already exceeded true costs) goes further up, so that some infra-marginal consumers stop buying it. But usually more contracts will increase rather than decrease competition (and rather cause economies of scale than diseconomies of scale) so that price (and production) externalities are more likely to be positive – in which case social benefits are maximized when the contract surplus of the two parties is maximized.

My point here is not so much to show how such assumptions could be justified (maybe even better justifications can be found). My point is to show that justifying these assumptions requires the balancing of many positive and negative effects. It requires, in other words, Kaldor–Hicks efficiency.

This means that economists who reject Kaldor–Hicks are not consistent. And since they are implicitly applying a criterion that is not made explicit, they are violating scholarly transparency norms.

Are Kaldor–Hicks statements also inconsistent or incomplete?

So far, I have argued that all alternatives to Kaldor–Hicks optimality are based on non-transparent reasoning. But some have argued that the Kaldor–Hicks criterion itself is internally inconsistent. So are those who apply the Kaldor–Hicks criterion also violating fundamental scholarly norms – specifically the duty to be consistent?

The Kaldor–Hicks criterion is sometimes believed to be internally inconsistent because of the Scitovsky (1941) Paradox. According to this paradox, a rule A, as well as its alternative, rule B, can be efficient if compensations do not effectively take place. Suppose a castle is worth $10 million to its owner, A (who is wealthy because she owns the castle). Person B has only a willingness-to-pay of $5 million (because her ability to pay is only $6 million). Since A's willingness-to-accept is larger than B's willingness-to-pay, Kaldor–Hicks dictates that the castle should remain in the hands of A. But suppose now that the castle is given to B without any form of compensation. Suppose that B (who is wealthier now that she owns the castle) now has a willingness-to-accept of $10 million, while the previous owner, A (who has become much poorer because of the uncompensated taking), has a willingness-to-pay of only $5 million. Kaldor–Hicks now dictates that the castle should remain in the hands of B. This paradox apparently shows that the Kaldor–Hicks criterion is internally inconsistent. It is inconsistent because it supports both the statement that A should own the castle and the conflicting statement that B should own the castle.

But this conclusion is incorrect. The Kaldor–Hicks criterion was used here in its narrow definition – of allocative efficiency given wealth distribution (and preferences) – because values were expressed in monetary terms. Allocative efficiency tells us only what is optimal given an existing wealth distribution. If a castle is taken away without compensation, two different things are done at the same time: the allocation of the good is changed (A loses his castle), and the wealth distribution is changed (A is impoverished). In the new situation (in which B has become wealthier than A), allocating the castle is optimal. The Scitovsky Paradox, at most, reminds us that the narrow version of Kaldor–Hicks is incomplete because it does not say anything about wealth optimality.[11]

Another criticism is that, in practice, Kaldor–Hicks analyses do not consider all (disadvantages) either. Many historical examples can be given of law and economics scholars who have taken normative positions based on a very incomplete analysis. It is definitely true that when analyses are incomplete, there may be some wisdom left in gut-feeling norms such as fairness maxims. But the imperfection of an application of a methodology should not lead to the rejection of the methodology itself.

A stronger criticism is that in some areas, certain aspects are deliberately and consistently left out. For instance, in areas outside tax law, redistributive effects are usually left out by law and economics scholars. In economic analysis of contract law, pollution costs or unemployment costs are consistently left out. But this does not mean that those other issues are ignored; it means that other fields of law are believed to have superior instruments to address them. One general principle of good policymaking is that N problems require N instruments (De Geest 2013). Therefore, considering one issue at a time (for instance, optimal care, optimal decisions to breach a contract, optimal payments to help the poor) is a good strategy for policymaking.

Concluding remarks

Kaldor–Hicks efficiency comes down to three imperatives: (1) reveal all advantages and disadvantages you have in mind; (2) reveal the meta-criterion you use for balancing them (and tell us if you know a better measure than dollars, utility, or happiness); and (3) reveal all your empirical information and assumptions when you make the best possible empirical guess of their magnitude.

Those who reject Kaldor–Hicks efficiency as a normative criterion either consider fewer types of (dis)advantages (categorically ignoring others), do not reveal their meta-criterion for solving conflicts of (dis)advantages, do not consistently apply their own criterion, or are unable to justify their assumptions. In short, they violate fundamental scholarly norms by being non-transparent, inconsistent, or incomplete.

While Kaldor–Hicks efficiency is often seen as a variant of Pareto efficiency, it is, at its core, a fundamentally different criterion. Moreover, the Pareto criterion, in its pure form, is a very unreasonable criterion. I am not aware of any scholar who consistently defends that changes should only be allowed if nobody on this planet is made worse off. Therefore, those who defend the Pareto criterion over the Kaldor–Hicks criterion do not reveal the criterion they truly apply – which means that they (unintentionally) violate transparency norms.

This leads us to a final question. If the ideas behind the Kaldor–Hicks criterion are so obvious, why is there so much resistance to Kaldor–Hicks? While the issue is complex (it involves, for instance, the relationship between utilitarianism and economics), there are two factors that may be mentioned in particular.

First, Kaldor–Hicks efficiency is often used in its narrow sense – as the optimal allocation of goods given distribution of wealth and given preferences. To find out what maximizes happiness, we should find out not only what is the optimal allocation given distribution of wealth and given preferences, but also the optimal distribution of wealth and the optimal preferences. The latter two are harder to study because utility and happiness are harder to measure, and therefore economists usually limit their analysis to the first one. But optimality statements based solely on the first one are obviously biased. Some mistakenly believe that this incompleteness is inherent, and therefore reject the criterion.

Second, the discussion is misleadingly framed as "fairness versus welfare" or "ethics versus economics" or "economic efficiency versus equity." This is misleading because efficiency is an attempt to define fairness or ethics rather than a rejection of it. The framing nearly comes down to asking the question, "Do you want economically optimal law or do you want good law?" If the question were framed like that, it would not be surprising if many people chose "good law." But one could actually argue that a scholar's duty to define terms also implies the duty to precisely define research questions. The lack of transparency with respect to the research questions may be partly responsible for the lack of success with respect to reaching a consensus on the answer.

If we would frame the question more accurately and less misleadingly as whether we should take all (dis)advantages of legal rules into account; whether we should reveal our meta-criterion for deciding conflicts between (dis)advantages; whether the meta-criterion should contain a fixed ranking of values or a balancing one; and whether someone knows a better (and still empirically verifiable) criterion for weighing conflicting values than dollars, utility, or happiness, the disagreement may quickly disappear.

Notes

* Charles F. Nagel Professor of International and Comparative Law and Director of the Center on Law, Innovation & Economic Growth, Washington University at St. Louis. I thank Adam Badawi, Jacob Francheck, Adam Rosenzweig, Brian Tamanaha, and Andrew Tucker for valuable comments. I thank Megan Laswell for research assistance.
1 (Dis)advantages here are defined as interpersonal (dis)advantages, which are allocated over multiple individuals. If an action requires only intrapersonal (dis)advantages (which is the case, for instance, when going to the beach has a benefit to me of +100 but also a transport cost of –20, so that it has an individual net benefit of +80 to me), I only consider the net advantage (or disadvantage).
2 A third idea is that we must check empirically whether these advantages or disadvantages really exist, and to what extent they exist. In this chapter, however, I will focus only on the first two ideas.
3 The notion of hypothetical compensation implicitly relies on a monetary measure because only money can be transferred from one individual to another – utility or happiness cannot be directly taken from one individual and given to another. See also (Kaldor 1939: 549–550), concurring with Robbins that interpersonal utility comparisons cannot be made on a scientific basis.
4 Kaplow and Shavell assume a reciprocal setting in which individuals do not know yet whether they will be the winners or losers of a change (somewhat analogous to Rawls's assumption that individuals are in an "original position"). The problem with this assumption is that it makes the difference between Pareto optimality and Kaldor–Hicks optimality disappear. Indeed, in an original position everyone can be made better off if and only if *ex post* the winners win more than the losers lose. To see which of these two criteria the scholar really applies, one should look at situations in which there is no perfect reciprocity. Note that in practice policymaking often takes place in such a non-reciprocal setting.

5 Completeness does not mean that scholars must have a position on all possible research issues. It only means that they need to consider all issues that could lead to inconsistent positions.
6 For attempts to derive a complete normative system built from only one fairness maxim, see, for instance (Van Dun 1983) (deriving a libertarian society from the "no slavery" premise) or Grotius (justifying all contract, tort, and property rules by deriving them logically from the "peace is good, war is bad" premise). Such normative systems obviously cannot determine many rules (e.g., the optimal length of intellectual property), which means that there must be some hidden premises.
7 This example is mine, not Scheler's, who focused on individual choices rather than on policy choices.
8 Since (dis)advantages have to be expressed in a common measure, a Kaldor–Hicks statement has an empirical component, even if it is a normative statement. Therefore, a normative conclusion such as, "the legal system should permit this activity" can be incorrect when it is based on an incorrect empirical estimate of the magnitude of the (dis)advantages.
9 I use the term "disadvantage" here in it social meaning. At an individual level, an activity with a net benefit for the individual may have individual costs too (for instance, effort costs) that are lower than the individual benefits.
10 Of course, we could try to give a reason why builder A is probably in the best position to build the house. We could argue, for instance, that the fact that builder A offered to work for a lower price probably means that builder A works more efficiently. But this is only "probably" true, not certainly true. There can be cases in which B could do the job more efficiently but did not get the contract because he underestimated his opponent. So the assumption that the one who asks the lowest price is also the one who can do it at the lowest cost can only be justified by the Kaldor–Hicks criterion, not by the Pareto criterion.
11 This point is also made in (Kaplow and Shavell 2002).

References

Buchanan, J.M. (1979) *What Should Economists Do?*, Indianapolis, IN: Liberty Fund.
Calabresi, G. and Melamed, A.D. 'Property rules, liability rules, and inalienability: one view of the cathedral', *Harvard Law Review* 85, 1972: 1089–1128.
De Geest, G. 'N problems require N instruments', *International Review of Law and Economics* 35, 2013: 42–57.
Kaldor, N. 'Welfare propositions in economics and interpersonal comparisons of utility', *Economic Journal* 49, 1939: 549–552.
Kaplow, L. and Shavell, S. 'Any non-welfarist method of policy assessment violates the Pareto principle', *Journal of Political Economy* 109, 2001: 281–286.
Kaplow, L. and Shavell, S. (2002) *Fairness versus Welfare*, Cambridge, MA: Harvard University Press.
Robbins, L. (1932) *Essay on the Nature and Significance of Economic Science*, London: Macmillan.
Robbins, L. 'Interpersonal comparisons of utility: a comment', *Economic Journal* 48, 1938: 635–641.
Samuels, W.J. and Schmid, A.A. (1981) *Law and Economics: An Institutional Perspective*, Boston, MA: Nijhoff.
Scheler, M. (1973 [1913]) *Formalism in Ethics and Non-Formal Ethics of Values*, Evanston, IL: Northwestern University Press.

Scitovsky, T. 'A note on welfare propositions in economics', *Review of Economic Studies* 9, 1941: 77–88.

Van Dun, F. (1983) *Het fundamenteel rechtsbeginsel*, Antwerp: Murray Rothbard Instituut.

11 Law and economics, the moral limits of the market, and threshold deontology

*Thomas S. Ulen**

Introduction

The academic world is awash with jokes that seem to capture the essence of those in the university's different disciplines. "How do you recognize an extrovert engineer? While he's talking to you, he looks at *your* shoes." Economists have been the object of these jokes for years, typically for being heartless.[1]

When I first came to the University of Illinois Department of Economics, my graduate school education had already acculturated me to the fact that a professional economist keeps his or her feelings about morals at bay in doing real economics. The principal criterion by which the microeconomist evaluates economic situations is allocative or Pareto efficiency.

In the early 1980s, when I began teaching in a law school, I could no longer assume that my colleagues or students shared the professional economist's devotion to efficiency and agreement to postpone talking about the moral aspects of situations. The law students, although interested in the new field of law and economics, were clearly uneasy about my not talking about distributive or fairness matters but were willing to defer to me because I was standing at the front of the room. I did include a short treatment of the literature on social choice and the Arrow Impossibility Theorem, hoping thereby to indicate that economists had given up on talking about social preferences for very respectable intellectual reasons (arguments that I briefly reprise later in this chapter).

None of those stratagems (nor any others that I have since tried, such as teaching law and economics not as a comprehensive doctrine that must be swallowed whole or not at all, but rather as a set of tools for analyzing the law) for deflecting interest in fairness, justice, distributive equity, and morality has lessened the uneasiness with which lawyers, law professors, judges, and law students approach law and economics.

So, I recently tried something new: I gave over an entire lecture to a description of some novel market transactions, such as selling space on one's body for tattooed advertisements, many of which transactions, I thought, would provoke discussion in the class. I was wrong. The students did not rise to this bait at all. They dutifully wrote down all the examples, perhaps expecting them to show up on the end-of-semester test. They later told me that they thought that my examples of odd or questionable market transactions were a trick, meant to catch them out. After all, they later told me in a syllogistic argument, you are an economist; economists love the market; so, we thought that you would like these examples of market transactions extending into previously unknown regions.

That experience was the genesis of this chapter. And it has led me to begin this investigation of the morality or fairness issue in economics and in law and economics from a novel starting point. In the third section I consider what the moral limits of the marketplace might be. I have long felt that there is such a limit, and over the years I have tried to give examples of market incentives that seem at odds with what is acceptable or moral – for example, tipping the hostess at a friend's house for the meal they have invited you to share (but, nonetheless, taking a bottle of wine or bouquet of flowers for that hostess), paying a friend who takes you to the airport as if he were a taxi driver (but offering to pay for her gas or parking), or paying one's spouse or partner for a loving kiss. But I have never tried to articulate why these and other examples cross the line between acceptable and unacceptable bargains, although in each of the instances just cited there are fairly obvious reasons, such as confusing friendship and an arm's-length market transaction. Beginning a discussion of morality in law and economics in these terms maps onto prior discussions of these matters, but not perfectly.

I am fairly certain that I will not succeed here in fully articulating the line that separates where the market ends and other social governance mechanisms begin. It happens, however, that there are both some older and some newer economic writings on this topic and that both help to throw some light on the moral limits of markets.[2]

In the fourth section I turn to a more conventional topic regarding morality in law and economics: the contrast between deontology and consequentialism as the basis for law. That section reviews some recent writing by two Israeli law-and-economics scholars – Eyal Zamir and Barak Medina – who propose an accommodation between consequentialism and deontology that they call "threshold deontology."

The fifth section outlines a modest proposal for incorporating considerations of morality and threshold deontology into the literature on law and economics. My proposal is modest because the topic is so complex that I cannot claim to encompass it.

A concluding section summarizes the argument.

The economist's case for ignoring morality

Economists – with an exception to be noted shortly – generally do not pay much attention to morality, fairness, or justice for several perfectly sound reasons. First, note that this lack of concern is certainly *not* due to the fact that economists do not care about fairness, justice, and morality, regardless of what the jokes about economists imply. They certainly *do* care. But, second, they believe that there is almost nothing in economics that allows them to say something meaningful about fairness, justice, or morality.[3] Those matters, economists have long maintained, are the domain of other disciplines, such as philosophy, sociology, history, and theology. The central normative concept for economists is efficiency, and with regard to that concept they have well-honed and well-known ideas.

Third, since the 1930s economists have been deeply committed to the notion that utility (or subjective well-being), which they presume that all consumers are seeking to maximize, is such a deeply subjective matter that it cannot be objectified into a measurable quantity that can then be compared between and among individuals. Ordinal, not cardinal, utility is at the heart of the modern theory of consumer behavior.[4] As a result, it is difficult for economists to give a precise account of when involuntary transfers (as through the taxation and benefit-creating activities of government) make the recipients better off than the donors. Insofar as there is an economic account of the benefit-creation aspect of these transfers, that account focuses on the fact that there is likely to be decreasing marginal utility of income and wealth so that a transfer from the rich to the poor is, all other things equal, likely to increase the well-being of the poor more than it diminishes that of the rich.[5]

Fourth, and perhaps most importantly, economists deeply believe in the separability of efficiency and fairness.[6] They believe that they can describe the conditions that will lead to general equilibrium – that is, the simultaneous consistency, in all markets, of quantity demanded and quantity supplied at a uniform price in each market – and the desirable properties of such an equilibrium – namely, that it is Pareto efficient (no one can be made better off without making at least one other person worse off). But once having reached an efficient outcome, the tax-and-transfer system can be used to move to any other point on the so-called "production possibilities frontier" to achieve a desirable distribution of income, wealth, and goods and services.

Because the expertise of economists is with the efficiency part of this separability, they focus on that topic in the belief that once efficiency has been achieved, then those adept at fairness can recommend principles of redistribution among the equally efficient outcomes to achieve their fairness goal.[7]

There is an economics literature that begins in the 1930s and continues through today that seeks to say more about fairness. That literature is called "social choice" and has become so vast and so complicated that it is beyond my ability to summarize it in its entirety.[8] However, I can give the sense of what a main topic of the literature is and what some of its principal points have been.

Shortly after the Hicksian revolution of the 1930s and its articulation of the individual utility function, Abram Bergson (1938) recognized that societies might also have a utility function that had some of the same well-defined properties (such as convexity to the origin) of the individual utility function. If so, that social welfare function would tell a policymaker, for instance, how to weight the utility of different policies and of different individuals into a unique, socially desirable outcome along the production possibilities frontier.[9]

Kenneth Arrow, however, demonstrated – in one of the most famous economic results of the twentieth century – that there is no method, such as democratic voting, by which to make social choices like those suggested by the social welfare function that does not violate one of five desirable properties.[10]

The literature since Arrow's famous 1951 result has sought to show that the Impossibility Theorem is not as restrictive as originally thought, or that one could relax one of the five conditions without dire consequence, or that there is some other corrective.[11] Nonetheless, none of these rehabilitative attempts has commanded enough acclaim to undo the Arrow result.

And there matters stand.

Some recent literature on morality and the market

In this section I first summarize and critique the writing of Michael J. Sandel on the limits of the market. Sandel is troubled by the increasing use of market instruments to make a profit and as solutions to public policy issues. He believes that these novel uses of the marketplace may violate arguments from moral and political philosophy.

In the last part of this section I turn to a consideration of some other recent economic writing on the relationship between morality and the market.

Sandel on the limits of markets

Michael J. Sandel, Professor of Government at Harvard, in a popular book – *What Money Can't Buy: The Moral Limits of Markets* (2012) – and in a summary article (Sandel 2013) has given some remarkable examples of situations in which market or market-like transactions have arisen in unusual circumstances:

1   In Santa Ana, California, nonviolent offenders who must spend time in jail can upgrade the cell to one with some better amenities by paying $82 per night.
2   In Minneapolis a solo driver can access the lanes reserved for high-occupancy vehicles (the "HOV" lanes) during rush hours by paying $8.
3   One can outsource the carrying of a fetus to term: For $6,250 one can hire a South Asian surrogate mother to bear a fetus to delivery for about one-third of the cost that one would pay in North America.
4   Those foreigners who would like to emigrate to the United States can jump to the front of the queue for visas by agreeing to invest $500,000 in an enterprise that creates at least ten new jobs in a high-unemployment area.
5   South Africa will allow one to shoot an endangered black rhino for a fee of $150,000, on the ground that this will encourage ranchers to raise the rhinos.
6   Rather than wait for an appointment with your doctor, you can pay $15,000 per year for an individual or $25,000 per year for a family to have "concierge medicine" through a group like MD^2 ("MD Squared"), a company founded in Seattle in 1996. The fee gives you access to your doctor at any time.

7 If you need some extra income, you can offer to stand in line for a seat at a Congressional hearing for a lobbyist at the rate of $15–20 per hour: www. linestanding.com.

8 You can rent out space on your forehead or elsewhere on your body for advertisements: "Air New Zealand hired 30 people to shave their heads and wear temporary tattoos with the slogan, 'Need a change? Head down to New Zealand.'" (Sandel 2012: 184)

9 You can buy the life insurance policy of an ill or elderly person – giving them immediate cash to help, for example, with medical payments – in exchange for being designated the policy's beneficiary when the person dies. (This "viatical settlement" industry, as it is called, is a $30 billion per year industry.)

10 Tongue-tied at how to apologize for something you did? You can hire the Tianjin Apology Society to write for you.[12]

11 If you have the responsibility to give a toast at a friend's wedding or retirement party, there's no need to agonize about what to say. Go, instead, to www.perfecttoast.com, fill out a questionnaire, pay $149, and within three days you will receive a script for a three- to five-minute toast.[13]

12 The internet has created some interesting examples of novel transactions. Consider "death pools." "For a $15 entry fee, contestants submit a list of celebrities they think are likely to die by year's end. Whoever makes the most correct calls wins the jackpot of $3,000; second place is $500." (See www.stiff.com.)

13 In 1991 a British novelist, Fay Weldon, agreed to mention the luxury company Bulgari a minimum of twelve times in her next novel for an undisclosed fee from the company.

14 Approximately 40 percent of all life-insurance polices written in the United States are so-called "spin life" or STOLI ("stranger-originated life insurance") policies. (These are now banned in many states.) For example, investors "have sponsored free cruises for seniors willing to undergo physical exams and apply for life insurance while on board" with the cruise sponsors paying the policy premiums and being designated as the policy beneficiaries.

15 Consider that some employers have taken out life-insurance policies on some of their employees or customers – sometimes referred to as "janitors's insurance" or "dead peasants's insurance."

16 And finally, Kari Smith, the mother of an 11-year-old special-needs son who required special education "auctioned commercial access to her forehead [in exchange for a] permanent tattoo advertisement on her forehead for a commercial sponsor willing to pay $10,000. An online casino met her price. Although the tattoo artist tried to dissuade her, Smith persisted and had her forehead branded with the casino's website address." (Sandel 2012: 184).

Some of these examples are cute, such as the apology society and the fee to acquire a perfect toast; some make us wonder if things might have gone too far, such as the permanent advertisement tattoo and the payment for an upgraded jail cell; and some suggest an interesting and possibly socially beneficial use of market reasoning to achieve a legitimate social end. For example, allowing solo drivers to pay to use HOV lanes strikes me as a potentially efficient transaction. If there is not overcrowding in those lanes, and if the fee paid by the solo drivers fully captures whatever congestion costs the additional car imposes, it is hard not to suspect that this may be an efficient transaction. It might, for instance, allow someone with a very important appointment to get to that meeting on time, which she would not be able to do if she could not access the HOV lanes. The transaction to purchase a wedding or retirement toast or to mention a paying customer several times in a novel are a little bit close to the line (wherever that line might be), but ultimately not terribly off-putting.

But other examples seem to go too far. The necessity of the mother of a special-needs student to have to sell a permanent advertisement on her forehead to finance her son's special education says, perhaps, something disturbing about our social priorities. Why should that child and his mother not have access to special education at either public expense or with substantial public subsidization? The poor mother's anxiety brings to mind the great nineteenth-century novels of Charles Dickens, Victor Hugo, and others that criticized the tragic choices facing the poor in a rapidly industrializing society.

The question, of course, is where do we draw the line between transactions that should and should not be allowed. Sandel has some interesting thoughts on this matter but no clear theory. Rather, he says that he is simply troubled by the growing role that money and markets play in "procreation and childrearing, health and education, sports and recreation, criminal justice, environmental protection, military service, political campaigns, public spaces, and civil life," realms in which they have not played significant roles before (Sandel 2013: 121). And, importantly, Sandel believes that in deciding where money and markets should and should not be allowed, "economics is a poor guide" (Sandel 2013: 122). We should look instead to moral and political philosophy for help in finding the moral limits of the marketplace.

Unfortunately, Sandel offers only the sparsest guidance as to how to use moral and political philosophy to answer the central question. Much of the time he relies on rhetorical questions that hint at outrage ("Should the United States sell the right to immigrate? What about allowing existing US citizens to sell their citizenship to foreigners and swap places with them? Should we allow a free market in babies up for adoption? Should people be allowed to sell their votes?" (Sandel 2013: 121). Or that "putting a price tag on children would objectify them, fail to respect their dignity, and erode the norm of unconditional love" (Sandel 2013: 123). Or that "there is something troubling about a system in which people buy and sell the right to have kids" (Sandel 2013: 130).

Nonetheless, Sandel raises interesting and important points. First, he says that some market transactions "corrupt or crowd-out non-market values worth caring about" (Sandel 2013: 123). So, for example, trying to buy a bride or a friendship may cause the buyer to think that there's no significant difference between

selfless love and a purchase and may make the person bought or befriended suspicious that someone may not really like them but simply "possesses" them.[14] To
put the matter starkly, when someone does something for you simply out of love
and without any particular idea of reciprocity – as when you arrange for an
anonymous present for your children or grandchildren, simply because you love
them – that is clearly a different and, I think we can agree, an admirable and
touching matter. In economic terms, we can effectively signal our affection for
someone by generosity and anonymity, by not seeking praise or reciprocity.

Relatedly, Sandel says that there is evidence that commodifying a good or
service – that is, allowing market transactions in some goods and services –
changes the nature of those goods or services, principally by crowding out nonmarket norms. (In contrast, economists typically assume that the transaction
itself does not change the nature of the thing being bought or sold.)

Consider the famous example of blood donation first discussed by Richard
Titmuss in *The Gift Relationship* (1971). Titmuss

> argued that turning blood into a market commodity eroded people's sense of
> obligation to donate blood, diminished the spirit of altruism, and under-
> mined the "gift relationship" as an active feature of social life. "Commer-
> cialization and profit in blood has been driving out the voluntary donor"

he wrote. "Once people begin to view blood as a commodity that is routinely
bought and sold," Titmuss suggested, "they are less likely to feel a moral
responsibility to donate it."[15]

Sandel has another striking example in which the confusion between public
spirit and a market transaction can change how people feel about a certain action:

> When residents of a Swiss town were asked whether they would be willing
> to approve a nuclear waste site in their community if the Parliament decided
> to build it there, 51 percent said yes. Then the respondents were offered a
> sweetener: Suppose the Parliament proposed building the nuclear waste
> facility in your community *and* offered to compensate each resident with an
> annual monetary payment. Adding the financial inducement did not increase
> the rate of acceptance. In fact, it cut it in half – from 51 percent to 25
> percent. ... 83 percent of those who rejected the monetary proposal
> explained their opposition by saying they could not be bribed.
>
> (Sandel 2013: 133)[16]

Sandel notes that these examples make an *economic* case – to which I shall
return – that public spiritedness, altruism, civic virtue, and the like are valuable
social assets. As with the voluntary blood donations and allowing the nearby dis-
posal of nuclear waste, these behaviors could have been motivated in other ways,
such as by eminent domain proceedings with compensation, tax holidays, and
otherwise. But being able to call on citizens's public spiritedness may be a very
inexpensive means of achieving desirable social ends.

While I stress the economic interpretation of this matter, Sandel cites an independent moral reason for relying on civic virtue when one can – namely, that public spiritedness, altruism, and generosity are habits that grow through being exercised. Thus, if the public is called upon to make an uncompensated sacrifice and does so, that may lead the public to make more such sacrifices in the future. Sandel's view is that there is not a fixed or limited supply of generosity but that it, like a muscle, increases and strengthens through frequent use. This is akin to Aristotle's view of virtue – that virtue is a habit and that we can become more virtuous by practicing virtuous habits (rather than, for example, by reasoning ourselves to be virtuous).

Second, Sandel says that "severe inequality can undermine the voluntary character of an exchange," raise issues of fairness, and foster corruption (Sandel 2013: 123). As examples, he points to the buying of votes, the market in nicer jail cells, and concierge medicine. The Nobel Prize winner James Tobin argued that there are some realms of social life, such as healthcare, education, and access to justice, where egalitarianism should prevail in the sense that in those areas, everyone should be treated precisely the same.[17] Perhaps Tobin believed (and Sandel believes) that there are moral arguments for these spheres of egalitarianism, but to my knowledge neither of them fleshed out those arguments.

Third, Sandel points to what Al Roth calls "repugnance" as a ground for disallowing some market transactions (Roth 2007). Roth gives examples such as the fact that it is illegal to eat horse or dog meat in California, to sell *foie gras* in Chicago, to enslave other humans or subject them to indentured servitude, to price-gouge consumers after disasters, to sell pollution permits, to toss dwarves, or to buy and sell organs for transplantation (Roth 2007: 37–38). He further notes that "some transactions that are not repugnant as gifts and in-kind exchanges become repugnant when money is added" (Roth 2007: 44). Examples are sex and a voluntary kidney donation.

Roth is well aware that there is a possible interaction between repugnance and the presence of negative externalities, without its being clear whether the principal reason for regulation is an attempt to internalize the externalities or to give effect to the widespread repugnance. He is also aware that sometimes what is repugnant changes – sometimes as tastes change, sometimes as consumers become educated and find that their repugnance is ill-justified and come to accept a market-like solution. He urges economists, when they find that the repugnance is misguided, not to "give up on the important educational role of pointing to inefficiencies, tradeoffs, and costs and benefits."[18]

There is no theory of what makes for repugnance, nor of what ought to be repugnant. Roth seems content to let widespread consumer sentiment define what is repugnant. He says that in his efforts to design markets or allocative mechanisms, he and his colleagues seek to defer to attitudes of repugnance. Roth recognizes, for example, that there is a widespread repugnance to cash transactions in transplantable organs. So, in trying to increase the supply of those organs, he has tried to design alternatives that defer to this repugnance. For instance, he and his co-authors have proposed "kidney exchanges" in which a patient with a willing donor who has an incompatible blood type (or who is incompatible for another reason) can exchange a kidney with another such incompatible patient–donor pair. (That is, the pairs are matched so that the donor from one pair is compatible with the patient from the other, and each patient receives a kidney from the other patient's donor.)[19]

Although Sandel does not have a complete or satisfying theory of what the moral limits of the marketplace are, he has raised some significant points. I take it that he has made a convincing case for the proposition that there are moral limits to the market and market-like transactions.[20] We shall have to feel our way a little further toward a theory of where those limits are and how we might implement those limits in implementing law and public policy based on those limits.

Other economic writing on morality

In this section I want to discuss several other recent attempts by economists to say something about the appropriate relationship between morality and economics.

The first is an article by Bruni and Sugden (2013) that urges that economists pay attention to virtue ethics, which they define as the "study of moral character." Bruni and Sugden characterize the field of virtue ethics, which begins with Aristotle's *Nicomachean Ethics*, as being extremely hostile to the market economy and to the academic field of economics:

> Expressed crudely, the charge sheet is this: The market depends on instrumental rationality and extrinsic motivation; market interactions therefore fail to respect the internal value of human practices and the intrinsic motivations of human actors; by using market exchange as its central model, economics normalizes extrinsic motivation, not only in markets but also in social life more generally; therefore, economics is complicit in an assault on virtue and on human flourishing.
>
> (Bruni and Sugden 2013: 141)

Bruni and Sugden disagree with this characterization. Most economists will defend economics and the market economy from the virtue-ethics criticism by asserting that the many material benefits (including the income and leisure to devote to nonmarket, intrinsically valuable activities) of capitalism are so much greater than the costs that the move to a market economy is justified. And economics survives criticism, the replies argue, because it explains the workings of the market economy that delivers this excess of benefits over costs.

But Bruni and Sugden undertake a more aggressive defense of the market and of economics, a defense that they are quick to point out, uses the language of virtue ethics:

Our central idea is that the public benefits of markets should be understood as the aggregate of the mutual benefits gained by individuals as parties to voluntary transactions, and that the market virtues are dispositions that are directed at this kind of mutual benefit. For a virtuous market participant, mutual benefit is not just a fortunate by-product of the individual pursuit of self-interest: He or she *intends* that transactions with others are mutually beneficial.... Our list of market virtues (which we do not claim is complete) includes universality, enterprise and alertness, respect for the tastes of one's trading partners, trust and trustworthiness, acceptance of competition, self-help, non-rivalry, and stoicism about reward. We will argue that these market virtues, grounded on ideas of reciprocity and mutual benefit, are closely associated with virtues of civil society more generally. It is, therefore, a mistake to think that the market is a virtue-free zone, or that the character traits that best equip individuals to flourish in markets are necessarily corrosive of virtue in other domains of life.

(Bruni and Sugden 2013: 143)[21]

There is, of course, something to this view. Markets can teach or enhance virtuous conduct. A merchant might take as his guiding principle to treat others as he (or she) would like to be treated. Indeed, that Golden Rule might be so strongly associated with successful commerce that it spreads and displaces a cruder pre-capitalist view that sees all rivals as inferior and all customers as objects of exploitation. And, further, successful capitalists may generously give substantial portions of their fortune to the public or to their communities. The library in my grandparents's small town in central Indiana had a Carnegie Library in which I spent many happy hours as a child. The Gates Foundation has given millions of dollars to worthy causes worldwide.

And yet, while the marketplace may foster generosity, cooperation, respect, and other virtues, there are also offsetting stories of capitalist exploitation, opportunism, rapaciousness of nations and peoples, callous disregard for the unfortunate, and the like.

I would like to endorse the Bruni–Sugden view of the consonance of the market and virtue ethics, but I cannot comfortably embrace that view wholeheartedly. I am fairly confident that a weaker version of what they argue for is true – namely, that the market economy is no worse than other forms of social organization (such as tyranny and the feudal society) and may be, in important regards, much better.

David Rose makes an important contribution to this literature in *The Moral Foundation of Economic Behavior* (2011). His central point is that as societies grow larger or trade across greater distances, people are engaged in transactions with strangers rather than with those who are family, neighbors, co-religionists, or tribe members. With the latter group there are many reasons of biology and repeat play that minimize opportunism in transactions. But with strangers the possibility of opportunistic behavior is much larger. Some alternative means of limiting opportunism must accompany the expansion of the market.

Rose's central point is that legal institutions are relatively ineffectual at controlling opportunism, but that morality and religion are highly effectual in controlling opportunistic behavior. As a result, Rose contends that the inculcation of moral and religious values through familial teaching, cultural transmission, and the like are a vital part of instilling trust among peoples who are strangers and that morality-instilled trust is a more effectual means of minimizing opportunism than any other social policy. That is, without a moral foundation, participants in market economies will so fear opportunistic behavior that the economy may not work well.[22]

Morality in law and economics

As I mentioned in the introduction, law and economics initially had a difficult time getting accepted in the legal academy. The central reason seemed to be its aggressive insistence on efficiency as a (or *the*) legal norm, an insistence that ran full-tilt into the widespread view that law was about justice and fairness. The debate about these seemingly competing norms by which to judge the law found one of its greatest expositions in the marvelous work of Louis Kaplow and Steven Shavell, *Fairness versus Welfare* (2002), which ringingly defended the efficiency norm, and in the many very critical reviews of that book.[23]

Instead of rehearsing that literature, I would like to review a recent contribution that I believe merits much more consideration than it has had – Eyal Zamir and Barak Medina's *Law, Economics, and Morality* (2010), and a companion article (Zamir and Medina 2008). I shall also briefly review some commentators's thoughts on Zamir and Medina in a Symposium in the *Jerusalem Review of Legal Studies* devoted to their book.

The central focus of Zamir and Medina is the difference between consequentialist and deontological justifications for law. Generally speaking, law and economics (and economics) takes a consequentialist view of legal principles. Consequentialism can be said to hold that acts, practices, intentions, behaviors, rules, and the like should be judged by their results. An act is bad if it has a bad result – diminishes well-being, say – and is good if it has good consequences – increases well-being, for example. So, a good result is morally acceptable, even if the means by which the result came about are questionable. There are different varieties of consequentialism, their differences depending, in part, on the particular results that count as desirable and undesirable.

Traditional legal analysis favors a deontological view. Deontology (the "study of duty") holds that actions cannot be deemed morally right or wrong according to their consequences. Rather, they are deemed right or wrong according to a theory (there are many options for this theory) that defines what is correct duty. A person who complies with that correct duty has satisfied his or her moral obligation, regardless of the outcome.

A handy means of distinguishing consequentialism and deontological theories is to recognize that deontology focuses on the *right*, while consequentialism focuses on the *good* (Alexander and Moore 2012).

Two famous examples of an important difference between consequentialism and deontology are called "Transplant" and the "Trolley Problem":

> A surgeon has five patients dying of organ failure and one healthy patient whose organs can save five. In the right circumstances, surgeon will be permitted (and indeed required) by consequentialism to kill the healthy patient to acquire his organs, assuming there are no relevant consequences other than the saving of the five and the death of the one. Likewise, consequentialism will permit ... that a fat man be pushed in front of a runaway trolley if his being crushed by the trolley will halt its advance towards five workers trapped on the track.
>
> (Alexander and Moore 2012)[24]

Deontological theories would not permit either interference – with the healthy patient or the fat man – on the ground that one person cannot, without his or her genuine consent, be used as a means to another person's benefit.

Law and economics and traditional law have wrestled with the question of whether laws are and should be premised on consequentialist or deontological theories. Consider tort liability. Consequentialism holds that the tort liability system ought to place its foundation on the premise that accident law should minimize the social costs of accidents. In contrast, deontological theories start from the premise that it is wrong to harm another person or her property and that someone who does so has a moral obligation, a duty, to right that wrong. The words and ideas may be different, but the standards they express amount to the same thing.

These different views of the tort liability system may not lead to large differences in the actual standards that courts apply in accident cases. For example, a consequentialist may excuse a defendant for harming another if he took all cost-justified care, and a deontologist may excuse that same defendant if he complied with the duty of care that he owed the victim.

But in other areas of the law, there may be important differences between these theories. For instance, the deontologist may hold that harming another has almost no justification (save perhaps in self-defense), while a consequentialist might hold that there are a broader range of circumstances in which harming another has excusable justification – as when killing one person would save five others.

A second common example has to do with breach of contract. A deontological view would be that it is wrong to break a promise. But a consequentialist view would hold that there are circumstances in which the results of breaking a promise are better than those from performing the promise and that, therefore, the promisor should be excused from performance, so long as she compensates the promisee and that there is no immorality that should attach to non-performance in those circumstances.

Zamir and Medina are bothered by the fact that there is an apparently unbridgeable gap between deontological and consequentialist theories of the law, and they hope to provide a bridge. The first step in their argument is to note that most currently prevailing deontological theories are *moderate* rather than *absolutist*. Moderate deontological theories admit that constraints have thresholds:

> A constraint may be overridden for the sake of furthering good outcomes or avoiding bad ones if enough good (or bad) is at stake. Thus, while consequentialism (at least presumably) approves the deliberate killing of one innocent person to save the lives of two, moderate deontology may justify such killing only for the sake of saving many more people, perhaps hundreds or thousands. Similarly, while consequentialism supports the breaking of a promise whenever it would produce slightly more net benefit than keeping it, moderate deontology would justify breaking a promise only to avoid very considerable losses (an absolutist would object to killing or breaking a promise under any circumstances). Moderate deontology conforms to prevailing moral intuitions ("commonsense morality").
>
> (Zamir and Medina 2008: 326)[25]

Zamir and Medina recognize that one of the most powerful criticisms of consequentialism is that it allows too much:

> It imposes no restrictions on attaining the best outcomes, thus legitimizing, and even requiring, harming people, lying, and promise breaking as means to achieve desirable results. Consequentialism does not recognize the moral rights of people over their body, labor, and talents. Thus, consequentialism arguably requires that we kill one person and harvest her organs to save the lives of five other people, or that we torture the baby daughter of a terrorist to force the terrorist to reveal information that may save lives.
>
> (Zamir and Medina 2008: 331)

Consequentialism does not seem to care how an agent brings about any given outcome. And that view (whether completely accurate) does not comport with commonsense morality, nor with deontological theories.[26] Deontology puts a great deal of emphasis on how one acts, drawing a "substantial moral difference between *actively harming* a person and *not aiding* her (often labeled the *doing/allowing* distinction)" (Zamir and Medina 2008: 332). And that distinction resonates with commonsense morality.

Zamir and Medina also find fault with deontological constraints. Even if it is wrong to harm another person or to use them as a means to an end, "it seems irrational to oppose such harming or such use when the outcome of not harming or not using the person is a greater amount of equally severe harming or using of other people" (Zamir and Medina 2008: 343). As a result, they would be comfortable altering the Biblical commandment from "Thou shalt not kill" to "Thou shalt not kill unless – all things considered – killing would enhance overall human welfare" (Zamir and Medina 2008: 335).

The upshot of their investigation is that analysis should begin with the deontological constraints that comport with commonsense morality but that those constraints should give way to consequentialist reasoning when the harm to be avoided or the good to be realized from violating the constraint are large enough. But what constitutes harms or benefits that are "large enough" to warrant violating the deontological constraints? Where, that is, does the threshold lie between deontological constraints and consequentialist reasoning?

Zamir and Medina cannot answer that question easily, although they canvas the possibilities for defining a "threshold function" admirably. They recognize that setting thresholds may be an incoherent exercise. Nonetheless, they believe that thresholds must exist and command our attention and respect. They hold that "there is nothing incoherent in maintaining that (contrary to consequentialism) the goodness of outcomes is not *the only* factor, and that (contrary to absolutist deontology) constraints may be outweighed by enough good outcomes" (Zamir and Medina 2008: 344–345).[27] They call this view "threshold deontology" or "deontologically constrained cost–benefit analysis."

The *Jerusalem Review of Legal Studies* hosted a symposium on Zamir and Medina's *Law, Economics, and Morality*. As might be expected, the critics focused on the administrability of threshold deontology and on the vexing issue of where to locate the threshold. Avishay Dorfman refers to Zamir and Medina's view as "humane consequentialism" and worries that a regulatory agency may have a difficult time locating and applying the threshold – so difficult a time that the agency might simply fall back on deontological theories of justice (Dorfman 2011: 66).

Larry Alexander, citing an earlier piece he wrote on deontological constraints in a consequentialist world, believes that the idea of deontological thresholds is manipulable and simply incoherent. His conclusion, quoted from the earlier piece, is a model of lucidity:

> In my opinion, the best conception of deontology would deem its core principle to be that one may never use another as a resource without his consent. In other words, a person's body, labor, and talents do not exist for others' benefit except to the extent that he freely chooses to benefit others.... The consequentialist, on the other hand, does view each of us as resources for others.... But deontology and consequentialism are incommensurable because they are fundamentally opposed conceptions of what morality is about. One sees the individual as inviolate, an end in himself, and the opposite of a resource for the betterment of the world. The other sees the individual in exactly the opposite way. The threshold deontologist would have us believe that we switch from not being resources for others to being resources for others when N is reached. When N is looked at like that, however, it seems downright implausible that the moral universe is so constituted. There may be thresholds at which new phenomena emerge, but it is quite another thing to have thresholds at which things become their opposites.

(Alexander 2011: 89–90, extending comments made in
Alexander 2000: 911–912)

Ariel Porat, a distinguished law-and-economics scholar, finds much to admire in Zamir and Medina's accommodation of consequentialism and deontology. But he also recognizes that there may be problems in implementing threshold deontology. First, there might be competing and inconsistent deontological theories with which to begin the analysis of a particular legal problem. Moreover, the threshold point with consequentialism could be different for these different deontological theories. So, how one comes out on a given legal issue might depend on which deontological theory one begins with. Finally, he notes that rather than using threshold deontology to examine most legal issues, it may prove more helpful to give preference to deontology in some areas of law and to consequentialism in others (Porat 2011).

A modest proposal

I think that it is possible to tease a coherent accommodation between morality and efficiency from this brief survey. Let me divide the task into two parts that correspond to the issues raised in the previous sections – the moral limits of the marketplace and the choice between deontological and consequentialist theories as a guide to the law.

When I introduced the marvelous Sandel examples of market transactions that seem to go too far, I noted that neither Sandel nor anyone else had provided a theory that would tell us where the moral limits of markets lie and command widespread acceptance. I cannot provide such a theory either; so, I cannot be too harsh in my criticisms of others who have failed to do so. But I can at least share my sense of what the problem is and identify the problems to which Sandel has alerted us. In entertaining the possibility of new markets, the obvious problem is that we would like to be able to distinguish between those new transactions that promise to do great good (and should, therefore, be encouraged) and those that either will not do much good or will do much harm (and should, therefore, be discouraged).

In drawing these distinctions, I take two important guiding principles from the literature that we saw in the third section. The first is Al Roth's identification of repugnant transactions. Some potential transactions so violate prevailing customs, morals, and norms that they seem repugnant. Because customs, morals, and norms are important aspects of social life, I find Roth's identification of this source of repugnance to be something to take seriously – with several caveats. One caveat is that, as Roth notes, ideas of what is repugnant change over time so that what was repugnant fifty years ago may be thought to be acceptable today. Same-sex relationships may be an example. The process by which the notion of repugnance alters is not well understood. Nonetheless, it happens, although the transition from repugnant to acceptable is not linear or smooth. What role law might play in this transition is a subject about which there has been much thoughtful writing.

The other caveat – one that Roth stressed – is that if the reason for the repugnance is misguided – as was the case with suggestions that there be a market for pollution permits and is still the case with respect to a market for unmatured tort claims (Cooter 1989) – then one hopes that lawyers and economists and others will do their best to educate the public that the repugnance is misguided.

There is no doubt that this education works. I recall, as an illustration, that when law and economics first began to work through the notion of "efficient breach of contract," the legal academy was skeptical. Some critics scoffingly compared the idea to "efficient commission of crime"; others noted the great difference between commonsense morality's view that there is a moral obligation to perform a promise and the economist's cavalier idea that the promisor could perform or not according to his or her cost–benefit analysis.[28] Now that we have had about three decades to examine the concept of efficient breach, it has become a commonplace view. Nearly every contracts casebook treats the concept as a central concept of contract law.[29]

There is a related matter on which I have touched at various points and that Bruni and Sugden noted: That is the importance of character and the difference between intrinsic and extrinsic motivation.

Let me give an example of what I mean by considering incentives within an academic enterprise. How should an academic department structure the incentives for rewarding the members of the department so as best to achieve the collective and individual goals of the department? This is not an easy or obvious management problem. First, there are many tasks that the academic department must undertake – teaching introductory, intermediate, and advanced undergraduate classes; teaching graduate classes; administering the affairs of the department through committees; gathering periodically to discuss mutual issues, such as who to hire and promote and to whom to award chairs and professorships; how to spend excess revenues; how to raise revenue; how to finance deficits; where to recruit students; how to reward faculty members for their research; and so on. Of course, some of these matters can be delegated to administrators, who then report back to the faculty how certain tasks will be handled. So, the issues with which the enterprise must deal are numerous, intertwined, and complex.

But let's focus on just one of them – how to incentivize and reward faculty members for their scholarly productivity. If you believe that extrinsic incentives are often effective, even in instances in which they have not been common, then you might seek to induce better and more scholarly output from your colleagues by promising them financial and other rewards for that output. But is that the right means to induce better and more scholarship?[30]

I believe that it is not. I think that we should be looking for colleagues who are *intrinsically motivated* to produce good scholarship. That is, they so enjoy or even love the process of discovery and communication that if given the choice between pursuing scholarship and doing almost anything else, they would devote their energies to that process. Let me not grow overly romantic or sappy about this. Everyone has got to have a concern for having enough income to live life in a manner they deem appropriate, and everyone must believe that his or her work is appropriately valued. But the larger point remains – intrinsically motivated scholarship is likely to be more highly desirable than scholarship produced solely for material rewards.[31]

The problem is a general one (Bénabou and Tirole 2003). There are some valuable habits and practices that might be encouraged by intrinsic or extrinsic motivation, and, for many of those, we prefer intrinsic motivation as the source of the habit and practice. For instance, we hope that children will come to enjoy reading and learning for the pleasure they give, not just because they are paid for good grades or for each book they read (Fryer Jr. 2010). Or that people will come to value the improved health and well-being that comes from regular exercise rather than being paid to go to the gym (DellaVigna and Malmendier 2006; see also DellaVigna 2009).

One of the difficulties with the view that intrinsic motivation is sometimes more desirable than extrinsic motivation through external incentives is that it is hard to measure intrinsic motivation. Moreover, there is a complicated relationship between intrinsic and extrinsic motivation: One may be intrinsically motivated but so off-put by the lack of extrinsic rewards that one becomes cynical, depressed, or non-productive. It is much easier to be intrinsically motivated if others recognize and reward that source of motivation.

There is another point that I should make about the example that I have just given and the topic of morality and efficiency. I have been speaking as if the choice between intrinsic and extrinsic motivation for a particular task is really a search for the most efficient means of achieving some end. If, for instance, we believe that intrinsically motivated scholars produce more and better scholarship than do those motivated by extrinsic rewards, then we are in favor of identifying intrinsically motivated scholars and of not using extrinsic rewards because they produce more and better scholarship, not because it is more moral to be intrinsically motivated.

This is a tendency that I simply cannot break away from easily. The line that I seek to draw regarding the limits of the market – that is, of where and when to use extrinsic rewards as incentives (Gneezy *et al.* 2011) – is not obviously about right versus wrong in a moral sense. This fuzziness about the distinction between right and wrong and effective and ineffective is, I believe, an inherent and central part of the confusion about this topic.

One last point. If people in an academic department only did things in response to extrinsic motivation, the department would not work very well. There have to be some people who are willing to do things for intrinsic motivational reasons. A wise dean once told me that in a faculty of about 40, there were about ten people – perhaps a few more than that – on whom he could count to do things for the good of the organization without explicit compensation. If given a job to do – chair a committee, write a report, sit as an adjudicator in an internal mess – they would do that job and do it well. They did not have to be induced to do so by a promise of summer research funds or a course off. And, this dean added, without these intrinsically motivated people, no amount or quality of scholarly output by the remainder of the faculty would be enough to make the enterprise work.

That observation leads me to my last point about the moral limits of markets. Sandel cites an important economic argument for relying on markets generally and for economizing on the use of morality, altruism, voluntarism, and the like for accomplishing social goals. Kenneth J. Arrow, in his review of Richard Tit-muss's book on blood donations, wrote that

> I do not want to rely too heavily on substituting ethics for self-interest. I think it best on the whole that the requirement of ethical behavior be confined to those circumstances where the price system breaks down.... We do not wish to use up recklessly the scarce resources of altruistic motivation.
>
> (Arrow 1972: 354–355)

That is, virtue, trust, the willingness to sacrifice one's well-being for that of strangers, altruism, and goodwill are in relatively short supply and must be used judiciously.[32] I noted earlier that Sandel disagreed with Arrow, that Sandel believes that "our capacity for love and benevolence is not depleted with use but enlarged with practice" (Sandel 2013: 137). I wonder. My own casual empiricism on the matter suggests that Arrow, Summers, and Robertson are closer to the truth than Sandel – virtue and goodwill are in shorter supply than we would wish and that until evidence demonstrates that Sandel's view is correct, society would be well advised to draw down that limited supply very cautiously.

Finally, what about consequentialism and deontology as guides to the law? Must one choose one or the other? Zamir and Medina have suggested that there is a middle course in which one can give credence to deontological theories of the *right* but accommodate consequentialist theories of the *good*. By beginning from principles of right – that, for example, it is wrong to harm another person – one can deal with many – if not most – of life's and the law's issues. But where the harms to be avoided or the good to be realized by violating those principles are large enough, one should switch to consequentialism. This hybrid philosophy – threshold deontology – has some problems of practicability (such as defining the threshold – if the lives to be saved from sacrificing someone are 100, the choice of what to do may be hard to implement but seems straightforward; but what if the lives to be saved are ten, five, or two?), but the general idea seems so appealing that it deserves careful thought.

Conclusion

Several years ago I had an unexpected episode of ill health. The matter was very serious and, as it turned out, involved a relatively rare disease that was difficult to diagnose but, if diagnosed, could be treated fairly effectively. My doctor, for whom I shall always be extremely grateful, was initially flummoxed by my symptoms but had the good sense to seek advice from a computerized diagnostic program. When the program told him the disease that best fit the symptoms and fit it so well that there was no doubt that I had it, he vaguely remembered hearing of the disease when he was in medical school. But he had never, in more than twenty years of practice, seen anyone with the disease. He skillfully ministered to me, and although I shall never be cured, the disease is at bay.

Although I expressed my gratitude to the doctor profusely, I wondered why I did not do something more material to show him how thankful I was and am.

Sure, my insurer nearly completely compensated him, the hospital, and the staff. But why didn't I send him a personal check for a substantial sum?[33] Or send him flowers or a gift card for a meal for him and his family at a fancy restaurant? Or make a donation to the hospital's foundation in his name?

In line with some of the thoughts of this chapter, I wondered whether some or all of those gestures were within the bounds of prevailing customs, norms, and morals. A direct payment to the doctor would, I thought, clearly violate prevailing norms. Moreover, it might indicate that I thought of the doctor not as a professional who would do his best for any patient, rich or poor, but as either someone, like a waiter, who works for wages and tips, or someone who might be induced to give better service to those willing to pay more. I did not believe either of these alternatives (being particularly mindful of Tobin's argument that healthcare should be available to all on the same terms). Nor did I want to chance insulting the doctor through a misunderstanding.

The gift to the hospital's foundation in honor of the doctor was, I believe, a different matter. Not being to the direct benefit to the doctor, that gift would not be subject to the same objections but would signify my gratitude to the hospital for having treated me so grandly. But I am still struggling with whether to give that gift now or as a death bequest (when there would be absolutely no thought of my getting better care for my gift).

I am sure that most readers and most economists have had similar episodes where considerations of gratefulness or generosity conflicted with those of the value of simple market-mediated exchanges. And as I have suggested in the previous example and earlier in this chapter, we all (or most of us) give weight to those nonmarket values and, typically, act in such a way as to comply with prevailing norms, as we understand them.

My very modest proposal for law and economics and economics more generally is to give weight and credence to nonmarket values in their analysis and their policy recommendations. Be sensitive to moral and ethical values that seem to find market transactions repugnant. Find alternatives, like Roth's kidney exchanges, that respect those nonmarket values but seek to serve the same end, such as increasing the supply of life-saving organ transplants. And when confronted with a deontological constraint on right and wrong, follow it unless by violating it one can avoid great harm or realize great good.

Notes

* Swanlund Chair Emeritus, University of Illinois at Urbana-Champaign, and Professor Emeritus of Law, University of Illinois College of Law. I would like to thank Nicholas Mercuro for his encouragement and enthusiasm for this project; Aristides Hatzis for his comments on an earlier draft; and Diego Proietti, LL.M. 2014, of the University of Illinois College of Law for his invaluable research assistance.
1 A man is waiting in the hospital for a heart transplant. His cardiologist comes to say, "There's good news. We have two hearts available for transplantation. The first belongs to a 23-year-old Olympic marathoner who was struck and killed by a taxi in front of the hospital a few minutes ago. The other belongs to a 90-year-old economist

who died in the hospital this morning." Without hesitation the patient says "I'll take the economist's heart." The doctor is stunned and asks, "Why?" The patient responds: "It's never been used."

2 As will become evident, I am greatly influenced by (Sandel 2013).

3 A notable exception to the contrary is (Young 1994).

4 The fascinating recent literature on happiness has made some progress toward rendering interpersonal comparisons of subjective well-being more comparable than has been the case under the Hicksian view of ordinal utility. See, for example (Frey and Stutzer 2002; Frey 2008; Bronsteen *et al.* 2010; Layard 2005; Di Tella and MacCulloch 2006).

5 There is, of course, a burgeoning literature on the efficiency aspects of income inequality (see, for example, Persson and Tabellini 1994; McAdams 2010). There is also a well-established literature that finds that income and wealth inequality is simply immoral (see, for example, Stiglitz 2012).

6 These are the topics of the First and Second Fundamental Theorems of Welfare Economics.

7 There is a bit of sleight of hand going on in this matter. Movements along the production possibilities frontier do not satisfy the Pareto criterion, although they are all equally efficient.

8 For an introduction, see (Sen 1970).

9 This social welfare function has typically been referred to as a "Bergson–Samuelson welfare function."

10 The result is known as the "Arrow Impossibility Theorem." See (Arrow 2012).

11 See (Sen 1999). With regard to legal implications of the social choice literature, see (Farber and Frickey 1991; Stearns and Zywicki 2009).

12 There's a good mystery novel that uses an apology-writing business as its focus (Drvenkar 2011).

13 Sandel asks if you were the person toasted, would you be upset to discover that the toast-giver had paid someone else to write the words? Note that we have had "ghost writers" for prominent people's books for decades, if not centuries. Think, too, of the love letters in *Cyrano de Bergerac*.

14 These are, of course, matters of degree and circumstance. Love can flourish even in arranged marriages or between purchaser of and purchased bride. And issues of suspicion about another's motives – even without explicit monetary transactions – are common in all human affairs.

15 (Sandel 2013: 135). There is another, more traditional, economic reason that paying for blood donations was not allowed till the mid 1980s – namely, that the cost of testing blood to see that it was drug- and communicable illness-free was very high. In the absence of the ability to test blood at a reasonable price (something that became possible in the mid 1980s), the thought was that if donations arose from altruism (or the desire to win a keg of beer for one's fraternity, which motivated my friends and me in college), then those most moved by that nonmonetary motivation – an intrinsic motivation – would be most likely to donate. By contrast, there was a fear that if the motivation was extrinsic, that fact might encourage a significant number of desperate people who might be ill or drug-addicted to give blood.

16 Sandel cites Frey and Oberholzer-Gee (1997). See also the famous study of Israeli day-care centers (Gneezy and Rustichini 2000).

17 See (Tobin 1970) cited in (Besley 2013).

18 (Roth 2007: 54). As an example of this possibility, Roth cites evidence to suggest that more people are coming around to a favorable view of the benefits of a carefully regulated market in transplantable organs.

19 (Roth 2007: 38) citing (Roth *et al.* 2004).

20 There is a good and generally favorable review of *What Money Can't Buy* at (Besley 2013).

21 See also (McCloskey 2006; 2010) and (Rapaczynski 2013).
22 For a marvelous example of these phenomena, see (Nunn and Wantchekon 2011).
23 See, for example (Farber 2003). See also this marvelous collection of articles about Kaplow and Shavell and other fairness topics in law and economics (Fennell and McAdams 2014).
24 See also (Thomson 1985; Cathcart 2013; Edmonds 2013).
25 See also (Scheffler 1994).
26 As Aristides Hatzis pointed out to me, Zamir and Medina are not being fair to modern conceptions of consequentialism. Modern consequentialists, Hatzis noted, rely on rule utilitarianism (to which rules all reasonable people would, by implication, agree *ex ante*), rather than on act utilitarianism, which only looks to the results of action.
27 Zamir and Medina (2008: 351) give an extended example of the sort of calculation that a practitioner of "threshold deontology" might undertake.
28 Of course, modern law and economics did not originate this view. Oliver Wendell Holmes, Jr., did. "The duty to keep a contract at common law means a prediction that you must pay damages if you do not keep it – and nothing else" (Holmes 1897: 995).
29 But, of course, scholarship moves on. See (Markovits and Schwartz 2011) but also see (Klass 2012).
30 I write of "better" scholarship, but that is a fraught term. My experience has been that we are all made uneasy by having to make judgments about the quality of our colleagues's work, no matter how important we take that matter to be. It is unfortunately much easier to measure the quantity of output than to measure its quality, and, therefore, compensation systems have a tendency to become more focused on what is more easily measured than on what is less easily measured but, perhaps, more important. As a early academic mentor of mine once advised me, "Not all your colleagues can read, but they can all count."
31 See (Wrzesniewski and Schwartz 2014) ("instrumental [or extrinsic] motives are not always an asset and can be counterproductive to success," as shown in a study of why more than 11,000 West Point cadets wanted to attend the academy and how they fared in their careers later: Those intrinsically motivated did better in their careers in every measurable regard), describing the results in Wrzesniewski *et al.* 2014).
32 Sandel (2013: 136–137) also cites a speech by Lawrence Summers, then president of Harvard, in which he made the same economizing-of-virtue point as Arrow and a passage from Sir Dennis H. Robertson of the University of Cambridge making a similar point.
33 Aristides Hatzis pointed out to me that this practice is common in Greece, the sum being placed in a distinctive red envelope.

References

Alexander, L. 'Deontology at the threshold', *San Diego Law Review* 37, 2000, 893–912.
Alexander, L. 'Deontological constraints in a consequentialist world: a comment on *Law, Economics, and Morality*', *Jerusalem Review of Legal Studies* 3, 2011: 75–90.
Alexander, L. and Moore, M. (2012) 'Deontological ethics', in *Stanford Encyclopedia of Philosophy*, available at http://plato.stanford.edu/entries/ethics-deontological (accessed July 20, 2014).
Arrow, K.J. 'Gifts and exchanges', *Philosophy & Public Affairs* 1, 1972: 343–362.
Arrow, K.J. (2012) *Social Choice and Individual Values*, 3rd edition, New Haven, CT: Yale University Press.
Bénabou, R. and Tirole, J. 'Intrinsic and extrinsic motivation', *Review of Economic Studies* 70, 2003, 489–520.

Bergson, B. 'A reformulation of certain aspects of welfare economics', *Quarterly Journal of Economics* 52, 1938: 310–334.

Besley, T. 'What's the good of the market? An essay on Michael Sandel's *What Money Can't Buy*', *Journal of Economic Literature* 51, 2013: 478–495.

Bronsteen, J., Buccafusco, C. and Masur, J.S. 'Welfare as happiness', *Georgetown Law Journal* 98, 2010: 1583–1641.

Bruni, L. and Sugden, R. 'Reclaiming virtue ethics for economics', *Journal of Economic Perspectives* 27, 2013: 141–164.

Cathcart, T. (2013) *The Trolley Problem, Or Would You Throw the Fat Guy Off the Bridge? A Philosophical Conundrum*, New York: Workman.

Cooter, R. 'Towards a market in unmatured tort claims', *Virginia Law Review* 75, 1989: 383–411.

DellaVigna, S. 'Psychology and economics: evidence from the field', *Journal of Economic Literature* 47, 2009: 315–372.

DellaVigna, S. and Malmendier, U., 'Paying not to go to the gym', *American Economic Review* 96, 2006: 694–719.

Di Tella, R. and MacCulloch, R. 'Some uses of happiness data in economics', *Journal of Economic Perspectives* 20(1), 2006: 25–46.

Dorfman, A. 'Humane consequentialism: a critical note on Eyal Zamir & Barak Medina, *Law, Economics, and Morality*', *Jerusalem Review of Legal Studies* 3, 2011: 54–74.

Drvenkar, Z. (2011) *Sorry: A Thriller*, New York: Vintage.

Edmonds, D. (2013) *Would You Kill The Fat Man? The Trolley Problem and What Your Answer Tells Us About Right and Wrong*, Princeton, NJ: Princeton University Press.

Farber, D.A. 'What (if anything) can economics say about equity?', *Michigan Law Review* 101, 2003: 1791–1823.

Farber, D.A. and Frickey, P.P. (1991) *Law and Public Choice: A Critical Introduction*, Chicago, IL: University of Chicago Press.

Fennell, L.A. and McAdams, R.H. (eds.) (2014) *Fairness in Law and Economics*, Cheltenham: Edward Elgar.

Frey, B.S. (2008) *Happiness: A Revolution in Economics*, Cambridge, MA: MIT Press.

Frey, B. and Oberholzer-Gee, F. 'The cost of price incentives: an empirical analysis of motivation crowding-out', *American Economic Review* 87, 1997: 746–755.

Frey, B.S. and Stutzer, A. 'What can economists learn from happiness research?', *Journal of Economic Literature* 40, 2002: 402–435.

Fryer, Jr., R.G. 'Financial incentives and student achievement: evidence from randomized trials', *NBER Working Paper* 15898, 2010.

Gneezy, U. and Rustichini, A. 'A fine is a price', *Journal of Legal Studies* 29, 2000: 1–17.

Gneezy, U., Meier, S., and Rey-Biel, P. 'When and why incentives (don't) work to modify behavior', *Journal of Economic Perspectives*, 25, 2011: 191–210.

Holmes, Jr., O.W. 'The path of the law', *Harvard Law Review* 10, 1897: 457–478.

Kaplow, L. and Shavell, S. (2002) *Fairness versus Welfare*, Cambridge, MA: Harvard University Press.

Klass, G. 'To perform or pay damages', *Virginia Law Review* 98, 2012: 143–158.

Layard, R. (2005) *Happiness: Lessons From A New Science*, London: Penguin.

McAdams, R.H. 'Economic costs of inequality', *University of Chicago Legal Forum* 2010, 2010: 23–41.

McCloskey, D.N. (2006) *The Bourgeois Virtues: Ethics for an Age of Commerce*, Chicago, IL: University of Chicago Press.

McCloskey, D.N. (2010) *Bourgeois Dignity: Why Economics Can't Explain the Modern World*, Chicago, IL: University of Chicago Press.

Markovits, D. and Schwartz, A. 'The myth of efficient breach: new defenses of the expectation interest', *Virginia Law Review* 97, 2011: 1939–1208.

Nunn, N. and Wantchekon, L. 'The slave trade and the origins of mistrust in Africa', *American Economic Review* 101, 2011: 3221–3252.

Persson, T. and Tabellini, G. 'Is inequality harmful for growth?', *American Economic Review* 84, 1994: 600–621.

Porat, A. 'Eyal Zamir and Barak Medina, *Law, Economics, and Morality*', *Jerusalem Review of Legal Studies* 3, 2011: 91–106.

Rapaczynski, A. 'The moral significance of economic life', *Capitalism and Society* 8(2), 2013: art. 1.

Rose, D.C. (2011) *The Moral Foundation of Economic Behavior*, New York: Oxford University Press.

Roth, A.E. 'Repugnance as a constraint on markets', *Journal of Economic Perspectives* 21(3), 2007: 37–58.

Roth, A.E., Sönmez, T. and Ünver, M.U. 'Kidney exchange', *Quarterly Journal of Economics* 119, 2004: 457–488.

Sandel, M.J. 'Market reasoning as moral reasoning: why economists should re-engage with political philosophy', *Journal of Economic Perspectives* 27, 2013: 121–140.

Sandel, M.J. (2012) *What Money Can't Buy: The Moral Limits of Markets*, New York: Farrar, Strauss and Giroux.

Scheffler, S. (1994) *The Rejection of Consequentialism: A Philosophical Investigation of the Considerations Underlying Rival Moral Conceptions*, 2nd edition, New York: Oxford University Press.

Sen, A. (1970) *Collective Choice and Social Welfare*, San Francisco, CA: Holden-Day.

Sen, A. 'The possibility of social choice', *American Economic Review* 89, 1999: 349–378.

Stearns, M.L. and Zywicki, T.J. (2009) *Public Choice Concepts and Applications in Law*, St. Paul, MN: West.

Stiglitz, J.E. (2012) *The Price of Inequality: How Today's Divided Society Endangers Our Future*, New York: Norton.

Thomson, J.J., 'The trolley problem', *Yale Law Journal* 94, 1985: 1395–1415.

Titmuss, R.M. (1971) *The Gift Relationship: From Human Blood to Social Policy*, New York: Random House.

Tobin, J. 'On limiting the domain of inequality', *Journal of Law & Economics* 13, 1970: 263–277.

Wrzesniewski, A. and Schwartz, B. 'The secret of effective motivation', *New York Times* July 4, 2014, available at www.nytimes.com/2014/07/06/opinion/sunday/the-secret-of-effective-motivation.html (accessed July 20, 2014).

Wrzesniewski, A., Schwartz, B., Cong, X., Kane, M., Omar, A. and Kolditz, T. 'Multiple types of motives don't multiply the motivation of West Point cadets', *Proceedings of the National Academy of Sciences* 2014, forthcoming.

Young, H.P. (1994) *Equity in Theory and Practice*, Princeton, NJ: Princeton University Press.

Zamir, E. and Medina, B. 'Law, morality, and economics: integrating moral constraints with economic analysis of law', *California Law Review* 96, 2008: 323–391.

Zamir, E. and Medina, B. (2010) *Law, Economics, and Morality*, New York: Oxford University Press.

12 Moral externalities

An economic approach to the legal enforcement of morality

Aristides N. Hatzis*

Morality arises from market failure.

David Gauthier[1]

Introduction

One of the major issues in moral, political, and legal philosophy is the question of legislating morality.[2] It is quite obvious why this has always been, and still is, a hot issue: law was inseparable from religious and social morality for the greatest part of human history – and it still is in some areas of the world. Legal rules regularly reflected conventional morality, used sanctions as a deterrent for anyone who didn't conform to society's moral standards and reinforced social morals by authentically "expressing" the society's general will and by educating citizens in the process of socialization. These expressive and educative functions of the law are still considered important by both politicians and lawyers (Sunstein 1996; McAdams 2000a; 2000b), even in legal systems where positivism is dominant. Legal positivism had never managed to wipe out the overwhelming influence of morality to law, especially to criminal law, but also in more unlikely areas such as contract or tort law (Dyzenhaus *et al.* 2007). Today, even in the most liberal criminal law systems, social morality still plays a major, if contained, role. A number of human acts, behaviors, lifestyles, and choices are still categorized as "crimes" despite the fact that the individuals involved have genuinely consented to these acts and there seems to be no harm to anyone involved or other reason related to the public interest for their criminalization – other than an explicit or implicit application to social morality.

This very close relationship of law and morality is not, of course, unreasonable. Even the staunchest positivist would admit that all the major crimes are also immoral acts: murder, rape, robbery, assault, blackmail, etc. are all crimes what are also considered immoral by the great majority of citizens in the liberal secular democracies. The consensus for the criminalization of such acts is so broad that one could be tempted to use it as a criterion that is both democratic and welfarist. An act that is considered immoral by the great majority of citizens in a democratic society should definitely be prohibited and criminalized if we are to respect the democratic (majoritarian) principle. Its prohibition will supposedly satisfy the same majority of citizens, thus increasing social utility by diminishing the disutility of people morally offended by certain types of behavior.

The democratic and the utilitarian arguments for the legal enforcement of conventional morality are interrelated and intuitive. They are also politically powerful. A moralistic public policy is usually popular, especially in more traditional societies. On the other hand, a liberal policy of acknowledging or establishing rights for minorities or individuals very often sounds counterintuitive and conflicts with moral intuition,[3] reflecting social morality. The opposition to liberal policies is fiercer where these rights protect behavior that is considered immoral by the society-at-large. These policies are treated as anti-democratic, especially if they have been promulgated by the courts in spite of referenda or the decisions of legislative majorities. The courts in all these cases are accused of being anti-democratic, activist usurpers of political power rightfully belonging to the legislator and the people (Bork 2003). On the other hand, the references to the utilitarian argument are not so common in everyday political discourse. It is mostly used indirectly, implicitly or in special cases with references to the concepts of "public interest" and (as unlikely as this may sound) "human dignity."[4] These two concepts are the two more popular vehicles for the enforcement of moralistic and paternalistic policies.

In this chapter I am going to briefly present the debate on the legal regulation of morality. I am going to present the harm principle as it was famously defined by John Stuart Mill, not only as a principle for a liberal objective criminal law, but as a guiding principle for political liberalism. I call Mill's principle the "liberal principle" to differentiate it from the "democratic principle" of majoritarian collective decision-making. Even though these two principles are antagonistic in contemporary liberal democracies, they also have a symbiotic relationship. After discussing briefly the critiques to the liberal principle by legal paternalists and legal moralists, I will introduce an additional argument in favor of a moralistic view of law, the "moral externalities" argument. As we are going to see, this is a quite powerful and interesting argument which is based on amoralistic grounds and it is defended by major law and economics scholars, among others. I am going to link this argument to the argument for the impossibility of Paretian liberal (Sen 1970; 1976) and the traditional moralistic arguments developed by philosophers and lawyers (Stephen 1993 [1873]; Devlin 1977). I will try to rebut these arguments by defending a narrow version of the right to self-ownership based on the Coase theorem as this was reconstructed and used by Richard Posner and Guido Calabresi.

From the harm principle to the paradox of liberal democracy

The harm principle was famously stated by J.S. Mill in his 1859 book *On Liberty*:

> [T]he sole end for which mankind are warranted, individually or collectively, in interfering with the liberty of action of any of their number, is

self-protection. That the only purpose for which power can be rightfully exercised over any member of a civilized community, against his will, is to prevent harm to others. His own good, either physical or moral, is not a sufficient warrant. He cannot rightfully be compelled to do or forbear because it will be better for him to do so, because it will make him happier, because, in the opinions of others, to do so would be wise, or even right. These are good reasons for remonstrating with him, or reasoning with him, or persuading him, or entreating him, but not for compelling him, or visiting him with any evil in case he do otherwise. To justify that, the conduct from which it is desired to deter him, must be calculated to produce evil to some one else. The only part of the conduct of any one, for which he is amenable to society, is that which concerns others. In the part which merely concerns himself, his independence is, of right, absolute. Over himself, over his own body and mind, the individual is sovereign.

(Mill 1859: I.9)

There is, of course, a rich literature which is trying to interpret harm (Feinberg 1984–1988; Wertheimer 2002). Does this include extreme offence? Does it include negative externalities? (Trebilcock 1993; Hatzis 2006, 2015). Could we add collective action problems to the cases where the government should limit liberty? Is this view compatible with social contract theories? Independently of the answer to these questions I should emphasize the essence of this argument: There is a presumption of personal freedom; the burden of proof for the necessity for restrictions to personal freedom always lies with the government.

One could restate this principle as the (Individual) Liberty Principle. According to Mill the real issue here is not to find a guideline for criminal law. The important question (the "vital question of the future") is what are the nature and the limits of "the power which can be legitimately exercised by society over the individual" (Mill 1859: I.1). This question is not as easy to answer in a democratic society where political decisions are taken collectively by a majority or a popular government. In these cases "the rulers should be identified with the people" and "their interest and will should be the interest and will of the nation. The nation did not need to be protected against its own will" (Mill 1859: I.3). When there is a disagreement, a decision by a majority ensures political legitimatization since the democratic decision-making process is the most compatible with freedom and political equality. This is called the democratic principle which, as is well known, was devised in ancient Athens (Schmidtz and Brennan 2010: 44–50).

However,

phrases as "self-government," and "the power of the people over themselves," do not express the true state of the case. The "people" who exercise the power are not always the same people with those over whom it is exercised; and the "self-government" spoken of is not the government of each by himself, but of each by all the rest. The will of the people, moreover, practically means the will of the most numerous or the most active *part* of the people; the majority, or those who succeed in making themselves accepted as the majority [...] "the tyranny of the majority" is now generally included among the evils against which society requires to be on its guard.

(Mill 1859: I.4)

Mill goes so far as to suggest that the tyranny of the majority (which he calls a social tyranny) "is more formidable than many kinds of political oppression, since, though not usually upheld by such extreme penalties, it leaves fewer means of escape, penetrating much more deeply into the details of life, and enslaving the soul itself." For Mill a limit should be set to "the legitimate interference of collective opinion with individual independence: and to find that limit, and maintain it against encroachment, is as indispensable to a good condition of human affairs, as protection against political despotism" (Mill 1859: I.5).

This limit ("between individual independence and social control") should be called the "liberal principle," a principle that is necessarily antithetical to the "democratic" (majoritarian) principle. There is an area where individuals should be free to decide for themselves even when their decisions have a direct or indirect impact on society. This area is protected by rights. These rights define the area of personal freedom and autonomy where society, the majority, the government cannot intervene. What's the extent of this area? Are there any established boundaries?

Actually, in all contemporary liberal democracies it is widely accepted that there is a personal domain protected by negative rights. This domain should be shielded not only from an authoritarian government, but also from a democratic majority. This domain should be under the protection of the rule of law and its most powerful institutional weapon: the Constitution. The rule of law, individual rights, and the Constitution are all instruments of protecting both principles – the democratic and liberal principle. However, they are also instrumental in defining the domain of personal freedom, the domain where the liberal principle takes over. The liberal principle was devised and introduced institutionally by James Madison (the main author of the US Constitution of 1787) with the Bill of Rights of 1789. The First Amendment is the best example of creating a well-shielded domain of personal freedom which cannot be usurped by the government or limited by the democratic process. The controversial Ninth Amendment is illustrative of Madison's philosophy for the protection of this domain of personal freedom from the power of the majority ("The enumeration in the Constitution, of certain rights, shall not be construed to deny or disparage others retained by the people."). It is not a coincidence that this right is still awkwardly treated by most American constitutional law scholars (Barnett 1989).

In the most developed and institutionally mature liberal democracies, the boundaries between democratic decision-making and individual self-determination are well settled but, at the same time, they are in a continuing state of flux. This is so because there is an inherent ongoing clash between the democratic and liberal principles. If collective decisions is the rule in a democracy, rights as "trumps" (Dworkin 1984) are the exception. Both principles tend to expand, one over the other. However, in most liberal democracies the liberal principle is advancing and the democratic principle is receding (for an opposing but not incompatible view, see Foley 2012). This is a movement which one could characterize as parallel, similar, or even identical with the one observed by Henry Sumner Maine two years after the publication of *On Liberty* by Mill: "[W]e may say that the movement of the progressive societies has hitherto been a movement from Status to Contract" (Maine 1861: 170). This whiggish approach to institutional development is reflected in the ongoing controversy about freeing individuals from society's authority and expanding the area of personal freedom. It is a similar movement of progressive societies from collective decisions to individual self-determination.

However, this movement cannot (and should not!) lead to the elimination or weakening of the democratic process. This would be destructive for a liberal democracy and thus detrimental to individual liberty. Even though there are a lot of cases of illiberal democracies around the world, there are no examples of liberal dictatorships or liberal "non-democracies" (whatever this might mean).[5] So a balance between these two antithetical principles should be attained. This balance is crucial for liberal democracies since it determines the quality of their rule of law (Hatzis 2014c). It is not a coincidence that countries with a high-quality rule of law and low levels of corruption have also the most extensive system of recognition and protection of individual rights and a well-functioning democratic process. I characterize this eccentric relationship of antithesis, symbiosis and balance as the "paradox of liberal democracy" (Hatzis 2014b).

Despite the fact that the boundaries between collective and individual decision making, i.e., between the domains of the democratic and liberal principle, are not given and any proposed boundaries are highly controversial, we can define a broad outline by using Mill's harm principle. Mill seems to recognize (Feinberg 1984–1988) four cases where boundaries should be drawn: harm, offence, harm to oneself, and harmless wrongdoing. This doesn't mean that there are no other instances where collective decision-making is advocated with powerful arguments (justice, need, and, most importantly, collective benefits – see Wertheimer 2002). I am not going to discuss these arguments. I am also not going to discuss, in this chapter, the related major issue of the boundaries between harm and extreme offence (but see Hatzis 2015). I will concentrate on the moralistic argument as this is curiously and interestingly connected to the democratic and welfarist (utilitarian) argument against individual self-determination.

Mill not only defined the area of permissible government interference with private choices, but also took for granted that there must be a presumption for personal freedom. Decisions by societies, majorities, and governments are residual. Even though I am quite sympathetic to (even though not totally persuaded by) this libertarian drawing of the boundaries – when individual self-determination is the rule and democratic decision-making the exception – I am not going to defend a strong libertarian position in this chapter but only a limited right to self-ownership. It is limited in the sense that I am not going to discuss the issue of the ownership of the fruits of labor (a far more controversial and complex subject) but only the issue of the control of the body.

I am going to elaborate on the most famous normative statement of Mill's formulation: "Over himself, over his own body and mind, the individual is sovereign." According to our own limited interpretation of this statement, a sovereign individual is one who is at least able to control her own body. It's an individual that owns her own body and who doesn't need the permission of a society for anything she does with it when she doesn't harm another person with her acts. She doesn't need the permission even when she "hurts" herself or "offends" society with her harmless acts.

Legal paternalism and legal moralism

There are basically two major objections to individual self-determination. The first is based on a critique of the ontological assumption of rational individuals (Becker 1976; 2002; Stigler and Becker 1977). A rational individual can decide, presumably, for herself better than any other individual or corporate actor can do on her behalf. Her welfare is based on her preferences and these preferences (and the manner of their formation) are not seriously disputed in a liberal society. This ontological view has been the target of attack by philosophers, sociologists, psychologists, even economists. However, if we accept the most elementary version of the premise of their critique we should conclude that, at least some times, in marginal cases, an individual might not be the best judge of her interests. Nonetheless, even then, it needs a big leap of faith to defend even the softest case of paternalism. Irrational or self-destructive preferences or actions do not justify paternalism in any case, under any circumstances. Nevertheless, one can easily understand the appeal of proposals for paternalistic policies that are particularly soft, even "libertarian" (Sunstein and Thaler 2003). The author of this chapter is very suspicious of any kind of paternalistic theory, even of those which are based on substantial scientific evidence[6] and promise to respect personal autonomy (Hatzis 2014a). On the other hand, we can't rule out a priori any form of soft paternalism, especially when this form is rigorously based on hypothetical consent and subjective well-being.

Moralism differs from paternalism in many respects – even though, quite often, the distinction is not so clear-cut (Hatzis 2009). According to moralistic theories, an act should be prohibited if it clearly violates morality. The strongest argument against "immoral" acts, liberties, and law is the one which defends conventional morality – the social morality shared by the majority of the population in a given society. This is the only kind of morality that one can persuasively argue that it should influence law. For conservative scholars, like James Fitzjames Stephen or Patrick Devlin, an act should be illegal if it grossly "offends" society's morals.

Stephen's arguments[7] are illustrative of this view:

If society at large adopted fully Mr. Mill's theory of liberty, it would be easy to diminish very greatly the inconveniences in question. Strenuously preach and rigorously practise the doctrine that our neighbour's private character is nothing to us, and the number of unfavourable judgments formed, and therefore the number of inconveniences inflicted by them, can be reduced as much as we please, and the province of liberty can be enlarged in a corresponding ratio. Does any reasonable man wish for this? Could anyone desire gross licentiousness, monstrous extravagance, ridiculous vanity, or the like, to be unnoticed, or, being known, to inflict no inconveniences which can possibly be avoided? [...] How can the State or the public be competent to determine any question whatever if it is not competent to decide that gross vice is a bad thing? I do not think the State ought to stand bandying compliments with pimps. [...] My feeling is that if society gets its grip on the collar of such a fellow it should say to him, "You dirty rascal, it may be a question whether you should be suffered to remain in your native filth untouched, or whether my opinion about you should be printed by the lash on your bare back. That question will be determined without the smallest reference to your wishes or feelings; but as to the nature of my opinion about you, there can be no question at all." [...] Most people, I think, would feel that the latter form of address is at all events the more natural. [...] [T]he object of promoting virtue and preventing vice must be admitted to be both a good one and one sufficiently intelligible for legislative purposes. [...] It is one thing however to tolerate vice so long as it is inoffensive, and quite another to give it a legal right not only to exist, but to assert itself in the face of the world as an "experiment in living" as good as another, and entitled to the same protection from law.

(Stephen 1993 [1873]: 11, 84–85, 96–97, 101)

In a similar vein, Lord Patrick Devlin emphasized the democratic element in his defense of the legal enforcement of morality. According to him, justice should be determined by the will of the majority; a consensus is necessary; if there is no fundamental agreement on good and evil a society will fail:

For society is not something that is kept together physically; It is held by the invisible bonds of common thought. If the bonds were too far relaxed the members would drift apart. A common morality is part of the bondage. The bondage is part of the price of society; and mankind, which needs society, must pay its price. [...] But if society has the right to make a judgement and has it on the basis that a recognized morality is as necessary to society as, say, a recognized government, then society may use the law to preserve morality in the same way as it uses it to safeguard anything else that is essential to its existence. If therefore the first proposition is securely established with all its implications, society has a prima facie right to legislate against immorality as such.

(Devlin 1977 [1965]: 74–75)

For Devlin, immoral acts are acts of treason since they are "harmful to the social fabric." According to him "[t]here are no theoretical limits to the power of the State to legislate against treason and sedition, and likewise I think there can be no theoretical limits to legislation against immorality" (Devlin 1977 [1965]: 77). Of course, Devlin didn't base his contentions on empirical observation but on the elusive concept of a "reasonable man": a representative of the moral majority in the sense that he is a right-minded man, holding commonly accepted views. Even Devlin uses this legal fiction with caution as he seems puzzled as to its ontological or even normative value.[8]

In both scholars we can discern at least two arguments (one explicit and another implicit) that are relevant to our discussion:

1   Social morality is shared by the majority of the population. In a democratic state this morality should be respected, especially if the disapproval is overwhelming. This is considered essential for a well-functioning society and polity (the explicit "democratic" argument).
2   The enforcement of widely accepted moral norms is imperative to the wellbeing of society. Not only because the non-enforcement could inconvenience the majority but because it could disintegrate society itself (the implicit "welfarist" argument).

One could adopt a less ominous argument that is also quite powerful: Acts that are considered immoral create negative externalities, "polluting" society morally and thus decreasing social welfare.

Moral externalities

The externality argument against "immoral" behavior which does not harm third parties directly (and against any "immoral" activity for that matter) goes something like this: a part of the cost of the voluntary but "immoral" activity spills over onto "moral" people, who are annoyed by the way of life of "immoral" people. Of course, every action and every transaction is likely to impose a cost on a third party. Even acts that are considered moral or amoral have negative external costs to third parties: An honest and active tax woman or a discount store will create negative externalities to small neighborhood businesses. However, the external cost is greater when this activity goes against conventional morality. Since individuals have preferences not only over their own choices but also about other individuals's actions, choices, and preferences, it is not surprising that the way of life or the acts of some people can be said to grossly offend the majority. Their acts or transactions have negative external effects of such magnitude that they can have detrimental effects to social order itself. Consequently, the argument goes, the state should intervene in order to protect the offended majority by making the "immoral" people internalize the cost of their "immorality", enhancing overall welfare.

According to the leading law and economics scholar Steven Shavell (2002: 255), "the existence of moral beliefs should itself influence the design of the law, given that moral beliefs constitute tastes the satisfaction of which raises individuals' welfare." Richard Posner connects this argument with the prevalence of the democratic principle:

> Constitutional rights are, after all, rights against the democratic majority. But public opinion is not irrelevant to the task of deciding whether a constitutional right exists. [...] [Judges] will have to go beyond the technical legal materials, of decision and consider moral, political, empirical, prudential, and institutional issues, including the public acceptability of a decision recognizing the new right. [...] That is the democratic way [...] [not] to ignore what the people affected by the issues think about them.[9]
>
> (Posner 1997: 1595–1587)

One could argue that such a "negative externality" could even satisfy John Stuart Mill's harm principle: "[T]he sole end for which mankind are warranted, individually or collectively, in interfering with the liberty of action of any of their number, is self protection" (Mill 1859: I.9). According to a certain interpretation of Mill's thought,

> it is no objection under the harm principle that a harmless action was criminalized, nor even that an action with no tendency to cause harm was criminalized. It is enough to meet the demands of the harm principle that, if the action were not criminalized, that would be harmful.
>
> (Gardner and Shute 2000: 216)

Amartya Sen has contributed to this discussion indirectly with the "liberal paradox." According to Sen (1970, see also 1976), censorship, under certain conditions, can maximize welfare by restricting individual rights. If Sen is right, then:

> [L]iberal values conflict with the Pareto principle. If someone takes the Pareto principle seriously, as economists seem to do, then he has to face problems of consistency in cherishing liberal values, even very mild ones. Or, to look at it in another way, if someone does have certain liberal values, then he may have to eschew his adherence to Pareto optimality. While the Pareto criterion has been thought to be an expression of individual liberty, it appears that in choices involving more than two alternatives it can have consequences that are, in fact, deeply illiberal.
>
> (Sen 1970: 157)

Sen, of course, did not advocate any kind of legal moralism. However, his paradox is illustrative of the existing tension between utility (utilitarianism) and rights (liberalism). Nevertheless, there are ways out of the paradox. For example, rule utilitarianism is more responsive to rights than act utilitarianism. Below we will also see that Sen's paradox is based on a rather narrow conception of liberalism which is perfectionist and not procedural.

Political and legal philosophers, especially Joel Feinberg (1985; 1988), tried to set the conceptual boundaries of harm since there is literally no imaginable kind of behavior, transaction, or relationship which cannot be considered as harmful to some. One criterion could be the magnitude of harm (Feinberg speaks of "extreme offence") and another the number of people harmed, but then the road to legal moralism is a one-way street.[10] Mill himself has given a tough-minded answer, which seems to preclude any kind of legal moralism:

> There are many who consider as an injury to themselves any conduct which they have a distaste for, and resent it as an outrage to their feelings [...]. But there is no parity between the feeling of a person for his own opinion and the feeling of another who is offended at his holding it; no more than between the desire of a thief to take a purse and the desire of the right owner to keep it.
>
> (Mill 1859: IV.12)

Economists seem to think that they do not have anything more to offer on this point. According to Trebilcock (whose discussion of moral externalities is very useful here), "[I]t is not clear to me that conventional economic theories of externalities have much, if anything, to offer on the problem" (Trebilcock 1993: 66 – referring to the negative externalities caused by pornography). Even in the simplest cases, Trebilcock feels that he should use concepts such as rights and autonomy (Trebilcock 1993: 75), which is fine but the point here is to find whether the concept of externalities itself can help by offering a clear-cut criterion, similar to that of Mill's or to Rawls's (1971: 13) mutual disinterest principle ("[people] are conceived as not taking an interest in one another's interests"). This is also important for the economic theory of externalities, since an uncontrolled expansion of the notion will make it trivial.

Richard Epstein's libertarian criterion is also very useful and it is compatible with the economic criterion I will be proposing:

> Seeking to respect all (but only) negative externalities by the legal system leads to a place where there is no decision for individual choice or personal self-control, a result that is wholly inconsistent with our ordinary intuitions about autonomy and self-control. So to avoid that situation we run to a world in which autonomy allows us to impose negative externalities on those with whom we refuse to deal but not on those upon whom we inflict force.
>
> (Epstein 1995: 700)

In his seminal article, Ronald Coase (1960) did not try to set boundaries for externalities since his main concern was to show that the problem is not externalities but transaction costs. According to David Friedman's reinstatement of the theorem:

> With externalities but no transaction costs there would be no problem, since the parties would always bargain to the efficient solution. When we observe

externality problems (or other forms of market failure) in the real world, we should ask not merely where the problem comes from, but what the transaction costs are that prevent it from being bargained out of existence.

(Friedman 2000: 40)

If it is a matter of bargaining in a low-transaction-cost environment one could identify the bargaining parties, their stakes, and, of course, a low-transaction-cost setting. With moral externalities this is more difficult than it sounds. The bargaining parties are apparently individuals and society, and as we will see, a low-cost environment can be identified. The problem is how to measure the willingness to pay when we deal with moral cost.

Scarce and non-scarce rights and the right to self-ownership

I believe that a distinction introduced by Meckling and Jensen (1980) in an unpublished paper and elaborated in another unpublished paper by Holderness *et al.* (2000) could be very useful for our analysis: External effects can be classified into physical and value effects. An example of the first is physical pollution of a neighbor's farm; an example of the second is the introduction of a product that reduces a competitor's profits. The first is a social cost, because options have been physically eliminated from someone else's opportunity set. The second is not a social cost (although the wealth of the competitor declines) because no options have been eliminated and no real resources have been consumed (Holderness 1989: 184, n9).[11] In the first case, it's a zero-sum game with distributive consequences. In the latter it is not.

In the second paper Holderness *et al.* (2000) discuss freedom of expression and connect the above distinction with the theory of rights by offering a criterion which is based on their treatment of externalities.[12]

To maximize freedom, one must differentiate between scarce and non-scarce rights. *Scarce rights* cannot be granted to everyone because of natural limitations caused by physical incompatibilities. When a scarce right is exercised, alternative actions that might have been taken are physically eliminated from the opportunity set, both for the person exercising the right and for all other individuals. When a scarce right is exercised, there is a cost because the right in this case is like a rival good: its use by one person diminishes or eliminates the use by another.

If one person burns a tree to keep warm, another cannot use the tree to build a house. Conflicts caused by such physical incompatibilities are resolved peacefully, by giving exclusionary rights in the physical use of the tree to a single, private party. These are scarce rights because more than one person cannot use the tree when there are physical incompatibilities.

Non-scarce rights, in contrast, can be granted to everyone. This class of rights is limitless, in the sense that granting a right to one person in no way precludes the opportunity to grant the same right to other people. The freedom to engage in an "immoral" non-harming activity does not forestall someone else from doing the same.

To maximize freedom, each scarce right must be assigned to specific individual persons, and all non-scarce rights should be assigned to everyone. Consequently, the right of self-ownership should be assigned to everyone individually and not only to the class of "moral" people – if they are the majority in a democratic society.

According to the self-ownership thesis "each person is the morally rightful owner of his own person and powers, and, *consequently*, that each is free (morally speaking) to use those powers as he wishes, provided that he does not deploy them aggressively against others" (Cohen 1995: 67).

Full ownership of an entity consists of a full set of the following ownership rights (Vallentyne 2014):

1   *control rights* over the use of the entity: both a liberty-right to use it and a claim-right that others not use it;
2   *rights to compensation* if someone uses the entity without one's permission;
3   *enforcement rights* (of prior restraint if someone is about to violate these rights);
4   *rights to transfer* these rights to others (by sale, rental, gift, or loan); and
5   *immunities to the non-consensual loss* of these rights.

According to this view of self-ownership, rights to transfer are as important as control rights. Thus we can see what Sen has missed. People can transfer their rights in order to maximize their utility. This transfer seems to limit their freedom but this is the essence of contract.[13] If we stick to an idea of inalienable rights that cannot be transferred even with the consent of their owners (and then self-ownership is a mirage) then every such transfer, if it happens, diminishes our liberty. This "perfectionist" version of liberalism (Raz 1986) is very problematic because it undermines self-determination and subjective well-being. According to a more neutral approach to liberalism (which I prefer to call "procedural liberalism"), if the process of transfer is based on genuine consent the result is fair and liberty-enhancing.[14] According to Brian Barry (discussing Sen's paradox): "Liberalism is, indeed, a principle that picks out a protected sphere, but one that is protected against unwanted interference, not against use in trading with others" (Barry 1986: 19).

A Coasean framework

One could then ask: Why should the value effects *not* be taken into account? Since society has a stake in the individual behavior (when this behavior has a social cost), why is there no right to interfere with another person's choices?

Using the wealth maximization criterion, can we imagine a world with no transaction costs where the majority of moral citizens would pay "immoral" people for the right of living the way they prefer? Putting it in a Coasean framework, if an "immoral" activity is legalized and there are no transaction costs, would it be possible for the legal entitlement to end up in the hands of the "moral majority" with the consent of rights-holders? Of course it would, but the question remains: What is the value of the right for the "moral majority" and the "immoral minority"?

First of all, the specification of the utility function of the third moral party that is offended is important here. It all depends on the assumptions about what is entering the third party's utility. It seems that there is some kind of nonlinearity in the "moral" component of the utility function of the representative individual. The representative individual is willing to tolerate such behavior up to a point/threshold. What complicates things here is that the idiosyncratic component in the utility function from individual to individual is very high. So talking about an average utility function (or a function of the representative individual) is not very helpful.[15]

For these and other reasons, in most cases the value of a right is indeterminate. Since the benefits and the costs are highly subjective and mostly psychological, there is great difficulty in assessing them, even where there are no serious incidents of moral hazard, adverse selection, and endowment effects – which are all quite common in cases of idiosyncratic preferences. Posner's famous solution (mimic the market) coincides with the normative version of the Coase theorem (Posner 1983: 71–72). When transaction costs are high, the rights should be vested initially in those who are likely to value them most so as to minimize transaction costs. According to Posner's own example, "this is the economic reason for giving a woman the right to determine her sexual partners" (Posner 1983: 71). If this right is assigned to strangers, it will generally be repurchased by the woman. However, the costs of the rectifying transaction should be avoided, thus the right should be assigned to the user who values it the most. In addition, since there is no reliable mechanism for identifying this *ex ante*, and thus vesting the right in the persons who value them most, the rights should initially be vested "in the natural owner" (Posner 1983: 72).

Another useful criterion could be Guido Calabresi's "best briber" solution to the normative Coase theorem, according to which the allocation of rights should be made in such a way "as to maximize the likelihood that errors in allocation will be corrected in the market" (Calabresi 1970: 150). In our case this comes to the following strategy: assign the right to the party from whom it could be transferred more easily. In all the self-ownership cases (organ-selling, surrogate motherhood, euthanasia) the interested parties are always a small minority (the "natural owners"). Their sheer number qualifies them since the right can be more easily moved from a small concentrated minority rather than from the dispersed and heterogeneous majority. However, as we will see in the next paragraph, there is an even stronger argument. Calabresi himself answers indirectly, since he discusses the reduction of primary costs in accidents: "The best briber may therefore be the activity that can enter into transactions with the least use of coercion" (Calabresi 1970: 151).

Minimizing transaction costs by recognizing individual rights

However, the most important problem is the amount of transaction costs involved if we assign the right to self-ownership not to the persons themselves, but to society at large. This is clearly illustrated by Clifford Holderness's treatment of positive externalities that are created by a contract. How can we distinguish between positive externalities and third-party beneficiary rights created by a contract? In my opinion, Holderness (1985) has provided the most satisfactory answer to the problem, discussing the issue of positive externalities from a contractual relationship. For Holderness, a necessary foundation for exchange is that the law assigns all rights to any resource to a closed class of clearly identifiable persons, each of whom is able to contract at any moment. A class is closed when persons can enter the class – and thus obtain the right – only by first purchasing the right from a current class member (Holderness 1985: 322). The rights, therefore, must lend themselves to voluntary transfer and this is not possible when the rights are assigned to open classes. If they are, then no voluntary transactions can take place and resources are blocked from moving to higher-valued uses.

Paraphrasing Holderness (1985: 324), we could say that an open class in negative externalities (value external effects) is created when there are at least some individuals who can enter the class, and thus obtain rights, without first purchasing them from the natural owners. "A class is open when entry to it is unrestricted" (Holderness 1989: 182).

If we give rights of moral protection to too many individuals (the whole society) by recognizing as harm the violation of conventional morality, the transaction costs for any hypothetical exchange will exceed the expected gains even if the rights are alienable. The larger the class of rights-holders, "the greater will be the transaction cost of arranging an exchange," because the prospective "immoral" person must negotiate with each individual who has been assigned rights to the life of third parties (cf. Holderness 1985: 326). This essentially means that a person can make decisions about his life only when he can identify all individuals who have been assigned rights to his life. One could argue that in a democracy this is not necessary: it is enough to persuade the majority. However, if the history of individual rights is an indication, the transaction cost is enormous in terms of time but most important in terms of human lives.

When the individual is unable to identify the other individuals who have been assigned rights to his life, "this calculation becomes impossible to make independent of the court." Accordingly, he is then put in the predicament of either not doing what he wants to do with his life or doing it and then subjecting himself to the court *ex post* rule (Holderness 1985: 327). The solution to the problem is to deny rights to an "indeterminate class" (Holderness 1985: 333) with unrestricted entry. Since these rights will be essentially inalienable, exchange would be futile. As Ronald Coase famously put it, "the delimitation of rights is an essential prelude to market transactions" (Coase 1960: 8).

This is also one of the problems of Sen's "liberal paradox." According to James Coleman, Sen's paradox "indicates the central position of externalities – either external diseconomies or external economies – in a theory of constitutions, for it is only in the presence of externalities that the most critical issues arise, those which distinguish different philosophical positions" (Coleman 1990: 341).

Conclusion

My goal in this chapter was twofold. One of my objectives was to try to rebut an economic argument for legal moralism by using another economic argument. My second objective was to show how law and economics literature can be fruitfully used in the discussion of issues that are considered *prima facie* irrelevant to the economic approach.[16] As we have seen, the theory of externalities can support the view that conventional morality should not be irrelevant for legislation if the increase of the welfare of society is one of law's legitimate goals. However, I also tried to demonstrate how the assignment of rights to the "moral majority" under the assumption that this would maximize total welfare undermines the Coasean dynamics because of the creation of open classes of right holders. The external effects that "immorality" can create are value effects, not physical effects. The right to an "immoral behavior" in particular is not a scarce right. Thus, exercising this right does not preclude anyone else from doing the same.

My conclusion is not a system of moral anarchy, but an appeal to the importance of "establishing closed and identified classes of rights holders" (Holderness 1985: 344). This can be achieved by assigning the right to self-ownership to individuals themselves, instead of making society, i.e., the "moral majority," a co-owner.[17]

Notes

* Associate Professor of Philosophy of Law and Theory of Institutions, Department of Philosophy & History of Science, University of Athens. I wish to thank Brian Bix, George Chortareas, Yulie Foka-Kavalieraki, Kenneth Einar Himma, Alain Marciano, Roland Kirstein, Richard Posner, and Michael Zouboulakis for their helpful comments, as well as the participants in various workshops and seminars where I have presented earlier drafts.
1 See (Gauthier 1986: 84).
2 For the rich literature in legal and moral philosophy see (Alexander 2003; Bix 2006: 157–166).
3 We are not going to discuss here more sophisticated views on moral intuitionism, moral realism, foundationalism, etc. In this text we are only going to discuss conventional (not critical) morality and the arguments for and against its influence on legal rules. Nevertheless, the author of this chapter feels obligated to stress that he does not subscribe to theories of moral subjectivism or moral nihilism.
4 See, e.g., (Kass 2002). Even the concept of autonomy can be used in a way that is paternalistic (see the survey by Fateh-Moghadam and Gutmann 2014).
5 I consider a liberal anarchist society as no realistic option. See (Nozick 1974) for more. See also (Friedman 1989) for an alternative view.

6 Mostly from psychology under the rubric of behavioral economics. However, see (Foka-Kavalieraki and Hatzis 2011).
7 Stephen's book is essentially a conservative rebuttal of Mill's *On Liberty*.
8 For a famous rebuttal see (Hart 1963).
9 See also (Posner 2003): "in a democratic society, powerful currents of public opinion deserve recognition even by the Supreme Court, at least in cases to which neither the Constitution nor any other authoritative legal text speaks with clarity." See, however, more recently (Posner 2013).
10 On this issue, see (Dworkin 1978: 255). According to Dworkin, "what is shocking and wrong is not his [Devlin's] idea that the community's morality counts, but his idea of what counts as the community's morality." I find this distinction to be far from satisfactory.
11 This is essentially the distinction between externalities and pecuniary externalities, which is much older (cf. Posner 1983: 96).
12 The following paragraphs draw heavily from (Holderness *et al.* 2000).

13   In a market exchange that leads to a contract, two (or more) rational actors promise to limit their future actions with the objective of deriving, from the present or future actions of the other party, a benefit that will be greater than the cost of restricting their actions.

(Foka-Kavalieraki and Hatzis 2009: 30)

14 This approach is not identical but it is not very far from Nozick's "justice in transfer."
15 I owe this point to George Chortareas.
16 See also (Donohue and Levitt 2001; Hatzis 2003; 2006; 2009; Karayiannis and Hatzis 2012).
17 Individuals should be free to trade their rights if they so wish. One way to do this might be a system of moral federalism, a system where individuals choose their residence and vote over a single-dimensional regulatory policy at the regional and national level (Janeba 2006).

References

Alexander, L. (2003) 'The legal enforcement of morality' in R.G. Frey and C.H. Wellman (eds.) *A Companion to Applied Ethics*, Oxford: Blackwell.
Barnett, R.E. (ed.) (1989) *The Rights Retained by the People: The History and Meaning of the Ninth Amendment*, Fairfax, VA: George Mason University Press.
Barry, B. (1986) 'Lady Chatterley's lover and doctor Fischer's bomb party: liberalism, Pareto optimality, and the problem of objectionable preferences', in J. Elster and A. Hylland (eds.) *Foundations of Social Choice Theory*, New York: Cambridge University Press.
Becker, G.S. (1976) *The Economic Approach to Human Behavior*, Chicago, IL: University of Chicago Press.
Becker, G.S. 'Nobel lecture: the economic way of looking at behavior', *Journal of Political Economy* 101, 2002: 385–409.
Bix, B. (2006) *Jurisprudence: Theory and Context*, 4th edition. London: Sweet & Maxwell.
Bork, R.H. (2003) *Coercing Virtue: The Worldwide Rule of Judges*, Washington, DC: AEI Press.
Calabresi, G. (1970) *The Costs of Accidents: A Legal and Economic Analysis*, New Haven, CT: Yale University Press.
Coase, R.H. 'The problem of social cost', *Journal of Law and Economics* 3: 1960 1–44.

Cohen, G.A. (1995) *Self-Ownership, Freedom, and Equality*, Cambridge: Cambridge University Press.

Coleman, J. (1990) *Foundations of Social Theory*, Cambridge, MA: Harvard University Press.

Devlin, P. (1977 [1965]) 'Morals and the criminal law', in R. Dworkin (ed.) *The Philosophy of Law*, Oxford: Oxford University Press.

Donohue, J.J. and Levitt, S.D. 'The impact of legalized abortion on crime', *Quarterly Journal of Economics* 116, 2001: 379–420.

Dworkin, R. (1978) *Taking Rights Seriously*, 2nd edition, Cambridge, MA: Harvard University Press.

Dworkin, R. (1984) 'Rights as trumps', in J. Waldron (ed.) *Theories of Rights*, Oxford: Oxford University Press.

Dyzenhaus, D., Reibetanz Moreau, S., and Ripstein, A. (eds.) (2007) *Law and Morality: Readings in Legal Philosophy*, 3rd edition, Toronto: University of Toronto Press.

Epstein, R.A. 'Are values incommensurable, or is utility the ruler of the world?', *Utah Law Review* 1995, 1995: 683–715.

Fateh-Moghadam, B. and Gutman, T. 'Governing [through] autonomy: The moral and legal limits of "soft paternalism"', *Ethical Theory and Moral Practice* 17, 2014: 383–397.

Feinberg, J. (1984) *The Moral Limits of the Criminal Law. Vol. 1: Harm to Others*, New York: Oxford University Press.

Feinberg, J. (1985) *The Moral Limits of the Criminal Law. Vol. 2: Offense to Others*, New York: Oxford University Press.

Feinberg, J. (1986) *The Moral Limits of the Criminal Law. Vol. 3: Harm to Self*, New York: Oxford University Press.

Feinberg, J. (1988) *The Moral Limits of the Criminal Law. Vol. 4: Harmless Wrong-Doing*, New York: Oxford University Press.

Foka-Kavalieraki, Y. and Hatzis, A.N. 'The foundations of a market economy: contract, consent, coercion', *European View* 9(1), 2009: 29–37.

Foka-Kavalieraki, Y. and Hatzis, A.N. 'Rational after all: toward an improved theory of rationality in economics', *Revue de Philosophie Economique* 12, 2011: 3–51.

Foley, E.P. (2012) *Liberty for All: Reclaiming Individual Privacy in a New Era of Public Morality*, New Haven, CT: Yale University Press.

Friedman, D.D. (1989) *The Machinery of Freedom: Guide to a Radical Capitalism*, 2nd edition, La Salle, IL: Open Court.

Friedman, D.D. (2000) *Law's Order: What Economics Has to Do with Law and Why It Matters*, Princeton, NJ: Princeton University Press.

Gardner, J. and Shute, S. (2000) 'The wrongness of rape', in J. Horder, *Oxford Essays in Jurisprudence: Fourth Series*, Oxford: Oxford University Press.

Gauthier, D. (1986) *Morals by Agreement*, Oxford: Oxford University Press.

Hart, H.L.A. (1963) *Law, Liberty, and Morality*, Stanford, CA: Stanford University Press.

Hatzis, A.N. (2003) ' "Just the oven": a law & economics approach to gestational surrogacy contracts', in K. Boele-Woelki (ed.) *Perspectives for the Unification or Harmonisation of Family Law in Europe*, Antwerp: Intersentia.

Hatzis, A.N. 'The negative externalities of immorality: the case of same-sex marriage', *Skepsis* 17, 2006: 52–65.

Hatzis, A.N. 'From soft to hard paternalism and back: the regulation of surrogate motherhood in Greece', *Portuguese Economic Journal* 49, 2009: 205–220.

Hatzis, A.N. (2014a) 'The good wolf, the libertarian paternalism and other fairy tales', University of Athens, working paper.

Hatzis, A.N. (2014b) 'The paradox of liberal democracy', University of Athens, working paper.

Hatzis, A.N. (2014c) 'Rule of law, individual rights and the free market in the liberal tradition: the case of Greece', in R. Meinardus (ed.) *Bridging the Gap: An Arab–European Dialogue on the Basics of Liberalism*, Cairo: Friedrich Naumann Foundation.

Hatzis, A.N. (2015) *An Economic Theory of Self-Ownership*, forthcoming.

Holderness, C.G. 'A legal foundation of exchange', *Journal of Legal Studies* 14, 1985: 321–344.

Holderness, C.G. 'The assignment of rights, entry effects, and the allocation of resources', *Journal of Legal Studies* 18, 1989: 181–189.

Holderness, C.G., Jensen, M.C., and Meckling, W.H. (2000) 'The logic of the first amendment', Harvard Business School, working paper.

Janeba, E. 'Moral federalism', *Contributions to Economic Analysis & Policy* 5.1, 2006: art. 32.

Karayiannis, A. and Hatzis, A.N. 'Morality, social norms and the rule of law as transaction costs-saving devices: the case of ancient Athens', *European Journal of Law and Economics* 33, 2012: 621–643.

Kass, L. (2002) *Life, Liberty and the Defense of Dignity: The Challenge for Bioethics*, San Francisco, CA: Encounter.

McAdams, R.H. 'An attitudinal theory of expressive law', *Oregon Law Review* 79, 2000a: 339–390.

McAdams, R.H. 'A focal point theory of expressive law', *Virginia Law Review* 86, 2000b: 1649–1729.

Maine, H.S. (1861) *Ancient Law: Its Connection with the Early History of Society, and Its Relation to Modern Ideas*, London: John Murray.

Meckling, W.H. and Jensen, M.C. (1980) 'A positive analysis of rights systems', University of Rochester, working paper.

Mill, J.S. (1859) *On Liberty*, London: J.W. Parker and Son.

Nozick, R. (1974) *Anarchy, State, and Utopia*, New York: Basic Books.

Posner, R.A. (1983) *The Economics of Justice*, 2nd edition, Cambridge, MA: Harvard University Press.

Posner, R.A. 'Should there be homosexual marriage? And if so, who should decide?', *Michigan Law Review* 95, 1997: 1578–1587.

Posner, R.A. 'Wedding bell blues', *New Republic*, December 22, 2003.

Posner, R.A. 'How gay marriage became legitimate', *New Republic*, July 24, 2013.

Rawls, J. (1971) *A Theory of Justice*, Cambridge, MA: Harvard University Press.

Raz, J. (1986) *The Morality of Freedom*, Oxford: Oxford University Press.

Schmidtz, D. and Brennan, J. (2010) *A Brief History of Liberty*, Oxford: Wiley-Blackwell.

Sen, A. 'The impossibility of a Paretian liberal', *Journal of Political Economy* 78, 1970: 152–157.

Sen, A. 'Liberty, unanimity and rights', *Economica* 43, 1976: 217–245.

Shavell, S. 'Law versus morality as regulators of conduct', *American Law & Economics Review* 4, 2002: 227–257.

Stephen, J.F. (1993 [1873]) *Liberty, Equality, Fraternity*, edited by S.D. Warner, Indianapolis, IN: Liberty Fund.

Stigler, G.J. and Becker, G.S. 'De gustibus non est disputandum', *American Economic Review* 67, 1977: 76–90.

Sunstein, C.R. 'Social norms and social roles', *Columbia Law Review* 96, 1996: 903–968.

Sunstein, C.R. and Thaler, R.H. 'Libertarian paternalism is not an oxymoron', *University of Chicago Law Review* 70, 2003: 1159–1202.

Trebilcock, M.J. (1993) *The Limits of Freedom of Contract*, Cambridge, MA: Harvard University Press.

Vallentyne, P. (2014) 'Libertarianism', in E.N. Zalta (ed.) *Stanford Encyclopedia of Philosophy*, http://plato.stanford.edu/entries/libertarianism (accessed October 18, 2014).

Wertheimer, A. (2002) 'Liberty, coercion, and the limits of the State', in R.L. Simon (ed.) *The Blackwell Guide to Social and Political Philosophy*, Oxford: Blackwell.

13 Engagement with economics
The new hybrids of family law/law and economics thinking

Brian H. Bix*

Introduction

This chapter offers a summary – inevitably incomplete, but, one hopes, suggestive – of the way that economics has been used in family law.[1] What follows is a critical overview of the way in which family law scholars have adopted, adapted, and resisted economic analysis (broadly understood) in response to the claims economic theorists have made regarding family law issues.

To many, the issues within family law seem as *in*apt as any for economic analysis. Family matters seem far from the commercial transactions that are usually the subject of economic analyses; the way we think about marriage and divorce, and love and children, seem far from the "rational choices" that economics analyzes; and few who have raised children would think of the experience as an instance of "wealth maximization."

This chapter considers the extent to which rational choice theory, in any of its many guises, offers us a clear understanding – or an *increased* understanding – of issues within the domain of family law. Ultimately, the chapter concludes that economic analysis can be far more useful in discussing family relations and family law than many of its critics allow, but that there are persistent limitations that those using economic analysis in this area should concede (and, where possible, compensate for).

The first section offers an overview of law and economics and raises some initial concerns relating to the application of economic analysis to family law issues. The second section focuses on issues relating specifically to the Coase theorem. The third part investigates the application of game theory to family law. The fourth section samples some of the main weak points in the application of law and economics to family law.

Engagement with economics

What is economics (and the economic analysis of law)?

To say that one is "applying economics" to family (law) matters is to assume that one has a clear notion of what "economics" is, though such knowledge is more often assume than explained. As one prominent economic theorist, Gary Becker, has discussed (Becker 1976: 3–8), many textbook and reference book definitions of economics often focus, unhelpfully, on the *subject matter* of economic discussions – the allocations of goods generally, or market goods in particular – when other disciplines can and do cover the same subject matter. If economics is to be understood – especially in its application to nonmarket behavior – it must be in terms of methodology and assumptions, not subject matter. Becker suggests the following:

> Everyone recognizes that the economic approach assumes maximizing behavior more explicitly and extensively than other approaches do.... Moreover, the economic approach assumes the existence of markets that with varying degrees of efficiency coordinate the actions of different participants ... so that their behavior becomes mutually consistent.... [And] preferences are assumed not to change substantially over time, nor to be very different between wealthy and poor persons, or even between persons in different societies and culture.
>
> (Becker 1976: 5)

I will largely adopt Becker's analysis for the purpose of the chapter, offering some modifications along the way (especially when discussing variations on the traditional economic approach, like game theory). Additionally, one must recognize that with economics – as with other disciplines, like sociology, anthropology, or philosophy – there is often a thin line between "an economic approach" and some version of "simple common sense" or "simple practical reasoning." Thus, for example, economists have no monopoly on understanding the effects of incentives or disincentives, or the way parties negotiate – though economists may have formalized such ideas to a greater extent than others have, and, in some cases, they have gone to greater lengths to investigate those ideas in real-world settings.

There are difficulties with discussing law and economics, or economic analysis of legal rules and practices, in a general way. While it is true that the category may seem monolithic and homogenous from a distance, from the perspective of the economically minded theorists who come at issues in quite different ways, there are important disagreements within the category. Starting from a (largely shared) assumption of rational choice, different economic approaches go off in different directions, on the basis of varying emphases or changes in the basic assumptions. For example, behavioral law and economics[2] emphasizes the cognitive biases and bounded rationality[3] of most individuals (particularly consumers), thus dissenting in part from one of the basic elements of the traditional (neoclassical) economic model[4] (e.g., Sunstein 2000). New Institutional Economics[5] also emphasizes bounded rationality, but mostly in the context of complex contracts, particularly the structuring of behavior within organizations[6] (Williamson 1998, 2000; Eggertsson 1998).

While a school of economic analysis that focuses on organizational behavior might not seem to have much to add to the analysis of domestic relations, a number of family law theorists have found this approach useful, directly or by analogy, in discussing relationships within the family. For example, one commentator has suggested that the members of a family are best seen as having the same sort of joint and overlapping interest that members of a firm have, and that this may explain aspects of their interactions that neither the assumption of self-interested pursuit of independent interests or the assumption of altruism could explain.[7]

Another variation of rational choice theory, game theory, considers the strategic behavior of people in games and other situations where each party's choices affect all the other participants. In comparison with traditional neoclassical economics, game theory emphasizes imperfect information, strategic behavior, and transaction costs (e.g., Aumann 1987; Ross 2010; Dau-Schmidt *et al.* 1997). In the context of the discussion of legal reform, game theory has the advantage that it is better placed than traditional economic analysis to consider the obvious point that "people ... make adjustments in the face of legal change" (Baird 1998: 193). On the other hand, game theory has the disadvantage (compared to traditional neoclassical economics) of frequently being unable to predict exact outcomes (Dau-Schmidt *et al.* 1997: 616–617).

While game theory, at its less sophisticated end (more sophisticated game theory analyses often look like calculus textbooks [e.g., Owen 1995]), is little more than bargaining theory with a little rigor, the potential application of game theory to analyzing the "negotiations" that precede marriage, divorce, and many important family events, is quite significant. Also, as I once heard mentioned by one feminist legal theorist, game theory allows feminists to speak about imbalances of power between the sexes without seeming to be making special pleading or mere ideological (conclusory) assertions. A later section will look in greater detail at some attempts to apply game theory to families and family law.

Application of classical economic analysis to family law

There is a sense in which one could now speak of the "engagement" of family law and law and economics: "engagement" in both its romantic sense (a close alliance, with promise of a closer one) and its military sense (a conflict). The list of those working recently in the overlap, or the battle zone, between the two, is large and growing.[8]

For a long time, economics and family law had little to do with one another.[9] Economics in its early development focused almost exclusively on commercial activity and price theory.[10] The basic idea of law and economics is that looking at legal problems in terms of individual preference satisfaction will offer insights into individual and social choices and behavior that would otherwise be unavailable.[11] The law and economics movement brought economic analysis to law and legal policy, but the focus initially remained far away from family law, in the incentives and disincentives for action[12] created by tort law and alternative regulatory regimes (Coase 1960; Calabresi 1970).

However, in due course, and with the prompting of Gary Becker and Richard Posner,[13] economic analysis of law extended to non-commercial behavior.

Economics was seen not merely as a way of discussing prices (narrowly understood), but as a way of understanding and predicting the exercise of choice. Economics was to be defined by approach rather than by subject matter. Becker focused on three elements: an assumption of utility-maximizing behavior; market equilibrium; and stable preferences (Becker 1976: 5). Posner similarly summarized the economic approach as a combination of choice among scarce resources, and a conception of people as rational maximizers of their self-interest (R. Posner 2011: 3–4).

Today, economic analysis dominates many doctrinal areas (and many law school faculties). However, it has only recently begun to get a foothold in family law. The first systematic application of economic analysis to domestic relations was offered by Gary Becker. Becker's most famous (or notorious) argument in his 1981 text (revised in 1991) (Becker 1991), developing ideas he had first published in the early 1970s (Becker 1973, 1974), was his portrayal of marriage as a kind of firm in which the two partners specialized – one in wage labor and one in household work – for greater overall efficiency (Becker 1991: 30–53).[14]

In some ways, the extension of economic analysis to domestic relations should not have been surprising. If one can analyze the way that tort rules and other regulations create incentives and disincentives that affect people's behavior in causing and preventing accidents, it is a natural step to wonder how our reaction to the incentives and disincentives of legal rules and other factors mold our domestic relations.

Certainly, there is no lack of subjects within family law awaiting possible discussion in terms of incentives and disincentives. Just to offer three examples: (1) Did the US welfare system (state benefits for the poor), prior to its recent reforms, created economic disincentives for marriage and economic incentives to have more non-marital children (Brinig 2000: 59–61)?[15] (2) Which set of rules would create the right set of incentives and disincentives for all the various parties involved in foster care, given the various and frequently conflicting interests of those parties?[16] (3) What incentive and disincentive effects were created by no-fault divorce?[17] As to this third category, commentators like Lenore Weitzman and Martha Minow – working outside of law and economics, but using ways of thinking familiar to that approach – have argued that no-fault divorce, combined with decisions regarding property division and spousal support, worked to penalize those (more often women than men) who "invest" in the marital relationship rather than "investing" in their own human capital (through education, job training, spending more time at the office, etc.)[18] (Weitzman 1985; Minow 1999).

Economic analysis has also considered a different sort of incentive analysis relating to marriage, in considering some of the effects of greater female participation in the workplace. This focus began early, with Gary Becker attributing much of the change in families, including the growth in the divorce rate and the rise in the number of non-marital children, to "the growth of earning power of women" (Becker 1991: 350). Becker's analysis was that, as women could make more in the labor force, a gendered division of labor (traditional marriage) had fewer advantages, and as marriage had fewer relative advantages over non-married life, divorce became relatively more attractive (e.g., as women became less dependent on husbands, and staying in bad marriages, for their economic survival) (Becker 1991: 350–358).[19]

Family law and the Coase theorem

It is too simple (and not very helpful) to equate economic analysis simply with incentive/disincentive analysis. In fact, arguably the seminal article for law and economics – and still one of the most influential publications in the field – worked to undermine a simple incentive and disincentive analysis for the effect of law on behavior. In "The problem of social cost," Ronald Coase argued against a welfare economics justification for state regulation (Coase 1960).[20] Some welfare economists had argued that businesses that impose costs on third parties, through pollution or other nuisances, should be forced to "internalize their externalities,"[21] either through taxes, fines, or tort law liability, for otherwise those businesses would be receiving a kind of subsidy that would lead to an inefficient distribution of goods and services. Coase argued that this view was based on a series of misunderstandings. What is now known as the Coase theorem is in fact an intermediate step in the article's analysis: that in a world without transaction costs, the distribution of legal rights (e.g., to pollute or to prevent pollution) would not matter, because the party who valued the entitlement the most could, and would, buy the right from a lower-valuing user, if the higher-valuing user did not have it to begin with (Coase 1960: 2–15). A later conclusion of the same analysis is that in a world *with* pervasive transaction costs (such as our world), the initial distribution of legal rights *does* matter, because high transaction costs may prevent a higher-valuing user from buying the right from a lower-valuing user (Coase 1960: 15–19).

One lesson some law and economics theorists learned from Coase was that law was – or at least *often* was – largely irrelevant to analysis, because parties could contract around the existing legal regime. A claim that law might be irrelevant to behavior would obviously be important for domestic relations, where much of the discussion is about how laws have allegedly changed behavior for the worse, and how other laws might undo some of the damage.[22]

This is certainly the focus of much discussion regarding divorce laws: Did the introduction of no-fault divorce speed the breakdown of marriage, and would the availability of covenant marriage[23] create changes in the opposite direction (see, e.g., Scott 2002)? The argument in terms of incentives would be that no-fault divorce has made divorce "cheaper"[24] and one should thus expect "demand" to go up. However, the Coase theorem seems to undermine that claim, and reinforce the conclusion that changes in divorce law should not affect behavior.[25] Thus, one might expect law and economics theorists to argue that the move from fault to no-fault divorce would have *no* effect on divorce rates: Whatever the rules governing divorce, if (say) the wife valued the ability to divorce more than the husband valued the ability to remain married, she would be able to "buy him out" and get the divorce she wanted; and the process should work the other way as well, if one party valued staying married more than the other wanted to leave the marriage, the parties should reach an agreement for staying together (Allen 2002).[26] It should not matter (transaction costs aside for the moment) whether the spouse has the right to seek a divorce unilaterally,[27] or must seek the open (or covert[28]) agreement of the other party.[29]

Some economic commentators, following the Coase theorem, *have* claimed that the move to unilateral divorce laws has had no effect on the divorce rates (cf. Wolfers 2006).[30] On the other hand, many commentators (both economists and noneconomists), with some support by the data, argue that no-fault *has* made a difference (Allen 2002; Brinig 2000: 153–158; Becker 1991: 15). How do economists in this second group deal with the Coase theorem? One simple way of asserting that no-fault laws have made a difference without denying the Coase theorem would be to point to transaction costs. As noted, Coase conceded (indeed insisted) that in situations of significant transaction costs, the distribution of legal rights *could* make a significant difference.

Economically minded scholars have offered different views about transaction costs and divorce, some pointing to the high percentage of divorces that are resolved, and relatively quickly, through separation agreements; while others note the high legal fees in many divorces and the lengthy litigation of some marital dissolutions.[31] One could, of course, also argue that the rise of the divorce rate is related to transaction costs in the more straightforward way, that no-fault divorce is itself a means of reducing the transaction costs of divorce.

Martin Zelder's suggestion for why there is not more "contracting around" no-fault divorce was that the major "good" in many marriages is the "public good" of children. "Public goods" are goods (e.g., clean air and safe neighborhoods) that can be enjoyed by one person without affecting others's access to the same good. This is in contrast to more traditional, transferable goods, where I can only have more of one thing if other people have (or potentially have) less. Zelder's point is that if the main "good" of many marriages was the "public good" of children, then there are fewer transaction possibilities.[32] Douglas Allen has offered a series of alternative explanations for why parties might enter "inefficient divorces" – ranging from significant assets (e.g., professional degrees, enhanced earning power, or pensions) that in the past have not been or are not now subject to property division at divorce (creating an opportunity for one spouse to exploit through divorce), to ineffective enforcement of property division, alimony (spousal support), and child support obligations, to domestic violence, to the unenforceability of spouses's agreements to stay married (Allen 2002: 194–197).

Some recent work has argued against a Coasean analysis for reasons other than transactions costs. These analyses (e.g., Rasul 2005; Mechoulan 2006) emphasize that a switch from mutual-consent divorce to unilateral divorce is not merely a change in the entitlement rules for divorce, but also acts to change the value of the "good" at the center of the "transaction": marriage. The change to unilateral divorce reduces the value of marriage,[33] which has two further consequences: (1) it makes divorce more likely among the couples already married at the time of the legal change; and (2) it makes divorce somewhat less likely among couples who marry subsequently, as they will only enter marriages with partners with whom they are better matched. Thus, a strict Coasean approach would be inappropriate, as what "bargains" will be made regarding entry and exit from marriage will be changed by the changed value of marriage, not (just) by the altered rules of entitlement.

If few now espouse a fully robust Coasean model (presuming that legal rules will have no effect), that model still has influence in making many economists look beyond changes in legal rules *alone* to explain changes in behavior.

Game theory and family law

As discussed above, there is now a group of related but distinct approaches based on economics's rational choice model of human behavior. This section will give some brief examples of how one of the variations on neoclassical economics – game theory – has been applied to family law. Game theory may seem a natural option among rational choice approaches in discussing the family and family law, as it is all about the interactions among people where their efforts to reach their objectives require taking into account the actions and strategies of others. Thus, as will be seen, game theory has been applied to couples who are dating and thinking about marriage, and also to couples within marriage trying to cooperate, or considering exit (divorce).

Arguably, the best example to date of applying game theory to family law issues is Amy Wax's work (Wax 1998).[34] Wax used game theory to show how, in today's world, the combination of women's preferences, workplace realities, and the rules of marriage and divorce combine to make equality of the sexes difficult and unlikely, especially within marriage. Another example is Eric Posner, who draws on ideas derived from game theory, like "signaling,"[35] to explain a wide range of behaviors, including (though not focusing especially on) domestic relations (E. Posner 2000: 68–87). At one point, Posner states that the "marital relationship can be modeled as a repeated prisoner's dilemma, in which each spouse deters the other from cheating by threatening to punish any transgression of the marital obligations" (E. Posner 2000: 72). Posner's model of signaling may be most transparent and most persuasive in the context of his discussion of courtship, where he explains expensive gifts, sexual celibacy or exclusivity, and engagement rings, as ways for partners to signal (1) their "low discount rate" (their ability to forego current satisfaction of preferences in favor of the satisfaction of long-term objectives); and (2) their ability to support the other partner, and eventual children, monetarily (E. Posner 2000: 70–72).

Weak points of economic analysis in family law

In talking about the limitations or weak points of economic analysis in the area of family law and policy, one can focus on a number of areas; among these are children, love, identification, bounded rationality, obligation, and development of preferences. This section will give a brief overview of these points of relative weakness, while also cautioning against overstating the problems of economic analysis.

Children

In economic analysis, as in much noneconomic analysis, it is hard to take proper account of the interest of children. Economists have tended to view children (when they have taken them into account at all) as something the family "produces," and have tried to figure out why parents would "selflessly" invest so many resources in them.[36] However, such armchair economics (or sociobiology and evolutionary psychology) aside, the main problem for legal and economic analysis regarding children is elsewhere. The legal system usually gives children little say in matters affecting their interests (and children – younger children especially – are in any event usually not able to make competent choices, and the legal system generally does not grant them the right to make legally binding decisions), and, in economic terms, children are mostly the subjects of (positive and negative) "externalities" from the choices of adults.

In considering dealings between parents, or potential parents, regarding marriage, divorce, and parenting decisions, the effects on the welfare of the children (or potential children) are externalities that, if sufficiently high, would justify state intervention under the economists's own terms.[37] However, we cannot know how or when to intervene in or restrict adult choices with repercussions on children until we have some notion of which effects on children we wish to encourage and which we wish to discourage. There is little choice in legal and policy analysis but to have *some* vision of what is best for children and which way(s) to raise children is best for society.[38] However, economic analysis, by nature, is about means to an end ("efficiency"), not about choosing ends (e.g., R. Posner, this volume: 5–7). Thus, economics seems to fall short in this crucial segment of family law. (Social norms analysis is the closest law and economics generally comes these days to full-fledged normative analysis.[39] However, that work tends to be only an attempt to *explain* within a rational choice model how norms can and do develop. It is not, strictly speaking, a normative argument; it is not *advocating* having particular norms, only an attempted explanation for why we have the norms we do.[40])

This is not to say that economic analysis has *nothing* of value to offer in matters relating to children and parenting. To the contrary: The standard price theories and incentive/disincentive analyses have offered a number of suggestive theories regarding parenting. For example, Gary Becker argued that changes in income, women's work habits, and the costs of raising children can explain differences in childbirth rates across communities and over time (Becker 1991: 135–178). From a different perspective, Allen Parkman has contended that as government has offered greater financial support for children, responsibilities that would formerly have been taken on by the parents, the lower cost of raising children has encouraged less responsible and less prepared people to become parents, to the detriment of children and society (Parkman 1997). The extent to which either claim, or others like them, is valid, is beyond the scope of this chapter, but the positions offered have an initial plausibility which warrants attention.

Love

"How much would I have to pay you to get you to love me for myself?"[41] As this quotation (attributed to Roland McKean) indicates, there seems to be a basic (and perhaps obvious) disconnect between love and the type of market transactions with which we associate economic thinking. At the same time, this chapter has recognized how Gary Becker and others have extended economic analysis – directly or by analogy – beyond market interactions to nonmarket behavior. The question is whether that extension can work to the far outlying domain of love.

As poets, novelists, and philosophers have had trouble explaining the nature of love, it is hardly surprising that economists, with their intentionally simplified models of human behavior, do not do a good job of dealing with that emotion. One could, of course, argue that economics should not be criticized for not understanding or explaining what no one else understands or explains, but the point remains that family relations and family law will resist economic analysis to the extent that love is central to much of what is going on, and economic analysis does poorly on that topic. The best economic analysis seems to be able to do is to translate love to a preference, a preference for the well-being of another person – that is, altruism (Estin 1995: 1013–1015, 1021–1022; Becker 1991: 277–278). This is at best a highly imperfect translation.

While it is important and perhaps obvious to note that economics is not well-placed to explain love (Brinig 2005: 451), economic analysis *can* speak to the incentives and disincentives that may affect the consequences of love (or its absence) on the margins.[42] For example, monetary considerations may affect the question of whether someone in love decides to follow-up on that feeling by getting married, or instead believes that this opportunity must be passed up because the financial security would not be sufficient; or, if the absence of love suggests that a marriage be ended and a new search for love begun, whether the likely post-divorce financial situation would be too severe to allow that option.[43]

Consider one of the most infamous "commodification" proposals: that of selling babies (Landes and Posner 1978). However much we believe that most parents do make, and should make, decisions about carrying a child to term as against having an abortion, and decisions about keeping the child as against giving the child up for adoption, based on love and responsibility, it is hard to believe that these decisions do not at least *sometimes* turn on parents's (perceived) economic ability to continue the pregnancy and to care for the child. So the argument that allowing substantial payments (above and beyond mere expenses) for the adoption of a child may lead to fewer abortions, and at least to some children ending up with parents who want the children more (and therefore will be better parents [Landes and Posner 1978: 337–339]) is hardly absurd. This is not to say that the proposal does not have significant difficulties and long-term disadvantages (e.g., Prichard 1984; Forum 1987),[44] only that the potential benefits should not be immediately dismissed.[45]

Also, while there may be a danger that too much emphasis on economic analysis could delude analysts (or readers) into believing that all marriage, divorce, and parenting are "rational" – in some meaning of that term (Estin 1995: 1064–1066), economics can add insights even into these sorts of decisions. One can concede that certain decisions in an individual's interaction with a spouse, or child, are irrational (however broadly that term is defined), while still asserting that analyses in terms of incentives and disincentives might be useful in discussing how different regulations might affect behavior at the margin, or summed over a large population. That is, domestic life may be like actuarial predictions: poor on individual cases, but much better on large groups.

Identification

Milton Regan has argued at length in his book *Alone Together* that economic analysis will never be sufficient for understanding marriage, because an important aspect of marriage – at least of successful marriages – is that the spouses think in terms of "we" instead of "I" (Regan 1999).[46] To the extent that law and economics is confined to an individualistic understanding of behavior (even one that has room for "altruism" and "interdependent utility functions"), it will miss something basic about the way people experience their intimate lives, and will mis-state the basis on which many decisions are made in this area (Brinig 2000: 83).

On the other hand, there are reasons for being wary of emphasizing too much (or celebrating too much) this form of identification. As both Naomi Cahn and Kate Silbaugh have pointed out, the way in which the wife may be more likely than the husband to take an "internal" perspective on the marriage can work to exacerbate inequalities both inside the marriage and in society generally (Cahn 2000: 1790–1796; Silbaugh 2000: 114–118).

Regardless of the merits of Regan's characterization of how people experience marriage, the meta-theoretical claim raises different issues. A "hermeneutic" failure to describe accurately how participants experience their lives is often taken as a significant disadvantage in a social theory (e.g., H.L.A. Hart's construction of his theory of law around an "internal point of view" is grounded on such considerations [Hart 2012: 54–57, 79–88; Bix 1999]). However, economists can argue that accurate reflection of people's self-perceptions is not a goal of economic analysis (or, if a goal, it is only one of secondary importance); economists would prefer that their models be judged a success or failure based on their ability *to predict behavior*. And if the models succeed in predicting behavior, the fact that they do so while seeming to be "untrue" to people's self-perception may be, to the economist, interesting, but no reason to reject the model.

Bounded rationality

Empirical studies have shown that most people's judgments and decisions do not conform to the ideal "rational actor" that is the central figure in most economic analyses: people are instead overly optimistic about some matters, and unduly pessimistic about others: they misperceive the likelihood of events, sometimes because they overstate the representative nature of events they hear about; and valuation is distorted by loss aversion, endowment effects, and the vagaries of mental accounting, etc.[47]

Among the places where our "bounded rationality"[48] seems to be most frequently and importantly present are in the consideration of long-term commitments like marriage, and especially for long-term commitments with negative consequences hidden in the distant future, as with divorce, which too frequently follows marriage. Soon-to-be spouses considering a premarital agreement[49] (through which one spouse usually waives his or her property or support rights upon divorce) are as unlikely to think rationally about that waiver of rights as employees entering a new employment arrangement would think rationally about the noncompetition clause that comes into effect after termination of the employment relationship.[50]

Of course, there is a sense in which parties entering premarital agreements are even *more* at risk to bounded rationality than those entering commercial agreements. "The distinctive expectations that persons planning to marry usually have about one another can disarm their capacity for self-protective judgment, or their inclination to exercise it, as compared to parties negotiating commercial agreements" (American Law Institute 2002: §7.02 cmt. c, p. 956). Forms of natural optimism and rationalization keep us from realizing the true extent of various risks – and, for those about to be married for the first time, the risk of divorce is highly likely to be one such underestimated risk.

As discussed earlier, if neo-classical economics has been criticized for being grounded on a view of "rationality" that mis-states the way people actually perceive their world and make decisions, alternative forms of economic analysis (and alternative forms of economic analysis *of law*) – New Institutional Economics, behavioral economics, and behavioral law and economics – have been developed with the purpose of incorporating a more realistic view of "rationality."[51] With the assistance of these new variations, the problems of applying economic analysis to family law may have been diminished, but it is (to date) too early to tell.

Obligation

As Ann Estin has pointed out, economics seems weakest at the two points perhaps most crucial to understanding family life: love and obligation (Estin 1995: 1082–1086). Economic analyses's relative silence on love was discussed in the prior section; law and economics scholars have not been similarly reticent about obligations, but their attempts to "explain" obligation are, for the most part, neither on point nor persuasive.

The law and economics literature on "social norms" has mostly been attempts to offer "just so" stories about how using the models of rational, maximizing behavior, obligations that do not always favor the believer's self-interest could have developed (e.g., Conference 1998; McAdams 1997). While the extent to which discussions of social norms have been, to date, inadequate, and may be fated always to remain so, is beyond the scope of this chapter,[52] it is worth noting that this historical-explanatory approach to norms no more takes obligation seriously than did the earlier law and economics approach, which treated individuals's responses to obligations as a matter of personal preferences, and potential sanctions as just one more cost to take into account. Neither the social norms analysis nor the earlier approach reflects the way most people *experience* obligations – as reasons for action different in kind, and more important than, mere preferences or mere incentives.[53] Additionally, Amartya Sen (1982) has argued at length that the economists's view of rationality is incomplete because it does not take account of the idea of commitment.[54]

Development of preferences

The main objective of economic analysis is to explain how people will behave, given their preferences and the available resources. Economic analysis generally accepts people's preferences as given.[55] However, theorists who are concerned that a current situation involves too much exploitation and irrationality might want more attention given to how we *came to have* the preferences we now have, and how those preferences might be reformed, where appropriate (Baker 2002: 502–510; R. Posner, this volume: 7–9). To the extent that we want to think about whether we want to change people's values and norms (as earlier mentioned, aspects of our character and our thought that operate at a higher level than mere "preferences"[56]), and how, if at all, such change can be effected (e.g., through the law or through other means), economics does not always seem well-placed to offer guidance.

One can combine the discussion of this section with the previous one, in that what may be most crucial to the long-term policy analysis is some understanding of how (if at all) behavior can be changed.[57] June Carbone has suggested in her work ways in which economic analysis can be incorporated into a larger analysis of the change in norms, while understanding the partial role economic analysis must play in that discussion (Carbone 2000). Her analysis points out that simple economic or legal incentives and disincentives can work to change behavior on the margins, but for significant changes one needs to change people's values and norms. It is hard to change people's norms either by simple incentives or by discussion in the utility-maximizing terminology favored by economic analysis. People's values and preferences are arguably more likely to be changed by analysis given in normative terms rather than commodified terms. That is, people may be more easily swayed to change their behavior by being told that a different approach is consistent with justice, fairness, or true liberty, than if they are told that the change would maximize individual utility or social wealth.

Conclusion

Economic analysis has become a pervasive force in legal academia and legal commentary, whether we like it or not, and family law is no longer the haven from this form of analysis that it once seemed to be. As law and economics theorists have explored the ways in which rational choice theory might extend fruitfully to the issues within family law, family law scholars have considered what of value can be learned from economic analysis. Many family law scholars seem to feel more comfortable with variations away from traditional forms of analysis: New Institutional Economics (transaction costs economic), behavioral law and economics, game theory, etc.

Economic analysis, in all its variations, is a tool whose usefulness cannot be denied. It is an approach which helps to remind us of unintended consequences and incentive effects we might otherwise overlook.[58] At the same time, economic analysis seems to fail us in the areas which concern us most: How can we understand love and obligation? What about situations where an individualistic analysis is out of place? How do we explain, predict, or effect changes in norms and values? While economic analysis, both narrowly construed and in its modern variations, can be *a part* of the discussion of these issues, it seems likely that traditional (noneconomic) normative analysis will continue to play a large role.

Notes

* Frederick W. Thomas Professor of Law and Philosophy, University of Minnesota. This chapter was originally written for this collection thirteen years ago. It has been modified in only minor ways since then. Earlier versions of the chapter were presented at the conference, "Commodification futures: retheorizing commodification," held at the University of Denver Law School, and at a faculty workshop at the University of California-Davis School of Law. I am grateful to Margaret F. Brinig, Naomi R. Cahn, June Carbone, Robert B. Chapman, Neil Duxbury, Joshua Getzler, Jill Elaine Hasday, Aristides Hatzis, Brett McDonnell, David McGowan, Nicholas Mercuro, Allen M. Parkman, Elizabeth S. Scott, and those taking part at the University of Denver conference and those attending the University of California-Davis workshop for their comments and suggestions; I am also grateful to Galen Lemei for his research assistance.
1 I am well aware that others before me have discussed this general topic or similar topics. Among my predecessors from whom I have learned a great deal are (Baker 2002), (Brinig 2000), (Estin 1995, 1996), (Fineman and Dougherty 2005), (Folbre and Weisskopf 1998), (Hasday 2005), (Morse 2001), (R. Posner 1992), (Regan 1999), (Singer 1992), and (Tsaoussi 2007). My own prior effort is (Bix 2001). Additionally, there are many useful articles collected in (Brinig 2007) and (Dnes and Rowthorn 2002).
2 Behavioral law and economics derives from, or at least strongly overlaps with, a similar approach within economics proper, behavioral economics, a movement which has received some national press attention (e.g., Uchitelle 2001; Lowenstein 2001). Behavioral economics (understood broadly) has also been the basis of two of the so-called Nobel Prizes in Economic Science (more precisely, "The Sveriges Riksbank Prize in Economic Sciences in Memory of Alfred Nobel"). See notes 6 and 47.
3 As described by one of the first theorists to develop the concept, "bounded rationality" entails the decision-making and problem-solving process of:

a person who is limited in computational capacity, and who searches very selectively through large realms of possibilities in order to discover what alternatives of action are available, and what the consequences of each of these alternatives are. The search is incomplete, often inadequate, based on uncertain information and partial ignorance, and usually terminated with the discovery of satisfactory, not optimal, courses of action.

(Simon 1985: 294)

4 The issue of bounded rationality, in connection with family law, is discussed further below.

5 Which seems to be identical with, or strongly overlap, what is called "transaction cost economics" (Williamson 1998; 2000).

6 The connection between bounded rationality and the distinctive type of decision making within organizations can be traced back to the work of Herbert A. Simon, who won the 1978 Nobel Prize in Economic Science for that work.

7 See, e.g., (Brinig 2000: 6, 73, 104–105). For other commentators analyzing the advantages and disadvantages of using transaction cost economics to understand (aspects of) family life, see, e.g., (Ben-Porath 1980), (Chapman 2000; 2002).

8 A partial list would include, among economists discussing family law, Gary Becker (e.g., Becker 1991), Allen Parkman (e.g., Parkman 1992), Eric Posner (e.g., E. Posner 2000), and Eric Rasmusen and Jeffrey Stake (e.g., Rasmusen and Stake 1998). The group of family law theorists seriously considering economic analysis would include Katherine Baker (e.g., Baker 2002), Margaret Brinig (e.g., Brinig 2000; 2005), June Carbone (e.g., Carbone 2000; Carbone and Cahn 2014), Ann Estin (e.g., Estin 1995), Rhonda Mahoney (e.g., Mahony 1995), Milton Regan (e.g., Regan 1999), Elizabeth Scott (e.g., Scott 1990), Katherine Silbaugh (e.g., Silbaugh 1996), Jana Singer (e.g., Singer 1992), Amy Wax (e.g., Wax 1998), and Joan Williams (e.g., Williams 2000).

9 See, e.g., (Becker 1991: 2) ("Aside from the Malthusian theory of population change, economic hardly noticed the family prior to the 1950s"). One should not overstate: There was economic analysis relating to domestic matters long before Gary Becker's work; it was just less systematic. Some of the economic work of the family prior to Becker is discussed and cited in (Estin 1995: 995–999, nn. 25–27). Additionally, one should take note of the work, some of it done by the earliest feminists, on valuing housework (e.g., Boydston 1990; State and Vincenti 1997; Cahn 2001; Silbaugh 1996).

10 I am excluding macroeconomics, which focuses on broader governmental policies and economic structures. Macroeconomics continues to have little interaction with family law and policy.

11 Some true believers have at times gone farther, and claimed that analysis of this sort is the only path to truth, and also the only measure of justice. See, e.g., (R. Posner 1981). Posner has more recently retreated from some of the more ambitious claims made in that book (e.g., R. Posner 2011: 35 – "there is more to notions of justice than a concern with efficiency").

12 "Incentives and disincentives" can be seen as a lay person's way of talking about the Law of Demand, the way that increased cost leads to decreased demand, and vice versa. See, e.g., (R. Posner 2011: 5–7).

13 (Becker 1976; 1991); (R. Posner 2011). Becker's work showing the way that rational choice theory can apply to nonmarket behavior eventually earned him the 1992 Nobel Memorial Prize in Economic Science. For Posner's own useful summary of the history of applying economic analysis to noncommercial behavior, see (R. Posner, this volume: 1–3).

14 Becker noted that the specialization was primarily along gender lines, but, at least in the 1991 edition of his book, he went out of his way to distance anything that might

seem to be an endorsement of patriarchy, or even a very strong endorsement of bio-logical determinism: "Rather ... the message is that even small amounts of market discrimination against women or small biological differences between men and women can cause huge differences in the activities of husbands and wives" (Becker 1991: 4). Becker is sometimes portrayed as assuming or asserting (in the course of discussing the advantages of specialization households) that households work to max-imize wealth or (in other characterizations of his work) to maximize children. In fact, the relevant text (Becker 1991: 30–53) takes economics's characteristic agnosticism to ultimate ends, emphasizing primarily that the parties (jointly) maximize *utility* (e.g., Becker 1991: 31). What maximizes utility for various couples will depend on their preferences – for some it may be wealth, for others children, for others a combination, etc.

15 As Brinig writes: "From a basic economic perspective, it might seem uncontroversial to suggest that public assistance results in increased unwed births. Subsidize some-thing and theoretically you will always get more of it" (Brinig 2000: 60).

16 See (Brinig 2000: 49–57). As Brinig points out, foster care creates a series of "princi-pal–agent problems," with many of the parties working in part for the interests of others, but with incentives to follow their own interests instead (thus "shirking" their duties). "To resolve the problems inherent in foster care because of its principal–agent problem, the law must make the players's incentives compatible" (Brinig 2000: 56).

17 See, e.g., (Parkman 1992: 91–138). For a discussion (grounded in an economically based bargaining theory) of how unilateral or no-fault divorce may have reduced family violence – or at least the suicides and homicides resulting from such violence, see (Stevenson and Wolfers 2006). For the related issue of joint custody, Margaret Brinig and Frank Buckley (Brinig and Buckley 1998a) found that divorce rates were lower in states which had joint custody. One theory for this correlation (though not one discussed by Brinig and Buckley) is that a greater obligation to share custody might make divorce "costlier" for the party most likely to get custody (wives are both the spouse most likely to get custody in most marriages and the spouse most likely to initiate divorce proceedings; on the last point, see Brinig and Allen 2000).

18 An economically minded theorist might put the same point by saying that a require-ment of consent or fault, or the provision of substantial alimony, would be required "to protect the wife's human capital investment in marriage" (Brinig 2000: 88; foot-note omitted).

19 At least one recent study by economically minded theorists has come to the opposite conclusion: "that increased labor participation by women *reduces* the divorce rate" (Brinig 2000: 94 [footnote omitted], citing [Brinig and Buckley 1998b]).

20 Coase was awarded the 1991 Nobel Memorial Prize in Economic Science for his work in this area.

21 "Externalities" is the shorthand for costs imposed on other parties (in principle, there can be "positive externalities" when one's activities have *benefits* for third parties, but the term "externalities" is usually a shorthand for *negative* effects).

22 While (Carbone 2000) does not focus on the Coase theorem, her general conclusion, that social norms are much more important than law in determining behavior in domestic matters, can be seen to derive in part from her reading of (and partial accept-ance of) economic analysis.

23 In the three states that currently have covenant marriage – Louisiana, Arizona, and Arkansas – couples can choose a "more binding" form of marriage, which purports to constrain the grounds and procedures for divorce. See *Ariz. Rev. Stat. Ann.* §§25–901 to 25–906; *La. Rev. Stat. Ann.* §§9:272 to 9:276; *Ark. Code Ann.* §§9–1–801 to 9–11–811.

24 Cf. (Parkman 2000: 4–5) (summarizing the negative short-term and long-term effects of making divorce easier, in the context of an economic analysis of marriage and divorce).

25 The reason, economically speaking, why a simple incentive/disincentive analysis will not work with marriage is that we are dealing with two parties whose interests are interconnected: an action by one, or an incentive for one, may affect the other. In economic terms, the parties could be said to be in a "bilateral monopoly" (Wax 1998: 538). This interdependence, combined with frequent asymmetries of information, indicates why game theory might be particularly apt for analyzing questions of marriage and divorce.

26 Of course, depending on the relevant laws, this might require some creativity in structuring the agreement. For example, the classical fault divorce regime in most American jurisdictions did not allow divorce by "mere agreement" and allowed later collateral challenges to divorces based on such agreements. See, e.g., *Fuchs* v. *Fuchs*, 64 N.Y.S. 2d 487 (Sup. Ct. 1946) (allowing a fault-based divorce judgment granted by default to be set aside on the basis that it had been obtained by agreement of the parties). An agreement to divorce in a system that allows later collateral challenges would thus have to be structured in such a way that the party who originally wanted to stay in the marriage has an ongoing incentive not to challenge the divorce judgment after it is granted.

27 (Ellman and Lohr 1997: 723 n.8) could only locate three states where unilateral divorce (divorce granted without either a finding of fault or the express agreement of the other spouse) was *not* available. And since that article was written, one of those states, New York, has changed its divorce law to make unilateral divorce available.

28 See note 27.

29 Cf. (R. Posner 2011: 191) ("Once the parties have arrived at mutually agreeable terms, they need only manufacture evidence of a breach that provides legal grounds for divorce in order to get around a law against consensual divorce.").

30 See, e.g., (Peters 1986: 437, 452); cf. (Becker 1991: 15, 324–341) (modifying the conclusion of an earlier edition, that the change in divorce laws should have *no* effect on divorce rates, but only to the conclusion that the change of divorce laws explains a *small part (only)* of the change in divorce rates). It should be noted that even if the Coase theorem applies fully, such that the initial entitlement regarding divorce has no effect on the divorce rate, the legal rules still have distributional effects deriving from the Coasean bargains: Thus, if there is a right to divorce, there will be payments from those wanting to stay married to buy off those with that right, and payments in the contrary direction if there are rights to remain married (that is, if divorce requires the consent of both parties. Cf. (R. Posner 2011: 65) ("The initial assignment of rights, even when transaction costs are zero so that efficiency is not affected, may affect the relative wealth of the parties").

31 For the low transaction cost argument, see (Brinig 2000: 154); see also (Zelder 1993: 245–257) (study purporting to show that no-fault has increased the divorce rate, but that this increase was *not* due to high transaction costs). June Carbone (Carbone 2000: 250–251 n. 13) suggests a contrary view.

32 See (Zelder 1993: 254) *("Within marriage,* [one spouse] cannot choose to have fewer children so that [the other spouse] can have more."); see also (Parkman 1993). Of course, while the good of *having* children is not divisible, the time one can spend with them obviously is.

33 (Choo and Siow 2006) have argued that the legalization of abortion in the early 1970s also affected the gains from marriage, creating repercussions in the marriage "market."

34 Wax summarizes her approach as follows: She "draws on game theory to model marriage as a bilateral monopolistic bargaining relationship between rational actors in which husbands and wives engage in a process of allocating the benefits and burdens of married life under conditions of conflict" (Wax 1998: 512–513). (Mahony 1995) and (Hirshman and Larson 1998) make similar sorts of points without invoking the terminology of game theory, through a sophisticated analysis of bargaining. (Rose

1992) used game theory to explain why women might systematically do worse than men in regards to acquiring wealth. Economists applying game theory models to family law issues include (Manser and Brown 1980) and (Lundberg and Pollak 1993).

35 Signaling is the process by which one shows others that one is a "good type," not a "bad type" ("bad types" being those likely to cheat, "defect," shirk) (E. Posner 2000: 19).

36 As summarized by one commentator: "Economists describe children either as 'producer durables' – a source of a stream of future income for their parents – or as 'consumer durables' – a source of a stream of future satisfactions for their parents" (Estin 1995: 1011 n.95).

37 See, e.g., (Brinig 2000: 44–79) (referring regularly to the externality problem in the course of offering economic analyses of parent–child relationships).

38 Depending on one's views, these two questions may or may not be identical.

39 See, e.g., (Conference 1998). For an example of an effort to offer a similar sort of analysis with assumptions about human nature more "relaxed" than those given in neoclassical economics, see (Sugden 1998).

40 For detailed discussion of social norms in the context of family law, see (E. Scott 2000).

41 Quoted by Guido Calabresi in his Plenary Lunch talk, AALS conference, Washington, DC, January 2006. Judge Calabresi attributes the quotation (or something similarly worded) to Rolan N. McKean, but I have not been able to find a published text where it was used.

42 If one moves from love to the slightly less mysterious emotion of caring for dependents, (Folbre and Weisskopf 1998) have a discussion, partly (but *only* partly) based on economics, for how the amount of "caring labor" in society can be increased.

43 Of course, it should also be reaffirmed that economic analysis, even or especially the economic analysis of love, need not be only about financial considerations, but in principle could take in all preferences.

44 There are certain nearly intractable problems that come with bringing certain matters into the market. Consider this comment from the related area of surrogacy: "If the surrogate has other children ... [h]ow do they know that Mommy will not decide to give them away if she needs money or if she feels that another couple needs them more than she does?" (Brinig 2000: 72; footnote omitted).

45 Cf. (Hasday 2005: 528–530) (arguing that allowing payments in the adoption process could maintain the specialness of parenting while alleviation some of the inegalitarian effects of "non-commodification"/anti-baby-selling rules).

46 While there is much to like about Regan's book, there are also some problems. Both the strengths and the weaknesses are well described in (Silbaugh 2000) and (Cahn 2000).

47 See generally (Kahneman *et al.* 1982), (Sunstein 2000), and (Simon 1987); see also *supra*, notes 2–6 and the accompanying text. Daniel Kahneman received the 2002 Nobel Memorial Prize in Economic Science for his experimental work on "irrational" decision-making. Oliver Williamson, who shared the 2009 Nobel Prize (with Elinor Ostrom), did his work on "the New Institutional Economics," which some would categorize with behavioral law and economics.

48 Sometimes the term "bounded rationality" is used narrowly to refer to the subset of deviations from "rational choice" described by Herbert Simon, see *supra* note 3. This narrow meaning refers to the limits on most people's abilities to analyze data and remember facts, and the (reasonable) methods we use to respond to these limitations. However, the term is also used more broadly, as it is in this chapter, to refer to the general category of systematic deviations from "rational choice." For a related set of criticisms of the economist's notions of "rationality," see (Sen 1982).

49 For the consideration of bounded rationality in the context of premarital agreements (and the enforceability of such agreements), see (Bix 1998: 193–200); (Eisenberg 1995).

50 In both cases, the problem is over-optimism, and understatement or self-delusion regarding the chance that things will work out poorly. Thus, in both cases, parties entering the agreement with recent bad experiences in similar circumstances (a divorce or a job termination) will likely be less susceptible to irrational thinking. Cf. *R.R.* v. *M.H. & another*, 689 N.E. 2d 790, 797 (Mass. 1998) (listing as one condition that would likely be important for finding a surrogacy agreement to be enforceable that the surrogate mother "have had at least one successful pregnancy").
51 See *supra* notes 2–6 and the accompanying text.
52 For an example of a critical analysis of the economic explanation of norms, see (Mitchell 1999). For an example of a critique of law and economics's treatment of the effects of laws on social norms, see (R. Scott 2000).
53 For a sympathetic appraisal by a law and economics scholar of the differences in the accounts of obligations, see Kornhauser (1999).
54 There is also sometimes a problem within economic analysis of implying a normative when none is properly intended. While economics purports to be, and usually is, descriptive, its use of terms like "rational," "efficient," and "optimal" confuse some readers into thinking moral judgments are being made, when this is (usually) not the case. (Leff 1974; see also R. Posner, this volume: 6); see also (Brinig 2000: 68) [referring to an "optimal" amount of fraud]).
55 See, e.g., (Becker 1976: 14) (summarizing the economic approach as one that sees "all human behavior … as involving participants who maximize their utility from a stable set of preferences"). In the same text, indeed on the same page, Becker concedes that other social sciences might be valuable in understanding "[h]ow preferences have become what they are" (Becker 1976: 14).
56 We can, and most of us regularly do, critique our current preferences based on our values and perceived obligations. We try to reform our preferences in line with our values and obligations (though we may not always succeed in the attempt).
57 Much of the discussion in the latter part of this section derives from discussions with June Carbone.
58 For example, the way that substantive and procedural protections meant to protect weak parties often work, over the longer term, against the interests of the group the rules were meant to protect. See, e.g., (R. Posner 2011: 645–648) (discussing protections in the landlord–tenant and housing context).

References

Allen, Douglas W. (2002) 'The impact of legal reforms on marriage and divorce', in Antony W. Dnes and Robert Rowthorn (eds.), *The Law and Economics of Marriage and Divorce*, Cambridge: Cambridge University Press: 191–211.
American Law Institute (2002) *Principles of the Law of Family Dissolution: Analysis and Recommendations*, Charlottesville, VA: LexisNexis.
Aumann, R.J. (1987) 'Game theory', in John Eatwell, Murray Milgate, and Peter Newman (eds.) *The New Palgrave Dictionary of Economics*, London: Palgrave Macmillan, vol. 2: 460–482.
Baird, Douglas G. (1998) 'Game theory and the law', in Peter Newman (ed.) *The New Palgrave Dictionary of Economics and the Law*, London: Palgrave Macmillan: vol. 2, 192–198.
Baker, Katherine K. 'Gender, genes and choice: a feminist analysis of evolutionary biology and law & economics', *North Carolina Law Review* 80, 2002: 465–525.
Becker, Gary S. 'A theory of marriage: part I', *Journal of Political Economy*, 81, 1973: 813–846.

Becker, Gary S. 'A theory of marriage: part II', *Journal of Political Economy*, 82, 1974: S11–S26.

Becker, Gary S. (1976) *The Economic Approach to Human Behavior*, Chicago, IL: University of Chicago Press.

Becker, Gary S. (1991) *A Treatise on the Family*, enlarged edition, Cambridge, MA: Harvard University Press.

Ben-Porath, Yoram 'The F-connection: families, friends, and firms and the organization of exchange', *Population & Development Review* 6, 1980: 1–30.

Bix, Brian H. 'Bargaining in the shadow of love: the enforcement of premarital agreements and how we think about marriage', *William & Mary Law Review* 40, 1998: 145–207.

Bix, Brian H. 'H.L.A. Hart and the hermeneutic turn in legal theory', *SMU Law Review* 52, 1999: 167–199.

Bix, Brian H. 'How to plot love on an indifference curve', *Michigan Law Review* 99, 2001: 1439–1454.

Boydston, Jeanne (1990) *Home and Work: Housework, Wages, and the Ideology of Labor in the Early Republic*, Oxford: Oxford University Press.

Brinig, Margaret F. (2000) *From Contract to Covenant: Beyond the Law and Economics of the Family*, Cambridge, MA: Harvard University Press.

Brinig, Margaret F. (2005) 'Some concerns about applying economics to family law', in Martha Albertson Fineman and Terence Dougherty (eds.) *Feminism Confronts Homo Economicus: Gender, Law, & Society*, Ithaca, NY: Cornell University Press: 450–466.

Brinig, Margaret F. (ed.) (2007), *Economics of Family Law*, vols. I & II, Cheltenham: Edward Elgar.

Brinig, Margaret F. and Allen, Douglas W. 'These boots are made for walking: why most divorce filers are women', *American Law & Economic Review* 2, 2000: 126–169.

Brinig, Margaret F. and Buckley, F.H. 'Joint custody: bonding and monitoring theories', *Indiana Law Journal* 73, 1998a: 393–427.

Brinig, Margaret F. and Buckley, F.H. 'No-Fault law and at-fault people', *International Review of Law and Economics* 16, 1998b: 325–340.

Cahn, Naomi 'Looking at marriage', *Michigan Law Review* 98, 2000: 1766–1796.

Cahn, Naomi (2001) 'The coin of the realm: poverty and the commodification of gendered labor', *Journal of Gender, Race & Justice* 5: 1–30.

Calabresi, Guido (1970) *The Costs of Accidents: A Legal and Economic Analysis*, New Haven, CT: Yale University Press.

Carbone, June (2000) *From Partners to Parents*, New York: Columbia University Press.

Carbone, June and Cahn, Naomi (2014) *Marriage Markets: How Inequality is Remaking the American Family*, Oxford: Oxford University Press.

Chapman, Robert B. 'Coverture and cooperation: the firm, the market, and the substantive consolidation of married debtors', *Bankruptcy Developments Journal* 17, 2000: 105–220.

Chapman, Robert B. (2002) 'Missing person: social science and accounting for race, gender, class, and marriage in bankruptcy', *American Bankruptcy Law Journal* 76, 2002: 347–444.

Choo, Eugene and Siow, Alysius 'Who marries whom and why', *Journal of Political Economy* 114, 2006: 175–201.

Coase, Ronald (1960) 'The problem of social cost', *Journal of Law and Economics* 3, 1960: 1–44.

Conference 'Social norms, social meaning and the economic analysis of law', *Journal of Legal Studies* 27, 1998: 537–823.

Dau-Schmidt, Kenneth, Rasmusen, Eric, Stake, Jeffrey Evans, Heidt, Robert H., and Alexeev, Michael 'On game theory and the law', *Law & Society Review* 32, 1997: 613–629.

Dnes, Antony W. and Rowthorn, R. (eds.) (2002) *The Law and Economics of Marriage and Divorce*, Cambridge: Cambridge University Press.

Eggertsson, Thráinn (1998) 'Neoinstitutional economics', in Peter Newman (ed.) *The New Palgrave Dictionary of Economics and the Law*, London: Palgrave Macmillan: vol. 2, 665–671.

Eisenberg, Melvin Aron 'The limits of cognition and the limits of contract', *Stanford Law Review* 47, 1995: 211–259.

Ellman, Ira Mark and Lohr, Sharon 'Marriage as contract, opportunistic violence, and other bad arguments for fault divorce', *University of Illinois Law Review* 1997, 1997: 719–772.

Estin, Ann Laquer 'Love and obligation: family law and the romance of economics', *William and Mary Law Review* 36, 1995: 989–1087.

Estin, Ann Laquer 'Can families be efficient? A feminist appraisal', *Michigan Journal of Gender & Law* 4, 1996: 1–33.

Fineman, Martha Albertson and Dougherty, Terence (eds.) (2005) *Feminists Confronts Homo Economicus: Gender, Law, & Society*, Ithaca, NY: Cornell University Press.

Folbre, Nancy and Weisskopf, Thomas E. (1998) 'Did father know best? Families, markets, and the supply of caring labor', in Avner Ben-Ner and Louis Putterman (eds.), *Economics, Values, and Organization*, Cambridge: Cambridge University Press: 171–205.

Forum 'Adoption and market theory', *Boston University Law Review* 67, 1987: 59–175.

Hart, H.L.A. (2012) *The Concept of Law*, 3rd edition, Oxford: Clarendon Press.

Hasday, Jill Elaine 'Intimacy and economic exchange', *Harvard Law Review* 119, 2005: 491–530.

Hirshman, Linda R. and Larson, Jane E. (1998) *Hard Bargains: The Politics of Sex*, Oxford: Oxford University Press.

Kahneman, D., Slovic, P., Tversky, A. (eds.) (1982) *Judgment Under Uncertainty: Heuristics and Biases*, Cambridge: Cambridge University Press.

Kornhauser, Lewis A. 'The normativity of law', *American Law & Economics Review* 1, 1999: 3–25.

Landes, Elisabeth M. and Posner, Richard A. 'The economics of the baby shortage', *Journal of Legal Studies* 7, 1978: 323–348.

Leff, Arthur Allen 'Economic analysis of law: some realism about nominalism', *Virginia Law Review* 60, 1974: 451–482.

Lowenstein, R. 'Exuberance is rational: or at least human', *New York Times*, February 11, 2001, Magazine Section, at p. 68.

Lundberg, S. and Pollak, Robert A. 'Separate sphere bargaining and the marriage market', *Journal of Political Economy* 101, 1993: 988–1010.

McAdams, Richard H. 'The origin, development, and regulation of norms', *Michigan Law Review* 96, 1997: 338–433.

Mahony, R. (1995) *Kidding Ourselves: Breadwinning, Babies, and Bargaining Power*, Boston, MA: Basic Books.

Manser, M. and Brown, M. 'Marriage and household decision-making: a bargaining analysis', *International Economic Review* 21, 1980: 31–44.

Mechoulan, Stéphane 'Divorce laws and the structure of the American family', *Journal of Legal Studies* 35, 2006: 143–174.

Minow, Martha (1999) 'Consider the consequences: review of Lenore Weitzman's The Divorce Revolution', in Martha Minow (ed.), *Family Matters: Readings on Family Lives and the Law*, revised edition, New York: New Press: 329–334.

Mitchell, Lawrence E. 'Understanding norms', *University of Toronto Law Journal* 49, 1999: 177–248.

Morse, Jennifer Roback (2001) *Love and Economics: Why the Laissez-Faire Family Doesn't Work*, Dallas, TX: Spence Publishing Company.

Owen, Guillermo (1995) *Game Theory*, 3rd edition, San Diego, CA: Academic Press.

Parkman, Allen M. (1992) *No-Fault Divorce: What Went Wrong?*, Boulder, CO: Westview Press.

Parkman, Allen M. 'Reform of the divorce provisions of the marriage contract', *BYU Journal of Public Law* 8, 1993: 91–106.

Parkman, Allen M. 'The government's role in the support of children', *BYU Journal of Public Law* 11, 1997: 55–74.

Parkman, Allen M. (2000) *Good Intentions Gone Awry: No-Fault Divorce and the American Family*, Lanham, MD: Rowman & Littlefield.

Peters, H. Elizabeth 'Marriage and divorce: informational constraints and private contracting', *American Economic Review* 76, 1986: 437–454.

Posner, Eric (2000) *Law and Social Norms*, Cambridge, MA: Harvard University Press.

Posner, Richard A. (1981) *The Economics of Justice*, Cambridge, MA: Harvard University Press.

Posner, Richard A. (1992) *Sex and Reason*, Cambridge, MA: Harvard University Press.

Posner, Richard A. (2011) *Economic Analysis of Law*, 8th edition, New York: Aspen Publishers (1st edition, 1973).

Prichard, J. Robert S. (1984) 'A market for babies', *University of Toronto Law Journal* 34, 1984: 341–357.

Rasmusen, Eric and Stake, Jeffrey Evans 'Lifting the veil of ignorance: personalizing the marriage contract', *Indiana Law Journal* 73, 1998: 453–503.

Rasul, Imran 'Marriage Markets and Divorce Laws', *Journal of Law, Economics, & Organization* 22, 2005: 30–69.

Regan, Milton C. (1999) *Alone Together: Law and the Meanings of Marriage*, New York: Oxford University Press.

Rose, Carol M. 'Women and property: gaining and losing ground', *Virginia Law Review* 78, 1992: 421–459.

Ross, Don (2010) 'Game theory', *The Stanford Encyclopedia of Philosophy*, edited by Edward N. Zalta. http//plato.stanford.edu/entries/game-theory (accessed October 8, 2014).

Scott, Elizabeth S. 'Rational decisionmaking about marriage and divorce', *Virginia Law Review* 76, 1990: 9–94.

Scott, Elizabeth S. 'Social norms and the legal regulation of marriage', *Virginia Law Review* 86, 2000: 1901–1970.

Scott, Elizabeth S. (2002) 'Marital commitment and the legal regulation of divorce', in Antony W. Dnes and Robert Rowthorn (eds.) *The Law and Economics of Marriage and Divorce*, Cambridge: Cambridge University Press: 35–56.

Scott, Robert E. 'The limits of behavioral theories of law and social norms', *Virginia Law Review* 86, 2000: 1603–1647.

Sen, Amartya (1982) '"Rational fools": a critique of the behavioral foundations of economic theory', in *Choice, Welfare and Measurement*, Cambridge, MA: MIT Press: 84–106.

Silbaugh, Katherine B. 'Turning labor into love: housework and the law', *Northwestern Law Review* 91, 1996: 1–86.

Silbaugh, Katherine B. 'One plus one makes two', *Green Bag* 4, 2000: 109–118.

Simon, Herbert A. 'Human nature in politics: the dialogue of psychology with political science', *American Political Science Review* 79, 1985: 293–304.

Simon, Herbert A. (1987) 'Bounded rationality', in John Eatwell, Murray Milgate, and Peter Newman (eds.), *The New Palgrave Dictionary of Economics*, London: Palgrave Macmillan: vol. 1, 266–268.

Singer, Jana B. 'The privatization of family law', *Wisconsin Law Review* 1992, 1992: 1443–1567.

State, Sarah and Vincenti, Virginia B. (eds.) (1997) *Rethinking Home Economics: Woman and the History of a Profession*, Ithaca, NY: Cornell University Press.

Stevenson, Betsey and Wolfers, Justin 'Bargaining in the shadow of the law: divorce laws and family distress', *Quarterly Journal of Economics* 121, 2006: 267–288.

Sugden, Robert (1998) 'Normative expectations: the simultaneous evolution of institutions and norms', in Avner Ben-Ner and Louis Putterman (eds.) *Economics, Values and Organization*, Cambridge: Cambridge University Press: 73–100.

Sunstein, Cass R. (ed.) (2000) *Behavioral Law & Economics*, Cambridge: Cambridge University Press.

Tsaoussi, Aspasia (2007) 'The economics of family law' (unpublished manuscript), available at papers.ssrn.com/sol3/papers.cfm?abstract_id=1116386 (accessed October 8, 2014).

Uchitelle, Luis 'Following the money, but also the mind: some economists call behavior a key', *New York Times*, February 11, 2001, Section 3 (Money & Business), p. 1, col. 2.

Wax, Amy L. 'Bargaining in the shadow of the market: is there a future for egalitarian marriage?', *Virginia Law Review* 84, 1998: 509–672.

Weitzman, Lenore (1985) *The Divorce Revolution*, Boston, MA: Free Press.

Williams, Joan (2000) *Unbending Gender: Why Family and Work Conflict and What to Do About It*, Oxford: Oxford University Press.

Williamson, Oliver E. 'Transaction cost economics: how it works; where it is headed', *De Economist* 146, 1998: 23–58.

Williamson, Oliver E. 'The New Institutional Economics: taking stock, looking ahead', *Journal of Economic Literature* 38, 2000: 595–613.

Wolfers, Justin 'Did unilateral divorce rates raise divorce rates? A reconciliation and new results', *American Economic Review* 96, 2006: 1802–1820.

Zelder, Martin 'Inefficient dissolutions as a consequence of public goods: the case of no-fault divorce', *Journal of Legal Studies* 22, 1993: 503–520.

14 The figure of the judge in law and economics

*Elisabeth Krecké**

The personage of the judge is at the heart of much of law-and-economics, and yet few scholars are relating their models to the complex professional reality of the man or woman in a black robe. What precisely is the status of the "judge" in the conceptual framework of the economic analysis of law (EAL)? The answer to this apparently simple question is surprisingly unclear. Theoretical construct, economic agent, psychologically and politically biased decision maker, de facto legislator... – can the judge be all this at once or simply, like a chameleon, change status according to the requirements of the model?

This chapter traces the evolution of the figure of the judge over the fifty years of existence of the law-and-economics movement, by exploring a range of paradoxes, starting with the fact that in the neoclassical EAL, judicial action is reduced to a strictly economic function (social wealth maximization/social cost minimization) and that, in order to be operational, the theory has, at least in its basic version, adopted assumptions concerning judges's knowledge and motivations that stand in sharp contradiction not only with judicial reality but, most of all, with its own conception of human rationality as self-interested behavior. The first section describes how in mainstream law-and-economics, since the beginning, the judge has been a central and, at the same time, absent (or self-contradictory) figure, as it amounts to an abstract, and hence malleable, hypothesis in a basic (stability and equilibrium seeking) microeconomic model which, in spite of its assumed (and theoretically justified) lack of realism, has clearly established normative pretensions.

The second part focuses on the recent behavioral amendments in law-and-economics that import analytical tools from cognitive psychology in order to reconsider the rationality of the model's actor. *Is there a psychology of judges* (Schauer 2010)? One would expect this to be a central question of the new behavioral developments; yet, as this chapter will argue, only a minority of works do address it and assume the risk of fragilizing the efficiency theory of law, once scope is left for cognitive biases of judicial actors.

It is Richard Posner who, in recent years, adopts a true change of perspective by proposing a realistic "reflection on judging" (Posner 2013). Already announced in a series of previous works,[1] Posner draws a wide-ranging, across-the-board, portrayal of what he calls the "pragmatic" adjudicator, which incorporates economic, cognitive, and legal facets of the figure of the judge. In this extended analytical framework, fundamental legal questions come up that so far the EAL (in its initial, neoclassical, as well as amended, behavioral, versions) had systematically eluded, such as judicial legitimacy. The third section raises the question of whether Posner's return to legal realism and sociological jurisprudence is susceptible either to undermine the very project of the EAL or, on the contrary, give it a new élan.

The neoclassical judge

From the start, the EAL has taken over the key rationality assumptions of the standard microeconomics framework. The behavioral conjecture of optimization under given constraints is applied to two basic categories of agents: first, private individuals (those governed by law), the focus being on how institutional constraints affect their decisions; and second, producers of law, in the large sense of the term, including judges, legislators, regulators, as well as any other officials operating within the legal system. It is here that a first paradox seems to come up concerning the expression of the rationality hypothesis. In the 1970s, the law-and-economics movement had largely adopted the assertions of the public-choice literature according to which rationality leads certain types of public decision makers (such as regulators or legislators) to maximize their own personal interests (career, prestige, money, power, etc.) rather than those of the community – an assumption which implies that the notion of general interest is to a large extent illusory. Underlining informational as well as motivational problems affecting those who are called to intervene in the economic or social sphere, and insisting on the direct and indirect costs of these interventions, but also the regulatory and legislative distortions created by the existence of a political market, Chicago celebrities such as Stigler, Becker, Peltzman, Coase, and Posner had succeeded in giving the economic theory of regulation an entirely new orientation. To the at-that-time prevailing economic theory of market failure (which recommended regulation to correct situations of market malfunctions), they had opposed a theory of regulation failure based precisely on the argument of economic rationality or, rather, a comparative institutional analysis of both market *and* government failures – a perspective that is nowadays widely acknowledged by economists as well as lawyers. What is amazing, however, is that, in the same years, the same rationality assumption had led more or less the same people (Richard Posner, among others) to elaborate a theory of law presenting an omniscient, fair-minded, perfectly disinterested judge whose assumed purpose is to impartially maximize a social welfare function rather than his own utility function. But by what miracle does rationality, in this particular case, no longer lead a public actor to pursue his personal interest, but those of the community or, more precisely, the wealth of society? On what ground can a theory consider that judges put their rationality in the service of the public good and, at the same time, maintain that other categories of public decision makers are rational if they pursue their private interests to the detriment of collective welfare? For a long time, the EAL has remained largely silent on this methodological issue.

The figure of the economically rational judge gives rise to a few more paradoxes. On one hand, at least in the initial version of the EAL, the judge had played a primordial role as a substitute for deficient or non-existing market mechanisms that he was supposed to mimic by maximizing social wealth. But on the other hand one could also say that this agent played no significant role at all, because he was supposed to act in a general equilibrium setting in which a priori, or by definition, there are no uncompensated costs, no externalities to internalize; in other words, no real problems to be solved, and hence, no scope for a judge. So this actor appeared to be all at once central and absent to the functioning of the model. Furthermore, the neoclassical judge who was supposed to balance social costs and benefits was, strictly speaking, not judging; he was above all calculating.

As a consequence, the contrast between the ideal judge of the basic neoclassical law-and-economics framework and the one of the real world seemed quite flagrant. It is even more intriguing (another paradox?) if we consider the fact that among those who have initiated this purposely reductionist model of judicial decision making, several scholars are (or have been) themselves professional judges. Posner, Easterbrook, Calabresi, and Bork, to quote just a few, are among the most reputed and influential judges of their generation in the United States. They certainly know better than anyone else the complex reality, the systematic biases, and all kinds of other constraints that weigh on judicial professions. How, then, to explain this apparent contradiction: be a judge oneself as a practitioner and, as a social scientist, elaborate such an unrealistic and simplifying account of this function?

The few methodological or founding texts of the law-and-economics movement provide some elements of answer to this enigma, to start with the well-known *Essays on Positive Economics* by Milton Friedman (1953), to which Posner relates since the very first editions of his *Economic Analysis of Law* (1973). Posner regularly quotes Friedman's formula, according to which the realism of the model's assumptions is without much importance. What counts is the formal coherence of the model, rather than the concordance between the model's hypotheses and social reality. For Friedman, it was obvious that the general equilibrium models were not destined to explain how markets work in reality, but only in a clearly defined theoretical framework. Thus, *Homo economicus* is not even an abstraction of real economic behavior but merely a theoretical solution to a theoretical problem of standard microeconomics. It is this assumption of rationality that allows the models to be operational. However, and this raises of course new ambiguities, the ultimate goal of neoclassical theories (including standard law-and-economics) is to lead to straightforward policy conclusions.

Initially, indeed, the economic approach to law had been developed as an extension of the mainstream market model. To quote again Posner from one of his early writings: "Law-and-economics can be defined as broadly as to be virtually coextensive with economics" (Posner 1987: 3). One might say that, at least in its beginnings, the EAL had been no more, no less, than a defense of the free market. In this sense, one could argue that there is no fundamental contradiction with the public-choice argument evoked earlier. In that theory as well, the purpose had been to emphasize the self-regulatory capacities of the market, precisely *in contrast* to the distortions that may result from a regulator's self-interested interference with market processes.

The conjecture of the social wealth-maximizing or cost-minimizing adjudicator was precisely what allowed the standard microeconomic theory of law to have all the elements at stake converge toward an optimum. The judge of this model is what permitted the market to achieve social optima even in case of failure (for instance, when too high transaction costs make it impossible to imagine an efficient exchange to take place). In this sense, the judicial agent, at least in the law-and-economics setting of the early days, appeared above all as a hypothesis, a mental construction, a function, rather than an abstraction (description) of a real-world public officer appointed to decide cases in a law court. It is a theoretical agent of the kind that Alfred Schutz (1967) would have called a "puppet"; Fritz Machlup (1978) might have preferred the term "heuristic fiction." Indeed, the figure of the neoclassical judge comes close in many respects to what the two Austrian methodologists had categorized as an "ideal type" (in contrast to a "real type"): a postulated actor, a rational entity, defined precisely by the problem it is supposed to clarify or solve;[2] in other words, a useful, if not indispensable "artificial device for the use of economic theorizing" (Machlup 1978: 298). Just like the firm had been reduced to a black box in the basic neoclassical price theory, the judge of the primitive EAL has been assimilated to a conceptual tool allowing the market model to work against all odds. In such a perspective, confusing the predicted actions of the imagined judge with the actual decisions of legal officials acting in the real world would be committing the same "fallacy of misplaced concreteness"[3] as confusing the neoclassical firm with existing enterprises or organizations.

Logically, issues fundamental for the understanding of the legal process, in particular those concerning the nature of judicial knowledge, have been assumed away by mainstream law-and-economics. The behavior of judges is treated in an ad hoc manner. The judge's sole mission, in this peculiar approach, is to push the law toward greater economic efficiency; therefore he is *supposed* to possess all the knowledge necessary to achieve this predetermined social goal. This is, of course, not a realistic assumption, but without it the neoclassical microeconomic model of law would not be workable.

Considering the judge as a conceptual device of social coordination is one of the true originalities of the EAL, a perspective that traces back to Coase's seminal work of the early 1960s. "The problem of social cost" (Coase 1960), one of the foundational texts of law-and-economics, provides indeed a few more elements of answer to the eventual paradox underlined earlier. Coase, too, had situated the judge on the side of the market and *not* of public intervention. In contrast to the regulator (an external authority who intervenes in, or interferes with, the market), the judge has been considered as a force internal to the market;

this actor was presented as a coordination mechanism *inside* the market, in other words, an element participating to the market's self-regulation. In this setting, questioning the judge's rationality (and considering his eventual personal motivations) would not have made much sense.

More precisely, Coase had argued that in the absence of transaction costs, conflicting parties will negotiate until they find a mutually satisfactory outcome (corresponding to a social optimum), which implies that, under conditions where the price system works correctly and there is a clear assignment of property rights, the market is capable of internalizing externalities without the intervention of any external authority. If, however, transaction costs are positive, as is usually the case in legal disputes, the judge comes into play and his mission is to simulate the outcome the market would have achieved if it had not failed because of too high transaction costs. In other words, in this perspective the judge acts as a substitute in a deficient market by deciding cases in a way that minimizes social costs or maximizes social wealth.

Is this unusual interpretation of the judicial mission not, above all, an attempt to overcome the traditional market failure argument? A way of saying: The market has its own institutions that help it overcome its eventual deficiencies? If so, one could wonder whether Coase's focus on the judicial mechanisms of dispute resolution had not been meant initially to be a contribution to *economic* rather than to *legal* theory. This could explain why, at times, Coase has been somewhat reluctant to be celebrated as one of the founding fathers of the EAL. Coase (1993) obviously did not fully adhere to the way his arguments were interpreted in a context of what was to become, with the EAL, a major contribution to legal scholarship rather than to economic theory. The EAL has indeed operated a methodological shift that could indeed be deranging from Coase's point of view. It is one thing to say that the judicial order can efficiently help the market to internalize externalities (Coase's argument), but it is another to praise the judge's capacities to enforce economic efficiency in legal cases (the EAL's extrapolation). In the latter perspective, the judge becomes a key decision maker intervening in the normative sphere. Moreover, the function of "market simulator" would require these actors to possess extraordinary competences and relevant information about all kinds of things, involving often very subjective data (in accident cases, for instance, they must be capable of outguessing *ex post* what could have happened *ex ante*, or which among the involved parties could have been the "cheaper cost avoider"). These quasi-omniscient judges do not seem to be affected by strategic motivations either.

And now, clearly, a contradiction has appeared with respect to the public-choice line, and the issue of the rationality of the judge (as an economic actor) matters.

The behavioral judge

In recent years, more and more authors within the law-and-economics movement have expressed their dissatisfaction with the standard neoclassical assumption of the hyper-rational decision maker. "As law and economics turns forty years old," some leading economic analysts of law regret, "its continued vitality is threatened by its unrealistic core behavioral assumption: that people subject to the law act rationally" (Korobkin and Ulen 2000: 1051). Challenging the traditional rational choice theory by introducing more realism into the models has become an important trend in modern law-and-economics, the purpose being to emphasize precisely the recurrent deviations of human behavior from the rationality standard of conventional microeconomic theory.

The idea is that because of a range of flaws, biases, and heuristics, on average, real people act far less rationally and efficiently than the neoclassical optimizer. For example, they tend to be either over-optimistic or too pessimistic; they are inclined to overemphasize short-term consequences or underestimate long-term effects; eventually, they are disposed to believe that small samples are representative; they are likely to assign greater importance to more recent experience, etc. As a consequence, they do not always correctly evaluate risks, especially with respect to low-probability events, nor are they capable of adequately comparing magnitudes such as, for instance, the utility of present consumption with future costs. Furthermore, while in some circumstances people might be more cooperative than the self-interested *Homo economicus*, in others they might be far more malicious than traditional economics would predict.[4]

How to bridge this gap between theory and reality? For a growing number of economic analysts of law, the only solution is to remove the neoclassical rationality assumption from law-and-economics.[5] In order to understand the complexity of real-world decision-making mechanisms, they prefer to turn to disciplines other than economics, such as cognitive psychology, whose experimental methods have been integrated into what was to become, within less than a decade, an extremely successful new framework for law-and-economics, most commonly labeled behavioral law-and-economics (BLE).

The empirical analyses conducted in BLE have noticeably lengthened the list of behavioral flaws and judgmental errors that had so far been identified by cognitive psychologists. More specifically, this new trend in law-and-economics has brought to the fore three major bounds on human behavior that seem to undermine the possibility of systematic utility maximization: bounded rationality (cognitive limits due either to limitations in information-processing capabilities or to a lack of adequate knowledge), bounded willpower (lack of self-control or weakness of will which explains why individuals often engage in actions that later they come to regret), and, last but not least, bounded self-interest (the fact that people care for others or simply act out of motives that appear as incompatible with the purely self-interested attitude of the rational, efficiency-seeking, economic man). Eventually, fairness is considered to be such a motive,[6] which may have intriguing repercussions on the way BLE would approach the nature of judicial duty. However, as critics have noted, "lumping fairness with cognitive quirks and weaknesses of will suggests that behavioral economics is merely the negative of rational choice economics – the residuum of social phenomena unexplained by it" (Posner 2001: 262).

What are the possible implications for law-and-economics of a fact-finding process that contradicts many of the general assumptions of conventional decision theory? In particular, does the argument that people do not always act according to the predictions of the economic standard of rationality imply that they do not always do what they *should* do? By addressing, at least implicitly, this psychological and to some extent moral issue, the recently emerged research program of BLE seems to reconnect (yet in quite different terms than did the original economic approach to law) with the jurisprudential tradition initiated in the late eighteenth century by Jeremy Bentham. The influential British philosopher, jurist and social reformer (in Posner's eyes one of "the most illustrious progenitors" of the EAL[7]) had indeed been among the first to attempt to predict and systematize people's behavioral defects[8] in a framework that we would today call a positive science of human conduct, in order to set up, in a next step, a so-called science of morals: a field whose primary purpose would be to provide criteria by which to judge whether a given conduct is right or wrong. Of the two facets – descriptive versus prescriptive – it was the second that appeared to Bentham to be the most important and also the most "scientific."[9] The idea was that ultimately, it is ethics that confers sense to scientific inquiry.

The modern BLE movement has not taken over this claim as such, but it seemed obvious from the start that this interdisciplinary literature would not content itself with the observation and description of a variety of cognitive illusions or biases that characterize ordinary decision makers. BLE would not just be about defining patterns of irrational (suboptimal) behavior in order to understand the origins of people's intellectual weaknesses and, eventually, to predict how these recurrent flaws come into play in relation to the prevailing social and legal frameworks. Rapidly indeed, a prescriptive dimension has been associated to the behavioralists's empirical findings. The founders of BLE have straightforwardly addressed the normative agenda of the theory when asking: "Is it possible for those involved in law to 'debias' people, in the process, perhaps, lengthening human lives?" (Sunstein 2000: 10). The purpose of this new experimental branch in law-and-economics is undeniably to work out procedures that should help individuals to overcome their common behavioral failures and get ahead, the endmost goal of such policies being to raise general welfare. In other words, BLE proposes to design so-called debiasing strategies referring to a host of cognitive methods that reach from education to behavior therapy,[10] over to psychiatry, and that are supposed to cure (or at least reduce) people's behavioral defects, precisely by increasing their incentives to make accurate judgments. Transform people into better calculators – that is how Bentham might, in his time, have formulated the same conjecture. Strictly speaking, any instructional device appears to be acceptable to BLE, as long as it helps people to take improved decisions. Providing individuals with more information, or at least putting them in a position to make more informed (and presumably better?) choices is considered as a fundamental task of law and policy and, above all, one that is concordant with the goal of efficiency. However, as psychologists also note, in a number of situations that are characteristic for systematic behavioral deficiencies, it is needless to urge citizens just to "try harder": a variety of biases that can be observed are in fact induced by processes of mental strategies; for example, implicit cognitive procedures that are mobilized to make judgments in hindsight (Rachlinski 2000: 98). In such cases, it is precisely upon those mental strategies that debiasing policies ought to act. They should attempt to restructure behavior so as to force people to "unlearn" their bad habits.

Overall, the modern-day BLE advocates appear more openly paternalistic[11] than the founder of classical utilitarianism had been himself (at times, Bentham had indeed expressed a certain anti-paternalism).[12] In reaction precisely against the anti-paternalism of standard (liberally oriented) law-and-economics, Sunstein and Thaler have launched in recent years a renewed debate on what they call "anti-anti-paternalism," a position they define as the conscious attempts by policymakers to alter the "choice architecture" that people face in their everyday lives, in order to get them to take decisions that will make them better off. They defend a soft form of interventionism that is meant to operate with "gentle nudges" rather than "hard shoves,"[13] the purpose being to help people improve "their decisions about health, wealth and happiness" (Sunstein and Thaler 2008). The idea is to push individuals to do what is best for them, and what eventually they would want to do, had they not been victims of their own weakness of will and/or their biased views on themselves and the world. In this context, the two co-founders of BLE came up with the controversial notion of libertarian paternalism,[14] a political doctrine that is presented as a new form of paternalism,[15] built on well-intended, reasonably weak, and overall not too intrusive public interventions in the private sphere of human action.[16] Let us again quote the two authors: "Equipped with an understanding of behavioral findings of bounded rationality and bounded self-control, libertarian paternalists should attempt to steer people's choices in welfare-promoting directions without eliminating freedom of choice" (Sunstein and Thaler 2003a: 1159).

Reinforced by a growing body of experimental research as well as policy recommendations, BLE is sometimes presented as the new scientific paradigm destined to amend or even replace mainstream law-and-economics.[17] It can be argued, however, that at least to some extent this new research agenda remains attached to two fundamental propositions of standard EAL: First, the assertion that policies and legal rules can be analyzed and evaluated in terms of their efficiency; and second, that it is desirable for policies and legal rules to be efficient (in the sense of creating incentives for individuals to act efficiently). In BLE, beyond doubt, rationality continues to be an ultimate referential norm for scientific inquiry, and efficiency a supreme value for guiding and evaluating the law.

What differs from the initial law-and-economics perspective is, of course, the content given to the normative conclusions. While in many policy contexts a typical rational-choice based perspective would argue that it is most appropriate to leave wide freedom of action to rational individual decision makers, the recent behavioral approaches could come to the exact opposite conclusion, namely that, if unrestricted choice was granted to individuals, they would (in many private as well as legal[18] contexts) end up acting against their own interests.[19] Thus, to the question of whether the legal system should always respect people's choices, the answer of prescriptive BLE appears to be an unambiguous "no." This movement away from the original perspective of law-and-economics is, above all, of an ideological nature. While integrating the behavioral paradigm, the new variant of law-and-economics has obviously drifted away from the initial, laissez-faire oriented spirit (Coase's framework) to an ever more dirigiste attitude[20] (the contemporary BLE framework).

It is, however, from a methodological point of view that BLE has operated the most far-reaching departure from the conventional law-and-economics framework. When rejecting the central assumption of the standard rational choice model, the economic approach to law seems to have moved from one extreme to another, trading its neoclassical standard of perfect rationality for a new assumption of "equal incompetence" (G. Mitchell 2002). As Mitchell remarks, "whereas law and economics treats all legal actors in all situations as if they were perfectly rational, behavioral law and economics treats all legal actors in all situations as if they were equally predisposed to commit errors of judgment and choice" (G. Mitchell 2002: 67). In this new (ideological as well as methodological) context, the question of the role of the judge in the law-and-economics framework all of a sudden takes an interesting turn. Where indeed does this agent stand between the reality of non-predictable, non-rational, behavior and the requests of paternalism?

First, one might argue that the knowledge requirements necessary to pursue the efficiency goal seem to be much higher for the BLE judge than for the neoclassical judge. In order to come to efficient decisions, a paternalistic decider would indeed have to take into account the various ways people make mistakes and to evaluate how this affects their own as well others's behavior, which would be a far more complex task than dealing with the flawless *Homo economicus* of the neoclassical model, whose actions are, after all, easily predictable. Nevertheless, even though, as Posner rightly argues, "judicial candidates are pretty carefully screened for honesty and basic professional competence," nothing exempts them "from the cognitive quirks, from weakness of will, or from concerns with fairness" (Posner 1994: 26; 2001: 287). So, to what extent is the judge also what Posner would call a "behavioral man, behaving in unpredictable ways" (Posner 2001: 287)?

Above all, does BLE provide us with a more comprehensive portrayal of a judge confronted with bounded rationality and uncertainty? In fact, it does so only in a rather limited way. As shown in a statistical study by Berggren (2012), focusing on research projects in behavioral economics published in the ten most highly ranked economic journals over the last ten years, 95.5 percent of the papers that propose paternalistic policies (which is the case of 20.7 percent of the studied articles) deal essentially with the behavioral flaws and the bounds of rationality of private individuals and almost not at all with those of policymakers – as if the "equal incompetence" affected everyone in society, *except them*.

In this context, a question imposes itself: How can such an unequal treatment of ordinary citizens versus political officials be interpreted? Does Berggren's result suggest that the paternalistically oriented branches of BLE feel no need to explore the biases of the second category of actors because, at least to some degree, they premise that the public decision maker is necessarily a "person of superior intelligence," capable of "delivering verdicts which will be more valid than those of the mass of men who presumably are on the average not in his class intellectually?"[21] Such a presumption would, of course, be incongruous. Given that in many situations, as psychologists argue, what people want is not necessarily what they choose, on what basis can we defend the idea that public decision makers are capable of identifying (and enforcing) what private individuals *really* want? How would regulatory or legal authorities manage to get access to the true preferences of those governed by law if, for a host of reasons (including lack of self-control), the latter had not acted according to them? How can a policymaker be supposed to know better than the concerned individuals themselves what is best for them?[22] Needless to insist that such a position is hardly tenable on scientific as well as political grounds.

Yet, some BLE authors advance an explanation. While admitting that error is likely to afflict "any" decision maker, they contend, for instance, that the simple awareness or comprehension by public authorities of the causes and consequences of misjudgment can be sufficient to steer clear of many easy answers and frequent policy pitfalls (Noll and Krier 2000: 351). Incidentally, does this imply that for this literature those who should have the final word in the designing of policies are the experts in psychology, economics, and the law – in other words, those who provide public decision makers with a more precise knowledge about citizen's behavior and misbehavior? As a matter of fact, the BLE framework assigns cognitive scientists an important role in the normative sphere. However, does this not merely move the bias issue from one level to another – yet, fundamentally, the problem would remain the same (how to avoid indeed that the scientist-expert's social purposes are not themselves biased, for example by political or personal motivations?).

This still does not explain the paradox that appears in Berggren's statistical study. Why indeed would a coherent behavioral approach be exempt from the requirement to confront the actions of both categories of agents (citizens *and* public decision makers) to the findings of conventional theory? Would such a task be simply too ambitious, as implied by some BLE scholars (Noll and Krier 2000: 326)? Concerned more precisely with the implications of risk regulation policies, the two authors decide on their account to proceed on a working hypothesis that may astonish: "while citizens behave according to the psychologists' description of the world, politicians do not" (Noll and Krier 2000: 352–353). Does this statement connote that only ordinary citizens (subject to biases) constitute a category of interest to psychologists, whereas political actors (supposedly rational in the economic sense of the term) do not, so that their actions could still be fittingly analyzed within the framework of conventional decision theory?[23] And, finally, is such an assumption a way to come to terms with Berggren's stupefying conclusion (asserting that, let us recall, 95.5 percent of the paternalistically oriented research papers published over the last decade in the major behavioral economics journals insist mainly on the cognitive illusions of private individuals, while only a negligible part of that literature is concerned with those of public decision makers)? This is far from certain.

And what about judges? Among the less than 4.5 remaining percent of the articles that treat the question of the cognitive limitations of the general category "policymakers," how many are devoted to the issue of misconduct observable in judicial professions? Berggren's study does not specify it. It appears, however, that in the rather young literature of behavioral economics (of which BLE is a sub-branch), the models that directly focus on adjudication are comparatively few. And, of those that do so, quite a few seem to be interested in the ways the "paternalistic judge" is anticipating and integrating the behavioral flaws of the conflicting parties that come to trial – a perspective which, as stated before, seems to presuppose that the efficiency-seeking judge of the BLE framework (the "libertarian paternalist") must be even smarter[24] than the one of the initial EAL model, and that his role is to become ever more extensive.

The limited but growing body of empirical research that veritably deals with the recurrent failings in judicial decision making concentrates on the psychology of jurors more than of judges. Among the systematic biases that are said to alter the judgment capabilities of juries, special attention is drawn to a "hindsight bias" which, generally speaking, refers to the propensity of people to overstate the predictability of past events (hence reinforcing their belief that what happened should have been foreseen). According to psychologists, this phenomenon is extremely hard to eliminate or even to attenuate.[25] In the courtroom, as argued by BLE, the hindsight bias may lead jurors to take unjust as well as inefficient decisions. For instance, in tort cases, by treating parties as if they were negligent (even though reasonable precautions had been taken), juries non-intendedly end up transforming the negligence standard into a "de facto system of strict liability" (Rachlinski 2000: 98) – with all this implies in terms of incentives (or, rather, disincentives). More specifically in punitive damages cases, the persistence of cognitive biases may explain why juries often produce erratic judgments. For example, in one case a jury awards millions of dollars to a plaintiff, while in another it grants nothing at all, even though both cases appear exactly similar, and both are argued in the same court, before the same judge (Sunstein *et al.* 2002). As shown by a large-scale experimental study in BLE,[26] jurors are inclined to set unpredictable (and obviously ever-higher) damages awards; as a consequence, their decisions often seem to amount to "a stab in the dark" (Sunstein *et al.* 2002: vii), much more than the result of a lucid collective reflection. In criminal cases a variant of the hindsight bias that is likely to have a negative influence on juries is a "pathology" that has been identified as the "sticky norms problem": the fact that sometimes jurors are tempted to follow popular misconceptions (for example, in rape cases the brainless idea that "no sometimes means yes"), rather than the prevailing law that eventually had intended to change such unfounded social norms (Kahan 2000). While, over the years, many legal systems throughout the world have substantially redrafted their rape laws, empirical studies seem to indicate that such reforms have nevertheless had little impact on juries (Kahan 2000: 607).[27]

Some BLE writings are concerned precisely with the various procedures or mechanisms that courts have developed over time to reduce the biases (in particular with respect to hindsight) affecting their juries (Kamin and Rachlinski 1995; Rachlinski 2000). Among the debiasing strategies supposed to help jurors to reach a "rational" decision, one can find tactics such as the suppression of evidence (that could be misleading), or the introduction of judicial instructions (Rachlinski 2000: 103). Yet, as psychologists insist, these generic remedies do not seem to have the excepted effect either. In many cases, juries seem indeed to ignore the instructions coming from the judges.[28] One reason might be that in particular areas they simply encounter difficulties in correctly understanding legal instructions. Eventually, according to this behavioral literature, more specific, so-called second-best strategies,[29] adapted to the particulars of the case at hand, appear as slightly more successful devices to cope with the fallacies of a given jury – all the same not conclusive enough to assert that courts are truly and durably able to help juries overcome their delusions and, eventually, correct their mistakes. Certain authors therefore call for a systematic replacement of jury decision making with that of judges.[30] The contention is that because of the obviously insurmountable behavioral flaws affecting jurors, the very institution of jury should be reconsidered (if not abandoned) in favor of a reinforcement of the judge's prerogatives.

This begs, of course, the question of whether judges are (or are not) themselves subject to the kinds of cognitive biases and judgmental errors that frequently influence juries. A common standpoint in the prevailing BLE literature is to claim that judges, even though they occasionally make some of the same mistakes as juries, are, in general, better equipped to decide a case.[31] This makes sense as the judge is a professional of the law while the juror (an eligible citizen) is, after all, a lay-person and, as such, an "amateur" (Robbenolt 2005: 470). Moreover, so the argument goes, judges (like any decision makers affected by bounded rationality) have learned to reduce the probability of error by using a variety of rules, presumptions, standards, heuristics, or routines. For behavioral economists, for example, courts reason by analogy precisely because this allows them to prevent unintended side-effects occurring "from large disruption" (Sunstein and Ullmann-Margalit 2000: 202). The authors further claim that:

> judges typically make narrow decisions, resolving little beyond the individual case; at least this is their preferred method of operation when they are not quite confident about the larger issues, not just in the common law but constitutional law too.[32]

Furthermore, it is often argued that judges know quite well how to overcome their own biases. In order to minimize the kinds of problems that could alter their decisional capacities in particular cases (such as partiality or favoritism), they may, for example, recuse themselves on their own initiative.

However, to what extent can judges adequately determine their own impartiality? The concern came up in a 2009 Supreme Court decision,[33] with respect to the refusal of a judge to recuse himself from a case in which one of the involved parties (as it happens, the CEO of a corporate defendant) had donated several million dollars in support of the challenged judge's election. In this important case, the Supreme Court states that the Due Process clause of the Fourteenth Amendment of the US Constitution requires the disqualification of a judge not only when an actual bias or obvious conflict of interest can be established, but also when "extreme facts" create a "probability bias" (for instance, when the judge clearly has an economic or personal interest in the outcome of the case).

Caperton addresses the issue of misjudging by insisting essentially on motivational aspects. What about cognitive and informational biases of which judges may be victims unwittingly? To what extent are their verdicts tainted by personal prejudices and misconceptions? A recent statistical study argues that in the behavioral literature on adjudication, there is a general tendency to focus above all on motivation rather than on cognition.[34] Insisting on the fact that even the most well-experienced, well-trained, and well-intended judges are vulnerable to cognitive illusions, the experimental studies conducted by Rachlinski, Guthrie, and Wistrich constitute in this respect noteworthy exceptions. This group of scholars, who work at the intersection of law, psychology, and social science, test for instance how common intellectual weaknesses such as anchoring, framing, hindsight bias, inverse fallacy, or egocentric bias, come into play in the judicial decision-making process (Guthrie *et al.* 2001; 2007; 2009; Wistrich *et al.* 2005; Rachlinski *et al.* 2009). Their explorations "inside the judicial mind"[35] bring up insightful, yet somewhat alarming, conclusions. Each of the above-mentioned quirks, the authors argue, has an undeniable impact on the outcome of judges's decisions. Another inquiry conducted by the same group of academics deals with a racial bias that may affect trial judges (Rachlinski *et al.* 2009). A distinction is made in this regard between explicit and implicit (or unconscious) biases.[36] The multi-part study, involving a large sample of trial judges that had been recruited from different parts of the United States, concludes that (1) judges hold implicit racial biases and (2) these biases actually influence their judgments. In the end, the authors moderate nevertheless the argument by claiming that, given sufficient motivation, judges can eventually overcome their biases (Rachlinski *et al.* 2009: 1197).

What is the significance of conclusions that seem to question, at least at first sight, the paternalistic project of BLE which, as said before, assigns the judge an important role as a "choice architect" (assuming that the judge is capable of imposing on disputants solutions that make them better off and of ensuring, at the same time, that resources are devoted to their best uses)? Empirical investigations that highlight important disparities among individual judges, resulting from factors such as personality and opinions,[37] seem to refute also the claim of standard law-and-economics according to which judging motivated by efficiency is to some degree objective and hence predictable. In other words, given the recently appearing psychological findings on judges's biases, is the efficiency approach to law still tenable?

For many BLE scholars there is obviously no major inconsistency. The empirical discoveries of flaws in judicial behavior, they tend to argue, serve essentially to elaborate normative suggestions for reducing the disparities in decision rates among individual judges – that is, reforms that aim at enhancing the efficiency of the court system (Sunstein *et al.* 2006). Furthermore, in one of their investigations on judicial independence,[38] Sunstein and his co-authors came to the conclusion that, contrary to expectations, ideology does not much affect legal judgments.[39] In the same vein, other scholars insist on the fact that the various studies on the psychology of judges are not necessarily meant to "criticize" judges and that, after all, "bad" or "corrupt" judges make up only a small minority of the trial bench; the point is merely to show that the vast majority of "good" judges are prone to "predictable blinders" which, eventually, could lead them to misjudge (Guthrie 2007: 455). But in case this happens, we are reassured, the process of appeals comes into play as a "means of error correction" (Guthrie 2007: 421). Does this suggest that, at least for this group of legal psychologists, the standard postulate of law-and-economics, according to which judges at large tend to push the law toward greater efficiency, remains valid, in spite of all?

Several challenges remain, however. For instance, as Bix (2013: 40) rightly points out, while wrong legal decisions are actually often reversed (either by the same court or by a higher court), it also happens that they are not overturned and then the legal mistake becomes part of the settled law. It may even occur that over a significantly long period of time, a majority of legal actors collectively reiterate the same fault, so that in the end the misconception transforms into what Bix calls a "global error."[40] It could be useful, in this context, to bring up the practical question of how common, how systematic, and how harmful misjudgment *really* is,[41] and eventually, whether it is possible to somehow measure this phenomenon in terms of scope and impact – impact not only on the lives of concerned disputants (judicial errors may indeed cause irreversible damage to them), but on the evolution of law at large. More generally, can there be relevant criteria for assessing, in the light of the recent psychological findings, the soundness (efficiency?) of a given system of adjudication? Fischman (2013) advances precisely three such potential standards – "inter-judge inconsistency,"[42] "legal indeterminacy,"[43] and "judicial error"[44] – in order to quantify the gap that can sometimes be observed between the way judges actually decide cases and the way they ought to do so. Other scholars prefer to evaluate judges with respect to their compliance with a series of prevailing normative standards.[45] Approaches differ, but the problem seems to remain the same, at least for those inquiries into the psychology of judicial decision making that embrace a normative dimension: How to bring together, in a coherent framework, empirical (quantitative) and conceptual (legal/philosophical) considerations? More fundamentally, how to appraise the "truth-aptness" (Bix 2013) of a legal system? And, with all the more reason, how to define "legal truth" (Bix 2009)? As Bix (2009) confirms, defining this concept is not less tricky than demarcating the one of legal error.

By focusing on the issue of negligently inflicted harm by judges, Tsaoussi and Zervogianni (2007) push further the analysis of judicial biases. "If judges are guardians of the law," they ask, "who is to protect the individual member of society from the occasional corrupt, malicious, or reckless judge?" (Taoussi and Zervogianni (2007: 333). Drawing on Herbert Simon's concept of bounded rationality, they elaborate a model of judicial misbehavior that describes judges as satisficers rather than maximizers. In complex situations (including uncertainty as well as imperfect or false information), all judges can do, so the authors conclude, is attempt to take acceptable decisions, given the constraints they have to face. This may to some extent explain the occurrence of judicial misbehavior and error. "Because their goal is not to optimize but to render opinions that are merely satisfactory," Tsaoussi and Zervogianni explain (Tsaoussi and Zervogianni 2007: 333), "judges often act as poor agents of their principals' interests. In this light, it becomes clearer why judges tend to engage in behavior that is 'improper,' especially under the circumstances of the currently overloaded judicial caseloads."

Bringing up the question of judicial liability for grave errors, the model by Tsaoussi and Zervogianni (applied essentially to cases of civil litigation) clearly offers a missing contribution to law-and-economics. Relying on analytical tools derived from economics as well as from psychology, it evaluates the impact of various incentive schemes on judicial behavior – among which is civil liability, a particularly efficient response, it is argued, to deter judges from committing what the authors call "inexcusable" errors. Many more studies applying the empirical methods of behavioral economics to judicial conduct (and misconduct) would be needed in order to overcome the aforementioned asymmetry (paradox?) in the literature concerning the unequal treatment of decisional structures of private versus public actors.

But maybe there is a plausible reason that could explain why a majority of behavioral economists persist in focusing essentially on the cognitive limitations and biases of individuals subject to law, while remaining amazingly evasive with respect to those of lawmakers. Is it not the validity (viability?) of the entire law-and-economics project that is at stake? As a matter of fact, the efficiency theory of law necessarily encounters conceptual difficulties as soon as it starts to integrate the flaws of producers of law. How, indeed, to justify and legitimate the fairly invasive role of the "paternalistic judge" when this figure appears itself as not perfectly reliable? So, is it not for fear of endangering the economic perspective of law that many BLE advocates are careful not to insist too much on the flaws of the judicial actor in their models, because this would unavoidably lead them to conclude that judges are not fully rational and, hence, not necessarily equipped to promote the goal of economic efficiency?

For now, as it seems, in BLE – with a few exceptions – nobody really wants the efficiency theory of law taken off the table.

The pragmatic judge

Since the 1990s, Richard Posner, certainly the most influential representative of the law-and-economics movement, has clearly distanced himself from the instrumental vision of the hyper-rational neoclassical judge – without, however, adhering to the methodology of BLE.[46] In many of his writings of the last two decades, he operates with a concept of the judge that is standing in sharp contrast to the mechanical judicial decision maker whose narrowly defined action (social wealth maximization) is formalized in the standard EAL setting – a model that Posner had himself contributed to elaborating some forty years ago.

For Posner, first of all, it was time to get to the bottom of a "mystery" that lies at the heart of the initial EAL (precisely the first of our aforementioned paradoxes) and that is, as is argued, "also an embarrassment": the divorce of judicial decision making from incentives. The author admits that so far, the economic analyst had "a model of how criminals and contract parties, injurers and accident victims, parents and spouses – even legislators and executive officials such as prosecutors – act, but falters when asked to produce a model of how judges act." However, "if economics is the science of rational choice," he takes up, "why shouldn't it be fully applicable to judges?" (Posner 1994: 1–2). Thus, in this new positive economic theory of appellate judges and justices, Posner proposes a complete revision of the judicial utility function, exploring the extent to which personal elements such as money income, but also the quest for popularity, prestige, public interest, reputation, or simply the desire to avoid reversal, come into play in judges's decisions. Although "the vast majority of judges are neither power seekers, like some politicians, nor truth seekers, like many scientists" (Posner 1994: 26) he writes, there are no valuable reasons to suppose that judges are not at all subject to self-interested behavior, or that they are perfectly insulated from external (in particular, political) pressure.

Given this reality, how can rational judicial behavior be defined? Landes and Posner (2009) have recently reconsidered the question within a strictly empirical perspective. Relying on Supreme Court and court of appeals data, they conducted a statistical study to evoke, among others, the ideological dimension inherent to judicial decision making.[47] So, to the decisive interrogation "what do judges and justices maximize?" Posner's new answer is unambiguous: "the same thing everybody else does."[48] In other words, the rational judge is no longer presented as a quasi-omniscient and fair-minded actor, maximizing a social welfare function; he ceases to be seen, to use Posner's terms, as a sort of genius, Promethean, or saint devoid of human weaknesses, quirks, and foibles. On the contrary, the adjudicator is described as an "ordinary person responding rationally to ordinary incentives" – a way for Posner (1994: 26) to "demystify" and "domesticate" this category of legal decision makers for economic analysis.[49]

Posner's uncompromising reconsideration of judges's rationality has been the first move in the direction of the elaboration of an extensive, voluntarily realistic approach to adjudication that clearly goes beyond a strictly economic framework. The term legal realism is defined here in the broadest sense of the term[50] as "everything in legal thought and practice that is not formalism" (Posner 2013: 5). The realist judge, Posner writes, is above all someone who is attentive to the "consequences of judicial rulings" and who, "in this regard, is pragmatic" (Posner 2013: 5). In a series of works published over the past twenty years,[51] Posner applies the notion of pragmatism all at once to the methods of the legal scholar (pragmatic jurisprudence) and those of the judge (pragmatic adjudication). In both cases, thinking pragmatically is understood in a commonsense manner as "looking at things concretely, experimentally, without illusions, with full awareness of the limitations of human reason, with a sense of the 'localness' of human knowledge ... the unattainability of 'truth' " (Posner 1993: 465).

Assessing which rules and decisions produce the best consequences in the world of facts,[52] pragmatic judges are thus still seeking efficiency, but they seem to be doing so in a rather loose sense. Indeed, the value of efficiency eventually acquires any meaning that individual judges wish to attribute to it (they may want to privilege systematic[53] or case-specific effects; they may focus on long-term or short-term consequences, etc.). Also, economic efficiency no longer appears to be that supreme legal goal to be defended at any cost, as was the case in the initial EAL. It has become a means rather than an end in itself; one criterion among others on which judges rely for evaluating the soundness of decisions, policies, or rules.

Pragmatism, Posner (2008: 9) argues, becomes a particularly valuable method of adjudication when judges "thrust into the open area" – precisely those areas of law where conventional sources of guidance (such as previously decided cases and clear statutory or constitutional texts) fail to generate acceptable answers to the questions they are required to solve. This standpoint makes clear that Posner has not, as one might think, moved from the paradigm of applied mainstream economics to the one of conventional legal theory. Posner remains deeply skeptical indeed about the basic contention of traditional American legal thought according to which judges do (and should) decide cases based on a straightforward application of pre-existing rules or precedents. Posner (1993: 455) emphasizes the fact that, on the contrary, legal rules are often "vague, open-ended, tenuously grounded, highly contestable, and not only alterable, but frequently altered," and, as a consequence, they are "more like guides or practices" to judges, rather "than like orders."

Above all, Posner (2001: 159) rejects the conventional views of judicial duty according to which "the past is, for lawyers and judges, a repository not just of information but of value, with the power to confer legitimacy on actions in the present."[54] He disagrees, for instance, with Paul Kahn (2000: 43) that legal arguments "begin from a commitment to the past" and that "the rule of law is for us the manner in which the authoritative character of the past appears" (Posner 2001: 159). He wonders on what grounds Ronald Dworkin (1986: 167) defends the idea that "the past must be allowed some special power of its own in court" (Posner 2001: 160). "Why *must*?" Posner (2001: 160) asks. Why *should* the past rule the present? (Posner 2001: 169). Why should the dead be ruling over the living? (Posner 2001: 154). Posner does not see any serious answer to these questions except, eventually, the fact that legal innovations may involve more or less heavy transitional costs. But he categorically refuses to admit that "our ancestors had a freshness of thought that is denied to us moderns" (Posner 2001: 154). Nothing allows concluding, according to him, that judges of the past had been better equipped to take good decisions than those of today. Posner acknowledges, of course, the fact that, in a number of situations, legal materials from the past constitute a precious source of information to judges about how to decide present cases, but at the same time, he points to what he thinks is a misleading confusion (frequently made by legal theorists) between the reliance on the past as a source of learning and the willingness to treat it as normative. Posner admits as well that the contemporary law is full of vestiges of ancient law (Posner 2001: 157), but these seem to hinder rather than enhance the efficiency of the legal process. This becomes clear in the following passage:

> Law is the most historically oriented – more bluntly the most backward-looking, the most "past-dependent" – of the professions. It venerates tradition, precedent, pedigree, ritual, custom, ancient practices, ancient texts, archaic terminology, maturity, wisdom, seniority, gerontocracy, and interpretation conceived of as a method of recovering history. It is suspicious of innovation, discontinuities, "paradigm shifts," and the energy and brashness of youth.
>
> (Posner 2001: 145)

In other words, blind idolatry of the past appears to have produced overall negative consequences for the evolution of law: Over decades and even centuries, legal doctrine has ended up being shaped by historical requirements rather than by current needs. "If we were starting from scratch" Posner (2001: 158) argues, "we could design and (even with due regard for political pressure) would adopt a more efficient system." And this appears to be the ultimate purpose of the pragmatic judge's action: forward- rather than backward-looking, he is not afraid of breaking with the past by overruling outdated statutes or obsolete precedents and by going his own way.

If judges are no longer bound by the past, pragmatism implies of course that there is a strong political element inherent to the judiciary (Posner 2008: 369); in other words, that judges (especially American appellate judges) exercise an important amount of discretion. They appear as legislators, at least as much as adjudicators (Posner 2008: 18). For Posner, this is obviously not a problem in itself, but merely the manifestation of the way the American legal system actually works. What is striking in Posner's new perspective is that, on one hand, the judge's mission appears to be much more far-reaching and intricate than most traditional approaches of judicial lawmaking would admit and, on the other, this personage is described as a quite ordinary person, influenced by all kinds of political and ideological opinions, as well as personal and professional values, notions of commonsense, and even intuition, sentiment, or idiosyncrasy. Legal pragmatism so understood (as "everyday pragmatism" [Posner (2005a)]) is not more than any other form of ordinary practical reasoning, because as Posner states, "there is no such thing as legal reasoning"; legal reasoning being no more than "practical reasoning deployed on legal problems."[55]

Nevertheless, and here Posner makes an interesting observation, judges tend to more or less skillfully hide this reality from the public.[56] More importantly, the entire process of precedent-following behavior by judges – a typical feature of the common law system – reflects, according to Posner, such a strategy of concealment of the pragmatic (and hence discretionary/political) nature of adjudication. In the same vein, courts would seize upon ancient "overarching" concepts of justice in order to motivate their decisions (Posner 1993: 460). The reasons why judges tend (or rather *pret*end) to invoke the authority of texts and legal material from the past are thus far more obscure than one might think at first sight. The use of history for legitimating present judicial decisions is, above all, rhetorical, Posner explains. Judges like to deify, for instance, the constitutional framers, because this allows them to keep back more easily the fact (difficult to admit openly?) that what they are doing is fabricating "a fictive history in the service of a contemporary, pragmatic project." In other words, concealment can be seen as an expression of judges's ingenuity. It is an adroit way of bringing up legal innovations without "breaching the judicial etiquette which deplores both novelty and a frank acknowledgment of judicial discretion" (Posner 2001: 154).

In fact, what judges want to keep confidential above all, so Posner states, is their difficulty to cope with a surrounding world that is becoming ever more complex. In this respect, Posner (2013) distinguishes between two kinds of complexity that affect judicial decision making: sources of complexity that are external to the law (including, among many others, scientific and technological evolution, risk of global catastrophes, and new strategic imperatives in corporate governance) and sources that are internal to the law, in other words, generated by the legal professions themselves (and exacerbated over the years by factors such as the growth of bureaucratic constraints,[57] massively increased caseload,[58] and, as a result, the expansion of the size of judges's staffs and the judiciary in general). Posner's point is that while the law is supposed to regulate external complexity, by doing so it creates its own *internal* complexity. In other words, judges tend to escape from one kind of complexity into another. But, as Posner also notes, judges to a large extent do so *deliberately*. They intensify internal complexity above all by overusing formalism. As Posner explains, some judges excessively evoke principles of statutory interpretation (so-called "canons of construction") that are sometimes far from clear and coherent;[59] others get literally obsessed with citation; still others persist in promoting judicial opinions that can be "verbose," "overly complex," "vague," and "poorly written" (Posner 2013: 15). In other words, sophisticated moral, jurisprudential, and constitutional theories, stylish principles of statutory interpretation, as well as obscure normative concepts inherited from the past, serve judges, in a way, to generate smoke screens that are destined to mask the indetermination arising out of the external complexity they have to face in their day-to-day decisions. Formalism and jargon are part of the tactics on which judges rely for deciding cases "without having to understand factual complexities" (Posner 2013: 4). But of course, by doing so, they end up complexifying ever more (and often needlessly) the legal process.

Posner thinks that the judges who are not aware of these strategic facets of judicial reality are victims of "self-deception."[60] It is in particular those judges who, convinced that what they are doing is not creating new rules but merely enforcing "immemorial custom" (Posner 2005a: 277), risk damaging most irreversibly the common law process. Posner therefore has a problem with legal theorists such as F.A. Hayek[61] who, he thinks, take such claims "literally" (Posner 2005a: 277), hence assigning judges a rather passive role by arguing that the essence of judicial duty is merely to enforce custom (Posner 2005a: 277). In contrast, the pragmatic adjudicator described by Posner is considered as far more active and creative than Hayek's rule-following judge. Rather than blaming judicial professionals for building a "carapace of falsity and pretense" (Posner 1993: 456) around the law, Posner insists on the context of radical uncertainty in which they often operate. Most of the time, they are forced "to exercise an uncomfortably large amount of discretion, casting them in the role of de facto legislators."[62] Especially in nonroutine cases, where the conventional legal materials are found lacking, "judges are on their own, navigating uncharted seas with equipment consisting of experience, emotions, and often unconscious beliefs."[63] Concealment is thus used to "feed a mystique of professionalism that strengthens the judiciary in its competition for power with the executive and legislative branches of government, the branches that judges like to call 'political' in asserted contra-distinction to the judicial branch."[64]

This unconventional portrayal of the judge could potentially lead to quite pessimistic conclusions about the substance and the evolution of law over time. Posner is aware of the harshness of eventual critiques to come when anticipating, already in the first volume of his series on pragmatism (and, more precisely, in his concluding *Pragmatist Manifesto*), that his colleagues might accuse him of having "announced the death of law" (Posner 1993: 461). But Posner refuses to succumb to the temptation of legal negativism which, he thinks, acts as a damper on useful propositions for reforming the law.[65] It is through a specific method based on a mix between sociological[66] and personalized analysis (drawing heavily upon his own experience as a federal judge)[67] that Posner seeks to overcome the problem. Convinced that we can learn much about judging from what judicial professionals have themselves written about the matter (rather than from some theoretical scholarship?), he proposes to offer his part to a literature that has been, much to his regret, neglected, despite the fact that, among its contributors can be found some of the most proficient judges in US history (such as Oliver Wendell Holmes, Louis Brandeis, Felix Frankfurter, Benjamin Cardozo, Roger Traynor, or Henry Friendly, to quote just a few of the judges and justices for whom Posner has expressed his admiration).

It is specifically in the line of some of the prominent jurists of the late nineteenth- and early twentieth-century, pragmatist tradition that Posner is situating his recent contribution to the judicial professions's "self-understanding." He links his view to the anti-formalist paradigm of American legal realism whose golden age was precisely at that period. More than an extended homage, he presents his work as a revival, in contemporary terms, of the sociological jurisprudence developed in the wake of legal realism by, among others, Holmes – except that he wants "to push the engine a bit farther along" (Posner 1999: vii).

The affinity of the EAL project with the early twentieth-century pragmatist school of legal realism seems almost natural. Yet, at the same time, it is only a partial kinship. One of the main characteristics of traditional legal realism had indeed been anti-conceptualism – in other words, the categorical rejection of legal formalism. If we consider the pronounced formalist turn (even if it is a mathematical rather than a legal formalism) taken by much of the mainstream law-and-economics movement from its very beginning, Posner's recent reconnection with legal pragmatism appears as a rupture rather than a continuity with standard (neoclassical) EAL. Nevertheless, his partly sociological, partly psychological and, to a large extent, personal experience-based description of the judicial profession, which displays a deep knowledge and understanding of the complex functioning of the contemporary American common law, has been attacked from the outside as well as from the inside of traditional law-and-economics.[68] Posner is said to do, at best, some anthropology or sociology of law, but that has no predictive power.

The refusal of many mainstream law-and-economics scholars to follow Posner on the new track of pragmatism may be symptomatic of their awareness of the negative impacts the framework of the pragmatist judge can have on the viability of the EAL project. Questioning the judge's rationality assumption (by conferring on the actor of the model more realism or plasticity – with all that this implies in terms of errors, ideological opinions, prejudices, strategic behavior, social and political pressure, but also a recognition of creativity, intuition, emotion, imagination in judging) could, as previously underlined in the context of BLE, undercut the conventional law-and-economics paradigm, at least in its basic (positive as well as normative) contention, according to which judges are (or should be) promoting social efficiency as a legal goal. While, in my view, Posner is willing to take the risk of undermining the efficiency theory of law, the majority of law-and-economics scholars (including obviously many advocates of BLE) are not.

In fact, Posner follows in many respects the path laid out by Holmes. Like the famous Harvard law professor and Justice of the US Supreme Court did a century ago, he argues that judges *make* rather than *find* law (Posner 1993: 457). Posner shares Holmes's conception of law according to which the "law is best described as the activity of the licensed professionals we call judges" (Posner 1993: 456–457). If, however, law is an activity rather than a "concept or a group of concepts," Posner (1993: 457) concludes, "no bounds can be fixed a priori on what shall be allowed to count as an argument in law." As law is shaped essentially by practical needs,[69] legal rules and their evolution over time are necessarily indeterminate. This explains the realists's interest in the concrete facts related to affairs brought to trial rather than in abstract principles of law or some deductive logic of some professed legal science. In the pragmatist perspective, the personality (psychology?) of the judge would necessarily become a determinant factor of the substance and quality (efficiency?) of law. Focusing on the motivational and behavioral aspects, and even the psychology of the judge, legal realism was in some sense a precursor movement of behavioralism, its main concern being the question: what do judges do and what are the effects of their decisions? In the Holmesian sociological jurisprudence, judicial decisions had themselves been treated as facts that have social repercussions.

Echoing Holmes's famous maxim "the life of law has not been logic, it has been experience," Posner is presenting the judge as a sort of satisficing agent who is doing as well as he can to find practical solutions to concrete problems – given his own cognitive and motivational limitations and, above all, given the uncomfortable circumstances generated by the "uncharted seas" he is navigating within a "dauntingly complex, uncertainty-riven legal system – featuring an antique constitution, an overlay of federal on state law, weak political parties, cumbersome and undisciplined legislatures, and executive-legislative tugs-of-war" (Posner 2008: 371).

By invoking the quirks and failures of the framers of the constitution and by arguing that judicial authorities cannot and should not be bound by the "will of the dead,"[70] Posner, as a matter of fact, frees the pragmatist judge from a whole range of constraints. If one believes, like Posner in the line of Holmes, that the law does not live in the statements of the legislator nor in the books of jurisprudence, and even less in some sacred texts,[71] but in the concrete day-by-day actions of the courts and in the behavior of judges who create the law (to which we must add the fact that most law is made, as Posner explains, "not by the tiny handful of great judges but by the great mass of ordinary ones" (Posner 1994: 3)), it could be only one step to conclude that, behind the decisions of courts, all there is to be found is the discretionary choices of judges in particular situations. Would this imply that, at least potentially, all judicial action is built on a form of arbitrariness? As detractors of pragmatism claim, such a conception of law might ineluctably lead to judicial activism and legal nihilism.[72]

Concluding remarks

Finally, the only way to overcome the (untenable?) posture of legal nihilism is by engaging the issue of judicial (and eventually democratic/constitutional) legitimacy. This issue is, however, almost never openly addressed in the EAL in general, its primary focus being on what judges do rather than why they should be obeyed. But a fundamental question remains: Can the pursuit of efficiency by judges be considered as an argument strong enough to confer validity to their decisions? In other words, can a criterion for evaluating the soundness of legal rules, decisions, or institutions (what initially the efficiency standard had been about) explain and justify why anyone should accept the verdicts of the man or woman in a black robe? The emphasis on the systematic flaws and biases that eventually reduce judges's capacity and willingness to pursue the goal of efficiency (the voluntarily under-explored research agenda of BLE?) should even more urgently call for consideration of the question of legitimacy. The systematic silence on this issue could eventually mean that, in law-and-economics, the legitimacy of judicial authority has simply been *assumed*. Nevertheless, with the significant extension of the scope of the pragmatist theory of law operated by

Posner and his repeated reference to judicial discretion, it seems no longer suitable for economic analysts of law to just elude the problem.

Posner's attempt to come to terms with the question of judicial legitimacy may again surprise. In one of the few texts situating the EAL within the various traditions of legal thought, he connects his own approach with Hans Kelsen's positivist theory of law, concerned precisely with the issue of the validity of legal norms. Rejecting, of course, arguments such as the autonomy of law as a discipline (brought to its paroxysm by the author of the *Pure Theory of Law* (Kelsen 1978)), Posner sees nevertheless several epistemological similarities,[73] especially with respect to the understanding of the judicial role within a legal system and, above all, with respect to the notion of lawfulness. Posner relates to Kelsen, who

> pictures the judge as either deriving a specific legal norm to resolve the case before him from a higher norm or, if there is no higher substantive norm to guide decision in the particular case, creating such a norm, as judges are authorized to do by the jurisdictional norm that authorizes them to decide cases. In either situation the judge is doing law; it is just that in the second he creates rather than derives the legal norm that he applies to decide the case.
>
> (Posner 2005a: 268–269)

By the same token, Posner disagrees with legal positivists such as H.L.A. Hart (1961) for whom the judge, in the latter scenario, would be clearly "stepping outside the law" and hence, "turn into a politician" (Posner 2005a: 269). Simultaneously, Posner suggests that a pragmatic conception of law like Kelsen's is indefensible without, at one point or another, referring to the rule of law whose role is precisely to set limits to judicial arbitrariness.

Can we suppose that for Posner, the same applies to his own perspective, based on a revival of legal realism? The fact is that, as pointed out earlier, he rejects the point of view of Hayek, for whom "custom is the only legitimate source of law and therefore a legal judgment that does not draw its essence from custom is not true law" (Posner 2005a: 280). For Posner, Hayek's attempt to limit judicial discretion as tightly raises a number of problems, such as the difficulty to ascertain what can be counted as custom[74] (and hence, as law). Above all, it could lead to the confusing presumption that "legislatures have superior competence to judges when it comes to prescribing rules of conduct" – a standpoint that, as Posner recognizes himself, Hayek would certainly not have defended since he was "so distrustful of legislatures" (Posner 2005b: 152). For Posner, Hayek has thus obviously missed some major points, in particular (and this may seem intriguing) with respect to fundamental distinctions such as the one between a formal and a substantial conception of law (Posner 2005a: 289).

Last but not least, Posner refutes the theory of constitutional legitimacy advanced by his law-and-economics colleague, Frank Easterbrook.[75] For the latter, it is indeed "only because (and if) the Constitution has a single meaning – the textual meaning" that federal judges should be obeyed,[76] whereas for Posner (in the line of Kelsen), judicial decisions, on the contrary, are obeyed "even when the textual basis for a decision is exceedingly tenuous" (Posner 2005a: 272). In other words, for Posner the propensity to obey judges is "unrelated to the textual basis for their decisions; it is much more closely related simply to their jurisdiction."[77] For it is precisely when founding legal documents such as the Constitution are unclear, and hence call for interpretation, that judges are needed. "If those documents were clear," Posner insists, "there would be fewer disputes, so fewer judges, and in a sense less law; if they were perfectly clear maybe we wouldn't need any judges" (Posner 2005a: 272).

Can we deduce from Posner's positioning within the established legal paradigms that, for the EAL (in its initial as well as amended version), the decisions of the efficiency-seeking judge, unbound by pre-existing norms or rules, are lawful – simply because he *is* a judge?

Notes

*   Professor of Economics, Aix Marseille Université, Faculté d'Economie et de Gestion, CERGAM. A first draft of this chapter has been presented at the *Colloquium on Market Institutions and Economic Processes* at New York University on January 25, 2013. Helpful comments from the participants of the colloquium, especially Mario Rizzo, are greatly acknowledged. I would also like to thank NYU and Earhart Foundation for support. Many thanks to Carine Krecké as well.
1   See, for instance, the trilogy (Posner 1993; 1995; 1999). See also (Posner 2005a; 2008).
2   Machlup (1978: 244), referring to Schutz (1967: 210–220).
3   To use the terms of Machlup (1967: 9).
4   Many more examples of frequent mistakes that contradict traditional decision analysis could be evoked. For an enumeration of a variety of biases and heuristics and how they come to affect human behavior see, for instance, (Sunstein 2000: 3–9).
5   Among others, see (Korobkin and Ulen 2000).
6   See (Jolls *et al.* 1998).
7   See, for example, (Posner 2001: 31).
8   For the pioneer of utilitarianism, people on average are incapable of calculating correctly "pleasures and pains" – the two sovereign magnitudes that, as he thought, govern human action in any context (Bentham 1907).
9   See (W.C. Mitchell 1967: 216).
10 A typical example is the printing of shock pictures on cigarette packs, supposed to deter people from smoking.
11 Some leading BLE scholars confirm: "Often people's preferences are ill-formed, and their choices will inevitably be influenced by default rules, framing effects, and starting points. In these circumstances, a form of paternalism cannot be avoided" (Sunstein and Thaler 2003a: 1159).
12 The author made clear on several occasions that the only laws he considered as legitimate were those that were designed to protect individuals from harm caused by others, whereas those that aimed to protect people against harm caused by themselves (not to speak of the so-called Good Samaritan laws, forcing people to help and assist others) had no legitimacy in his eyes (Bentham 1907).
13 To use the terms of (Kahan 2000: 607–645).

14 On several occasions they argue that "libertarian paternalism is *not* an oxymoron" (Sunstein and Thaler 2003a; 2003b). Critiques have argued that, on the contrary, it is the perfect incarnation thereof (G. Mitchell 2005).

15 Some authors distinguish *old* forms of paternalism "which sought to make individuals behave consistently with the (often moralistic or religious) preferences of policy makers," from *new* forms of paternalism, which seek to "help individuals maximize their own welfare as they see it themselves" (Rizzo and Whitman 2009a: 685–686).

16 See (Sunstein and Thaler 2003a: 1162).

17 See (Korobkin and Ulen 2000: 1051).

18 In BLE, this idea is indeed applied to private behaviors such as driving, drinking, smoking, over-eating, drug use, money management, etc., but also to numerous settings of law, including crime, family, tort, contract, bankruptcy, diverse regulatory schemes, etc.

19 See (Jolls *et al.* 1998: 1471).

20 Even though, principally, BLE supports relatively non-invasive forms of paternalism, such policies are nonetheless seriously "vulnerable to expansion," as argued by critiques of behavioral economics, as they easily end up following a path of "slippery slopes that can lead from modest (or 'soft') paternalism to more extensive (or 'hard') paternalism" (Rizzo and Whitman 2009b: 684, 687).

21 To refer, once again, to Bentham's terminology. See E.C. Mitchell (1967: 222) on Bentham.

22 In particular, economists from the Austrian tradition have addressed powerful critiques against the use of behavioral economics to justify even soft paternalistic policies. It is argued, for instance, that "policymakers may lack the knowledge necessary to craft beneficial paternalist policies" (Rizzo and Whitman 2009b: 686–687).

23 The authors suppose indeed that "while cognitive theory accurately describes how citizens make decisions about risks to life and health, traditional decision theory can be aptly applied to the political actor's problem of calculating the best response to citizen demands for action" (Noll and Krier 2000: 326).

24 This comes out, for instance, in the following statement by the advocates of soft paternalism: "It is possible to show how a libertarian paternalist might select among the possible options and to assess how much choice to offer" (Sunstein and Thaler 2003a: 1159).

25 Empirical studies show, for example, that "simple remedies, such as informing people about the bias or giving them repeated attempts to make judgments with feedback, have no effect" (Rachlinski 2000: 98).

26 Involving more than 8,000 jury-eligible citizens.

27 Kahan refers in this context to studies which show that, in many cases, juries still "continue to treat verbal resistance as equivocal evidence of nonconsent," and that oftentimes prosecutors "remain reluctant to press charges unless the victim physically resisted the man's advances." Similarly, in cases involving drunk driving or domestic violence, juries tend to play down, as stated by Kahan (2000), the seriousness of the problems at hand.

28 Some psychologists have observed that debiasing judicial instructions had no ostensible effect in most cases brought before trial (Kamin and Rachlinski 1995). The aforementioned experiment confirms this finding: In punitive damages cases, juries obviously tend to ignore instructions given by judges (Sunstein *et al.* 2002).

29 Among examples of such "second-best strategies," one can count, for instance in tort cases, the compliance of the defendant with prevailing regulations and/or some given customary practices (Rachlinski 2000). Compliance with such *ex ante* norms could be considered as a form of evidence for a judge who must determine whether a defendant has been negligent or not. Also, as Rachlinski argues, in order to minimize the hindsight bias of the jury, judges sometimes prefer opting for a no-liability rule instead of a negligence rule.

30 This scholarship insists that judges, not juries, should set punitive damages (Robbe-nolt 2005).
31 For example, when it comes to deciding punitive damages (Sunstein *et al.* 2002).
32 This kind of "small steps" approach is, to the authors, the "hallmark of Anglo-American common law" (Sunstein and Ullmann-Margalit 2000: 189).
33 *Caperton* v. *A.T. Massey Coal Co.* (129 S.Ct. 2252).
34 Engel (2013) relies on descriptive statistics to quantify statements with respect to behavioral papers published in the *Journal of Empirical Legal Studies* from 2004 (when the journal was founded) to the end of 2012. Among the 227 published papers, seventy-seven enter into the framework of BLE. It appears that fifty-seven of these papers deal with the problematics of motivation, while only twenty focus on cognition.
35 To refer to the title of one of their studies which involved a sample of 167 federal magistrate judges (Guthrie *et al.* 2001).
36 By explicit bias, the authors mean the types of bias that "people knowingly – some-times openly – embrace." By implicit bias they mean "stereotypical associations so subtle that people who hold them might not even be aware of them" (Rachlinski *et al.* 2009: 1196–1197).
37 For example, (Sunstein *et al.* 2006).
38 The question of whether judges are "political" (and, if so, to what extent) has been the starting point of this enquiry (Sunstein *et al.* 2006).
39 This is the case, it seems, at least in areas where the law is clear (Sunstein *et al.* 2006).
40 According to Bix (2013: 35), the persistence of such "long-term" errors explains in part why the law is, to a large extent, indeterminate.
41 A point that is addressed, among others, by Guthrie (2007).
42 This concept refers to the disparities that can be observed among judicial decisions, depending precisely on the identity of the selected adjudicator.
43 This term relates to the proportion of cases in which the legal system is unsuccessful in requiring a unique outcome.
44 In Fischman's model, the term "error" denotes the proportion of cases where the judge's decision is in conflict with the outcome required by law.
45 For example (G. Mitchell 2010; Wistrch 2010; Mitchell and Tetlock 2010).
46 For an exhaustive critique of BLE, see Posner (2002).
47 The purpose of the study by Landes and Posner (2009) is to correct a series of system-atic errors prevailing in the ideological classification of Supreme Court as well as court of appeals decisions, as elaborated respectively by the so-called Spaeth and Songer databases (Spaeth, concerning Supreme Court decisions from 1953 to 2000, and Songer, concerning decisions of appellate courts from 1925 to 2002). As Posner and Landes explain, a large number of studies, dealing with the issue of the influence of ideology on judicial voting, rely precisely on these inaccurate databases. The cor-rection by Landes and Posner brings to the fore unexpected features of judicial behav-ior such as an "ideology shift" in Supreme Court decisions: While some Justices tend to become more conservative, others seem to become more liberal during their time on court. Another example emphasized by the authors is the fact that for appellate judges, a "conformity effect" and a "group polarization" can be identified, an effect that is not observed, however, on the Supreme Court level.
48 In reference precisely to the title of (Posner 1994).
49 In a next step, Posner's model discusses the impacts and relevance of prevailing incentive structures in judicial professions such as life tenure, compensation systems, etc.
50 Posner's definition obviously goes beyond a simple reconnection with the early twentieth-century American movement of legal thought labeled "legal realism."
51 See, among others, (Posner 1993; 1995; 1999), as well as (Posner 2005a; 2008).

52 Posner (1993: 467) writes: "The soundness of legal interpretations and other legal propositions is best gauged ... by an examination of their consequences in the world of facts."

53 When referring to the systematic consequences of a given judicial decision, Posner (2013: 5) evokes, among others, its influence on the predictability of law, but also on administrability, on the various branches of government and, eventually, the expectations of those governed by law.

54 Posner (2001) is quoting Kronman (1990: 1029, 1032, 1039).

55 An insight that Posner has found in the tradition of the early twentieth-century American pragmatism, as incarnated by, among others, John Dewey. See (Posner 1993: 459; 2005a: 270).

56 "The secrecy of judicial deliberations," Posner writes, "is an example of the tactics used by the judiciary to conceal the extent to which such deliberations resemble those of ordinary people attempting to resolve disputes in circumstances of uncertainty" (Posner, in conversation with Masur 2008: 1).

57 The perfect emblem of the excessive bureaucratization of the American legal system being the *Bluebook* citation manual (Posner 2013: 13).

58 Posner (2013: 13–15) shows how, in order to face increased caseload, judges tend to delegate opinion drafting to clerks, trial court judges, jurors, or administrative agencies. All this, he argues, complexifies the judiciary.

59 In this respect, Posner is particularly critical of Justice Scalia's textualist view on how judges interpret the law (Scalia and Garner 2012).

60 Posner (2001: 155) worries, for instance, that

> some judges fool themselves into thinking that history really does deliver the solutions to even the most consequential legal issues and thus allows them always to duck the really difficult question – the soundness of the solution as a matter of public policy.

61 Posner (2005a) refers, among others, to Hayek (1973).

62 See (Posner, in conversation with Masur 2008: 1).

63 See (Posner 2008: Book Description).

64 See (Posner, in conversation with Masur 2008: 1).

65 Posner (1993: 441). "Moral and legal nihilism," Posner writes, "is as untenable as moral realism and legal formalism" (Posner 1993: 459).

66 > There is a name for the scholarly niche that this book occupies, and the name – some readers will be surprised to hear *me* say this – is sociology. This is a book about a profession – or rather professions, not only the law at large.
> (Posner 1999: xiii)

67 Posner (2013) draws most openly on his experience of over thirty years as a judge (and for a long time, chief judge) on the United States Court of Appeals for the Seventh Circuit. Posner's "recent reflections on judging" (to refer to the book's title) meticulously traces the evolution of the judiciary since his nomination on that court in 1981.

68 Critics of Posner's new pragmatism have argued, for example, that it is endorsing a "visceral, personalized, rule-less, free-wheeling, unstructured concept of judging" (Rosen 1995: 581).

69 Posner (1993: 465).

70 To use the expression of Easterbrook (1998: 1119).

71 Posner (1993: 467, 460) writes: "Law is not a sacred text ... but a usually humdrum social practice vaguely bounded by ethical and political convictions.... "Law is functional, not expressive or symbolic either in aspiration or in effect."

72 This is indeed what happened to several late twentieth-century projects of resuscitation of the tradition of legal realism (reaching from Critical Legal Studies to postmodern legal theories of deconstructivism or anti-foundationalism).

73 Many of the features that Posner attributes to Kelsen's theory may apply to his own as well, such as the "rejection of natural law," the "emphasis on jurisdictional at the expense of substantive norms," the "claim that the application of law is not mechanical but often involves the creation of a 'lower norm on the basis of a higher norm,'" the "acknowledgement that sometimes the only preexisting law that a court can apply to decide a case is the law that confers the power of decision on the court," the "concept of interpretation as a frame rather than an algorithm" (Posner 2005a: 267).

74 Kelsen's theory of law being "content-neutral," whereas Hayek's is "interested only in content" (Posner 2005a: 280).

75 Easterbrook is also a judge at the US Court of Appeals for the Seventh Circuit (where he has, a few years ago, replaced Posner as chief judge).

76 Posner (2005a: 272), referring to Easterbrook (1998).

77 Posner (2005a: 273). "Judicial role," he also argues, is just another name for "the judge's jurisdiction" (2005a: 267).

References

Bentham, J. (1907) *An Introduction to the Principles of Morals and Legislation*, Oxford: Clarendon Press (first edition 1823).

Berggren, N. 'Time for behavioral political economy? An analysis of articles in behavioral economics', *Review of Austrian Economics* 25, 2012: 199–221.

Bix, B.H. 'Global error and legal truth', *Oxford Journal of Legal Studies* 29(3), 2009: 535–547.

Bix, B.H. (2013) 'Linguistic meaning and legal truth', in M. Freeman and F. Smith (eds.) *Law and Language*, Oxford: Oxford University Press.

Coase, R.H. 'The problem of social cost', *Journal of Law and Economics* 3, 1960: 1–4.

Coase, R.H. 'Coase on Posner on Coase and concluding comment', *Journal of Institutional and Theoretical Economics* 96, 1993: 360–361.

Dworkin, R.M. (1986) *Law's Empire*, Cambridge, MA: Harvard University Press.

Easterbrook, F.H. 'Textualism and the dead hand', *George Washington Law Review* 66, 1998: 1119–1126.

Engel, C. 'Behavioral law and economics: empirical methods', *Preprints of the Max Planck Institute for Research on Collective Goods* 1, 2013: 1–19.

Fischman, J.B. 'Measuring inconsistency, indeterminacy, and error in adjudication', *American Law and Economics Review* 15(2), 2013: 2–46.

Friedman, M. (1953) *Essays in Positive Economics*, Chicago, IL: University of Chicago Press.

Guthrie, C. 'Misjudging', *Nevada Law Journal* 7, 2007: 420–456.

Guthrie, C., Rachlinski, J.J., and Wistrich, A.J. 'Inside the judicial mind', *Cornell Law Review* 86, 2001: 777–830.

Guthrie, C., Rachlinski, J.J. and Wistrich, A.J. 'Blinking on the bench: how judges decide cases', *Cornell Law Review* 93, 2007: 1–43.

Guthrie, C., Rachlinski, J.J., and Wistrich, A.J. 'The hidden "judiciary": an empirical examination of executive branch justice', *Duke Law Journal* 58, 2009: 1477–1530.

Hart, H.L.A. (1961) *The Concept of Law*, Oxford: Clarendon Press.

Hayek, F.A. (1973) *Law, Legislation and Liberty: Rules and Order*, Chicago, IL and London: University of Chicago Press.

Jolls, C., Sunstein, C.R., and Thaler, R.H. 'A behavioral approach to law and economics', *Stanford Law Review* 50, 1998: 1471–1550.

Kahan, D. 'Gentle nudges vs. hard shoves: solving the sticky norms problem', *University of Chicago Law Review* 67, 2000: 607–645.

Kahn, P.W. (2000). *The Cultural Study of Law: Reconstructing Legal Scholarship*, Chicago, IL: University of Chicago Press.

Kamin, K.A. and Rachlinski, J.J. 'Ex post ≠ ex ante: determining liability in hindsight', *Law and Human Behavior* 19, 1995: 89–104.

Kelsen, H. (1978) *Pure Theory of Law*, Berkeley and Los Angeles, CA and London: University of California Press (first edition 1934 by Deuticke, Vienna).

Korobkin, R.B. and Ulen, T.S. 'Law and behavioral science: removing the rationality assumption from law and economics', *California Law Review* 88, 2000: 1051–1144.

Kronman, A.T. "Precedent and tradition," *Yale Law Journal* 99, 1990: 1029–1068.

Landes, W.M. and Posner, R.A. 'Rational judicial behavior: a statistical study', *Journal of Legal Analysis* 1, 2009: 775–831.

Machlup, F. 'Theories of the firm: marginalist, behavioral, managerial', *American Economic Review* 57, 1967: 1–33.

Machlup, F. (1978) *Methodology of Economics and Other Social Sciences*, New York, San Fransisco, CA and London: Academic Press.

Masur, J. 'How judges think: a conversation with Judge Richard Posner', *University of Chicago Law School, the Record Online*, spring 2008, available at www.law.uchicago.edu/alumni/magazine/spring08/posnerhowjudgesthink (accessed April 5, 2014).

Mitchell, G. 'Why law and economics' perfect rationality should not be traded for behavioral law and economics' equal incompetence', *Georgetown Law Journal* 91, 2002: 67–167.

Mitchell, G. 'Libertarian paternalism is an oxymoron', *Northwestern University Law Review* 99, 2005: 1245–1277.

Mitchell, G. (2010) 'Evaluating judges', in D. Klein and G. Mitchell (eds.) *The Psychology of Judicial Decision Making*, New York and Oxford: Oxford University Press.

Mitchell, G. and Tetlock, P.E. (2010) 'Cognitive styles and judging', in D. Klein and G. Mitchell (eds.) *The Psychology of Judicial Decision Making*, New York and Oxford: Oxford University Press.

Mitchell, W.C. (1967) *Types of Economic Theory: From Mercantilism to Institutionalism* (Vol. 1), New York: Augustus M. Kelly, Publishers.

Noll, R.G. and Krier, J.E. (2000) 'Some implications of cognitive psychology for risk regulation', in C.R. Sunstein (ed.) *Behavioral Law and Economics*, Cambridge: Cambridge University Press.

Posner, R.A. (1973) *Economic Analysis of Law*, Boston, MA and Toronto: Little, Brown and Company.

Posner, R.A. 'The law and economics movement', *American Economic Review* 77, 1987: 1–13.

Posner, R.A. (1993) *The Problems of Jurisprudence*, Cambridge, MA: Harvard University Press (first edition 1990).

Posner, R.A. 'What do judges and justices maximize? (The same thing everybody else does)', *John M. Olin Law & Economics Working Paper* no. 15. University of Chicago Law School 1–26. Reprinted in *Supreme Court Economic Review* 3, 1994: 1–41.

Posner, R.A. (1995) *Overcoming Law*, Cambridge, MA: Harvard University Press.

Posner, R.A. (1999) *The Problematics of Moral and Legal Theory*, Cambridge, MA: Harvard University Press.

Posner, R.A. (2001) *Frontiers of Legal Theory*, Cambridge, MA: Harvard University Press.

Posner, R.A. 'Behavioral law and economics: a critique', *Economic Education Bulletin of the American Institute for Economic Research* XLII(8), 2002: 1–40.

Posner, R.A. (2005a) *Law, Pragmatism and Democracy*, Cambridge, MA: Harvard University Press (first edition 2003).

Posner, R.A. 'Hayek, law and cognition', *NYU Journal of Law and Liberty* 1, 2005b: 147–165.

Posner, R.A. (2008) *How Judges Think*, Cambridge, MA: Harvard University Press.

Posner, R.A. (2013) *Reflections on Judging*, Cambridge, MA: Harvard University Press.

Rachlinski, J.J. (2000) 'A positive psychological theory of judges in hindsight', in C.R. Sunstein (ed.) *Behavioral Law and Economics*, Cambridge: Cambridge University Press.

Rachlinski, J.J., Johnson, S.L., Wistrich, A.J., and Guthrie, C. 'Does unconscious racial bias affect trial judges?', *Notre Dame Law Review* 84, 2009: 1195–1246.

Rizzo, M.J. and Whitman, D.G. 'Little brother is watching you: new paternalism on the slippery slopes', *Arizona Law Review* 51, 2009a: 685–739.

Rizzo, M.J. and Whitman, D.G. 'The knowledge problem of new paternalism', *Brigham Young University Law Review* 4, 2009b: 905–968.

Robbenolt, J.K. 'Evaluating juries by comparison to judges: a benchmark for judging?', *Florida State University Law Review* 32, 2005: 469–509.

Rosen, J. 'Overcoming Posner', *Yale Law Journal* 105, 1995: 581–596.

Scalia, A. and Garner, B.A. (2012) *Reading Law: The Interpretation of Legal Texts*, Eagan: West Publishing Company.

Schauer, F. (2010) 'Is there a psychology of judging?', in D. Klein and G. Mitchell (eds.) *The Psychology of Judicial Decision Making*, New York and Oxford: Oxford University Press.

Schutz, A. (1967) *The Phenomenology of the Social World*, Evanstan, IL: Northwestern University Press.

Sunstein, C.R. (2000) 'Introduction', in C.R. Sunstein (ed.) *Behavioral Law and Economics*, Cambridge: Cambridge University Press.

Sunstein, C.R. and Thaler, R.H. 'Libertarian paternalism is not an oxymoron', *University of Chicago Law Review* 70, 2003a: 1159–1202.

Sunstein, C.R. and Thaler, R.H. 'Libertarian paternalism', *American Economic Review* 93, 2003b: 175–179.

Sunstein, C.R. and Ullmann-Margalit, E. (2000) 'Second-order decisions', in C.R. Sunstein (ed.) *Behavioral Law and Economics*, Cambridge: Cambridge University Press.

Sunstein, C.R., Hastie, R., Payne, J.W., Schkade, D.A., and Viscu, K.W. (2002) *Punitive Damages: How Juries Decide*, Chicago, IL: University of Chicago Press.

Sunstein, C.R., Schkade, D.A., Ellman, L.M., and Sawicki, A. (2006) *Are Judges Political? An Empirical Analysis of the Federal Judiciary*. Washington, DC: Brookings Institution Press.

Thaler, R.H. and Sunstein, C.R. (2008) *Nudge: Improving Decisions about Health, Wealth and Happiness*. New Haven, CT: Yale University Press.

Tsaoussi, A. and Zervogianni, E. 'Judges as satisficers: a law and economics perspective on judicial liability', *European Journal of Law and Economics* 29, 2007: 333–357.

Wistrich, A.J. (2010) 'Defining good judging', in D. Klein and G. Mitchell (eds.) *The Psychology of Judicial Decision Making*, New York and Oxford: Oxford University Press.

Wistrich, A.J., Guthrie, C., and Rachlinski, J.J. 'Can judges ignore inadmissible information? The difficulty of deliberately disregarding', *University of Pennsylvania Law Review* 135, 2005: 1251–1341.

15 Behavioral law and economics

Its origins, fatal flaws, and implications for liberty

*Joshua D. Wright and Douglas H. Ginsburg**

Introduction

Behavioral economics is one of the most significant developments in economics over the past thirty-six years. The field combines economics and psychology to produce a body of evidence that individual choice behavior departs from that predicted by neoclassical economics in a number of decision-making situations. These departures from rational choice behavior are said to be the result of the individual's "cognitive biases," that is, systematic failures to act in one's own interest because of defects in one's decision-making process. The documentation of these cognitive biases in laboratory experiments has been behavioral economics's primary contribution to microeconomics. These biases, behavioral economists assert, demonstrate systematically irrational choice behavior by individuals and firms. This irrational behavior, in turn, breaks the link between revealed preference and individual welfare upon which neoclassical economic theory depends.

Emerging close on the heels of behavioral economics over the past thirty years has been the "behavioral *law and* economics" movement, which explores the legal and policy implications of cognitive biases. The legal academy has widely disseminated the body of experimental evidence documenting irrational behavior and is largely responsible for the behaviorists's foothold in regulatory policy circles,[1] in and out of the Obama Administration, and, more recently, the government of the United Kingdom as well. Behaviorist proposals include mandates requiring the supply of more or better information in an attempt to "debias" individual decision makers, altering legal default rules, and imposing "sin" taxes upon or even banning disfavored products.

Despite its remarkably broad scope, covering nearly every area of law and human behavior, the behavioral law and economics regulatory agenda reflects a common philosophical source – so-called libertarian paternalism. That seemingly oxymoronic phrase, coined by proponents Richard Thaler and Cass Sunstein, is intended to describe legal interventions that both (1) increase the individual's economic welfare by freeing him from the limitations of his cognitive biases, and (2) change the individual's behavior without limiting his choices (see Sunstein and Thaler 2003). In other words, the promise of behavioral law and economics is to regulate so as to improve economic welfare by more closely aligning each individual's actual choices with his "true" or unbiased preferences without reducing his liberty, at least as it is represented by the choices available to him.

We agree with Thaler and Sunstein's implicit premise that the behavioral law and economics enterprise is properly evaluated by how successfully it solves this constrained optimization problem of maximizing welfare while respecting liberty. The behaviorists's economic welfare claims have been questioned by economists and some law professors on a variety of disparate theoretical, empirical, and institutional grounds, but the behaviorists's claim that their proposed policy interventions do not entail a significant reduction in liberty and individual autonomy has been less scrutinized.

The full implications of the behaviorist regulatory agenda for liberty are the focus of our analysis. Those implications have not been fully appreciated, at least in part, either because legal scholars have excluded libertarian considerations from their regulatory calculus altogether or because they have accepted the behaviorists's conception of liberty as the mere preservation of choices.[2] Alas, the behaviorists's libertarian claims fail on even these narrow terms. Nonetheless, as we show later, the behaviorists's narrow conception excludes the broader liberty interest in what Mill, Hayek, Sen, and others taught about the "process aspect of freedom."[3] We argue that so long as libertarian paternalism ignores the economic welfare and liberty value of allowing individuals the freedom to err, it will fail to achieve its goal of increasing welfare without reducing liberty and will pose a significant risk of reducing both.

First, we provide a brief history of the economics of irrational behavior and describe the research program of modern behavioral economics. Then we describe the major categories of cognitive biases documented in the behavioral economics literature. We also evaluate the robustness of those findings and their appropriateness for policy implementation in light of a variety of theoretical, experimental, and empirical critiques. Next, we discuss the incorporation of behavioral economics into the legal academy and subsequently into policy discourse; document the remarkable intellectual distance between the regulatory interventions proposed by behaviorists in the legal academy, and the policy interventions, if any, justified by existing theory and empirical evidence; and examine existing welfare-based critiques of behavioral law and economics. We then argue behavioral law and economics poses a significant and underappreciated threat to liberty. Finally, we analyze the present appeal and future prospects of behavioral law and economics in the legal academy.

From bounded rationality to predictably irrational: a brief history of the economics of irrational behavior

Irrationality and economic theory

The neoclassical economic edifice is built upon the foundational assumption that economic agents – individuals as well as firms – are rational maximizers. Indeed, within the model of "perfect competition," economic agents do not make mistakes or commit errors of any kind. Sellers are homogenous. Transaction and information costs, including the costs of processing information required to make economic decisions, are zero. It follows that resources instantaneously flow to their highest valued use.[4]

That these assumptions are counterfactual is not a critique of price theory. After all, the model of perfect competition was not designed for the purpose of describing the competitive activities of economic agents. Indeed, as Harold Demsetz has pointed out, the neoclassical model has little to say about competitive activities at all and is better described as a model of "perfect decentralization" (Demsetz 1988). The purpose of the model was to demonstrate the relative efficiency of decentralized allocation of resources.

With the academic battle over the relative virtue of market versus governmental allocation of resources largely settled by the 1950s, economists devoted their efforts to extending the neoclassical framework to explain real-world phenomena observed in markets. Beginning with George Stigler's *The Economics of Information*, economists began to consider the costs of obtaining and processing the information required for economic decision making (Stigler 1961). The cost of information and the roles of error and of irrational behavior in consumer decision making also attracted the attention of Armen Alchian, Gary Becker, and Milton Friedman, who demonstrated that the tools of price theory were both consistent with and valuable for analyzing observed irrational behavior (see Friedman 1953: 3–16; Alchian 1950: 220–221; Becker 1962: 12–13).

While the price-theoretic framework was expanding to address irrationality from one direction, Herbert Simon offered insights from another, planting the seed of what would become the modern behavioral economics literature. Simon's work began with the observation that humans do not possess the cognitive capacity to execute all the functions necessary to maximize their welfare; instead, human decision making is better explained by "satisficing" behavior (Simon 1979: 495).[5] He explained the role of mental shortcuts or "heuristics" in economizing upon limited cognitive capacity. This form of bounded rationality, as Simon described it, generated predictions for economic behavior by both individuals and firms that often differed from those offered by price theory (see, e.g., Cyert and March 1992: 10).

In the 1970s, psychologists Daniel Kahneman and Amos Tversky built upon Simon's insights to generate an alternative to the rational choice model, which they called "prospect theory" (Kahneman and Tversky 1979: 274–284). Their work provided the intellectual foundation for the modern literature on behavioral economics. Based upon a series of laboratory experiments, Kahneman and his various co-authors identified departures from rationality and categorized these departures by attributing them to one of three sources of bias: "representativeness," "availability," and "adjustment or anchoring" (see, e.g., Kahneman *et al.* 1990: 1329–1336; Kahneman and Frederick 2002: 49; Kahneman and Tversky 1979: 265–273; Tversky and Kahneman 1973: 208–209; Tversky and Kahneman 1982: 3).

The modern research program of behavioral economics, which continues to use the approach introduced by Kahneman and Tversky, has proceeded largely along two lines. The first line has expanded the set of documented cognitive biases, cataloging the systematic departures from rational choice observed in experimental and field settings.[6] The second line of research has tested whether these biases, initially documented in experiments within a controlled laboratory setting, are generalizable to markets.[7]

In a series of academic articles, Sunstein and Thaler,[8] individually and together, made significant contributions to what is now a vast literature documenting cognitive biases in a variety of laboratory settings and in some field experiments (see, e.g., Kuran and Sunstein 1999; Sunstein 2004; Sunstein and Thaler 2003; Thaler 1996; 1985; 1980; Thaler and Benartzi 2004; Thaler and Dawes 1992). Sunstein and Thaler are best known for introducing the concept of "libertarian paternalism," which they define as "an approach that preserves freedom of choice but that authorizes both private and public institutions to steer people in directions that will promote their welfare" (Thaler and Sunstein 2003: 179; Thaler and Sunstein 2008: 4–6). Sunstein and Thaler distinguish libertarian paternalism from classic paternalist philosophies on the grounds that the former seeks to develop legal rules that encourage individuals to maximize their welfare as those individuals subjectively define it (Thaler and Sunstein 2003: 175). As discussed below, the concept of libertarian paternalism has served as a catalyst, facilitating the creation of a behavioral law and economics movement in the legal academy and beyond.[9] Sunstein and Thaler thus attempt to provide an intellectual link between the behavioral economics literature – mapping the conditions under which economic decision makers err – and a theory of when and how the government should regulate their errors (Thaler and Sunstein 2003: 179).[10]

Behavioral economics as a theory of errors

As has long been observed, the assumption of rationality in price theory is not meant to characterize the actual decision-making process of economic agents.[11] Rather, rationality is a simplifying assumption made to render modeling of economic interactions among firms and consumers tractable and to harness the powerful mathematical tools of optimization. Therefore, if behavioral economics is to outperform price theory, its superiority must be proven by its greater predictive power, not merely by the assertion that its underlying assumptions are more "realistic."

The behaviorists appear to embrace this challenge. The fundamental link holding together the various strands of behavioral economics – or behavioral decision theory, as it is sometimes called – is the identification of errors in decision making, each of which is independently costly. Thus, behavioral economics research is overtly empirical. Behaviorists believe a market theory that incorporates "more realistic" psychological accounts of economic actors is a means of generating predictive power greater than that of economic accounts grounded in the assumption of individual rationality.

The first stage of the behavioral economics research program is best described as developing a comprehensive theory of errors. The theory-building exercise thus far has focused largely upon the effort to catalog circumstances in which economic decision makers appear systematically to depart from rational choice behavior.[12] The second step required to make the theory of errors relevant to policy is to map the conditions under which specific errors are more or less likely to affect decisions and then to generate estimates of the social costs imposed by those errors. This step is particularly important when the incidence of a particular decision-making error is context specific, unevenly distributed throughout the population, and likely to interact systematically with other errors. The third step is to compare the costs of any proposed corrective intervention against the social benefits produced by reducing the rate of error. At present, however, research in behavioral economics does not appear to have moved much beyond the first step.[13]

The lack of an integrative theory of errors has not discouraged ambitious attempts to leverage the biases documented in the first stage of the research program into specific regulatory applications.[14] Indeed, the mere identification of systematic decision errors leads behaviorists seemingly without hesitation to ask: How can government "correct" those errors with "choice architecture" or other forms of "libertarian paternalism?"

The minimum required to correct recurring and systematic errors is an accounting of their social costs and benefits. The behavioral law and economics literature exhibits a strong tendency to ignore the social benefits of error. At the same time, it tends to overestimate the social costs of errors or at least implicitly to assume the social benefits from reducing identified errors will be greater than the social costs of interventions aimed at correcting those errors.[15] This tendency explains the current condition under which "virtually every scholar who has written on the application of psychological research on judgment and choice to law has concluded that cognitive psychology supports institutional constraint on individual choice" (Rachlinksi 2003: 1166).[16]

Identifying cognitive errors and knowing when they arise

Although the literature documenting cognitive biases continues to develop, much of the behavioral law and economics agenda is based upon two well-documented and long-recognized categories of cognitive bias: contextualization effects and self-control errors. After describing these biases, we explain why the research underlying them is not as sound as behavioral economists claim.

The biases

Contextualization errors: framing, prospect theory, and endowment effects

Contextualization errors are those departures from rational choice that arise from the context in which the individual makes his decision (Mitchell 2005: 1255).

Biases of this type are frequently described as "framing effects" (see Jolls *et al.* 1998: 1536–1537). These effects are seen when an individual faced with an identical set of choices in different contexts makes different choices, thereby implying an underlying inconsistency in his preferences, denominated "preference reversals" (see, e.g., Thaler and Tversky 1992: 79–81).

Kahneman and Tversky's prospect theory is most commonly associated with framing effects. Prospect theory posits that decision makers evaluate and maximize expected outcomes not in isolation, but rather relative to an initial reference point (Kahneman Tversky 1979: 265–273).[17] While this effect is uncontroversial, prospect theory adds the empirical observation that decision makers weigh losses from the reference point more heavily than gains, a phenomenon described as "loss aversion." The key experimental finding of prospect theory is that individuals are, in many cases, reluctant to sell a good endowed to them when offered a sum greater than they are willing to pay to acquire the good (Thaler 1980: 43–44; Tversky and Kahneman 1991: 1041–1042).

This "endowment effect" is the most celebrated, and certainly the most discussed, of the cognitive biases in the behavioral law and economics literature, in part because behavioral economists and legal scholars claim it as the most robust of the biases,[18] and in part because of its significant policy implications. The principal implication of the endowment effect is that the Coase theorem does not apply,[19] and thus market transactions may not lead to an efficient allocation of resources, which in turn has implications for virtually every area of substantive law.[20] Legal scholars have certainly not missed many opportunities to elaborate on these implications.[21] For example, they have relied upon failures of Coasean bargaining caused by the endowment effect to reexamine areas of property law (see, e.g., Fischel 1995: 187; Rachlinski and Jourden 1998: 1542–1546), tort law (see, e.g., Knetsch 2007: 684–685; McCaffery *et al.* 1995: 1351–1354), contract law (see, e.g., Korobkin 1998: 630–633), and intellectual property.[22]

Self-control problems: hyperbolic discounting and optimism bias

The behavioral economics literature focuses upon two types of biases affecting self-control. The first involves systematic errors in decisions allocating resources over time. In other words, individuals place so much weight upon immediate gratification that they regularly make decisions they will later come to regret. Stable, time-consistent preferences require a constant exponential discount factor; hyperbolic discounting generates time-inconsistent preferences, sometimes described as present bias (see Frederick *et al.* 2003: 24–26). Rather than discounting the future exponentially, as is done when calculating present value, hyperbolic discounting entails placing an extremely high weight upon the present, after which future values decline exponentially (see Frederick *et al.* 2003: 24–26). Behavioral economists have relied upon hyperbolic discounting to explain a wide array of self-control problems, ranging from overeating, to incurring excessive debt, to gambling and other forms of addiction.[23]

The second type of self-control error is optimism bias (Weinstein 1980: 806–807). Behavioral economists have identified circumstances in which individuals appear to underestimate the likelihood of their experiencing a loss. Jolls *et al.* describe optimism bias as "[a] common feature of human behavior" characterized by people tending to "think that bad events are far less likely to happen to them than to others" (Jolls *et al.* 1998: 1524). The tendency to underestimate the likelihood of a bad outcome leads decision makers to take on too much risk.[24] Accordingly, this bias is often blamed for an individual's impulsive or high-risk choices that might indicate a lack of self-control.[25]

Empirical shortcomings: robustness and data interpretation

While the experimental findings of cognitive biases are interesting, it does not necessarily follow that they are useful for policy purposes. One need not (and we do not) reject the existence of behavioral biases in order to raise doubts about the policy relevance of purely experimental results. A significant concern for the behavioral law and economics policy agenda is that biases documented in experimental settings may not prove robust when exposed to market institutions.[26] Indeed, as others have pointed out, many (but not all) of the behaviorists's findings are fragile and disappear when exposed to market discipline and the profit motive, which create incentives for participants to specialize and to learn to reduce their errors.[27] These incentives are not present in the laboratory (see Arlen *et al.* 2002: 4; Wright 2007: 471–472).[28] To support a policy intervention, however, experimental research must (1) yield data that are robust and (2) be interpreted carefully to distinguish irrational behavior from efficient mistakes. The current research agenda fails to meet either requirement.[29]

Experimental evidence and data accrual

Behaviorists propose to alter the regulatory regime in broad and fundamental ways. It is a bedrock principle of both law and science that such advocates of change bear the burden of demonstrating the superiority of their theories. The existing data marshaled in support of behaviorist proposals generally, however, fail to meet this standard for several reasons. First, much if not most of the data suggesting that cognitive biases affect individual decision making are drawn from experimental settings and the bias has not been shown to persist in the presence of market institutions.[30] This limitation is especially significant because some biases found in the laboratory have been shown not to survive exposure to real-world settings (see Smith 1994: 118).[31] Second, even within the confines of the laboratory, results may be sensitive to relatively small changes in experimental procedures. Finally, and perhaps most importantly, the evidence supporting the behaviorist regulatory regime has not been subjected to comparative institutional analysis; there is little to no evidence that any particular behavioral regulation would reduce errors more efficiently than would market institutions. Nonetheless, a regulator faced with behaviorist advocacy, even if unsupported by empirical data sufficient to reject alternative theories, may readily embrace the behaviorist model because it produces outcomes closest to his own preconceptions.

Behavioral economists are, of course, aware of the need for experiments that isolate and identify biases that persist in market environments as a precondition to regulation designed to mitigate those biases; nevertheless, the available data frequently fall short of that standard because they fail to account for the possibility of multiple and simultaneous biases (see Lambert 2004: 1054–1055), do not adequately control for experimental procedures that might bias studies in favor of finding bias (Plott and Zeiler 2007: 1454–1456; Plott and Zeiler 2005: 532–535), or cannot rule out rational behavior as an explanation for the observed conduct.

This is true even of the bias most cited in support of the behaviorist agenda – the endowment effect (Plott and Zeiler 2007: 1454; Plott and Zeiler 2005: 532). As mentioned above, prospect theory is based upon the purported gap between willingness to accept (WTA) and willingness to pay (WTP) – the idea that individuals will report a lower WTP for a particular good than their WTA after they have been given the same good (Plott and Zeiler 2005: 530–531). As economist David Levine explains, however, it is not at all clear that evidence of a WTA–WTP gap implies a preference reversal:

> On the surface [the appearance of a gap] is not much of a paradox: we all know to buy low and sell high. However: the elicitation of values is done using a method called the Becker-DeGroot-Marschak [1964] elicitation procedure. A willingness to pay or accept payment is stated, and then a random draw is made. If the random draw is lower than the stated value (in the willingness to pay case) then the item is sold at the randomly drawn price. If the draw is higher than the stated value then no transaction takes place.
>
> Is it obvious to you that when this procedure is used that the unambiguously best course of action is to bid your true value and not buy low and sell high? It is true, and subjects are often informed of this fact. So: is there a paradox here, as some behavioral economists and psychologists would argue, or, … is it simply the case that people have trouble understanding a complex and unfamiliar procedure?
>
> (Levine 2012: 81)

A critical precondition to acting upon the purported WTA–WTP gap is to know, rather than to assume, the reason it arises. Charles Plott and Kathryn Zeiler demonstrate that observed gaps can be explained by misconceptions about experimental protocols and the experimental task; when those misconceptions are dispelled and a full set of experimental controls is employed to eliminate them, contrary to prospect theory, such gaps disappear (Plott and Zeiler 2007: 1462; Plott and Zeiler 2005: 531–532).

Plott and Zeiler's results do not eliminate the possibility that prospect theory is the best explanation of the WTA–WTP gap observed in some improved experimental settings (Plott and Zeiler 2007: 1462).[32] That finding would encourage further inquiry and elicit a serious scholarly discussion of the origins of WTA–WTP gaps, skeptically approached, as would any theory contradicted by robust evidence. Indeed, experimental economists continue to study the conditions under which WTA–WTP gaps might appear independent of the subjects's misconceptions and whether any such gaps are explained by the reference-dependent preferences contemplated by prospect theory (see, e.g., Knetsch and Wong 2009: 408; Ericson and Fuster 2011: 1879–1883).[33] Although the debate rages on in economics, the legal academy has leapt to the conclusion that individuals act irrationally in actual market transactions. Over 1,000 articles in legal periodicals reference the "endowment effect."[34] Of the 396 articles published after Zeiler's and Plott's first two articles appeared, only thirty-four cite either one of them.[35]

The scientific method obliges behaviorist scholars to disclose and to discuss alternative theories for explaining observed facts. The methodological commitment – in Jolls *et al.*'s words, to produce a "higher R^2" (Jolls *et al.* 1998: 1487)[36] – reflects acceptance of both scientific rigor and the pursuit of objectively verifiable knowledge. That only 10 percent of the legal articles citing the endowment effect even refer to the leading contrary literature suggests that in the legal academy, pursuit of the behaviorist policy agenda is only minimally constrained by the norms of scientific inquiry.

Similar problems plague the literature on framing effects. As Gregory Mitchell has observed, though the existence of framing effects is not disputed – indeed, such effects have long been noticed in public opinion polling[37] – the effects are not robust to even small changes in experimental settings (see Mitchell 2005: 1256, n. 40). For example, small manipulations in the decision-making context, such as asking subjects to think about the possible success or failure of their options, to give reasons for their choices, or to deliberate more analytically, can reduce or eliminate the influence of framing effects (Mitchell 2005: 1255–1256). Mitchell also highlights evidence that stable preferences prevail in settings where choices are made frequently and involve less emotion, more deliberation or reflection, or a smaller number of options, or where the subject is well informed (Mitchell 2005: 1253). These findings suggest framing effects can be reduced or eliminated at low cost without the extensive interventions proposed by libertarian paternalists (Mitchell 2005: 1255–1260).[38] As we will discuss later, a fundamental problem with the behaviorists's regulatory agenda is that its proposals are not calibrated to the costs of "debiasing" behavioral biases as evidenced by experiments; to the contrary, behaviorist proposals frequently assume that the social costs of cognitive error are large and presumptively greater than the cost of the regulatory solution designed to reduce them.

Data interpretation and rational error

Even if there were robust evidence of irrationality in markets, such evidence would have to be interpreted with care; the challenge would be to distinguish truly irrational behavior from rationally made and therefore efficient mistakes. Efficient mistakes occur because rational economic actors economize on both information and transaction costs. In short, not all errors imply irrationality because perfect decision making would be costly. To miss subtle distinctions between rational and irrational decision making will almost certainly lead to erroneous conclusions about legal policy. The data required to distinguish rational mistakes from irrational mistakes, much less to estimate the magnitude of any welfare loss caused by the latter, are significant and may be unavailable.

The behavioral law and economics literature nonetheless fails to distinguish between rational and irrational errors, assuming instead that error reduction is always efficient. Where there are information and transaction costs, however, the efficient level of error is not zero.[39] For example, if a consumer could switch from credit card *A* to credit card *B* at a transaction cost of $10, but credit card *B* is only $5 superior to credit card *A*, then the consumer's failure to switch is not evidence of his irrationality. Consider the problems encountered if a behavioral economist tries to interpret the following stylized facts from an empirical study of consumers's selection of credit cards following a natural experiment in which a card company offers them two cards: (1) one card has a higher interest rate but no annual fee; and (2) the other has a lower interest rate and an annual fee. What do the behavioral theories of consumer credit predict?

Oren Bar-Gill, who, along with Elizabeth Warren, championed creation of the new Consumer Financial Protection Bureau (CFPB), argues that consumers consistently underestimate their future borrowing due to a potpourri of behavioral biases such as imperfect self-control, hyperbolic discounting, and systematic underestimation of the probability of negative consequences (Bar-Gill 2004: 1395–1411). Rather than viewing "teaser rates," zero annual fees, and rewards programs as signs of intense and healthy competition among credit card issuers, they and others have argued that card issuers design such products and contracts to exploit the behavioral biases of consumers.[40] Bar-Gill argues that competition on these margins leaves consumers worse off because their expressed credit choices do not reflect their true preferences (see Bar-Gill 2004: 1411–1412).

This "predatory lender" interpretation of the credit market gives rise to several testable hypotheses about the underlying behavioral theories. First, we should expect to see a significant majority of consumers selecting the wrong card – that is, the card that does not maximize interest-cost savings net of any annual fee paid. Second, we should expect the consumers's error rate, if it is the product of irrationality, to remain invariant to the cost of the error. Third, we should expect consumers who carry monthly balances instead of paying them off to hold cards with high rewards and no annual fee. This third hypothesis is the heart of the Bar-Gill "seduction by plastic" argument that consumers who revolve debt are irrationally optimistic about their financial prospects, leading them to select the card better suited for nonrevolvers (see Bar-Gill 2004: 1400).

The data bear out none of these expectations. Agarwal *et al.* found that approximately 60 percent of consumers selected the "optimal" card (Agarwal *et al.* 2006: 4). Of the 40 percent who did not, many corrected their errors with some experience and only "a small minority of consumers persist[ed] in holding substantially sub-optimal contracts without switching" (Agarwal *et al.* 2006: 5). The authors found these errors were bounded in magnitude by the level of the annual fee (typically around $25) (Agarwal *et al.* 2006: 4–5, 7).[41] Further, and consistent with neoclassical economic theory, the probability of selecting the optimal credit card increased both with the cost of the error and with repeat decisions, which suggests that learning mitigates the effects of the relevant biases (Agarwal *et al.* 2006: 15). All of these findings are consistent with rational (but, of course, not perfect) decision making and, more specifically, with price theory. Further, contrary to the behaviorist model, "more nonrevolvers than revolvers" carried "cards with average minimum APRs greater than 10 percent" (Brown and Plache 2006: 80). "This result does not support the hypothesis that hyperbolic discounting results in consumers bearing credit card debt at high interest rates" (Brown and Plache 2006: 80).

The available data strongly suggest consumers make rational choices in the credit card market. The upper bound of the initial error rate suggests switching costs would outweigh any potential gains consumers might realize from changing cards – the error rate is efficient. How would a behaviorist interpret these same data? Warren explains her approach as follows:

> What's the point of offering two different products, except to hope that the number of consumer [*sic*] who get it wrong will exceed in dollar volume the number who get it right. Or, from an informed consumers' [*sic*] perspective, perhaps the optimal system is one in which they make good decisions and hope for cross-subsidization from less-clever consumers who help keep credit cards highly profitable and easy to use in a variety of settings (e.g., grocery stores, cabs, pizza deliveries, etc.).
>
> I realize it is heresy in many circles to ask if consumers should have fewer choices. But at some point the empirical studies about high error rates bring into question the assumptions that underlie the claim that more choice is always good.
>
> (Warren 2006)

Professor Warren's answer is simple: A high error rate implies irrationality, and irrationality implies the need for choice-reducing regulation. It is also simplistic.

Warren's interpretation – the behaviorist interpretation – of the data reveals her methodology, which results in three significant errors. First, the initial error rate of 40 percent is evaluated without reference to the costs of switching; therefore, no attention is paid to the fundamental challenge of identifying the efficient rate of error. Second, no weight is assigned to the finding that the error rate decreases both with the cost of error and with repeat decision making, facts that are consistent with rational choice but difficult to reconcile with the models of consumer behavior in credit markets put forth by Bar-Gill and others. Third, Warren describes the errors as "staggering" (Warren 2006), but does not address the finding that the magnitude of these costs is bounded by the size of the

typically small annual fee. While the initial error rate is indeed high, her evaluation of the rationality and welfare properties of the choice occurs in a vacuum
where the costs of error or of investment to correct the error are ignored and thus
effectively assumed to be zero. Warren's leap from identifying the error rate to
questioning whether "more choice is always good" illustrates what Harold
Demsetz famously called the Nirvana Fallacy – the failure to ask: compared to
what? (See Demsetz 1969: 1–3.)[42]

Our point is not merely that we disagree with Warren's interpretation of this
single study. The more general point is that Warren's analysis ignores fundamental economic concepts and threatens to subject consumers to a serious policy
error by conflating rational choice with irrational behavior – that is, by ignoring
switching and other costs incurred everywhere except in Nirvana – and by avoiding comparative institutional analysis.

Compounding the shortcomings of the research with policy error

As previously discussed, behavioral economics research has largely consisted of
identifying, documenting, and classifying apparent errors in decision making. What
has thus far eluded the researchers is a theoretical mapping of the real-world conditions under which individual decisions will be fettered by these cognitive biases
and when they will not (see Klick and Mitchell 2006; Mitchell 2005). This gap in the
behavioral theory of errors is critical because it makes it inevitable that, in attempting
to correct for cognitive biases, behavioral interventions will lead to policy errors.

The inevitability of policy errors derives from the insurmountable theoretical
and empirical obstacles to identifying any one person's, let alone the distribution
of all persons's, "true preferences." One type of policy error will occur when a
behavioral intervention is aimed at seemingly irrational behavior that is, in fact,
rational for the decision maker in question. In other words, the social costs of this
type of policy error flow from encouraging behavior the paternalist inaccurately
believes will make individuals better off and concomitantly discouraging acts that
satisfy their actual preferences. A second type of policy error will occur when an
intervention designed to improve the decision making of truly irrational economic
agents imposes costs, as it inevitably will, upon all those who are not irrational
and for whom the same decision is not an error. In this case, it is erroneous beliefs
about the distribution of true preferences that lead to the policy error. For
example, even if a particular default rule meant to offset a cognitive bias will
reduce some individual errors in decision making, failure to calibrate the default
rule to the distribution of true preferences may impose social costs upon rational
decision makers that are greater than any benefits in error reduction.

The risk of policy error is significant, however, even if consumers's error rate
is 100 percent. For example, behaviorists repackage the "sin tax" as a means to
reduce hyperbolic discounting by consumers of certain goods, such as cigarettes,
that often have deleterious health effects in the long run. But even if all consumers in the market exhibit present bias in consumption and the intervention is
successful in reducing the rate of consumption, the question remains of whether

the social costs saved are greater than the social costs of intervention. In the case of a sin tax, the likelihood of this type of policy error is exacerbated because regulators do not, and surely cannot, have accurate knowledge of every consumers's, or even the average consumer's, "true" preferences or the discount rate necessary to calculate the optimal tax. The expanding behavioral law and economics agenda largely disregards these risks.

From behavioral economics to behavioral law and economics

The quest to translate the insights of behavioral economics, such as they are, into public policies intended to improve decision making and welfare has achieved a remarkable degree of momentum. In addition to Thaler and Sunstein's recent book, *Nudge: Improving Decisions About Health, Wealth, and Happiness*, a popular summary of the behavioral approach to law, and Dan Ariely's similarly oriented *Predictably Irrational*, there is abundant evidence that behavioral law and economics is affecting public policy. Indeed, a recent account in the popular press describes behavioral economics as "the governing theory" of the Obama Administration's regulatory agenda, in part because President Obama appointed Cass Sunstein to head the Office of Information and Regulatory Affairs in the Executive Office of the President, which reviews proposed regulations before they can be issued (Ferguson 2010: 18).[43] To give concrete examples, behavioral economics provided the intellectual blueprint for the CFPB, which the Congress created at the urging of the Obama Administration,[44] and a member of the Federal Trade Commission has discussed taking a more behavioral approach to enforcing the antitrust laws (Rosch 2010: 12–15).[45] Regulatory proposals informed by behavioral law and economics span the law school curriculum, ranging from antitrust and consumer protection to discrimination and employment law. The depth and breadth of the behaviorist agenda is in no small part due to its success in the legal academy.

The rise of behavioral law and economics in the legal academy

The legal academy is the driving force behind the rise of behavioral law and economics and its growing influence in policy debates. Legal academics have discovered in the behavioral economics literature a rich supply of empirical findings they can marshal in support of paternalistic regulatory interventions. Indeed, law professors have produced hundreds of such articles in a relatively short time.[46] From 1980 through 1984, across all legal publications, only a single article mentioned the term "behavioral economics." From 2005 through 2009, however, 988 articles mentioned the term.[47] This dramatic increase has been duplicated in books. As Figure 15.1 shows, the terms "behavioral economics," "endowment effect," and "cognitive bias" have experienced an equally dramatic increase in usage over the same time period.

The increasing footprint of behavioral law and economics in the legal academy extends beyond legal scholarship, via law school faculties, into the law

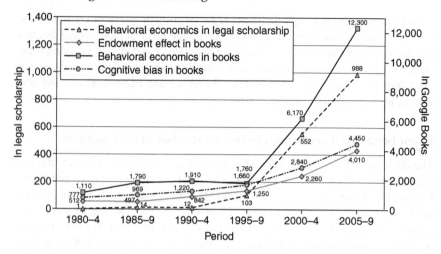

Figure 15.1 References to "behavioral economics."

school curriculum. For example, ten of the top twenty law schools in the United States have offered at least one course in behavioral law and economics in the past five years.[48]

There has also been a concerted effort to transplant the research agenda of behavioral economics overseas, particularly to Europe. In April 2004, the European Network for the Advancement of Behavioural Economics (ENABLE), a joint venture between European universities with nascent behavioral institutes and established programs at Harvard and Princeton, undertook a mission to "advance this emerging field of behavioural economics in Europe" by facilitating the "development of a critical mass of the brightest young researchers by concentrating the currently highly fragmented expertise in Europe" (Centre for Economic Policy Research, n.d.).[49]

Some behavioral law and economics regulatory proposals

Behaviorist regulatory proposals run the gamut from gentle attempts to encourage retirement savings to outright bans of certain products.[50] Common to each of these proposals is the claim that the intervention will improve individuals's decision making by reducing errors attributable to cognitive biases and bounded rationality, thus making each individual better off as measured by his own preferences (see, e.g., Jolls *et al.* 1998: 1536–1537; Thaler and Sunstein 2003: 178–179). Some proposals would modify legal default rules; others invoke "choice architecture" to manipulate framing effects. Some behaviorist proposals do not directly restrict the set of choices available to consumers but impose a cooling-off period or some other burden placed upon producers that, in turn, results in higher prices, reduced variety, or both.[51]

Choice architecture and retirement savings

The most frequently discussed example of a behavioral intervention invoking choice architecture is default enrollment in employer-sponsored savings plans. Sunstein and Thaler have argued that a law "requir[ing] employers to provide automatic enrollment and allow[ing] employees to opt out" would be consistent with libertarian paternalism (Sunstein and Thaler 2003: 1176). Others less concerned with preserving the opportunity to opt out have suggested that firms be required by law to make enrollment automatic (see Camerer *et al.* 2003: 1227–1230).

The most common behavioral argument in support of automatic enrollment is that, freed of the "status quo bias" and the "sticky" nature of defaults, many more employees would enroll in a savings plan than actually enroll at present.[52] Sunstein and Thaler contend that if employees only thought more carefully about the enrollment decision, they would act upon, and hence reveal, their true preference, causing enrollment rates to rise (Sunstein and Thaler 2003: 1172–1173).[53] The "Save More Tomorrow" plan – a defined-contribution retirement savings plan in which the contribution rate of those who do not opt out increases automatically when an enrollee receives a pay raise – was designed to "help those employees who would like to save more but lack the willpower to act on this desire" (Thaler and Benartzi 2004: S170). Sunstein and Thaler describe Save More Tomorrow as "successful libertarian paternalism in action" because it has resulted in increased enrollment and savings rates at the handful of firms that have implemented it (Sunstein and Thaler 2003: 1185).[54] Paradoxically, this claim of a successful behavioral intervention is based upon the failure of employees to opt out of the new default (Sunstein and Thaler 2003: 1191).[55] That is, in order to evaluate the success of the behavioral intervention in terms of employees's welfare, the behaviorists point to the preferences revealed by subjects's actual behavior – in this case, their failure to opt out of the default – while simultaneously justifying the intervention on the ground that status quo and other biases render defaults "sticky" and revealed preferences therefore untrustworthy evidence of true preferences.[56] The only meaningful difference is the preference of the would-be regulators for one outcome over the other.[57]

Regulation of consumer credit

Behavioral law and economics has provided the intellectual foundation for the new CFPB and a new approach to the regulation of consumer credit. The proponents argue the Bureau can promulgate rules and regulations that improve consumers's decision making by altering the design of consumer credit products, mandating various disclosures, restricting consumers's choices, and instituting default rules in favor of standardized products approved by the Bureau (see Evans and Wright 2010: 319–320).[58]

The Bureau's approach to regulating consumer credit is a direct outgrowth of the behavioral law and economics movement – indeed, the Bureau itself is the outgrowth of a 2008 article written by law professors Elizabeth Warren and Oren Bar-Gill (Bar-Gill and Warren 2008). Another law professor, Michael Barr, who was an Assistant Secretary of the Treasury in the Obama Administration, contributed to a second article laying out a series of proposals to regulate consumer credit, including the requirement that a lender offer every customer a basic or "plain vanilla" product before trying to sell him a product with additional features (Barr *et al.* 2008a: 7–9).[59] The behavioral premise of these proposals is that "[m]any consumers are uninformed and irrational" (Bar-Gill and Warren 2008: 21) and therefore make "systematic mistakes in their choice of credit products" (Bar-Gill and Warren 2008: 26) and require behaviorally informed policy interventions in order to reduce those mistakes and hence increase consumers's welfare. Other behaviorist proposals concerning consumer credit include banning credit cards altogether (Loewenstein and O'Donoghue 2006: 196–198) and requiring credit card companies to unbundle transaction and financing services so that consumers could not use the same card to make a purchase and to finance it (Bar-Gill 2004: 1421–1422). The Bureau has broad powers, perhaps sufficient to implement these or similar behavioral interventions in the consumer credit market.[60]

Sin taxes

Behaviorists also propose using taxes to improve individual decision making and to offset the effects of behavioral biases. For example, Botond Kőszegi and Jonathan Gruber contend consumers would be made better off with higher taxes on goods towards which they exhibit time-inconsistent preferences (see Gruber and Kőszegi 2001: 1293–1294; 1980–1981; Gruber and Mullainathan 2005: 2). While Kőszegi and Gruber have focused upon the theoretical and empirical case for higher taxes on tobacco products, other behaviorists have proposed sin taxes aimed at reducing errors committed by consumers who discount hyperbolically, especially with respect to the consumption of potentially unhealthful products, such as fatty foods, alcoholic beverages, and sugary sodas (see O'Donoghue and Rabin 2003: 190–191).

As discussed above, hyperbolic discounting invokes the concept that people value immediate gratification so much that they make decisions they will come to regret.[61] The behaviorists often bundle this concept with the idea of "multiple selves" to argue that time-inconsistent preferences result in lower lifetime well-being for consumers because they regularly make decisions today that their future "self" will regret. Paralleling the economic concept of externalities,[62] the behaviorists describe these costs as "internalities." The case for sin taxes based upon the logic of internalities requires both an aggregate loss of total welfare when one sums up the utilities of all one's selves across time, and some assumption about which of one's multiple selves represents one's true preferences. As we show below, however, there is neither a theoretical nor an empirical basis for the behaviorists's implicit privileging of a future self who may or may not ever come into existence, depending upon the individuals's age at death.[63]

Behavioral law and economics and economic welfare

Sunstein and Thaler are clear in stating the goals of the behavioral approach: to make individuals better off. But what is meant by "better off" in a world where individuals's revealed preferences cannot be relied upon for inferences about their own welfare? Again, Sunstein and Thaler provide a clear answer: The appropriate measure of welfare is economic well-being as it would be expressed by the preferences of each individual if he were free of behavioral biases (see Thaler and Sunstein 2003: 176). Thus, the promise of behavioral law and economics lies in its potential to increase economic welfare according to each individual's "true" preferences. As we have seen, the behavioral literature often appears to assume a reduction in errors is conclusive evidence of a move toward true preferences and hence of an increase in welfare. Much of this literature, in our view, overestimates the expected welfare benefits of behavioral interventions while underestimating some costs and altogether failing to take account of others.

An economic analysis of the effects of a behavioral intervention requires not only an agreed-upon metric of welfare, but also information sufficient to measure its effects. At its core, the promise of behavioral law and economics's theory of errors is to design interventions that will make each individual better off by more closely aligning his choices with his "true preferences." Once one assumes an individual's decisions do not align with his own preferences, however, evaluating the behaviorists's welfare claims becomes difficult, if not impossible.[64]

To date, critiques of behavioral law and economics and its promise of increasing welfare have raised three types of concerns: The behaviorists (1) as we discussed in the previous section, have no way to identify irrational decisions, (2) cannot reliably discern an individual's "true preferences," and (3) fail consistently to account adequately for the social costs of a proposed intervention. Each of these concerns raises significant doubt both about the presumption that error reduction alone increases welfare and about the potential for behavioral interventions to improve welfare. Having considered the first problem above, we now direct our attention to the other two concerns.

The search for true preferences

Behavioral law and economics's claim to welfare-increasing intervention requires one to disregard the neoclassical assumption that actual behavior reveals evidence of welfare. How, then, do behavioral economists identify true preferences?

In rejecting the standard understanding among economists that, by choosing x, an actor reveals he expects to be better off with x,[65] the behaviorist conflates welfare and happiness. This critical difference concerning conceptions of economic welfare leads to a methodological divide: When the neoclassical economist finds an economic agent's actual behavior departs from the prediction of his economic model, he suspects the model is to blame; when a behavioral economist observes a gap between actual and predicted behavior, he concludes the agent is acting against his own best interests.

The neoclassical critique of the behaviorists's view of the relationship between preferences and welfare is illuminated by examining the behaviorists's model of the individual as multiple and distinct sequential selves with conflicting interests owing to different time perspectives. But the multiple-self model fails both in theory and in practice.[66] The theoretical failure is simple: Economics does not provide a basis for identifying which of the multiple selves's decisions expresses the individual's "true" preferences for the purposes of welfare analysis. The convention in the behavioral literature, in order to make utility trade-offs among the various selves possible, has been to adopt the long-run *ex ante* preference (see, e.g., Gruber and Kőszegi 2001: 1287; O'Donoghue and Rabin 2003: 190). Nothing, however, either in standard economic theory or in behavioral economics, justifies this approach to identifying "true" preferences.[67]

The manipulation of the standard welfare criterion in favor of long-run *ex ante* preferences, and thereby the behaviorists's preferred alternative, is not a defensible basis upon which to claim departures from those preferences represent defects justifying a legal intervention. Untethered from the standard economic approach to welfare, the behaviorist's approach becomes "both an opportunity and a rationale for activism," and implicitly assigns to the economist the task of convincing individuals to improve their own decision making and the welfare of their future selves or, alternatively, persuading a third party to intervene on behalf of the future selves (Gul and Pesendorfer 2005: 39).[68]

As Rizzo and Whitman observe, a similar problem arises more generally with claims of welfare-reducing choices biased by context dependence, such as those affected by the status quo bias or the endowment effect (see Rizzo and Whitman 2009a: 703). Once again, the behaviorist theory claims empirical proof of internal inconsistency of choices but cannot offer an empirical basis for identifying which choice represents one's "true" preferences. With respect to framing, the question is not how to resolve conflicts between multiple selves but rather how to determine which context-dependent choice expresses the preference that maximizes welfare. After ruling out revealed preferences as expressions of true preferences, the behaviorist lacks a coherent principle to identify welfare-maximizing choices. Indeed, without revealed preferences, economic science simply cannot do so. The behaviorists can only declare by fiat what they expect a rational individual would or should do – thereby justifying the imposition of correct choices by a third party, contrary to the behaviorist promise to maximize economic welfare by the individuals's own lights and undermining the behaviorist claim to the prefix "libertarian."

Errors of omission in behavioral cost–benefit analysis

Another concern regarding behavioral law and economics is that it proceeds from premises that ignore the often significant costs of intervention. We identify three types of omitted costs.

The default rule

Sunstein and Thaler claim choice architecture, or selection of a default rule,[69] is "inevitable" (Sunstein and Thaler 2003: 1174). This may be so, but it neither requires nor implies that the state – or anyone else – must always select the default rule.[70] It is even less apparent that the state will select a default rule more closely aligned with an individual's true preferences (as defined by the central planner) than what the individual himself would choose to do. As Mitchell points out, the inevitability claim regarding "manipulation of choices by central planners" holds only "so long as individuals remain subject to these irrational influences" (Mitchell 2005: 1250–1251 [emphasis omitted]).[71] Mitchell demonstrates the claim of inevitability is not justified by the psychological literature, which identifies conditions under which individuals are not likely to be affected by framing (see Mitchell 2005: 1251–1252).[72] We can reject Sunstein and Thaler's inevitability hypothesis on the ground that a less intrusive measure is often sufficient to eliminate the framing effect without exposing individuals to the risks of policy errors.

Relatedly, behaviorist analyses of policy interventions often underestimate or ignore the cost of opting out of the default rule. The claimed "libertarian" aspect of behavioral interventions is that the manipulation of choice frames still respects freedom of choice; the individual can always reject the regulator's preferred choice in favor of expressing his own preference, even if irrational. Many of the proposed behavioral interventions, however, simply do not live up to the claim of "choice-neutrality," for they ultimately reduce or constrain available choices. For example, sin taxes raise the cost of opting out, while product bans go further, eliminating entirely the ability to opt out; the number of choices practically available is reduced, respectively for some or for all individuals.

Other proposed interventions, such as the plain vanilla requirement or the cooling-off period, impose significant costs upon those who would like to opt out. The behaviorally inspired Model Employment Termination Act, which Sunstein and Thaler support on the ground that it respects freedom of choice, would switch the legal default rule from employment "at will" to termination "for cause" only, but would require the employer to pay a substantial price to opt into the "at will" regime.[73] Thus, the choice set of mutually agreeable employment contracts initially available to employers and employees is restricted, and opting out entails significant costs. These costs would be borne in part by employers and in part by employees, who are the intended beneficiaries of the scheme, because employers's willingness to pay for labor will decline to reflect the additional risk they assume by hiring new employees subject to the penalties of the Act. Behaviorist policy analysis simply assumes these costs of opting out are at or near zero, thereby skewing regulators in favor of an intervention that reduces welfare.

The cost of government intervention

In addition to underestimating or ignoring the social cost associated with manipulating choice frames through legal default rules, behaviorists tend to underestimate the costs of implementing proposed policies – an error we term the "government intervention bias." If one believes individuals are predictably irrational and will commit decision-making errors, then the relevant policy question is whether society is better off if error correction is supplied by individuals in markets or by individuals in the government.[74] It is unclear that either bounded rationality or outright irrationality supports a larger role for government as opposed to greater private investment in error correction, but more government is inevitably the policy prescription favored by the behaviorist agenda (Rachlinski 2006: 224).[75] Answering this question requires comparative institutional analysis in order to identify the lower-cost source of "error reduction." The pro-government position suffers from two underlying problems.

First, we question the behavioral economist's implicit assumption that regulators are rational. As Judge Posner pertinently inquired: "Behavioral economists are right to point to the limitations of human cognition, [b]ut if they have the same cognitive limitations as consumers, should they be designing systems of consumer protection?" (Posner 2009) In response to Judge Posner's question, Thaler posits that regulators's bounded rationality has indeterminate conclusions for behavioral regulation. He explains:

> The premise of behavioral economics is that humans are not perfect decision-making machines.... Even Judge Posner is human, and given the number of books he has written, he must have made a few mistakes in print. But our legal system needs judges, and one of the reasons we have a layered judicial system is so that mistakes by one judge can be corrected by others. Should we abolish our legal system because judges are known to make mistakes?
>
> No government agency (or judge) will be error-free. The goal of the Nudge agenda sketched out in my co-authored book of that title was to create decision-making environments in which it is easier for error-prone human decision makers to choose well. The [CFPB] proposed by the administration is a good example of this kind of thinking. Even imperfect experts can help us achieve better outcomes, just as imperfect judges can help us enforce the law fairly. Until we invent the perfect human (or computer decision-making device), we have no good alternatives.
>
> (PBS Newshour 2009)

Thaler's response proceeds from the Nirvana Fallacy and hence misses the critical point: Neither governments nor individuals can make error-free choices. Perhaps, as Thaler says, "[e]ven imperfect experts can help us achieve better outcomes," but the pertinent question is their comparative performance. How costly will government policy errors be if government actors suffer from, say, hyperbolic discounting or status quo bias, or are subject to framing effects? What will be the frequency and magnitude of those errors relative to relying upon private decision makers to correct their own errors to the extent they can do so? Can we trust behavioral regulators suffering from confirmation bias reliably to identify the true preferences of individuals, as they would have to do in order to implement successful behavioral polices?[76] By casting the issue as whether people err – which no one could dispute – Thaler ignores the more subtle and fundamental points about the consequences of the choice to rely upon the government rather than private decision makers to correct errors.[77] The counterintuitive presumption that irrationality among regulators is irrelevant consistently biases cost–benefit analysis in favor of government intervention.

Second, the behaviorists's government intervention bias depends upon their systematic underestimation of information costs. Behaviorist prescriptions for intervention assume regulators are able to recognize, gather, and process the data required to identify each individual's "true preferences" (Rizzo and Whitman 2009b: 910). Their implicit assumption is that regulators enjoy a comparative advantage over private economic actors in acquiring information. Professors Mario Rizzo and Douglas Whitman describe this obstacle to welfare-increasing behavioral interventions as the "knowledge problem" of behavioral law and economics, derived from F.A. Hayek's well-known critique of central planning (Rizzo and Whitman 2009b: 910; Hayek 1945). Rizzo and Whitman describe the dilemma facing behaviorists:

> *If* well-meaning policymakers possess all the relevant information about individuals' true preferences, their cognitive biases, and the choice contexts in which they manifest themselves, *then* policymakers could potentially implement paternalist policies that improve the welfare of individuals by their own standards. But lacking such information, we cannot conclude that actual paternalism will make their decisions better; under a wide range of circumstances, it will even make them worse. New paternalists have not taken the knowledge problems that are evident from the underlying behavioral and economic research seriously enough.
> (Rizzo and Whitman 2009b: 910)

The assumptions required to overcome the knowledge problem are both heroic and impossible. Behaviorists must assume regulators will be able simultaneously to (1) identify the distribution of individuals's true preferences, (2) access reliable empirical data sufficient to identify departures from rational choice, (3) interpret those data accurately, and (4) design and implement policies so the reduction in errors works a net increase in welfare. The failure of any one of these assumptions is fatal to the behavioral enterprise; disregard of the knowledge problem biases the perceived costs of behavioral interventions.

The knowledge problem necessarily invites regulators to misuse behavioral economics. The behavioral literature does not offer clear predictions of individual behavior when multiple cognitive biases infect decision making. The interaction of biases is poorly understood even in controlled settings, much less in markets. Because behavioral economics generates indeterminate predictions in many settings, central planners have myriad opportunities to substitute their preferences (or the preferences of special interest groups) for those of the public. Furthermore, because behavioral economics produces a range of possibilities open to a regulator considering a proposed intervention, behavioral economics entails a much greater risk of policy error than would reliance upon the relatively narrow predictions of price theory.[78] Any rigorous evaluation of the costs and benefits of behavioral intervention must account for the potential abuse or simply mistaken use of behavioral economics by regulators.

Consider, for example, the recent policy decision to implement the Making Work Pay income tax credit as a slow and recurring decrease in withholding rather than a one-time lump-sum reduction. Behavioral economists, including Sunstein and Thaler (see Surowiecki 2009; Sahm *et al.* 2010 citing Sunstein and Thaler 2009), predicted that one-time tax cuts, such as the 2008 tax rebate, would be less effective in stimulating economic activity than would recurring payments, because individuals would be more likely to treat the latter as disposable income (see Schwartz 2009). The limited available evidence, however, suggests their prediction was incorrect (Sahm *et al.* 2010: 1–3). Claudia Sahm, Matthew Shapiro, and Joel Slemrod found, contrary to the behaviorist prediction, 25 percent of households reported that the one-time economic stimulus payment in 2008 would lead them to mostly increase their spending, while only 13 percent reported that the extra pay from the lower withholding in 2009 would lead them to mostly increase their spending (Sahm *et al.* 2010: 29).[79]

Either of these classes of objections – the default rule fallacy or the government intervention bias – is sufficient to undermine dramatically or to reject altogether the welfare-based case for behavioral law and economics. Even if, however, we assume the behavioral economics research and policy programs can avoid all such problems and would be justified on pure economic welfare grounds, the behaviorist calculation of the net increase in societal welfare ignores the significant but underappreciated threat to individual liberty posed by government interventions predicated upon behavioral law and economics.

Beyond welfare: behavioral economics and liberty

In the brave new world contemplated by the advocates of government policies informed by behavioral law and economics, many more aspects of each individual's life would be regulated, or more stringently regulated, than at present. This would be true even if the behaviorists's agenda were limited to matters of health and finance, the two major subdivisions of Thaler and Sunstein's book (see Thaler and Sunstein 2008), each of which they define capaciously; the former, for example, includes smoking, nutrition, and medical insurance (Thaler and Sunstein 2008: 157–196), while the latter includes credit cards, investing, and saving for retirement (Thaler and Sunstein 2008: 101–156).

Assuming, again, the behavioral law and economics regulatory agenda could be implemented in a manner that avoids the problems discussed above in *From behavioral economics to behavioral law and economics*, and in a manner that increases or at least does not reduce economic welfare, that agenda would still present a substantial threat to the liberty of the individual. The current literature, however, assigns no weight to liberty beyond the narrow focus upon choice preservation; it is nearly devoid of thinking about the implications of behavioral law and economics for individual autonomy and about the social significance of autonomy's further diminution (Mitchell 2005: 1260–1264). How should one evaluate a regulatory intervention that would increase welfare but also diminish liberty? What are the mechanics of trading off welfare and liberty when the two are in tension? To be sure, a minor reduction in liberty should not be sufficient to reject an intervention with significant welfare benefits just as an intervention generating only modest welfare benefits is not justified regardless of its negative effect upon liberty.

In close cases it will be necessary to consider such tradeoffs in order to fully assess the desirability of a proposed policy intervention.[80] Assigning a precise value to liberty in the regulatory calculus is an impossible task given that individuals value their liberties to different degrees and policymakers have no way of knowing those valuations or their distribution. Even without assigning a precise weight to a loss of liberty, however, it is inevitable that such losses, if taken into account, will sometimes – perhaps often – defeat the case for intervention.[81] We believe the best approach to evaluating these potential tradeoffs is to establish a presumption against behaviorist regulation that reduces liberty, rebuttable only by demonstrating that the regulation is likely to generate significant gains in economic welfare. It is to those liberty concerns that we now turn.

Autonomy

John Stuart Mill followed Immanuel Kant (see Kant 1785: 97–98) in noting explicitly the value of autonomy in its own right, that is, apart from what one does with one's autonomy or the consequences of its exercise.[82] Mill's point was that a fully realized human being is one who makes the important decisions in his own life:

> If a person possesses any tolerable amount of common sense and experience, his own mode of laying out his existence is the best, not because it is the best in itself, but because it is his own mode. Human beings are not like sheep; and even sheep are not undistinguishably alike.... If it were only that people have diversities of taste that is reason enough for not attempting to shape them all after one model. But different persons also require different conditions for their spiritual development.
>
> (Mill 1859: 75)[83]

On the related topic of unthinking conformity to a tradition or custom, which he acknowledges may embody the teachings of experience, Mill's observation is a cautionary note with equal application for those who would relieve the citizen of the need to decide things for himself:

> [T]o conform to custom, merely as custom, does not educate or develop in him any of the qualities which are the distinctive endowment of a human being. The human faculties of perception, judgment, discriminative feeling, mental activity, and even moral preference, are exercised only in making a choice.
>
> (Mill 1859: 65)

And finally, in words that fortuitously seem to anticipate Thaler and Sunstein's ideas on manipulating the default rule for enrolling employees in payroll savings plans (see Thaler and Sunstein 2008: 103–117), Mill exhorts:

> He who chooses his plan for himself, employs all his faculties. He must use observation to see, reasoning and judgement to foresee, activity to gather materials for decision, discrimination to decide, and when he has decided, firmness and self-control to hold to his deliberate decision.
>
> (Mill 1859: 65)

More than a century later, Friedrich Hayek, in *The Constitution of Liberty*, made a slightly different point about the value of having more rather than fewer choices:

> [T]he importance of our being free to do a particular thing has nothing to do with the question of whether we or the majority are ever likely to make use of that particular possibility.... [T]he less likely the opportunity, the more serious will it be to miss it when it arises, for the experience it offers will be nearly unique.
>
> (Hayek 1960: 83)

As Amartya Sen would later point out, this consideration relates to "the process aspect of freedom," which "includes considerations that may not figure in the accounting of the opportunity aspect [of freedom]" (Sen 1993: 523–524). In particular, Sen identifies

> (i) decisional autonomy of the choices to be made, and (ii) immunity from interference by others. The former is concerned with the operative role that a person has in the process of choice, and the crucial issue here is self-decision, e.g., whether the choices are being made by the person herself – not (on her behalf) by other individuals or institutions.
>
> (Sen 1993: 524)[84]

Behaviorists in general do not place any value upon "the process aspect of freedom" or "decisional autonomy."[85] Sunstein and Thaler in particular claim to preserve the choices now open to people by, for example, merely altering default rules without preventing the determined individual from opting out; as we have seen, however, that is not always the case, and it is never without cost to the person whose preference is different from theirs. Indeed, the proposals they advance are libertarian only in the limited sense that they "do not block choice" altogether (Qizilbash 2009: 23). As Mozaffar Qizilbash observes, Sunstein and Thaler do not address the deeper anti-paternalist objection that their proposals deny the inherent value individuals place upon autonomy (Qizilbash 2009: 23). Autonomy – "deciding for oneself" – has value that "run[s] contrary to even the weak form of paternalism" favored by Sunstein and Thaler, rendering "the idea of 'libertarian paternalism' as they define it … potentially incoherent" (Qizilbash 2009: 23).

Sometimes Sunstein and Thaler obscure their coercive instinct from view, as in the example with which they begin *Nudge*. There they instance the "director of food services for a large city school system" who has "formal training in nutrition" (Thaler and Sunstein 2008: 1). She can have food presented in the schools's cafeterias in any sequence, including the sequence that is best for the children and the one that will maximize profits (Thaler and Sunstein 2008: 1–3). Sunstein and Thaler mean to point out the inevitability of some choice being made and of that choice influencing the children's preferences. Their choice of setting, however, defeats this implication. In their hypothetical illustration, the nutritionist ultimately influences children, who have less autonomy than do adults – which is why most of them are in school. The "choice architect" works for a public school system, not a for-profit enterprise, the mission of which school system is to educate children, perhaps even on the subject of nutrition. What the nutritionist's choice, inevitable or not, has to do with the case for the government manipulating adults, who are sovereign in the marketplace, remains obscure.[86]

Limiting the range of decisions to be made by individuals or burdening those who would make an officially disfavored choice – not saving enough, eating unhealthful foods, etc. – tends to infantilize the public. Effective decision making is acquired through trial and error, that is, by making a decision and either getting verbal feedback about or directly observing the success or failure of one's decision as a means of reaching one's goal (Byrnes *et al.* 1999: 1122).[87] Moreover, "when people are motivated to be accurate, they expend more cognitive effort on issue-related reasoning, attend to relevant information more carefully, and process it more deeply, often using more complex rules" (Kunda 1990: 481).

The lesson, which is, ironically, ignored in the prescriptive behavioral law and economics literature, is clear: The more palpable the consequences of one's decisions, the more indelible the imprint of experience.[88] Indeed, there is reason to think experimental results such as these tend to understate significantly the value of experience gained outside the confines of the experiment, i.e., in the marketplace. As Glaeser has pointed out, the subjects enrolled in an experiment face limited incentives, which are much stronger in the real world than in the laboratory. In experiments, individuals have few tools with which to improve their reasoning, and their only real method of responding to incentives is to think harder. Outside of the lab, people have access to advisers, books, the Internet, and more time. Their willingness to spend time and money to use these resources will surely depend on the stakes involved in the decision.

(Glaeser 2006: 140)

It is precisely because individuals invest more effort when making more important decisions that paternalistic policies relieving them of responsibility for those decisions will have the most corrosive effect upon their decision-making ability (see Klick and Mitchell 2006: 1635–1636). Klick and Mitchell describe this cost of libertarian paternalism as a type of moral hazard, which in the long run would raise error rates because people would invest less in error correction (Klick and Mitchell 2006: 1626). Nor is it reasonable to think the adverse effect will be felt with respect only to a narrow class of similar decisions; a muscle that has atrophied is rendered incapable of any strenuous activity, regardless of the particular purpose of that activity.

If individuals are to realize their full potential as participants in the political and economic life of society, then they must be free to err in large ways as well as small. The fatal flaw of libertarian paternalism is to ignore the value of the freedom to err. Interestingly, Hayek said as much in making the inherently anti-paternalistic case for *The Constitution of Liberty*: "Man learns by the disappointment of expectations" (Hayek 1960: 82). "Liberty not only means that the individual has both the opportunity and the burden of choice; it also means that he must bear the consequences of his actions and will receive praise or blame for them. Liberty and responsibility are inseparable" (Hayek 1960: 133). In a passage that, if heeded, would have saved the behaviorists a great deal of effort, he wrote:

> The justification for assigning responsibility is thus the presumed effect of this practice on future action; it aims at teaching people what they ought to consider in comparable future situations…. This does not mean that a man will always be assumed to be the best judge of his interests; it means merely that we can never be sure who knows them better than he.
>
> (Hayek 1960: 139)

James Buchanan also emphasizes the relationship between liberty and responsibility (Buchanan 2005: 23),[89] and in particular, individuals's demand for institutions that insulate them from responsibility: "Relatively few persons are sufficiently strong, as individuals, to take on the full range of liberties and their accompanying responsibilities without seeking some substitute or replacement of the parental shelter" (Buchanan 2005: 24). The role of economists is to remedy the "widespread failure to understand that the independence offered by the entry and exit options of the market offsets the *dependence* on others when markets are closed or displaced" (Buchanan 2005: 27). Hayek and Buchanan illustrate that the political and economic value of the freedom to err derives from the exercise of individuals's liberty, but requires sufficient independence from the state that individuals bear the costs of their choices.

Thinking about the implications of paternalism – soft or hard, libertarian or totalitarian – both for individuals and for the society they compose, yields some testable hypotheses. For one, we would expect people who were raised in a paternalistic state, and hence relieved of the need to make many important decisions for themselves, to have less well-developed decision-making skills and to be more risk averse. As it happens, there is a body of literature in cognitive psychology that tends to support this hypothesis; it proceeds from an understanding of the characteristics associated with entrepreneurship.

In general, "entrepreneurs ... exhibit a particular mode of information processing, or cognitive style" (Licht 2007: 819). They are more alert to opportunities that require linking previously unrelated information (Licht 2007: 824–825).[90] Indeed, the experimental literature strongly tends to validate Israel Kirzner's description of the Austrian tradition, which "postulates a tendency for profit opportunities to be *discovered* and *grasped* by routine-resisting entrepreneurial market participants" (Kirzner 1997: 71).

In a socialist state, however, resistance is futile. Uncritical acceptance of the party line is essential to survival, much less advancement. Of course, there are choices to be made: Shall I read Pravda or Izvestia? Yet the choice set has been limited by the state in a way that serves the state's ends, not those of the individual.[91] As Milan Simecka so graphically recounted from his personal experience after the Prague Spring of 1968, the Communist Party of Czechoslovakia controlled the citizenry by depriving individuals of their decisional autonomy in only three respects: The state determined their housing, their occupation, and their children's education (see Simecka 1984). That is why this professor of mathematics in mid-career became an operator of construction equipment. Perhaps it is not a coincidence that his book was published in 1984 (see Simecka 1984: 18).[92]

The end of the Soviet era in Russia and the Eastern European states it dominated, and the very substantial movement in China toward a market economy, provide useful comparisons. The Soviet experience uniquely spanned the lives of three generations over a period of seventy-four years (see Aidis *et al.* 2008: 658). The experience of Eastern Europe with communism lasted about forty-five years and in most places did not entail as comprehensive a form of state control over the economy;[93] unlike in Russia, therefore, at the end of the communist era there were many small business owners as well as people with pre-communist business experience who could rekindle the entrepreneurial spirit. China began to shift to a more privatized economy even in the late 1970s, after only thirty years of economic totalitarianism, again during the lifetime of pre-communist-era business people (Putterman 1996: 86).[94]

Transnational comparisons using data from the Global Entrepreneurship Monitor[95] produce strong evidence that, even after controlling for relevant variables, all countries with a communist past have a lower rate of entrepreneurship activity than do other countries (see Aidis *et al.* 2008: 658–659, 662). A recent study concludes that even now those unfortunate countries have "low levels of entrepreneurial human capital that have been engendered by decades of existence under a central planning system that tended to blunt individual incentives" (Robson 2007: 890). As one would expect, however, the level of entrepreneurship is "significantly lower in Russia" (Aidis *et al.* 2008: 657, 670).[96] A study conducted jointly by Russian and US scholars concludes that "[t]he absence of freedom of decision-making in the most important resource – the workforce – and the 'no-choice' employment situation were two fundamental obstacles to the development of entrepreneurship" during the communist era (Ageev *et al.* 1995: 369). After the fall of communism, moreover, Russian entrepreneurs tended to be younger than was typical elsewhere;[97] only the young were unscathed by their nation's paternalistic history.

A slippery slope

Of course, no proponent of regulation based upon the findings of behavioral economics espouses a regime remotely as encompassing and restrictive as even the least oppressive of the late, unlamented communist regimes. There is reason to believe, however, they would put us on a slippery slope – or push us that much further down the slope than we have already slid.[98]

Paternalistic policies are, by nature, likely to be slippery.[99] Such policies are expressed in regulations specifically adopted, at least initially, for the benefit of those regulated and, if those individuals do not want to be regulated for their own good – which is hardly unusual – the regulators will likely deem ever more stringent measures necessary. The federal laws protecting the occupants of automobiles provide a familiar historical example.[100] Initially, the regulators merely required manufacturers to install seatbelts in all automobiles. As the Supreme Court has recounted: "It became apparent, however, that most occupants simply would not buckle up their belts," so the regulators turned to requiring various passive restraints, including airbags, automatic seat belts, and briefly even an "ignition interlock" device that prevented a car from starting if an occupant had not fastened his seatbelt.[101] "But the interlock and buzzer devices were most unpopular with the public."[102] Then the regulators threatened the states with sanctions if they did not adopt laws requiring that seat belts be used (Huntington 2002: 101–102).[103]

Each of these mandates imposed a cost upon the manufacturers and the purchasers of automobiles, but not upon the government officials who formulated them. On the contrary, each successive measure tended to insulate the regulators from legislative and bureaucratic reprisals. Risk regulators – whether they supervise financial institutions, protect the environment, or certify foods and drugs as fit for use – face asymmetrical incentives that inevitably put them on a slippery slope: They stand to be criticized if their initial measures are insufficient to prevent all harms of the sort they are tasked (or have tasked themselves) with preventing; they will not be fully rewarded until they have fully accomplished their mission.

Also, regulatory missions tend to expand;[104] "mission creep" (Jenkins 2011: 805 n. 212)[105] assures that the government agency will require more money and more staff over time, forestalling any danger of the agency accomplishing its mission and becoming redundant (see, e.g., Djankov *et al.* 2002: 3; McChesney 1987: 117). Just as the development of a vaccine for polio threatened to put the March of Dimes charity out of business (see Greenwald 2008: 369; Sills 1957: 253–254) (and caused it to adopt a mission that could never be fully achieved, namely "improv[ing] the health of babies" worldwide [March of Dimes 2014]), government agencies are always on the lookout for conduct that needs to be regulated. Mission creep is a concern regardless of whether an agency's purpose is paternalistic, but with a mandate to regulate conduct for the benefit of the regulated individuals, there is no end to the good an agency may attempt to do at the expense of those individuals's freedoms.[106]

Once a regulation is in place it may well come to be accepted as the new norm. Extension of the regulation then seems like a modest and indeed logical next step (see Whitman and Rizzo 2007: 441).[107] Smoking bans are a case in point (see Rizzo and Whitman 2009a: 720–723). The federal government first determined that cigarette smoking is bad for the smoker's health and so advised the public. When the public's behavior did not conform to the regulators's expectations for what rational people would do, i.e., give up smoking, they ratcheted up the regulatory intervention: warnings were required on cigarette packages, tobacco advertisements were prohibited from television, and sin taxes were imposed upon the purchase of cigarettes (Rizzo and Whitman 2009a: 720). The regulators's preferences notwithstanding, millions of people continued to smoke cigarettes (see Centers for Disease Control and Prevention 2013). The federal government then publicized the hazard smoking posed to nonsmokers, which provided a new, externality-based rationale for banning smoking (see Rizzo and Whitman 2009a: 720). This rationale was flawed, of course, because there was no gap in the relevant property rights: Patrons of restaurants and bars who did not want to be exposed to secondhand smoke could take their custom elsewhere. The expressed concern for employees of those establishments was similarly flawed in that, unlike the unfortunate subjects of the Soviet system, they were free to change their place of employment. Eventually, the ban on smoking in bars and restaurants was generalized by many local governments to all indoor spaces and recently has spawned proposals to ban smoking out-of-doors in some localities,[108] notwithstanding the lack of any reason to be concerned with the welfare of third parties there.

As the assault on smoking proceeded down the slope, the justification for each new step zigged and zagged between the paternalistic and fallacious externality-based rationales. In fact, once smoking was deemed unhealthful to smokers and bystanders alike, the actual rationale for each next step became unimportant.[109] The previous step had established the new normal, and the next step was but a small effort to perfect implementation of the norm.

It is upon similarly flawed grounds that the historical concept of "public health" evolved from a concern with contagious disease (Turnock 2012: 4)[110] into a paternalistic, all-encompassing concern with the health of the public.[111] If smoking is unhealthful, that is now enough to deem it a matter of public health. So, too, with obesity[112] and other self-determined and noncontagious harms – if harms they are in the eyes of the individual who smokes or overeats.

The theoretical and empirical problems that make the case for behaviorally inspired regulation so weak also increase the probability that, once adopted, such a regulation will have an even more pronounced tendency to expand. If the regulation is justified on the ground that there is a divergence between the expressed preference and the "true preference" of the regulated persons, and assuming that, based upon experimental data worthy of reliance, the degree of that divergence can be estimated for each individual, the regulator will initially have to make his best guess as to the degree of debiasing pressure to exert. Suppose, for example, my true preference is to save more tomorrow for retirement – specifically, $100 more per month – or to eat a less fattening diet – specifically, enough less to lose one pound per month for twenty-five months. How much must the regulator burden my poor choices to spend rather than save and to indulge rather than abstain in order to goad me into making choices aligned with my true preferences? The answer, alas, is blowing in the wind and hence out of reach.

If the burden the regulator imposes initially does not produce the expected result, then it will seem self-evidently insufficient; the obvious, self-serving, and hence nearly inevitable response will be to ratchet up the pressure as many times and as much as needed, not to reexamine whether there is really a gap between the expressed and the true preference, whether it is of the magnitude estimated, and whether there are other explanations for the initial or successive burdens's failure to work as expected. Perhaps my true preference for saving, as detected in the laboratory, changed when a member of my family developed a health problem that made a more immediate demand upon my income. Perhaps I shifted my consumption of fattening foods, when they were taxed highly enough, to consumption of unhealthful quantities of foods that would not be fattening in the recommended serving size. As long as the regulator can tax only the inputs, and not the output in the form of a tax based upon my weight, it can only continue to cumulate the burdens in the hope of getting lucky. As the king might have said upon learning all his men and all his horses could not put Humpty Dumpty together again, this "simply proves to me that I must have more horses and more men" (Fradon 1978).

On the other hand, suppose the burden initially established by the regulator over-corrects the bias at which it is aimed. I start saving too much for retirement – that is, more than my true preference – because I would rather forgo present gratification than have my money go to the government in taxes; and I consume insufficient calories because I do not substitute healthful foods for the sweets I consumed before the sin tax took the pleasure out of eating. For all that appears to the regulator, the taxes it imposed upon unsaved income and fattening foods will have been a success. It will have no incentive to learn whether the regulation overshot the mark and induced an unexpected adaptation; doing so could only cause it to confess its error and ratchet down the tax. To admit to overregulating is more embarrassing than to confess to having underregulated, for the public is somewhat grudging about being regulated at all.[113]

Why this, why now?

Behavioral law and economics is produced primarily by law professors. As we have seen, the number of articles on behavioral law and economics appearing in law reviews has grown exponentially over the last ten years.[114] What, we now ask, accounts for the great and increasing attraction of the subject to legal academics?

For at least the last forty years, legal scholarship has been swept along by waves of fashion in academia, and the amplitude of those waves has been increasing. Starting around 1970, the Realist school that had dominated the legal academy for decades gave way increasingly to the newer field of economic analysis of law; particularly after Richard Posner published his treatise on that subject in 1973 (Posner 1973), scores of articles analyzing the economics of a particular legal doctrine appeared in law journals every year (see, e.g., Breit and Elzinga 1973; Epstein 1975; Goetz and Scott 1977; Kronman 1978; Posner 1977; Priest 1978; Schwartz and Wilde 1979). They contributed greatly to our understanding of the law as an instrument of social control and as a force for the promotion or diminution of economic growth. Articles and books in this genre continue to be published (see, e.g., Vandenberghe 2004; Temple *et al.* 2010), but they no longer have as large a share of the market.

In something of a reaction to the growing interest in economic analysis, a small but prolific cadre of law professors created the Critical Legal Studies (CLS) movement,[115] which in turn inspired cognate sub-schools such as Critical Race Theory,[116] Critical Feminism,[117] and Queer Theory.[118] CLS, which had a significant following, particularly among faculty at elite law schools, advanced the idea that all law, including court-made law, is indistinguishable from politics, particularly class politics (see, e.g., Horwitz 1977; Kelman 1987 ; 1979: 676–677; 1983 ; Unger 1975; Kennedy 1970; 1982: 591–592; 1985; 1987).[119] As recounted by Harvard Law School Professor Duncan Kennedy, a leading figure in the CLS movement, one of its early projects was to "produce a critique of mainstream economic analysis of law" (Kennedy 1998: 465).

Overtly a leftist movement (Kelman 1987: 1; Kennedy 1985: 1014, 1017), CLS turned out to be little more than a warmed-over species of Marxism, as it had evolved in the hothouse of radical European social theorists such as Herbert Marcuse, Jürgen Habermas and others of the Frankfurt School of neo-Marxist critical theorists, Antonio Gramsci, a leader of the Communist Party in Italy, and Michel Foucault, Jacques Derrida, and other "poststructuralist" philosophers (see Caudill 1987: 299–304; Gordon 1984: 102 n. 102). The self-declared purpose of the CLS movement was "to provide a critique of liberal legal and political philosophy" that would show the "liberal embrace of the rule of law is actually incompatible with other essential principles of liberal political thinking" (Altman 1990: 3).[120]

Key to the CLS analysis was the notion of "false consciousness,"[121] meaning the "holding of false or inaccurate beliefs that are contrary to one's own social interest and which thereby contribute to the maintenance of the disadvantaged position of the self or the group" (Jost 1995: 400).[122] Like the presumed gap between revealed preferences and "true preferences," assuming a wedge between reality and the perceptions of others provides a space to be filled by some combination of reeducation and outright coercion.[123] Duncan Kennedy encapsulates these Maoist[124] tendencies in his proposal that professors and janitors at the Harvard Law School be required to trade places for one month each year.[125] Kennedy described the ultimate goal of CLS as "building a left bourgeois intelligentsia that might one day join together with a mass movement for the radical transformation of American society" (Kennedy 1982: 610).

The end of the communist era in Russia and Eastern Europe dealt a blow to CLS, as it did to all leftist movements. The worldwide triumph of socialism, which had long seemed inevitable to so many, now seemed more improbable than ever. That is not to say that CLS surrendered or even went underground; the leading authors are still publishing (see Kennedy 2007; Lukes 2011), but new recruits are scarce.[126]

With interest in CLS and other "critical" movements waning, young legal scholars were in danger by the mid 1990s of being remitted to further work in economic analysis of law or even more traditional doctrinal exegesis. The widespread excitement and productive fervor of law and economics scholarship in the 1970s and 1980s, however, could not be recovered. Whereas the pioneering work had been done by academic lawyers who were autodidacts in economics, such as Richard Posner, Robert Bork, Henry Manne, Gordon Tullock, and Guido Calabresi (see, e.g., Bork 1978; Calabresi 1961 ; 1970; Posner 1973; Calabresi and Melamed 1972; Manne 1965; Tullock 1967), and by collaborations between those same academics and their economist colleagues (see, e.g., Calabresi and Klevorick 1985; Landes and Posner 1976),[127] by the mid 1990s all the leading law schools had appointed to their faculties one or more Ph.D. economists, many of whom also had a law degree. In other words, the field had grown up; the creative and talented amateurs gave way to highly trained professionals using the formal tools of economics and statistics. An assistant professor without significant formal training in economics could not hope to distinguish himself in law and economics, let alone write something to warrant his promotion to a tenured position.[128] What to do?

The answer came: Behavioral law and economics, for which a more than sophomoric understanding of economics was not required. Just as the first wave of law and economics scholarship had provided hundreds of opportunities to revisit plowed ground and turn up new insights, behavioral law and economics offered a reason to return to the same ground with confidence that the new approach would yield new results – results that could be published in one of the more than 750 non-peer-reviewed, student-edited law reviews.[129] Much of the early law and economics work had explored the hypothesis that a particular common law rule was efficient (see, e.g., Calabresi 1970: 311–318; Landes and Posner 1980: 517; Polinsky 1980: 1079–1080)[130] or, in the public choice variation, that a particular statutory provision served some special interest and was inefficient (see, e.g., Becker 1983: 394–396; Easterbrook 1984: 15–16; McChesney 1987: 101–103; Peltzman 1976: 240; Stigler 1971: 3–4).[131] In the new behavioral scholarship, the author would inevitably conclude the prevailing rule should be reformed to take account of the cognitive biases of the individuals subject to the rule[132] or to regulate some as yet unregulated conduct in order to protect individuals from their tendency to err as they pursue their self-interest.[133]

Because behavioral law and economics scholarship yields proposals for law reform less radical than what CLS had produced, it appeals to a larger segment of the legal professoriate than CLS ever did. At the same time, behavioral law and economics shares with CLS the paternalistic premise that the poor wretches to be benefited by the insights of their governors suffer from a form of "false consciousness." Behavioral law and economics scholars never use that term – the connotation would not be helpful – but they have built their entire enterprise upon its foundation. Indeed, we doubt legal academics would have seen the appeal of appropriating the fruits of cognitive research had they not first been exposed by CLS to the idea that individuals routinely fail to act in their own best interest as they themselves express it.

False consciousness is a hearty perennial, much like the notion that there is a "third way" of social organization that suffers from neither the arbitrary nature of government nor the unforgiving ways of the market. The staying power of the idea reflects the romantic notion that government can help individuals overcome their own frailties and conform their behavior to their stated goals.

The full effect the behaviorists's new formulation of this old idea will have upon policy is yet to be determined. Academic lawyers and economists who studied regulation and the economic analysis of law had a profound impact upon the government of the United States, starting in the Carter Administration. In those four years, the Congress passed significant deregulatory legislation affecting energy,[134] transportation,[135] and other sectors of the economy.[136] The Congress was less obliging during the Reagan Administration, but the president's appointees did much administratively to deregulate telecommunications,[137] finance,[138] energy,[139] and other sectors.[140] Reagan also appointed to the federal courts a number of law professors prominent in the economic analysis of law, including such luminaries as Richard Posner and Frank Easterbrook of the University of Chicago, Robert Bork and Ralph Winter of Yale, and Stephen F. Williams of the University of Colorado.

The Obama Administration has now made behavioral law and economics the foundation for its re-regulatory program (see Ferguson 2010: 18; Grunwald 2009: 29; Dorning 2010: 19).[141] The president appointed the leading proponent and popularizer of the behavioral approach, Cass Sunstein, to oversee the regulatory output of the executive branch (Ferguson 2010: 18). Whether this Administration will be able to work a substantial change in the government's approach to regulation is uncertain at best. Enduring changes of this magnitude cannot be made in a mere eight years, in large part because a change in political leadership does not effect a change in the composition of the bureaucracy;[142] the Administration's challenge is to educate the permanent staff in how to initiate regulatory proposals based upon the new behaviorism.

Conclusion

Even the least paternalistic version of behavioral law and economics makes two central claims about government regulation of seemingly irrational behavior: that (1) the behavioral regulatory approach, by manipulating the way in which choices are framed for consumers, will increase welfare as measured by individuals's own preferences; and (2) a central planner can and will implement the behavioral law and economics policy program in a manner that respects liberty and does not limit the choices available to individuals. Some economists and law professors have focused, in their disparate ways, upon these two claims, offering critiques grounded in microeconomic theory, empiricism, and public choice. The crux of their critiques, with which we agree, is that the behaviorists's welfare claims are in some cases misspecified and, in the others, unsupported by robust data; such data as exist are misinterpreted in support of a paternalist objective; and the behaviorists's cost–benefit analysis is woefully incomplete. While behavioral economics broadly, and behavioral law and economics in particular, are too new to support bold predictions about what future laboratory and field evidence might show, the theoretical and empirical infirmities plaguing the behavioral welfare claims suggest these faults will prove to be enduring limitations. Further, the chasm between the aggressive policy interventions proposed in the behavioral *law and* economics literature and the interventions (if any) warranted by existing behavioral economic theory and empirical evidence is a warning sign of a discipline far overextended.

Our primary goal in this chapter has been to draw attention to the second and less scrutinized of the behaviorists's claims, namely that behavioral law and economics poses no significant threat to liberty and individual autonomy. One need not await further evidence to conclude that this claim fails. The behaviorists's regulatory toolkit includes not only overt coercion, but also subtler forms of control, including interventions that would directly or indirectly either reduce the choices available to individuals or penalize individuals for pursuing their own preferences rather than following those of a regulator. Despite having adopted a narrow conception of liberty as consisting only of "choice preservation," the behaviorists's libertarian claims fail on their own terms. What Mill, Hayek, Friedman, and others taught about the "process aspect of freedom" – the liberty interest of a public that is not infantilized, has entrepreneurial spirit, and can learn effective decision making through experience – has no place in the behaviorists's regulatory calculus. So long as behavioral law and economics continues to ignore the value to economic welfare and individual liberty of leaving individuals, the freedom to choose and hence to err in making important decisions, libertarian paternalism will not only fail to fulfill its promise of increasing welfare while doing no harm to liberty; it will pose a significant risk of reducing both our welfare and our liberty.

Notes

* Joshua D. Wright is a Commissioner on the US Federal Trade Commission and a Professor of Law (on leave) at George Mason University School of Law. Douglas H. Ginsburg is a Senior Judge on the United States Court of Appeals for the District of Columbia Circuit and a Professor of Law at George Mason University School of Law. We thank Angela Diveley, Elyse Dorsey, Lisa Madalone, Judd Stone, Dana Brusca, and Bryan Heckenlively for research assistance, and workshop participants at George Mason University School of Law and Columbia University Law School for comments. This chapter was initially published by *Northwestern University Law Review* 106(3), 2012: 1033–1090.

1 We refer to adherents of behavioral law and economics as "behaviorists," but their work is not to be confused with the "radical behaviorism" of John Watson and B.F. Skinner. See, generally, (Skinner 1965), advocating a science of psychology focused upon external human behavior to the exclusion of consciousness and other internal phenomena, and (Watson 1913), defending the scientific study of human behavior.

2 Our analysis focuses upon Thaler and Sunstein's libertarian paternalism because their apparent commitment to "choice preservation" evinces a greater concern about liberty than do other behaviorists. For example, the "asymmetric paternalism" of Camerer prefers paternalism that "helps those whose rationality is bounded from making a costly mistake and harms more rational folks very little" (Camerer *et al.* 2003: 1254). This asymmetric paternalism makes no commitment to avoiding infringements upon individual autonomy. See (Camerer *et al.* 2003: 1219), which focuses upon paternalism justified because the benefits of error prevention to irrational decision makers would exceed the harm imposed upon rational individuals. As discussed *infra* in the section *Some behavioral law and economics regulatory proposals*, a number of behaviorist regulatory proposals would prohibit or tax certain products, reduce consumer choice, or otherwise reduce liberty. Thus, Thaler and Sunstein's libertarian paternalism represents a lower bound on the threat to liberty presented by the behaviorist regulatory agenda.

3 See *infra*, *Autonomy*, in which we contrast the "process aspect of freedom," which is focused upon means, with the "opportunity aspect of freedom," which is focused upon ends.

4 See (Alchian and Allen 1972: 114), which explains that in the model of perfectly competitive markets, "no unexploited opportunity of trade remains to enable any person to reach still more preferred situations by revision of the allocation of goods." Also see (Knight 1921: 76–87). For the history and implications of the model of perfect competition, see (Stigler 1957).

5 See also (Simon 1955), which suggests, based upon modern psychological insights, revisions to the traditional assumption of rationality in economic theory.

6 For a recent review of the literature, see (Jolls 2007: 115).

7 Articles exploring the quantitative and other relevant differences between laboratory and market conditions with respect both to study results and to cognitive biases include, e.g., (Haigh and List 2005; Levitt *et al.* 2010; List 2003; 2004; Gneezy and List 2006), which discuss the sensitivity of laboratory results to market environments where competition, expertise, and learning might be expected to ameliorate any biases.

8 Sunstein was formerly Administrator of the Office of Information and Regulatory Affairs, US Office of Management and Budget, which oversees the regulatory activity of the executive branch of the government, and is currently a law professor at Harvard Law School.

9 See *infra, From behavioral economics to behavioral law and economics.*

10 Thaler and Sunstein write: "Our goal here has been to defend libertarian paternalism, an approach that preserves freedom of choice but that authorizes both private and public institutions to steer people in directions that will promote their welfare." (Thaler and Sunstein 2003: 179).

11 See (Friedman 1953: 13), stating "Truly important and significant hypotheses will be found to have 'assumptions' that are wildly inaccurate descriptive representations of reality, and, in general, the more significant the theory, the more unrealistic the assumptions."

12 See (Klick and Mitchell 2006: 1627–1628, n. 20), stating:

> The dominant research program within behavioral decision theory, the heuristics and biases program, consists of a collection of robust empirical findings bound together by high-level concepts rather than an integrative theory that can predict how particular features of the mind and environment are likely to interact in particular cases.

13 Some notable early efforts to craft a general theory of errors include (Kőszegi and Rabin 2006) and (Kőszegi and Rabin 2007).

14 See *infra, Some behavioral law and economics regulatory proposals.*

15 See *infra, Empirical shortcomings: robustness and data interpretation.*

16 See also (Mitchell 2002b), which characterizes the policy prescriptions of behaviorists as relying upon the empirically false assumption that people uniformly suffer from certain cognitive biases.

17 In this narrow sense, prospect theory implicates rational choice behavior. As discussed, however, the reference-dependent preferences against which economic agents maximize generally arise from a form of cognitive bias such as "loss aversion."

18 See, e.g., (Issacharoff 1998: 1735), stating "[T]he endowment effect is the most significant empirical observation from behavioral economics"; (Kahneman *et al.* 2000: 159, 170), which describes the robustness of the endowment effect as "part of our endowment, and we are naturally keener to retain it than others might be to acquire it"; and (Korobkin 2003: 1229), stating "The endowment effect is undoubtedly the most significant single finding from behavioral economics for legal analysis to date."

19 Compare (Hoffman and Spitzer 1993: 99), which illustrates how a difference between a person's willingness to pay to purchase a good and the price the same person is willing to accept to sell the same good could prevent Coasean bargaining; and (Jolls *et al.* 1998: 1427), stating "[A]n important aspect of law and economics is the Coase theorem, which says that the assignment of a legal entitlement will not influence the ultimate allocation of that entitlement."

20 See (Buccafusco and Sprigman 2010: 13), stating "Recognition of the systematic discrepancy between owner and purchaser valuations has caused legal scholars to reevaluate many areas of the law where Coasean bargaining has been influential"; and (Sunstein 2002: 112), stating:

> The Coase Theorem fails to account for the fact that the initial allocation seems to create an endowment effect. When the endowment effect is at work, those who initially receive a legal right value it more than they would if the initial allocation had given the right to someone else (footnote omitted).

21 As of June 19, 2012, a search of the Westlaw Journals & Law Reviews (JLR)

database reveals 1,094 articles in legal periodicals referencing "endowment effect." The same search on Google Scholar shows 1,030 references in legal periodicals and court opinions. According to one legal scholar, a broader search for "endowment effect" *or* "status quo bias" revealed that the terms were referenced in only two legal periodicals in 1990 but in 373 by 2003 (Korobkin 2003: 1229).

22 See, e.g., (Buccafusco and Sprigman 2011: 51–52), which argues evidence of an endowment effect in experiments simulating intellectual property markets "undermine[s] the normative justification for an IP law structured around strong property rules"; and (Buccafusco and Sprigman 2010: 2–4).

23 See, e.g., (Bar-Gill 2004: 1375), which relies upon hyperbolic discounting to explain why people incur extensive credit card debt; (Gruber and Kőszegi 2004: 1960), which uses hyperbolic discounting to explain cigarette smoking; and (Weiss 1991: 1275), which discusses how imperfect self-control results in insufficient saving for retirement.

24 Optimism bias can be characterized as contextual; individuals reach inordinately optimistic conclusions due to their failure to process information that would give them an accurate risk perception. Nevertheless, most behaviorist commentators group optimism bias with irrational failures of self-control.

25 See (Bar-Gill 2004: 1376), which explains how optimism bias could cause consumers to underestimate the occurrence of a future event that might necessitate borrowing. On the other hand, pessimism bias occurs when an individual overestimates the occurrence of adverse events (Sunstein 2003: 773). Sunstein observes, "With respect to some low-probability events, including life-threatening risks such as AIDS, people actually tend to overestimate their own susceptibility, and in that sense seem to show pessimistic bias" (Sunstein 2003: 773).

26 See, generally, (Levitt and List 2007), which analyzes properties of human behavior that limit the power of inferences drawn from laboratory results in markets.

27 See (Glaeser 2006: 140), stating "In experiments, individuals have few tools with which to improve their reasoning, and their only real method of responding to incentives is to think harder."

28 See also sources cited *supra* note 7.

29 The most obvious failure is to attribute all errors to irrational behavior when rational economic agents would not reduce their error rate to zero because the gains to error reduction are small relative to its cost. For example, consumer errors in selecting the best credit card from among several choices are often attributed to irrational behavior despite the low cost of making an error that can readily be corrected with experience, the relatively high cost of analyzing competing offers, and evidence that the error rate declines as the cost of errors increases. See *infra, Data interpretation and rational error*.

30 See, e.g., (Buccafusco and Sprigman 2011: 51), which advocates various intellectual property reforms on the basis of experimental evidence.

31 Also see sources cited *supra* note 7.

32 Plott and Zeiler write, "While we do challenge the general accuracy of endowment effect theory, we do not challenge prospect theory" (Plott and Zeiler 2007: 1462). Others have also found prospect theory to have limited power in explaining WTA–WTP gaps. See (Kovalchik *et al.* 2005: 85–87), which finds results consistent with Plott and Zeiler on the endowment effect.

33 One recent study replies to Plott and Zeiler's findings and has elicited a response from them (see Isoni *et al.* 2011; Plott and Zeiler 2011).

34 A search on May 31, 2012, of the Westlaw JLR database for the term "endowment effect" resulted in 1,087 articles that include the term.

35 These results are based upon the search referenced *supra* note 34, with the results restricted to articles written after September 1, 2007.

36 Jolls, Sunstein, and Thaler write, "Behavioral law and economics, in short, offers the

potential to be law and economics with a higher 'R^2' – that is, greater power to explain the observed data" (Jolls *et al.* 1998: 1487).

37 See, generally, (Payne 1951; Rugg and Cantril 1944), which discuss how varying the wording of a question can affect survey outcomes.

38 Libertarian paternalists have relied upon framing effects, and particularly the endowment effect, to justify significant policy interventions, including switching the legal default rule from "at will" to "for cause" termination, redistributing various property rights, and preferring liability rules over property rules. See, e.g., (Korobkin 2003: 1259–1269, 1283–1287), which discusses proposals to redistribute property rights relying upon the endowment effect and favoring liability rules over property rules; and (Sunstein and Thaler 2003: 1187), which advocates the Model Employment Termination Act.

39 This point is doubly salient when one considers that behaviorists often assert the inapplicability of the Coase theorem due to the mere presence of transaction costs. See *supra, Contextualization errors: framing, prospect theory, and endowment effects.*

40 E.g., (Barr *et al.* 2008a: 12), stating "Credit card companies have fine-tuned product offerings and disclosures in a manner that appears to be systematically designed to prey on common psychological biases – biases that limit consumer ability to make rational choices regarding credit card borrowing"; (Bar-Gill and Warren 2008: 46–52), which provides examples of numerous product design features that can be used to exploit consumer biases; and (Warren 2010: 391), stating: "Businesses have learned to exploit customers' systematic cognitive errors, selling complex credit products that are loaded with tricks and traps."

41 That potential consumer irrationality is bounded by the level of the relevant cost is potent indirect evidence for the proposition that even relatively minor market pressures will dissipate behavioral errors made in a laboratory.

42 Demsetz wrote,

> The view that now pervades much public policy economics implicitly presents the relevant choice as between an ideal norm and an existing 'imperfect' institutional arrangement. This *nirvana* approach differs considerably from a *comparative institution* approach in which the relevant choice is between alternative real institutional arrangements.
>
> (Demsetz 1969: 1–3)

43 *Time Magazine* described the Obama Administration's advisers as a "behavioral dream team" that would rely upon behavioral economics to "transform the country" (Grunwald 2009: 29).

44 Warren, a prominent behaviorist in her own right, was charged with setting up the CFPB. For examples of her writing on behavioral economics and consumer choice, see (Bar-Gill and Warren 2008: 39) and (Warren 2007). Sendhil Mullainathan, a leading behavioral economist, was appointed CFPB Assistant Director for Research. For a criticism of the behavioral approach to regulating consumer credit, see (Evans and Wright 2010). The CFPB and its roots in behavioral law and economics are discussed *infra* in *Regulation of consumer credit*.

45 For a skeptical account of the implications of behavioral economics for antitrust, see (Wright and Stone 2012).

46 As of May 31, 2012, a search of the Westlaw JLR database finds 2,281 articles in legal periodicals referencing "behavioral economics." A search on Google Scholar turns up 2,190 legal opinions and articles referencing the same term.

47 Based on data that first appeared in (Ginsburg and Moore 2010: 93–96), which Figure 15.1 updates. The number of references in the Google Book search was compiled by the authors at books.google.com on December 22, 2010. The *y*-axis on the left-hand side of Figure 15.1 measures the number of times the term "behavioral

economics" appears in the Westlaw JLR database in the relevant time period. The *y*-axis on the right-hand side of Figure 15.1 measures the number of times each of the three terms appears in Google Books.

48 Data compiled by authors. The law schools are those of Yale University, Harvard University, the University of Chicago, New York University, Columbia University, Vanderbilt University, the University of California at Los Angeles, the University of Virginia, the University of Pennsylvania, and Georgetown University.

49 The ENABLE network, funded in part by the European Commission, completed its work in March 2008 (European Network for the Advancement of Behavioral Economics 2014a). The research training network enlisted several prominent figures in behavioral economics, including Daniel Kahneman of Princeton University and David Laibson of Harvard University (European Network for the Advancement of Behavioral Economics 2014b).

50 Descriptions of the behaviorist approach similarly vary, from Sunstein and Thaler's preferred "libertarian paternalism" to the more restrictive "asymmetric paternalism" and the more constraining "new paternalism." See (Camerer *et al.* 2003: 1212), stating: "A regulation is asymmetrically paternalistic if it creates large benefits for those who make errors, while imposing little or no harm on those who are fully rational"; and (Rizzo and Whitman 2009b: 908), stating:

> The new paternalism, by contrast, takes the individual's own subjective preferences as the basis for policy recommendations. New paternalist policies allegedly help the individual to better achieve his own subjective well-being, which cognitive impediments prevent him from attaining on his own.

51 See discussion *infra, The default rule.*

52 Behaviorists also rely on present bias and hyperbolic discounting in support of nudges that would increase savings (see, e.g., Laibson 1997).

53 Sunstein and Thaler write, "[E]mployers think (correctly, we believe) that most employees would prefer to join the 401(k) plan if they took the time to think about it and did not lose the enrollment form" (Sunstein and Thaler 2003: 1172–1173).

54 Accord (Thaler and Benartzi 2004: S186).

55 Sunstein and Thaler write, "The fact that very few participants choose to opt out supports (though it does not prove) the claim that they are helped by a system that makes joining easy" (Sunstein and Thaler 2003: 1191).

56 For a discussion of this point, see (Mitchell 2005: 1252, n. 24).

57 Recent evidence also supports skepticism concerning the claim that manipulating the choice architecture for retirement savings will "nudge" the decisions of those whose welfare will be increased while allowing nearly costless opt out by those whose welfare would not. See (Tergesen 2011), which discusses findings that while total 401(k) savings increased moderately due to greater participation at specified default rates, participants's average savings rates fell after adoption of auto-enrollment because individuals who would have opted for higher savings rates in the absence of auto-enrollment accept the lower auto-enrollment default rate.

58 See also (Barr *et al.* 2008a: 12–15), which discusses the potential structure of such rules and regulations.

59 This is consistent with the behaviorists's preference for legal requirements to call attention to particular risks in order to offset consumers's optimism bias, which causes them to underestimate the likelihood that they will personally suffer bad outcomes (see Jolls and Sunstein 2006: 212–213).

60 The CFPB has the broad authority to

> ensure that the features of any consumer financial product or service, both initially and over the term of the product or service, are fully, accurately, and effectively disclosed to consumers in a manner that permits consumers to

understand the costs, benefits, and risks associated with the product or service

(12 U.S.C. § 5532(a) (2006))

This provision may authorize, for example, a plain vanilla requirement, at least if the CFPB interprets the statute to mean all or nearly all consumers must understand disclosures before it authorizes a product. See, e.g., (Evans 2011), which explains that, even without explicit authority to do so,

> the [CFPB] can also steer financial services companies toward offering plain vanilla products designed by the CFPB by either banning products that don't conform to the CFPB view or by making it legally risky and expensive to deviate too far from the products that the CFPB wants;

and (Wright and Zywicki 2009: 41–44), which discusses the vague mandates of the Consumer Financial Protection Act.

61 See *supra, Self-Control problems: hyperbolic discounting and optimism bias*. The original analysis of such time-inconsistent preferences in economics is (Strotz 1955).
62 See (Schelling 1984: 84), stating:

> [P]eople act as if there were two selves alternately in command.... [T]he ways that people cope, or try to cope, with loss of command within or over themselves are much like the ways that one exercises command over a second individual (emphasis omitted).

63 See infra, *The search for true preferences*.
64 In the *Why this, why now?* section of this chapter, where we focus upon the underappreciated threat behavioral law and economics poses to individual liberty, we will assume for the sake of the argument that any given behavioral intervention offers a Pareto-superior alternative to the status quo.
65 See (Varian 2010: 121), which describes the core economic concept of revealed preference, whereby "[i]f a bundle X is chosen over a bundle Y, then X must be preferred to Y."
66 We discussed *supra*, in *Empirical shortcomings: robustness and data interpretation*, the empirical obstacles facing behaviorists relying on hyperbolic discounting models.
67 See (Rizzo and Whitman 2009b: 701), stating "[T]he normative standard inherent in any attempt to 'help' agents with hyperbolic preferences is *inherently vague*. We do not know where 'reasonable' impatience ends and 'excessive' patience begins." See also (Gul and Pesendorfer 2005: 38–39), stating:

> Economists often note the arbitrariness of using $U0$ as a welfare criterion in the multiselves model. It is not clear what hedonic utility calculations have led neuroeconomists to decide that $U0$ represents the right trade-off among the hedonic utilities of the various selves.

68 Gul and Pesendorfer describe this stance as "therapeutic" and "paternalistic," and "similar to the position of medical professionals who attempt to cure a patient's addiction" (Gul and Pesendorfer 2005: 39); accord (Becker and Murphy 1988: 681), which defines addiction as current behavior positively influencing future behavior.
69 In contract law, a default rule is a right that acts as the standard unless waived by the party it benefits (see Sunstein 2002: 107).
70 One alternative to the selection of a default rule may be to require that the individual make a choice – for example, about whether to participate in a payroll savings plan.
71 See also (Rachlinski 2006: 224–226), which discusses how "[t]he presence of significant individual variation in [cognitive] vulnerability" weakens the common cognitive psychology arguments supporting paternalistic interventions.

72 For a fuller explanation of the circumstances under which framing effects are likely to dissipate, see *supra, Experimental evidence and data accrual.*

73 Model Employment Termination Act §§ 3, 4(c), 7A U.L.A. 71, 312–313 (2002); (Sunstein and Thaler 2003: 1187).

74 See (Glaeser 2006: 134), stating "[I]f psychological errors are understood to be endogenous, then there are good reasons why we might think that public decision-making is likely to be more flawed than private decisionmaking."

75 Rachlinski writes, "The most common use of cognitive psychology in legal scholarship is to support paternalistic legal interventions" (Rachlinski 2006: 224).

76 For a discussion of the confirmation bias in the context of behavioral law and economics and its proponents, see (Mitchell 2002a).

77 Nor do Sunstein, Thaler, or other behaviorists appear to be concerned with a research program or policy agenda intended to "nudge" regulators and judges to more rational evaluation of data or improved decision making free from behavioral biases. For example, the behavioral literature does not appear to include cooling-off periods for regulatory decisions made in haste, or a plain vanilla requirement for novel applications of behavioral interventions that would require the government decision maker to be informed of the risks of policy error and the potential costs of unintended consequences. But see (Wright 2010).

78 See (Ginsburg and Moore 2010: 96–97), stating "[Behavioral economics] is almost the opposite of price theory, which narrows significantly the range of outcomes a court may reach"; instead it "increases the degrees of freedom with which a court may pursue personal, idiosyncratic goals."

79 Sahm, Shapiro, and Slemrod use survey data based upon telephone interviews to assess the impact of the tax rebates (Sahm *et al.* 2010: 6, n. 9).

80 Regulatory proposals that reduce welfare for the reasons described in the section *From behavioral economics to behavioral law and economics* of this chapter will necessarily reduce liberty. The theoretically plausible set of "close calls" involves interventions that would increase welfare while posing a significant threat to liberty.

81 For example, these liberty concerns are likely to dominate behaviorist regulatory proposals with positive, but trivial, expected welfare benefits.

82 Compare, e.g., (Locke 1960: 306), stating:

> [T]he end of Law is not to abolish or restrain, but *to preserve and enlarge Freedom....* Freedom is ... a *Liberty* to dispose, and order, as he lists, his Person, Actions, Possessions, and his whole Property, within the Allowance of those Laws under which he is; and therein not to be subject to the arbitrary Will of another, but freely follow his own.

83 Accord (Griffin 1986: 67), stating:

> One component of agency is deciding for oneself. Even if I constantly made a mess of my life, even if you could do better if you took charge, I would not let you do it. Autonomy has a value of its own.

84 Compare (Friedman and Friedman 1980: 27), which notes that "[s]elf-interest is not myopic selfishness. It is whatever it is that interests the participants, whatever they value, whatever goals they pursue," including their altruistic goals.

85 Sunstein and Thaler would assign zero weight to decisional autonomy unless it is linked with a welfare-based preference for decision making (Sunstein and Thaler 2003: 1198–1199). Sunstein and Thaler write, "Freedom of choice is itself an ingredient in welfare. In some situations people derive welfare from the very act of choosing.... But much of the time, especially in technical areas, people do not particularly enjoy the process of choice" (Sunstein and Thaler 2003: 1198–1199). In practice, they ignore it altogether.

86 Sunstein clarified the connection in an earlier work, instancing "the cafeteria at some

organization" and rather lamely suggesting that if the cafeteria's goal is profit maximization, then even

> those cafeterias that face competition will find that some of the time, market success will come not from tracking people's preferences, but from providing goods and services that turn out, in practice, to promote their welfare, all things considered. Consumers might be surprised by what they end up liking.
>
> (Sunstein 2005: 178–179)

Clearly Sunstein and Thaler have little to offer when they move from a coercive to a market environment, where consumers are sovereign.

87   See also (Byrnes 1998: 27–28), which relies upon the approach used in the field of artificial intelligence in formulating the self-regulation model for rational task analysis and observing "[n]o one would disagree with ... my claim that decision making requires the[se] four processes." The experimental literature shows that subsequent decisions are more likely to be improved by experiencing success or failure than by being told one's decision was a success or a failure and why (Byrnes *et al.* 1999: 1137). Experimental studies suggest "adults could progressively learn to make better decisions if they received relatively clear feedback from outcomes" (Byrnes *et al.* 1999: 1125, 1137). Byrnes *et al.* cite two studies in support of the general proposition adults will make better decisions as a result of clear feedback and two studies that conclude older children are more likely to exhibit improved decision making as a result of feedback than are young children (Byrnes *et al.* 1999: 1125, 1137). Klick and Mitchell have expanded somewhat upon Byrnes's findings, concluding that, because feedback is obtained "[t]hrough education, experimentation, experience, and observation," increased activity or opportunity in these areas will likewise lead individuals to "select the option that will lead to the most favorable outcomes" (Klick and Mitchell 2006: 1629). A related body of studies in experimental psychology shows that individuals better remember and more closely analyze unfavorable feedback than they do favorable feedback. See, e.g., (Ditto *et al.* 1998: 65).

88   Consistent with this inference, Vernon Smith and James Walker's review of the experimental literature on the effect of incentives on decision making finds that "[s]ome studies report observations that fail to support the predictions of rational models, but as reward level is increased the data shift toward these predictions" (Smith and Walker 1993: 259–260). Consequences need not be serious, however, for the effect of a choice to provide valuable feedback; studies show the repetition of feedback that accompanies making similar decisions may be useful to the decision-making process. See (List 2003: 70), stating, "I find strong evidence that individual behavior converges to the neoclassical prediction as trading experience intensifies"; and (Smith 1994: 118), which notes that rational behavior tends to emerge "in the context of a repetitive market institution."

89   Buchanan observes that the academy has "failed to emphasize sufficiently, and to examine the implications of, the fact that liberty carries with it *responsibility*" (Buchanan 2005: 23).

90   See also (Gaglio and Katz 2001: 96–98).

91   See (Verdery 1996: 26), which explains that the purpose of socialism was "to accumulate means of production" in order "to redirect resources to a goal greater than satisfying the population's needs."

92   See also (Devlin 1982).

93   See, e.g., (Judt 2005: 428), which notes that Hungary under János Kádár implemented economic reforms in 1968 to promote a "mixed economy" with some local autonomy and private ownership; and (Lipton and Sachs 1990: 80–82), which notes that farmers in Poland "retained their private land after World War II," and a larger though still restricted "private sector ha[d] been allowed to operate under the reforms in Hungary and Poland" during communism.

94 Putterman writes, "The period from 1978 to the early 1990s was marked by a massive shift ... with significant new participation by foreign and domestic private firms" (Putterman 1996: 86). See also (Alsén 1996: 20–21), which details the shift to more private ownership in China beginning in 1978; and (Cudahy 2010: 53–56), which notes "[t]he flexibility of the Chinese in economic matters seemed to far exceed the Soviets" and discusses China's cautious shift toward privatization.

95 Global Entrepreneurship Monitor, www.gemconsortium.org (last visited June 27, 2014).

96 Aidis *et al.* attribute the difference in part to weak institutions to support entrepreneurial development (Aidis *et al.* 2008: 657, 670).

97 See (Ageev *et al.* 1995: 374), which finds entrepreneurs in Russia are younger than their counterparts in Poland and Hungary.

98 See (Whitman and Rizzo 2007: 412), stating:

> A slippery slope argument is one suggesting that a proposed policy or course of action that might appear desirable now, when taken in isolation, is in fact undesirable (or less desirable) because it increases the likelihood of undesirable policies being adopted in the future.

99 See (Rizzo and Whitman 2009a: 691–705), stating "slippery slopes flourish in the presence of a gradient or continuum," and "[t]he new paternalist paradigm ... relies on discarding sharp distinctions in favor of gradients."

100 For a brief history of federal seat belt laws, see (Huntington 2002: 101–104).

101 See *Geier* v. *Am. Honda Motor Co.*, 529 U.S. 861, 875–77 (2000) (discussing the history of federal regulations requiring passive restraints).

102 See *Geier* v. *Am. Honda Motor Co.*, 529 U.S. 861, 876 (2000).

103 States without mandatory seatbelt laws also receive reduced federal funding for highway maintenance (Huntington 2002: 102).

104 See (Friedman 1993: 9), stating

> The general rule is that government undertakes an activity that seems desirable at the time. Once the activity begins, whether it proves desirable or not, people in both the government and the private sector acquire a vested interest in it. If the initial reason for undertaking the activity disappears, they have a strong incentive to find another justification for its continued existence.

See also (Rizzo and Whitman 2009a: 717–723), which argues that the adoption of a moderate paternalist policy makes the adoption of further policies more likely because the proponent can argue the now-accepted justification for the first policy also provides a foundation for the new policy.

105 Jenkins writes, "Mission creep refers to an organizational phenomenon in which entities inadvertently, over time, stray from their fundamental mission by engaging in activities or behaviors less closely related to the core ... purpose" (Jenkins 2011: 805, n. 212).

106 See *Olmstead* v. *United States*, 277 U.S. 438, 479 (1928) (Brandeis, J., dissenting):

> Experience should teach us to be most on our guard to protect liberty when the Government's purposes are beneficent. Men born to freedom are naturally alert to repel invasion of their liberty by evil-minded rulers. The greatest dangers to liberty lurk in insidious encroachment by men of zeal, well-meaning but without understanding.

107 Compare (Lessig 1998: 666–672), which describes work by scholars concluding law can regulate social norms; and (Sunstein 1996: 964), stating:

> Many laws have an expressive function. They "make a statement" about how much, and how, a good or bad should be valued. They are an effort to constitute

and to affect social meanings, social norms, and social roles. Most simply, they are designed to change existing norms and to influence behavior in that fashion.

108 See, e.g., (Chan 2009), which discusses the New York City Health Commissioner's proposal to ban smoking at city parks and beaches.

109 See (Rizzo and Whitman 2009a: 722), stating "[F]urther restriction of public smoking became acceptable with little or no evidence of significant harm to bystanders.").

110 Turnock notes the "clear intent" of creating state public health agencies in the late nineteenth century was that their "powers be used to battle epidemics of infectious diseases" (Turnock 2012: 4).

111 For example, the Office of the Assistant Secretary for Health – formerly the Office of Public Health and Science, 75 Fed. Reg. 53,304 (August 31, 2010) – currently comprises eleven public health offices with missions ranging from "improv[ing] the quality of healthcare across the United States" to "[c]oordinat[ing] adolescent health promotion and disease prevention" (United States Department of Health and Human Services 2014). The World Health Organization, the objective of which is "the attainment by all peoples of the highest possible level of health," defines "health" as "a state of complete physical, mental and social well-being and not merely the absence of disease or infirmity" (World Health Organization 2006). Similarly, the mission of the US National Institutes of Health is "to enhance health, lengthen life, and reduce the burdens of illness and disability" (National Institutes of Health 2013).

112 The legal effort to promote more healthful eating started in 1990 with the enactment of the Nutrition Labeling and Education Act, which authorized the Food and Drug Administration to issue rules requiring that food bear nutrition labels. See Pub. L. No. 101–535, 104 Stat. 2353 (1990); see also 21 C.F.R. pt. 101 (implementing regulations). This effort has evolved into outright bans on the use of trans fats in restaurants. N.Y.C. Admin. Code § 81.08 (West 2006). The Centers for Disease Control refers to obesity as an "epidemic" (Centers for Disease Control and Prevention 2009: 2). The Centers for Disease Control writes,

> American society has become 'obesogenic,' characterized by environments that promote increased food intake, nonhealthful foods, and physical inactivity. Public health approaches that affect large numbers of different populations in multiple settings – communities, schools, work sites, and health care facilities – are needed.

113 In addition, as pointed out by (Rizzo and Whitman 2009a: 717), "rent-seeking activities impart a particular direction to slippery slopes.... As a result, we are unlikely to observe 'backward' slippage toward more laissez-faire policies" (emphasis omitted).

114 See *supra* Figure 15.1. See also (Ginsburg and Moore 2010: 94), which catologs the number of law review articles discussing behavioral economics.

115 See (Kelman 1987: 1), stating:

> [T]he first annual Conference on Critical Legal Studies in 1977 gave little hint as to what the organizers thought 'critical legal studies' (CLS) was or might become.... [T]he organizers were simply seeking to *locate* those people working either at law schools or in closely related academic settings [who were] ... something akin to New Leftists.

116 See (Delgado and Stefancic 2000: xvi), which notes that Critical Race Theory "has predecessors – Critical Legal Studies, to which it owes a great debt."

117 See, generally, (Rhode 1990: 617–619), which charts the relationship between CLS and feminist theories, identifying "crosscutting objectives, methodologies, and concerns" between the two fields and observing a "growing body of feminist and critical

race scholarship … developed along lines that paralleled, intersected, and challenged critical legal theory."

118 See (Valdes 1995: 29), stating "[T]his project endeavors to enlist critical legal theories and theorists in an effort to create a space and a framework for holistic and contextual critiques of sex, gender, and sexual orientation as legal (and social) concepts." See also (Kotkin 1998: 101–102), stating:

> Critical jurisprudence also finds expression in feminist legal theory, critical race theory, and queer theory. These movements are alternatively viewed as offshoots of CLS or independent schools of legal thought that changed the focus of CLS. In either case, by the late 1980s, critical scholarship had shifted to some degree from exclusively economic analysis to the exploration of how issues of race, gender, and sexuality determine legal outcomes.

119 For a more complete bibliography of the CLS movement, see (Kennedy and Klare 1984).

120 Accord (Kelman 1987: 1–8).

121 This phrase is often attributed directly to Marx. But see (McCarney 2005), which questions whether Marx ever actually described ideology as "false consciousness." The phrase, if not the concept, seems actually to derive from an early translation of a letter Friedrich Engels wrote to Franz Mehring (see Barrett 1991: 5–6).

122 Accord (Delgado 1993: 653, n. 57), which defines "false consciousness" as the "phenomenon in which the oppressed come to identify with their oppressors, internalize their views, and thus appear to consent to their own subordination."

123 As one student of Kennedy's put it, the phrase "implies that all those who disagree with you are stupid" (Kahlenberg 1999: 166).

124 See (Froomkin 2003: 768), which notes that under Habermas's theory of self-deception, "[e]xplanation, education, discussion, and even therapy may serve to allow everyone except those suffering from the worst forms of self-delusion to understand (or, at least, better understand) their true interests"; and (Munro 2002: 103), stating:

> [I]f we use class education and political-line education to profoundly re-educate the mentally ill in the proletarian worldview … and raise their awareness of the class struggle, the struggle over political line and the need to continue the revolution under the dictatorship of the proletariat … and dig out the roots of mental illness by overthrowing the concept of private ownership and implanting the principle of public ownership … then the overwhelming majority (90%) of mentally ill people can be completely cured.
>
> (Quoting Jia Rubao, a psychiatrist from Shaanxi Province, April 1977)

125 See (Kennedy 1982: 615), which proposes legal education be reformed by

> equaliz[ing] all salaries in the school (including secretaries and janitors), regardless of educational qualifications, 'difficulty' of job, or 'social contribution'" and encouraging every university employee or faculty member to "spend one month per year performing a job in a different part of the hierarchy from his normal job, [so that] over a period of years everyone [is] trained to do some jobs at each hierarchical level.

See also (Beck 1988: 447), stating "Among [Kennedy's] more familiar proposals is his suggestion that law schools allocate positions in the starting class by lottery to all students possessing minimum qualifications and that janitors and law professors periodically switch jobs."

126 See (Sunstein 2001: 1255), which discusses the disappearance of Critical Legal Studies from law schools. In 2007, Brian Leiter compiled a list of the most cited faculty members by specialty, including Critical Theories, which includes Critical

Legal Studies, Critical Race Theory, and Feminist Legal Theory. The ages of the top twenty members ranged from mid forties to sixties, showing a lack of young entrants in the field (Leiter 2007). More recently, the 2010–2011 edition of the *Association of American Law Schools Directory of Law Teachers* listed only ninety-nine professors with one to five years of experience currently teaching Critical Theories, which also includes Critical Legal Studies, Critical Race Theory, and Feminist Legal Theory (Association of American Law Schools 2011: 1627–1628, 1669–1670).

127 Pioneering examples include (Buchanan and Tullock 1962; Bork and Bowman 1965; Director and Levi 1956).

128 See, generally, (Manne and Wright 2008: 10–11), which discusses the shift toward the modern, formal, mathematical approach to economics and its implication for law and economics and legal education.

129 The Berkeley Electronic Press law review submission service, ExpressO, includes more than 750 student-edited law reviews and journals. See *List*, ExpressO, http:// law.bepress.com/expresso/list.html (last visited August 13, 2012).

130 Compare (Langbein and Posner 1980: 77–96), which argues conventional investment practices of trusts are inadequate with the portfolio theory and therefore yield inadequate returns.

131 Easterbrook writes,

> People demand laws just as they demand automobiles, and some people demand more effectively than others. Laws that benefit the people in common are hard to enact because no one can obtain very much of the benefit of lobbying for or preserving such laws. Smaller, more cohesive groups are more effective lobbyists. These groups can obtain a greater share of the benefits of laws targeted to assist people who have common characteristics, and so they will raise more money and campaign for legislation more effectively.... It also turns out that small, cohesive groups can get more for themselves by restricting competition and appropriating rents than by seeking rules that enhance the welfare of all. Thus we should expect regulatory programs and other statutes to benefit the regulated group – they need not "capture" the programs, because they owned them all along. The burgeoning evidence showing that regulatory programs increase prices for consumers and profits for producers supports this understanding.
>
> (Easterbrook 1984: 15–16)

132 See, e.g., (Barr *et al.* 2008b: 197–198), which argues for a default option of plain vanilla mortgages.

133 Nutrition labeling on menus exemplifies well the creeping nature of paternalism. Initially required by only a few cities and states – most notably, New York City, Philadelphia, and the state of California – the House of Representatives proposed to bring nutrition labels to restaurant menus nationwide in its first three drafts of the Affordable Health Care for America Act. See (Wang 2010). See also Affordable Health Care for America Act, H.R. 3962, 111th Cong. § 2572 (2009) (as introduced to the Senate on November 16, 2009). The labeling provision did not survive the Senate, Preservation of Access to Care for Medicare Beneficiaries and Pension Relief Act of 2010, Pub. L. No. 111–192, 124 Stat. 1280, but it is unlikely we have seen the last of the nutrition-labeling proposal.

134 See, e.g., Natural Gas Policy Act of 1978, Pub. L. No. 95–621, 92 Stat. 3350 (codified as amended in scattered sections of 5, 12, 15, 16, and 42 U.S.C.) (phasing out price regulations); Emergency Natural Gas Act of 1977, Pub. L. No. 95–2, 91 Stat. 4 (codified at 15 U.S.C. § 717).

135 See, e.g., Staggers Rail Act of 1980, Pub. L. No. 96–448, 94 Stat. 1895 (codified as amended in scattered sections of 5 and 49 U.S.C.); Motor Carrier Act of 1980, Pub. L. No. 96–296, 94 Stat. 793 (codified in scattered sections of 49 U.S.C.); Airline

Deregulation Act of 1978, Pub. L. No. 95–504, 92 Stat. 1705 (codified in scattered
sections of 49 U.S.C.); Air Cargo Deregulation Act of 1977, Pub. L. No. 95–163, 91
Stat. 1278 (codified as amended in scattered sections of 26 and 49 U.S.C.).
136 See, e.g., Depository Institutions Deregulation and Monetary Control Act of 1980,
Pub. L. No. 96–221, 94 Stat. 132 (codified in scattered sections of 12, 15, 22, 38,
and 42 U.S.C.) (preempting various state restrictions on mortgages).
137 See, e.g., Revision of Programming & Commercialization, Policies, Ascertainment
Requirements, & Program Log Requirements for Commercial Television Stations, 6
FCC Rcd. 5093 (1991) (eliminating ascertainment requirements and programming
guidelines for commercial television); Syracuse Peace Council, 2 FCC Rcd. 5043,
5052 (1987) (invalidating "fairness doctrine" as unconstitutional and contrary to
public interest), *aff'd*, Syracuse Peace Council v. FCC, 867 F.2d 654 (D.C. Cir.
1989); Amendment of Part 73 of the Comm'n's Rules & Regulations in Regard to
Section 73.642(a)(3) & Other Aspects of the Subscription Television Serv., 90
F.C.C.2d 341 (1982) (abolishing various programming and other restrictions for subscription television); *In re* Deregulation of Radio, 84 F.C.C.2d 968 (1981).
138 See, e.g., Shelf Registration, Securities Act Release No. 33–6499, 48 Fed. Reg.
52,889 (November 23, 1983) (codified as amended at 17 C.F.R. § 230.415) (reducing registration requirements for mortgage-related securities); (Turner 1986: 1744),
which describes the willingness of the Comptroller of the Currency in the Reagan
Administration to charter "nonbank banks," thereby allowing companies to escape
restrictions of various banking laws and regulations.
139 See, e.g., Exec. Order No. 12,287, 46 Fed. Reg. 9909 (January 30, 1981) (eliminating oil price controls immediately rather than phasing out over time).
140 See Improvement of TOFC/COFC Regulation, 46 Fed. Reg. 14,348, 14,352 (1981)
(exempting "piggyback" services from certain railway and trucking rules); (Wallace
1988: 938–941), which describes the Commission's largely successful efforts at
deregulating the transportation industry in the 1980s.
141 Dorning writes,

> [T]he behavioralists could be influencing regulations long after [Peter] Orszag
> leaves [OMB]. Their ideas have been seeded in numerous initiatives, just as the
> regulatory state is poised for a dramatic comeback following decades of
> retrenchment. Other promoters include Michael S. Barr, the Assistant Treasury
> Secretary for Financial Institutions, who helped draft Obama's Wall Street
> reforms.
> (Dorming 2010: 19)

The first chairman of President Obama's Council of Economic Advisers was Austan
Goolsbee, who is sympathetic to (but not himself a practitioner of) behavioral economics (see Montgomery 2010).
142 Indeed, the CFPB is perhaps the only major behavioral law and economics initiative
that was realized during the president's first term.

References

Agarwal, S., Chomsisengphet, S., Liu, C., and Souleles, N.S. (2006) 'Do consumers
choose the right credit contracts?', unpublished manuscript, available at http://papers.
ssrn.com/sol3/papers.cfm?abstract_id=843826.
Ageev, A.I., Gratchev, M., and Hisrich, R. 'Entrepreneurship in the Soviet Union and
post-socialist Russia', *Small Business Economics* 7, 1995: 365–376.
Aidis, R., Estrin, S., and Mickiewicz, T. 'Institutions and entrepreneurship development
in Russia: a comparative perspective', *Journal of Business Venturing* 23, 2008:
656–672.

Alchian, A.A. and Allen, W.R. (1972) *University Economics*, 3rd edn, Belmont, CA: Wadsworth Publishing Company.

Alchian, A.A. 'Uncertainty, evolution, and economic theory', *The Journal of Political Economy* 58, 1950: 211–221.

Alsén, J. 'An introduction to Chinese property law', *Maryland Journal of International Law and Trade* 20, 1996: 1–60.

Altman, A. (1990) *Critical Legal Studies: A Liberal Critique*, Princeton, NJ: Princeton University Press.

Arlen, J., Spitzer, M., and Talley, E. 'Endowment effects within corporate agency relationships', *The Journal of Legal Studies* 31, 2002: 1–37.

Association of American Law Schools (2011) '2010–2011 directory of law teachers'.

Bar-Gill, O. 'Seduction by plastic', *Northwestern University Law Review* 98, 2004: 1373–1434.

Bar-Gill, O. and Warren, E. 'Making credit safer', *University of Pennsylvania Law Review* 157, 2008: 1–101.

Barr, M.S., Mullainathan, S., and Shafir, E. (2008a) *Behaviorally Informed Financial Services Regulation*, Washington, DC: New America Foundation.

Barr, M.S., Mullainathan, S., and Shafir, E. (2008b) 'Behaviorally informed home mortgage credit regulation', in N.P. Retsinas and E.S. Belsky (eds.) *Borrowing to Live: Consumer and Mortgage Credit Revisited*, Washington, DC: Brookings Institution Press.

Barrett, M. (1991) *The Politics of Truth: From Marx to Foucault*, Stanford, CA: Stanford University Press.

Beck, R. 'The faith of the "crits": critical legal studies and human nature', *Harvard Journal of Law and Public Policy* 11, 1988: 433–459.

Becker, G.S. 'Irrational behavior and economic theory', *The Journal of Political Economy* 70, 1962: 1–13.

Becker, G.S. 'A theory of competition among pressure groups for political influence', *The Quarterly Journal of Economics* 98, 1983: 371–400.

Becker, G.S. and Murphy, K.M. 'A theory of rational addiction', *The Journal of Political Economy* 96, 1988: 675–700.

Bork, R.H. (1978) *The Antitrust Paradox: A Policy at War with Itself*, New York: Basic Books.

Bork, R.H. and Bowman, Jr., W.S. 'The crisis in antitrust', *Columbia Law Review* 65, 1965: 363–376.

Breit, W. and Elzinga, K.G. 'Antitrust penalties and attitudes toward risk: an economic analysis', *Harvard Law Review* 86, 1973: 693–713.

Brown, T. and Plache, L., 'Paying with plastic: maybe not so crazy', *University of Chicago Law Review* 73, 2006: 63–86.

Buccafusco, C. and Sprigman, C.J. 'The creativity effect', *University of Chicago Law Review* 78, 2011: 31–52.

Buccafusco, C. and Sprigman, C. 'Valuing intellectual property: an experiment', *Cornell Law Review* 96, 2010: 1–45.

Buchanan, J.M. 'Afraid to be free: dependency as desideratum', *Public Choice* 124, 2005: 19–31.

Buchanan, J.M. and Tullock, G. (1962) *The Calculus of Consent: Logical Foundations of a Constitutional Democracy*, Ann Arbor, MI: University of Michigan Press.

Byrnes, J.P. (1998) *The Nature and Development of Decision Making: A Self-Regulation Model*, Mahwah, NJ: L. Erlbaum Associates.

Byrnes, J.P., Miller, D.C., and Reynolds, M. 'Learning to make good decisions: a self-regulation perspective', *Child Development* 70, 1999: 1121–1140.

Calabresi, G. 'Some thoughts on risk distribution and the law of torts', *Yale Law Journal* 70, 1961: 499–553.

Calabresi, G. (1970) *The Costs of Accidents: A Legal and Economic Analysis*, New Haven, CT: Yale University Press.

Calabresi, G. and Klevorick, A.K. 'Four tests for liability in torts', *The Journal of Legal Studies* 14, 1985: 585–627.

Calabresi, G. and Melamed, D.A. 'Property rules, liability rules, and inalienability: one view of the cathedral', *Harvard Law Review* 85, 1972: 1089–1128.

Camerer, C., Issacharoff, S., Loewenstein, G., and O'Donoghue, T. 'Regulation for conservatives: behavioral economics and the case for asymmetric paternalism', *University of Pennsylvania Law Review* 151, 2003: 1211–1254.

Caudill, D.S. 'Disclosing tilt: a partial defense of critical legal studies and a comparative introduction to the philosophy of the law-idea', *Iowa Law Review* 72, 1987: 287–358.

Centers for Disease Control and Prevention (2009) *Obesity: Halting the Epidemic by Making Health Easier*, available at www.cdc.gov/chronicdisease/resources/publications/AAG/pdf/obesity.pdf.

Centers for Disease Control and Prevention (2013) 'Trends in current cigarette smoking among high school students and adults, United States, 1965–2010', www.cdc.gov/tobacco/data_statistics/tables/trends/cig_smoking/index.htm (last visited June 27, 2014).

Centre for Economic Policy Research (n.d.) 'First European summer symposium in behavioural economics', available at www.cepr.org/meets/meetings/meetdesc.asp?meetno=5525 (last visited August 13, 2012).

Chan, S. '"No smoking" could be rule outdoors, too', *New York Times*, September 15, 2009: A1.

Cudahy, R.D. 'From socialism to capitalism: a winding road', *Chicago Journal of International Law* 11, 2010: 39–65.

Delgado, R. 'Rodrigo's sixth chronicle: intersections, essences, and the dilemma of social reform', *New York University Law Review* 68, 1993: 639–674.

Delgado, R. and Stefancic, J. (eds.) (2000) *Critical Race Theory: The Cutting Edge*, 2nd edition, Philadelphia, PA: Temple University Press.

Demsetz, H. 'Information and efficiency: another viewpoint', *The Journal of Law and Economics* 12, 1969: 1–22.

Demsetz, H. 'The theory of the firm revisited', *Journal of Law, Economics, & Organization* 4, 1988: 141–161.

Devlin, K. (1982) *How Normal is Normalization?*, Munich, Germany: Radio Free Europe, available at www.osaarchivum.org/files/holdings/300/8/3/pdf/139-4-7.pdf.

Director, A. and Levi, E.H. 'Law and the future: trade regulation', *Northwestern University Law Review* 51, 1956: 281–296.

Ditto, P.H., Scepansky, J.A., Munro, G.D., Apanovitch, A.M., Lockhart, L.K., and Kruglanski, A.W. 'Motivated sensitivity to preference-inconsistent information', *Journal of Personality and Social Psychology* 75, 1998: 53–69.

Djankov, S., La Porta, R., Lopez-De-Silanes, F., and Shleifer, A. 'The regulation of entry', *Quarterly Journal of Economics* 117, 2002: 1–37.

Dorning, M. 'A beachhead for the behavorialists [sic]', *Business Week*, June 28, 2010: 19.

Easterbrook, F.H. 'Foreword: the court and the economic system', *Harvard Law Review* 98, 1984: 4–60.

Epstein, R.A. 'Unconscionability: a critical reappraisal', *Journal of Law and Economics* 18, 1975: 293–315.

Ericson, K.M.M. and Fuster, A. 'Expectations as endowments: evidence on reference-dependent preferences from exchange and valuation experiments', *Quarterly Journal of Economics* 126, 2011: 1879–1907.

European Network for the Advancement of Behavioral Economics (2014a) 'Enable', http://dev3.cepr.org/Research/Networks/enable/www.cepr.org/research/networks/enable/ (last visited June 27, 2014).

European Network for the Advancement of Behavioral Economics (2014b) 'People', http://dev3.cepr.org/Research/Networks/enable/people_new.htm (last visited June 27, 2014).

Evans, D.S. (2011) 'Who's watching the watchmen? Oversight of the consumer financial protection bureau: hearing before the subcomm. on tarp, financial services & bailouts of public and private programs of the house committee on oversight and government reform', 112th Cong. 50.

Evans, D.S. and Wright, J.D. 'The effect of the Consumer Financial Protection Agency Act of 2009 on consumer credit', *Loyola Consumer Law Review* 22, 2010: 277–335.

ExpressO (2014) 'List', http://law.bepress.com/expresso/list.html (last visited June 27, 2014).

Ferguson, A. 'Nudge nudge, wink wink: behavioral economics – the governing theory of Obama's nanny state', *The Weekly Standard*, April 19, 2010: 18–23.

Fischel, W.A. 'The offer/ask disparity and just compensation for takings: a constitutional choice perspective', *International Review of Law & Economics* 15, 1995: 187–203.

Fradon, D. 'Gentlemen, the fact that all my horses and all my men couldn't put Humpty...', *New Yorker*, July 24, 1978: 29.

Frederick, S., Loewenstein, G., and O'Donoghue, T. (2003) 'Time discounting and time preference: a critical review', in G. Loewenstein, D. Read, and R.F. Baumeister (eds.) *Time and Decision: Economic and Psychological Perspectives on Intertemporal Choice*, New York: Russell Sage Foundation.

Friedman, M. (1953) 'The methodology of positive economics', in M. Friedman, *Essays in Positive Economics*, Chicago, IL: University of Chicago Press.

Friedman, M. (1993) *Why Government is the Problem*, Stanford, CA: Hoover Institution Press.

Friedman, M. and Friedman, R. (1980) *Free to Choose: A Personal Statement*, New York: Harcourt Brace Jovanovich.

Froomkin, M. 'Habermas@discourse.net: toward a critical theory of cyberspace', *Harvard Law Review* 116, 2003: 749–873.

Gaglio, C.M. and Katz, J.A. 'The psychological basis of opportunity identification: entrepreneurial alertness', *Small Business Economics* 16, 2001: 95–111.

Ginsburg, D.H. and Moore, D.W. 'The future of behavioral economics in antitrust jurisprudence', *Competition Policy International* 6, 2010: 89–98.

Glaeser, E.L. 'Paternalism and psychology', *University of Chicago Law Review* 73, 2006: 133–156.

Gneezy, U. and List, J.A. 'Putting behavioral economics to work: testing for gift exchange in labor markets using field experiments', *Econometrica* 74, 2006: 1365–1384.

Goetz, C.J. and Scott, R.E. 'Liquidated damages, penalties and the just compensation principle: some notes on an enforcement model and a theory of efficient breach', *Columbia Law Review* 77, 1977: 554–594.

Gordon, R.W. 'Critical legal histories', *Stanford Law Review* 36, 1984: 57–125.

Greenwald, H.P. (2008) *Organizations: Management Without Control*, Los Angeles, CA: Sage Publications.

Griffin, J. (1986) *Well-Being: Its Meaning, Measurement, and Moral Importance*, Oxford: Oxford University Press.

Gruber, J. and Kőszegi, B. 'Is addiction "rational"? Theory and evidence', *Quarterly Journal of Economics* 116, 2001: 1261–1303.

Gruber, J. and Kőszegi, B. 'Tax incidence when individuals are time-inconsistent: the case of cigarette excise taxes', *Journal of Public Economics* 88, 2004: 1959–1987.

Gruber, J.H. and Mullainathan, S. 'Do cigarette taxes make smokers happier?', *Advances in Economic Analysis & Policy* 5, 2005: 1–43.

Grunwald, M. 'How Obama is using the science of change', *Time*, April 13, 2009: 28–32.

Gul, F. and Pesendorfer, W. (2005) 'The case for mindless economics', unpublished manuscript, available at http://economics.uchicago.edu/pdf/Pesendorfer040306.pdf.

Haigh, M.S. and List, J.A. 'Do professional traders exhibit myopic loss aversion? An experimental analysis', *The Journal of Finance* 60, 2005: 523–534.

Hayek, F.A. 'The use of knowledge in society', *The American Economic Review* 35, 1945: 519–530.

Hayek, F.A. (1960) *The Constitution of Liberty: The Definitive Edition*, edited by Ronald Hamowy, Chicago, IL: University of Chicago Press.

Hoffman, E. and Spitzer, M.L. 'Willingness to pay vs. willingness to accept: legal and economic implications', *Washington University Law Quarterly* 71, 1993: 59–114.

Horwitz, M.J. (1977) *The Transformation of American Law: 1780–1860*, Cambridge, MA: Harvard University Press.

Huntington, B.L. 'Welcome to the Mount Rushmore state! Keep your arms and legs inside the vehicle at all times and buckle up … not for safety, but to protect your constitutional rights', *South Dakota Law Review* 47, 2002: 99–133.

Isoni, A., Loomes, G., and Sugden, R. 'The willingness to pay–willingness to accept gap, the "endowment effect," subject misconceptions, and experimental procedures for eliciting valuations: comment', *American Economic Review* 101, 2011: 991–1011.

Issacharoff, S. 'Can there be a behavioral law and economics?', *Vanderbilt Law Review* 51, 1998: 1729–1745.

Jenkins, G.W. 'Who's afraid of philanthrocapitalism?', *Case Western Reserve Law Review* 61, 2011: 753–822.

Jolls, C. (2007) 'Behavioral law and economics', in P. Diamond and H. Vartiainen (eds.) *Behavioral Economics and its Applications*, Princeton, NJ: Princeton University Press.

Jolls, C. and Sunstein, C.R. 'Debiasing through law', *The Journal of Legal Studies* 35, 2006: 199–242.

Jolls, C., Sunstein, C.R., and Thaler, R. 'A behavioral approach to law and economics, *Stanford Law Review* 50, 1998: 1471–1550.

Jost, J.T. 'Negative illusions: conceptual clarification and psychological evidence concerning false consciousness', *Political Psychology* 16, 1995: 397–424.

Judt, T. (2005) *Postwar: A History of Europe since 1945*, New York: Penguin Press.

Kahlenberg, R.D. (1999) *Broken Contract: A Memoir of Harvard Law School*, Amherst, MA: University of Massachusetts Press.

Kahneman, D. and Frederick, S. (2002) 'Representativeness revisited: attribute substitution in intuitive judgment', in T. Gilovich, D. Griffin, and D. Kahneman (eds.) *Heuristics and Biases: The Psychology of Intuitive Judgment*, Cambridge: Cambridge University Press.

Kahneman, D. and Tversky, A. 'prospect theory: an analysis of decision under risk', *Econometrica* 263, 1979: 274–284.

Kahneman, D., Knetsch, J.L., and Thaler, R.H. 'Experimental tests of the endowment effect and the Coase theorem', *The Journal of Political Economy* 98, 1990: 1325–1348.

Kahneman, D., Knetsch, J.L., and Thaler, R.H. (2000) 'Anomalies: the endowment effect, loss aversion, and status quo bias', in D. Kahneman and A. Tversky (eds.), *Choices, Values, and Frames*, Cambridge: Cambridge University Press.

Kant, I. (1785) *Groundwork for the Metaphysics of Morals*, edited by L. Denis, T.K. Abbott (trans), 2005 edition, Peterborough, Canada: Broadview Press.

Kelman, M. 'Consumption theory, production theory, and ideology in the Coase theorem', *Southern California Law Review* 52, 1979: 669–698.

Kelman, M. 'Misunderstanding social life: a critique of the core premises of "law and economics"', *Journal of Legal Education* 33, 1983: 274–284.

Kelman, M. (1987) *A Guide to Critical Legal Studies*, Cambridge, MA: Harvard University Press.

Kennedy, D. 'How the law school fails: a polemic', *Yale Review of Law and Social Action* 1, 1970: 71–91.

Kennedy, D. 'Legal education and the reproduction of hierarchy', *Journal of Legal Education* 32, 1982: 591–615.

Kennedy, D. 'Psycho-social CLS: a comment on the Cardozo symposium', *Cardozo Law Review* 6, 1985: 1013–1032.

Kennedy, D. (1987) 'Toward a critical phenomenology of judging', in A.C. Hutchinson and P. Monahan (eds.) *The Rule of Law: Ideal or Ideology*, Toronto: Carswell.

Kennedy, D. (1998) 'Law-and-economics from the perspective of critical legal studies', in P. Newman (ed.) *The New Palgrave Dictionary of Economics and the Law*, New York: Stockton Press.

Kennedy, D. 'Teaching from the left in my anecdotage', *New York University Review of Law and Social Change* 31, 2007: 449–454.

Kennedy, D. and Klare, K.E. 'A bibliography of critical legal studies', *Yale Law Journal* 94, 1984: 461–490.

Kirzner, I.M. 'Entrepreneurial discovery and the competitive market process: an Austrian approach, *Journal of Economic Literature* 35, 1997: 60–85.

Klick, J. and Mitchell, G. 'Government regulation of irrationality: moral and cognitive hazards', *Minnesota Law Review* 90, 2006: 1620–1663.

Knetsch, J.L. 'Biased valuations, damage assessments, and policy choices: the choice of measure matters', *Ecological Economics* 63, 2007: 684–689.

Knetsch, J.L. and Wong, W. 'The endowment effect and the reference state: evidence and manipulations', *Journal of Economic Behavior and Organization* 71, 2009: 407–413.

Knight, F.H. (1921) *Risk, Uncertainty and Profit*, 2006 edition, New York: Cosimo, Inc.

Korobkin, R. 'The status quo bias and contract default rules', *Cornell Law Review* 83, 1998: 608–687.

Korobkin, R. 'The endowment effect and legal analysis', *Northwestern University Law Review* 97, 2003: 1227–1293.

Kőszegi, B. and Rabin, M. 'A model of reference-dependent preferences', *Quarterly Journal of Economics* 121, 2006: 1133–1165.

Kőszegi, B. and Rabin, M. 'Reference-dependent risk attitudes', *American Economic Review* 97, 2007: 1047–1073.

Kotkin, M.J. 'Creating true believers: putting macro theory into practice', *Clinical Law Review* 5, 1998: 95–115.

Kovalchik, S., Camerer, C.F., Grether, D.M., Plott, C.R., and Allman, J.M. 'Aging and decision making: a comparison between neurologically healthy elderly and young individuals', *Journal of Economic Behavior and Organization* 58, 2005: 79–94.

Kronman, A.T. 'Specific performance', *University of Chicago Law Review* 45, 1978: 351–382.

Kunda, Z. 'The case for motivated reasoning', *Psychological Bulletin* 108, 1990: 480–498.

Kuran, T. and Sunstein, C.R. 'Availability cascades and risk regulation', *Stanford Law Review* 51, 1999: 683–768.

Laibson, D. 'Golden eggs and hyperbolic discounting', *Quarterly Journal of Economics* 112, 1997: 443–477.

Lambert, T.A. 'Two mistakes behavioralists make: a response to professors Feigenson *et al.* and professor Slovic', *Missouri Law Review* 69, 2004: 1053–1060.

Landes, W.M. and Posner, R.A. 'Legal precedent: a theoretical and empirical analysis', *The Journal of Law and Economics* 19, 1976: 249–307.

Landes, W.M. and Posner, R.A. 'Joint and multiple tortfeasors: an economic analysis', *The Journal of Legal Studies* 9, 1980: 517–555.

Langbein, J.H. and Posner, R.A. 'Social investing and the law of trusts', *Michigan Law Review* 79, 1980: 72–112.

Leiter, B. (2007) 'Most cited law professors by specialty, 2000–2007', Brian Leiter's Law School Rankings, December 18, 2007, available at www.leiterrankings.com/faculty/2007faculty_impact_areas.shtml#CriticalTheory.

Lessig, L. 'The new Chicago school', *The Journal of Legal Studies* 27, 1998: 661–691.

Levine, D.K. (2012) *Is Behavioral Economics Doomed? The Ordinary Versus the Extraordinary*, Cambridge: Open Book Publishers.

Levitt, S.D. and List, J.A. 'Viewpoint: on the generalizability of lab behaviour to the field', *Canadian Journal of Economics* 40, 2007: 347–370.

Levitt, S.D., List, J.A., and Reiley, D.H., 'What happens in the field stays in the field: exploring whether professionals play minimax in laboratory experiments', *Econometrica* 78, 2010: 1413–1434.

Licht, A.N. 'The entrepreneurial spirit and what the law can do about it', *Comparative Labor Law and Policy* 28, 2007: 817–862.

Lipton, D. and Sachs, J. 'Creating a market economy in Eastern Europe: the case of Poland', *Brookings Papers on Economic Activity* 21(1), 1990: 75–147.

List, J.A. 'Does market experience eliminate market anomalies?', *The Quarterly Journal of Economics* 118, 2003: 41–71.

List, J.A. 'Neoclassical theory versus prospect theory: evidence from the marketplace', *Econometrica* 72, 2004: 615–625.

Locke, J. (1690) *Two Treatises of Government*, edited by Peter Laslett, 1988 student edition, Cambridge: Cambridge University Press.

Loewenstein, G. and O'Donoghue, T. '"We can do this the easy way or the hard way": negative emotions, self-regulation, and the law', *University of Chicago Law Review* 73, 2006: 183–206.

Lukes, S. 'In defense of "false consciousness"', *University of Chicago Legal Forum* 2011: 19–28.

Manne, H.G. 'Mergers and the market for corporate control', *The Journal of Political Economy* 73, 1965: 110–120.

Manne, H.G. and Wright, J.D. (2008) 'The future of law and economics: a discussion', George Mason University Law and Economics Research Paper, available at http://papers.ssrn.com/sol3/papers.cfm?abstract_id=1145421.

McCaffery, E.J., Kahneman, D.J., and Spitzer, M.L. 'Framing the jury: cognitive perspectives on pain and suffering awards', *Virginia Law Review* 81, 1995: 1341–1420.

McCarney, J. (2005) 'Ideology and false consciousness', *Marx Myths and Legends*, available at http://marxmyths.org/joseph-mccarney/article.htm.

McChesney, F.S. 'Rent extraction and rent creation in the economic theory of regulation', *The Journal of Legal Studies* 16, 1987: 101–118.

March of Dimes (2014) 'Global programs', www.marchofdimes.com/mission/globalprograms.html (last visited June 27, 2014).

Mill, J.S. (1859) 'On liberty', in J. Gray (ed.) *On Liberty and Other Essays*, Oxford: Oxford University Press.

Mitchell, G. 'Taking behavioralism too seriously? The unwarranted pessimism of the new behavioral analysis of law', *William and Mary Law Review* 43, 2002a: 1907–2181.

Mitchell, G. 'Why law and economics' perfect rationality should not be traded for behavioral law and economics' equal incompetence', *Georgetown Law Journal* 91, 2002b: 67–167.

Mitchell, G. 'Libertarian paternalism is an oxymoron', *Northwestern University Law Review* 99, 2005: 1245–1278.

Montgomery, L. 'New economic face, still familiar', *Washington Post*, September 11, 2010: A12.

Munro, R.J. 'Political psychiatry in post-Mao China and its origins in the Cultural Revolution', *The Journal of the American Academy of Psychiatry and the Law* 30, 2002: 97–106.

National Institutes of Health (2013) 'Mission', www.nih.gov/about/mission.htm (last visited June 27, 2014).

O'Donoghue, T. and Rabin, M. 'Studying optimal paternalism, illustrated by a model of sin taxes', *The American Economic Review* 93, 2003: 186–191.

Payne, S.L. (1951) *The Art of Asking Questions*, Princeton, NJ: Princeton University Press.

PBS Newshour 'Thaler responds to Posner on consumer protection', July 28, 2009, available at www.pbs.org/newshour/businessdesk/2009/07/thaler-responds-to-posner-on-c.html.

Peltzman, S. 'Toward a more general theory of regulation', *The Journal of Law and Economics* 19, 1976: 211–240.

Plott, C.R. and Zeiler, K. 'The willingness to pay–willingness to accept gap, the "endowment effect," subject misconceptions, and experimental procedures for eliciting valuations', *The American Economic Review* 95, 2005: 530–545.

Plott, C.R. and Zeiler, K. 'Exchange asymmetries incorrectly interpreted as evidence of endowment effect theory and prospect theory?', *The American Economic Review* 97, 2007: 1449–1466.

Plott, C.R. and Zeiler, K. 'The willingness to pay–willingness to accept gap, the "endowment effect," subject misconceptions, and experimental procedures for eliciting valuations: reply', *The American Economic Review* 101, 2011: 1012–1028.

Polinksy, A.M. 'Resolving nuisance disputes: the simple economics of injunctive and damage remedies', *Stanford Law Review* 32, 1980: 1075–1112.

Posner, R.A. (1973) *Economic Analysis of Law*, Boston, MA: Little, Brown.

Posner, R.A. 'Gratuitous promises in economics and law', *The Journal of Legal Studies* 6, 1977: 411–426.

Posner, R.A. 'Treating financial consumers as consenting adults', *Wall Street Journal*, July 23, 2009: A15.

Priest, G.L. 'Breach and remedy for the tender of nonconforming goods under the uniform commercial code: an economic approach', *Harvard Law Review* 91, 1978: 960–1001.

Putterman, L. (1996) 'The role of ownership and property rights in China's economic transition', in A.G. Walder (ed.) *China's Transitional Economy*, Oxford: Oxford University Press.

Qizilbash, M. (2009) 'Well-being, preference formation and the danger of paternalism', Max Planck Institute of Economics Papers on Econonomics and Evolution, available at ftp://papers.econ.mpg.de/evo/discussionpapers/2009-18.pdf.

Rachlinksi, J.J. 'The uncertain psychological case for paternalism', *Northwestern University Law Review* 97, 2003: 1165–1225.

Rachlinksi, J.J. 'Cognitive errors, individual differences, and paternalism', *University of Chicago Law Review* 73, 2006: 207–229.

Rachlinski, J.J. and Jourden, J. 'Remedies and the psychology of ownership', *Vanderbilt Law Review* 51, 1998: 1541–1582.

Rhode, D.L. 'Feminist critical theories', *Stanford Law Review* 42, 1990: 617–638.

Rizzo, M.J. and Whitman, D.G. 'Little brother is watching you: new paternalism on the slippery slopes', *Arizona Law Review* 51, 2009a: 685–1097.

Rizzo, M.J. and Whitman, D.G. 'The knowledge problem of new paternalism', *Brigham Young University Law Review* 2009, 2009b: 905–968.

Robson, M. 'Explaining cross-national variations in entrepreneurship: the role of social protection and political culture', *Comparative Labor Law and Policy Journal* 28, 2007: 863–892.

Rosch, J.T. (2010) 'Behavioral economics: observations regarding issues that lie ahead, remarks before the Vienna Competition Conference', speech, available at http://ftc.gov/speeches/rosch/100609viennaremarks.pdf.

Rugg, D. and Cantril, H. 'The wording of questions', *The Journal of Abnormal and Social Psychology* 37, 1942: 469–495 reprinted in H. Cantril (1944) *Gauging Public Opinion*, Princeton, NJ: Princeton University Press.

Sahm, C.R., Shapiro, M.D., and Slemrod, J. (2010) 'Check in the mail or more in the paycheck: does the effectiveness of fiscal stimulus depend on how it is delivered?', National Bureau of Economic Research Working Paper, available at www.nber.org/papers/w16246.pdf.

Schelling, T.C. (1984) *Choice and Consequence*, Cambridge, MA: Harvard University Press.

Schwartz, A. and Wilde, L.L. 'Intervening in markets on the basis of imperfect information: a legal and economic analysis', *University of Pennsylvania Law Review* 127, 1979: 630–682.

Schwartz, B. 'On the economic stimulus package: the "packaging" counts', *Psychology Today*, February 1, 2009, available at www.psychologytoday.com/blog/the-choices-worth-having/200902/the-economic-stimulus-package-the-packaging-counts.

Sen, A. 'Markets and freedoms: achievements and limitations of the market mechanism in promoting individual freedoms', *Oxford Economic Papers* 45, 1993, 519–541.

Sills, D.L. (1957) *The Volunteers: Means and Ends in a National Organization*, Glencoe, IL: Free Press.

Simecka, M. (1984) *Restoration of Order: The Normalization of Czechoslovakia 1969–1976*, A.G. Brain (trans.), London: Verso.

Simon, H.A. 'A behavioral model of rational choice', *The Quarterly Journal of Economics* 69, 1955: 99–118.

Simon, H.A. 'Rational decision making in business organizations', *The American Economic Review* 69, 1979: 493–513.

Skinner, B.F. (1965) *Science and Human Behavior*, New York: Free Press.

Smith, V.L. 'Economics in the laboratory', *The Journal of Economic Perspectives* 8, 1994: 113–131.

Smith, V.L. and Walker, J.M. 'Monetary rewards and decision cost in experimental economics', *Economic Inquiry* 31, 1993: 245–261.

Stigler, G.J., 'Perfect competition, historically contemplated', *The Journal of Political Economy* 65, 1957: 1–17.

Stigler, G.J. 'The economics of information', *The Journal of Political Economy* 69, 1961: 213–225.

Stigler, G.J. 'The theory of economic regulation', *The Bell Journal of Economics and Management Science* 2, 1971: 3–21.

Strotz, R.H. 'Myopia and inconsistency in dynamic utility maximization', *The Review of Economic Studies* 23, 1955: 165–180.

Sunstein, C.R. 'Social norms and social roles', *Columbia Law Review* 96, 1996: 903–968.

Sunstein, C.R. 'Foreword: on academic fads and fashions', *Michigan Law Review* 99, 2001: 1251–1264.

Sunstein, C.R. 'Switching the default rule', *New York University Law Review* 77, 2002: 106–134.

Sunstein, C.R. 'Hazardous heuristics', *University of Chicago Law Review* 70, 2003: 751–782.

Sunstein, C.R. 'Moral heuristics and moral framing', *Minnesota Law Review* 88, 2004: 1556–1597.

Sunstein, C.R. (2005) *Laws of Fear*, Cambridge: Cambridge University Press.

Sunstein, C.R. and Thaler, R.H. 'Libertarian paternalism is not an oxymoron', *University of Chicago Law Review* 70, 2003: 1159–1202.

Sunstein C. and Thaler, R. 'How behavioral economics could show up in the new stimulus package', *Nudge Blog* January 20, 2009, available at http://nudges.org/2009/01/20/how-behavioral-economics-could-show-up-in-the-new-stimulus-package.

Surowiecki, J. 'A smarter stimulus', *The New Yorker*, January 26, 2009: 25.

Temple, J.A., White, B.A., and Reynolds, A.J. 'Cost-effective crime prevention: economic analysis of the Chicago child–parent centers early education program', *Public Interest Law Reporter* 15, 2010: 181–197.

Tergesen, A. '401(k) law suppresses saving for retirement', *Wall Street Journal*, July 7, 2011: A1.

Thaler, R. 'Toward a positive theory of consumer choice', *Journal of Economic Behavior & Organization* 1, 1980: 39–60.

Thaler, R. 'Mental accounting and consumer choice', *Marketing Science* 4, 1985: 199–214.

Thaler, R.H. (1996) 'Doing economics without *Homo economicus*', in S.G. Medema and W.J. Samuels (eds.) *Foundations of Research in Economics: How Do Economists Do Economics?*, Cheltenham: Edward Elgar.

Thaler, R.H. and Benartzi, S. 'Save more tomorrow™: using behavioral economics to increase employee saving', *Journal of Political Economy* 112, 2004: S164–187.

Thaler, R.H. and Dawes, R.M. (1992) 'Cooperation', in Thaler, R.H., *The Winner's*

Curse: Paradoxes and Anomalies of Economic Life, Princeton, NJ: Princeton University Press.

Thaler, R.H. and Sunstein, C.R. 'Libertarian paternalism', *American Economic Review* 93, 2003: 175–179.

Thaler, R.H. and Sunstein, C.R. (2008) *Nudge: Improving Decisions About Health, Wealth, And Happiness*, New Haven, CT: Yale University Press.

Thaler, R.H. and Tversky, A. (1992) 'Preference reversals', in Thaler, R.H., *The Winner's Curse: Paradoxes and Anomalies of Economic Life*, Princeton, NJ: Princeton University Press.

Tullock, G. 'The welfare costs of tariffs, monopolies, and theft', *Western Economic Journal* 5, 1967: 224–232.

Turner, D.W. 'Nonbank banks: congressional options', *Vanderbilt Law Review* 39, 1986: 1735–1775.

Turnock, B.J. (2012) *Essentials of Public Health*, 2nd edn, Sudbury, MA: Jones & Bartlett Learning.

Tversky, A. and Kahneman, D. 'Availability: a heuristic for judging frequency and probability', *Cognitive Psychology* 5, 1973: 207–232.

Tversky, A. and Kahneman, D. (1982) 'Judgment under uncertainty: heuristics and biases', in D. Kahneman, P. Slovic, and A. Tversky (eds.) *Judgment Under Uncertainty*, Cambridge: Cambridge University Press.

Tversky, A. and Kahneman, D. 'Loss aversion in riskless choice: a reference-dependent model', *Quarterly Journal of Economics* 106, 1991: 1039–1061.

Unger, R.M. (1975) *Knowledge and Politics*, New York: Free Press.

United States Department of Health and Human Services (2014) 'Public health offices, U.S.', www.hhs.gov/ash/public_health/indexph.html (last visited June 27, 2014).

Valdes, F. 'Queers, sissies, dykes, and tomboys: deconstructing the conflation of "sex," "gender," and "sexual orientation" in Euro-American law and society', *California Law Review* 83, 1995: 1–377.

Vandenberghe, A. (2004) *An Economic Analysis of Employment Law*, Northampton, MA: Edward Elgar Publishing.

Varian, H.R. (2010) *Intermediate Microeconomics: A Modern Approach*, 8th edition, New York: W.W. Norton & Co.

Verdery, K. (1996) *What Was Socialism, and What Comes Next?*, Princeton, NJ: Princeton University Press.

Wallace, M.A. 'Interstate commerce commission', *George Washington Law Review* 56, 1988: 937–959.

Wang, S.S. 'Menu Labeling to Go National, Thanks to Health Bill's Passage', *Wall Street Journal Health Blog*, March 22, 2010, available at http://blogs.wsj.com/health/2010/03/22/menu-labeling-to-go-national-thanks-to-health-bills-passage.

Warren, E. 'Economic model almost working or broken?', *Credit Slips*, December 26, 2006, www.creditslips.org/creditslips/2006/12/economic_model_.html.

Warren, E. 'Unsafe at any rate', *Democracy* 5, 2007: 8–19.

Warren, E. (2010) 'Redesigning regulation: a case study from the consumer credit market', in E.J. Balleisen and D.A. Moss (eds.) *Government and Markets: Toward a New Theory of Regulation*, Cambridge: Cambridge University Press.

Watson, J.B. 'Psychology as the behaviorist views it', *Psychological Review* 158, 1913: 248–253.

Weinstein, N.D., 'Unrealistic optimism about future life events', *Journal of Personality and Social Psychology* 39, 1980: 806–820.

Weiss, D.M. 'Paternalistic pension policy: psychological evidence and economic theory', *University of Chicago Law Review* 58, 1991: 1275–1319.

Whitman, D.G. and Rizzo, M.J. 'Paternalistic slopes', *New York University Journal of Law and Liberty* 2, 2007: 411–413.

World Health Organization (2006) 'Constitution of the World Health Organization', pmbl., art. 1, available at www.who.int/governance/eb/who_constitution_en.pdf.

Wright, J.D. 'Behavioral law and economics, paternalism, and consumer contracts: an empirical perspective', *New York University Journal of Law and Liberty* 2, 2007: 470–599.

Wright, J. 'A "plain vanilla" proposal for behavioral law and economics', *Truth On The Market*, July 16, 2010, available at http://truthonthemarket.com/2010/07/16/a-plain-vanilla-proposal-for-behavioral-law-and-economics.

Wright, J.D. and Stone, J.E. 'Misbehavioral economics: the case against behavioral antitrust', *Cardozo Law Review* 33, 2012: 1517–1533.

Wright, J.D. and Zywicki, T.J. 'Three problematic truths about the Consumer Financial Protection Agency Act of 2009', *Lombard Street*, September 14, 2009: 1.

Index

normative economic analysis of law:
difficult cases 6; reforms category 6;
utility maximization 7–10; wealth
maximization 9–11, 13
norms: Ancient Roman example 47–8; the
dominance of 43–63; examples of
47–50; Ik tribe example 49–50;
interpreting the examples 50–4; material
self-interest maximizing as Western
modernity's prevailing norm 54–9;
Mediaeval Europe example 48–9;
prevailing norms and the social norms
literature 59–63; prevailing norms in
other societies 45–6
norms and values: in the economic
approach to law 1–14; in the study of
law 32–41
novel transactions, moral perspective
206–11
*Nudge: Improving Decisions About
Health, Wealth, and Happiness* (Thaler/
Sunstein) 309, 321

On Liberty (Mill) 227, 230
the open-access resource sector, as a
system of social control 135
opportunistic behaviour, David Rose on
212–13
optimism bias 302–3
ordinality, and Pareto 108
Ostrom, E. 134
ownership rights, typology 237

paradox of liberal democracy 230
Paretianism 22
Pareto, V. 108
Pareto efficiency: benchmarking problem
193–4; definition 12, 91, 193; vs
Kaldor–Hicks 110, 136, 159, 184,
192–8; ordinality and 108; speculativity
of 194–8
the Pareto principle: the argument for
utilitarianism 176–8; vs autonomy
171–3; autonomy, welfare and 159–80;
and bounded rationality 169–71; and
changing circumstances 165–6;
changing values and tastes 166–7;
choice versus welfare 161; cognitive
limitations 168–9; Cooter on 159;
criticisms 108; *ex-post* vs *ex-ante*
175–6; and individual welfare 161–2;
issues relating to "preferences" 161–71;
and the legal centralist approach to
public policy 136; the "Paretian

dilemma" 165; policy-induced changes
in values and tastes 167–8; Robinson
Crusoe analogy 161; Sen on the conflict
of liberal values with 234; Sen's
conclusion 172–3; and social welfare
162–4; systems of social control and
124; technical difficulties 163–4; and
the temporal problem 164; two
justifications 159; welfarist and
utilitarianist perspectives 173–6
Parisi, F. 115
Parkman, A. 252
paternalism 169, 173, 231, 274–5, 321,
323; *see also* legal paternalism;
libertarian paternalism
personal freedom: Mill's view 230; and the
US Constitution 229
philosophy, Adam Smith's view 17
Pigou, A.C. 1, 70
Pitcairn Island 62
Plato 16–18, 24
Plott, C.R. 304
political parties 122–3, 125, 127–30, 133,
137
political stability, wealth maximization
and 76
Porat, A. 217
pornography, Trebilcock on 235
positive externalities 133, 239
Posner, E. 251
Posner, R.A. 17, 26, 32–3, 40–1, 62,
69–71, 73–5, 78–80, 89–90, 105–6,
111–14, 234, 238, 269, 275, 281–8, 316,
328
Predictably Irrational (Ariely) 309
preference maximizers 98
preference reversals 169–70, 302, 304
preferences: development of 256;
distinction between action and 24;
endogeneity of 16–17, 23; *ex-post* vs
ex-ante 165–7; framing and 170;
happiness and 161; interpretations of
159–60; Law and Economics' treatment
24; neoclassical critique of the
relationship between welfare and 314;
and the Pareto principle 161–71;
revealed preference 9, 97; revelation of
as decision criterion 114–15; the search
for true preferences 313–14; *see also*
choice
pregnancy, economic analysis 253–4
price fixing 5–6
price theory 70, 80, 247, 299–300, 307,
318

utility, and well-being 18
utility maximization 7–10, 36, 111–13, 115, 272

values and tastes, changing 166–7
veil of ignorance, Rawlsian 117n17
Viner, J. 80

Warren, E. 306–8, 312
Warren court 38
Wax, A.L. 251
wealth maximization: Calvinism and 56; criticisms 111; fundamental objection to 10–11; judges' role in promoting 75; vs natural rights 114; Posner's defence 41, 76; as a social value 112–13; supportive arguments 113; utility maximization vs 10, 111–13
The Wealth of Nations (Smith) 57; publication 92
Weber, M. 38, 55, 61
welfare, choice vs 161, 167
welfare economics 5, 13, 108, 163, 192, 194; fairness and 173–4
welfarism, *ex-post* vs *ex-ante* 174–6

well-being 20–1, 26, 54, 108, 110–11, 122, 159, 161–2, 173, 205, 213, 219–20, 253
What Money Can't Buy: The Moral Limits of Markets (Sandel) 206
Whitman, D.G. 314, 317
Will, G. 152n8
Williams, S.F. 329
Williamson, O. 3
willingness-to-accept 10, 198
willingness-to-pay 198
Winner-Take-All Politics (Hacker/Pierson) 153n28
Winter, R. 329
Wistrich, A.J. 279
WTA–WTP gaps 304–5

Xu, C. 152n8

Yale School, Chicago School vs 80, 104–6

Zamir, E. 213–15, 217, 220
Zeiler, K. 304
Zeisel, H. 250
Zelder, M. 250
Zervogianni, E. 280–1

For Product Safety Concerns and Information please contact our
EU representative GPSR@taylorandfrancis.com Taylor & Francis
Verlag GmbH, Kaufingerstraße 24, 80331 München, Germany